THE WORLD IN A C.

Edited by Paul Anisef and Michael Lanphier

Toronto is arguably the most multicultural city in the world. The process of settlement and integration in modern-day Toronto is, however, in many ways more difficult for recent immigrants than it was for those arriving in previous decades. Newly settled immigrants face a multitude of challenges, including access to health care, education, employment, housing, and economic and community services.

The World in a City explores Toronto's ability to sustain a civic society in the face of profound demographic change. The essays in this collection highlight the need to pay more attention to certain at-risk groups and stress the importance of adapting policy to fit the changing settlement and clustering patterns of newcomers. Throughout the volume the concepts of social exclusion and integration are examined and employed to analyse the various challenges facing newcomers. The authors' research findings demonstrate that there are many obstacles to providing opportunity for immigrants, such as low resource bases and inadequate service delivery. Together the authors make a convincing case that by providing a level 'playing field' for its newly arrived inhabitants, and recognizing the particular needs of new communities, the city of Toronto can encourage social and economic growth that would be of immense benefit to the community as a whole.

PAUL ANISEF is a professor of sociology and associate director of the Centre of Excellence for Research in Immigration and Settlement (CERIS) at York University.

MICHAEL LANPHIER is professor emeritus of sociology and senior scholar at the Centre for Refugee Studies at York University.

THE WORLD IN A CITY

Edited by Paul Anisef and Michael Lanphier

UNIVERSITY OF TORONTO PRESS
Toronto Buffalo London

© University of Toronto Press Incorporated 2003
Toronto Buffalo London
Printed in Canada

ISBN 0-8020-3560-4 (cloth)
ISBN 0-8020-8436-2 (paper)

∞

Printed on acid-free paper

National Library of Canada Cataloguing in Publication

The world in a city / edited by Paul Anisef and Michael Lanphier.

Includes bibliographical references and index.
ISBN 0-8020-3560-4 (bound).   ISBN 0-8020-8436-2 (pbk.)

1. Immigrants – Ontario – Toronto Region – Social conditions.
2. Toronto Region (Ont.) – Emigration and immigration – History –
20th century.   3. Multiculturalism – Ontario – Toronto Region.
I. Anisef, Paul, 1942–   II. Lanphier, C. Michael, 1937–

FC3097.9.A1W67 2003   305.9'0691'09713541   C2003-900682-4
F1059.5.T689A28 2003

University of Toronto Press acknowledges the financial assistance to its publishing program of the Canada Council for the Arts and the Ontario Arts Council.

University of Toronto Press acknowledges the financial support for its publishing activities of the Government of Canada through the Book Publishing Industry Development Program (BPIDP).

Contents

ACKNOWLEDGMENTS vii

Introduction: Immigration and the Accommodation of Diversity   3
Paul Anisef and Michael Lanphier

1 Becoming an Immigrant City: A History of Immigration into Toronto since the Second World War   19
   Harold Troper

2 Immigrants in the Greater Toronto Area: A Sociodemographic Overview   63
   Clifford Jansen and Lawrence Lam

3 Towards a Comfortable Neighbourhood and Appropriate Housing: Immigrant Experiences in Toronto   132
   Robert A. Murdie and Carlos Teixeira

4 Immigrants' Economic Status in Toronto: Stories of Triumph and Disappointment   192
   Valerie Preston, Lucia Lo, and Shuguang Wang

5 Immigrant Students and Schooling in Toronto, 1960s to 1990s   263
   Carl E. James and Barbara Burnaby

6 Diversity and Immigrant Health   316
  Samuel Noh and Violet Kaspar

7 Images of Integrating Diversity: A Photographic Essay   354
  Gabriele Scardellato

8 Integrating Community Diversity in Toronto: On Whose Terms?   373
  Myer Siemiatycki, Tim Rees, Roxana Ng, and Khan Rahi

9 World in a City: A View from Policy   457
  Meyer Burstein and Howard Duncan

Epilogue: Blockages to Opportunity   474
Michael Lanphier and Paul Anisef

REFERENCES   479

CONTRIBUTORS   523

INDEX   529

Acknowledgments

We wish to acknowledge the research assistance of Lynn Winter, Jadranka Bacic, Colleen Burke, Suzanne McFarlane, Tomoko Mizuguichi, Elizabeth Rossick, Denise Tom-Kun, and Kelliebeth Hand. Martha Ayim provided early proofing assistance while Andrea Knight copy-edited the near final manuscript and Irinel Bradisteau prepared the index. Susan Rainey offered secretarial assistance in producing the first iteration of the manuscript. Technical assistance in assembling the final tables and figures was provided by Stephen Young.

This book would not have been possible without a Major Research Initiatives grant from the Joint Centre of Excellence for Research on Immigration and Settlement-Toronto (CERIS). Both Morton Beiser and Kenise Murphy Kilbride of CERIS warrant special mention for their advice throughout the process of developing *The World in a City*. We are also grateful for the research funding provided by Canadian Heritage for this and other related projects. Funding for final editing and index construction was generously provided by the Office of the Dean, Faculty of Arts, the Vice-President, Research and Innovation, at York University; the Associate Vice-President, Academic (Research and International Development) at Ryerson University; and the Executive Head of the Metropolis Project.

Virgil Duff of the University of Toronto Press recognized the value of the book and supported us throughout. Several anonymous readers offered suggestions, which we believe helped us to strengthen the manuscript. Finally, we would like to thank the following persons who were asked to review and comment upon specific chapters: William R.

Avison, Gerald Tulchinsky, June Beynon, Dan Hiebert, Brian Ray, Roderic Beaujot, and Daiva Stasiulis. The editors are most appreciative of the encouragement and sustained support from their spouses – Etta Baichman and Caroline Lanphier – and from their families throughout the months and years as this project grew to fruition.

THE WORLD IN A CITY

Introduction: Immigration and the Accommodation of Diversity

Paul Anisef and Michael Lanphier

At the end of June 2001, a reporter asked Mel Lastman, mayor of Toronto, for his comment on the Mombasa meeting of the Association of National Olympic Committees of Africa he was to attend in support of the Toronto Olympic bid. Lastman quipped, 'Why the hell would I want to go to a place like Mombasa? I just see myself in a pot of boiling water with all these natives dancing around me' (James 2001). As soon as his remark hit the press, his effort at humour turned into a firestorm of controversy. In spite of his repeated apologies, the remarks led to increased public questioning of the mayor's leadership style. Others assessed the damage his remark had done to Toronto's Olympic hopes. Most importantly, the mayor's comment ignited soul-searching debate on the state of racial harmony and intergroup relations in Toronto, a city where the public culture has long trumpeted the success of its planned pluralism and exemplary mutual respect among diverse cultural groups.

Events such as the Lastman incident raise a series of challenges regarding the capacity of a racially and ethnically pluralist Toronto to sustain a civic society. It is true that Toronto is among the most, if not *the* most, pluralist of the major cities in the Western world. Indeed, in this era of emergent globalism, Toronto may be the first global city to sustain ethnic diversity. Consider that, as of 1996, 42 per cent of Toronto's population was foreign-born, in contrast to 23 per cent in New York, 31 per cent in Los Angeles, 39 per cent in Miami, and 34 per cent in Sydney. Furthermore, the Toronto metropolis currently attracts almost half of all newcomers to Canada. Some 70,000 immigrants arrive in the city annually from approximately 170 countries. Almost half of these new immigrants speak neither English nor French upon arrival; as a result, over one hundred languages are commonly spoken in the city.

It is therefore understandable that Lastman's comment should refocus public attention on issues of exclusion and inclusion in such a multiethnic and multiracial urban society. *The World in a City* explores the challenges with respect to the accommodation of immigrants in Toronto, employing the critical lenses of social exclusion and inclusion as a key theoretical perspective. Beginning with a historical overview of how Toronto emerged in the late twentieth century as an important destination for immigrants from all over the world, *The World in a City* goes on to analyse the impact of racial and ethnic pluralism on areas of critical importance to public life in the city: housing, education, health, economic well-being, and the dynamics of community and group life. The contributions in this volume, individually and severally, add to our understanding of how the diverse origins in a major city become the shaping factor in developing a workable civic society. While each of these analyses is written within the conventions of the various academic disciplines represented among the authors – history, sociology, political science, demography, geography, and education – all of the essays wrestle with the central question of the extent to which the social structure includes or shuts out immigrants in the Toronto region.

INTEGRATION PERSPECTIVES

Several factors may render the process of settlement and integration more difficult for many immigrants than in previous decades. Rapid social change, globalization, and persistently high unemployment rates, especially among newcomers, have produced a less-than-warm welcome for immigrants who strive to do well for themselves and their children. In addition, many recent immigrants who choose Toronto as their new home arrive from non-European countries and represent ethnic and racial groups that are minorities in Toronto and in Canada. Although racism has traditionally appeared to be a less prominent issue in Canada than in the United States or Great Britain, increases in racial conflict and systemic forms of discrimination have undermined the image of Canada as a multicultural country. These factors pose settlement difficulties for minority immigrants and increase the likelihood of social exclusion. Complaints of numerous forms of discrimination have occurred with some frequency and are discussed throughout this book.

Many experiences with forms of exclusion stem from informal agreements or structural arrangements embedded in the everyday institutional processes in the life of a metropolis, rather than from formal stipulations or restrictive covenants. As a result, such cases of discrimination are among the most difficult of human rights violations to investigate, even though the grounds for the complaints are well founded (Frideres and Reeves 1989). However intractable such claims may be in litigation, the struggles against exclusion of some groups by other interests in the community or the state are important issues for *The World in a City* to explore.

Throughout this work, and in much research on the settlement of newcomers, we speak of the end result as the integration of newcomers into the ongoing community and society. Integration is defined as the process by which newcomers become part of the social, cultural, and institutional fabric of the community or society (Breton 1992), a process comprising three dimensions. The first dimension refers to the structural or institutional environment that moderates the terms and styles of integration, such as the prevailing levels of rights and the existing economic conditions. The second is the agency among the people resettling; that is, those who resettle exercise individual choice directed at influencing their life conditions and their personal environment. The third dimension includes the process or processes by which agents of resettlement engage with the structural and institutional environment.

Integration is a generic process of creating long- and short-term arrangements between an immigrant group and the host society. Weinfeld and Wilkinson (1999) outline three perspectives on integration, the first being the perspective of the immigrant group on the fulfilment of its needs and interests upon resettlement. These may range from short-term immediate concerns, such as orientation to the community, housing, acquisition of a new language, employment, education of children, establishing a social network, to long-term interests such as concern for family members, development of a subcommunity of people from a similar background, representation of collective interests in associations and government. For long-time residents of the metropolis, however, integration may imply the assimilation of standards already established in the wider community for language use, family relationships, consumption patterns, and entitlement to places in the occupational and social structure. These expectations may be at variance with those that newly arrived community members have for themselves. And governments may assume a third set of criteria for the interpretation of integration: official indicators of belonging to the new society such as acquisition of citizenship, financial contribution to the state through taxes, and relatively low rates of welfare use. In addition, governments are particularly interested in conventional forms of active civic participation, such as representation in local community organizations, contacts with government officials and members of Parliament, and campaigning for political office.

The common denominator running through these three perspectives is the two-way exchange between the newcomer group and the host society. With this exchange comes a sense of expectation from one group that the other will act not only out of its own interests but also out of concern for the wider community. Integration as a concept, therefore, assumes that the interests of the various parties will complement one another and add to the development of a civil society without blurring the identities of the participants.

Weinfeld and Wilkinson (1999) also note that the onus of integration is borne disproportionately by the newcomer group, whatever the norm of tolerance for diversity within Canadian society and the official policy of multiculturalism may be. At the same time, changes in technology now permit everyone, including newcomers, to reach across Canada, across North America, and well beyond by means of the telephone and the Internet. Contact with the homeland culture remains strong and can be continually renewed through electronic means and international travel. Multicultural patterns, then, will persist regardless of pressures for conformity. Moreover, they will be reinforced by sustained contacts with friends and relatives in the former homelands. Transnational exchanges have become woven into the fabric of multicultural orientation at the millennium.

SOCIAL EXCLUSION AND INCLUSION

The origin of social exclusion as an explanatory concept can be traced back to the response in France in the early 1970s to the problem of sustaining adequate living conditions for people left behind by economic growth (Ebersold 1998). Many researchers have used the term interchangeably with poverty and/or unemployment, but it is important to understand social exclusion as a concept that is broader than either of those terms. Thus, in 1989, the European Economic Community (EEC) began to link social exclusion to the inadequate realization of social rights. And, in 1990, the European Observatory on National Policies to Combat Social Exclusion was established to examine 'the social rights of citizenship to a basic standard of living and to participation in major social and economic opportunities in society' (Cousins 1999, 127). Duffy (1995) defines social exclusion as the lack of material means and the inability to participate effectively in economic, social, and cultural life that results in alienation or distance from mainstream society. Room (1995) adds a new dimension to the definition by stating that social exclusion is the denial or non-realization of civil, political, and social rights of citizenship. Byrne (1999) further refines the concept by characterizing social exclusion as a dynamic process that impedes healthy participation in social, economic, political, and cultural institutions.

Paugam (1996) cautions that there is no 'right/wrong' or 'good/bad' meaning attached to social exclusion and writes:

> On questions as socially and politically sensitive as poverty and exclusion, sociologists must first of all recognize the impossibility of finding exhaustive definitions. These concepts are relative, and vary according to time and circumstance. It is unreasonable to expect to find a fair and objective definition, which is distinct from social debate, without falling into the trap of putting unclearly defined populations into clumsily defined categories (4).

Klasen (1998) asserts that the goal of an *inclusive* society, by contrast, is for 'people to have equal access to basic capabilities such as the ability to be healthy, well-fed, housed, integrated into the community, participate in community and public life, and enjoy social bases of self-respect' (1). This view implies that the inability to participate in mainstream society is a violation of a basic right of all citizens and thereby places a burden on society to ensure that it supports the participation and integration of all its members (2). Alexander (1997) develops a conception of civil society that extends the traditional notion of collective or public consciousness to one that analyses the interpersonal, intergroup, and institutional ties required to create cohesion through abstract notions (e.g., rights and peoplehood). Achieving civil society in this sense will, in all likelihood, be accompanied by a protracted struggle for inclusiveness.

A metropolis as complex as Toronto exemplifies the notion of a civil society. As an area that receives large numbers of newcomers, the city contains many social arrangements that predetermine an individual's social and economic status. The outcomes of differences in social backgrounds among newcomers are sometimes (mis)construed as group inferiority. Consequently, this type of social perception results in newcomers encountering difficulties in their resettlement that exacerbate the normal process of integration.

The main *sources* of social exclusion – which Klasen (1998) lists as economic, social, birth or background, and societal/political – are closely related to the multiple risk factors that inhibit the healthy development of individuals in society; the *process* of social exclusion further leads to various forms of economic, social, and cultural disadvantage. If, as is believed by many social scientists and mental health practitioners, children who experience social exclusion pose a threat to society because they grow up with little stake in the existing social order, then the explanation lies in their being subjected to multiple risk factors.

Applying this view of social exclusion to the experience of immigrants in the City of Toronto, a report commissioned for social agencies and municipal governments documented considerable evidence. Ornstein (2000) carefully demonstrated through a detailed series of 1996 census tabulations the pervasive extent of social and economic disadvantage newcomers experienced. His data analysis indicates that a number of newly arrived ethnic groups suffer simultaneous obstacles in overlapping areas of completed formal education, individual and household income, lower occupational status, and greater periods of unemployment (122–33). Despite variations in the disadvantage profiles, from one group to another, there is sufficient overlap to infer that certain groups experience pervasive structural discrimination in the Toronto region (and more broadly in Canadian society). Moreover, these disadvantages, especially with respect to income, have widened to some extent since 1990.

A dynamic and multidimensional process, social exclusion encompasses economic, social, cultural, and political realms, touching on aspects of power and identity, as well as on the labour market. As a concept, social exclusion highlights the variety of ways in which people may be denied full participation in society and full effective rights of citizenship (Lister 2000, 38). It takes into account relations of power and the process of marginalization experienced by the excluded. In deploying this concept, the intersection of social class and sociocultural aspects of marginalization are brought to the forefront of the analysis.

Social exclusion is the opposite of social integration, which stresses the importance of being part of a society (Freiler 2000). In restricting the life chances of individuals and groups, social exclusion commonly leads to a process of marginalization, polarization, and social disintegration. This is perhaps most obvious in the case of children, where the decisions, choices, and opportunities will shape the social, economic, and civic position that children will later assume as adults (Klasen 1998). But the applicability to the case of newcomers is no less cogent. Decisions, choices, and opportunities available to newcomers will similarly project onto their life course as well as their children's.

In a recent critical examination of the concept of social exclusion, Sen (2000) stresses that its importance lies 'in emphasizing the role of relational features of deprivation of capability and thus in the experience of poverty' (6). Accordingly, Sen distinguishes between the 'constitutive relevance' of exclusion and the instrumental aspects of exclusion. Being excluded from participating in the activities of a community can itself be a form of deprivation and directly impoverish a person's life. As such, it is a loss on its own, in addition to whatever further deprivation this may indirectly generate. Sen refers to this scenario as a case of the constitutive relevance of social exclusion. But there may also be instrumental deprivations that result from causally significant exclusions. For example, not having access to credit markets is not automatically impoverishing, although it may lead to income poverty (13). Sen's distinction is useful in that it moves beyond a strict theoretical focus on the material dimensions of poverty and segregation to include non-material dimensions, such as cultural factors that shape relationships and choices both within community and larger society. In Sen's words, 'We must look at impoverished lives and not just at depleted wallets' (3).

Sen also makes a distinction between active and passive social exclusion, thereby accounting for intentional and non-intentional aspects of deprivation. He writes:

> When, for example, immigrants or refugees are not given a usable political status, it is an active exclusion, and this applies to many of the deprivations from which minority communities suffer in Europe and Asia and

elsewhere. When, however, the deprivation comes about through social processes in which there is no deliberate attempt to exclude, the exclusion can be seen as a passive kind. A good example is a sluggish economy and a consequent accentuation of poverty. Both active and passive exclusions may be important, but they are not important in the same way. (Sen 2000, 15)

In considering Sen's discussion, along with the works of Klasen, Ornstein, and the other writers discussed above, it becomes clear that the concept of social exclusion opens up promising ways to analyse the various challenges facing newcomers to Toronto.

In summary, Rodgers (1995) suggests that the value of social exclusion theory lies in its diagnostic powers. 'Social exclusion, then,' he writes, 'is seen as a way of analyzing how and why individuals and groups fail to have access to or benefit from the possibilities offered by societies and economies' (45). According to Rodgers, the 'pattern of exclusion' affects individuals or groups in six key areas, all of which will be considered in the essays contained in this volume:

1 Exclusion from goods and services, including material goods and services such as education and health care.
2 Labour market exclusions, including both unemployment and unstable, low-wage employment.
3 Exclusion from land, including unstable housing and homelessness.
4 Exclusion from security, including risk to physical safety.
5 Exclusion from human rights, including racist or discriminatory treatment; non-acceptance by the mainstream society and culture.
6 Exclusion from macroeconomic development strategy, referring to adverse impact of market-driven economic and political restructuring reducing public services and supports. (Rodgers, 44)

To this comprehensive list we add one more important type of exclusion:

7 Exclusion from (regaining) identity, including problems of mental health and loss of community.

The above concerns take us well beyond the consideration of ethnic particularities in the Toronto region, towards an examination of the processes of inclusion and exclusion in the context of a metropolis integrally linked to all parts of the contemporary world. Given the current trends of emergent pluralism and globalism, one would hope that negative characterizations of peoples in other lands would be in decline. However, utterances such as that of the mayor of Toronto are piercing reminders of the everyday relationship between discourses of exclusion and the invidious social arrangements that block the road to integrating diversity.

ORGANIZATION OF THIS BOOK

This volume is designed to provide an introductory overview of the key issues of resettlement and integration outlined above. Successive publications in this series will address specific questions and additional concerns in each domain area. The present study represents the first effort towards the portrayal of Toronto as a complex metropolis as we enter the new millennium. The research initiative is intended to extract the main lessons of the experiences of the Toronto region with respect to immigration and settlement and present them in a series of monographs that offer a multidisciplinary perspective on the dynamics of Toronto's civic culture. The researchers address the reciprocal impact of successive waves of immigration from diverse origins on the development of Toronto since 1970 and, correspondingly, the effects of the metropolis as a social form on the collective lives of those who have newly arrived, as well as on their descendants. Some of the major themes discussed in each domain are institutional transformation; peak moments for various immigrant groups; adaptation problems; segregation; institutional completeness; integration; interdependency; systematic discrimination; and future trends, challenges, and policy implications. In addition, the editors agreed that a photo essay would visually capture a few moments of the richness of Toronto's development as a diverse, multicultural metropolis. It provides yet another dimension in the complex appreciation of the city.

While this volume attempts to incorporate three decades of immigration into the composite, the authors can only speculate on ways in which future immigration and policy will alter social arrangements. We can only hypothesize about how increased population intake from a range of origins will affect each domain and only estimate the impact of larger developments in Canadian society, regional alignments, or globalization on the local organization of the Toronto region as Canada continues to widen its role in trade and other transnational activities.

New types of occupations may arise while others wither. Certain newcomers may find a niche, while others may see their jobs disappear because of structural changes or adjustments in society. It is important to note that only present conditions and the history of those conditions are available from which to make inferences regarding future directions. Though one hesitates to predict outcomes, the authors will assess possible scenarios of change. The clarity of these assessments depends on the adequacy of available research. While, in many areas, the chapters that follow leave no doubt about the extensiveness of our findings to date, others leave some questions unexplored or unanswered and await further contributions from researchers and members of the many diverse groups constituting the greater Toronto community.

The objective of this volume is to explore the settlement and integration of immigrants in Toronto within the social exclusion/ inclusion framework outlined in the previous section. *The World in a City* is organized under specified domain areas (i.e., economy, housing and neighbourhoods, education, health, and community) as established by the Joint Centre of Excellence for Research on Immigration and Settlement (CERIS). Research in each of these areas provides a provocative and insightful investigation of how immigration-intake affects structural arrangements within the metropolis and the effect of those arrangements on the lived experience of immigrants and their social networks. The first two chapters survey immigration and ethnic groups in the Toronto metropolis, in each successive chapter the discussion turns to ways in which the process of integrating diversity takes shape in a particular domain.

In chapter 1, Harold Troper provides a historical overview of immigration to Toronto since the Second World War, focusing on the manner in which immigrants have been envisioned as fitting into Canadian cities. One example of this is the widespread public support for Prime Minister Mackenzie King's national immigration policy that targeted only 'desirable future citizens' – code words for light-skinned Europeans. Changes to this policy occurred with the unfolding of the 1950s, when post-war prosperity in Western and Northern European countries slowed Canadian-bound immigration to trickle; only then did Canada begin accepting Italian immigrants and members of other groups previously deemed unworthy of citizenship. The 1960s brought the federal government's white paper on immigration, a document that called for removing racial criteria while simultaneously attempting to restrict regulations on family reunification. But by this time, Toronto was home to significant numbers of Jewish, Italian, and Eastern European immigrants, and their community leaders successfully mobilized against the regressive aspects of the policy document. Taking his historical analysis to the end of the century, Troper pays close attention to settlement and integration issues such as employment, housing, education, family, multiculturalism, and social services. While Troper's chapter emphasizes the Greater Toronto Area, it also makes comparisons to both Montreal and Winnipeg.

In chapter 2, Clifford Jansen and Lawrence Lam examine the same period, but focus their survey on the changing nature of immigrant settlement in the Toronto region through a sociodemographic analysis of those individuals and groups who chose to make the city their home. The authors demonstrate not only the expanding diversity of ethnic and cultural origins over some three decades but also the widening gaps in social equality – especially in the cases of more recently arrived newcomers from world regions who do not have a history of settlement in Canada or North America. Noting the different rates of unemployment among the twenty-one birthplace groups listed in the survey data, the authors ask, 'What cost in terms of social value and market value do groups have to pay for being "immigrants" who make Toronto their home, especially if they are from countries in Asia, the Middle East, and Africa?' While Jansen and Lam remain cautiously optimistic about Toronto's future, they show that, at present, discrepancies exist across a number of demographic and cultural categories, including country of birth, gender, marital status, and education.

Each of the following chapters profiles how the process of integrating diversity plays out in a particular sphere of social life. In chapter 3, Robert Murdie and Carlos Teixeira examine issues related to the residential patterns of immigrant groups and the success that these groups have had in gaining access to good quality, suitable, and affordable housing. The chapter includes a historical overview of the changing spatial patterns of immigrant settlement, thereby complementing Troper's review of the history of immigration in Toronto. Particular attention is given to the way in which many groups entering the city after 1970 have bypassed inner-city reception areas and have either opted for or been restricted to initial settlement in the suburbs.

The emphasis on choice and constraint underscores the diversity of immigrants who arrived in the city during this period, ranging from relatively affluent business immigrants to more impoverished refugees. These variations in settlement patterns have been influenced by changes at the global and national levels as well as at the local level, especially by shifts in Toronto's housing market. The much more restrictive opportunities in the rental market, particularly in the 1990s, mean that many lower-status immigrants and refugees have been excluded from appropriate housing and struggle to make advances in their housing careers. The authors conclude that without serious efforts by various levels of government towards expanding the supply of low-income housing, there is little possibility of improving the housing circumstances of Toronto's newest and most impoverished immigrant groups.

In chapter 4, Valerie Preston, Lucia Lo, and Shuguang Wang investigate the economic domain and provide an overview of the ethnocultural composition of Toronto, as well as the federal legislative and policy changes that resulted in increasing numbers of immigrants. The authors use both government-collected administrative and census data and independently collected information from the period 1971 to 1996. In analysing a number of pertinent issues, such as unemployment and poverty rates, the period of immigration, and socio-economic status, Preston, Lo, and Wang provide insight into the economic activities of immigrants and their effects on the Toronto economy. They highlight the experiences of various immigrant groups, some relatively successful and others still struggling The chapter begins by describing the make-up of Toronto's immigrant communities, differentiating them by immigration classes as well as by the usual categories of ethnic origin and time of arrival, and then goes on to examine immigrants' economic contributions through a tax-benefits analysis of the workers and the job-generating abilities of the entrepreneurs.

In examining recent data on jobs created in Toronto by Somali and Chinese immigrants, Preston, Lo, and Wang debunk the myth that immigrants 'take away' jobs from native-born Canadians. Subsequent sections of the chapter examine the industrial division of labour among immigrants, taking into account their entrepreneurial activities, earnings, unemployment, and poverty rates, and comparing them with those of the native-born population. The authors find that long-standing patterns of stratification are mirrored in employment data that show the high concentration of immigrant women in service industries and the overrepresentation of immigrant men in fields such as construction and transportation. Since there is a high concentration of new Torontonians of both genders in the manufacturing sector, one can see the relative vulnerability of certain groups in an environment marked by industrial restructuring, economic recession, and social exclusion. The authors' suggestions on policy realignment and future research should be considered within the context of these findings.

In chapter 5, Carl James and Barbara Burnaby explore ways in which immigrants and refugees have been inserted into the Toronto educational system, and the ways immigrants have inserted themselves in their efforts to become established in Canada. Subjects of particular importance in their account are English as a second language (ESL) courses, school and community relations, institutional adaptation, and the impact of racial and/or ethnic differences in educational attainment. The authors discuss, within a four-decade time frame, the educational participation, experiences, aspirations, and outcomes of immigrants and, where information allows, of refugees. Examining trends of educational outcomes for immigrant learners, particularly young immigrants, James and Burnaby draw a number of conclusions. They find that governments and institutions have changed considerably in favour of including the perspectives and participation of all stakeholders, especially those of immigrants and refugees themselves. Information is readily available about programs and policies from the policymakers' point of view, but is scarce in terms of how they affect participants, much less the general public. Research implications, then, are that more research must be done on the impact of programming. However, truly informative research of this sort is difficult and time-consuming. Linking cause and effect in these cases is challenging, indeed. Finally, such research must take into account the dynamic nature of immigration, immigrant groups, and the lives of immigrants themselves.

In chapter 6, Samuel Noh and Violet Kaspar review empirical findings of research into the relationship between immigration and health. They examine overall immigrant health and changes to immigrants' health status over time, using a comprehensive array of indices of both physical health (e.g., life expectancy, morbidity, disability) and mental health (e.g., depression, somatic symptoms, and general psychological distress). The overall conclusion is that immigrants arrive in good health, but lose their health advantage. And further, the second generation (Canadian-born children of immigrants) appears to have more health problems than their parents. The authors discuss how such declines in health are often attributed to acculturation – a claim that is based on the assumption that the second generation must be better acculturated to American and Canadian life than the first generation of immigrants, who most often arrive with a limited understanding of official languages and with limited occupational, professional, and cultural resources. However, Noh and Kaspar caution that there is a tautology in many studies of acculturation and health: the association between acculturation and cultural behaviours (e.g., smoking, alcohol consumption, sexual behaviours, diet, drug use) as health outcomes. Nonetheless, research to date on adult and youth health seems to imply that Canada (and Toronto) may not have been successful in accommodating the health needs of immigrants.

In chapter 7, Gabriele Scardellato provides the reader with a photographic essay designed to illustrate the growing diversity of the Greater Toronto Area, and to show the significant contributions that immigration has made to that diversity. Scardellato illustrates visually and in chronological order the history of immigration and shows how immigrant groups followed one another to Toronto – though rarely in linear progression. The other important criteria for the inclusion of photographs are their ability to address themes covered by other chapters in *The World in a City*, including immigrant enterprise, education, health, community life, and social exclusion. These photographs signal both continuity and change in the cultural features that characterize Toronto.

In chapter 8, Myer Siemiatycki, Tim Rees, Roxana Ng, and Khan Rahi examine the terms and conditions of immigrant community integration in Toronto. A variety of historical and latter-day factors contributing to 'differential incorporation' and social exclusion are discussed: the pattern of twentieth-century migration to Toronto, the current socio-economic status of newcomers to Toronto, manifestations of immigrant community civic mobilization, and local government responses to immigrant diversity. The chapter begins by exploring the settlement experiences of four immigrant communities (Jews, Italians, Caribbeans, and Chinese) whose large-scale arrival sequentially challenged the prevailing definitions of who qualified as a Torontonian. As the authors demonstrate, marginalization and exclusion proved to be recurring experiences for each community of newcomers. A socio-economic analysis of contemporary Toronto reveals that stark differentiation and polarization between European and non-European residents have not disappeared. But immigrant communities in Toronto have not passively acquiesced to their accorded place in Toronto society. Rather, a discussion of mobilization in four immigrant communities –

anti-racism campaigns, immigrant women's organizing, access and equity efforts, and political representation campaigns – illustrates the civic determination and activism of many newcomers. Finally, after analysing problems in the responses of municipal government to immigrant diversity, the authors conclude that unfinished business remains before Toronto fulfils its claim to modelling inclusive, immigrant integration.

In chapter 9, Meyer Burstein and Howard Duncan draw on the observations and conclusions of authors in the preceding chapters to point to avenues in the formulation of research and policy. Burstein and Duncan begin by noting the difficulties that accompany terms like 'integration,' which is nevertheless preferable to the now-discredited 'assimilation.' Moving into the discussion of policy, the authors suggest that governments can help the integration process in a number of ways: by encouraging positive social values through laws, community policies, public debates, and educational systems; by creating expectations that refugees and immigrants will be supported by individuals and institutions, including neighbourhoods, social services, and the workplace; by fostering a social climate in Canada and abroad that encourages immigrants and refugees to accept Canadian citizenship; and by supporting housing and settlement services, language training, and other programs of assistance. These policy recommendations affect not only local government but also extend to provincial and federal jurisdictions. The chapter then discusses when, if at all, governments should intervene in the process of integrating diversity. The authors then go on to summarize research findings, such as the need to pay more attention to certain subpopulations at risk and the importance of adapting policy and understanding to fit the changing settlement and clustering patterns of newcomers to Toronto. Some conclusions may suggest that greater attention be paid to specific areas, such as the renewal of low-cost housing especially for newcomers, while other findings may converge into a more general issue, such as the need to strengthen anti-racist principles and practices in civil society.

In their conclusion, the editors offer a brief summary and synthesis of the chapters in this volume, paying particular attention to the variety of interpretations that researchers and federal policy analysts have for findings concerning the unequal distribution of resources, goods, and services to newcomers in the Toronto area. The authors suggest that the metropolis does not provide a level 'playing field' for newly arrived immigrants and, consequently, the state's concern with equality of opportunity over equality of outcome is misplaced; the findings reported in this volume repeatedly demonstrate that there are definite blockages in opportunity through low resource bases and inadequate service deliveries.

1 Becoming an Immigrant City: A History of Immigration into Toronto since the Second World War

Harold Troper

In 1999, a Canadian immigration museum was inaugurated at Pier 21 in Halifax. It stands as a testament to the historic contribution of immigrants to Canadian society. The site is well-chosen: in just over forty years – from 1928 to 1971 – tens of thousands of European immigrants arriving by ship first set foot on Canadian soil at Pier 21. Unsure of exactly what awaited them in their land of second chance, the new arrivals were processed by immigration authorities and left Pier 21 to begin new lives in Canada.

If this museum honours Canada's immigration past, it also shows how much immigration has changed since the processing facilities at Pier 21 were finally closed in 1971. Halifax's Pier 21 looks eastward, out over the Atlantic towards Europe. In 1971, the number of immigrants entering Canada from Europe dipped below 50 per cent; since then, that percentage has continued to fall. What is more, Pier 21 was designed to process immigrants arriving by ship. Today, the vast majority of immigrants arrive by air and relatively few land in Halifax. The single most important port of immigrant entry into Canada is Toronto's Pearson International Airport. And not only do immigrants land in Toronto: unlike the vast majority of those who once arrived in Halifax, many stay there. Toronto is not only an immigration port of entry, it is also an immigration destination. It has become home to more than one-third of all immigrants arriving in Canada.

For Toronto, now Canada's largest city, so large an infusion of immigrants raises understandably important issues about settlement services, urban planning, the place of immigration in shaping the city's culture, economy, and institutions, and about how best to accommodate and integrate immigrants from many different origins while avoiding the scourge of racism. Even as the city and its surrounding suburban ring continue to wrestle with these issues, there can be no doubt that immigration is reshaping the city's self-perception. Indeed, the city's boosters like to point out that the United Nations has proclaimed Toronto the most multicultural city in the world (J. Berridge 1995). No small accolade, this point of municipal pride is said to set Toronto apart from its North American sister cities. But despite all the backslapping hullabaloo, there is no United Nations proclamation. It is an urban myth. Nonetheless, Torontonians, working by the dictum that some events are so real it doesn't matter that they never happened, have willed the myth into a functioning reality.

By any measure, Toronto is indisputably a multicultural city. If we could take an aerial photo of the Greater Toronto Area at the millennium, we would be looking at a sprawling urban complex of approximately four million people. According to the 1996 Canadian census, just over 17 per cent of all Canadians were born outside Canada, but more than 40 per cent of those in Toronto were born outside Canada. Indeed, almost three-quarters of all heads of households in Toronto were either born outside Canada or had at least one parent who was. That inflow of immigration has come from every corner of the globe. Once a parochial Protestant town – the Ulster of the North – where the Sunday blue laws, Draconian liquor legislation, and the Orange Order held sway, Toronto now trades on its cultural diversity as a draw for tourists. More than one hundred different languages are commonly spoken in this city, and many children born in Toronto enter public schools each year not able to speak English well enough to avoid remedial English classes. Included in the Greater Toronto Area multiethnic mix are an estimated 450,000 Chinese, 400,000 Italians, and 250,000 African Canadians, the largest component of which are of Caribbean background, although a separate and distinct infusion of Somalis, Ethiopians, and other Africans is currently taking place. There are almost 200,000 Jews, and large and growing populations from the Indian subcontinent, Greece, Portugal, Poland, Vietnam, Hispanic America, and Central and Eastern Europe, to name but a few.

The Protestant majority is long gone. As a result of immigration, Toronto now has a Catholic plurality and there are more Muslims in the city than Presbyterians. Nor is the city the almost exclusively white enclave it was only a generation ago. As the city ushered in the millennium, a major proportion – and likely soon to be the majority – of those living in this urban complex are people of colour. The simple fact is that Toronto remains a magnet for immigration. With the federal government promising to keep annual immigration into Canada at or near 1 per cent of the total population, more than triple the per capita American immigration level, both the number and diversity of this immigration show no sign of lessening. Compared with tomorrow, the Toronto of today may be recalled as a city of relative cultural homogeneity (Siemiatycki and Isin 1997).

Although Toronto is Canada's leading immigrant-receiving centre, city officials have neither a hands-on role in immigrant selection nor an official voice in deciding immigration policy. In Canada, immigration policy and administration is a constitutional responsibility of the federal government, worked out in consultation with the provinces. Cities, as creatures of the provinces, are officially kept at arm's-length from immigration policy discussions. Yet, if Toronto does not have an official role in determining immigration policy, immigration policy determines much about Toronto. As the city continues to be the destination of choice for so many immigrants, immigration has become a singular force shaping and reshaping its streetscape, residential housing construction patterns, economy, neighbourhood continuity, and delivery of municipal services, including education and health care.

In order to fully appreciate the impact of immigration on Toronto, it is important to understand the history of federal immigration policy and how that policy has affected the city. It is also important to understand that immigration was often a controversial area of public policy. Advocates and opponents repeatedly tussled over immigration policy, and immigrants and would-be immigrants have not sat passively like pawns on some policy chessboard waiting to be moved here and there. They have been actors on their own behalf, working to further agendas shaped by their own needs and expectations. How the often separate interests of the state, immigration activists, and immigrants play off one another is also part of the Toronto immigration story, a story deeply rooted in the past.

THE PRE–SECOND WORLD WAR IMMIGRANT PAST

Toronto was not always one of the world's major immigrant-receiving centres. During the late nineteenth century and through to almost the mid-twentieth century, Toronto was a major and bustling business and commercial centre, but it was also a city deeply respectful of British Protestant ascendancy, values, and traditions. While there was a considerable Roman Catholic minority, municipal political, economic, and social levers were firmly in the hands of an Anglo-Protestant élite. Their vision afforded little or no room for urban-bound immigrants, particularly those who did not speak English.

That is not to say that Toronto and other major Canadian cities of the day – Montreal, Winnipeg, and Vancouver – did not each have significant enclaves of 'foreigners,' as they were commonly labelled. On the contrary. In the years before the Second World War each city had its foreign neighbourhoods. Best known are The Main in Montreal, Vancouver's Chinatown, Winnipeg's now-legendary North End, and the Kensington Market area of Toronto. Each of these immigrant settlement areas had its own particular tone and texture, even its own neighbourhood identity, institutions, and sense of how it fit into the larger urban social and economic complex. But each of these different immigrant neighbourhoods was also regarded by many in the mainstream as an area apart from the city, in the city but not really an organic part of its urban core. Many mainstream Torontonians hoped their city would be no more than a stopover for foreigners who would quickly move on to rural Canada or the United States. But if these foreigners insisted on staying in Toronto, it was assumed that they would know their place. In effect, this meant they would remain in the social and economic shadows, relegated to a corner of the larger urban landscape reserved for the immigrant underbelly of the urban labour force, doing jobs that 'real' Canadians preferred not to do.

Thus, while there were immigrants in pre–Second World War Toronto, Toronto was not a city of immigrants in the way that urban geographers and historians might talk about American cities like New York, Chicago, Pittsburgh, St Louis, New Orleans, Galveston, or Los Angeles. Going back to well before the turn of the century, as the American agricultural frontier was being aggressively depleted of new agricultural land and the burgeoning urban-based industrial sector demonstrated an almost insatiable appetite for cheap labour, Americans came to regard cities, especially in the industrial northeast, as contact points between immigrant workers and domestic capital. Cities were places where unskilled and semi-skilled immigrants stoked the furnaces of American growth in the decades following the Civil War.

From Confederation through to the turn of the century and beyond, no Canadian city, except perhaps Montreal, could claim the same urban status as New York or Chicago. For the most part, Canadian cities – with notable exceptions like Hamilton, Ontario, and Sydney, Nova Scotia – were less industrial hubs than they were regional administrative and commercial centres feeding off an agricultural or extractive industrial hinterland. In Toronto, few could envision any good coming out of immigrants piling up in their city, especially those of a non-Anglo-Saxon lineage. It is true that immigration officials at the national level actively sought out immigrants, but Canadian immigration policy of the day deliberately and systematically sought to stream non-British and non-American immigrants away from cities into non-urban and labour-intensive industries like railway construction, mining, lumbering, and, most particularly, farming. Indeed, until well after the First World War, farming and the wealth it generated were regarded as not just the bedrock of Canadian economic and social development, but the very raison d'être for encouraging large-scale immigration – the immigration of agriculturalists (Gates 1934).

Farming was hardly an easy life. The unforgiving Canadian climate, unstable markets for farm produce, and marginal lands unyielding to the plough too often drained immigrant muscle, resources, and hopes. As a result, in spite of hard work, it was not unusual for farm incomes to fall far short of that necessary to sustain a family on the land. Conditions were often so difficult that in the years before the turn of the century, tens of thousands of immigrant farmers and Canadian-born agriculturalists alike, unable to find alternative employment, turned their backs on Canada and took refuge in factory jobs or sought out more congenial lands in the United States. So pronounced was the outflow of population to the United States that one wag claimed Canada's story was foretold in the books of the Bible: 'It begins in *Lamentations* and ends in *Exodus*' (Hamilton 1952, 69; Hansen and Brebner 1940).

This changed with the turn of the century. The completion of the first Canadian transcontinental railway, built with borrowed capital and cheap imported labour, opened the vast Canadian prairie to expansive agricultural settlement. The time was right. A seemingly unquenchable European market for Canadian raw materials and agricultural products, especially grains, coincided with a major population upheaval in Central, Southern, and Eastern Europe that cut millions of people loose to seek homes in the New World. The result was unprecedented Canadian economic expansion propped up by a huge wave of immigration that the government streamed into labour-intensive extractive industries like mining and lumbering and, most of all, into settling the vast expanse of agricultural lands in Western Canada. Wheat was king and, from the government's point of view, immigration afforded an opportunity not to be missed – an opportunity to further economic and population growth by settling farmers without land in a land without farmers.

The name most associated with this peak period of Canadian immigration is Clifford Sifton, Canada's forceful minister of the interior. Working in collusion with industry and railway interests, Sifton revitalized Canada's immigration recruitment program. The priority continued to be fixed on aggressively promoting the immigration of farmers and farm families. But, initially, this was not the only criterion for preferred admission. Unabashedly colonial, the government defined those from outside the British Isles as foreign and, unabashedly North American, it excluded white, English-speaking American immigrants from this foreign category. In their source-country preference, Sifton and the Canadian government were no more racist in their thinking than the culture of their times. Nonetheless, Canadian immigration policy remained as racially selective as it was economically self-serving.

With an insatiable demand for agricultural labour as well as for workers for expanding industrial sectors, and confounded by a shortfall in the number of settlers of the 'preferred types,' Sifton and his immigration authorities were forced to set aside their racial concerns, at least as far as Euro-ethnics were concerned. In their active search for more and more agricultural and bush workers, Sifton reluctantly agreed to admit other European agricultural settlers in a descending order of ethnic or racial preference. At the top remained British and white American agriculturalists, followed closely by Northern and Western Europeans. Then came Eastern Europeans – the fabled peasants in sheepskin coats. Closer to the bottom of the list came those who, in the minds of both the public and the government, were less assimilable and less desirable; these were made up largely of Southern Europeans. Slotted in at the very bottom were Asians, Blacks, and Eastern European Jews who showed little inclination for farming. At first, the government was unsure how to deflect urban-oriented Eastern European Jews from Canadian shores while beating the bushes for other Eastern Europeans. That would take time to work out. But it was clear what to do about Asians and Blacks. Laws were passed and immigration regulations strictly enforced that tightly controlled Asian immigration and effectively barred Blacks from Canada (Munro 1971; Troper 1972, 1987).

Government programs encouraging agricultural immigration worked. Between the turn of the century and the First World War, Western Canada soaked up immigrants. While immigration into Canada never reached the absolute numbers into the United States, the ratio of foreign-born to Canadian-born population was far higher. These non-English- or non-French-speaking settlers, most arriving in family units, gradually filled the geo-economic niches reserved for them in prairie agriculture or wage labour on the rugged mining and lumbering frontier. They fuelled Canadian economic expansion; they also raised social anxiety. For many English-speaking Canadians, the continuing influx of strange peoples speaking strange languages – people until recently loyal to foreign kings, czars, and kaisers, who prayed to alien gods and seemed so distant and indifferent to Canadian values – generated fears that these foreigners might never be assimilated into Canadian society. They would always be the strangers in our midst.

French-Canadian leaders had a different and almost diametrically opposite fear. They feared that these foreigners would indeed assimilate and assimilate into English-speaking society. In so doing, they would tip the national political and demographic balance even further in favour of *les anglais*. But many English- and French-Canadian leaders at least agreed on one thing: Immigration was a boon to the economy and, in balancing economic benefits against social costs, they agreed that so long as these foreigners were content to remain in the rural hinterland, so long as they continued to play the subservient economic and social role reserved for them, then immigration should continue.

Not all immigrants were content to play this game. To the unease of many mainstream Canadians, the number of foreigners leeching out of rural areas into waiting jobs in Canadian cities, including Toronto, increased. As immigrant numbers in Toronto increased so did anti-immigrant sentiment. But why were there immigrants working in Toronto at all? Wasn't there an unspoken agreement between immigration boosters and the urban polity that the foreigners would stay put in rural Canada? Yes. But, the prosperity that opened Canada's western agricultural, mining, and lumbering frontier and attracted so many immigrants to Canada in the first place also spurred industrial development and an enlarged job market in cities like Toronto. Immigration policy might still trumpet agricultural settlement as a national priority, but it was not long before new immigrants were joined by older immigrants or their Canadian-born children in abandoning the isolation of the bush or escaping the vagaries and insecurities of life on the land in favour of wage labour in cities. Immigrants rebounded into Toronto, where the men found jobs in the expanding urban economy – paving streets, laying trolley tracks, labouring in the expanding textile factories, and tunnelling the sewer systems – while women worked as household domestics, took in boarders, or performed various kinds of piecework.[1]

Regardless of how willingly immigrants – men and women – filled waiting jobs in Toronto and other Canadian cities, by the early 1920s there was a growing urban mind-set that regarded the 'foreigners' in the city as an intrusive threat. Many Toronto gatekeepers charged that immigration was hastening the onset of municipal blight, political corruption, and miscegenationist race suicide that they associated with cities south of the border. The signs seemed to be there. Weren't these foreigners starting to cram into Toronto slums in seeming defiance of Canadian immigration policy? And didn't these foreigners, largely Catholics and Jews, cleave to their Old-World ways and to one another, showing precious little inclination to assimilate? It might be one thing if foreigners were content to spend their lives in sweat labour; it was another to find some of them starting to successfully compete with skilled native-born artisans and small businessmen. And what about the children of immigrants? With legislation requiring universal and compulsory school attendance, they were present in classrooms and the brightest among them were demanding access to universities, to professions, and to the political arena. No. If these foreigners did not know their place – and their place certainly wasn't Toronto – they should be denied admission to Canada.

As xenophobia in Toronto and other cities inched upward, the federal government could not ignore demands for cuts to immigration. By the mid-1920s, Canadian immigration laws and regulations were revised so as to restrict immigrant entry into Canada along racial and ethnic lines. Rules against Asian admission were already tight; now the admission of Eastern Europeans was made much more difficult and the immigration door was pushed shut on Southern Europeans and all Jews, irrespective of country of origin, except those few who might come to Canada from the United Kingdom or the United States (Troper 1982).

Following the economic collapse of 1929, with mass unemployment in urban Canada and a withering away of farm income, any residual appreciation for immigrants evaporated. The door was sealed. Immigration officials who had once competed with other countries for immigrants now stood vigil against any breach in the Canadian wall of restriction (Abella and Troper 1982).

POST-WAR IMMIGRATION POLICY

The Second World War and its aftermath are a critical watershed in the history of Canadian immigration and of immigration into Toronto. While many policy planners initially feared that the end of the war would throw Canada back into the job-hungry Depression of the 1930s, the exact opposite took place. A surprisingly smooth transition from wartime to peacetime production found a new urban industrial base – the product of massive wartime industrial investment – retooling to satisfy pent up consumer demand for goods and services that had been denied to Canadians as far back as the beginning of the Depression. In addition, a huge export market quickly opened up as Western Europe began its massive post-war reconstruction. Rather than a shortage of jobs, within a year or so after the war's end, Canada faced a surging demand for labour. Labour-intensive industry, much of it in and around cities like Toronto, demanded that Canada's doors to immigration be reopened.

In truth, however, when immigration was first reopened, the government sought to hold the line against the wholesale entry of non-British or non-Western Europeans. Prime Minister Mackenzie King was only reflecting the national mood when he observed that 'the people of Canada do not wish to make a fundamental alteration in the character of their population through mass immigration.' Discrimination and ethnic selectivity in immigration would remain. 'Canada is perfectly within her rights in selecting the persons whom we regard as desirable future citizens. It is not a "fundamental human right" of any alien to enter Canada. It is a privilege. It is a matter of domestic policy' (House of Commons, Debates, 1 May 1947: 2644–7). Nor was Ottawa congenial to the notion of renewed immigration by people who were regarded to be least likely to fit in. Immigration officials – who still understood their duty to be to guard the Canadian gate against all comers – were particularly unsympathetic to any liberalization of guidelines when it came to allowing in the groups against whom immigration barriers had been carefully erected in the first place: Asians, and Southern and Eastern Europeans. The officials, who could not see beyond their own hierarchy of ethnic preferences, asked what would be gained by filling a short-term labour gap if it meant a permanent infusion of Jews and Slavs – those who stood first in Europe's exit line (Abella and Troper 1982; Luciuk 1984).

The public seemed to agree. Just over a year after the guns fell quiet in Europe, a public opinion poll found that Canadians would rather see recently defeated Germans allowed into Canada than Eastern and Southern Europeans, and, in particular, Jews. Only the Japanese fared worse. Thus, even a grudging willingness to reopen immigration in late 1947 was very much predicated on holding to the ethnically and racially based immigration priorities of the 1920s (Canadian Institute of Public Opinion, 1946).

British, American, and Northern European, particularly Dutch, immigrants, were actively courted. Legislated bars against Asians remained in place and administrative tinkering assured that Southern and Eastern Europeans, especially Jews, would find it difficult to get into Canada. The government of Ontario was so concerned that it receive only the 'right' type of immigrant that it flexed its jurisdictional muscle in immigration matters and inaugurated a highly publicized airlift of British families into the province. When British currency regulations threatened to choke off the flow of applicants, special transportation tariffs were negotiated to stimulate the inflow (Richmond 1967). When currency regulations similarly hobbled the immigration of other desirable Western European groups, especially the Dutch, the federal government intervened. In 1948, a three-year bilateral agreement was signed with the Netherlands to ensure the smooth transplanting of approximately 15,000 Dutch farmers and farm workers – family units – to Canada, many of them taking up farming immediately to the north of Toronto (Peterson 1955).

If labour-intensive and increasingly urban-based industry was generally pleased by the government's building commitment to immigration, it was less pleased with restrictions against importing cheap labour from outside the government's narrow ethnic circle of acceptability. Pleading that it must have access to a continuing supply of imported labour willing to assume low-wage and low-status positions rejected by both the preferred immigrants and native-born Canadians, business warned that the economic boom was in jeopardy. They pressed Ottawa to skim off the cream of the almost one-million-strong labour pool languishing in the displaced person (DP) camps in Germany, Austria, and Italy before other labour-short nations – including the United

States and Australia – beat Canada to the punch. Largely as a result of this pressure, the federal government gradually began to sift through DP camps for acceptable settlers, while carefully monitoring the public mood at home for any negative reaction to their arrival (Abella and Troper 1982; Momryk 1992).

Most of the displaced persons were former citizens of Eastern European states who refused repatriation to countries of origin now dominated by the Soviet Union. Others were Jews, a tattered remnant of Europe's pre-war Jewish community who had somehow survived the Holocaust. Hoping to rebuild lives shattered by the war, many men and some women accepted Canada's calculated kindness and accepted work in assigned industrial, service sector, or domestic jobs as the price of admission to Canada. And one should not confuse Canada's intake of displaced Europeans with the United Way; this was not a humanitarian effort. It was a labour-importation scheme, plain and simple. There can be little doubt that, if there were no Canadian labour shortages, few DPs would have been admitted to Canada and, certainly, few Jews or other Eastern Europeans. As they sorted through the existing and available European labour pool, immigration officials gave preference whenever possible to refugees from the Baltic republics, highly prized as hard working 'Nordic types.' Only as jobs remained unfilled did the Canadian government cautiously agree to lift barriers against Jewish and Slavic settlers (Abella and Troper 1982).

Along with racial and ethnic reservations about reopening immigration, the government had another domestic reason for a its go-slow approach. Through the 1950s, government immigration and policy planners expected the economic bubble to burst and the demand for labour to subside. Again they were wrong. What is more, while demand for labour remained high, especially in and around booming centres like Toronto, Canada was not the only immigration game in town. Labour shortages in the United States, Australia, and elsewhere forced Canadian officials to continually scramble for their share of a shrinking labour pool. It was not long before candidates who might previously have been rejected as undesirable became valued prospects. In the face of the continuing demands of a robust economy, remaining barriers to Jews and Slavic immigrants slipped away, especially for the families of those already in Canada and for immigrants with skills demanded by labour-starved Canadian industries (Abella and Troper 1982; Luciuk 1984; Aun 1985; Danys 1986).

By the time the DP admission program ended, tens of thousands of new immigrants had resettled in Canada – many in Toronto, home to more displaced persons per capita than any other Canadian city – and aggressive immigration recruitment in Europe remained the order of the day. The old backwater of Ottawa bureaucracy, the Immigration Branch of the Department of Mines and Resources, was revitalized and, reflecting its new profile, was upgraded in 1950 as the new Department of Citizenship and Immigration. Old-school restrictionist immigration officers were also replaced with a new breed of pro-immigration personnel. Canada was finally back in the immigration importation business, and Toronto became a major immigration destination.

AN URBAN-FRIENDLY IMMIGRATION POLICY

As part of its revamped activist mandate, the new immigration bureaucracy set about preparing a new immigration law. The existing legislation had been enacted before the First World War and, with its emphasis on agricultural settlement, it was a stretch to make the new industrial and urban labour recruitment priorities fit within its parameters. Recognizing this, in 1952, the government passed a new immigration act designed to attract a continuing stream of industrial and urban-bound immigrants without casting an ethnic or racial immigration net beyond Europe's borders. The subtext of the 1952 legislation might have been drawn from Mackenzie King's previous caution against immigration undermining the social structure of Canadian society. Affirming what had long been Canadian immigration policy, the 1952 act allowed the minister of immigration and his officials sweeping powers to set such regulations as they felt necessary to enforce the act. At the discretion of the minister, individuals or groups could be rejected because of nationality, geographic origin, peculiarity of custom, unsuitability to the climate, or because of an omnibus provision that allowed for the rejection of any individual or group who demonstrated an inability 'to become assimilated.' In effect, this meant a continuation of some sort of hierarchy of preference among European-origin applicants and an almost total ban on non-white applicants, especially Asians (Hawkins 1972).

Furthermore, in keeping with the deepening Cold War climate of the day, security checks were required of would-be immigrants. Security personnel, working under the umbrella of the RCMP, functioned as something of a separate estate; a cone of secrecy was drawn over their activities and procedures. Canada's Cold War gatekeepers focused on the Communist threat. But many non-Communists and even anti-Communists on the left – trade unionists, socialists, social democrats – were also denied entry. Individuals barred from Canada on security grounds had few avenues of appeal and often were not even told the true cause of their rejection. Unfortunately, while standing guard against Communists, Canada allowed or abetted the entry of others whose Second World War records should have set off alarms in Ottawa. Most were not even questioned about Nazi skeletons in their closets. But even if there had been reason to suspect individuals of having a Nazi past or pro-Nazi sympathies, in the eyes of Canadian security authorities, they had the virtue of being proven anti-Communists (Whitaker 1987; also Commission of Inquiry on War Criminals 1986; Matas and Charendoff 1987; Troper and Weinfeld 1989).

At least there was positive change in one area. Through the 1950s, concern for ethnically biased selectivity gradually receded, at least as far as Euro-ethnics were concerned. One might see this racial leavening as the 'whiting' of Euro-ethnics, spurred on by a repudiation of eugenically based notions of racial boundaries and by public revulsion at the excesses of Nazi racism. Perhaps. More likely it was triggered by a combination of the continuing heavy demand for labour and the surprising level of comfort Canadians, particularly in cities, seemed to have with the new immigration. As long as the economy remained buoyant and immigrants were regarded as essential to keep the economy moving forward, immigration was tolerated, if not welcomed.

The wall of restriction against people of colour started to show a first tiny crack. Former British colonial holdings were achieving independence in a reconfigured British Commonwealth and, in 1951, hoping to gain an economic toe-hold in the developing world, Canada set aside a small but symbolically important immigrant quota for its non-white Commonwealth partners, India, Pakistan, and Ceylon. If the actual numbers admitted to Canada were small, the symbolism of the government-sanctioned admission of even a small group of non-white immigrants should not be minimized (Hawkins 1972).

The question now for government was whether the economy would be able to sustain still more immigration. To the surprise of many economists and immigration officials who had warned that the Canadian economy would cool and unemployment increase through the 1950s and into the early 1960s, the Canadian economy generally remained strong, as did the labour market. Jobs in Toronto's labour-intensive industries were going begging and there was a particular pressing need for immigrant workers to service a massive boom in residential housing construction and in the expanding urban infrastructure. Where would the necessary immigrant labour force come from? There weren't that many options. As prosperity gradually returned to Northern and Western Europe in the late 1950s and early 1960s, the pool of applicants from those areas gradually dried up. The DP camps had been emptied of all but the hard-core cases – displaced persons who were physically or mentally disabled or infirm. The lowering of the Iron Curtain locked Europeans in the Eastern bloc in place and no one in government could conceive of recruiting immigrants from the non-white world.

With business interests cautioning that continued prosperity was at stake and pressing for more and more labour, immigration officials had little choice but to expand their focus to include Europe's southern rim. Labour-intensive industries such as the construction trades were particularly interested in Italy and other Mediterranean countries, where population increase and land dislocation sapped the absorptive capacity of war-ravaged local economies. The result was an unskilled, rural labour pool that could easily be redirected to waiting employment in Canada. After some hesitation, the government agreed. Restrictions against the admission of Italians, recently barred as former enemy aliens, were lifted and, with security personnel on guard against Communist infiltration, immigration offices were opened in Italy.

Ottawa may have hoped at first to attract the more 'Germanic' northern Italians, but, almost immediately, southern Italians dominated the immigrant flow. By the mid-1960s Italian immigration climbed into the hundreds of thousands (Iacovetta 1992). In the industrial heartland of Southern Ontario and in urban Canada more generally, Italian labourers, many of them former agricultural workers from the rural farm villages that dotted central and southern Italy, soon became a mainstay of the thriving construction industry, much as Slavic immigrants had been in breaking the prairie sod and Jews had been in the needle trades.

So extensive was the influx of Italian immigrants that, in the decade of the 1950s, Canada's Italian-origin population grew threefold – from approximately 150,000 to 450,000. Toronto received the lion's share of these new arrivals. Indeed, almost half of all Canadians of Italian origin soon lived in Toronto and, unlike the pre-war Italian migration, there were comparatively fewer sojourners among them. The post-war Italian immigration was largely made up of permanent settlers arriving in family units or, if the male head of household was the first to migrate, of men who made reunification with family a first priority (Iacovetta 1992).

Unschooled in large city ways, most Italian immigrants to Toronto located in residential working-class pockets along major public transportation arteries and took up lower-status manual – but often unionized – labouring jobs in construction and related industrial sectors. For many immigrants from Italy, residential property acquisition and organizing chain migration to ensure reunification with kin were their twin priorities. Home ownership and a widening circle of kin also served to prop up the integrative process. Family often took in family and together the extended family formed a social and economic unit, pooling capital and resources, networking together for jobs, caring for one another's children, sharing information, and serving as a secure base for personal interaction and emotional strength. As the numbers of Italians in Toronto increased, so did their institutional presence. Italian grocery stores, cafés, food wholesalers, and newspaper publishers, along with Italian parishes and social clubs, gave Italian neighbourhoods a distinctive flavour and streetscape, and even a distinctively ethnic subeconomy.

Other immigrant groups followed suit. As Italian immigration continued, Greeks, Portuguese, and the peoples of the Balkan peninsula began arriving in Toronto in large numbers. Each group was unique in its historical self-definition, cultural traditions, institutional organization, and economic priorities; at the same time, each adopted many of the same family-based economic and social integrative strategies so characteristic of post-war Italian immigrants (Iacovetta 1992; Harney 1998).

THE NEW PLURALISM

Immigrant resourcefulness and integrative patterns were hardly noticed by federal government officials. Their priorities were elsewhere. With bureaucratic tunnel vision, many persisted in regarding immigration as little more than the importation of labour to capital, workers to jobs. The impact of this immigration on the Toronto urban landscape and mind-set, however, was far more than economic; post-war immigrants gradually reshaped urban life and attitudes. Whether they were Southern or Eastern Europeans, these immigrants altered the city's religious balance, gradually undermining the long-standing Protestant hegemony while invigorating existing Roman Catholic, Orthodox, and Jewish communities in Toronto. They also brought with them a richness of cultural forms and a diversity of social expression that Toronto had never seen before.

At first, Toronto wore this new cosmopolitanism like a new and somewhat uncomfortable pair of shoes. Mainstream Torontonians understood that immigration played into the city's growth, but they still felt a little pinched and thrown a little off balance by the changes that immigration was bringing to the world around them. They felt the city they had known beginning to slip away and some were cautious about stepping into an ethnically pluralist future. Old ways died hard. Difficult as it is to believe in retrospect, in the late 1950s, Toronto police descended on picnicking Italian immigrants for having a glass of wine in a public park, let alone for allowing their children take a sip. Municipal health authorities were suspicious of new European-style cafés that violated city ordinances by serving food at sidewalk tables. And what could they make of the smells and tastes of foods so alien to the fare that most Torontonians were used to? Even espresso coffee, new to Toronto, smacked a little too much of the exotic – maybe even of the subversive.

And when would these foreigners learn to be like us? It was not uncommon for immigrants speaking their mother tongue in the street or on public transit to be made to feel out of place and told to 'Speak white!' School teachers and administrators, thinking they were liberating immigrant children from narrow Old-World parochialism or protecting them from the schoolyard bully, took liberties with many an immigrant child's most personal possession – his or her name. Gabriella became Gail, Luigi became Louis, Olga became Alice, and Hershel became Harold. All the while, some members of the press and some local politicians warned against the evils of immigrant overcrowding, ghettoization, and crime. But not all. Slowly at first, Torontonians became more and more comfortable with the new foods, the polyphony of languages, and the new neighbourhoods that immigrants brought in their wake. And for some, comfort gradually turned to pride in Toronto's new-found sophistication and cosmopolitan image.

And what became of the bedrock of vitriolic and politically acidic xenophobia that so dominated Canadian and Toronto thinking only a few years earlier? What of that mainstream certitude that, almost as a sacred trust, Toronto must stand guard over British values in North

America? How was it that in less than one generation Toronto's public face shifted from the defence of Anglo-conformity to a celebration of the mosaic? Put simply, by the late 1960s, the past was cut loose, made dysfunctional both by the onslaught of city-bound immigration and the mediating force of governments awakened to the fact that political power was increasingly in the hands of a new and pluralist urban electorate that was made up more and more of immigrants and their children. If it would take time for its importance to soak in, the election of Nathan Phillips – a Jew and a child of immigrants – as the first mayor of the 1960s Toronto was a telling barometer of the effect that immigration was having on the municipal polity; it represented something of a civic revolution of the mind.

The revolution was of many parts, but had its genesis in the late 1940s with the redefining of community through the introduction of a distinct and separate Canadian citizenship. Until 1947 there was no such thing as Canadian citizenship; people living in Canada were legally designated British subjects who were residents of Canada, not Canadians. Pressure for change began in the post-war period and the name most associated with that change was Paul Martin, a Liberal backbencher who was appointed secretary of state towards the end of the war. In his autobiography, he claimed to have previously flirted with the notion of a distinct Canadian citizenship, but his total conversion to the necessity of separate citizenship came during an official visit to recently liberated Europe in 1945. In France he visited the Canadian military cemetery at Dieppe where, walking amid the rows of graves, some still fresh with wooden markers, he reported being deeply moved by the incredible diversity of names found among the Canadian fallen – names which spoke to the pluralism of origins that even then made up Canadian society. Martin later wrote, 'Of whatever origin, these men were Canadians.' They had fought and died for Canada; they deserved to be remembered as Canadians. In their memory, Martin claimed, he championed the creation of a Canadian citizenship (Martin 1983, 437).

Without negating Martin's contribution, it has to be acknowledged that other factors prodded the government towards instituting a separate Canadian citizenship. Certainly, there was desire to build on pride at Canada's major contribution to the Allied war effort – distinct from that of Britain's – but there was also a desire by Ottawa to carve out an independent place for Canada in the post-war United Nations and in the family of nations. An independent Canadian voice would be well-served by having a separate Canadian citizenship. On the domestic level, it was hoped that Canadian citizenship would become a focal point for a national unity that all – Canadian-born and immigrant, French- and English-speaking – could share (Martin 1983; Brown 1996).

It took several years but Canadian citizenship became a reality on January 1, 1947. The adoption of Canadian citizenship turned out to be far more than simple post-war patriotic puffery or flag-waving sentimentalism; it proved a far-reaching act. By rejecting the notion of layered citizenship, a citizenship of degrees, Canada pronounced itself inclusive. Henceforth, individual Canadian citizens were promised that, under the law, all would be treated the same, irrespective of whether they were Canadian- or foreign-born, no matter their heritage, religion, or national origin, and irrespective of any proprietary claim that one group might make to being more Canadian than another. It would take time for reality to match rhetoric, but with post-war immigration just building up a head of steam, the introduction of an inclusive Canadian citizenship paved the way for all subsequent human rights initiatives that became so important to immigrants to Canada.

The inauguration of a distinct and separate Canadian citizenship was only the first step towards a major expansion of human rights legislation in Canada. If anything, the implementation of Canadian citizenship raised expectations about more openness in civic society and about unprecedented equality of access to public institutions for all Canadians, and fuelled the demand for legislated equality before the law. This human rights agenda was soon being driven by a coalition of organized labour, liberal churches, the Co-operative Commonwealth Federation (CCF), and older Canadian ethnic communities who had embraced the Canadian war effort, sent their children off to fight, and, in the aftermath of war, refused to ever again accept second-class status for themselves or their children. Alive with expectations raised by Canadian citizenship, the coalition was also swept along by a number of contributing forces: revulsion at the racial excesses of Nazism; a popularization of the new social sciences and the consequent academic-led assault on social Darwinist and eugenic thinking; a growing sense of the disfunctionality of the Anglo-centric urban Canadian world-view now rendered an anachronism by the erosion of colonialism and the British imperial dream; a spillover of social justice ideology from the nascent Black civil rights struggle in the United States; and, of major importance, a recognition that civic society had to clear away encumbrances to smooth the social, economic, and political integration of immigrants moving into cities like Toronto.

Canadian human rights activists pushed for legal protections against racial, religious, or ethnic discrimination. If few believed social attitudes could change overnight, all worked to ensure that the law would. And the law did. In the first decade after the war, Canadian provinces followed Saskatchewan's lead and enacted fair employment and accommodation legislation barring discrimination on account of race, religion, or country of origin. In the international forum, Canada's signing of the Universal Declaration of Human Rights added symbolic urgency to the new Canadian human rights agenda. Canadian courts were soon responding to the more progressive spirit of the day by using their powers to expand society's human rights thrust (Walker 1997).

This embrace of a singular citizenship and the legal guarantees of human rights for all Canadians mirrored a new spirit in urban Canadian thinking. It even remade language. Immigrants were no longer foreigners; they were 'New Canadians.' And, for that matter, they were no longer part of cities like Toronto by sufferance. They were there by right, and now by right of law. It was only a matter of time before the domestic human rights upheaval impacted on Canadian immigration legislation and administration.

In Toronto, where most immigrants lived, the revitalization of the notion of citizenship and human rights reinforced the realization that yesterday's immigrants and their children were becoming tomorrow's taxpayers and voters. Urban politicians, once leery of 'foreigners,' now reached out to New Canadians. Issues that were important to immigrant communities were being taken up by city hall. Most important to many immigrants, boards of education that had long been home to assimilationist, if not nativist, assumptions about the place of the foreign-born and their children in Canadian society were being forced to reinvent themselves as open and inclusive. Public expressions of racism shifted from being normative to being anti-social and from being anti-social to being legally punishable violations of community-wide standards. Toronto's urban polity had changed.

Immigration showed no sign of slowing. While Southern Europeans continued to dominate the stream of European immigrants entering Canada through the 1950s and into the 1960s, in 1956 the Cold War unexpectedly increased immigration from Central Europe. When the Soviets crushed the Hungarian uprising, they unleashed a flood of refugees westward into Austria. This first major European refugee crisis of the Cold War came at a fortuitous moment for Canada. The economy was still strong and the plight of exiled Hungarian 'freedom fighters' moved Canadians. At first, Ottawa was cautious. Canadian security personnel warned that the Soviets might salt this refugee movement with secret agents seeking entry into unsuspecting Western countries. For its part, the Canadian government seemed less concerned with Communists than with costs. Unlike the earlier DP movement, in which labour-intensive industry, ethnic communities, and families shouldered much of the financial burden, any Hungarian resettlement program promised to be largely Ottawa's responsibility.

As the government dithered, public sympathy and media pressure grew. Press editorials, savaging the government for inaction, demanded that Canada take the lead in welcoming victims of Soviet aggression. Under withering pressure, the Cabinet finally cut a path through immigration red tape. Normal immigration procedures, including pre-embarkation medical and security checks, were sidestepped or postponed until after arrival in Canada. Jack Pickersgill, the minister of immigration, hurried to Vienna and hard on his heels came immigration teams authorized to scoop up the best of the well-educated and highly motivated Hungarian refugees before other countries got them.

The Hungarian refugee resettlement program ran remarkably smoothly in spite of its lurching start and a lack of preparedness on the part of education and social service officials to deal with the influx. In Toronto, after some initial confusion, government officials at all levels joined forces with non-governmental organizations to help settle the new arrivals. And, in the end, Canada did well by doing good. The refugee resettlement program brought almost 37,000 Hungarians to Canada, with Toronto soon becoming home to the largest community. Many of these refugees were established professionals who, once they received orientation and English-language training, gradually found employment in the retail, commercial, or white-collar sectors. But, successful as this refugee resettlement exercise was, it was hardly a routine immigration program. Immigration officials regarded it as a one-time initiative, a singular exception to the procedural guidelines they so closely guarded. Time would prove them wrong (Dirks 1977; Dreisziger 1982).

THE WHITE PAPER

After two decades of almost uninterrupted growth, Canada's economy began to weaken in the early 1960s. With insistent 'I-told-you-so' warnings from many economists and government planners that Canada now faced serious industrial burnout, demand for new immigrant labour took a nosedive. Toronto's economy flagged along with the rest of the national economy, federal immigrant recruitment was curtailed, and immigration numbers soon fell by half. As the number of immigrant arrivals dropped off, some officials, convinced that immigrant absorptive capacity of the Canadian economy had been reached if not exceeded, called for a permanent cap on immigrant inflow. Responding to the chorus of naysayers, Ottawa commissioned a review of Canadian immigration with an eye towards redefining immigration priorities.

A white paper on immigration was released in 1966. The policy document attempted to walk a tightrope between the still-vocal pro-immigration lobbyists and a growing body of immigration opponents. For immigration advocates the white paper was infused with the liberal rhetoric of the day, even though it called for a complete overhaul of Canadian immigration law, regulations, and procedures, including a final purge of every last hint of racial or ethnic discrimination. While these were hailed as long overdue reforms, some immigration advocates viewed other white paper policy recommendations with alarm. Perhaps reflecting the larger public debate in the 1960s on optimum population size, the white paper questioned the long-term wisdom of taking in so many job-hungry immigrants at the prime of their fertility cycle. The white paper's recommendations were far from the Malthusian warnings of an earlier time and were certainly not endorsing the then-fashionable zero population growth, but they did offer a blueprint for capping immigration numbers. This stirred up a hornets' nest of controversy. Particularly controversial was the document's plan for tightening regulations on family reunification, which accounted for almost half of all immigrant entries into Canada, in favour of more skilled, independent immigrants. The white paper recommended that landed immigrants, those who were not yet citizens, be restricted to sponsoring only immediate dependents, the closest of family, while those who were Canadian citizens only be allowed to sponsor relatives who satisfied the educational and occupational qualifications in place for the admission of independent immigrants. If implemented, these moves would sharply restrict the possibility of sponsoring family, especially for immigrants who had come to Canada from Southern Europe.

Perhaps still unaware of the depth of controversy brewing over the family reunification issue, Cabinet referred the white paper to the Parliamentary Committee on Immigration for public input and discussion.

The committee soon got an earful. Italian, Jewish, and Eastern European ethnic leaders, particularly in Toronto – now home to large and increasingly resourceful post-war immigrant and ethnic communities – were outspoken in their hostility to any reduction in family sponsorship. They warned politicians that enraged ethnic voters would neither forgive nor forget any political party that slammed the door on their kith and kin. Mainstream churches and the Canadian Labour Congress joined the chorus of those demanding a broadening, not a narrowing, of family reunification provisions of the immigration regulations. Members of Parliament from Toronto, especially those from immigrant-heavy ridings, who feared that campaign contributions and ethnic votes would go elsewhere, waded in on the side of family sponsorship.

Ducking the political buckshot, the federal government set aside the proposed changes, at least as recommended in the white paper. Instead, Ottawa tinkered with the regulations. The list of those family members entitled to entry into Canada as first-degree relatives was narrowed. At the same time, however, a new class of immigrant, a nominated class, was announced. Nominated immigrants, primarily non-dependent family members who seemed likely to integrate well, were given priority in immigration processing. Their Canadian sponsor or nominator was also relieved of some of the legal and fiscal liability assumed in the case of sponsorship of immediate family. As a result, family migration was not curtailed. It was restructured and, to some degree, expanded. For years to come, the largest single subset of immigrants arriving in Toronto would continue to be family or other sponsored categories (Statistics Canada 1990).

There was another and, conceivably, more significant impact of the sponsorship battle. Thoughtful political observers of the day may have sensed the emergence of a newly empowered urban immigrant and ethnic political constituency, largely based in Toronto. In the white paper debate, that constituency seemed to be serving notice that it was prepared to take its place as a player on the Canadian political stage. But was this particular political victory an aberration, a one-time single-issue success by a coalition of otherwise disparate ethnic groups? Political commentators were unsure and began discussing a possibly fundamental and far-reaching shift in urban politics. One thing was certain, though, in Toronto, yesterday's immigrants were emerging as political, social, and economic powerbrokers in their own right – a 'third force' whose origins were neither English nor French (Porter 1972; Burnet 1976, 1979; Troper 1978; Breton 1979; Lupul 1983).

FROM ETHNIC TO RACIAL PLURALISM

Several other white paper recommendations were implemented, including the final expunging of racial and ethnic barriers to Canadian entry. A few years earlier, in 1962, in line with human rights initiatives at the provincial and federal levels, Cabinet approved the lifting of racial and ethnic restrictions on the processing of independent applicants. But the government stopped short of universalizing the policy change. To assuage public concerns about any sudden influx of dependent Chinese or other Asians, especially in British Columbia, racial restrictions remained in place for Asian family reunification cases. Nonetheless, even if the direction of public policy seemed clear, de facto racial and ethnic discrimination lingered for a time under administrative guise: the resources of the immigration bureaucracy were almost exclusively concentrated in areas of traditional immigrant preference – the United Kingdom, the United States, and Western Europe.

By contrast, few on-site immigration services were available and little immigration promotion money was spent in the developing world. In 1960, for example, Canada operated twenty-seven immigration offices outside North America. Twenty-four were in Europe and three were in Asia (one of which was in Israel). There was not one in all of black Africa, the Caribbean, or South America. But change would not be denied. In 1967, as a result of one of the key white paper recommendations, all vestiges of racial and ethnic discrimination were finally and officially expunged from Canadian immigration regulations and procedures, including all those relating to sponsored and nominated immigration. The privilege of applying to bring in family was extended to all Canadian citizens and landed immigrants alike, including family from the developing world (Ramcharan 1982).

Canada's network of immigration offices abroad were gradually expanded. A Canadian immigration office was opened in Egypt in 1963; in Japan in 1967; and in Lebanon, the Philippines, the West Indies, and Pakistan in 1968. And, as part of the package in which Ottawa restructured family reunification regulations and ended racial and ethnic preferences, the government also overhauled the procedures by which independent immigration applicants were admitted into Canada. Again, without enacting new legislation, the government both reined in the discretionary powers of immigration officials to reject an applicant and brought immigration admissions more exactly into line with domestic economic fluctuations. The point system, as it came to be known, was instituted to calibrate the desirability of each independent applicant. Simply stated, points were granted each applicant for specific skills, for their background, or for Canadian links. In addition to education and employment experience, points were assigned for character, market demand for skills, English- and French-language proficiency, age, proposed Canadian destination, and pre-arranged employment. Should Canadian economic conditions or skill demands change, the point system could be quickly adjusted to reflect these new priorities.

While the interviewing immigration officer still influenced approvals, the approved system was now more governed by the iron laws of mathematics rather than by the vagaries of subjective assessment. Some argued that a point system that rewarded education, professional status, and English- or French-language skills disadvantaged most potential applicants from the developing world, but few would argue that the kind of bedrock racism that was so inherent in the previous selection system was still operative (Hawkins 1972; St John-Jones 1973; Stasiulis 1985; Satzewich 1989).

REFUGEES

By affirming universality in its immigration policy, Canada took a big step towards further routinizing immigration procedures. But in another area – the issue of refugee policy – there were still no routine procedures. If there was a policy at all it seemed to be one of non-commitment. As had been the case with displaced persons and the Hungarian refugees, Canada's response to refugees who had well-founded fears of being persecuted in their homeland remained largely ad hoc. Even with Canada's high-profile role at the United Nations and its 1969 signing of the 1951 United Nations Convention on Refugees, for most of the next decade, Canada made no legislative commitment to guarantee sanctuary for those seeking asylum. Indeed, the DP and Hungarian episodes, which brought so many immigrants into Toronto, were understood by government as exceptional cases, outside normal and routine Canadian immigration activity.

Another such exception came in 1968. The end of the Prague Spring sent thousands of Czechoslovakian refugees westward in what seemed a repeat of the Hungarian exodus a decade earlier. But this time there was no Canadian stalling. Moved by a mixture of humanitarianism, Cold War posturing, and the opportunity to enhance Canada's human capital, Ottawa moved quickly to gather up its share of the new homeless. The Canadian economy was on the mend, events had produced a pool of well-educated and available immigrants to be picked over, and Canadian immigration teams swung into action. Not even the usually cautious Canadian security service raised strong objections to the Czech resettlement scheme. In short order, immigration authorities set aside regular immigration procedures to bring approximately 12,000 Czech refugees into Canada. Again, disproportionate numbers of the new arrivals eventually settled in Toronto (Dirks 1977).

The fortuitous mixture of altruism and economic self-interest that drove the Canadian resettlement effort in the case of Czech refugees did have limits and, like the refugee problem itself, these limits also appeared to be grounded in politics. Refugee advocates repeatedly attacked the government for favouring refugees from Communist or other high-profile and unpopular regimes over victims of equally repressive right-wing persecution. The charge was not without merit. For example, there was a glaring discrepancy between the government's response to Ugandan Asian refugees expelled by Idi Amin in 1972 and to Chilean refugees from the 1973 right-wing coup d'état against Salvador Allende's democratically elected left-wing government. In the case of the approximately 50,000 Asians with British passports expelled from Uganda, the British, fearing a domestic backlash against the sudden influx of so many Asians, appealed to Canada and other countries for assistance. Canada responded positively. Just as it was winding down its Czech resettlement program, as if to underscore the non-racial thrust of revamped Canadian immigration practice, authorities swung into action and quickly admitted 5,600 Ugandan Asians who, it was judged, could do well in Canada.

The Ugandan program stands in sharp contrast to the Chilean experience a year later. The Canadian government may have become colour-blind to race, but not to ideology; when it came to Chileans, immigration and security personnel saw red. After the fall of Allende's socialist government in an American-supported coup, Canada, protective of major Canadian investment in Chile, was among the first to recognize the new Pinochet regime. The Pinochet government may have been hospitable to Canadian investment, but was less so to those it had recently ousted from power. Arrests, 'disappearances,' and political repression were the order of the day. Canadian officials regarded this reign of political terror as a regrettable, but still an internal, problem of post-coup Chilean political adjustment. They would have continued to do so were it not for a small group of terrified Chileans who refused to leave the Canadian Embassy in Santiago, begging for sanctuary and political asylum in Canada. Ironically, while Chilean authorities respected the right to sanctuary in the embassy, Canada did not (Immigration 1974). As external affairs officials and embassy staff scrambled to dislodge the unwelcome guests, in Canada a vocal lobby group, including high-profile academics and labour leaders, coalesced under the umbrella of the Canadian Council of Churches to pressure Ottawa into accepting significant numbers of Chileans facing torture or imprisonment for their political views (Carroll 1974).

In contrast with Ugandan Asian refugees or with the earlier Czech and Hungarian resettlement programs, the Chileans did not fare nearly so well. Perhaps Canada was uneasy about accepting any large group of potentially left-leaning immigrants, or perhaps it was concerned about a negative American or Chilean government reaction. In any case, it proceeded with deliberate caution – too much caution in the eyes of some. While, by special arrangement with Chilean authorities, many of those camped in the embassy were allowed to leave for Canada, Canadian immigration authorities did not rush to process other applications. Just the opposite. They showed a marked reluctance to wave immigration regulations and, in spite of continuing pressure from pro-refugee advocates, immigration officials were slow in setting up shop in Chile.

Two years after the fall of Allende, in the face of continuing protests at the wholesale abuse of civil liberties – or worse – by the Pinochet regime, less than 2,000 Chileans were processed for entry into Canada, most of whom came to Toronto. Many were educated, white-collar professionals who, under other circumstances, might well have been granted entry as independent immigrants. This is not to argue that Chilean refugees were any more or less deserving of admission to Canada on humanitarian grounds than were Ugandan Asians. But, it does underscore that there was more to Canadian refugee policy than humanitarian concern. And if humanitarian concerns might sometimes take second place to economic self-interest, economic self-interest could also take second place to political considerations (Dirks 1977).

MULTICULTURALISM

By the early 1970s, three separate but interrelated phenomena had combined to reshape the immigrant experience in Canada and, in particular, in Toronto – multiculturalism as federal policy, a major shift in immigration demographics, and a downturn in the economy. With immigration continuing to expand the mosaic of peoples who constituted urban Canada, in 1971 the federal government announced its support for a policy of multiculturalism, a policy that symbolically recognized the positive and enduring impact of past immigration on Canadian society and that put forward a pluralist model for nation-building. While observers debated the complex political pressures that nudged the Liberal government of Pierre Elliott Trudeau towards adopting multiculturalism, there is no doubt that the policy, as articulated by government, suggested a radical reconstruction of Canadian cultural definitions. It eschewed formal recognition of any overriding or primary national cultural tradition. In so doing, the multicultural policy statement affirmed English and French as the two official national languages, but rejected biculturalism – a notion of Canada as a product of the nation-building efforts of two charter groups, the English (British) and the French, in which these two groups retained both a proprietorial right to determine the boundaries of Canadian identity and a custodial prerogative to preserve the primacy of their respective cultural heritages. Instead, multiculturalism espoused respect for diversity and acceptance of pluralism as the true and only basis of an inclusive Canadian identity.

In another context, it might be interesting to speculate as to whether multiculturalism was good policy, or, for that matter, how and whether it made any appreciable difference in the lives of individual Canadians. But, for this discussion, what is most important is that the Canadian government, with wide provincial support in English-speaking Canada, was conceding that no overriding national cultural consensus had taken root through more than one hundred years of national development. As the policy statement asserted, 'there is no official culture, nor does any ethnic group take precedence over any other. No citizen or group of citizens is other than Canadian, and all should be treated fairly.' Instead, the government declared that the binding force in the Canadian social compact would henceforth be articulated as a function of mutual respect rooted in cultural diversity, the same cultural diversity that was now the reality of the urban Canadian street. Nowhere was that diversity more visible to the eye than in the greater Toronto area, the destination of more than one-in-three post-war immigrants to Canada.

Multiculturalism has recently been under attack as a detriment to the development of a singular and bonding Canadian identity and a diversion from more pressing issues – that it ignores issues of racial and economic disparity in favour of funding folk dancing in church basements – but, at the time, multiculturalism struck a positive chord especially in urban English-speaking Canada. Whatever else multiculturalism did or did not do, it symbolically rounded the circle begun with the implementation of a separate and distinct Canadian citizenship. If multiculturalism was not the Magna Carta for group rights that some ethnic activists hoped for and their detractors feared, it was a clear statement to Canadians of all backgrounds that individual or group cultural affinity exercised in accord with Canadian law was neither antithetical to the common good, nor should it be allowed to encumber citizen participation in the civic society. Stripped of its policy rhetoric and political puffery, for many Canadians in the early 1970s, multiculturalism simply translated as 'live and let live.'

It is easy in retrospect – maybe even fashionable – to be cynical about official multiculturalism, and it is certainly appropriate to chastise politicians for attempting, without much success, to spin multiculturalism into a vote-buying device. It is also true that, for some, multicultural rhetoric rang hollow in the face of ongoing economic disparities and human rights abuses. It is similarly all too easy to find gaps in the net of Canadian human rights protections, especially as they relate to racial discrimination affecting immigrants and refugees. Few would claim that the lot of immigrants and refugees in urban Canada is anything close to problem-free. Not by a long shot. All of this notwithstanding, multiculturalism as government policy did make a difference. Canadian urban experience is now an immigrant and ethnic experience and, equally important, it is accepted as such in spite of the fact that less than a generation ago, the very idea of urban-bound immigration – let alone immigration of non-Europeans – would have been rejected as a nightmare vision. Any government that advocated large scale urban-bound immigration would have been driven from office by the wrath of voters. That is not true today. There can be no doubt that Canadians generally, and Torontonians in particular, acknowledge that theirs is a pluralist society in which equality remains an important social goal. For all its flaws, multiculturalism helped frame that view (Troper 1999).

THE GREEN PAPER

Multiculturalism was not the only public policy initiative to affect public attitudes towards pluralism in the 1970s; there was a shift in immigration policy itself. From the early 1950s to the late 1970s, immigration authorities laboured under the 1952 Immigration Act. The legislation had been amended a number of times and the immigration regulations that shaped day-to-day immigration operations were forever being reviewed, but Canada of the 1970s was a very different place from that of early 1950s. The social and economic priorities that shaped the 1952 legislation were no longer operative; a law that was designed to attract a large pool of unskilled agricultural and industrial workers seemed out of place in one of the most urban and technologically advanced Western states. Revisions to the old legislation, including the abandoning of racial and ethnic discrimination and the adoption of a point system, attempted to bridge the yawning gap between life in 1952 and the social and economic realities of the 1970s. But there was a difference between papering over the flaws in the 1952 legislation and designing a new act. To successfully meet the demands imposed by changing domestic and international world markets, government again hoped to move immigration away from its emphasis on family reunification towards a policy that would encourage the immigration of people with immediately employable skills and capital-productive potential. Along with new immigration priorities, new thinking was required; a new immigration law was overdue.

The first step towards tabling new legislation was an announcement by the minister of manpower and immigration in September 1973 that a federal commission would undertake yet another review of Canadian immigration policy that would be subject to public debate. After almost eighteen months of study and hearings, of collecting expert testimony and weighing suggestions for reform of immigration law and procedures, in late 1974, the commission issued its four-volume *Report of the Canadian Immigration and Population Study*.[2] Described more as a discussion paper than a blueprint for the future, the green paper on immigration, as the report was commonly known, put forward a number of recommendations that the commission hoped would encourage wide and thoughtful public debate.

But if the review was timely, the public debate misfired; not all of it proved to be thoughtful. Some people dismissed the green paper recommendations as little more than a retread of existing practice. To the surprise of no one, the document affirmed the need for a close relationship between immigration and labour supply. In opposition to the earlier white paper, however, recommendations in the 1974 document called for very tightly controlled population growth through increased immigration. Without sustained population growth, particularly among those in their wealth-generating years, the green paper warned, declining Canadian fertility rate and low mortality rate could hasten a time when the number of people generating wealth would be outstripped by those requiring support. The commission posited that the number of immigrants admitted would not only determine Canada's population growth, it would also be the key factor determining the pace of that growth (Department of Manpower and Immigration 1974).

On the other hand, the green paper advised that the duel problems of runaway urbanization and slippage in the percentage of francophones in the population were also a direct result of immigration. As a result, the paper recommended that Canada should both raise the skills bar for immigrants and cut back on the admission of family-class immigrants, while, at the same time, encouraging immigrants to settle in areas of designated need, rather than allowing them to congregate up in Canadian cities, particularly in the greater Toronto area (Department of Manpower and Immigration 1974; *Canadian Ethnic Studies* 1975).

Unfortunately for the commission, it could not have been a worse time for debate on the green paper recommendations. Just as a parliamentary committee geared up to hold hearings, the Canadian economy went into a tailspin triggered by the 1973 Middle East oil embargo. With economists talking about stagflation in the face of a steep rise in unemployment and a sharp jump in interest rates, thoughtful discussion of immigration among ethnic, business, and labour leaders in the media and the academy were almost drowned out in the flurry of finger pointing over who was to blame for Canada's faltering economy and the fearmongering that immigrants were poaching jobs from 'real' Canadians. Few people seemed prepared to entertain the argument that immigration was important to national population renewal or that immigration created jobs. As long as there were so many unemployed in Canada, many Canadians – including former immigrants threatened with job loss – saw little good in allowing job-hungry immigrants into the country.

But was this spike in anti-immigration sentiment just a reflection of a poor economy? Some immigration advocates felt that the talk about jobs and Canada's economic carrying capacity was a thinly veiled cover for racism. Charging that any upward adjustment of the immigration skills bar, restrictions on sponsorship or family reunification, or demands that immigrants be streamed into designated areas was a transparently crude attempt to reinstitute a preference for country of origin and ethnic or racial selectivity, many ethnic leaders cried foul. If some of these leaders were overstating the case, they were not entirely wrong. Home-grown racists, lurking beyond the margins of respectable discourse, needed no prodding to denounce the increasing immigration of non-whites (Barrett 1987). Their racist ranting found few receptive ears, but it was no secret that the racial and ethnic composition of immigration was changing. After the removal of racial selection criteria and the opening of immigration offices in previous areas of non-traditional Canadian immigration, the admission of persons of colour – visible minorities primarily from the developing world – increased. In 1967, shortly after Canadian immigration operations were upgraded in Asia and the Caribbean, less than 15 per cent of immigrants into Canada were of African or Asian descent, but in the early 1970s, economic pressures in the Caribbean and South Asia induced more people to grab at the chance of relocating abroad. By 1975, as the green paper debate raged, members of visible minorities constituted the majority of immigrants entering Canada each year. Ethnic pluralism, already the hallmark of urban centres like Toronto, was gradually being paralleled by racial pluralism (Richmond 1976).

NEW LEGISLATION

In 1976, the clamour over the green paper had subsided and, although the economy was still sluggish, the government was prepared to wait no longer. It pressed ahead with its own immigration agenda, including new immigration legislation. The preamble to the immigration bill submitted to Parliament that year promised a new vision of immigration. The bill did reaffirm the close tie between immigration and Canada's economic needs in tough economic times and, in a preamble that also reflected heightened concern for the welfare of individual immigrants, the government's continued commitment to family reunification. But for some people, the government's words sounded a little tinny. In spite of the progressive tone in the bill's preamble, when it came to delivering on family reunification, generosity of heart seemed to have worn thin. In practice, to be eligible for reunification with kin in Canada, other than a spouse or dependent child under ten, the new legislation gave priority admission to family members from abroad who could satisfy government personnel that their education, employment record, or skills were an immediate asset to Canada. This was hardly an open door.

The bill did break new ground in other areas. For the first time, immigration authorities began working with a form of quota system. In consultation with the provinces, Ottawa established a yearly target for the number of immigrants of various categories it hoped to admit the following year. The Canadian immigration target, more a guideline allowing provinces and urban municipalities to plan for immigrant arrivals than a fixed commitment, could be shifted up or down depending on prevailing conditions at home and abroad. But it was hoped that by agreeing on a target figure, including one for refugees and family sponsorships, the resources necessary for the smooth integration of immigrants would be in place as they arrived. As a rule of thumb, in recent years, the immigration target has been set at about 1 per cent of the total Canadian population each year or, by the late 1990s, about 300,000 immigrants per year. On a per capita basis, the 1 per cent target is almost three times the immigration rate of the United States.

Unfortunately, the federal-provincial consultation process was not always smooth. The issue was not so much the number of immigrants, but the number of dollars. Who was going to put up the money to pay for immigrant-related services? For the greater Toronto area, a magnet for almost one-third of all immigrants entering Canada, the often fractious debates between federal and provincial officials over who would cover what costs and for how long was critical. After all, it is the city and its agencies, together with the province, that deliver the essential grass-roots services immigrants need and that the municipal property taxes are often strained to provide. But Toronto was not officially part of these consultations. No doubt federal and provincial officials who discussed immigration options were well-briefed on the special needs of the Toronto immigration catchment area. But being briefed and making Toronto's needs a priority were not one and the same. As a result, Toronto politicians, public servants, social agency officials, and ethnic leaders worried that shrinking resources would force a reduction in services to new arrivals. Stretched thin, Toronto immigrant-service providers always seemed to be waiting for a cheque from either the federal or provincial levels that, when it came, was seldom enough (Statistics Canada 1990).

The new immigration act also opened the door to a new class of immigrant: business-class immigrants, who were divided into several categories, including entrepreneur and investor classes. As part of their admissions process, would-be entrepreneur-class immigrants were required to submit to Canadian authorities a business plan that offered promise of employing a number of Canadians, while investor-class immigrants were required to show a net worth of $500,000 and be ready to invest half of that amount in a job-creating project. While there were those who attacked the business-immigrant scheme as little more than 'Canadian citizenship for sale,' it is important to remember that government never confused immigration with charity. Whatever the agenda of the individual immigrant, for government, immigration has always been regarded as serving national economic development. From this perspective, how is the current juggling of the immigration point system going to favour applicants who will best serve Canadian economic and business expansion in any way different from the previous ingathering of immigrants who promised to prime the national economic pump – not with money or professional training, but with raw muscle?

In the years after the business category was initiated, entrepreneurial immigration jumped by 600 per cent and Canada became a favourite destination for capital in flight (Statistics Canada 1990). Before 1997, many business-class immigrants who came to Canada were from Hong Kong. With the impending Chinese takeover of the British colony, many Hong Kong businesspeople, looking for a safe harbour for family and money, welcomed the opportunities being offered for capital investment in Canada, particularly in Vancouver and Toronto. The previously small Toronto Chinese community now constitutes the largest ethnic community in the greater Toronto area, almost half a million strong, and includes immigrants from mainland China, Taiwan, and the Chinese diaspora (Cannon 1989; DeMont and Fennell 1989; Lai 1992).

For independent immigrants – those not blessed with a pool of available capital to invest or without a sponsoring Canadian family – getting into Canada might prove somewhat more difficult. Under immigration regulations that applied during the early 1980s, applicants with more modest resources and no family sponsor would find it difficult to enter Canada unless they had a job waiting for them. This was not easy to arrange. Before offering employment to a would-be immigrant, a prospective employer had to be prepared to satisfy immigration officials that no satisfactory Canadian candidate was available or willing to take the job.

REFUGEE POLICY

The new Immigration Act did underscore a Canadian humanitarian commitment in one area: refugees. Of course, Canada had accepted refugees in the past – displaced persons, Hungarians, Czechoslovakians, Ugandan Asians, Chileans – but they had always been regarded as special cases admitted by special permission, exceptions to the normal and administrative routine of Canadian immigration procedure. Under the new immigration legislation, for the first time, Canada agreed that people who were 'displaced or persecuted,' who, as defined by the 1951 United Nations Convention on Refugees, had 'a well-founded fear of persecution,' were declared a class eligible for admission to Canada even though, as individuals or as a group, they might not meet Canada's usual selection standards.

But what did this mean in reality? With a world increasingly awash in refugees and the end of one refugee crisis all too often the beginning of the next, official Ottawa struggled to institute a policy to replace the ad hoc response to refugees that had characterized the previous decades. In practice, as part of its annual immigration consultations with the provinces, the government set aside a specified number of refugee admissions as part of the total number of immigrants Canada expected to admit during the coming year. The cost of refugee integration would be covered by the government, but with provision for private groups to sponsor refugees as well. It was expected that refugees, in the main, would be selected and processed abroad from among those who had already been judged by international refugee officials to fit within the definition of the UN Convention. However, Canada reserved for itself the prerogative of expanding the definition or designating specific groups as special cases, eligible for Canadian admission as refugees, even though they might not technically fit the definition. And, while Canada did not envision itself as a first haven for refugees – the first country a refugee might reach after leaving his or her home country – Canada left open the possibility of individuals or groups arriving in Canada and making an inland claim to refugee status. This internal route demanded that Canada establish domestic procedures for determining the legitimacy of individual refugee claims.

The new Immigration Act's refugee provisions, which came into effect in 1978, were quickly put to the test during the Vietnamese 'boat people' crisis. Stirred by press and television reports of desperate refugees fleeing Vietnam by sea in tiny boats, sometimes hardly more than rafts, the strength of the pro-refugee sympathy in Canada took Ottawa by surprise. While some people in government and among the larger civic society may have harboured private doubts about the wisdom of Canada accepting a large number of the boat people, influential public and media demands for action grew louder. Across Canada, friend joined with friend, neighbour with neighbour, and church group with church group in applying to sponsor the arrival and settlement of Vietnamese refugees under the refugee sponsorship provisions of the new legislation. Ottawa responded to these sponsorship groups with both humanity and dispatch. The government promised that it would work with private sponsorship groups and match the sponsorships refugee for refugee.

By the end of 1980, the government had agreed to the admission of more than 60,000 Vietnamese, Cambodian, Laotian, and ethnic Chinese from Southeast Asia in a blend of government and private sponsorship programs unique in Canadian history. By the time this refugee crisis subsided, Canada was distinguished by having the highest per capita boat people resettlement of any country. Toronto soon became home to the largest number of Southeast Asian refugees, adding yet another layer to the city's remarkable ethnic and racial mix (Adelman 1980; Canada Employment and Immigration Commission 1987; Adelman 1982).

Since the boat people episode, refugee admissions have continued to be an important, if often controversial, part or Canada's immigration program. In 1980, at the height of the crisis, slightly more than 28 per cent of all immigrants admitted to Canada were refugees. During the subsequent ten years, the percentage hovered between 14 and 20 per cent (Statistics Canada 1990). But the core of the controversy regarding refugees had little to do with the number of refugees admitted to Canada. That number moved up or down on a year-by-year basis, depending on federal negotiations with the provinces and the state of international refugee supply. The problem for government and the source of much heated public and media debate was the issue of inland applicants – those who, instead of being selected and processed abroad by Canadian authorities and, if acceptable, granted Canadian admission, entered Canada one way or another and claimed refugee status once they were in Canada. Canada did not pick them; they picked Canada.

While Canadian immigration regulations made provision for inland refugee claims, Canadians and Canadian officials had likely given little thought to the notion that refugees would arrive on the national doorstep seeking admission. It was certainly not easy for refugees to get to Canada – the only land border is with the United States and the country is otherwise sheltered from large-scale refugee movements by vast oceans. Indeed, compared with Western European countries – closer by distance and communication links to countries of persecution than Canada – the number of refugees who arrived in Canada remains small.

Nevertheless, officials were initially ill-prepared for people who found some way to enter Canada and claim refugee status. It was not long before the existing inland refugee determination process was clogged; hearing a claim and getting a decision sometimes took months or even a year or more. And until each claimant was individually assessed and a decision rendered, the legal status of these people remained in limbo.

This was most problematic in Toronto, where so many refugee claimants settled as they awaited their refugee hearing. Questions as to the municipality's responsibilities to the refugees remained to be answered. Were they entitled to social assistance or municipal housing? If not, who would pay their living expenses until their status was decided? What about educating refugee children? Were children of refugee claimants entitled to be in public school before refugee status was decided? Again, who would pay the costs – the federal government, the province, the municipal ratepayer, individual refugee claimants? Would claimants be allowed to work? And what would become of those who were eventually judged not to be refugees? Would they be sent home? Easier said than done. By making a refugee claim in Canada, a claimant was asserting that he or she had been persecuted at home. True or not, after making such a claim how would claimants who were denied refugee status in Canada be received if they were deported back to their home country?

While these issues were being resolved and refugee processing procedures streamlined, there were still issues of public perception that had an effect on refugee policy. While advocates of a progressive refugee policy were actively lobbying government, others warned that Canada was being hoodwinked, that refugee policy was a back door into Canada for those who would otherwise be rejected. There were rumours of unscrupulous refugee consultants and travel agents abetting fraudulent refugee claimants from people who had no 'well-founded fear of persecution.' The press was rife with discussions of false claimants taking advantage of so-called lax Canadian refugee procedures to jump the immigration queue or otherwise bypass regular immigration procedures. It was not long before government critics began calling for a wholesale overhaul of refugee regulations. For some, the issue of refugees may also have been clouded by whispered fears over the growing presence of visible minorities in Canadian cities. In 1985 non-European immigration topped 60 per cent (Canada Employment and Immigration 1987). And while most Canadians continued to reject racism, there is no doubt that they were increasingly aware of the changing ethnographic face of Canada, especially urban Canada.

In 1985 the Supreme Court ruled in *Singh v. Minister of Employment and Immigration* that once they were in Canada, refugee claimants, like everyone else in Canada, are protected by the Canadian Charter of Rights and Freedoms. Specifically, the court held that any government attempt to bypass its own regulations for refugee claimant hearings was a violation of the Charter. If the government wanted to speed up the determination process, it had to change the regulations within the framework of the Charter. Better still, from the government's point of view, the court would welcome mechanisms to stem the flow of refugees claimants before they could get to Canada and be protected by the Charter.[3]

While the government was considering options for tightening up Canadian inland refugee procedures, the issue heated up again. Two ships illegally stranded their respective refugee cargoes on Canadian shores in the dead of night – 155 Tamils in Newfoundland in 1986, and 174 Sikhs in Nova Scotia in 1987. Refugee claims were not unknown in Newfoundland. The airport in Gander, a regular refuelling stop for flights on the route from Eastern Europe to Cuba, was often the site of numerous requests for Canadian asylum. Nevertheless, the arrival of the Tamils was a surprise and the Canadian public and media responded as much with curiosity as with concern. The landing of the Sikhs a year later was another thing altogether. Public attention became riveted on the refugee issue as the government hinted that boatloads of additional refugees might be on their way to Canada. Over the protests of pro-refugee advocates who warned against overreacting, Parliament was recalled and passed legislation that, among other things, threatened sanctions against anyone who aided people who entered Canada illegally for the purpose of making a refugee claim. The legislation also tightened up regulations by, for example, denying refugee status to individuals who had passed though another country where a refugee claim might have been made, such as the United States. This move alone could sharply curtail the number of Latin American claimants who could be eligible for Canadian consideration.[4]

The proposed changes in refugee regulations produced a firestorm of debate both in and out of Parliament. Some people charged that the government's hidden agenda was not so much control of refugee admissions as another attempt to curtail non-white arrivals in Canada. Others argued that the government legislation contained provisions that again flew in the face of the Canadian Charter of Rights and Freedoms. Nevertheless, the changes were approved.

This was not the end of Canada's effort to control the flow of inland refugee claimants. In 1992, in the midst of the sharpest economic slump since the 1930s, the government introduced yet another package of major revisions to the Immigration Act, which it hoped might further check the flow of refugees entering Canada. Pro-refugee lobbyists encouraged government to withdraw several of the more Draconian provisions of its proposed immigration legislation, but the essential features of the package passed through Parliament in December 1992. Pending legal challenges that could be raised against the legislation, it became still more difficult for inland refugee claimants to reach and make refugee claims in Canada (Kelly and Trebilcock 1998).[5]

In spite of legislative and regulatory changes, refugees continued to arrive and Canadian immigration and refugee policy continued to be a political hot potato. In the federal election of 1993, the Reform Party of Canada, using tactics that some in the media thought bordered on racist, turned immigrant and refugee policy into an election issue. It is hard to know how much the playing on concerns that immigration was being out of control helped the Reform Party, but the party did come from being almost non-existent to being only one seat short of forming the official Opposition. In Toronto, however, where pluralism is a municipal fact of life, the Reform Party came out of that election with no seats in the city and its suburbs. But if the Reform Party was frozen out of Toronto, its willingness to incite public anxiety over immigration as a political tool and its suddenly powerful voice in Ottawa could not help but give pause to individuals and groups in the city who look to Ottawa for leadership and financial assistance in addressing municipal immigration and intergroup issues (Soberman 1999).

In 1999, with Reform in the official Opposition and Canada's refugee policy still a flashpoint of controversy, yet another refugee crisis exploded. Late that summer almost 400 illegal Chinese migrants, including women and children, were apprehended while smuggling themselves into Canada aboard three small and dangerously overcrowded vessels. The crews of the vessels were arrested and charged with various violations of the Canadian Criminal Code. The migrants faced a different and uncertain future: once in Canadian custody, most of the migrants claimed to be refugees fleeing persecution in China. In accord with established Canadian immigration procedures, as soon as an individual makes a refugee claim on Canadian soil, a review process is set in motion designed to determine the legitimacy of the individual's claim. While there was talk of fast-tracking the refugee determination process for these migrants, the process promised to be difficult and lengthy. It also promised to be controversial. But in the end, claimants who eventually satisfied officials that they did indeed have a well-founded fear of persecution in China were granted refugee status and allowed to stay in Canada. Those whose claims were rejected could be deported back to China.

With the review process under way, some of the Chinese migrants were released from custody pending their hearings before a refugee review panel and warned not to work without a special permit. Unable to work legally and without financial resources, most of the refugee claimants would likely require public support until their claims were decided. A number of those who were released were reported to have disappeared, likely secreted across the American border and headed for New York City, to the world of sweat labour reserved for illegal immigrants.

The media were generally unsympathetic to the migrants, but no more so than many Canadians. If radio talk shows and letters to the editor are in any way reflective of the public mind, than the Chinese migrants sparked widespread Canadian anger. The anger was not only directed at the migrants for attempting to smuggle themselves into Canada, but also at the government for its seeming laxity in dealing with people who enter Canada illegally. Many Canadians resented that the country's sovereignty had been violated, fearing that Canadian immigration and refugee regulations were little more than a sieve that allows almost everyone and anyone to slip into Canada. No other country, some people charged, would stand for this kind of wholesale violation of its borders. If these illegal Chinese migrants were allowed to remain, they warned, Canada would become an international laughingstock. And to make matters worse, weren't Canadian tax dollars paying the bills to feed, house, and cloth these migrants, let alone pay for all the legal and administrative overhead involved in processing their refugee claims? Some critics argued that there were many needy Canadians who were being denied assistance while undeserving foreigners – illegal immigrants – were quick to get government handouts.

As time passed, the controversy subsided. Media and public attention focused elsewhere. However, the events of September 11, 2001, and the repercussions have implications for Canadian immigration and refugee policy. The potential for immigration and refugee issues to erupt again in the public discourse remains high.[6]

TORONTO-BOUND IMMIGRANTS

In the late 1990s, thousands of inland refugee claimants awaited hearings in Toronto and many immigrants found it difficult to access affordable housing, employment matching their skill levels or experience, and language training. Policy debates on immigration continued and so did immigration. Indeed, as the Canadian economy started to improve, the flow of immigration into Canada and into the Greater Toronto Area, in particular, showed no signs of slowing. The measure of that immigration is not just its continuity, but also its diversity and impact – an impact that not even the most far-seeing policy planner of an earlier era could have predicted. Toronto, the hub of Canadian economic development, has been a draw for immigrants. This is unlikely to change. As I mentioned at the beginning of this chapter, Toronto's Pearson International Airport remains the major port of arrival for immigrants into Canada and many immigrants are sticking very close to that port of arrival. Numbers continue to tell a story. Almost 40 per cent of all those living in Toronto were born outside Canada. The foreign-born, together with their Canadian-born children, now constitute a majority of the city's residents, a majority of the urban polity. Almost three-quarters of immigrants moving into Toronto in recent years have been of non-ethno-European origin and most of them are in or are just preliminary to their birthing cycle.

Accordingly, immigration has not only transformed community definitions, it has also transformed urban space. Since the Second World War, Anglo Toronto has given way to a rich montage of ethnic villages, an urban complex where variegated ethnic and racial core zones nuzzle up against one another in an overlapping pattern that stretches from the inner city well into the outer suburban ring. These villages may be characterized by vast stretches of single family homes or, in recent years, by vertical villages, high-rise developments dominated by one or another ethnic or racial community. These villages are commonly replete with ethnic shopping, business, and cultural areas, where any one of many home languages or dialects coexist alongside English. Here one can find a sometimes uneasy middle ground between adopted mainstream Canadian ways and an effort to withstand the forces of homogenization. And at the cutting edge of discourse between the immigrant's memories of the old country and hopes for the new, there are the worlds of children and of the infill of popular culture, the impact of the marketplace, and the often painful realization that change, sometimes unwelcome change, is the inevitable price exacted for survival in the new urban home.

What of interethnic and interracial tension in Toronto? For all the potential for intergroup conflict to be found in Toronto's cultural and racial mix, and in spite of the kind media-influenced outburst witnessed on the landing of Chinese migrants in British Columbia in the late summer of 1999, it might be argued that the level of public civility in Toronto remains remarkably high. This is not to say that there are not areas of interracial or interethnic tension. There are many. Some tensions swirl around a growing distancing of the city from the larger Ontario hinterland, a distancing shaped at least in part by different visions of what Toronto has become after several decades of large-scale immigration. While Toronto publicly boasts of being a cosmopolitan and pluralist city, a multicultural if not transnational city, this vision holds little or no appeal to those who distrust the city as a crude and alien space, home to foreigners and foreign ways, distant from their orderly sense of what and who is Canadian.

Other immigration-related tensions are found much closer to home. As a new immigrant community begins to move into an established neighbourhood, shifting the existing racial or ethnic balance, turf wars are sometimes the result. This phenomenon is as much a feature of Toronto's suburban ring as it is of the inner city. For example, in Toronto's suburban northeast corridor, part of the up-market 905 region, a sizable infusion in the early 1990s of often well-heeled Hong Kong immigrants caused alarm among some members of the previously dominant community. Struggles sometimes took place over high-profile community anchors. When several large neighbourhood shopping centres adopted an all-Chinese language format, the reaction from some non-Chinese speakers was anger. Controversy also dogged new arrivals who purchased 'tear-down' homes on large lots and built what came to be called 'monster homes.' Charges of Chinese neighbourhood-busting were met with countercharges of anti-Chinese racism.

Closer to the city core, there have been confrontations and even shootings involving police and youth, particularly Black youth and so-called Asian youth gangs. Sometimes problems are one-on-one and may seem trivial, but they are worrying nonetheless. Recently, two Toronto neighbours settled a much-publicized dispute over the smell of ethnic cooking. One neighbour sued the other over what were claimed to be 'disagreeable' cooking odours vented out of the kitchen of the other. While the problem was eventually resolved by an agreement to extend and redirect the vent, the whole affair was played out on a canvas of intergroup interpretation.

With so much possibility for ethnic and racially based misunderstanding, municipal officials in Toronto continue to wrestle with ways and means of adapting municipal services to accommodate the pluralist reality. For example, in order to stay on top of Toronto's shifting demographic reality, the police have had to rethink their role and public profile. Among other things, this is precipitating a process of more vigorous race-sensitivity training for police and an accelerated minority-hiring program. The police are not alone. Other street-level services – the courts, non-governmental organizations, and social welfare agencies like children's aid societies, hospitals, and schools – are also attempting to offer culturally and racially sensitive services. But this is not as easy as it seems. It may be possible to offer multilingual services, or even to make agency staff more reflective of the demographics of the larger civic society, but how far should public agencies and services bend to accommodate the different cultural norms, values, gender relations, religious beliefs, and family structures reflected in so diverse a community? Should ethnic or racial groups be encouraged to organize services to serve their own and, if so, at whose expense?

Adding to concerns in the late 1990s and in the new millennium, the government of Ontario has downloaded the cost of many public programs onto municipalities and, in the case of Toronto, began siphoning educational dollars out of the city's schools to support schools in the more distant suburban and rural ring. Relying on its property tax base, Toronto found it increasingly difficult to sustain adequate services without driving up taxes to impossible levels. Faced with less money, the public sector had been forced to make triage-like decisions about competing needs. Services essential to immigrant integration have not escaped the chopping block. In Toronto schools, for example, programs of English as a second language for children were severely cut back and those for adult learners eliminated almost completely. Low-end rentals have disappeared, and legal aid for refugee claimants has been cut back. All the while, immigrant and refugee arrivals continued. The implications of downloading by federal and provincial governments and a consequent downsizing in community-based services for the long-term integration and economic health of new arrivals to Toronto has yet to be seen.

For all these problems and the potential for tension, nothing so defines Toronto at the millennium as its cultural and racial pluralism. But it remains a pluralism of contradictions. Some might say Toronto loves pluralism, but is uneasy about immigrants. If this is a contradiction, it is one Torontonians seem destined to live with.

Notes

1 One of the truly great Canadian novels, Michael Ondaatje's *In the Skin of a Lion*, is about Macedonian labourers in urban Canada in the 1920s.
2 The *Report of the Canadian Immigration and Population Study* (Ottawa: Manpower and Immigration, 1974) was issued in four volumes: *Immigration Policy Perspectives*; *The Immigration Program*; *Immigration and Population Statistics*; *Three Years in Canada*. All volumes were published simultaneously in French.
3 The 1951 Convention Relating to the Status of Refugees to which Canada subscribes defines refugees as 'any person who ... owing to a well-founded fear of being persecuted for reasons of race, religion, nationality, membership of a political social group or political opinion, is outside his country of nationality and is unable or ... unwilling to avail himself of the protection of that country.'
4 In 1988, Employment and Immigration Canada issued a press release noting that Canada had a backlog of 85,000 claims for refugee status (Employment and Immigration Canada 1988).
5 In one important area, the Canadian categories for determination of refugee status have been expanded. Beginning in 1993, Canadian guidelines were issued regarding women refugee claimants claiming gender-related persecution. These guidelines were an important step in recognizing that women refugee claimants often suffer from gender-based persecution and have served as a model for other countries, including the United States and

Australia, which have adopted similar versions to protect women who do not qualify as refugees under the 1951 UN Convention relating to the Status of Refugees (Valji 2001).
6 Media reports about the two boat loads of Chinese migrants were a mainstay of the front pages of Canadian newspapers from early August through to September 1999. While the tone and texture of editorial comment, news, and feature articles may not have been uniform from paper to paper, an examination of the four Toronto-based dailies, the *Globe and Mail*, *National Post*, *Toronto Star*, and *Toronto Sun*, show that, on the whole, the papers raised alarm at both the arrival of the Chinese migrants and the state of Canadian immigration and refugee policy.

2 Immigrants in the Greater Toronto Area: A Sociodemographic Overview

Clifford Jansen and Lawrence Lam

Chapter 1 describes how Toronto moved from a predominantly British Protestant society to what we know today as a multicultural one. Like much of Canada's history and culture, this change came about, in large part, as the result of successive waves of immigration. Many people can trace their roots back several generations in this country, but the reality is that immigration has been on the Canadian agenda for decades. Each generation of Canadians has had to deal with immigration problems relevant to their time and, as Harold Troper points out, events outside Canada, such as two world wars and their aftermaths, persecution in foreign countries, changes in emigration policies in countries that had formerly restricted emigration, and Third World poverty have all had an effect on Canadian immigration policy. In other words, as we approached the beginning of the twenty-first century, we could look back and realize that in every decade of the century some decision has had to be made about whether to admit immigrants, the numbers to admit, and who to admit. Every generation believes that their problems concerning immigrants are unique, yet Canada has always had to deal with integrating diversity, even if the nature of that diversity is constantly changing.

In this chapter, we hope to illustrate, by using numbers, the effects of the constantly changing global circumstances and Canada's specific policy reactions to them. Immigration to Canada is shown in figure 2.1, which shows numbers in five-year periods from 1871 (four years after Confederation) to 1998. Despite the belief that in the recent past Canada has been increasing the number of people admitted, the chart shows that between 1911 and 1915, the period just before the First World War, more immigrants were admitted to Canada than in any other five-year period. One can only imagine what kind of situation the country had to face, accommodating almost 1.3 million immigrants in a total population of 7.5 million. In contrast, as the chart indicates for the period 1991 to 1995, just under 1.2 million immigrants were coming into a total Canadian population that, by 1996, was over 28 million. The problems of integrating diversity today may be different, but they are not unique. In terms of actual numbers of immigrants, the chart also indicates that periods of relatively little immigration include the last thirty or so years of the nineteenth century and the years of the Great Depression through to the end of the Second World War. However, since 1946, the numbers in five-year periods have remained above 400,000.

As Troper points out, the Second World War and its aftermath was a critical watershed in the history of Canadian immigration, with profound effects on the city of Toronto. Between 1946 and the end of the twentieth century, the origins of immigrants to Canada changed constantly (fig. 2.2). While immigrants with European origins dominated the ten years immediately following the war, after the mid-1950s the proportion of immigration from this source declined at a constant rate. The proportion from the United States, on the other hand, was fairly constant until the 1990s, when there was a decline. While all immigration from non-European countries of origin showed a steady growth after 1956, the Asia- and Pacific-origin groups increased the most quickly: from 1.2 per cent of immigrants in the first ten years after the war to 53 per cent since 1995. In this latest period, immigration from Africa and the Middle East represented 17 per cent of the total; South and Central America 9 per cent; and the United States just under 3 per cent. In contrast, the proportion of immigrants from Europe had dropped from 91 per cent in the decade immediately following the war to 19 per cent between 1995 and 1999.

As Troper has also noted, Toronto had become the preferred destination for immigrants to Canada, although the two other major cities – Vancouver and Montreal – received their share as immigration concerns shifted from agricultural settlement to new industrial and urban labour recruitment priorities. By 1996, of all the foreign-born in Canada (4,914,439), 37 per cent were living in Toronto – just 1 point less than the percentage in all of Canada outside the three major cities (38 per cent); 13 per cent were living in Vancouver; and 12 per cent in Montreal (fig. 2.3).

Figure 2.1
Immigration to Canada, 1871–1998 (Five-year periods)

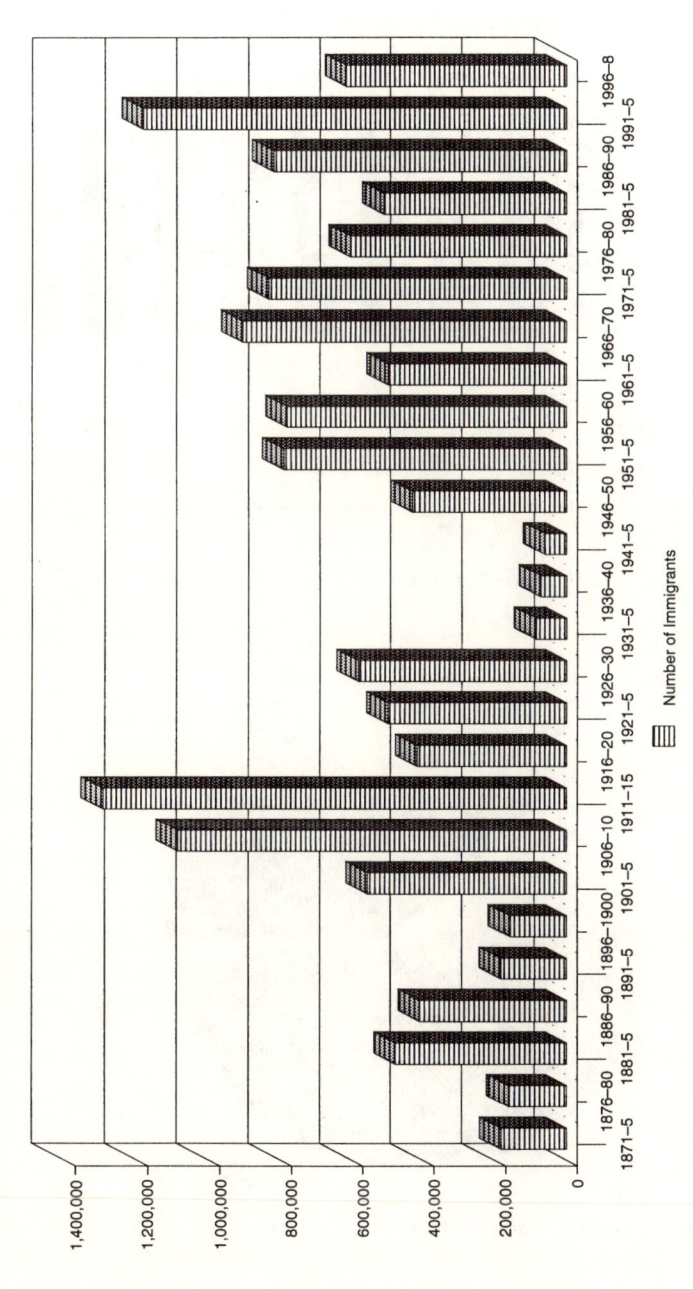

Sources: 1871–1979: Immigration, Department of Citizenship and Immigration; 1980–1998, Citizenship and Immigration Canada, Landed Immigrant Data System.

66 Clifford Jansen and Lawrence Lam

Figure 2.2
Origins of post-war immigrants, Canada, 1946–1999

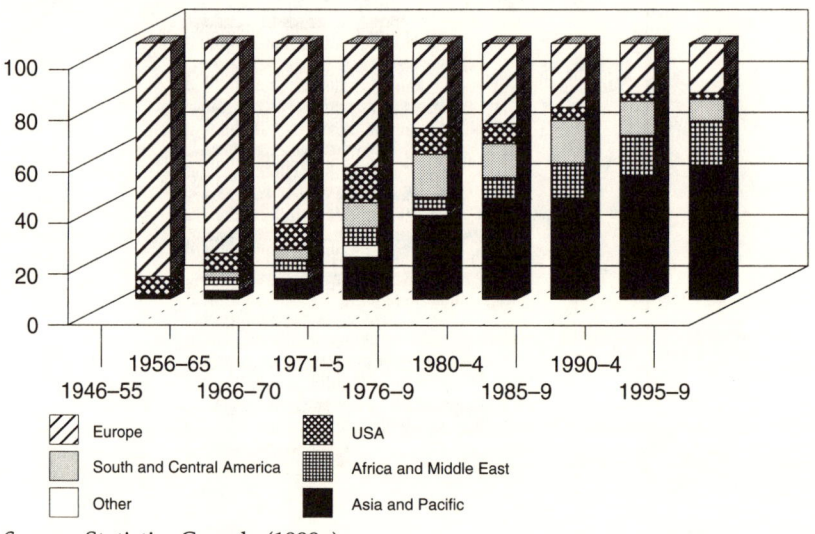

Sources: Statistics Canada (1999a).

Figure 2.3
Share of Foreign-born: three major cities, 1996

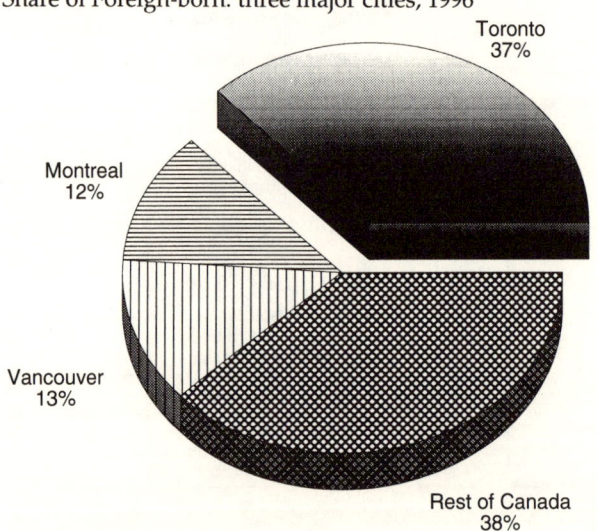

Sources: Statistics Canada (1999a).

If we look at the total population of the three cities represented in figure 2.3, the impact of immigration is even more dramatic. In Toronto, the foreign-born represented between 42 and 43 per cent of the total population; in Vancouver, 36 per cent; in Montreal, 19 per cent. In the rest of Canada, the foreign-born represented only 10 per cent of the total population. These trends have continued in recent years. Citizenship and Immigration Canada data reveal that for the three years following the census – 1997, 1998, and 1999 – Toronto's share of all immigrants was 46, 44, and 44 per cent respectively (Citizenship and Immigration Canada 1999b). The magnitude of the increase in the number of immigrants to Toronto prompted the former minister of citizenship and immigration, Lucienne Robillard, to acknowledge that 'her officials take into account the stresses that immigration levels put on major urban centres like the Greater Toronto Area ... [and] it would be better if newcomers were dispersed more evenly across the country' (Carey 1997, A1). And not only have the numbers of immigrants changed, the origins of those immigrants have transformed a city whose roots were predominantly British and European to such an extent that, by 1996, Toronto was home to 42 per cent of the more than three million Canadians who identified themselves as members of a 'visible minority.'

Inevitably, resources are an issue, particularly in the areas of education, housing, and social assistance. Officials at various levels have raised concerns about the capacity of the receiving society, and of immigrants themselves, to contribute to their integration. Toronto-area school boards complain that they do not have the resources to teach English and provide appropriate programs to so many newcomers from such diverse backgrounds. During its mandate, the Ontario government's own Education Improvement Commission lamented that inadequate funds for cities and schools – funds that would enable them to ease newcomers into society – have resulted in 'starving the Toronto school board that must deal with students from 170 countries speaking 70 languages' (Siddiqui 1999). Toronto city council has expressed concern about a shortage of housing and social assistance. The mayor of Toronto, Mel Lastman, has openly charged that providing social assistance and shelters to some of the newcomers – a cost of about $200 million – would force the city to increase property taxes. While school boards and the city point the finger at the provincial government, the province, in turn, blames the federal government for not providing it with sufficient funds to run the immigrant settlement programs. Queen's

Park pointed out that, while Ontario attracts almost two-thirds of immigrants, it receives only $102 million for settlement services, in contrast to Quebec's guaranteed $90 million a year regardless of how few immigrants it attracts – less than 15 per cent in recent years.

In the second part of this chapter, we document post-war changes in immigration policy and consider the effect these have had on the numbers, origins, and types of immigrants coming into Canada in general, and into Toronto in particular. Our principal focus will be on the period from 1970 to 2002 because, as Troper describes in the previous chapter, cities like Toronto only shifted from an emphasis on *ethnic pluralism* to one of *racial pluralism* following the 1966 white paper on immigration. In the third section of this chapter, we focus on the degree to which Toronto has been able to integrate its diverse immigrant groups. In particular we address the questions of *inclusion* and *exclusion* that are raised in the introduction, supporting our findings with data from the census and similar sources.

CANADIAN IMMIGRATION POLICY, 1945–2002

1945 to 1971

Harold Troper has already outlined much of this period of Canada's immigration history in chapter 1. Here, we will only sketch in as much as is necessary to underpin our analysis in the remaining sections of this chapter. In the immediate post-war period, labour shortages in Canada's primary and secondary industries were met by encouraging farmers from the Netherlands to emigrate, facilitating the immigration of Polish army veterans, selecting displaced people from European refugee camps, and encouraging British immigrants to work in mines and manufacturing industries (Petersen 1955; A. Richmond 1967; Satzewich 1991). The obverse of a strong preference for British and Western European immigrants was discrimination against African, Asian, and Caribbean migrants who were then subject to quota restrictions and their immigration was largely confined to those who already had close relatives in the country.

The creation of the Department of Citizenship and Immigration in 1950 and the enactment of the new, consolidated Immigration Act of 1952 gave the minister of immigration considerable power to draft regulations governing admission to Canada. A set of preferential categories was established that remained in force until 1962, when race or nationality ceased to be used as selection criteria, although the distribution of Canadian immigration offices abroad continued to give de facto approval to applicants from Britain, Europe, and the United States (Hawkins 1988). At the same time, efforts were made to integrate settlement services and citizenship education with immigration selection and administration.

During the Second World War, annual immigration never exceeded 17,000, but in 1945 it jumped to just under 23,000, and continued to increase steadily, so that the average for the period from 1946 to 1953 was 108,985 per year. Then, in 1956 and 1957, respectively, the Soviet invasion of Hungary and the Suez Crisis caused a peak in the flow of Hungarian refugees and politically motivated British immigrants. In 1957, 282,164 immigrants came to Canada, a number that has never been exceeded in any year since. However, economic conditions in Canada at that time were not conducive to rapid absorption. Consequently, the numbers admitted in the following five years were significantly reduced. Italian immigrants, mainly sponsored by close relatives already in Canada, moved into second place behind immigrants from the UK, followed by Americans, some of whom saw Canada as a 'safe haven' from being drafted into the Vietnam war. The crisis in Czechoslovakia in 1968 resulted in the admission of refugees from that country.

By 1966, there was a growing recognition of the need to relate immigration to labour force requirements and, following the publication of a white paper, a new Department of Manpower and Immigration was created. The Citizenship Branch was moved to the Secretary of State's office, where it tended to be subordinated to the government's growing concern with integrating Canada's French-speaking population (in Quebec and other provinces) into a federal Canada that was being threatened by growing separatist sentiments. The selection of immigrants was geared to economic needs through the adoption of a points system that gave considerable weight to education, occupational qualifications, and a knowledge of English, French, or both official languages, although the precise weight given to these factors has varied over the years. Family reunion also continued to be a high priority for churches and ethnic communities and, as a gesture to these bodies, applicants could earn extra points if they had relatives in Canada who were prepared to accept some financial responsibility and ensure that the sponsored immigrant would not become a 'public charge.' As a result, the largest single group of immigrants admitted into Canada has

Figure 2.4
Proportion foreign-born, Toronto, 1961–1996

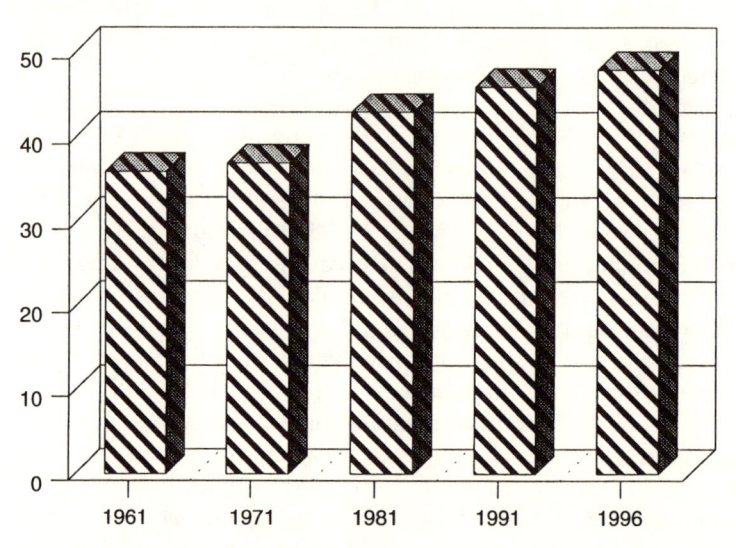

Sources: Statistics Canada (1996a).

continued to be in the family and other sponsored categories (Troper 1993).

Changes made in 1967 to the 1952 Immigration Act ended the last remnants of racial and ethnic discrimination in Canada's immigration policies and opened the door to a massive shift in Canadian immigration patterns as shown in figure 2.2. Since then, Third World countries have become an increasingly important source of temporary and permanent workers admitted to Canada (Simmons 1990, 1993; Burstein 1991). A study by Michael Lanphier (1979) showed that the proportion of permanent immigrants from these countries had increased from 8 per cent in the early 1960s to more than 50 per cent by the end of 1975. There was also an increase in annual migration: while, the annual average was just under 109,000 in the period from 1945 to 1953, this had increased to 143,438 in the period from 1954 to 1971; in total, 2.6 million immigrants came into Canada during that period. As Toronto became a major destination for immigrants, the proportion of foreign-born in the city also increased at a steady rate, from 33 per cent in 1961 to 43 per cent by 1996 (fig. 2.4).

However, while the amended regulations and procedures ameliorated the situation after 1967, the reality was that the Canada of the 1970s was very different from the Canada of the early 1950s, and the social and economic priorities that had shaped the 1952 legislation were out of place. It had become evident that papering over the flaws in the legislation was not enough; to compete in changing domestic and international markets, a new immigration act was imperative.

1972–1977

Among the precipitating events that finally led the government to introduce a new immigration act was the backlog of cases before the independent Immigration Appeal Board that was created when an unusual number of visitors to Canada applied for landed immigrant status and appealed the decision when the application was denied. By the end of May 1973, the number of cases had increased to 17,472, while the board was only able to handle about 100 cases a month. After revoking the right to change status within Canada in November 1972 and implementing a sixty-day Adjustment of Status program in July 1973, the minister of manpower and immigration announced in September 1973 that a major public review of Canadian immigration policy was to take place. The *Report of the Canadian Immigration and Population Study*, published by the Department of Manpower and Immigration, upheld the crucial relationship between immigration and labour supply and raised important questions about the need for population growth through increased immigration (1974a). The report concluded that 'the number of immigrants Canada admits may progressively become, not only the main determinant of eventual population size, but also the chief factor responsible for the pace at which growth occurs' (1974a, Vol. 3).

As we have already seen in the previous chapter, the debate on the issues raised by the report took place against a backdrop of economic slowdown caused mainly by the Middle East oil embargo. At a time when Canada was experiencing a severe unemployment crisis and when the percentage of visible minorities among Canadian immigrants had more than doubled by 1975 (Richmond and Rao 1977), few people seemed prepared to enter into any discussions about opening the doors to increased immigration. Despite the clamour over the report, however, the government went ahead with its own immigration agenda and the new Immigration Act was passed by Parliament in 1976, becoming law on April 10, 1978. The economic and social implications of the future size, rate of growth, and structure of the Canadian population underscored the legislation's three main objectives:

1 To facilitate the reunion of Canadian citizens and permanent residents with their close relatives from abroad.
2 To foster the development of a strong and viable economy and the prosperity of all regions in Canada.
3 To fulfil Canada's international legal obligations with respect to refugees and uphold its humanitarian tradition with respect to the displaced and the persecuted.

The new Act affirmed the principle of universality in its immigration policy, but it also established three categories of immigrants – family class and assisted relatives, economic migrants, and refugees. For the first time, the minister of immigration and employment was mandated, in consultation with the provinces, to submit to Parliament a yearly target for the number of immigrants for each of the three categories. Other significant changes were the adoption of the distinct category of refugee into the classification of immigrants and the provisions relating to the refugee sponsorship plan, allowing Canadian citizens or permanent residents to undertake sponsorship of refugees. This provision proved to be invaluable for Canada's involvement in resettling the Indochinese refugees after the fall of Saigon in 1975 (Adelman 1980, 1982; Neuwirth et al. 1985; Hawkins 1988). However, it was the introduction and implementation of an internal refugee status determination that greatly influenced the subsequent changes in Canada's immigration policies. In the six-year period from 1972 to 1977, just under one million immigrants came into Canada, averaging 162,800 per annum. These shifts in Canada's immigration policy after the mid-1960s must certainly have led to major changes in the countries of origin of immigrants and refugees. Reflecting on the new policies, Simmons (1993) argued that 'they initially opened the doors to Third World immigrants and subsequently the door to Third World refugees' (285).

The number of immigrants from European and U.S. origins continued to shrink, while those from non-European origins increased. The impact of the move from traditional to non-traditional sources resulted 'not so much from the magnitude of the flows but from their concentration in a small number of receiving communities since the majority of newcomers tend to settle in the major urban sectors' (Burstein 1991, 1),

A Sociodemographic Overview 73

Table 2.1
Number of countries from which Toronto has received immigrants, 1996 Census

Region	No. of Countries	Region	No. of Countries
America		Africa	
North America	1	Western Africa	15
Central America	8	Eastern Africa	16
Caribbean and		Northern Africa	6
Bermuda	24	Central Africa	6
South America	13	Southern Africa	5
Total American	46	Total African	48
Europe		Asia	
Western Europe	9	West Central and	
Eastern Europe	5	Middle East	17
Ex-Soviet Europe	8	Ex-Soviet Asia	8
Northern Europe	7	Eastern Asia	7
Southern Europe	7	South East Asia	10
Former Yugoslavia	5	Southern Asia	5
Total European	41	Total Asian	47
		Oceania	12

Total Countries 194

Source: Statistics Canada (1999a). Immigrant Population by Place of Birth.

such as Toronto, Montreal, and Vancouver. From special runs of the 1996 census, we were able to identify 194 distinct countries of birth among immigrants in Toronto (see table 2.1). These origins are broken down by regions within continents. The boast that almost every country on the globe has a representative in Toronto does not appear that far from the truth. Among immigrants arriving in Toronto before 1961, the top ten countries of birth represented 79 per cent of all immigrants, while in the period from 1991 to 1996 they represented only 57 per cent. This is indicative of the growing number of origins of Toronto's immigrants. The top ten countries of those arriving before 1961 were all European (including the United States), while only one of the top ten from 1991 to 1996 was European.[1]

1978-1990

This period was characterized by the resettlement of Indochinese refugees; the magnitude and subsequent breakdown of the Canadian refu-

Table 2.2
Class of immigrants coming to Toronto in five-year periods, 1980–1999

Class	1980–4 (n = 158,732) (%)	1985–9 (n = 266,351) (%)	1990–4 (n = 481,525) (%)	1995–9 (n = 378,430) (%)
Family	51	37	43	31
Skilled workers	31	44	27	49
Business	4	5	5	5
Refugees	11	13	10	9
Other	3	1	16*	6

*A backlog of immigrants in this period accounted for 10 per cent.
Source: Special runs from Citizenship and Immigration Canada.

gee determination system; the 'uninvited refugee claimants' whose applications for refugee status from within Canada led to the passage of Bill C-55 and the establishment of an Immigration and Refugee Board; and the growth of business immigration.

Considering the main classes in five-year periods, we note that the number of immigrants in the family class declined from just over half in the first period to less than a third in the last period (see table 2.2). The trend, however, was not constantly downwards, since the proportion was higher in the third period than in the second. The number of immigrants who were skilled workers increased from 31 to 49 per cent, while those in the business class remained constant at 4 and 5 per cent. The proportion of refugees ranged between 13 and 9 per cent. The figures are somewhat distorted by the fact that a backlog of 46,431 people already in the country accounted for 10 per cent of immigrants in the period from 1990 to 1994.

Nonetheless, family class immigration remained an important component of Canada's immigration intake, constituting about 40 per cent of the yearly intake. The peak years were 1983 and 1984, with 54.6 per cent and 58 per cent respectively of the total immigration intake being classified under this category. The number of 'kinship bonus points' available to assisted relatives was increased in July 1988 from ten to fifteen.

The acceptance of refugees during the decade was marked by the welcoming to Canada of Indochinese refugees. The admission of these refugees was granted under a provision of the 1976 Immigration Act that gave authority to the government to accept people who were in a 'refugee-like' situation – 'designated classes of refugees' – and who were in need of resettlement, though they might not meet the strict definition of 'convention refugee.' Notwithstanding Canada's expressed traditional humanitarian concerns, the admission of over 60,000 refugees from Southeast Asia between 1979 and 1980 marked the beginning of a new era in Canada's refugee policy in two important respects (Dirks 1985; Neuwirth et al. 1985; Hawkins 1988, 1991; Simmons 1990, 1992). First, it constituted the largest single group of refugees from developing countries ever to have been resettled in a Western nation. Second, their resettlement was made possible by the active participation of the private sector. This combined government and private sponsorship programs distinguished Canada for having absorbed for resettlement the highest number of 'boat people' per capita of any nation (Adelman 1982; Troper 1993).

Of all immigration-related issues, none remained more complex, controversial, costly, or contentious than that of refugees. While the majority of refugees were selected abroad for resettlement in Canada, an increasing number of asylum-seekers arrived in Canada by sea or air and claimed refugee status after arrival. The number of people seeking refugee status in Canada increased from 500 claims in 1977 to 6,100 in 1983. By the end of 1989, the backlog had reached over 95,000 claims and had clogged a refugee determination system that had not been designed to handle such a heavy caseload (Burstein 1991).

The refugee issue took a dramatic turn, as pointed out in chapter 1, when two ships illegally stranded their refugee cargoes on Canada's East Coast in the dead of night. In 1986, 155 Tamils arrived in Newfoundland, and in 1987, 174 Sikhs arrived in Nova Scotia from refugee camps in Germany, which led to fears that more boatloads of refugees may be on their way to Canada. In addition, it was feared that migrants from other source countries (such as El Salvador, Guatemala, and the Caribbean) entering Canada would claim refugee status (Contenta 1986; Malarek 1986; Ruimy 1986). Reacting to this situation, the government recalled Parliament and passed emergency legislation in the summer of 1987. In addition to imposing a transit visa for some nationals making stops in Canada en route to other countries, Bill C-55 and Bill C-84, concerning refugee status determination and deterrent measures, included substantially increased penalties for smugglers of refugee claimants and their accomplices, and for the transportation companies bringing undocumented people to Canada.

Measures in the new laws allowed immigrants who arrived without proper documentation to be detained until their identities could be established, and those who posed a criminal or security threat to be removed. Any individuals who had passed through another country deemed to be 'safe' and where a refugee claim might have been made, would not be allowed to make a refugee claim in Canada. (This provision of the legislation, the so-called safe third country, provision, if proclaimed and enforced, could have reduced the number of the claims made after the claimants' arrival in Canada since one-third of the claimants came to Canada via the United States. As of 1993, the Canadian government continued negotiations with the United States under the auspices of another piece of legislation – Bill C-86 – for a bilateral agreement whereby refugee claimants could be sent back to the United States.) The 'safe third country' provision had still not been finalized in the 2001 Immigration and Refugee Protection Act.

The census does not include information on immigrant and refugee categories that would allow us to match up census data with immigration data. This is particularly regrettable in the case of refugees, since, as we pointed out above, the refugee situation has become a focal point of public and private debate, despite the fact that refugees represent 13 per cent[2] or less of all immigration. Available immigration sources do indicate that, in the recent past, Toronto has had the 'lion's share' of refugees. In 1999 Toronto had 8,000 and Montreal had 5,000, while no other Census Metropolitan Area had as many as 2,000 (Citizenship and Immigration Canada 1999b). Using countries of origin data from the above source and classifying these origins into birthplace categories, we can see that between 1997 and 1999 the largest number of refugees came from the former Yugoslavia (in particular, from Bosnia-Herzegovina), the Middle East, and South Asia (fig. 2.5).

Along with changes affecting refugees, another noted change in Canada's immigration policy during this period was one of deliberately encouraging the migration of 'business immigrants' – immigrants who brought with them substantial capital for investment and who planned to start a business that would create employment for Canadians. Statistics indicate that the immigration of this group, including their dependents, increased from 15,112 in 1988, to 17,564 in 1989, and to 18,126 in 1990, an increase that was entirely attributable to the investor class. Hong Kong was the largest single source country in 1984, supplying 31 per cent of the business immigrants (Burstein 1991). They reportedly invested a total of $817 million in Canada in 1984 and created more than 8,000 jobs. In 1987, business immigrants brought an estimated $1.9 billion to Canada and, in 1988, the figure rose to $2.9 billion. Again,

Figure 2.5
Main source countries of refugees in Canada, 1997–1999

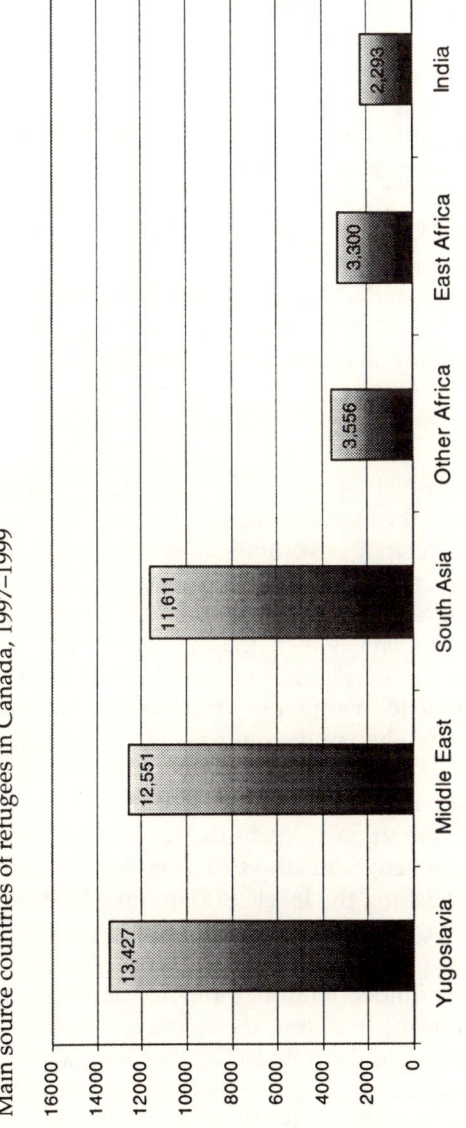

Yugoslavia	13,427
Middle East	12,551
South Asia	11,611
Other Africa	3,556
East Africa	3,300
India	2,293

Source: Citizenship and Immigration Canada, *Facts and Figures: Immigration Overview, 1999.*

Hong Kong was the largest single source, accounting for 28 per cent of all business immigrants, followed by Korea, Taiwan, and the United States (L. Wong 1984, 1991; A. Richmond 1991). However, there was much controversy over this program, concerning charges of abuse of the system by those merely endeavouring to obtain entry into Canada without fulfilling their obligations (Malarek 1987; Nash 1987; Cannon 1989; Fennel and DeMont 1989; Lai 1992). In 1989, the minister of employment and immigration put a monitoring program in place that was designed to track entrepreneurs until they had complied with the terms and conditions of their landing (A. Richmond 1991; Employment and Immigration Canada 1992).

During the above period, average annual immigration dropped to 122,118 (compared to 162,815 in the previous period); during the period 1983 to 1985, immigration totals were well below 90,000.

1991–2002

In 1990, the government presented a five-year immigration plan – which it developed through a nation-wide consultation process with provincial and municipal governments, special interest groups, individuals, and organizations – rather than a yearly program as mandated by the 1976 Immigration Act (Employment and Immigration Canada 1990). The five-year plan, which took effect in 1991, provided for a moderate increase in immigration levels to 220,000 in 1991 and to 250,000 in each of the following four years, while maintaining a reasonable balance between the family, refugee, and independent immigrant categories.

However, actual immigration fell short of the announced levels. Employment and Immigration Canada explained that the discrepancies were due to the fact that, while the 1976 Immigration Act provided the authority for establishing the levels of immigration deemed appropriate, it did not give the government the 'tools to manage the immigration system' effectively (1992, 1993). For example, without the authority to set limits on the number of immigrant applications accepted for each category, any applicant who met the relevant statutory requirements and selection criteria had the right to land in Canada, regardless of how many applications had already been received. Hence, lengthy delays and backlogs in processing applications resulted in discrepancies in the planning figures and the actual landings.

There were also specific causes for the shortfalls. The business immigrant shortfall was attributable, in part, to the political climate in Hong Kong, a recession in Canada, and changes in the effective monitoring, reporting, and enforcement of conditions set under the program (ibid.). Changes in world conditions in Eastern Europe, Southeast Asia, and Latin America resulted in fewer people being accepted under the designated classes of refugees.

Notwithstanding these changes, immigration in the 1990s was distinctly marked by the massive legislative amendments in Bill C-86, passed by the government in 1992 and enacted in January 1993. Previous amendments made in Bill C-55 and Bill C-84 did not achieve what the government intended (reducing the number of people entering Canada and claiming refugee status). The government's overall concern – fuelled by media reports of refugees making multiple welfare claims, of criminals entering Canada and making refugee claims, of convicted terrorists winning refugee status, and of organized smuggling of illegal aliens – was to retain effective control over the types and the numbers of immigrants entering through Canada's borders.

The most significant change under Bill C-86 was the legislative power given to the government to control and streamline the internal refugee determination process. To prevent refugee claimants from asylum-shopping (making multiple refugee claims in different countries), in accordance with the Dublin Convention in Europe, and from making multiple applications for welfare and social assistance while waiting for a hearing in Canada, Bill C-86 empowered the government to fingerprint and photograph the claimants and to make agreements with other countries whereby refugee claimants could be sent back to the 'safe third countries' to make their claims. This reduced the pressure on Canada's refugee determination system and reduced the costs of social assistance, medical care, and education provided to claimants pending their hearings.

Furthermore, Bill C-86 eliminated the initial hearing stage in view of the fact that over 95 per cent of the claimants who went through this stage were able to establish that their claim did have a prima facie credible basis, in contrast to the original expectation envisaged in Bill C-55 that one-third of the claimants would be rejected and then removed. Bill C-86 gave authority to the senior immigration officer at ports of entry to make a decision as to whether the claim had credible basis. Rejected claimants could appeal, with leave, for a judicial review to the Trial Division of the Federal Court, where cases are heard by one judge, as opposed to the Federal Court of Canada, where cases are heard by three judges (this was stipulated in Bill C-55 in 1989 and created a large backlog of cases before the Federal Court – sometimes as long as several years). Access to the Appeal Division only exists in situations that have been identified by a Trial Division judge as involving a serious question of law (Employment and Immigration Canada 1992, 1993). The new legislation also allowed the government to increase its efforts to intercept 'illegal migrants' overseas before they arrived in Canada by providing training and technological assistance to airlines to help them identify passengers with fraudulent documents and by increasing fines to airlines that did 'not undertake reasonable precautions' in screening the passengers they brought to Canada.

In late 1996, the Legislative Advisory Group under Lucienne Robillard, then minister of citizenship and immigration, was appointed to conduct an independent review of the existing Act. The ministry's final report, *Not Just Numbers: A Canadian Framework for Future Immigration* (1997), proposed 172 recommendations for changing the Canadian immigration policy. In 1998, another document, *Building on a Strong Foundation for the Twenty-first Century: New Directions for Immigration and Refugee Policy and Legislation*, outlined measures to update the current policy 'to respond to the challenges of the new domestic and international environments; to address the legitimate expectation of potential immigrants and their sponsors that their rights and obligations will be presented in a clear and comprehensive way; to update Canada's approach to refugee selection abroad, and to refugee determination, in Canada; and to ensure that the legislation provides the tools that allow immigration to maintain its positive role in the social and economic development of the country.'

In June 2000, Elinor Caplan, the then minister of citizenship and immigration, tabled Bill C-11 – the Immigration and Refugee Protection Act. The current act, critics argued, was 'burdened with a 20-year accumulation of layered-on, statutorily entrenched, administrative and procedural provisions' and 'legislative amendments.' Though the proposed act deals with much of the same subject matter as the current one – applications for permanent residence, permits, inadmissibility, refugee claims, appeals, enforcement, and removals – it reiterates that 'immigration has proven to be an essential social, cultural, and economic lever for Canada in the past. It will be equally vital in the future. New legislation is needed to ensure that Canada can preserve immigration as a source of diversity, richness and openness to the world' (Citizenship and Immigration Canada 2000a).

The objectives of the proposed Immigration and Refugee Protection Act and the main classes of immigrants who will be accepted for settlement remain essentially the same as those stipulated in the 1978 Immigration Act. According to the minister, 'Bill C-11 renews our commitment to family reunification so that Canadian citizens, permanent residents, and refugees can be reunited with their families as soon as possible and provides a fair, efficient, and adaptable process for welcoming those immigrants who will help Canada grow.' Meanwhile, the proposed act aims to do what the minister has described as 'closing the backdoor' by giving immigration officers the 'tools they need to bar entry to foreign nationals who, as part of organized crime, are encouraging transnational crimes such as trafficking in people' (Citizenship and Immigration Canada 2000b).

Essentially, the new Act, which was passed in 2002, and its regulations are designed to make the system more efficient. Applications for immigration to Canada must be complete before processing, so applicants who cannot meet the requirements will save money by not submitting their application. Provisions have been simplified for the following categories: refugee claimants seeking work permits; students coming to Canada to take courses for less than six months; performance artists and after-sales personnel for global corporations (who become business visitors); and frequent border-crossers (using a 'Canpass' system).

Independent Migrants ('Points System')
One of the significant changes in the 'points system' is its reference to 'work' rather than 'employment,' which is usually referred to as 'paid work.' This allows the self-employed to count their work as points, as can people who come to Canada to work as interns or in some other form of (often unpaid) work. People may thereby 'test out' work situations for a few months and may gain 'points.' They may remain in Canada to take work-upgrading and language courses to enhance the chances of being accepted. As well, employers can recruit whole classes of workers to work temporarily in Canada. Since there is 'credit' accrued for this work experience, this may mean more 'internal' sourcing of immigration, as these workers may apply for permanent residency from within Canada after such a temporary work experience.

The former 'skills rating' for occupations has been eliminated. Instead, rating for the 'points' system disproportionately falls upon completed (formal) education. Education includes skills training as well as undergraduate training. The rationale for this change involves a judgment call by Canada that specific skills can be learned in Canada more easily for persons with higher levels of completed education. Likewise, specific skills take time to recruit – often up to five years, by which time, demand patterns in Canada may have changed and the skilled persons do not find the jobs their immigration was intended to fill.

By using these 'objective' indicators (education, language), the administrative decision-making burden on immigration officers is expected to be easier. They can award up to ten points for 'objective adaptability' but cannot give any points for the largely subjectively assessed 'personal adaptability' under the existing system.

A large 'points system' category is work experience. Applicants are rated on their skill levels and for the skill type relative to the degree of need for the *general* type, rather than *specific* type, of occupation. In this connection, an applicant may gain up to twenty points for trade certificates and diplomas under the 'education' category. A trade certificate based on three years of training is given the same value as a university bachelor's degree.

If the applicant is between the ages of twenty-one and forty-four years, he or she gains ten points. These points are systematically subtracted for older independent immigrants.

Language proficiency gains up to twenty points. This refers to a *mastery* of English *or* French, not a smattering of words and phrases in one or both languages.

The pass mark was originally set at eighty points and applies to all applications received after the Act comes into force as well as to cases not having received a selection interview. While there is much controversy about far back a 'grandfather' (old rules) clause should apply and for whom, Citizenship and Immigration Canada seems intent to make allowances by lowering the admissions threshold to seventy points for cases already in the system. The pass mark for applicants under the new regulation is seventy-five points.

Business (Entrepreneur and Investor) Classes
These groups bypass the 'points system' their requirements remain about the same. Entrepreneurs need $300,000, while investors with demonstrated business experience must have at least $800,000 in net

capital, of which half must be available for investment. These classes are monitored after arrival to ensure compliance.

Caregiver Program
Prospective employers must enter into a formal contract with the caregiver in an effort to forestall possible abuse. Yet this contractual situation means that women may not be able to change employers until they have received a new offer of employment, have that offer validated by an immigration officer, and enter into a new (formal) contract. So the procedure is even more complicated for the caregivers.

Family Class
The definition of family has been altered to include same-sex and common-law partners. Under some conditions – a degree in higher education, for example – the principal (independent) applicant can gain an additional five points that can be applied both to the applicant and the partner.

Sponsorship is reduced from ten to three years. Some screening has been introduced to detect spouse-abusers. If sponsors default on support within the three-year period, a collection agency will pursue the sponsor in the early stages of default.

Also, the dependent child must be single and not in a consensual union. To accompany the parents, the child can be as old as 22 or older if he or she is still a dependent (e.g., a student or a person with a disability).

Humanitarian Class
This class has been broadened to include those refugees selected abroad and those making a claim within Canada, as well as those who are subject to capital punishment in their home country and who seek to stay in Canada for humanitarian reasons. Immigration in this category are subject to a Pre-Removal Risk Assessment by the Immigration and Refugee Board (IRB), and if they are not judged to be inadmissible (criminal, torturer, terrorist, rejected refugee claimant), then they gain the right to remain in Canada. If a claimant is held because he or she may have tortured or exploited someone in the country of origin, his or her case is assessed under the restrictive criteria of the Convention against Torture.

The criterion that potential refugees must be able to 'successfully establish themselves' has been relaxed to include a social, rather than a strictly economic, meaning. Those refugees applying from abroad may include their dependents in the same application and bring them over within a year after their arrival in Canada.

For claimants within Canada, the removal procedures have been tightened to assess the risk these rejected cases might pose. They may have another hearing if there is new evidence.

Two new issues have emerged for refugee claimants. A Refugee Appeal Division has been set up, where rejected refugee claimants can appeal the decision made by the IRB instead of seeking leave for a judicial review from the Federal Court of Appeal. However, as reported by the Canadian Council for Refugees (2002), the implementation of the Appeal Division was postponed by at least a year when the new Act came into force on June 28, 2002.

The other issue is the continuing debate on the implementation of the 'safe third country.' Since 1989, Canada has been trying to negotiate a reciprocal agreement with the U.S. to allow Canada to turn back refugee claimants who arrive each year via the United States. If implemented, there could be a substantial reduction in the numbers of refugee claimants entering Canada via that country. While the basic premise of a 'safe third country' agreement is that Canada and the United States would recognize each other as a safe place for refugee claimants to seek asylum, it is contested and challenged by human rights and refugee advocates because the U.S. determination system is much politicized and does not meet Canada's expectations. This was demonstrated by the large numbers of Salvadoran refugees accepted by Canada and not the United States in the 1980s.

The assistant deputy minister, Citizenship and Immigration, told the Senate Committee that 'close to 40% of people who claim refugee status in Canada come to Canada from the U.S.' (Canadian Council for Refugees, 2001). According to data reported in the Montreal *Gazette* of September 29, 2001, 'asylum seekers who file their refugee claims upon entering Canada are far more likely to do so after travelling overland via the U.S. ... The data reveal that a decade ago, 37% of all asylum seekers who filed claims upon entering Canada did so after travelling here overland through the United States. By last year, that figure had risen to 63%' (qtd. in CCR 2001).

The United States may be reluctant to strike a deal, fearing they might end up with more claimants than Canada does. Canada's deputy prime minister has said that 'talks are under way again and we're making progress' (A. Thompson 2002, A6). On May 6, 2002, it was reported that 'Canada has reached a draft agreement that would allow Ottawa to turn back at the border thousands of refugee claimants who arrive each year via the U.S.' (MacCharles 2002, A6). The deputy prime minister repeated that 'statistics indicate that, so far this year, 72% of the total number of refugee claimants here came through the U.S. Last year, about 60% did so' (ibid.). While the details of the agreement have not been announced, it is likely that there would be some provisions allowing refugee claimants to make their claims in Canada because some countries, including most in Latin and Central America, cannot get direct airline flights – most make an American stopover.

However, we should keep in mind the following questions: Will this act serve to 'strike a balance between Canada's tradition of protecting refugees and welcoming immigrants' and 'respond quickly to a rapidly evolving environment and to emerging challenges and opportunities' as Canada enters a new century? Will it help Canada to meet its announced target of accepting between 225,000 and 250,000 immigrants a year? Will it provide the necessary tools and resources to allow the minister of Citizenship and Immigration to increase the annual intake of immigrants to 1 per cent (about 300,000) of Canada's population in order to sustain its demographic and economic growth?

THE INCREASING DIVERSITY OF TORONTO'S IMMIGRANT POPULATION

Having covered the main points of changes in legislation immediately following the Second World War, with an emphasis on the last thirty of those years, we now want to consider how this legislation has affected the characteristics of immigrants coming to Canada, in general, and to Toronto, in particular. The information that follows comes from various censuses held between 1971 and 1996; in some cases, we have information for 1961 as well.

A group's mother tongue gives a fair indication of their cultural origin. However, because of a colonial past, many non-European countries had adopted the language of their colonizers, thus making it their own mother tongue. This was particularly true for English and French. In 1961, the proportion of Toronto's population that did not have English or French as a mother tongue was only 23 per cent, but by 1996 this had risen to 38 per cent (see figure 2.6). In 1996, the most important mother tongues in Toronto were Chinese (7 per cent) and Italian (5 per

86 Clifford Jansen and Lawrence Lam

Figure 2.6
Non-English/French mother tongues, Toronto, 1961–1996

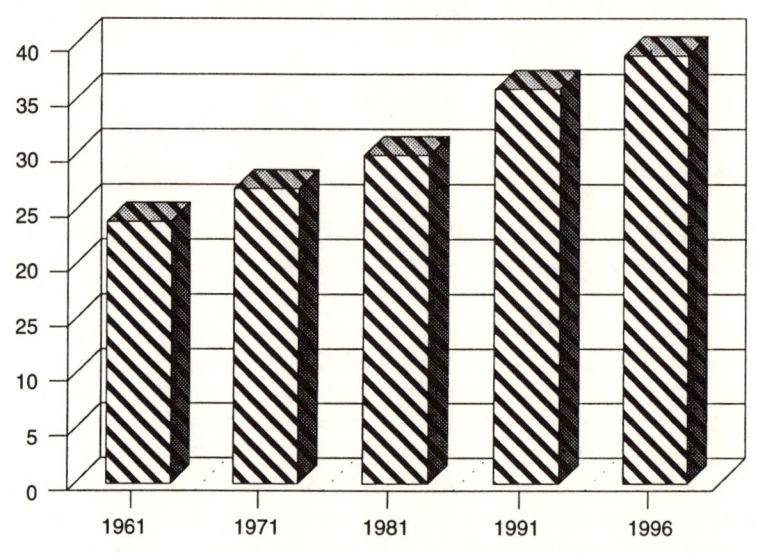

Source: Statistics Canada, *Census 1961–1996, Public Use Microfiche Files.*

cent); other significant mother tongues (in order of importance) were Portuguese, Indo-Iranian, Polish, Spanish, Punjabi, Greek, and German (all accounting for over 1 per cent) while the mother tongues of 14 per cent of the city's population were classified as 'other.'

The census information on the 'language usually spoken in the home' can give us a good idea of the variety of languages one can hear on the streets of Toronto. As was to be expected, in 1996, just under three-quarters (73 per cent) of the population spoke either English or French in the home. Chinese accounted for 6 per cent, and Italian, Portuguese, and Indo-Iranian languages each accounted for 2 per cent. The remaining 15 per cent of the population spoke a variety of other languages in the home. Given that 266 immigrants a day were coming to Canada in 1996, one can imagine the kinds of problems schools, employers, institutions, and immigrant agencies faced in attempting to integrate an everchanging population, so many of whom had a scant knowledge of English.

Religion is another aspect of the changing diversity of Toronto. In the census, a question about the religion of Canadians is only asked every

TABLE 2.3
Major religious categories in Toronto, 1971–1991

	1971 (%)	1981 (%)	1991 (%)
Catholic	36	40	39
Protestant	49	44	36
Jewish	4	4	4
Non-Christian	5*	4*	7
No religion	6	9	14

Source: Statistics Canada, Censuses 1971–1991, Public Use Microfiche Files.
*These are classified as 'other' and might include non-Christian religions.

ten years, in the census years ending in '1.' Our comparisons are thus limited to the years 1971, 1981, and 1991. In 1971, the number of religious categories was twelve, plus one category for 'no religion.' In 1981, this had increased to thirteen, with 'none/other' classified in one category. By 1991, there were twenty categories for religion and one assigned to 'no religion.'

These data give us an indication of how Toronto has changed over the past three decades and the necessity for adding more categories to include non-Christian religions. The major categories could be regrouped as Catholic (Roman, Ukrainian, and Greek and Eastern Orthodox), Protestant (Anglican, Baptist, Jehovah's Witness, Lutheran, Mennonite/Hutterite, Pentecostal, Presbyterian, United Church, and other Protestant), Jewish, and non-Christian (Buddhist, Hindu, Muslim, and Sikh). Table 2.3 indicates the changes in these major groups for Toronto.

It is interesting to contrast Canadian-born and immigrants, as far as non-Christian religions are concerned. Among Canadian-born Torontonians, 3 per cent of the total were non-Christian, while among immigrants, non-Christians represented 13 per cent. In actual numbers, this meant that 61,071 Torontonians born in Canada were non-Christians, while the number of non-Christian immigrants was 209,321. By period of immigration, non-Christian religions accounted for only 3 per cent of the total of immigrants arriving in Toronto until 1965. These religions have increased steadily since then, representing larger and larger proportions of total immigrants. Table 2.4 shows the proportions by period of immigration.

One can only assume that this trend has continued since 1991 and,

TABLE 2.4
Percentage of non-Christian religions by immigration period

Dates	Percentage
Before 1966	3
1966–70	5
1971–5	16
1976–80	18
1981–5	23
1986–91	26

Source: Statistics Canada, *1991 Census of Canada, Public Use Microfiche Files.*

thus, as we move into the twenty-first century, more and more immigrants are coming into Toronto with non-Christian religions.

Canadians have always been defined by ethnic origin. The diversity of Toronto could be analysed by looking at the ethnic composition of the population in different periods. However, the definition of ethnicity has changed from one census year to the next, making perfect comparison between periods impossible.

In 1961, ethnically,[3] Toronto was predominantly British (61 per cent) and European (35 per cent). Among the 640,730 Europeans, 140,378 were Italian, 80,300 were German, and 61,421 were French. There were only slight variations in the decade that followed, since changes in immigration laws had not yet had an effect on the ethnic composition of the city. The predominant ethnic groups in Toronto, in 1971, were British (56 per cent) and Italian (10 per cent). Germans and Jews accounted for just over 4 per cent each, while French accounted for just under 4 per cent. Allowing for a few regroupings so as to be comparable to later censuses, the population of Toronto in 1971, could be broken down as follows: 60 per cent were charter groups (British and French); 28 per cent were of European origins; 3 per cent were of non-European origins; with the remaining 9 per cent classified as 'other' (see figure 2.7).

The definition of ethnic origin was changed again by 1981 and people could give more than one ethnic origin, thus creating two major categories: single and multiple. British was the number one single-origin ethnic group (50 per cent) in Toronto. The Italian proportion of those listing a single origin was 11 per cent, while the Jewish proportion was 4 per cent, and the German had dropped to 3 per cent. Other single groups with 3 per cent or more included Chinese and Portuguese;

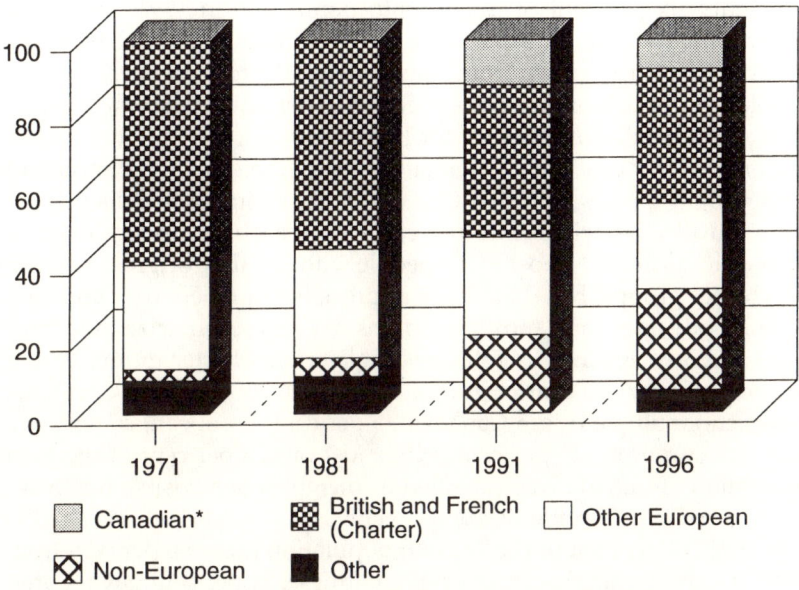

Figure 2.7
Major ethnic origins, Toronto, 1971–1996

- Canadian*
- British and French (Charter)
- Other European
- Non-European
- Other

Source: Statistics Canada, *Census 1961–1996, Public Use Microfiche Files*.
*'Canadian' was a new category in 1991.

Caribbeans were just under 3 per cent. Multiple origins accounted for only 7 per cent. Most of these involved charter-group origins, so that in reclassifying respondents, we could summarize the ethnic breakdown of Toronto as follows: single charter, 49 per cent; multiple charter, 7 per cent; European, 29 per cent; non-European, 5 per cent; and other single and multiple, 10 per cent.

By 1991, still more changes were included in the definition of ethnicity. Most important of these was a separate classification of Canada's peoples into a group called 'visible minority' when compared with the rest of the population. This allowed for the definition of the population not only by European and non-European origin but also by the descendants within each of these groups. Another important change was the fact that people could use 'Canadian' as an ethnic origin. In Canada as a whole, just under 3 per cent gave Canadian as their ethnic origin, while for Toronto the proportion was just under 7 per cent. Since it is not clear how many people who had previously defined themselves as having a non-Canadian ethnicity were now being classified as Canadian, comparisons with earlier years is not possible.

Seventy-six per cent of the Toronto population in 1991 declared a single ethnic origin. Multiples – people who identified more than one ethnic origin – had grown from 7 per cent in 1981 to 24 per cent in 1991. People with British origins accounted for 26 per cent of the single-origin ethnic group; Italians accounted for 11 per cent; and, as mentioned above, just under 7 per cent gave Canadian as their ethnicity. Other important single-origin groups included Chinese, 8 per cent; South Asian, 7 per cent; and Black/Caribbean, 6 per cent; the Jewish group remained at 4 per cent. As in 1981, most of the people with multiple origins involved the charter groups, but there were appreciable numbers of 'Canadian' among both single and multiple origins. We can summarize the ethnic breakdown of Toronto as follows: single-origin charter group, 21 per cent; multiple-origin charter group, 20 per cent; single-origin Canadian, 7 per cent; multiple-origin Canadian, 5 per cent; European, 26 per cent; and non-European, 21 per cent. While just over 9 per cent of the total population of Canada was classified as members of a 'visible minority,' the proportion in Toronto was 26 per cent.

In 1996, 70 per cent of the Toronto population (down 6 per cent from 1991) declared a single-ethnic origin. Of these, 11 per cent gave 'Canadian' as their ethnicity. British single origins accounted for only 16 per cent; Italians and Chinese for 11 per cent; South Asian for 10 per cent; Caribbeans for 6 per cent; Portuguese for 4 per cent; and Jewish and Polish for 3 per cent each. If we include people with multiple origins, we can summarize the ethnic breakdown of Toronto in 1996 as follows: single-origin charter group, 12 per cent; multiple-origin charter group (including British, French, and Canadian), 24 per cent; single-origin Canadian, 8 per cent; European, 23 per cent; non-European, 27 per cent; and others with multiple origins, 6 per cent. By this time, the visible minority population in Toronto had increased to 32 per cent from 26 per cent in 1991.

While the above breakdown describes the increase in Toronto's ethnic diversity since the 1960s, it does not take into account the degree to which people of different ethnic origins were 'mixing.' By allowing respondents in the census to give more than one ethnic origin, one could use the proportion of people with multiple origins as an indicator of this. As we noted above, the proportion of respondents who had multiple ethnic origins increased from 7 per cent in 1981 to 24 per cent in 1991, and to 30 per cent in 1996. This would indicate that more and

Table 2.5
Proportions of identified ethnic groups who have multiple origins,
Toronto, 1996

Group	%	Group	%
French	85	Latin/South American	34
German	75	African	32
Dutch	67	Caribbean	31
British	66	Italian	25
Ukrainian	60	Greek	24
Spanish	57	West Asian	21
Hungarian	55	Portuguese	20
Polish	49	South Asian	19
Lebanese	48	Vietnamese	18
Jewish	38	Filipino	15
		Chinese	12

Source: Statistics Canada (1999a).

more intermarriages were taking place between people of different ethnic origins, and their children's origins were becoming more diversified. By 1996, the proportion of all origins naming British plus one other origin (including French and Canadian) totalled 20 per cent. In fact, origins that included British, French, or Canadian accounted for 19 per cent of all origins, while multiple origins that did not involve the above groups accounted for only 6 per cent. (When comparing multiple origins, it is obvious that double counting will take place. If someone has British and French origin, then they will appear in the British and French category as well as in the French and British category.)

Despite the potential for double-counting, by looking at specific ethnic groups, we can compare the proportions of the total population who have multiple origins. Groups with a high proportion identifying multiple origins are, no doubt, mixing more than those who a have low proportion. There are many possible reasons for the differences, including length of time the group has been immigrating to Canada, cultural or religious reasons for marrying mainly within one's own group, the size of the ethnic population and possibility of mixing with one's own group, and, perhaps, prejudicial attitudes of some groups towards others.

Table 2.5 shows the proportion of multiples in each of the twenty-one groups identified by the census in order of highest to lowest proportion of multiple origins. The proportions of groups with multiple origins compared with totals in a given ethnic group range from 85 per cent for people of French ethnic origin to 12 per cent of Chinese origin. This means that people of French origin are most likely to come from mixed parentage, and people of Chinese origin are least likely to do so. In the case of the Chinese, many would have married before immigrating to Toronto and, of those who did not, most still tend to marry within their own group.

INCLUSION AND EXCLUSION AT THE END OF THE TWENTIETH CENTURY

Before considering the degree to which the diversity of immigrants has been integrated into Toronto society, we need to comment on the use of the term 'immigrant' in daily language and in the media. Some groups, such as Ukrainians, Italians, Greeks, and Portuguese, are often considered to be immigrants whether or not they were, in fact, born in Canada. Members of visible minorities are always considered to be immigrants. When any individuals of these origins excel in sports or in the arts, they are immediately claimed to be 'Canadian.' When they are involved in negative activities like crime, however, emphasis is placed on the fact that they are immigrants. The reality is that many members of various ethnic groups are Canadian-born and have no other experience than that of Canada, but because of their racial and/or cultural background, they continue to be labelled as immigrants.

Table 2.6 lists a number of ethnic groups in which a significant proportion is born in Canada. Of course, the Aboriginal people are all Canadian-born and people who define their ethnicity as Canadian are 98 per cent Canadian-born. This is also true for about 90 per cent of people with multiple British and French origins, as well as for people with French single-ethnic origins. Among people with British single-ethnic origins, however, the proportion born in Canada is 70 per cent; more than half of those whose origins are Ukrainian (64 per cent), Jewish (63 per cent), Italian (53 per cent), Dutch, or 'other multiple' (51 per cent each) are Canadian-born. Other East and Southeast Asians (38 per cent) had a higher proportion of Canadian-born than several European-origin groups, including Balkan (33 per cent), Portuguese (32 per cent), other European (32 per cent), Hungarian (28 per cent), and Polish (27 per cent). It is important not to assume that all people of a given ethnic group are necessarily immigrants.

In considering the extent to which the diverse groups have been

Table 2.6
Proportions of ethnic groups born in Canada, Toronto, 1996

Group	%	Group	%
Aboriginal	100	Balkan	33
Canadian	98	Portuguese	32
French multiple	91	Other European	32
British multiple	90	Caribbean	32
French single	90	Hungarian	28
British single	70	Polish	27
Ukrainian	64	Other single origins	27
Jewish	63	Lebanese	26
Italian	53	South Asian	24
Dutch	51	Vietnamese	21
Other multiple	51	Other Arabic	20
Greek	48	Latin, Central, South American	20
Other Western European	39	Chinese	19
Other E & SE Asian	38	Filipino	19

Source: Statistics Canada (1999a).

socially accommodated or 'included' in Toronto society, we will focus on birthplace and on single-origin ethnic groups. Because of the problem of double-counting, it would not be appropriate to include people with multiple ethnicities. We can go as far as to assume that people who have identified multiple origins are more likely to be included in the society because they are descendants of previous mixes. When we compare respondents of multiple ethnicity to those of single, we find that 10 per cent of the former are under 18 years of age, another 9 per cent are classified as children, 10 per cent have never been married, 36 per cent are Canadian citizens by birth, and almost all (93 per cent) speak English or French in the home, compared with 65 per cent for respondents of single-origin ethnicity.

The concept of social inclusion/exclusion – like that of diversity – is difficult to measure. Normally, we would take one group as the standard or reference group to which all others could be compared. For Canada, as a whole, this may well be the two groups that we consider to be the charter groups, namely the British and French. However, as we have seen, while our institutions may still be predominantly based on British and French culture, in a city like Toronto, the importance of the British (especially English) influence has been in constant decline; as we have seen, by 1991, the British accounted for only 26 per cent of the single-origin ethnic groups and French influence was, for all intents and purposes, non-existent.

New immigrants coming into Toronto today would certainly not be aware that the British are or should be the reference group to which they should aspire. In fact, Toronto City Council may well be the reference group for many new immigrants since their lives are directly affected by this political institution. In the year 2000, we endeavoured to identify the approximately fifty city councillors by ethnic origin.[4] Quite a few had multiple ethnic origins, but taking their first-mentioned ethnicity as the dominant one, we found that 16 per cent were English, 14 per cent were Irish, 10 per cent were Scottish, and 2 per cent were Welsh, for a total of 52 per cent. However, Italians (18 per cent), Jewish (10 per cent), Chinese (6 per cent), and a variety of others, made up the remaining 48 per cent.

In the end, we concluded that we had to consider the characteristics of the *total population of Toronto* as the norm, and to consider the characteristics of subgroups of this population in terms of their deviance from the norm.[5] For example, in table 2.7, while 31 per cent of people 15 years old and over in Toronto had less than secondary education, the proportion in the Vietnamese ethnic group was 55 per cent (or 24 percentage points higher than the 'norm.')

Since we could not expect subgroups to have an exact correspondence with the total population, we decided to only identify situations where a subgroup differed by plus or minus 5 per cent or more from the total. This criterion has been applied to all tables that refer to (1) demographic, (2) educational/occupational, and (3) income characteristics. Data for those categories where a subgroup differed by less than plus or minus 5 per cent have not been included in the tables. In each of the tables, the percentages in each category of the total population of Toronto is given and then differences between these percentages and those of the subgroups are compared. The subgroups include all foreign-born, foreign-born from Europe-U.S., and foreign-born from other origins. After that, immigrants born in twenty-one distinct countries or regions are compared with the results for all of Toronto. Finally, twenty-eight single-origin ethnic groups are compared with the Toronto proportions.

Inclusion or exclusion of groups could well depend on factors other than ethnic discrimination. Some of these include the average age of groups, family status (for example, families with lone parents may exclude more than two-parent families), family size, marital status, and language spoken in the home. We discuss these and other details in the next three sections. In the first section, we provide a sociodemographic profile of foreign-born and ethnic groups. In the second section, we focus directly on education and occupation, because the types of education or skill levels with which some groups arrived in Canada could have an influence on their social inclusion or exclusion. In the third, we focus on income characteristics – the most important indicator of exclusion/inclusion for all immigrants. Within the latter two sections, we also consider differences by gender.

A SOCIODEMOGRAPHIC PROFILE

This profile takes into consideration age groups, gender differences, family status, household size, marital status, home ownership, foreign citizenship, and language spoken in the home (table 2.7). Age groups were broken down into the following categories: 5 years and under, 6–13, 14–18, 19–45, 46–64, and 65 and over. The reason for these categories is to identify pre-school children and to distinguish them from primary- and secondary-school children. The category 19–45 represents younger people in the labour force (and corresponds closely to ages used to gain points in the point system of immigration), while the category 46–64 corresponds to older people in the labour force and, of course, the 65 and over category represents those in retirement age. While most other categories are obvious, when considering census family status, we considered only male and female single parents and their children because, for the most part, there were no differences in the other categories. For the same reason, when considering marital status, we limited the comparison to singles and divorced/separated.

Age Groups

When we compared all foreign-born to the total Toronto population, the foreign-born were less likely to include people age 13 or younger and more likely to include people in the 46–64 age category. The big difference was found when we compared European with the non-European immigrants: 30 per cent of Europeans were over age 45, as compared with less than 5 per cent of non-Europeans. Non-Europeans also had 12 per cent more than the total population in the 19–45 age category.

Table 2.7
Demographic characteristics of subgroups compared with percentages of total population, Toronto, 1996

	Age							Lone parent		
Group	-5 %	-13 %	-18 %	-45 %	-64 %	65+ %	Feml %	Male %	Feml %	Child %
Toronto	9	11	6	44	20	10	51	1	4	7
All foreign-born		-8	-6			+9				
Born Europe-US	-8	-8		-10	+17	+13				-5
Born non-European					+12					
Born In										
USA	-6									
UK	-9	-10		-10		+16				-5
Germany	-9	-9		-24	+31	+16				-6
Italy	-9	-11	-6	-21	+31	+15				-7
Netherlands	-9	-10	-5	-26	+29	+20				-7
Poland	-9					+11				
Portugal	-9	-7		+7	+11					-5
Former USSR	-8	-6		-15		+30				
Former Yugoslavia	-7	-5		+15	+15	+6				
Other European	-9	-8		-12	+21	+13				-5
Middle East	-6			+7			-6			
India	-9	-8		+10	+9					
S. Asia	-7			+15						
China	-9	-9		-9	+15	+15				-5
Hong Kong	-7			+18	-5	-6				
Philippines	-8	-5		+13			+9			
Vietnam	-9	-7		+27	-7					
Other E&SE Asia	-8	-5		+10						
East Africa	-8			+18		-5				
Other Africa	-7			+11			-6			
Central/South America & Caribbean	-8	-6		+12	+5				+7	
Single Ethnic Origin										
British	-6	-6			+8	+13				
French	-6	-7		+6	+8					
Dutch	-7	-7		+5	+6	+7				
German	-7	-9	-5	-5	+13	+13				
Other W. European	-9	-9		-6	+11	+17				-6
Hungarian	-6	-6		-9	+13	+12				
Polish										
Ukrainian	-6	-6		-8		+20				
Balkan					+5					
Greek	-5				+7					
Italian					+5					
Portuguese										
Spanish				+6		-5				
Jewish				-10		+10				
Other European	-6	-6			+7	+13				
African	+6			+6	-11	-8				+14
Lebanese	+5									
Other Arab					-5	-5				
West Asian				+6	-5	-5				
South Asian										
Chinese										
Filipino				+5			+7			
Vietnamese	+5			+11	-11	-5				+6
Other E & SE Asia										
Latin, Central, South America				+7	-5	-6				
Caribbean						-5			+7	+13
Aboriginal				+9		-5	-6		+5	
Canadian					-5					

Source: Statistics Canada (1999a).

A Sociodemographic Overview

Household size						Marital		Own home	Forgn citizp	Home lang English
1 %	2 %	3 %	4 %	5 %	6+ %	Sing %	Div./Sep %	%	%	%
8	19	19	27	15	12	44	6	66	13	74
						−19			+18	−26
	+9				−5	−28	+5	+12	+13	−18
	−6				+9	−10		−13	+23	−32
	+10					−9		−6	+43	+22
+7	+16		−8	−8	−8	−27		+11	+9	+24
+8	+20		−8	−10	−10	−32		+8	+7	+7
						−39		+27	+5	−37
+8	+24		−13	−9	−8	−34		+10	+5	+13
	+8			−7	−8	−21		−17	+12	−48
+7			+5			−28		+11	+28	−46
	+15		−5	−11	−10	−26		−10	+18	−46
	+5					−22		−5	+23	−44
	+10		−5	−5	−7	−31			+6	−19
	−6			+6	+8			−26	+24	−43
−6	−10	−7			+21	−25			+31	−42
−6	−8			+7	+13	−8		−36	+40	−48
	−6		−5		+12	−29		+8	+25	−67
−5	−9		+5		+7			+20	+25	−63
−5	−6		−7		+18	−12		−21	+25	−36
−6	−9	−5	−6	+5	+23			−20	+11	−65
						−7		−5	+26	−46
					+7			−31	+23	−32
						−12		−24	+22	−9
						−10	+6	−22	+18	+8
+6	+14		−7	−6	−8	−16			−6	+26
+8	+14		−10	−7	−8	−17		−12	−10	+26
	+14		−8	−5		−19		+9	+21	
+7	+17		−5	−10	−9	−23		+7	+15	
+15	+22		−15	−10	−10	−25	+6	+5	+12	
+5	+20			−11	−9	−20		−5	−17	
			+5	−5	−7	−10		−14	+7	−38
+5	+12		−6	−5	−9	−17		+8	−7	
						−7		+10	+10	−31
				+8				+12	−7	−23
						−8		+25	−8	
−5	−8		+7	+5				+11	+14	−33
	−5							−35	+21	−44
	+6			−8		−5		+10	−5	+11
+5	+12	+5	−5		−9	−19		−45	+6	−11
	−5		−7		+8	+16	+5	−28	+23	−15
	−7	−5		+8	+11					−36
	−7	−5		+9	+17	+5		−28	+22	−48
	−6							−29	+20	−26
−6	−11	−5		+6	+16			−11	+21	−53
−5	−9				+10			+13	+16	−28
−5	−8				+17			−20	+19	−63
−7	−10				+20	+10		−29	+10	−30
	−12		+8					−12	+13	−48
	−8		+7	+5				−35	+22	+25
						+10		−25	+8	+20
+7				−9		+10		−37		+26
						+10				

In looking at individual countries of birth, we found that every origin category had fewer people in the 5 years and under category, which is understandable because the youngest are most likely born in Canada. For the same reason, fourteen birthplaces had fewer people in the age category 6–13, while not one place had more than 5 per cent. It was in the 14–18 age category that groups from different birthplaces were most similar to the overall Toronto population, with only those born in Italy (–6 per cent) and the Netherlands (–5 per cent) standing out. In the age group 19–45, we noted large differences and these continued into the higher age groups. With the exception of Poland, Portugal, and the former Yugoslavia, all European-origin immigrants had considerably fewer people in the 19–45 age category and considerably more in the 45 and over age categories. All non-European origins, except China, had substantially more in the younger age group and fewer in the 45 and over age groups. For example, if we look only at those in the 65 and over age group, the overrepresentation among European birthplaces, compared with the total population of Toronto, ranged from +6 per cent for those born in the former Yugoslavia to +30 per cent for those born in the USSR. Among non-European origins, China was overrepresented by +15 per cent, but all other birthplaces had about the same or less than the Toronto population.

In the single-origin ethnic groups in the 5 years and under age category, African, Lebanese, and Vietnamese had overrepresentations of 5 per cent or more, while most other groups were either similar to the Toronto population or had fewer people. In the 6–13 categories, no group had more than the Toronto average, but eight European-origin ethnic groups had less, while in the age group 14–18, only the German group differed strongly from the norm, with 5 per cent fewer. Again, when we consider differences in the older age categories, some groups had really high proportions. In the 46 and over categories, the German proportion was 26 per cent higher than the norm, followed by the Hungarian (25 per cent), the British (21 per cent), and Dutch (13 per cent). A category embracing other Western Europeans had 28 per cent more than the norm, while among Ukrainians, the proportion was similar in the 45–64 age category, but, in the 65 years and over category, there were 20 per cent more than the norm.

Gender Differences

For the most part, the proportions of males to females were within the plus or minus 5 per cent range of the Toronto total, which was almost evenly split between male and female. However, for two birthplace origins – the Middle East and other Africa – were significantly male-dominated, each having 6 per cent fewer females than the norm, while the Philippines had 9 per cent more females than the norm. Similarly, other Arabs and West Asians had more than 5 per cent fewer women than the norm and Filipinos had 7 per cent more. Aboriginals also had 6 percent fewer females than the Toronto proportion of 51 per cent.

Family Status

When considering family status, male and female single-parent proportions did not differ much from the norm. However, those born in Central and South America had 7 per cent more female single parents, as did those with ethnic origins from the Caribbean (+7 per cent) and Aboriginals (+5 per cent). Interestingly, when considering children in single-parent families, the Toronto proportion of 7 per cent was similar for most birthplace groups, although seven of the groups had 5 to 7 per cent fewer than the Toronto average. On the other hand, three groups had considerably more children in single-parent families: Africans (+14 per cent), Caribbeans (+13 per cent), and Vietnamese (+6 per cent).

Household Size

Among all people in Toronto, 19 per cent were in households of three people. The groups who differed from this norm in any significant way were only those born in India (–7 per cent) and in Vietnam (–5 per cent). Similarly, among ethnic groups, only the Lebanese, other Arab, and South Asian groups differed from the norm (–5 per cent each). When we look at the higher end of the scale (six-or-more-person households), all European-born Torontonians had 5 per cent fewer than the norm of 12 per cent, but the non-European-born had +9 per cent. All European-born groups had lower proportions than the norm, but for people born in Vietnam, the percentage was 23 per cent higher and for India, 21 per cent higher; the Philippine-born followed closely with 18 per cent higher. Among ethnic groups, a similar pattern existed. The Vietnamese ethnic group had 20 per cent more than the norm, followed by Filipinos and other Arabs (17 per cent each), and South Asian (16 per cent). To conclude, the older immigrants, mainly of European origin, tended to live in significantly smaller households than the newer, non-European immigrants.

Marital Status

Because the proportions of married (and common-law) couples were very similar, we concentrated on single and divorced/separated respondents. For Toronto as a whole, 44 per cent of the population was single, while the proportion for all foreign-born was 19 per cent lower, with those born in Europe being 28 per cent lower and those born in non-European countries being 10 per cent lower. It is only natural, that, as a whole, the foreign-born would have a lower proportion of singles because of the emphasis put on family migration. Italian-born Torontonians had 39 per cent fewer singles, followed by those born in the Netherlands (–34 per cent), Germany (–32 per cent), other European-born (–31 per cent), China (–29 per cent), Portugal (–28 per cent), the USSR (–26 per cent), and India (–25 per cent). Only people born in the Middle East, Hong Kong, Vietnam, and East Africa had proportions of singles that were similar to the norm. Of course, a different pattern emerges when we look at ethnic groups, since many people within these were born in Canada. The groups that had higher proportions of singles than the norm were the African (+16 per cent), Caribbean, Aboriginal, and Canadian groups (+10 per cent each), and the Latin, Central, and South American groups (+5 per cent). Ten ethnic groups had proportions of singles similar to the norm, while twelve, especially other Western Europeans (–25 per cent), Germans (–23 per cent), and Hungarians (–20) had lower proportions. The proportion of the total who were divorced or separated was 6 per cent, but those born in Europe had 5 per cent more and those born in Central and South America had 6 per cent more. Among the ethnic-origin groups, the only two groups that had higher proportions of the divorced/separated were other Western Europeans (+6 per cent) and Africans (+5 per cent).

Home-Ownership

While 66 per cent of census respondents in Toronto in 1996 were living in owned homes, the figures were 12 per cent higher for people who were European-born and 13 per cent lower for those who were non-European-born. The group with by far the most members living in owned homes was the Italian-born (+27 per cent). This was followed by people born in Hong Kong (+20 per cent), Portugal (+11 per cent), and the Netherlands (+10 per cent). Groups least likely to be living in owned homes included those born in South Asia (–36 per cent), East Africa (–31 per cent), the Middle East (–26 per cent), other African countries (–24 per cent), and those born in Central and South America (–22 per cent). Similar patterns were found among ethnic groups, with those of Italian ethnic origin having 25 per cent more members living in owned homes. Their closest rivals were the Greeks (+12 per cent), the Portuguese (+11 per cent), and the Jews (+10 per cent). Among people of Spanish ethnic origin, however, 35 per cent fewer lived in owned homes, exceeded only by Africans (–45 per cent) and Aboriginals (–37 per cent), while Caribbeans (–35 per cent), Vietnamese and West Asians (–29 per cent each), and Lebanese and other Arabs (–28 per cent each) were also among those least likely to be living in homes that they owned.

Foreign Citizenship

Only 13 per cent of the population of Toronto had foreign citizenship. Naturally, these proportions were high among all foreign-born groups, with 23 per cent more of people who were non-European-born having foreign citizenship. However, despite the fact that U.S.-born people have been immigrating to Canada for a considerable period, it was this group that had the largest proportion (+43 per cent) of all groups. Even among those born in the UK, 9 per cent more had foreign citizenship. After the U.S., those born in South Asia (+40 per cent), India (+31 per cent), Portugal (+28 per cent), and other Eastern and Southeast Asian countries (+26 per cent) all had high proportions of foreign citizenship. Among ethnic-origin groups, the British, French, Greek, and Jewish groups had lower proportions than the norm, while other Western European-born groups had similar proportions. Africans (+23 per cent), other Arabs, Central and South Americans (+22 per cent each), and Spanish and South Asians (+21 per cent each) also had high proportions with foreign citizenship.

Language Spoken in the Home

Among all foreign-born people living in Toronto, 26 per cent fewer than the 74 per cent total spoke English in the home. In the case of those born in non-European countries, the number was 32 per cent fewer. Obviously, using the English language at home is an indicator of integration for those who are foreign-born. But as many as 67, 65, and 63 per cent fewer people born in China, Hong Kong, and Vietnam, respectively, spoke English in the home. Among those born in Poland and South Asia, 48 per cent fewer spoke English at home, while the number among those from the USSR, the former Yugoslavia, and other East and Southeast Asian countries was 46 per cent for each. In the ethnic-origin groups, the British (+26 per cent), French (+26 per cent), Dutch (+21 per cent), German (+15 per cent), and other Western European (+12 per cent) ethnic groups all had high proportions of people using English in the home. Among non-European ethnicities, people from the Caribbean (+20 per cent), from Central and South America (+25 per cent), and Aboriginals (+26 per cent) also had proportions considerably higher than the norm. The ethnic groups who were least likely to speak English in the home were Filipinos (–63 per cent), South Asians (–53 per cent), West Asians, as well as other East and Southeast Asians (–48 per cent each), and the Spanish (–44 per cent).

EDUCATIONAL AND OCCUPATIONAL CHARACTERISTICS

In this section, we consider the highest levels of education, the proportions of unemployed, self-employed, and part-time workers, major industries of the employed, and occupational status. Among these categories, we also look at comparisons for birthplaces and ethnic groups as a whole, and whether there are strong differences by gender of the respondents.

Comparison of Total Groups

Highest Level of Education
In the total population of Toronto, 31 per cent have less than a secondary school education; the figure is 10 per cent higher among people born in Europe. This is not surprising because most of the Europeans came to Canada in the immediate post–Second World War period, when unskilled labourers were in high demand. But the two European groups who stood apart in this category are followed closely by two non-European groups: 36 per cent more of the Italian-born had less than secondary education, 40 per cent more of the Portuguese, 27 per cent more of the Vietnamese, and 18 per cent more of the Chinese (table 2.8). In contrast, people born in the U.S. and the Philippines had low proportions (–18 and –17 per cent, respectively). Both of these birthplace groups had a high proportion of members with a bachelor's

degree (BA) and, in the case of the U.S., 11 per cent more than the norm had higher than a BA degree.

Among ethnic groups, the Portuguese were the worst off in terms of having less than secondary education (+32 per cent), followed by the Vietnamese (+24 per cent), and the Italians (+15 per cent). At the other end of the scale, among Jews, 15 per cent more than the total population had a BA and those with education higher than a BA represented 6 per cent more than the total.

Unemployment
In Toronto, 9 per cent of people in the labour force had been unemployed in the year preceding the 1996 census. Those from the two birthplaces of South Asia and East Africa (both +11 per cent) had the highest unemployment. The rate was also relatively high for those born in Vietnam (+8 per cent), the Middle East (+7 per cent), and other African countries (+6 per cent). Naturally, this was reflected when considering ethnic groups: those of African ethnic origin had 16 per cent more than the total; for those of other Arab and Vietnamese origin, the figures were +13 per cent and +12 per cent, respectively.

Self-Employment
In Toronto as a whole, 8 per cent of the population was self-employed. Those born in the Netherlands had 8 percent more, but those born in the Philippines and Vietnam had 6 per cent fewer self-employed. In terms of ethnic background, the Jewish group had 10 per cent more self-employed than the total for Toronto, while other East and Southeast Asians had 7 per cent more; Filipinos and Vietnamese, in contrast, had considerably fewer (–6 per cent each).

Part-time Employment
Just over one-fifth (21 per cent) of the Toronto workforce were employed part-time. Among the foreign-born population, however, not one group had a proportion that was higher by 5 per cent or more. Those who were least likely to be part-time workers included people born in Italy (–9 per cent), Portugal and India (–8 each per cent), and the former Yugoslavia and Vietnam (–7 per cent each). However, when we look at part-time work among ethnic groups, we find that Jews and Africans both had 5 per cent more part-time workers than the Toronto proportion, while Vietnamese (–9 per cent), other Western European (–8 per cent), Lebanese (–7 per cent), and German (–5) groups had less.

Table 2.8
Education and occupation of subgroups compared with percentages of total population, Toronto, 1996

Group	–2nd %	2nd %	Col %	Un–Un %	Self-BA %	Part-+BA %	empl %	empl %	Time %
Toronto, total pop.	31	14	25	11	15	4	9	8	21
All foreign-born									
Born Europe-US	+10				–5				–5
Born non-European									
Born In									
USA	–18		–12	+5	+17	+11	–5		
UK	–5		+9						
Germany	–11		+18						
Italy	+36		–5	–8	–8	–11			–5
Netherlands			+9		–6		–6	+8	–9
Poland					–7	+5			
Portugal	+40		–11	–9	–13				–8
Former USSR						+6			
Former Yugoslavia									–7
Other European	+5				–5			+5	
Middle East			–7				+7		
India			–8		+7				–8
S. Asia							+11		
China	+18		–12						
Hong Kong	–8				+9				–6
Philippines	–17	–6		+13	+16			–6	–5
Vietnam	+27		–10		–9		+8	–6	–7
Other E & SE Asia	–7		–6	+6	+9			+5	
East Africa							+11		
Other Africa	–13		+5	+9			+6		
Central/South America & Caribbean			+12		–8				
Single Ethnic Origin									
British									
French									
Dutch	–9		+11				–5		
German	–10		+14						
Other W. Europe	–9	–5	+16				–6		–5
Hungarian			+10						–8
Polish	–6								
Ukrainian									
Balkan									
Greek	+14				–5				
Italian	+15				–6				
Portuguese	+32		–8	–7	–12				
Spanish	+8				–9		+5		
Jewish	–8		–7		+15	+6		+10	+5
Other European	–7								
African			+5		–6		+16		+5
Lebanese			–8				+9		–7
Other Arab			–11		+10		+13		
West Asian	–6	+5	–8				+8		
South Asian							+5		
Chinese			–8						
Filipino	–15		–5	+12	+14			–6	
Vietnamese	+24		–11		–7		+12	–6	–9
Other E & SE Asia	–9		–7	+7	+8			+7	
Latin, Central, South America			+5		–8				
Caribbean			+13		–10		+7		
Aboriginal	+7				–9				
Canadian	–6								

Definitions:
Education: –2nd: less than secondary; 2nd: secondary; Col: college; –Un: university-no degree; BA: bachelor's degree; +BA: higher than bachelor's.
Industry: Prm: primary (Agric. and mining); Man: manufacturing; Con: construction; Tpt: transport; Com: communication; WhS: wholesale; Ret: retail; Fin: finance; Bus: business; Gvt: government; Edu: education; Hth: health; Acc: accommodation-food; Oth: other.

A Sociodemographic Overview

Industry														Occupation		
Prm %	Man %	Con %	Tpt %	Com %	WhS %	Ret %	Fin %	Bus %	Gvt %	Edu %	Hth %	Acc %	Oth %	Upp %	Lwr %	Man %
1	16	5	4	4	7	12	9	10	4	6	8	6	8	18	64	18
		+5													−5	+6
		+6														+5
	−7							+6		+9				+18	−6	−11
																−7
	+5		+12					−7		+5				−10	−8	+18
																−5
	+7															+13
	+9	+13						−6				+6		−14	−10	+24
														+6	−6	
	+14													−5	−8	+14
					+8						+6					
	+15														−12	+16
	+9										+8			−7		+9
	+9										+11					
						+7								+7		−8
											+10		+6	−6		+8
	+35					−5		−6			−5			−10	−25	+25
						+7										
														+7		−9
														−7		+7
								+7						+7		−6
															−6	
															−5	+9
									+6					+8		−6
	+8															+8
	−6										+13			−9	+9	
			+8								−7			−7		+6
	+6		+10			+5							+5	−13		+19
	+12							−5				+6	+5	−10		+13
	−8													+19		−14
						+7								−7		+12
						+11					−6					
						+6										
						+8					+7					
	+11										+5					+11
											+10	+5	+6	−7	+9	
	+37					−5		−6						−8	−27	+36
						+9									+5	−5
	+7												+8	−11		−10
											+7			−7		+7
						−6			+9							

Occupation: Upp: upper non-manual (senior managers, professionals); Lwr: lower non-manual (middle manager, technician, supervisor clerical-sales-service, supervisor crafts-trades, admi-senior clerical, skilled sales-service, clerical, intermediate sales-service, other sales-service) Man: manual (skilled crafts-trades; semi-skilled manual, other manual).
Source: Statistics Canada (1999a).

Industry

We identified fourteen categories in the industrial section, with manufacturing accounting for 16 per cent of the Toronto workforce; retail trade, 12 per cent; business, 10 per cent; and finance, 9 per cent. Most foreign-born Torontonians appeared to be concentrated in the manufacturing sector. Leading the way were those born in Vietnam (+35 per cent), India (+15 per cent), and the former Yugoslavia (+14 per cent), while those born in Portugal, South Asia, and China (+9 per cent each), Poland (+7 per cent), and Germany (+5 per cent) also had more than the overall population. All other foreign-born groups, with the exception of those born in the U.S. (–7 per cent) were close to the Toronto norm.

Other industrial sectors also had high concentrations of specific foreign-born groups. In construction, people born in Portugal (+13 per cent) and Italy (+12 per cent) were most overrepresented. In the retail trade, Middle Eastern-born (+8 per cent) and other East- and Southeast-Asian-born (+7 per cent) were well represented. In education, people born in the U.S. had 9 per cent more than the overall Toronto population. In health, the proportion of those born in the Philippines was 10 per cent higher. In the accommodation/food sector the proportion of those born in China was 11 per cent higher. In terms of ethnic groups, the patterns were similar. Vietnamese (+37 per cent), Spanish (+12 per cent), and South Asians (+11 per cent) were highly concentrated in manufacturing; Jews (–8 per cent) and Greeks (–6 per cent) were the only two groups with proportions that were considerably below the norm. Italians and Portuguese were highly concentrated in construction; Lebanese, and other East, Southeast, and West Asians in the retail trade; Aboriginals in government, Filipinos in health; and Greeks in the accommodation/food sector. All of the above had proportions that were at least 8 per cent higher than the Toronto proportion.

Occupation

We regrouped the 1991 census classification of occupations into three categories: upper non-manual, lower non-manual, and manual. Occupations included in these categories are given in table 2.7. For Toronto as a whole, 18 per cent each of the occupations could be classified as upper non-manual and manual, while the remainder (64 per cent) were in the lower non-manual category. There were large variations in these categories by birthplace. Only people born in the U.S. (+18 per cent), Hong Kong (+7 per cent), other Africa, which includes South Africa

(+7 per cent), and the USSR (+6 per cent) had proportions significantly higher than the Toronto proportion in upper non-manual jobs. At the other end of the scale, those born in Portugal (–14 per cent), Italy, and Vietnam (–10 per cent each), and South Asia, Central and South America, and the Caribbean (–7 per cent each) had significantly lower proportions. People born in Vietnam had 25 per cent fewer than the Toronto proportion in lower non-manual jobs, and in manual occupations, they had 25 per cent more.

Other groups concentrated in manual occupations were those born in Portugal (+24 per cent), Italy (+18 per cent), India (+16 per cent), the former Yugoslavia (+14 per cent), and Poland (+13 per cent). The ethnic group with the highest concentration in upper non-manual jobs was the Jewish group (+19 per cent); only two other groups, the Ukrainians (+8 per cent) and the other Western European-born (+7 per cent), were significantly above the Toronto norm. In the manual sector, the Vietnamese were overrepresented by 36 per cent and the Portuguese by 19 per cent, while the Spanish (+13 per cent), Africans (+12 per cent), South Asians (+11 per cent), and Latin, Central, and South Americans (+10 per cent) were also concentrated in this sector.

Comparisons by Gender

Table 2.9 considers percentage differences between the sexes in the subcategories. Females are taken as the reference point and compared with males. For Toronto as a whole, the differences were minor when we took into consideration the highest level of education, unemployment, and self-employment. In terms of labour-force activity, 12 per cent more females were likely to be in part-time jobs than males. Females were underrepresented in manufacturing (–8 per cent) and construction (–7 per cent), and overrepresented in finance (+4 per cent), education (+5 per cent), and, especially, in health (+11 per cent). In all other industries, the difference was plus or minus 3 per cent or less. Finally, when we looked at occupations, we could see that while there were no differences in proportions in higher non-manual occupations, the proportion of women in lower non-manual occupations was 20 per cent higher than that of men and in manual occupations, which was 20 per cent lower.

We also compared differences between male and female proportions within subgroups of the Toronto population. In cases where these dif-

Table 2.9
Differences in proportions of females compared with males in education and occupations by subgroup, Toronto, 1996

Group	–2nd %	2nd %	Col %	–Un %	BA %	+BA %	Un-empl %	Self-empl %	Part-time %
Toronto	–1	+2	–1	0	–1	–2	+2	–3	+12
All foreign-born		+4							+9
Born Europe-US	+5		–6						+15
Born non-European		+4		+2			+8	–7	
Born In									
USA		–5				–6			
UK	+6	+5		–3	–4				
Germany	+13	+9	–13	–4			–2	–6	+15
Italy	+12	+4	–14						+16
Netherlands	+8	+12	–7		–8				+28
Poland	+2	+5	–5				+8		+18
Portugal	+2		–7						
Former USSR	+6						+6		
Former Yugoslavia	+13	+5	–15					–8	
Other European	+6		–7					–7	+16
Middle East	+6					–5	+6	–8	+19
India	+10					–6	+10	–6	
S. Asia	+7		–4		–4		+19		
China	+8				–4	–4	–1		
Hong Kong	+4		+6		–5	–5			
Philippines									
Vietnam			+3	–4			+5		
Other E & SE Asia	+3		+3						
East Africa	+8	–1	+3	–4			+10		
Other Africa	+6	+6		–3	–6	–4	+8		
Central/South America & Caribbean			+4						
Single Ethnic Origin									
British		+6							
French			–6	+4					
Dutch	+3	+8	–7					0	+23
German	+7	+8	–9						+16
Other W. European		+11	–8		–5		+7		+20
Hungarian	+8	+5	–8			–5		+2	+17
Polish		+5	–4				+5	–6	+15
Ukrainian	+10	+5	–6	–5				–6	+17
Balkan	+8		–9					–6	
Greek	+4	–3	–5					–11	+16
Italian	+3		–8						+16
Portuguese									
Spanish	+9	–4		–5			+6	+1	
Jewish	+4				–9			–8	+19
Other European				+3					
African	+8		+3	–5			+9	–6	+15
Lebanese	+5	+5	–9	+4			+13	–15	
Other Arab	+5				–4	–5	+13		
West Asian	+6					–7		–8	+20
South Asian	+8				–4		+8		
Chinese	+5				–4				+9
Filipino							–1		+1
Vietnamese		+6	+3	–4	–4		+7		
Other E & SE Asia	+5	–2							
Latin, Central, South America			+3		–4		+5		
Caribbean	–4	–4	+6						+5
Aboriginal	–5	+9	+13	–12	–6		–7		
Canadian									

Definitions
Education: –2nd: Less than Secondary; 2nd: Secondary; Col: college; –Un: university–no degree; BA: bachelor's degree; +BA: higher than bachelor's.
Industry: Man; manufacturing; Con: construction; WhS: wholesale; Ret: retail; Fin: finance; Bus: business; Edu: education; Hth: health; Oth: other.
Occupation: Upp: upper non-manual (senior managers, professionals) Lwr: lower non-manual (middle manager, technician, supervisor

A Sociodemographic Overview

Industry									Occupation		
Man %	Con %	WhS %	Ret %	Fin %	Bus %	Edu %	Hth %	Oth %	Upp %	Lwr %	Man %
−8	−7	−3	+2	+4	−1	+5	+11	+3	0	+20	−20
	−14									+23	
	−3										−16
−2	−3		−1			+1		−1	−3	−9	+6
					−4				−7		−12
−20			+6			+9					−23
+3	−22		+5				+7			+25	−24
−5		−8	+6				+17		−7		−12
	−15					+1	+14			+31	−31
−16		−7									
								+12	−8	+26	−16
−5	−13							+7	−4	+23	
	−10										
											−17
	−1						+7	+6	−3	+11	−9
	−2	+1	−2							+11	−10
+10			−1			+1			−4	−4	+8
−2	−2				−5		+6	0	−8	+11	−2
−21	−1					+1	+15	+12		+26	−27
−17	−3	+1				+1	+5			+9	−11
−5	−2		−1				+6	+1	−7	+14	−6
	−3		−3			+3	+15	−1			
	−3						+6		−5	+17	−12
−15						+1	+18			+27	−27
				+2		+8		−2			
−5		−7	0			+14			+8	+11	
−17						+8					
−2	−10	+5	+10		+2	+16	−1		+3		−25
−11	−12		+7		+2	+4			+8	+11	
	−13									+27	−29
				+1				0	−6		−14
	−12				+2	+2		+6			
−4			−1							+16	
−5	−18		+5	+7	+2		+6			+24	−26
−2	−23			+7	+2	+2		+10		+31	−32
−13				0	+4	−1		+9	−3	+33	−30
−3	−3				−10	+10			−12	+16	−4
−11	−10		+7								
−11	−2	0				+1	+16	0		+25	−27
	−4	−7		+7		+9	+4	−2	+3	+25	−28
			−2	+10	+8	+2			−5		−14
	−4	0	+1						−3		−18
	−2	0								+14	−12
0	−2					+2	+6	−4	−5	+7	−2
−21	−1					+1	+14	+12		+25	−26
−15	−2	+3				+1	+7	0		+16	−15
	−1			+1		+1	+7	+6	−9	+17	−8
−19		+2				0			+3	+25	−28
−14			−2			+2	+20		+6	+24	−30
+1	−10	+9	+7	0			0		−7	+34	−27
											−24

clerical-sales-service, supervisor crafts-trades, Admi-Senior clerical, skilled sales-service, clerical, intermediate sales-service, other sales-service); Man: manual (skilled crafts-trades; semi-skilled manual, other manual).

How to read the table: The row for Toronto shows the difference in female proportions compared to males. For example, 3 per cent fewer females are self-employed and 12 per cent more are in part-time occupations. All other rows are compared to the differences for Toronto. Only those with differences plus or minus 3 per cent or greater are given. For example, considering all foreign-born the difference in female proportions compared to males in part-time work is only 9 per cent.

Source: Statistics Canada (1999a).

ferences were less than 3 per cent (plus or minus) from the difference found among the sexes for Toronto as a whole, we considered the subgroup to be close to the Toronto norm, and these figures do not appear in the table; where differences between sexes were higher, they do appear on the table. For example, while 1 per cent fewer Toronto females had less than secondary education, among all foreign-born the proportion was 4 per cent higher for females than for males. Similarly, while females in Toronto as a whole had 12 per cent more part-time work than males, among all foreign-born the differences was only 9 per cent more for females.

Education
In all but four of the birthplaces of immigrants, women had a higher proportion with less than secondary education. We found strong differences between the sexes among those born in Germany and the former Yugoslavia (+13 per cent each), Italy (+12 per cent), and India (+10 per cent). In other words, among these groups, levels of female education lagged considerably behind those of males. In terms of ethnic groups, the differences were not as sharp as they were among the foreign-born. Nonetheless the Ukrainian (+10 per cent), Spanish (+9 per cent), Hungarian, Balkan, African, and South Asian (+8 per cent each), and German (+6 per cent) groups still had considerably higher proportions of females with less than secondary education than the males in their groups.

Unemployment
In Toronto as a whole, the rate of unemployment among females was only 2 per cent higher than that of males, while among the European foreign-born it was 8 per cent higher. Those born in South Asia (+19 per cent), India and East Africa (+10 per cent each), and Poland and other Africa (+8 per cent each), as well as in the Middle East (+6 per cent) showed differences in proportions that were much higher than the norm. In only one birthplace (China) was female unemployment lower than that of males by 3 per cent or more. Ethnic groups in which the female proportion of unemployment exceeded that of males to a considerable degree included Lebanese and other Arab (+13 per cent each), African (+9 per cent), South Asian (+8 per cent), other Western European and Vietnamese (+7 per cent each), and Spanish (+6 per cent). Among Aboriginal peoples, the female rate of unemployed was 7 per cent lower than that of the male.

A Sociodemographic Overview   111

Self-Employment
The proportion of females who were self-employed in Toronto was 3 per cent lower than that of males. In most other birthplace subgroups, it was similar or lower for females. The range was between –6 per cent each for German- and Indian-born women, and –8 per cent each for women born in the former Yugoslavia and the Middle East. Among ethnic groups, the Lebanese (–15 per cent), Greek (–11 per cent), and Jewish and West Asian (–8 per cent each) had strong differences, but among Hungarians (+2 per cent) and Spanish (+1 per cent), females had proportions at least 3 per cent higher than their male counterparts.

Part-time Employment
Differences among the sexes were really strong when we looked at part-time employment. In Toronto as a whole, 12 per cent more females were in part-time employment; in *no* subgroup did the proportion of males working part-time exceed that of females by plus or minus 3 per cent or more. Within foreign-born groups, 15 per cent more females born in Europe were in part-time jobs, led by the those born in the Netherlands (+28 per cent), Poland (+18 per cent), Italy and other Europe (+16 per cent each), and Germany (+15 per cent). Among those born in non-European countries, only the Middle Eastern-born had a considerably higher proportion for females (+19 per cent). When we consider ethnic origins, the Dutch (+23 per cent), other Western Europeans and West Asians (+20 per cent each), Hungarians and Ukrainians (+17 per cent each), Germans, Greeks, and Italians (+16 per cent each), and African (+15 per cent) all had proportions of females in part-time employment that were significantly higher than those of their male counterparts.

Industry
The three types of industry in which there were strong differences between the sexes – for Toronto as a whole, as well as for subgroups – were manufacturing (8 per cent fewer females in Toronto), construction (7 per cent fewer), and health (11 per cent more). In all other industrial sectors the differences were much smaller, although in one or two cases – for example, among the Portuguese (+10 per cent), Spanish (+9 per cent), and Filipino (+12 per cent) groups – a larger number of females had to be classified as being in 'other' industries. In manufacturing, the differences between the sexes were noted mainly among those born in the Philippines, where we found 21 per cent fewer females than males, Germany (–20 per cent), Vietnam (–17 per cent),

Portugal (−16 per cent), and Central and South America and the Caribbean (−15 per cent). The one major exception occurred among people born in China, where 10 per cent more females than males were found in manufacturing. In all ethnic groups, the proportions were similar to or lower than the Toronto norm for females in manufacturing. Leading the way were the Filipinos (−21 per cent), the Central and Latin Americans (−19 per cent), the Germans (−17 per cent), the Vietnamese (−15 per cent), and the Caribbeans (−14 per cent).

As was to be expected, the construction industry was predominantly male. The largest differences with females were found among those born in Italy (−22 per cent), Poland (−15 per cent), the former Yugoslavia (−13 per cent), and other European countries (−10 per cent). In fact, among all Torontonians born in Europe, 14 per cent fewer females were in construction than males. Similar differences were found among ethnic groups. The Portuguese led the way, with 23 per cent fewer females in construction, followed by the Italians (−18 per cent), the Poles (−13 per cent), the Hungarians and the Greeks (−12 per cent each), and other Europeans and Aboriginals (−10 per cent each).

The health industry, on the other hand, was dominated by females. While many among the foreign-born had fewer females in health than the Toronto norm, among people born in Central and South America and the Caribbean, 18 per cent more females than males were in the health industry, and they were followed by those born in the Netherlands (+17 per cent), Vietnam and East Africa (+15 per cent each), and Poland (+14 per cent). Among ethnic groups, Caribbeans (+20 per cent), other Western Europeans and Africans (+16 per cent each), and the Dutch and Filipinos (+14 per cent each) led the way in the overrepresentation of females.

Occupations

In terms of actual occupations, most groups were similar or only slightly different from the Toronto norm when comparing females to males in upper non-manual occupations. However, while females in nearly all groups were concentrated in lower non-manual occupations (20 per cent more females in Toronto as a whole), males were concentrated in manual occupations. Foreign-born groups that differed more than plus or minus 3 per cent from the Toronto norm in lower non-manual jobs included those born in Poland (31 per cent more females), Central and South America and the Caribbean (+27 per cent), the USSR and the Philippines (+26 per cent), Italy (+25 per cent), and the former Yugoslavia (+23 per cent). Among ethnic groups, the largest differences were found among Aboriginals (34 per cent more females in non-manual occupations), and among the Spanish (+33 per cent), Polish (+27 per cent), African, Lebanese, Filipino, and Latin (+25 per cent each), and Italian and Caribbean (+24 per cent each) groups. Naturally, where proportions of females were high in non-manual occupations, they were low in manual occupations, as can be seen in table 2.9.

While we are not addressing the question of integration directly, by comparing differences between the sexes within groups to the differences for Toronto as a whole, we can consider those groups close to the Toronto norm as being less likely to have strong variation within the group, and, to that extent, to be more integrated in terms of gender differences. The differences among the sexes show up much more in the next section, which deals with incomes.

INCOME CHARACTERISTICS

In all likelihood, income is the most important indicator of integration for all immigrants. Other than family reunion and fleeing dangerous situations (refugees), the majority of immigrants leave their own countries and come to another in order to improve their socio-economic status. In North America, that means improving their incomes. While Canada is seen as one of the countries in which to achieve this improvement, strong differences in incomes persist, and these are not always related to the length of time a group has been in Canada. Other factors, such as language, qualifications, skills, and discrimination also influence one's socio-economic well-being. In this final section we compare subgroups to the Canadian 'norm' by major source of income, proportions living below the 1996 poverty line, household incomes, and average wage incomes. In general, women have lower wage incomes than men, quite often even when they have similar qualifications, which translates into lower total incomes and, often, a greater reliance on government support. We also consider differences by gender in these areas of incomes.

Comparison of Total Groups

Major Source of Income
When considering various major sources of income, we focused on those who depended on government as their primary source. On the

whole, this was the case for 15 per cent of the population of Toronto (table 2.10). For people who were born in Europe, the U.S., and non-European countries, the proportion was at least 5 per cent higher. And while the proportion among immigrants from twelve different birthplaces was similar to the Toronto norm, and the proportions among those born in the U.S. and in Portugal were 6 to 7 per cent lower, immigrants from the USSR (+22 per cent), South Asia (+21 per cent), and East Africa (+17 per cent) depended heavily on government income. When we look at ethnicity, Africans (+23 per cent), Vietnamese (+20 per cent), and Aboriginals (+19 per cent) had the highest number of dependents, followed closely by the Spanish (+14), while around 10 per cent more Hungarians, other Arabs, West Asians, and Caribbeans than the norm depended on government income.

Proportions Living below the 1996 Poverty Line
Just over one-fifth (21 per cent) of the Toronto population was living below the poverty line in 1996. The proportion of those who were non-European-born and living in poverty was 14 per cent higher than the Toronto norm; in particular, among the highest proportions of all foreign-born living below the poverty line were people born in South Asia (+31 per cent), East Africa (+28 per cent), the Middle East (+25 per cent), the USSR (+18 per cent), and other East and Southeast Asian countries (+15 per cent). The only foreign-born people who had proportions that were lower by more than 5 per cent than the norm were those born in the U.S., the UK, Germany, and the Netherlands, although those born in Italy, Portugal, other European countries, and the Philippines had proportions that were similar to the norm. Among ethnic groups, a good many had high proportions living below the poverty line. These included Africans (+37 per cent), West Asians (+29 per cent), Spanish (+25 per cent), other Arab (+24 per cent), Lebanese (+23 per cent), Vietnamese (+20 per cent), Aboriginals and Latins (+17 per cent each), and Caribbeans (+16 per cent).

Household Incomes
Just over one-quarter (27 per cent) of Torontonians were living in households where the annual income was under $35,000, while the same proportion were in households of $86,000 and over. In the categories of $35,000–$59,000 (21 per cent) and $60,000–$85,000 (25 per cent), most of the various groups were fairly close to the norm. Hence, it would seem that the real differences between groups were reflected mainly at the

Table 2.10
Incomes of subgroups compared with percentages/averages of total population, Toronto, 1996

Group	Gvt. maj. source $ %	Below poverty %	Household income. 000's (by age) -35 %	35–59 %	60–85 %	86+ %	Av. wage income $	Av. total income $
Toronto	15	21	27	21	25	27	18,971	25,898
All foreign-born	+5	+7	+8			−6	−2,832	−3,272
Born Europe-US	+6	−8					−1,224	+819
Born non-Europe	+5	+14	+11			−8	−4,334	−6,760
Born In								
USA	−6	−7	−6			+20	+8,029	+10,821
UK		−8		−5		+10	+3,875	+7,293
Germany		−6				+8	+3,927	+8,519
Italy	+12					+5	−3,069	−1,623
Netherlands		−8	+7				+742	+5,701
Poland	−7	+8	+14	+7		−9	−5,848	−4,254
Portugal						−6	−2,677	−4,349
USSR	+22	+18	+26		−6	−16	−9,237	−5,095
Former Yugoslavia	+10	+7	+12		−7	−9	−5,296	−4,385
Other Europe			+6			−5	−2,661	−497
Middle East	+14	+25	+22			−13	−7,907	−9,255
India					−7		−2,817	−5,057
S. Asia	+21	+31	+27		−9	−19	−9,111	−12,597
China		+14	+11			−9	−8,620	−10,264
Hong Kong		+14	+11			−7	−4,171	−6,629
Philippines							−1,870	−5,785
Vietnam	+11	+13	+7		−5	−8	−6,019	−9,630
Other E & SE Asia		+15	+13		−8	−5	−4,972	−6,318
East Africa	+17	+28	+26	−6	−7	−11	−4,041	−6,762
Other Africa		+12	+13				−819	−413
C/S America & Carib		+10	+11			−14	−2,384	−5,150

Table 2.10 (Concluded)

Group	Gvt. maj. source $ %	Below poverty %	Household income. 000's (by age) -35 %	35-59 %	60-85 %	86+ %	Av. wage income $	Av. total income $
Single Ethnic Origin								
British		-6					+2,314	+5,617
French							+6,005	+6,274
Dutch		-10					+5,127	+6,494
German		-7					+3,410	+6,884
Other W. Europe	+5	-6		+6		-10	+2,145	+5,076
Hungarian	+10		+13			-8	-2,027	-50
Polish		+6	+9	+6	-7	-11	-3,302	-3,620
Ukrainian	+8		+7	-7			-337	+3,521
Balkan			+4			-6	-3,680	-4,106
Greek				+6		-8	-4,416	-6,047
Italian		-7	-6		+5		-742	-1,408
Portuguese						-7	-3,148	-5,453
Spanish	+14	+25	+22		+5	-16	-7,342	-10,441
Jewish	-5	-8	-6	-7		+16	+1,850	+11,661
Other European			+6				-1,235	+1,289
African	+23	+37	+35	-11		-19	-9,046	-11,822
Lebanese	+5	+23	+20	-6		-8	-3,791	-5,738
Other Arab	+11	+24	+20	-10		-8	-6,437	-7,337
West Asian	+10	+29	+27	-10		-15	-8,585	-10,444
South Asian		+11	+7			-7	-4,945	-8,139
Chinese		+11	+7			-5	-5,570	-7,825
Filipino							-2,761	-6,934
Vietnamese	+20	+20	+14		-5	-11	-6,276	-10,218
Other E + SE Asia		+10	+9		-7		-4,508	-4,652
Latin, Central, S. America	+8	+17	+17		-5	-14	-6,264	-9,588
Caribbean	+10	+16	+16			-13	-3,943	-6,987
Aboriginal	+19	+17	+19		-6	-12	-2,591	-4,660
Canadian		-5					+2,356	+1,775

Source: Statistics Canada (1999a).

lower and higher ends of the household income scale – the higher the proportion in the under $35,000 category, the lower it was in the $86,000 and over category. We will focus on differences in the under $35,000 group.

Among all foreign-born residents of Toronto, four groups had really high proportions in the under $35,000 category: South Asia (+27 per cent), the USSR and East Africa (+26 per cent each), and the Middle East (+22 per cent). While people from six birthplaces were close to the norm, only those born in the U.S. had more than 5 per cent lower than the norm, earning under $35,000 (–7 per cent), and this was reflected in the proportion born in the U.S. who had incomes $86,000 and over (+20 per cent). Except in the case of the Vietnamese ethnic group (+14 per cent), all groups with high proportions living below the poverty line were also those with household incomes under $35,000. These included Africans (+35 per cent), West Asians (+27 per cent), Spanish (+22 per cent), Lebanese and other Arabs (+20 per cent each), Aboriginals (+19 per cent), Latins (+17 per cent), and Caribbeans (+16 per cent).

Average Wage Incomes

In 1996, the average annual wage income in Toronto was $18,971. The differences for subgroups are best illustrated in figures 2.9 and 2.10. All foreign-born had lower average wage incomes, but, while the average for those born in Europe and the U.S. was $1,224 less, for the non-European-born, it was $4,334 less. Only those born in three countries – the UK, Germany, and the U.S. – had averages higher than the norm, and, in the case of the U.S.-born, this was considerably higher (+$8,029). People who were born in the Netherlands and other Africa (most likely Southern Africans) were within $1,000 of the norm. Birthplaces that were associated with wage incomes well below the norm included the USSR (–$9,237), South Asia (–$9,111), China (–$8,620), the Middle East (–$7,907), Vietnam (–$6,019), and Poland (–$5,848). Among ethnic groups, the British, French, Dutch, German, other Western European and Jewish groups had wage incomes above the norm. In the case of French Torontonians, the average wage income was $6,005 higher; for the Dutch, it was $5,127 higher. Ukrainians and Italians were both within $1,000 of the norm, but Africans (–$9,046), West Asians (–$8,585), Spanish (–$7,342), other Arabs (–$6,437), Vietnamese (–$6,276), and Chinese (–$5,570) had average wages that were considerably below the norm.

Figure 2.8
Differences by birthplace in average annual wage income (Toronto = $18,971)

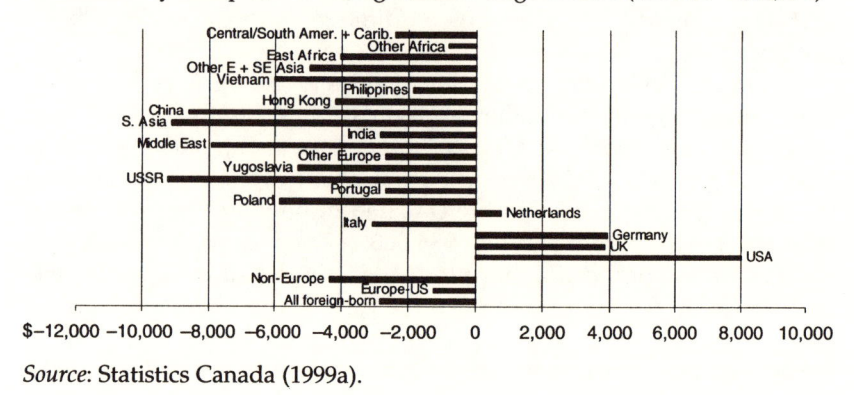

Source: Statistics Canada (1999a).

Figure 2.9
Differences by ethnic group in average annual wage income (Toronto = $18,971)

Source: Statistics Canada, *Census 1961–1996, Public Use Microfiche Files.*

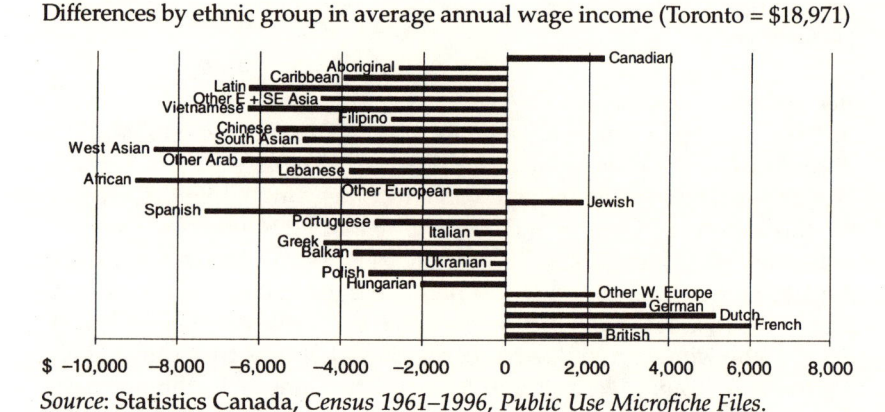

Average Total Incomes
Total income includes income from all sources. In many cases, it includes incomes in addition to wage incomes, such as income from investments, interest, renting out property, and so on. It would appear that the total income of more recent immigrants is largely based on their wages, whereas more established groups are more likely to have other sources of income. The average total income for all individuals in Toronto was $25,898 (see figs. 2.10 and 2.11). The average total income for non-European foreign-born Torontonians was $6,760 less than the

Figure 2.10
Differences by birthplace in total income (Toronto = $25,898)

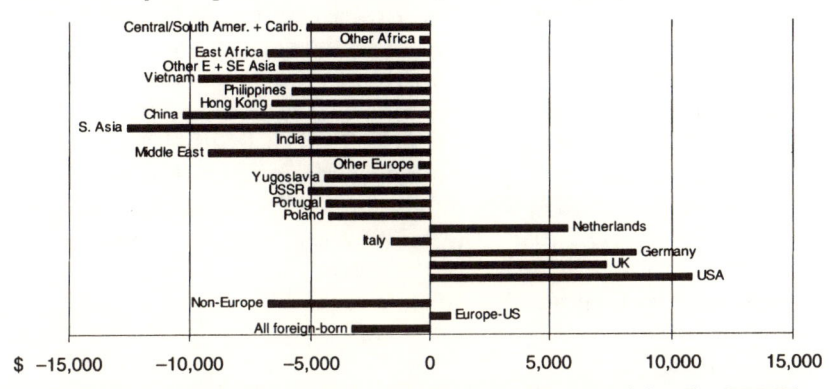

[Bar chart showing income differences by birthplace, with values ranging from approximately -$15,000 to $15,000. Groups shown include: Central/South Amer. + Carib., East Africa, Other Africa, Other E + SE Asia, Vietnam, Philippines, Hong Kong, China, S. Asia, India, Middle East, Other Europe, Yugoslavia, USSR, Portugal, Poland, Italy, Netherlands, Germany, UK, USA, Non-Europe, Europe-US, All foreign-born]

Source: Statistics Canada, *Census 1971–1996, Public Use Microfiche Files* (PUMF).

Figure 2.11
Differences by ethnic group in total income (Toronto = $25,898)

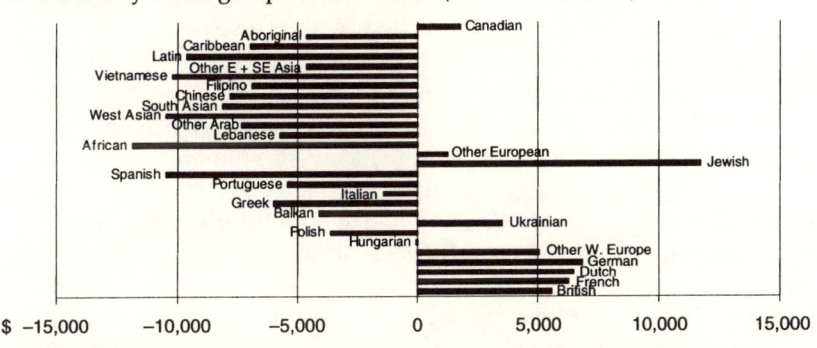

[Bar chart showing income differences by ethnic group, with values ranging from approximately -$15,000 to $15,000. Groups shown include: Aboriginal, Caribbean, Latin, Other E + SE Asia, Vietnamese, Filipino, Chinese, South Asian, West Asian, Other Arab, Lebanese, African, Spanish, Other European, Jewish, Portuguese, Greek, Italian, Balkan, Polish, Hungarian, Ukrainian, Other W. Europe, German, Dutch, French, British, Canadian]

Source: Statistics Canada, *Census 1971–1996, Public Use Microfiche Files* (PUMF).

norm, while for European-born residents, it was just slightly higher than the norm. Only three birthplace groups – French, Dutch, and German – had average total incomes higher than the norm, and, in the case of the U.S.-born, the average was well over $10,000 higher. Other Europeans and other Africans were within $1,000 of the norm.

The poorest groups included people who were born in South Asia (–$12,597), China (–$10,264), Vietnam (–$9,630), the Middle East (–$9,255), East Africa (–$6,767), Hong Kong (–$6,629), and other East and Southeast Asian countries (–$6,318). Differences by ethnic group were even more marked. The British (+$5,617), French (+$6,274), Dutch (+$6,494), German (+$6,884), other Western European (+$2,145), and Jewish (+$11,661) groups were well above the norm, while Hungarians were just $50 below the norm. Four ethnic groups, however, had total incomes that were more than $10,000 below the Toronto average: Africans (–$11,822), West Asians (–$10,444), Spanish (–$10,441), and Vietnamese (–$10,218). Other groups who had significantly lower total incomes were Latins (–$9,588), Chinese (–$7,825), other Arabs (–$7,337), Caribbeans (–$6,987), Lebanese (–$5,738), and Portuguese (–$5,453).

Comparisons by Gender

Major Source of Income
For Toronto as a whole, 2 per cent more females than males depended on government for their major source of income (table 2.11). Among all immigrants, whether European-born, U.S.-born, or non-European-born, differences were within a range of plus or minus 3 per cent of the Toronto proportion. For people from eleven of the specific birthplaces, the proportion was also similar to that of Toronto as a whole, but for those from three birthplaces – the Netherlands, other Europe, and India – the proportions were lower than the Toronto population. Birthplaces with the highest proportions of female dependence on government when compared with that of males were Vietnam (+9 per cent), Central and South America and the Caribbean (+8 per cent each), and East Africa (+6 per cent). When we looked at ethnic groups, however, only one group stood out from the rest: Aboriginals (+19 per cent). The other ethnic groups closest to that rate were Vietnamese (+9 per cent), Lebanese (+8 per cent), and Spanish and Caribbean (+7 per cent each). For all other ethnic groups, the differences in proportions were comparable to the Toronto ratio.

Proportions Living below the 1996 Poverty Line
Similarly, in Toronto as a whole, only 2 per cent more females than males were living below the poverty line. And whether immigrants were born in Europe, in the U.S., or in non-European countries, on the whole, none of the differences from the Toronto ratio were greater than plus or minus 3 per cent. However, among immigrants who were born in the USSR, the difference was 9 per cent higher for women than for men. Other significant variations showed up among those who were

Table 2.11
Female compared to male percentages/averages: incomes: Toronto, 1996

Group	Gvt. maj. source $ %	Below poverty %	Household Income. 000's (by age) −35 %	35–59 %	60–85 %	86+ %	Av. wage income $	Av. total income $
Toronto	+2	+2	+4	−1	−2	−2	−9,431	−11,826
All foreign-born							−8,770	−11,164
Born Europe-US							−11,600	−10,764
Born non-Europe							−6,614	−5,239
Born In								
USA							−18,530	−24,267
UK		+5	+8	+3		−6	−13,831	−18,603
Germany	+5		+1			−6	−14,312	−17,880
Italy	+5						−12,696	−15,646
Netherlands	−3	+7	+14			−9	−17,929	−24,729
Poland		+7		−4			−8,543	−11,659
Portugal					+1		−10,963	−13,537
USSR		+9					−8,412	−11,747
Former Yugoslavia		−1	+1		+2		−7,551	−11,672
Other Europe	−1				−5	+1	−9,482	−12,620
Middle East		−2	−2		+3	+2	−5,168	−8,372
India	−1		+1				−10,009	−12,127
S. Asia	+5						−8,494	−10,365
China		−2	0			+1	−5,201	−6,176
Hong Kong		−1	0		+3		−3,866	−5,907
Philippines		+6					−3,954	−4,388
Vietnam	+9	+7	+7				−8,757	−8,727
Other E & SE Asia		−1	−1			+1	−6,726	−9,453
East Africa	+6		0			+2	−9,612	−9,317
Other Africa	+5		+1			+1	−8,204	−11,913
Central/South America & Carib.	+8	+8	+9	−4			−6,987	−7,227

Table 2.11 (Concluded)

Group	Gvt. maj. source $ %	Below poverty %	Household Income. 000's (by age) −35 %	35−59 %	60−85 %	86+ %	Av. wage income $	Av. total income $
Single Ethnic Origin								
British			+9				−13,365	−16,462
French	−2						−13,835	−14,918
Dutch	−2	+5				−8	−15,710	−19,244
German			+8	+4			−13,370	−16,592
Other W. Europe			+17		−7		−13,311	−9,945
Hungarian					+2	−6	−9,894	−13,168
Polish	−1		+1				−6,857	−9,590
Ukrainian		+7					−10,634	−16,729
Balkan		−2	+1			+1	−6,872	−9,911
Greek	−3				+1		−5,323	−7,899
Italian							−10,019	−12,567
Portuguese							−9,368	−11,530
Spanish	+7	+19	+16	−9		−5	−9,562	−9,757
Jewish	−1	−3			+1	+1	−10,389	−20,847
Other European	−1	+5					−9,001	−12,890
African			+1	+2			−4,447	−4,493
Lebanese	+8	−5	−4	+6		+2	−10,434	−13,730
Other Arab				−5		+4	−5,356	−9,149
West Asian			0				−4,149	−6,533
South Asian			0			+2	−8,605	−10,464
Chinese		−2					−5,132	−6,572
Filipino		+5					−3,177	−3,755
Vietnamese	+9	+10	+8		−7		−9,505	−9,396
Other E & SE Asia			+1				−7,554	−10,951
Latin, Central, S. America		+5			+2		−7,207	−7,690
Caribbean	+7	+6	+9	−4			−4,529	−4,145
Aboriginal	+19	+14	+19	−10	−5	−5	−6,731	−5,046
Canadian							−10,486	−11,960

Source: Statistics Canada, *1996 Census* (1999a).

born in Central and South America and the Caribbean (+8 per cent), the Netherlands, Poland, and Vietnam (+7 per cent each), and the Philippines (+6 per cent). Among ethnic groups, the Spanish displayed the most marked contrast, with a difference of 19 per cent more females than males living below the poverty line. The other two groups with considerable differences in ratios included Aboriginals (+14 per cent) and Vietnamese (+10 per cent).

Household Incomes
In the overall Toronto population, 4 per cent more females than males were living in households where the income was under $35,000. Most of the differences between males and females tended to be in this income category. Among birthplaces, the greatest contrasts were among those who were born in the Netherlands (+14 per cent), Central and South America and the Caribbean (+9 per cent), the UK (+8 per cent), and Vietnam (+7 per cent). When we compare ethnic groups, the most significant variations were among Aboriginals (+19 per cent), closely followed by other Western Europeans (+17 per cent), and Spanish (+16 per cent); considerably further back were the British and Caribbeans (+9 per cent each), and the Germans and Vietnamese (+8 per cent each).

Average Wage Incomes
In not one of the twenty-one birthplace groups or the twenty-eight ethnic groups did females have higher wage incomes than males. For Toronto as a whole, the female average wage was $9,431 lower than that of males. When we look at birthplaces, it appears that that the more traditional immigrant birthplace groups displayed more inequality between the sexes than recent foreign-born groups. Among immigrants who were born in Europe and the U.S., females had average wage incomes that were $11,600 lower than those of males (see figs. 2.12 and 2.13). Among immigrants born in non-European countries, females earned an average $6,614 less than males. Leading the way in the first group were the U.S.-born immigrants with females making an average $18,530 less than males, followed by those who were born in the Netherlands (–$17,929), Germany (–$14,312), the UK (–$13,831), Italy (–$12,696), and Portugal (–$10,963). The non-European-born groups with the highest variations were from India (–$10,009), East Africa (–$9,612), Vietnam (–$8,757), and South Asia (–$8,494). Similar differences were found among ethnic groups. The Dutch led with a dif-

Figure 2.12
Female/male average wage differences by birthplace (Toronto = –$9,431)

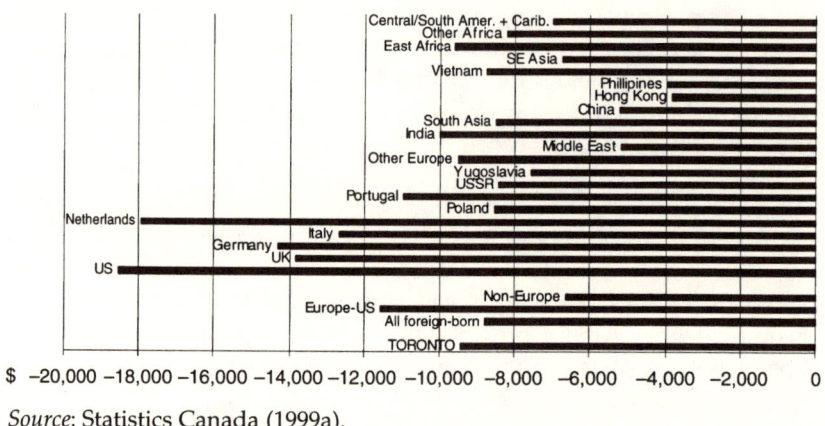

Source: Statistics Canada (1999a).

Figure 2.13
Female/male average wage differences by ethnic group (Toronto = –$9,431)

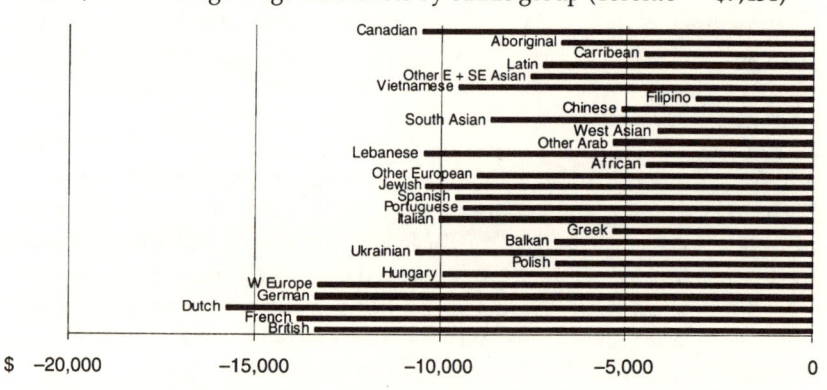

Source: Statistics Canada (1999a).

ference of $15,710 in favour of males, while the British, French, German, and other Western European males had average wage incomes that were more than $13,000 higher than those of females. At the other end of the spectrum, the smallest differences in average wages between the sexes were found among Filipinos (–$3,177), West Asians (–$4,149), Africans (–$4,447), and Caribbeans (–$4,529).

A Sociodemographic Overview   125

Figure 2.14
Female/male average total income differences by birthplace
(Toronto = –$11,826)

[Figure 2.14: horizontal bar chart showing income differences by birthplace, with bars for Netherlands, US, Germany, UK, Italy, Other Europe, Yugoslavia, USSR, Portugal, Poland, Other Africa, Central/South Amer. + Carib., E Africa, SE Asia, Vietnam, Phillipines, Hong Kong, China, S Asia, India, Middle East, Europe-US, All foreign-born, Non-Europe, TORONTO; x-axis from –$30,000 to 0]

Source: Statistics Canada (1999a).

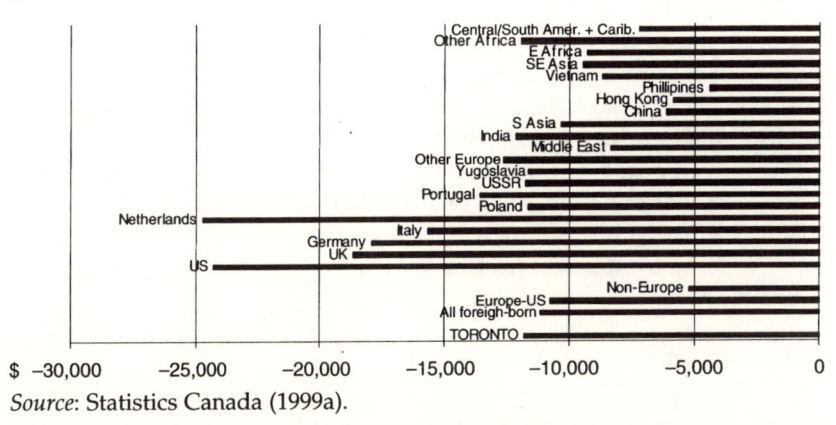

Figure 2.15: Female/male average total income differences by ethnic group,
(Toronto = –$11,826)

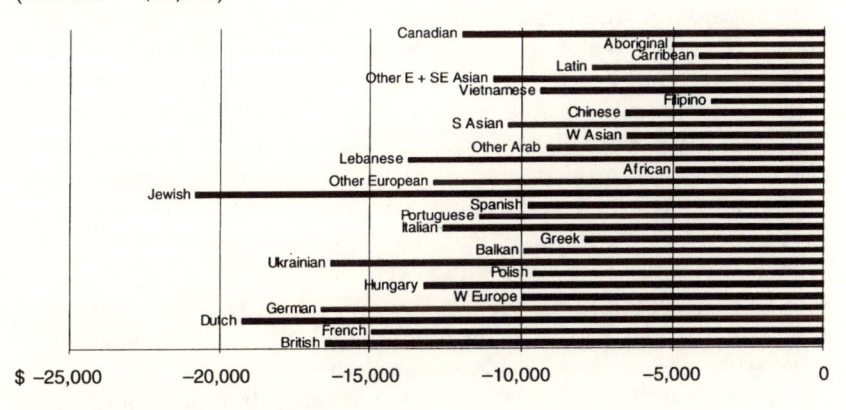

[Figure 2.15: horizontal bar chart showing income differences by ethnic group, with bars for Jewish, Dutch, British, French, German, Ukrainian, Hungary, W Europe, Polish, Balkan, Greek, Italian, Portuguese, Spanish, Other European, Lebanese, Other Arab, S Asian, W Asian, Chinese, Vietnamese, Other E + SE Asian, Filipino, Canadian, Latin, African, Aboriginal, Carribean; x-axis from –$25,000 to 0]

Source: Statistics Canada (1999a).

Average Total Incomes
The above pattern was repeated when we look at total incomes in Toronto. In this case, overall, women earned $11,826 less than men. Among European- and U.S.-born immigrants, women earned $10,764 less than men; among the non-European-born, they made $5,239 less (see figs. 2.14 and 2.15). With one or two exceptions, differences in

average total incomes in favour of males were even greater than they were for wages. Females who were born in the Netherlands (–$24,729), the U.S. (–$24,267), the UK (–$18,603), Germany (–$17,880), Italy (–$15,646), Portugal (–$13,537), and other European countries (–$12,620) were the most disadvantaged. Among women who were born in non-European countries, those who suffered the greatest liabilities were from India (–$12,127), other Africa (–$11,913), and South Asia (–$10,365). The ethnic groups that experienced the most marked deficits in total incomes for women were Jewish (–$20,847), Dutch (–$19,244), German (–$16,592), British (–$16,462), French (–$14,918), and Hungarian (–$13,168). Groups with the smallest differences were Filipinos (–$3,755), Caribbeans (–$4,145), Africans (–$4,493), and Aboriginals (–$5,046).

CONCLUSION

For the most part, we depended on statistics from government sources to analyse the situation of immigrants and ethnic groups. As is well known, statistics can be unreliable – respondents to census questions may not answer truthfully, some may underreport their incomes, and so on. However, when we found really wide discrepancies between groups, we had to accept them; even though the data was not absolutely perfect, the trends were strong enough to be real. One thing that was clear from our statistical findings was that there were some birthplace and ethnic groups who were well below the norm on many indices of 'success.' For the most part, these were immigrants from Third World countries or ethnic groups who were considered to be 'visible minorities.' Of course, they were also, for the most part, Canada's newest immigrants. Based on this fact, we suggest that, with time, they will also participate in the success that other immigrant groups have achieved.

Our analysis of the 1996 census data has certainly yielded some very interesting findings. Despite being among the most recent immigrants, people born in the former Soviet Union included 30 per cent more than the average number who are 65 years and over. Forty-six per cent fewer of these immigrants spoke English in the home, although in this they were joined by the Portuguese, the Poles, and immigrants from the former Yugoslavia. These proportions, however, were nowhere near those of Third World immigrants. Among people born in Hong Kong, the Philippines, and other East and Southeast Asia, close to 70 per cent more than the norm did not speak English at home.

When it came to citizenship, we expected older immigrants to be least likely to have retained foreign citizenship. Yet, immigrants from the U.S. had the highest proportion of all foreign-born groups who were not Canadian citizens. The next closest group was that from South Asia. Quite often, citizenship was used as an indicator of integration, but despite being among the most successful in terms of income, occupation, and education, many immigrants from the United States did not give up their American citizenship (this may be, at least in part, because it was only recently that the United States allowed their citizens to carry dual citizenship, to become Canadian citizens without losing the right to hold U.S. citizenship). U.S. immigrants were also remarkably successful in terms of education: 28 per cent more than the norm held a BA or a higher degree, unlike Italian immigrants: 19 per cent fewer than the norm held a BA or higher degree, as did 13 per cent fewer Portuguese. By contrast, as many as 29 per cent of immigrants from the Philippines had a higher proportion than the norm with a BA or higher degree. Yet, while U.S. immigrants had wage and total incomes that were $8,029 and $10,821 higher than the norm, Philippine-born immigrants had wage and total incomes that were $1,870 and $5,785 *below* the norm. This could, in part, be due to the fact that among Philippine immigrants, 9 per cent more than the norm were female.

As we mentioned, the contrast between male and female incomes in all immigrant and ethnic groups was striking. However, the differences in incomes appeared to be much larger between males and females in older immigrant groups than among newer, Third World immigrants. For example, American and Dutch immigrant women in the labour force earned $19,000 and $18,000, respectively, less in wage incomes than their male counterparts, while the largest male-female difference of $10,000 in wage incomes occurred among women from India.

Ethnic groups that seemed to be at a great disadvantage when compared with the Canadian norm were Africans, Vietnamese, and Aboriginals, among whom large proportions depended on government for their major source of income and among whom significant proportions (more than 15 per cent above the norm) lived below the poverty level. In this, they were accompanied by the Spanish, West Asians, Lebanese, and other Arabs. In particular, immigrants from South Asia and East

Africa had proportions well above the norm for living below the poverty line.

Canada is entering the 'post-industrial' age of a globalized, highly competitive, knowledge-based economy, and the need to develop a highly skilled workforce is more important now than ever before. As immigration continues to play a vital role in developing such a workforce, debates about the number of immigrants Canada should accept, the balance among the categories of immigrants, the settlement and integration of immigrants, and the factors affecting the distribution of immigrants across Canada will continue.

The Canadian record is largely a story of successful immigrant integration – at least in terms of how the world views Canada. This largely positive portrayal has conveyed a message that immigrant groups have become integrated despite their specific sociodemographic profiles at the time of their arrival in Canada and that they have been able to gain access to relevant opportunities.

However, while all references to ethnic origin, race, or religion as selection criteria have been absent from immigration policy since the 1960s, our analysis indicates that high educational and occupational status helped many of the non-European immigrants gain admission to Canada, but failed to produce economic rewards commensurate with their qualifications. Like the studies by Ornstein (2000), Reitz (1999), and Kalbach and Kalbach (1999), we find that ethnic and racial discrimination might account for these differences.

Regardless of Canada's endorsement of official multiculturalism, human rights and non-discrimination legislation, and Toronto's motto – 'Diversity Our Strength' – there is an implicit assumption that immigrants must adapt their behaviour to that of the native-born, whose performance serves as a benchmark. Still, we must ask, What is integration? Is this necessarily a one-way process? Or should integration be accepted as a two-way process of accommodation between native-born Canadians and immigrants. Weinfeld and Wilkinson (1999) argue that the term 'integration' is ambiguous because immigrants themselves, native-born citizens, and the government all see integration as encompassing different processes.

For immigrants, integration involves locating suitable housing, adjusting to a new climate, securing employment, making friends, learning more about Canadian culture, and helping children to adapt to the 'Canadian way of life.'

Native-born Canadians see integration quite differently. For some

Canadians, successful integration means that immigrants must abandon their culture and language in order to conform to the Canadian way of life. For other Canadians, integration is perceived as a two-way process of accommodation. It involves a general acceptance of all immigrant cultures, languages, behaviour, and norms, with the understanding that Canada is a country open to cultural diversity.

While the government pledges to aid in the integration process, nowhere does the government articulate a policy of integration that includes the active participation of native-born Canadians. In reality, while the Ontario government spent millions in partisan advertising, funding for settlement programs has been greatly reduced, if not totally eliminated (Siddiqui 1999).

Ideally, to facilitate the full and meaningful integration of immigrants, the receiving society should be prepared to adjust to the emerging diversities by offering facilities that would enhance the ability of the newcomers to participate in all aspects of their new and changed socioeconomic and sociocultural milieu. This requires the provision of appropriate ethno-specific services and opportunities for people to upgrade their trades and professions in order to participate in social and economic activities. More importantly, there is the need for the Canadian society to promote the acceptance of the newcomers by other Canadians through education and the dissemination of reliable and accurate information that promotes the contributions immigrants and refugees make to Canadian society.

On the basis of our analysis, there is evidence that highlights the disadvantages in income and occupation of many ethnic groups in Toronto. The analysis does not give a positive picture of the integration of the immigrants, but, rather, gives a picture of social and economic marginalization. Racism is alive in Canada, not just in Toronto. Minority job applicants are refused interviews more often than white applicants. The glass ceiling often deprives minorities and immigrants, particularly those with accents, of job mobility.

In view of the fact that the admission of people of colour – visible minorities from the Third World – has been increasing in the past decades, 'racists, lurking beyond the margins of respectable discourse, needed no prodding to denounce the growing immigration of non-whites' (Troper 1993, 277). Worries about the erosion of cherished traditions and values, about problems in schools swamped by pupils learning English or French as a second language, about an immigration system that seems out of control, and about social assistance programs being abused by immigrants and refugees will provide racists with a forum to denounce Canada's immigration program. The challenge for Canada in the years ahead is to put in place effective measures to deal with non-economic issues associated with the changing ethnic mix brought about by immigration. More action to combat prejudice is needed. The litmus test of Canadian equality and of the success of integrating diversities in Toronto will be the degree to which the Canadian-born children of immigrants, particularly those who are non-white, are able to break through the social and economic barriers to achieve full equality.

As Kralt (1990) puts it, the ethnic data collected in the census have a very definite impact on how Canadians have perceived their society. While the reporting of multiple ethnic origins was encouraged in subsequent censuses after 1981 and the data on ethnic origin (ethnic self-identification as opposed to ethnic roots) have provided a much fuller and clearer picture of the actual ethnic composition of the Canadian population, the question remains: How are we going to deal with certain physical, demographic and cultural characteristics that are associated with people at birth and that are defined as their 'ethnic origin' without attributing any social significance to them? What cost, in terms of social value and market value, do groups have to pay for being 'immigrants' who make Toronto their home, especially if they are from countries in Asia, the Middle East, and Africa? The ultimate challenge for all Canadians is to live up to what they have so proudly and readily accepted – that Canada is a land of opportunity for all people regardless of differences in race, national or ethnic origin, colour, religion, or sex. For Torontonians, the challenge is to show that diversity is indeed the city's strength.

Notes

1 The top ten countries in order of numbers were, before 1961: Italy, United Kingdom, Germany, Poland, Greece, Netherlands, Hungary, Ukraine, United States, and Austria; between 1991 and 1996 they were Hong Kong, Sri Lanka, China, Philippines, India, Poland, Jamaica, Guyana, Vietnam, and Trinidad.
2 The proportion of 13 per cent could be higher, since refugees waiting to have their situation recognized, are most likely classified as 'other.'
3 'Ethnicity' at this time, as well as prior to this, was defined as the 'cultural

group to which one's male ancestor belonged on coming to the North American continent.'
4 A good deal of this information came from the City of Toronto Web page 'Members of Toronto City Council 2000–2003' at http://app.city.toronto.on.ca/im/council/councillors.jsp, and from the help of an individual city councillor.
5 This is similar to comparisons of ethnic groups in Porter (1965), table 1, 87.

3 Towards a Comfortable Neighbourhood and Appropriate Housing: Immigrant Experiences in Toronto

Robert A. Murdie and Carlos Teixeira

The acquisition of an appropriate house in a comfortable neighbourhood is particularly important in defining immigrant integration. As Ray (1999) notes, both neighbourhood and house 'make a statement, whether intended or not, about an economic position,' and, as well, they 'affirm a social and/or cultural identity' (66). The nature and location of the neighbourhood and the availability of suitable accommodation also affect social inclusion. As well, what is considered to be an appropriate house in a comfortable neighbourhood will differ according to the expectations and cultural norms of the immigrant group. A comfortable neighbourhood is one in which the newcomer feels at home. It offers a safe environment and provides good access to shopping, employment opportunities, community-based services, and friends and relatives. Often, this is a neighbourhood that contains other members of the same ethnic group, as well as ethnic businesses and institutions that cater to the needs of the group. For some, these enclaves act as important catalysts in the integration process, while for others they may act as barriers to successful integration. An appropriate house is a good quality dwelling that is spacious and affordable. It also provides privacy, identity, and safety. The latter is important to everyone, but especially to immigrants and refugees, many of whom have experienced considerable disruption in their move from one country to another. Thus, like a comfortable neighbourhood, an appropriate house is one where the family feels at home.

These themes are developed in this chapter by using two overarching research questions that focus on immigrant experiences in Toronto. The first looks at the ways in which Toronto's social landscape has been changed by the diverse array of immigrant groups that have entered the city, especially following the Second World War. Immigrant groups no longer settle exclusively in inner-city ports of entry. Instead, many groups that initially settled in these enclaves have moved outwards to the suburbs, while others have settled directly in suburban neighbourhoods, bypassing the inner city altogether. The second question concerns the extent to which immigrants have been successful in obtaining appropriate housing in Toronto and the degree to which they have attained home-ownership. For many immigrant families, the attainment of home-ownership is the ultimate dream. Like language acquisition and labour market mobility, home-ownership is usually viewed as the final step in a successful housing career, and an important indicator of integration into the receiving society.

The chapter is divided into four major sections. The first provides a brief conceptual overview of the importance of neighbourhood and housing to immigrant groups. In this section we raise questions about the advantages and disadvantages of the spatial concentration of immigrants, outline the Canadian government's position on adequate, suitable, and affordable housing, and review the assumed importance of home-ownership for immigrant groups.

The second section focuses on the settlement patterns of immigrant groups. Here, we use a modified chronological perspective to discuss the settlement patterns of a cross-section of Toronto's ethnic communities. The discussion is guided by two principal questions, both of which concern the very substantial ways in which Toronto's social landscape has been changed by the inflow of immigrant groups during the past century. The first question concerns the extent to which the spatial assimilation model defines the reality of immigrant settlement in Toronto – especially at the beginning of the new millennium. Have most immigrant groups assimilated spatially with the rest of Toronto's population, as predicted by the model, or do some groups remain spatially concentrated? If certain groups remain concentrated, what are the dominant spatial patterns and how do these vary between groups? Also, have these patterns changed over time and are there new factors that account for the concentration of ethnic groups? The second – and related – question concerns the continued relevance of inner-city reception areas as the sole ports of entry for newly arrived immigrant groups.

Have certain groups bypassed the inner city and settled directly in other parts of the city? If so, what factors determine the residential choices and constraints of these groups?

In order to set a context, the second section begins with a brief overview of immigrant ports of entry into the inner city prior to the Second World War. The movement of these immigrant groups outwards to the suburbs in succeeding generations is also noted. This is followed by a discussion of European immigrant settlement from 1945 to the early 1970s, with emphasis on the formation of ethnic neighbourhoods by Southern European immigrants such as Italians, Portuguese, and Greeks. We then turn our attention to the settlement patterns of immigrant groups from Asia, the Caribbean, and Africa who entered Canada from the early 1970s to the present. These highly diverse groups include relatively affluent business immigrants, as well as refugees and other lower status immigrants. As might be expected, these two groups live in quite different residential environments and occupy very different kinds of housing. Their overall spatial pattern, however, differs from earlier groups in that many have bypassed inner-city reception areas in favour of first residing in the suburbs.

The third section concerns the contemporary position of immigrants in Toronto's housing market. Data for this section were obtained primarily from the 1996 census using the individual Public Use Microdata File. Two somewhat related questions guide the discussion in this section. The first concerns the extent to which various immigrant groups occupy adequate, suitable, and affordable housing. Are there differences between recently arrived immigrant groups and more established groups? Which groups are most disadvantaged in Toronto's housing market? Given the lack of new rental construction and increased rents in the private rental sector, what is the prospect of the most disadvantaged groups achieving a progressive housing career? The second question focuses on home-ownership. As indicated earlier, this is a particularly important issue, given the significance of home-ownership in Canadian society, the opportunities that ownership offers for accumulating equity, and its importance as an indicator of immigrant integration.

As a background to the discussion, we consider the supply and demand aspects of housing. Supply is important because this determines the housing opportunities that are available to new immigrants. We place particular emphasis on changes that have taken place in the 1990s, especially in the private and public rental markets. This is important because many newly arrived immigrants and refugees do not have the necessary resources to enter the home-ownership market. In contrast to supply, housing demand is primarily determined by the living arrangements of households as identified by household size, type, and family structure. Housing demand is also constrained by the financial resources available to individual households and, in some instances, the discriminatory practices of various gatekeepers in the housing market.

The fourth section of the paper addresses research gaps and policy issues concerning the spatial concentration of immigrants and their access to appropriate housing. Despite the increased amount of research that has been conducted in this area, much remains to be done. Also, given the disadvantaged position of many new immigrants and the shortage of low-cost rental housing in Toronto, much more consideration needs to be given to the ways in which these families can be accommodated in appropriate, secure, and permanent housing.

CONCEPTUAL FRAMEWORK

The integration of immigrants and refugees into a new society is based on the successful attainment of several basic needs (fig. 3.1).[1] Of these, access to a neighbourhood where the newcomer feels comfortable and to housing that is adequate, suitable, and affordable are particularly important, especially in the initial stages of settlement. Indeed, it could be argued that immigrants first seek a neighbourhood in which to live and housing for their families. Subsequently, they and their children enter the educational system for language training, schooling, and job training, and finally, their experiences with training and schools (in addition to education and skills from their home country) influence employment and level and source of income. However, although this may be the general scenario, the links between factors need not be as linear as portrayed above. Thus, we have used double-headed arrows in figure 3.1 to convey the potential complexity of these relationships.

For many immigrant groups, integration also takes place over a relatively long time. Ideally, during this period, immigrants better their economic position and are able to make improvements in neighbourhood location and housing circumstances. The arrow linking income with neighbourhood and housing in figure 3.1 illustrates the dynamic nature of this process. This, of course, is the ideal situation. Reality suggests that some immigrant groups are more successful than others in achieving a comfortable neighbourhood and appropriate housing.

Figure 3.1
The importance of neighbourhood and housing in immigrant and refugee integration

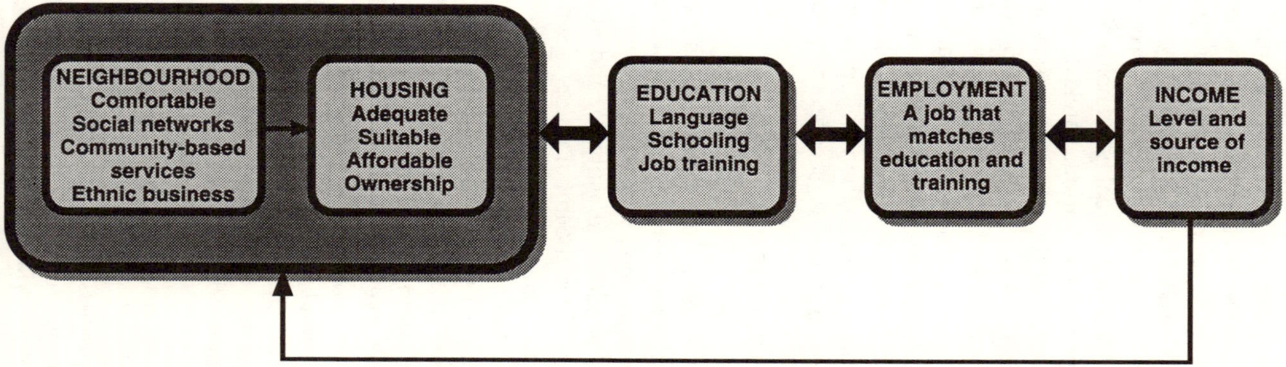

Some experience a greater degree of social exclusion than others do. In many instances, obstacles to success relate to various structural and cultural barriers that new immigrants encounter in the labour and housing markets.

Towards a Comfortable Neighbourhood

When immigrants first arrive in a large city like Toronto, they seek a neighbourhood that is comfortable – a place where they feel they belong. Often these neighbourhoods contain a relatively large number of people from the same ethnic background. Social networks develop that provide moral support and help newcomers find jobs and housing. Institutions that are more formal in character provide community-based information and services that enhance opportunities for new immigrants and act as a cushion to soften the full impact of social exclusion from the larger society. A business infrastructure often develops, offering goods and services that are familiar to newcomers in their own language. Consequently, the formation of an ethnic neighbourhood is valuable for many immigrant and refugee groups, especially in the initial period of settlement, and ultimately eases their integration into the new community.

While this is the ideal model, it is important to acknowledge that not all immigrants form compact ethnic neighbourhoods and have access to well-established social networks and a vibrant community infrastructure. The type of social networks available, the use that newcomers can make of these, and the nature of information and help obtained will vary depending on the immigrant group and in many instances the gender of the immigrant (Hagan 1998). Social networks can also strengthen or weaken over time, thus affecting immigrant integration. With respect to community infrastructure, such as retail businesses and socio-cultural and religious institutions, some immigrant groups are better equipped than others are. As with social networks, these services can change over time, thereby affecting the immigrant settlement experience. The outcome is that, while most immigrants seek a comfortable neighbourhood, not all are successful in finding an area where they feel they belong, at least in the initial stage of settlement.

Following the initial period of settlement, many immigrant groups remain spatially concentrated, while some become more integrated with the existing population. Still other groups achieve spatial assimilation from the outset. The role of ethnic concentration in enhancing or inhibiting educational, economic, and linguistic integration is much debated. One view maintains that ethnic enclaves play a significant role in minimizing social exclusion and encouraging the successful integration of newcomers. Some scholars, however, believe that these enclaves reinforce the persistence of social inequalities. In the latter context, the general argument, both in the United States and Europe, is that continued spatial concentration of immigrant groups can impede language acquisition, educational achievement, and labour market integration (e.g., Clark 1998; Musterd and Ostendorf 1998). In contrast, Canadian scholars (e.g., Ley and Smith 2000; Germain and Gagnon 1999; Kazemipur and Halli 2000) have found little support for this perspective in the country's largest metropolitan areas. Instead, there has been more emphasis on the positive role of ethnic concentration in enhancing the institutional completeness and ultimate integration of immigrant communities. In part, these divergent perspectives relate to the different histories of racialization, immigration policies, and urban development in Canada and the United States. Extreme forms of ghettoized African-American neighbourhoods in American cities are quantitatively and qualitatively different from ethnic enclaves in large Canadian cities.

In Search of Appropriate Housing

As we have noted, in addition to a comfortable neighbourhood, immigrants seek adequate, suitable, and affordable housing when they first arrive in a new city. These are the three components of appropriate housing that have been adopted by Canada Mortgage and Housing Corporation (CMHC) in its Core Housing Need Model. *Adequacy* refers to the physical quality of the dwelling; *suitability* to the appropriateness of the dwelling for accommodating a particular size and type of household; and *affordability* to the maximum proportion of before-tax household income that a household 'should' spend on shelter.[2] When households fall below a minimum standard of housing, as defined by CMHC, and cannot afford to rent housing locally that meets the standards, they are said to be in 'core need.' There is considerable debate about the measurement of these components and the policy contexts within which they have been used (e.g., Hulchanski 1994). There is much less debate, however, about their utility in comparing the housing situations of different households.

Along with a basic minimum standard of housing, it is assumed by many policy analysts, and confirmed in numerous polls, that most Canadian households wish to achieve home ownership at some point during their housing career. The acquisition of home-ownership is also important, if not more so, for immigrant households.[3] Indeed, the extent to which and the speed at which immigrants achieve home-ownership has been identified as an important element of immigrant integration. Home-ownership satisfies an inherent need for social prestige, allows maximum control over one's dwelling, and provides an investment opportunity that renting does not. It also provides accommodation for families with children who may have difficulty finding suitable housing in the rental sector. In addition to the reasons mentioned above, home-ownership is particularly significant for immigrants because it provides a sense of identity, security, and permanency, and a commitment to the new country.

IMMIGRANTS AND NEIGHBOURHOOD FORMATION

Toronto has been an immigrant reception centre since the beginning of the last century. However, the shift in the city's immigrant settlement patterns has been especially evident during the past three decades. Immigrant groups who arrived in Toronto prior to the 1970s, such as the Chinese, Eastern European Jews, Italians, Portuguese, and Greeks, tended to settle initially in the traditional inner-city immigrant reception areas, where they formed institutionally complete ethnic neighbourhoods.[4] These areas tended to be compact sociospatial units where a large number of immigrants from the same ethnic background lived and where most of their cultural and religious institutions, businesses, and services were located. Paraphrasing Breton (1964), we contend that, due to the number and diversity of their social organizations, these groups created institutionally complete communities. However, institutional completeness, as manifested by these groups, was neither uniform nor static over time. In fact, the visibility and longevity of these self-contained communities depended not only on the development of social networks, but also on the continued construction of an institutional structure.

Over time, these groups moved to the suburbs, usually in some form of segregated resettlement. In contrast, many immigrants who arrived in Toronto following the 1970s circumvented inner-city reception areas and settled directly in the suburbs. By 1996, recent immigrants were spread across the City of Toronto and beyond, with older post-war suburbs such as Etobicoke, North York, and Scarborough becoming major areas of settlement (fig. 3.2). This settlement pattern is more complex than the traditional spatial assimilation model that is characterized by initial location in inner-city reception areas and subsequent diffusion to the suburbs as immigrants improve their economic position (Mandres 1998; Ray 1998; Teixeira and Murdie 1997). The newcomers also make up a diverse group that includes both refugees and other poor immigrants, mainly from developing countries, and business immigrants, mainly from various Asian countries.

In this first section of the chapter, we explore the ways in which immigration has altered Toronto's social space, especially the shift from inner-city ports of entry to direct settlement in suburban reception areas, focusing attention on a sample of various immigrant groups who settled in Toronto under different circumstances in the twentieth century. We consider three identifiable periods in Toronto's immigrant history: the pre–Second World War inner-city ports of entry and the subsequent outward movement of these groups; post-war European settlement; and the increased internationalization of Toronto's population following the 1960s. Discussion of the pre-war period concentrates on the three immigrant groups (Eastern European Jews, Italians, and Chinese) who first settled in inner city ports of entry but subsequently moved upwards in social status and outwards spatially to suburban areas of Toronto. There, especially after the war, immigrants from the same ethnic background joined them and reinforced these patterns.

In the post-war period, Toronto became what can be best described as a city of 'homelands,' as waves of new immigrants established ethnic enclaves and attempted to reproduce many of the features and traditions that they left behind in their countries of origin. The discussion about this period provides more details about the post-war Italian, Portuguese, and Greek settlers who initially arrived in Toronto during the first two decades after the war. The discussion on the third period looks at the diversity of immigrant groups that have settled in Toronto since changes were made to Canada's immigration policy in the 1960s. The focus here is on the way in which these groups have altered Toronto's suburban neighbourhoods.

Pre- and Post-war Inner-city Ports of Entry

Most immigrants arriving in Canada in the first half of the twentieth century settled in agricultural areas of the West. Three groups of immi-

Figure 3.2
Settlement pattern – recent immigrants to the City of Toronto, 1991–1996

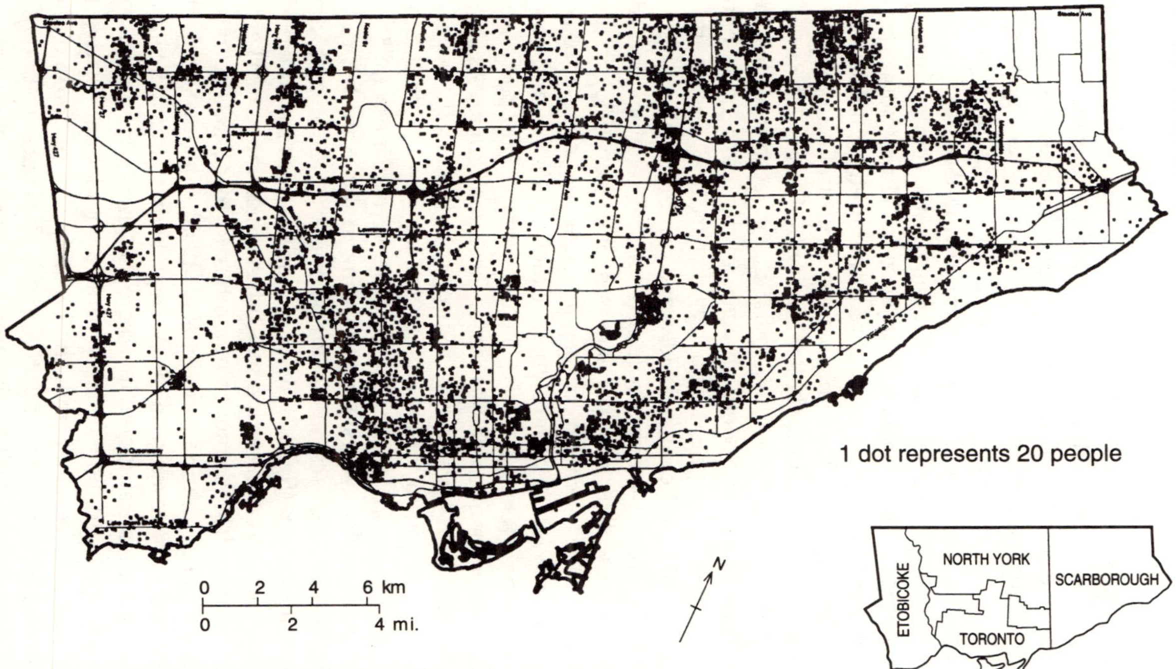

Source: Urban Planning and Development Services, City of Toronto (1998)

grants, however – the Jews, the Italians, and the Chinese – located primarily in urban areas, and Toronto was one of their main destinations. When these groups first settled in Toronto at the beginning of the 1900s, the city was a 'mere extension of Great Britain' with a predominantly British character – in 1911, 87 per cent of Toronto's population was of British descent, a figure that did not decline very much until after the Second World War (R. Harney 1983; Lemon 1985).

In Toronto, many members of these immigrant groups lived in St John's Ward in close proximity to Old City Hall and the commercial downtown (fig. 3.3). St John's Ward (or the Ward as it was popularly known) was the city's original immigrant reception area, providing newcomers with a 'focus and an anchor.' Throughout the period between the two world wars, several more ethnic enclaves appeared; nonetheless, in 1945 Toronto remained – culturally, racially, and linguistically – an overwhelmingly British city (R. Harney 1983).

St John's Ward was initially the major reception area for Eastern European Jews, who were attracted by its inexpensive housing and proximity to the garment industry (Hiebert 1993; Speisman 1985). This area became a self-contained Jewish community with a high degree of institutional completeness including cultural, religious, and educational facilities, as well as Jewish businesses (Speisman 1985). In the first two decades of the twentieth century, an increasing number of Jewish residents of the Ward became owners of their residences and proprietors of their business (Dennis 1997). The ownership of property was of great social and economic significance for these immigrants. As Dennis (1997) notes: '[P]roperty was a way to propriety, both in the sense of "being proper" – acquiring respectability and status – and in the meaning of "proprietorship" – becoming the owner of a business' (393).

In the next few years, overcrowding in the Ward led to the Jewish invasion of nearby residential areas, primarily the area of Kensington/ Spadina Avenues (fig. 3.3). By 1915, this area was the core of the Jewish community and Kensington was transformed into a market that sold a wide range of food and commodities to the 15,000 Jews who lived within a fifteen-minute walk (Hiebert 1993). The development of a self-contained infrastructure in the Ward and what came to be known as the Kensington Market served to isolate the Jewish immigrants physically and culturally from the rest of Toronto's population. Positive and negative outcomes resulted from the identification of Toronto's Jews with these two locations. In a positive sense, the concentration of Jews fostered the growth of a Jewish community, but from a negative perspec-

Figure 3.3
Toronto ethnic neighbourhoods, 1900–1970

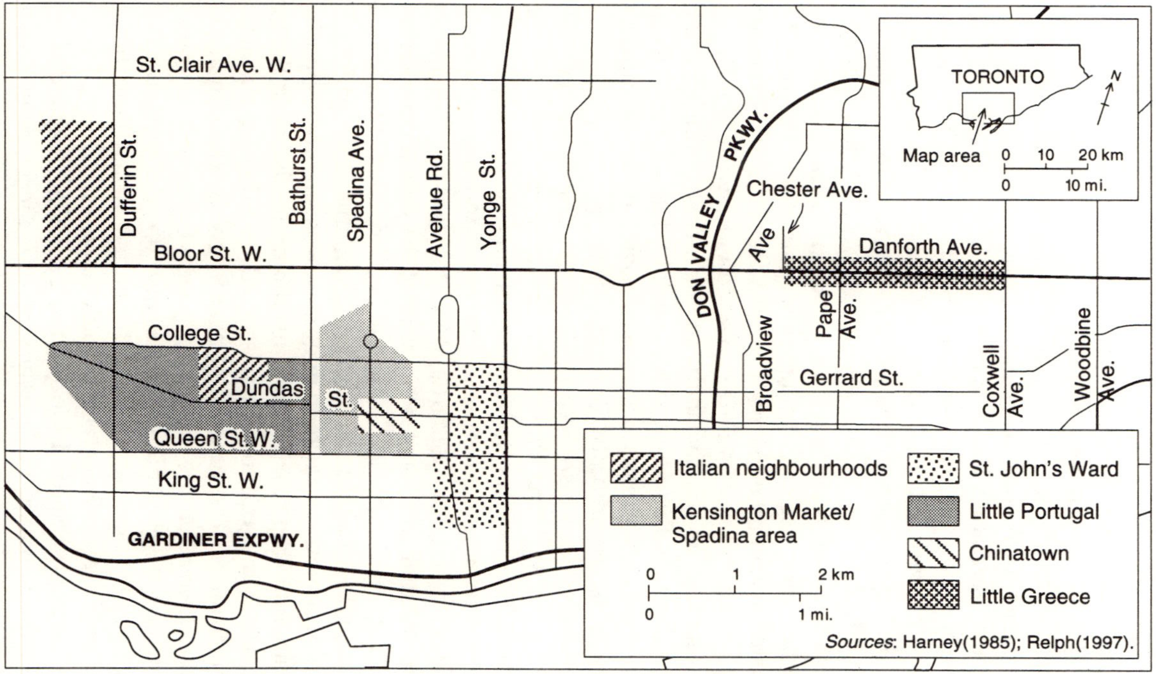

Sources: Harney(1985); Relph(1997).

tive, it also provided a visible target for anti-Semitism, particularly in the 1930s (Dennis 1997).

Jewish settlement and residential patterns in Toronto changed dramatically after the Second World War. Beginning in the early 1950s, most Jews left the inner city and moved in a sectoral and highly segregated fashion towards the suburbs. There they concentrated in identifiable neighbourhoods, especially along Bathurst St (known as the 'Bathurst corridor'), but also in the York Mills/Bayview and Steeles/Leslie areas, and further north beyond the City of Toronto in Thornhill and Richmond Hill. According to Weinfeld (1999), the Jews 'have retained a high degree of often self-imposed residential segregation' (865), largely due to the high level of 'survivalism' that characterized the Jewish community during immigration historically driven by pogroms and the Holocaust. Interestingly, a revitalization of Toronto's inner-city Jewish community is taking place, which is, to a significant degree, the result of an influx of a new generation of Jewish families – the baby boomers who used to live in the suburbs. The vibrant life and amenities of the centre of the city, and a renewed interest in their roots, culture, and religion, may explain their rediscovery of the old downtown core of the Jewish community (Kenridge 1998).

St John's Ward also became Toronto's first Little Italy (R. Harney 1983). After the First World War, however, the Italians established a second Little Italy centred on College and Grace Streets, primarily in response to urban renewal in the Ward and the prospect of better-quality housing elsewhere (fig. 3.3). This working-class area remained the residential and commercial core of the Italian community into the period immediately following the Second World War (Sturino 1999; Zucchi 1988). Labour recruitment programs (the 'padroni' system), kinship networks, and chain migration were largely responsible for the formation of these early Italian neighbourhoods. As in the case of the Jews, the Italian community possessed well-defined cultural and economic features. The practice of boarding was common among Italian families living in Little Italy, with lodgers being an important source of income for many families. Italians also opened their own businesses, which catered mainly to compatriots and which brought a sense of Latin ambience to the streets of Little Italy.

Following the Second World War, the Italians expanded northward and formed another Little Italy west of Dufferin Street between Bloor Street and St Clair Avenue (fig. 3.3). By the 1960s, this neighbourhood had, to a great extent, replaced the one on College Street. The residential mobility of the Italian immigrant group did not stop there, however. Always in search of better neighbourhoods and better housing conditions, Toronto's Italians continued to move, first to the older suburban municipalities of York and North York, and then, in the early 1970s, to the newly developed Woodbridge area in the City of Vaughan (N. Harney 1998), which has been interpreted as a sign of their drive to attain a middle-class standard of living (Sturino 1999; Evenden and Walker 1993). Today, they form the majority of the population in Woodbridge and show high levels of home-ownership.

The Jews and Italians thus shared initial settlement patterns, gave high priority to property ownership, and constructed institutionally complete communities. The early Italian immigrants moved into reception areas previously occupied by Jewish immigrants, but in their move to the suburbs the Jews and Italians took different directions. Both groups assumed distinctive directional movements, the Jews north along Bathurst Street and the Italians north along Dufferin and Keele Streets, west of the Jewish corridor. The Italian group, however, assumed a wider residential dispersion and is less segregated than the Jews.

In contrast to the Jews and the Italians, the Chinese faced much greater overt discrimination upon arrival in Canada. Thus, they quickly formed ethnic enclaves ('Chinatowns') where immigrants could live and carry on business transactions without fear of discrimination. As noted by Lai (1988), these areas were physically and functionally a 'town within a city.' Before the 1940s, it was not easy for Chinese to move into better residential areas. While it has been argued, therefore, that the Chinese created Chinatowns for self-protection, these areas may also be seen as physical manifestations of racism (Olson and Kobayashi 1993; K. Anderson 1991).

Before the beginning of the twentieth century, Toronto's Chinese immigrants were scattered around the city. Many were engaged in hand laundries and lived at their places of work. By the early 1900s, however, discernible clusters of Chinese businesses appeared both east and west of the downtown core, especially along Queen Street. Self-employment in laundries, restaurants, and small retailing businesses provided an alternative means of economic survival (P. Li 1988). At the same time, concentration in these specialized economic niches reinforced cultural exclusiveness (R. Thompson 1989). Gradually, between the First and Second World Wars, Chinatown was established in the southern part of St John's Ward, and came to be known as Old

Chinatown or Chinatown Proper. By 1955, plans for construction of a new City Hall in the core of this area forced the community to establish another Chinatown, this time in the former Jewish neighbourhood of Kensington Market/Spadina Avenue (fig. 3.3). Known as Chinatown West, this area flourished and, by the 1960s, became an important business district and an important source of employment for members of the Chinese community. Nonetheless, the rapid growth of the area can be attributed to the new immigration of Chinese in the 1950s and 1960s rather than to the migration from Old Chinatown (Watson 2001).

In the post–Second World War period, the continued immigration of the Chinese to Toronto, and especially to Toronto's suburbs, led to the emergence of several discernible Chinatowns, both inside and outside the central city. Although Chinatown West near the downtown core remains the largest and most important Chinese commercial area in Toronto, it has lost many of the functions that it once performed for Chinese residents (P. Li 1988; Lo and Wang 1997). Today, there are indications that Toronto's major Chinatown is primarily a commercial district and tourist attraction, rather than an ethnic neighbourhood. Many new Chinese immigrants have the education, occupational skills, and economic resources necessary to avoid Chinatown West as a port of entry, and buy housing in newer and more expensive suburban areas of the city.

In this section, discussion has focused on the succession of Jewish, Italian, and Chinese immigrant groups in Toronto's early immigrant reception areas. It should be noted, however, that although ports of entry such as St John's Ward may have been dominated by each of these groups at various points in time, most of these areas were inherently multiethnic. In short, they were heterogeneous social worlds characterized by considerable ethnic and social complexity. It should also be noted that the city's substantial British majority was itself residentially concentrated, which had important implications for Toronto's ethnic geography. Given this concentration, and the prevailing negative attitude of the city's British Protestant majority towards 'foreigners,' it was understandable that these areas were 'regarded by the mainstream as an area apart' and that 'if foreigners insisted on staying, mainstream Torontonians hoped they would know their place' (Troper 2000, 5). Thus, these ports of entry provided newcomers with a 'focus and an anchor' in their adopted city, but also kept them away from the British majority, many of whom hoped that they would move on to other areas of the country or, perhaps, to the United States.

Post-War European Settlement, 1945 to the 1970s

Between 1945 and the 1970s, most of Canada's immigrants came from Britain and continental Europe, initially from Northwestern Europe and then increasingly from Southern Europe. During the 1960s and 1970s, Italians, Portuguese, and Greeks were among the most significant groups to arrive in Toronto. These immigrants relied extensively on chain migration, which encouraged the formation of discernible neighbourhoods with ethnic businesses and cultural and religious institutions (Anderson and Higgs 1976; Chimbos 1980; Sturino 1990; Iacovetta 1992). Indeed, Iacovetta has estimated that family members sponsored more than 90 per cent of post-war Italian immigrants in Toronto. Relatives and friends from the same ethnic background, especially co-villagers, played a crucial role in helping these Southern European immigrants become established by finding a comfortable neighbourhood, as well as finding good housing and a job.

Southern Europeans also attached considerable importance to home-ownership and used several strategies to achieve this goal (A. Richmond 1972; Teixeira 1995; Ray 1998; Harris 2000). Typically, they started by buying relatively inexpensive housing in downtown Toronto's immigrant reception areas. Private sources of finance (particularly second mortgages) facilitated undercapitalized purchases (Murdie 1991). As well, many families occupied one part of the house and rented the other part, often to relatives and co-villagers (A. Richmond 1972; Teixeira 1995; Sturino 1999). The boarding-house system was a transitional phase both for the boarders, who were saving to become home-owners themselves at a later stage, and for the families who owned the house and wanted to pay off the mortgage as soon as possible. Dwellings were often overcrowded, with two or more families sharing the same house or flat. The boarding system also affected the gender relations of these immigrants, as it was one of the major industries that 'employed' Italian women (Ramirez and Del Balzo 1981; Zucchi 1988; Iacovetta 1992).

The desire to own property was particularly strong among first-generation Southern Europeans. By investing in housing, which was perceived as a stable investment, immigrants also acquired a sense of permanence, a symbolic security in the New World. Later, housing in the suburbs provided a means by which Southern Europeans attained social inclusion independent of their low socio-economic status. This improved housing situation reflected both the aspirations towards and achievement of upward mobility and provided an effective base from which to integrate into Canadian society without fully assimilating. By investing extensively in housing, Southern Europeans not only changed the ethnic make-up of many of Toronto's neighbourhoods, they also had an impact on the city's housing market and its economy.

Southern Europeans also contributed substantially to maintaining the vitality of older inner-city neighbourhoods in Toronto (Caulfield 1994; Buzzelli 2000). The renewal that took place in these working-class neighbourhoods was defined by the tendency of ethnic groups to rely extensively on strong social networks (friends, relatives, and community ties) for help, advice, and labour. Many Southern European immigrants, particularly Italians and Portuguese, were employed in the construction industry and used these skills in home renovation. In addition, retail buildings on streets such as St Clair Avenue were modernized and given a Southern European appearance, with little or no financial assistance from the government (Ley 1993; Teixeira 1995). Southern Europeans later continued this practice of urban rejuvenation in their move to the suburbs (Holdsworth 1993; Ley 1993).

Southern European immigrants have had a visible influence on Toronto's inner-city landscapes. For example, in the core of Little Italy and Little Portugal, it is common to find houses that have been 'Mediterraneanized,' that is, they have been given an architectural style characterized by angel-brick façades and porches with grillwork rails or brick arches (Caulfield 1994). Also common, particularly among the Portuguese, is the use of bright colours (red, green, blue, and yellow, which are common colours in Portugal) to decorate their houses and the growing of flowers, vegetables, and vineyards in their front yards. Saints and religious figures are often depicted on glazed tiles mounted beside the main door of the house, with statues (in particular, those of the Madonna or Our Lady of Fátima) placed in ornamental front yards. Similar transformations have occurred along commercial streets like St Clair Avenue, where original Georgian architecture has been overlaid with Italian features such as stucco, arches, and café windows (Buzzelli 2000).

In many respects, the Portuguese are typical of the Southern European immigrants of the early post-war period. In the 1950s and 1960s, Portuguese immigrants bought relatively inexpensive houses in the Kensington Market/Spadina Avenue area, replacing the Jews and Italians from a previous era. The Portuguese home-owners undertook extensive renovations, including the creation of basement apartments, that became a key factor in increasing the quality and value of housing in a neighbourhood once labelled a slum and scheduled for demolition and expropriation (Caulfield 1994). In addition to housing renovations, the establishment of many Portuguese businesses revitalized the commercial streets of Kensington Market.

More than one-third of Toronto's Portuguese population lives in Little Portugal, an area bounded by Bathurst Street, Queen Street, College Street, and the CNR/CPR railways (fig. 3.3). This residential neighbourhood has remained intact and contains most of the community's social, cultural, and religious institutions, as well as the two most important commercial strips: Dundas and College Streets (Teixeira 1998). In the past two decades, however, two new patterns of Portuguese settlement have emerged. First, the Portuguese have expanded to the northwest of the city, replacing earlier waves of Italian settlement. The second pattern, as illustrated in figure 3.4, has been a resettlement of the Portuguese in the western suburbs of Toronto, especially in the City of Mississauga (Teixeira and Murdie 1997). Some of these families (most are first generation) live within, or in close proximity to, existing nuclei of Portuguese concentration, while others (perhaps the most assimilated) are more dispersed.[5]

In part, this resettlement in particular areas of Mississauga has occurred because of Portuguese home-buyers' heavy reliance on ethnic sources of information, especially Portuguese real estate agents, who have played a vital role as cultural intermediaries in the home-buyers' relocation process (Teixeira and Murdie 1997). Indeed, the use of ethnic sources of information may be viewed as one of the Portuguese immigrants' strategies in adapting to a new society. Resettlement was also possible because of Toronto's extensive transportation networks, which allow suburbanized minorities such as the Portuguese to return relatively quickly to their original ethnic neighbourhoods to shop for special ethnic goods and participate in the institutional life of the community. Thus, distance from inner-city ethnic concentrations is less of a constraint on residential mobility for these suburban dwellers than it would have been for their predecessors.

The neighbourhood of Riverdale, especially the Greek-dominated section of Danforth Avenue (from Chester to Coxwell Avenues), is also typical of an ethnic neighbourhood in transition. This neighbourhood became an important reception area for Greek immigrants in the 1960s,

150 Robert A. Murdie and Carlos Teixeira

Figure 3.4
Portuguese population in the cities of Toronto and Mississauga, 1971 and 1996.

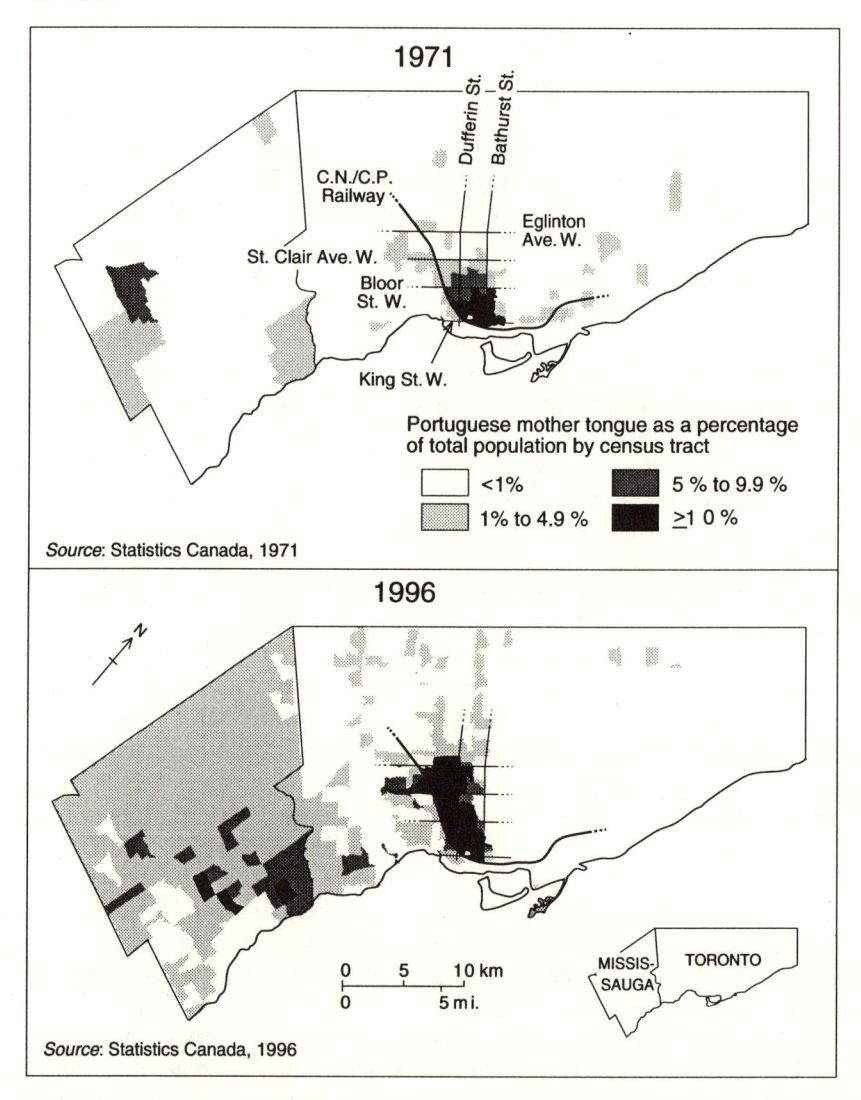

and although it remains a significant area of Greek settlement in Toronto, many Greek families have left the area for the suburbs. Recent home-buyers tend to be young non-Greek professionals in search of well-located residential units. Despite these changes, however, a thriving ethnic economy remains. Danforth Avenue, or the Danforth, continues to be known as Little Greece, a busy, vibrant, and colourful area known for its Greek restaurants and specialty stores (fig. 3.3). By promoting the Danforth, attracting non-Greek customers, and encouraging suburban Greeks to return and shop in the area, Greek entrepreneurs have so far prevented the economic decline of Little Greece.

The movement of Italians, Portuguese, and Greeks to suburban areas of Toronto raises a question about the eventual viability of these inner-city ethnic neighbourhoods. The future of both the ethnic niche markets that many Southern European entrepreneurs have created and the ethnic neighbourhoods within which they conduct their businesses, remains uncertain. With the new generation's shift in tastes and residential location, as well as a dramatic decrease in immigration from Italy, Portugal, and Greece that began in the early 1970s, ethnic entrepreneurs may have to look to the non-ethnic market for survival. This problem has been exacerbated by the invasion of ethnic neighbourhoods by gentrifiers, primarily from the baby-boom generation. Their considerable disposable income has led to increases in residential and commercial real estate prices and, ultimately, to the fragmentation and dispersal of ethnic businesses in Toronto (Carey 1999c; Sanati 1999).

Toronto's ethnic groups have attained varying degrees of involvement and success in small businesses, but they are not all confined to a spatially restricted coethnic market. For example, although Portuguese businesses are primarily oriented towards the Portuguese community, Italian and Greek entrepreneurs have established a more diverse ethnic economy by moving into businesses outside the retail sector and targeting a more varied clientele. In Toronto, Italian and Greek restaurants on College Street and Danforth Avenue, respectively, have been able to attract a culturally diverse clientele, thus becoming successful businesses as well as icons for their communities. These ethnic restaurants are not only neighbourhood institutions and sites for maintaining ethnic contacts, but are also major centres of attraction for people from other ethnic groups and for visitors to the city. The iconic status of these businesses, based on the commodification of ethnic cultures for a wider society, characterizes Toronto as well as other Western metropolises.

The Emergence of a Suburban Immigrant Landscape, 1970s to the Present

As we indicated in the previous two sections, immigrants arriving in Toronto before 1970 settled first in an immigrant reception area close to the downtown core of the city. They built institutionally complete communities and later moved to the suburbs in search of single-family dwellings. For most groups, home-ownership was a major goal and the move to the suburbs was both an expression of upward economic mobility and a way of showing that mobility. Some groups became more spatially integrated into the existing population than others. Their initial settlement patterns took two major forms: (1) corridor expansion with relatively little retention of their original inner-city residential neighbourhoods (for example, the Jews and Italians), and (2) relocation to the suburbs while retaining a relatively strong residential and commercial presence in the central city (for example, the Portuguese and, to a lesser extent, the Greeks).

The most recent source of large immigrant groups coming into Toronto is Asia. This is a highly differentiated group, including refugees from Vietnam ('boat people') and Sri Lanka, relatively well-educated immigrants from India and mainland China, and wealthy Chinese from Hong Kong and Taiwan. Their presence has altered both the ethnic make-up and the physical landscape of Toronto and its suburbs. Toronto's Chinese community, with its 360,000 members, is a heterogeneous group with various regional backgrounds, languages, and dialects. These subgroups concentrate in different neighbourhoods and socialize within their own communities. We have already noted that, while the pre-war Chinese community in Toronto was 'ghettoized' in the inner city, recent Chinese immigrants show a more dispersed pattern with pockets of concentration in both central and suburban Toronto (Lo and Wang 1997).

Recent Chinese immigrants, especially the Hong Kong Chinese, have been welcomed for their financial resources, their educational attainment, and their occupational skills. They are often business or professional people who have the economic resources to start businesses and buy expensive housing in suburban communities such as Scarborough, Markham, Richmond Hill, and Mississauga (fig. 3.5). Once there, they form compact ethnic clusters and self-sufficient communities, what Wei Li (1998) in her study of Chinese settlement in Los Angeles termed 'ethnoburbs.' In contrast to the Chinese born in Hong Kong, those born in mainland China are concentrated in the oldest Chinatown in central Toronto, as well as in areas of northwest Scarborough occupied by the Hong Kong–born Chinese. Finally, the much smaller and more recently arrived Taiwan-born Chinese are scattered throughout the city. As Lo and Wang (1997) note, the spatial patterns of these three groups of Chinese immigrants show both convergence and divergence. Convergence is explained by cultural similarity, while divergence relates to differences in economic status and exposure to Western culture.

The influx of Asians into Toronto's suburbs, and the physical changes they have brought to existing suburban neighbourhoods by building 'monster homes' and 'Asian theme' malls has led to racial tensions (Denovan 1986; T. Wong 1988; Preston and Lo 2000). For example, the growth of the Chinese presence in Agincourt (Scarborough), Markham, and Richmond Hill has provoked confrontations between the new Chinese entrepreneurs and long-time residents and storeowners. It has also precipitated a Canadian version of 'white flight,' with some residents moving to more distant suburbs (Denovan 1986; T. Wong 1988). The two largest Chinese malls in the Toronto area, Market Village and Pacific Mall, have also been criticized for being too insular and for causing too much traffic congestion. Therefore, in spite of the major economic contribution of these malls to the local economy, as well as the economic achievements and occupational mobility of Chinese immigrants, their image remains largely negative because of racism or cultural misunderstanding (P. Li 1994). Residential discrimination continues in the suburbs of Toronto, leading ultimately to residential segregation in specific neighbourhoods. The culturally homogeneous clusters of Chinese seem to act as 'homelands' – places where they feel protected from outsiders, places they can call home!

Unlike Chinese immigrants from Hong Kong, who arrived as skilled labour or business immigrants and settled directly in large numbers in the suburbs, the Vietnamese came in the 1980s as refugees and, later, as family-class immigrants. With few economic resources, this group settled first in inner-city Chinatowns where relatively inexpensive rental housing was available (Lo and Wang 1997; Carey 1999b). Between 1981 and 1996, however, the Vietnamese group gradually shifted to outlying areas of Toronto such as North York, Mississauga, and Brampton (fig. 3.6). In 1986, more than half of all Vietnamese in the Toronto area lived in the former City of Toronto, while by 1996 this figure had dropped to one-third. Recently arrived Vietnamese immigrants have settled in sev-

Figure 3.5
Selected Chinese subgroups in the Toronto area by place of birth, 1996

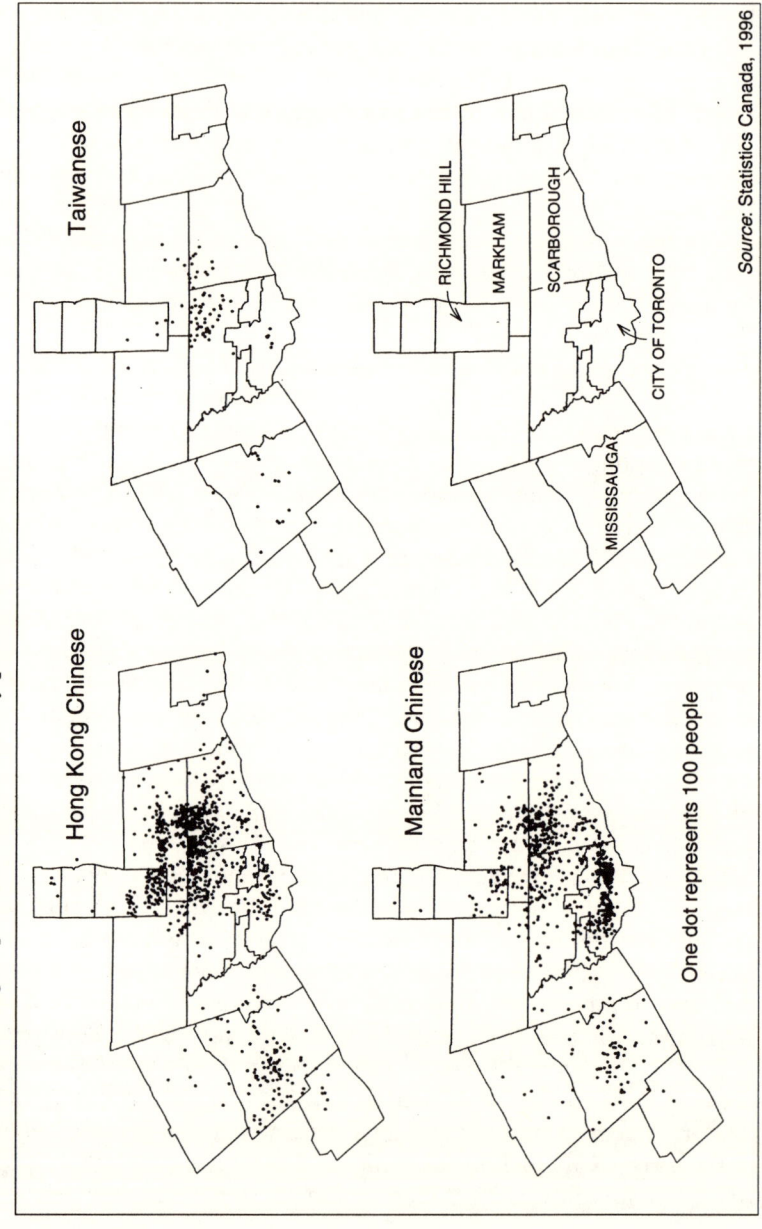

One dot represents 100 people

Source: Statistics Canada, 1996

eral neighbourhoods throughout the Toronto area. These include some areas in the central city (Parkdale in Toronto's west end, as well as Regent Park and Chinatown East), and some in outlying areas (the Jane and Woolner neighbourhood of the former City of York, the Jane-Finch area of Downsview, and the Bloor and Dixie and Cooksville neighbourhoods of Mississauga). In the outlying areas, Vietnamese are purchasing inexpensive housing; in the central city and inner suburbs they are locating in clusters of relatively low-rent, high-rise apartments (Pfeifer 1999).

The remaining groups of new immigrants and refugees have arrived from diverse geographic regions including the Caribbean, Africa, and Latin America. As they had for the Asians, the suburbs of Toronto have become the main areas of settlement for these groups, although members of some groups are also concentrated in the central city (City of Toronto 1998). For most of these groups, there were no pre-existing ethnic enclaves to receive and assist them with their integration into the new society.

Pockets of concentration of Caribbean immigrants are evident in both the inner city and the suburbs (Ray 1998; Ley and Smith 1997; Murdie 1996). This spatial diversity arises in part because the Caribbean community is a highly varied group originating from many different countries (e.g., Jamaica, Trinidad and Tobago, Barbados, and Guyana) and ethnic backgrounds (e.g., African-Caribbean, South Asian). Until recently, it was not possible to disaggregate the Caribbean population by country of origin using published census data. In the older parts of Toronto, Caribbeans are located in the Eglinton Avenue and Vaughan Road areas and the Bathurst and Bloor Streets areas, often occupying relatively inexpensive private rental apartments. The highest concentration of Black and West Indian businesses in Toronto is also located in a Little Caribbean district along Eglinton Avenue, with the heart of the strip situated between Marlee and Oakwood Avenues (Infantry 1995).

Caribbean immigrants have found an economic niche, but, unfortunately, self-employment for this group has been stimulated in large part by racial discrimination in the labour market (Henry 1994). Indeed, racial discrimination seems to be the major barrier preventing the integration of Caribbean as well as African Blacks in Toronto (Carey 1999a). A recent survey by *The Toronto Star* reveals that Blacks (both Caribbean and African) feel more discriminated against than any other group in

156 Robert A. Murdie and Carlos Teixeira

Figure 3.6
Residental distribution of Vietnamese households in the cities of Toronto, Mississauga, and Brampton, 1986 and 1997

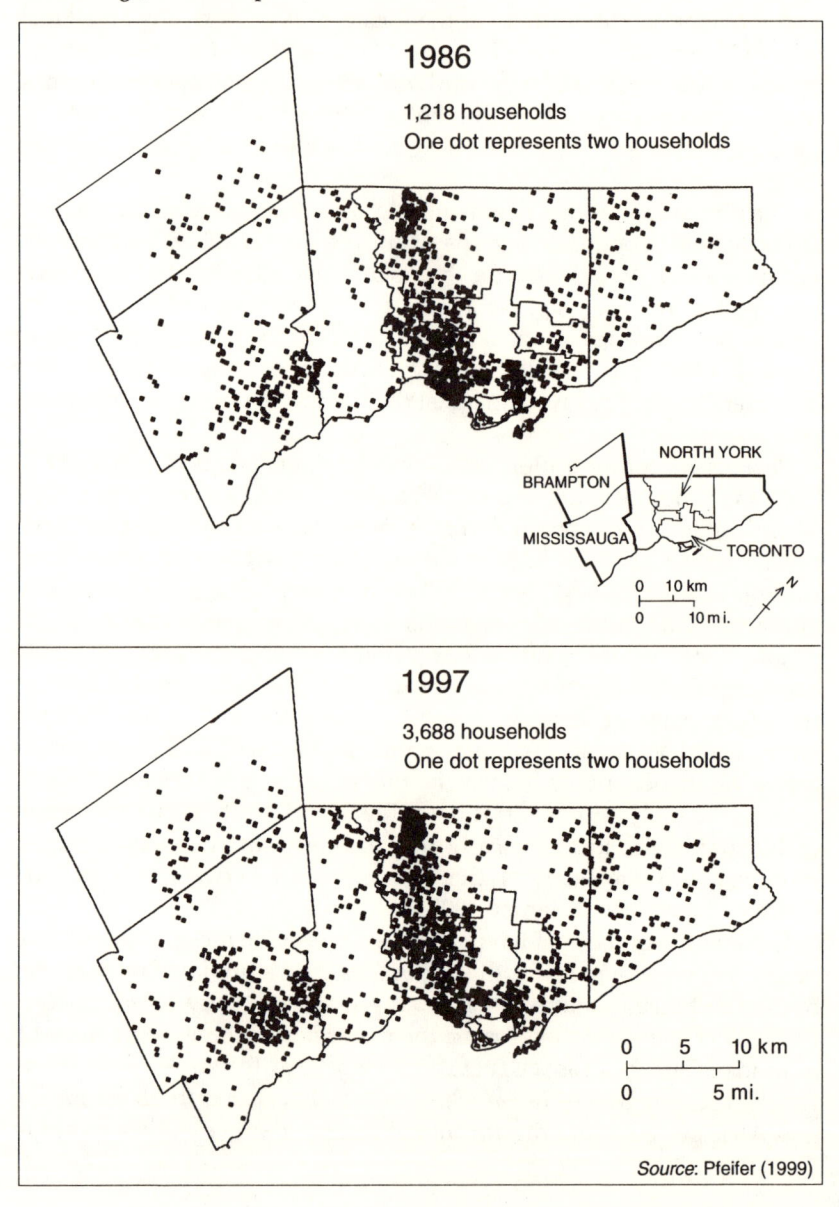

the city, with 71 per cent indicating that racism is a major concern (Carey 1999d).

As the Caribbean community became larger and more established, families moved first to outlying areas of the City of Toronto, and later to Mississauga and Brampton. This outward movement was paralleled by the concentration of relatively large numbers of African-Caribbean families in public housing provided by the Metropolitan Toronto Housing Authority (now part of the Toronto Community Housing Corporation) (Murdie 1994). In part, the increased number of African-Caribbeans and other visible minorities in public housing is due to low household income, compounded by supply, cost, and discriminatory constraints in Toronto's private rental market (Murdie 1996). African-Caribbeans are also constrained in their search for housing by gender and type of household. The majority of African-Caribbeans in Toronto are women, many of whom are heads of single-parent (single-income) households. These factors present further barriers to this group in Toronto's housing market.

Many African immigrants and refugees who have arrived recently from countries such as Somalia and Ghana are located in Toronto's older suburbs, especially in parts of Etobicoke, North York, and York. According to the 1996 census, there are approximately 17,000 Somalis in Toronto.[6] Undoubtedly, this is an underestimation of the numbers; some estimates place the Somali population as high as 35,000 to 40,000 (Farah 1999). When they first arrived in Toronto in the late 1980s, Somalis tended to concentrate in the Dixon Road and Islington Avenue area, also known as Little Somalia. There, large households, together with a tendency to concentrate in order to create a sense of security, have led to overcrowding in apartments that has contributed to cultural clashes and harassment by building managers and property owners (Sorenson 1999). Although the Somali population is still highly segregated, many have moved away from these areas of high concentration to other parts of Toronto (Opoku-Dapaah 1995).

The Ghanaians, like the Somalis and other recent immigrant groups, have also tended to locate in Toronto's older suburbs, especially in North York (Owusu 1996, 1999) (see fig. 3.7). This suburban orientation, and the tendency to concentrate in relatively few high-rise apartment buildings, results from a combination of factors, including the availability of relatively low-cost housing in these areas, the role of highly structured social networks in the housing search process, and opportunities for employment in manufacturing firms that are increasingly located in Toronto's suburbs (Owusu 1999).

The residential geographies of the Somalis and Ghanaians are more diffuse and complex than the settlement patterns of groups such as the Italians, Portuguese, and Greeks who arrived in Toronto before the 1970s. As recent immigrant groups, they have not only bypassed Toronto's traditional immigrant reception area, but have not yet built institutionally complete ethnic neighbourhoods. Instead, they display tendencies to reside in highly segregated pockets of concentration dispersed throughout Toronto. None of these areas can be described as a ghetto, however, in the sense of the large-scale ghettos that are characteristic of American cities (Henry 1994; Ley and Smith 1997). In contrast to American ghettos, they exist in both the inner city and in the surrounding suburbs, are dispersed rather than compact and concentrated, and are often situated adjacent to middle-class or stable working-class neighbourhoods. Nevertheless, concern has been expressed about these pockets of poverty that are associated with poorly maintained private-rental complexes and public-housing developments (Carey 2001). The question remains whether these groups need an institutionally complete ethnic neighbourhood as a survival strategy to counteract discrimination and to establish themselves as a community in Toronto's diverse mosaic.

As a result of these new immigrant geographies, it may be argued that we need to add another pattern to those used already to describe the residential concentration and movement of post–war immigrants. For these groups (Asian, Caribbean, and African), the inner city does not seem to have the same relevance as an immigrant reception area.[7] Instead, most members of these groups settle directly in outlying suburban areas, with their residential location determined by a combination of economic, cultural, and discriminatory factors. Thus, Hong Kong Chinese have settled in upper-middle-class neighbourhoods, while Vietnamese, as well as immigrants of African-Caribbean or African origin, are usually limited to areas of lower-cost suburban housing.

An 'EthniCity' at the Beginning of the New Millennium

The settlement patterns of ethnic groups in Toronto have changed considerably in the last century. Some groups, such as the Jews, Chinese, Italians, Portuguese, and Greeks, who arrived prior to the 1960s, settled initially in inner-city immigrant reception areas. There, they

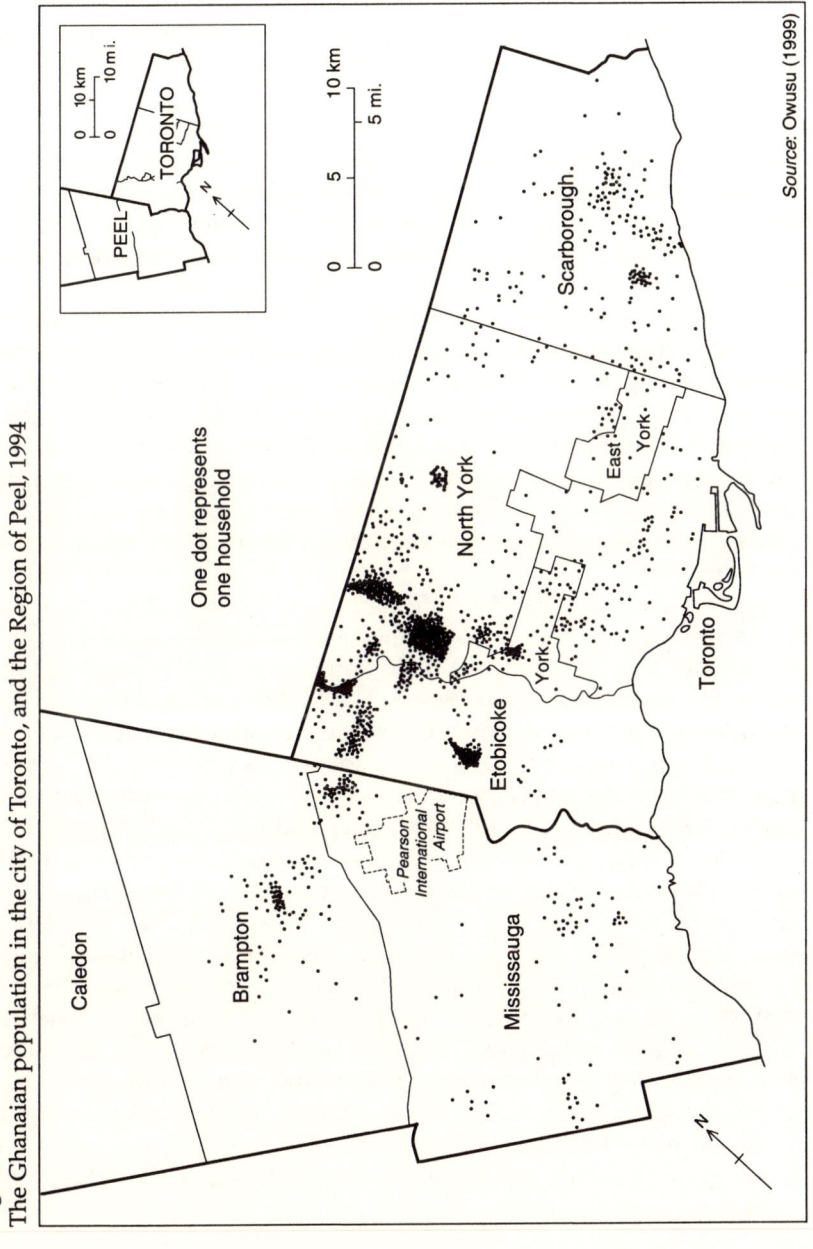

Figure 3.7
The Ghanaian population in the city of Toronto, and the Region of Peel, 1994

Source: Owusu (1999)

formed distinctive, culturally compact and institutionally complete ethnic neighbourhoods. Later, these groups moved to the suburbs, with most retaining some form of segregated settlement pattern. Some groups, such as the Jews and Italians, moved outwards in a sectoral fashion taking their commercial cores and institutional structures with them. Others, like the Portuguese, resettled in the suburbs, but retained a strong visible presence, both residentially and commercially, in the inner city. Still others, such as the Chinese, developed a nucleated pattern of Chinatowns initially in the inner city and, more recently, in the suburbs.

The direct settlement of recent Hong Kong Chinese immigrants in Toronto's suburbs highlights a significant shift in the residential patterns of immigrants to Toronto. They, as well as other post-1960 immigrant groups have largely bypassed the traditional inner-city immigrant reception areas in favour of immediate settlement in Toronto's suburbs. Their economic status and the nature of Toronto's housing market determine the residential choices of these groups, as well as the constraints and relative exclusion that they face in Toronto's restrictive rental market.

These important changes in Toronto's ethnic geography have not taken place in a vacuum. Instead, they have been affected by the major demographic, social, and economic trends that have transformed the city's geography in the post–Second World War period. These changes include dramatic population growth fuelled both by immigration and in-migration from other parts of Canada, the development of Toronto as Canada's most important financial and business centre, and the accompanying professionalization of the labour force (Murdie 1998).

Spatially, these changes have had several consequences that affect the neighbourhood choices open to immigrants of various origins and socio-economic status. For example, the Toronto region's population more than doubled from 1961 to 1996, creating a substantial demand for the construction of new and relatively expensive housing on the suburban fringe. Some of this housing is within financial reach of some new immigrants, such as Asian entrepreneurs, but, for other newly arrived groups, it is not. At the same time, more established immigrant groups, including Italians and Portuguese, have achieved sufficient economic mobility to be able to afford this new suburban housing and many have done so by moving to Vaughan and Mississauga, respectively.

There have also been major changes in the central city that have affected the potential settlement patterns of immigrants. The locus of manufacturing activity and routine office functions has shifted to the suburbs, while executive jobs in the financial sector have remained in the central city. One outcome, encouraged by city planning policies from the 1970s, has been the gentrification of the central city (Ley 1993). The result of the accompanying demolitions, renovations, and luxury condominium construction has been the displacement of low-income households, including immigrant households, to other areas of the city.

These other areas are typically in parts of of the city now referred to as the inner suburbs – the former municipalities of Etobicoke, North York, and Scarborough that were built up between the end of the war and the 1970s. It is these areas that offer some of the most affordable rental opportunities in a city where rents are high and vacancy rates low. These are also the areas where a considerable amount of public and relatively low-cost private-rental housing was built on greenfield sites in the 1960s and 1970s. These areas have been declining in physical quality and social status over the last three decades and are now attracting new immigrants and refugees from a wide variety of countries. It is these immigrants and refugees who have experienced the greatest degree of social exclusion in Toronto's housing market.

At the beginning of the new millennium, Toronto has become a microcosm of the world. It does not draw its immigrants equally from all parts of the world, however, and its residential patterns defy easy classification. Instead, the social geography of contemporary Toronto reveals the limitations of the traditional spatial assimilation model of immigrant settlement. Toronto, at the beginning of the new millennium, reflects the complexity and heterogeneity of its immigrant populations.

IMMIGRANTS AND THE HOUSING MARKET: OPPORTUNITIES AND CONSTRAINTS

Housing serves numerous functions, all of which are important for immigrant households and some of which assume greater importance for immigrants than non-immigrants. At its most basic level, housing is shelter, a place to live. In some societies, this is all it is. In most Western, industrialized societies, however, housing takes on a social as well as a physical meaning. In this sense, it is a home or a refuge from the outside world that offers privacy and is a safe and enjoyable place in which to be. For those who achieve home-ownership, housing is also an investment that has the potential to increase in value. The success of immigrants in accessing appropriate housing is determined to a considerable extent by the nature of the local housing market – the opportunities that are available within the constraints of household resources. In addition to housing supply, housing need is important. Many immigrant households have different living arrangements than non-immigrant households. While the trend for most non-immigrants is towards smaller households and less doubling up, immigrants are often part of a shared arrangement in large households. Frequently, this involves two or more families living in the same dwelling.

Toronto's Housing Market in the 1990s

Housing in the Toronto area consists of three basic tenure types: home-ownership, private rental, and public rental. Ownership housing accounts for about 60 per cent of the total stock. Of the remaining 40 per cent, about three-quarters is private rental and the rest is some form of public or social housing. For lower-income immigrants, housing opportunities are restricted to the rental market, especially low-cost private-rental accommodation.

The home-ownership sector is the most sought after segment of Toronto's housing market. As noted earlier, home-ownership is highly valued in most areas of Canada. Throughout the late 1980s, however, home-ownership in Toronto became less accessible to lower-income immigrants as average house prices increased from about $100,000 in the mid-1980s to more than $250,000 by the end of the decade (Ley and Tutchener 2001). Thereafter, prices declined, but the average rose again to over $250,000 at the turn of the century, primarily due to lower interest rates. Ley and Tutchener suggest that the increase in the late 1980s would have been much lower had it not been for the demand for home-ownership from relatively well-off immigrants during the recession of the early 1990s. They also suggest that this is why the development industry has lobbied for sustained levels of immigration, especially for immigrants with job skills and/or financial resources. The implication of this trend is a sharp polarization of recent immigrants by tenure between those who can afford home-ownership and those who have no option but to start their housing career in Toronto's rental market.

Toronto's rental-housing market is very diverse. About half the rental stock is conventional (purpose-built) apartments in the private-rental sector, while the rest is distributed among rented houses, apartments in houses, rented condominium units, and social housing (Metropolitan Toronto Planning Department 1993). In recent years, the development of purpose-built private-rental housing has declined, while less conventional sources of rental housing have increased. The latter include rented houses and rental condominium units at the upper end of the market and apartments in houses at the lower end. Since the mid-1990s, very little new rental housing has been built in Toronto. Vacancy rates in the City of Toronto are very low, less than 1 per cent through most of the 1980s, increasing to just above 2 per cent in the early 1990s, and then falling back to 0.6 per cent by October 2000, as reported by the Ontario Non-Profit Housing Association and Co-operative Housing Federation of Canada – Ontario Region (1999 and 2001). Vacancy rates are also lowest for the largest units, the kind of accommodation that is most in demand by relatively large immigrant households. The result of the tight vacancy rate has been a 'bidding war' for apartments, resulting, in turn, in higher rents. The severity of the problem is indicated by the dramatic decrease in the number of low-cost apartments in the conventional-rental sector between 1990 and 1995 (Golden et al. 1999).[8] Also, between 1994 and 1998, rents in Toronto increased at almost twice the level of inflation (Ontario Non-Profit Housing Association and Co-operative Housing Federation of Canada – Ontario Region 1999). Recently, rents have further increased because of the removal of rent controls from vacated apartment units. Now, when a tenant vacates an apartment, landlords can charge whatever the market will bear. In Toronto, between October 1999 and October 2000, the average rent for a two-bedroom unit increased by 6.5 per cent (Ontario Non-Profit Housing Association and Co-operative Housing Federation of Canada – Ontario Region 2001).

Public or social housing accounts for about 11 per cent of the total stock in the Toronto region. Of this, a little more than half is rent-geared-to-income housing. Public and social housing are often used interchangeably to refer to any housing developed and operated by the government or non-profit sectors. In a more specific context, however, public housing refers to rent-geared-to-income housing that was developed by government agencies, primarily between 1950 and 1975, and social housing is used to describe the more mixed-income housing that was developed between 1975 and 1997. Because of the substantial withdrawal of funding by both the federal and provincial governments, no new social housing has been built in Toronto since 1997.[9] And because of high demand and limited supply, the waiting list for social housing is very long – upwards of 60,000 households are on the list with a waiting time of ten years or more.

There are a variety of public-sector housing providers in Toronto. Public housing is now administered by the Toronto Community Housing Corporation, an agency of the City of Toronto.[10] Except for higher-income areas such as North Toronto and parts of North York and Etobicoke, there are 124 public-sector developments scattered throughout the City of Toronto. Much of this housing was built in less attractive and/or accessible areas, including on land on the suburban fringe that private developers did not want for more luxurious housing. These developments are primarily high-rise, high-density buildings with relatively small units. They tend to be occupied by a high proportion of low-income households, single-parent families, and Black minority groups, especially African-Caribbeans. As we indicated earlier, concern has been expressed about the creation of social ghettos, especially the disproportionate number of African-Caribbeans in public housing and their segregation within specific developments. Evidence indicates, however, that the concentration is not as high as public perception suggests (Murdie 1994). The most likely explanation for the observed concentration of African-Caribbeans in suburban public housing is a form of 'constrained choice' that emerged in the 1970s when newly built public-housing units in the suburbs corresponded with a demand from recently arrived Caribbean immigrants for low-cost rental housing.

In the early 1970s, the public-housing program was terminated and replaced by public and private non-profit developments and co-operatives. The major objective was to achieve a greater mix of incomes within individual developments. Some of these developments were built as senior citizens' residences under the sponsorship of various immigrant groups, especially those of European origin. Examples of such projects are Casa del Zotto and Caboto Terrace (Italian), Vilnius Manor (Lithuanian), Hellenic Home for the Aged (Greek), and Sts Peter and Paul (Ukrainian). Others, such as the Tamil Housing Co-operative and the Salvador Del Mundo Co-operative (Latin American) cater to a broader range of age groups.

Because of the difficulties in accessing public-sector housing, many newly arrived immigrants with limited financial resources have sought accommodation in Limited Dividend Housing that is owned and managed by private developers (Murdie 1992; Owusu 1998; Pfeifer 1999). As the name implies, developers were given financial incentives such as high-ratio mortgages at low interest rates in return for providing low-cost rental housing and accepting a relatively low return on investment. Limited Dividend Housing was developed primarily in the 1960s and 1970s, often on surplus sites in close proximity to public housing. In Toronto, these units are concentrated in North York and Scarborough, and are frequently adjacent to public-housing developments. Although Limited Dividend Housing is often thought of as public housing, it is owned by individual developers and does not have the same strong administrative control as public housing. The physical quality of the buildings is usually inferior to public housing and the units are deteriorating quickly because of low maintenance and excessive overcrowding. Also, as Limited Dividend owners paid out their outstanding mortgages with Canada Mortgage and Housing Corporation (CMHC), they were released from their obligations under the operating agreements; in some cases, rents shifted from below-market level to market level. A high proportion of recent immigrants occupy Limited Dividend Housing (Murdie 1992). Indeed, these areas of the city have become modern-day immigrant reception areas for newcomers with limited financial resources and relatively large families.

Immigrant Resources and Living Arrangements

Because Toronto has a limited supply of rent-geared-to-income housing with extremely long waiting lists, most immigrants must purchase or rent market housing upon first arriving in the city. The result is that household resources determine the kind and quality of housing that the immigrants can afford. Unfortunately, the census does not provide information on resources, and a measure of household income must be used as an imperfect surrogate. As Ley (1999) notes in the context of business immigrants in Vancouver, an immigrant can be asset-rich, but income-poor. Income, by itself, is not a perfect indicator of housing affordability. Nevertheless, for many groups it is suggestive of the kind of housing that they can afford.

Figure 3.8 provides information from the 1996 Public Use Microdata File (Individual File) on the percentage of individuals in low-income economic families by immigration status and place of birth.[11] It is likely that these families will experience difficulty finding decent housing in

166 Robert A. Murdie and Carlos Teixeira

Figure 3.8
Per cent of individuals in low-income economic families by immigration status and place of birth, Toronto CMA, 1996

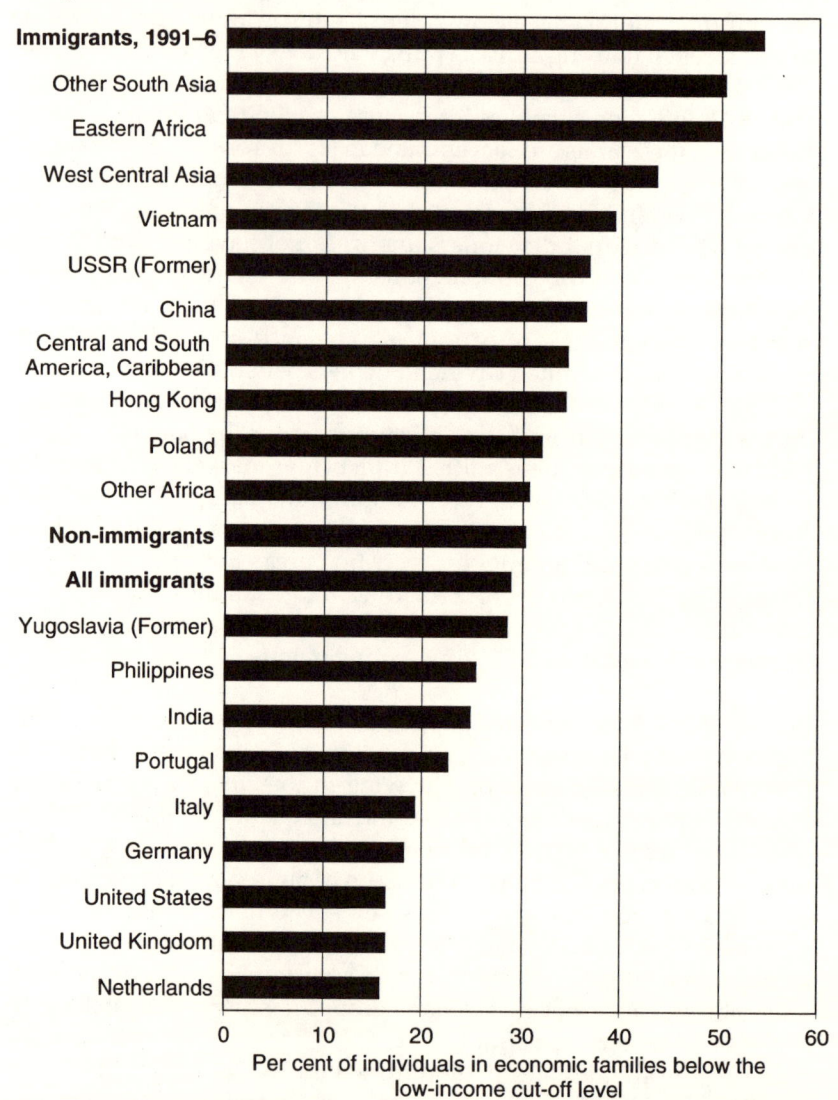

Source: Statistics Canada, *Census of Canada, 1996*, Public Use Microdata File (Individual File).

Toronto's expensive home-ownership and tight rental markets. (The groups in this and subsequent charts are limited to those for whom data are available from the Public Use Microdata File on individuals.) About 30 per cent of non-immigrants and an almost equal percentage of immigrants live in families that are below the low-income cut-off. In contrast, over 50 per cent of immigrants who arrived in Canada between 1991 and 1996 fall into this category. Seven of the ten countries or groups of countries with the largest proportion of individuals in low-income families are economically less developed.[12] Immigrants from these countries first entered Canada in large numbers in the 1970s after changes in Canadian immigration policy and many are also refugee-producing countries. In contrast, six of the nine countries with relatively few individuals in families below the low-income cut-off are European. On the basis of income, immigrants from these countries will likely experience less difficulty accessing good quality housing.

In addition to relatively low incomes, many immigrant households may have difficulty obtaining appropriate housing because of their large size. This is especially true for immigrants who cannot afford to purchase a home. On average, immigrant families are larger than non-immigrant families and immigrant households are more likely to have additional persons or multiple families. Figure 3.9 indicates that almost 20 per cent of immigrants live in households with five or more persons compared with less than 10 per cent of non-immigrants. For immigrants arriving between 1991 and 1996, the average exceeds 20 per cent. As with income, those countries in the top half of the chart tend to be economically less developed and the immigration stream to Canada more recent, while those in the bottom are more likely to be European in origin and the immigrant flow less recent. The relationship between income and household size is not perfect, however. Over 35 per cent of immigrants from India, for example, live in households with five or more persons, but immigrants from India also live in households (economic families) with comparatively high incomes. The same is true for immigrants from the Philippines and China. In contrast, immigrants from Vietnam, other South Asia, and West Central Asia are characterized by a disproportionately large number of individuals in economic families below the low-income cut-off and a relatively high number of individuals in large households.

Combining income and household size, immigrants from other South Asia (primarily Sri Lanka, Pakistan, and Bangladesh), Vietnam, and West Central Asia (primarily Iran and Iraq) are likely to experience the

Figure 3.9
Per cent of individuals in large households by immigration status and place of birth, Toronto CMA, 1996

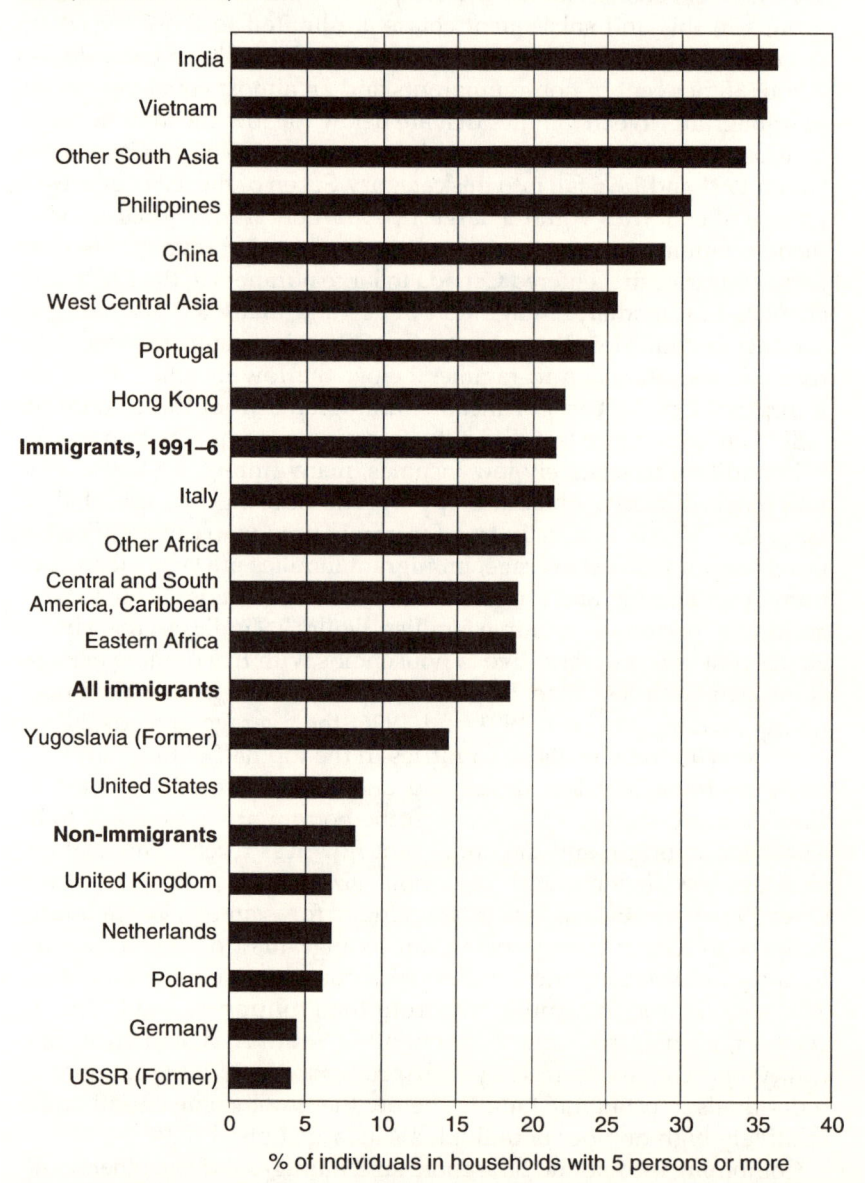

Place/Status	%
India	~36
Vietnam	~35
Other South Asia	~34
Philippines	~30
China	~28
West Central Asia	~25
Portugal	~24
Hong Kong	~22
Immigrants, 1991–6	~21
Italy	~21
Other Africa	~19
Central and South America, Caribbean	~19
Eastern Africa	~19
All immigrants	~18
Yugoslavia (Former)	~14
United States	~9
Non-Immigrants	~8
United Kingdom	~7
Netherlands	~7
Poland	~6
Germany	~5
USSR (Former)	~4

% of individuals in households with 5 persons or more

Source: Statistics Canada, *Census of Canada, 1996*, Public Use Microdata File (Individual File).

greatest difficulty finding appropriate housing in Toronto. These groups all include a relatively sizable number of recent immigrants, and all have comparatively low incomes and large households. In contrast, immigrants from the Netherlands, Britain, the United States, and Germany are likely to experience few problems. Most immigrants from these countries have been in Canada for a long time and, generally, have relatively high incomes and small households.

Immigrant Housing Outcomes: Adequacy, Suitability, and Affordability

As noted earlier, adequate, suitable, and affordable housing encompass the three components of decent housing adopted by CMHC as the basis of its Core Housing Need Model. Adequate housing is usually defined by the condition of the dwelling, identified here as the percentage of individuals living in dwellings needing major repair.[13] Interestingly, as indicated in figure 3.10, housing conditions are slightly better, on average, for immigrants than for non-immigrants. The dwelling adequacy conditions of recently arrived immigrants (1991–6) are about the same as non-immigrants. Overall, relatively few dwellings in Toronto are in need of major repair and the range between immigrant groups is not large, from a low of 4 per cent for Italian immigrants to just over 10 per cent for Vietnamese. Immigrant groups with a relatively high percentage of individuals living in dwellings in need of major repair tend to be those with a high percentage of low-income households. Immigrant groups that exceed the average for non-immigrants also tend to be recent immigrants. In order of rank, these include Vietnam, Central and South America and the Caribbean, other South Asia, other Africa, the Philippines, and West Central Asia. The United States also appears in this list, for which there is no easy explanation.

Although some immigrants undoubtedly live in quite deteriorated housing, the housing conditions of recent immigrants are not any worse, on average, than non-immigrants and for all immigrants they tend to be marginally better. The explanation may relate to the shift in immigrant-settlement patterns, both 'old' and 'new,' from inner-city reception areas to newer suburban housing that, on balance, is in better physical repair than much of the older stock in the central city. While some suburban rental housing has not been maintained to a high standard, it does not yet have defective plumbing or wiring and is not in need of major structural repairs.

Suitability, the second component of the Core Housing Need Model,

170 Robert A. Murdie and Carlos Teixeira

Figure 3.10
Per cent of individuals in dwellings needing major repair by immigration status and place of birth, Toronto CMA, 1996

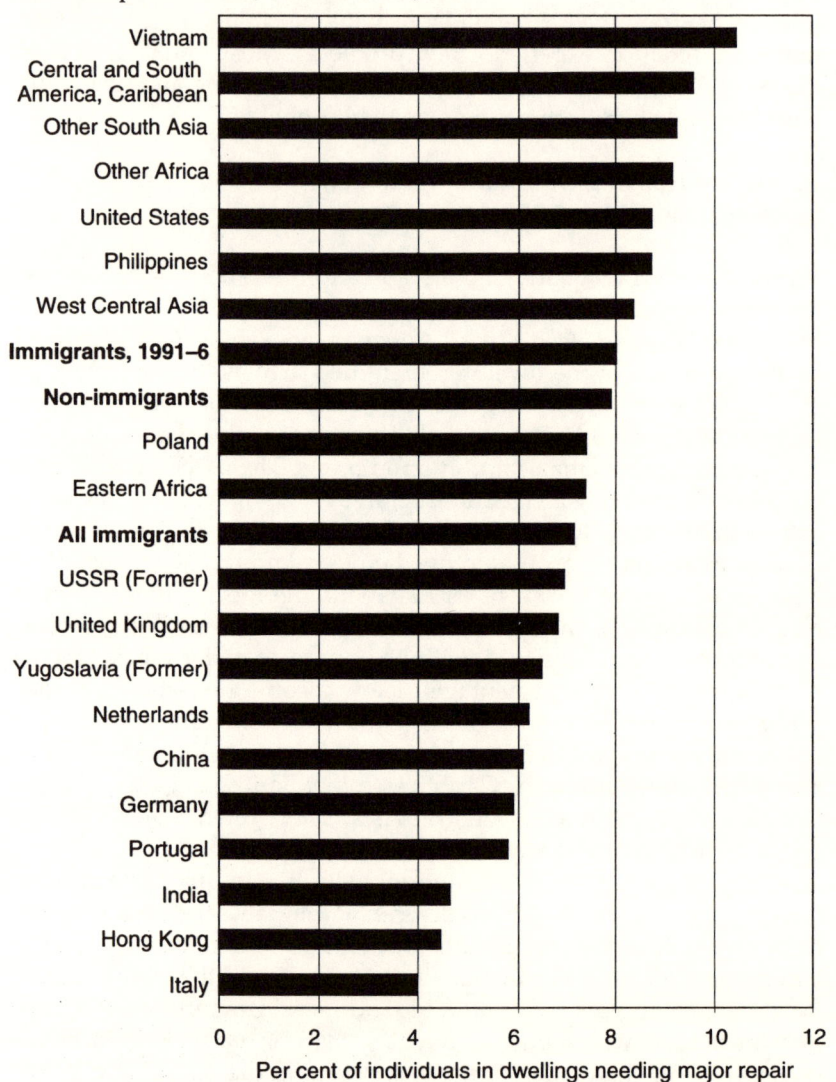

Source: Statistics Canada, *Census of Canada, 1996,* Public Use Microdata File (Individual File).

relates to the appropriateness of the dwelling for accommodating a particular size and type of household. This is defined by CMHC as enough bedrooms for the size and make-up of the occupying household (1999). It is not possible to obtain this measure from the published census, so we have opted for a more general measure: the average number of persons per room. Given their relatively large households, it is not surprising that immigrants have a higher average number of persons per room than non-immigrants (fig. 3.11). This is especially true for recent immigrants, for whom the average figure is twice that of non-immigrants. And, not surprisingly, there is a strong correlation between household size and average number of persons per room. For the most part, immigrant groups with large households tend to live in relatively crowded conditions. There is also a strong correlation between the incidence of low income and average number of persons per room, indicating those groups with low incomes and large households are likely to live in crowded conditions. This is especially true for people from other South Asia, Vietnam, the Philippines, India, and West Central Asia. India, in fourth position, does not score as highly as predicted on the basis of household size, probably because many immigrants from India have sufficient incomes to purchase relatively spacious housing.

The third component of the Core Housing Need Model concerns affordability. For renters, CMHC uses shelter cost.[14] From the published census, however, it is only possible to obtain information on rent. Therefore, we use median per cent of household income spent on rent. As indicated in figure 3.12, immigrants, on average, spend more of their income on rent than non-immigrants. This is especially true for immigrants from West Central Asia, other South Asia, the former USSR, and East Africa, who, on average, spend more than 30 per cent of their income on rent. And, not surprisingly, there is again a relatively strong correlation between this variable and the percentage of immigrants in households (economic families) below the low-income cut-off.

The median rent-to-income ratio is higher for recent immigrants than for all immigrants; recent immigrants spend almost one-third of their income on rent. For recently arrived Hong Kong immigrants, this figure exceeds 50 per cent, reaffirming the relatively low-income status of new Hong Kong immigrants compared with their overall wealth. Newly arrived immigrants from West Central Asia and the former USSR also spend, on average, more than 40 per cent of their income on rent, while immigrants from East Africa and elsewhere in South Asia spend just under 40 per cent, on average.

Figure 3.11
Average number of persons per room by immigration status and place of birth, Toronto CMA, 1996

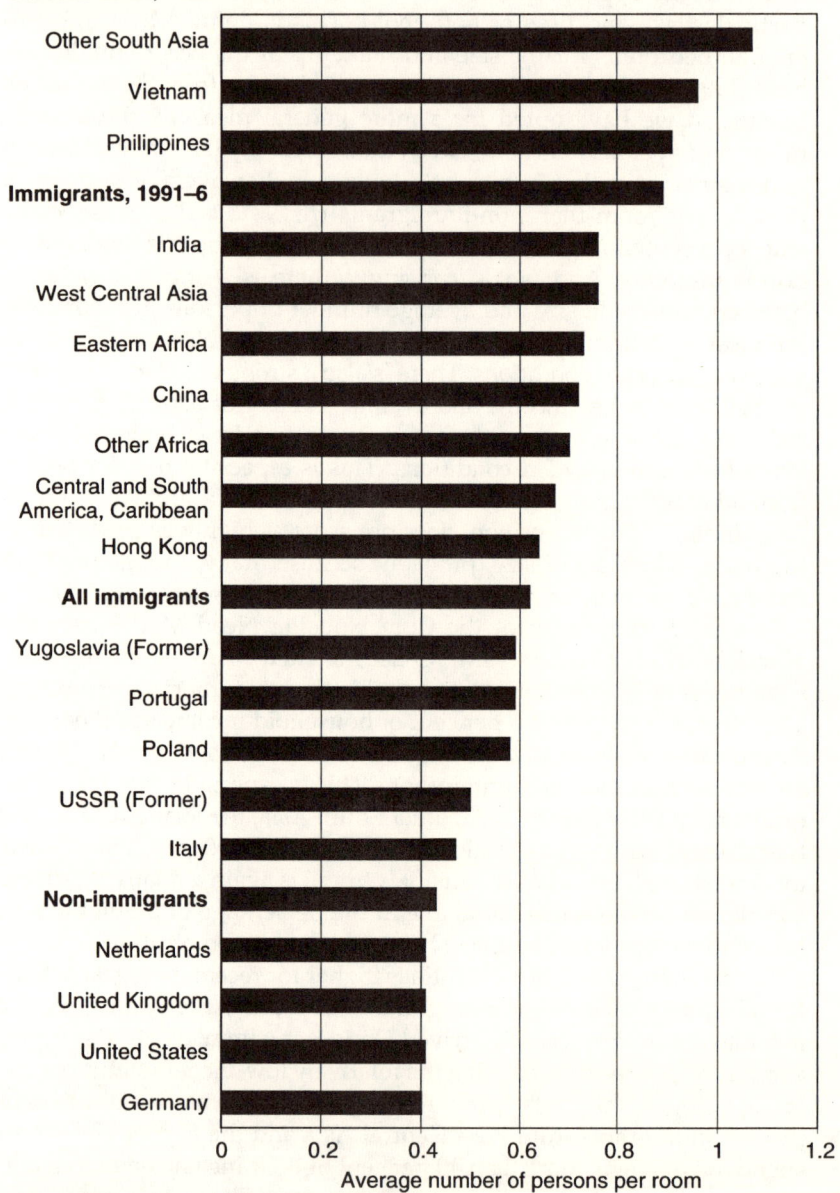

Place of birth / status	Average number of persons per room
Other South Asia	~1.05
Vietnam	~0.95
Philippines	~0.90
Immigrants, 1991–6	~0.88
India	~0.77
West Central Asia	~0.76
Eastern Africa	~0.73
China	~0.72
Other Africa	~0.70
Central and South America, Caribbean	~0.67
Hong Kong	~0.63
All immigrants	~0.62
Yugoslavia (Former)	~0.59
Portugal	~0.58
Poland	~0.57
USSR (Former)	~0.50
Italy	~0.47
Non-immigrants	~0.43
Netherlands	~0.42
United Kingdom	~0.41
United States	~0.41
Germany	~0.40

Average number of persons per room

Source: Statistics Canada, *Census of Canada, 1996*, Public Use Microdata File (Individual File).

Figure 3.12
Rent-to-Income ratio by immigration status and place of birth, Toronto CMA, 1996

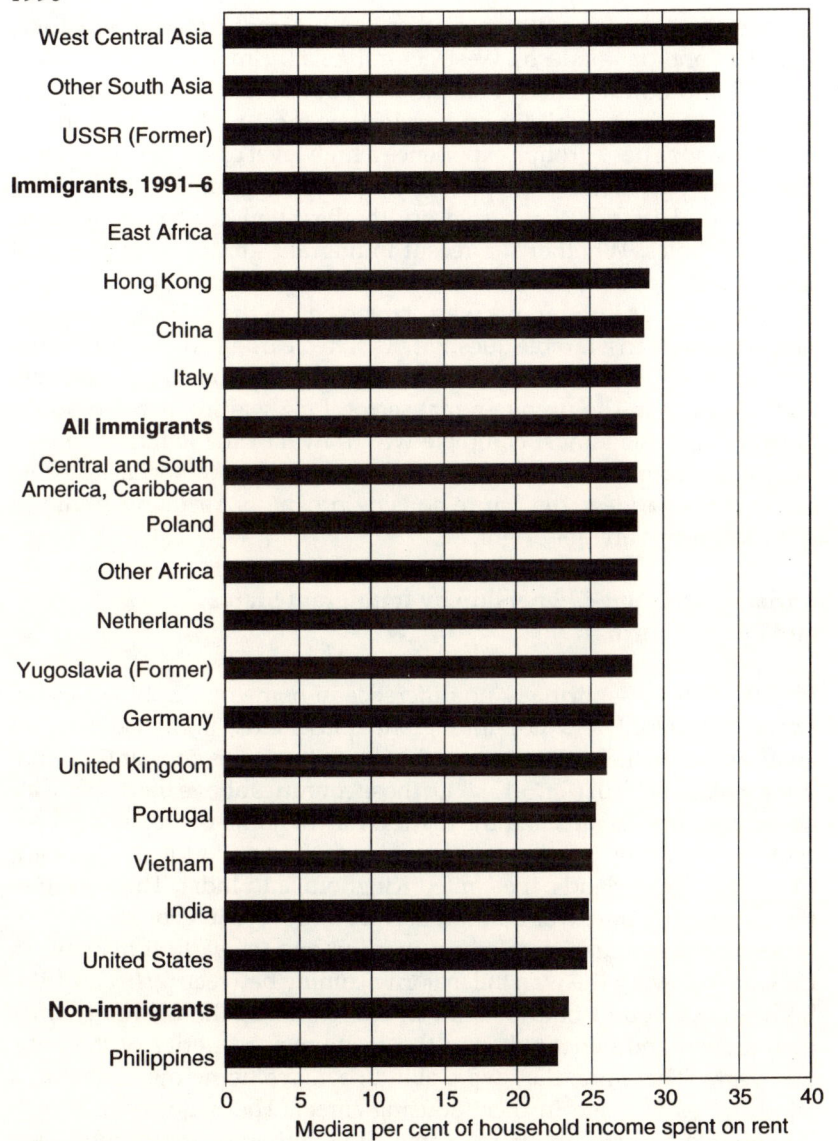

West Central Asia	
Other South Asia	
USSR (Former)	
Immigrants, 1991–6	
East Africa	
Hong Kong	
China	
Italy	
All immigrants	
Central and South America, Caribbean	
Poland	
Other Africa	
Netherlands	
Yugoslavia (Former)	
Germany	
United Kingdom	
Portugal	
Vietnam	
India	
United States	
Non-immigrants	
Philippines	

Median per cent of household income spent on rent

Source: Statistics Canada, *Census of Canada, 1996*, Public Use Microdata File (Individual File).

Combining housing conditions, crowding, and percentage of income spent on rent, immigrants from other South Asia (primarily Sri Lanka, Pakistan, and Bangladesh), West Central Asia (primarily Iran and Iraq), Central and South America and the Caribbean, East Africa, Vietnam, and other Africa exhibit (in rank order) the most problematic housing conditions.[15] These groups experience a high level of social exclusion in the housing market. Not surprisingly, immigrant groups from the early post–Second World War period are the best-housed, based on these three variables. Whether the recent immigrant groups with the most problematic housing conditions will ultimately achieve the same quality of housing as immigrants who arrived before the 1970s is an important and yet unanswerable question. As stated earlier, Toronto's housing market in the 1990s was characterized by high housing prices, low vacancy rates in the private-rental sector, long waiting lists for public housing, and the almost complete withdrawal of the federal and provincial governments from the development of new social housing. Given this overview, the future housing prospects for many members of these groups are not bright.

Variation in Home-Ownership by Immigrant Status and Place of Birth in 1996

In 1996, there was virtually no difference in home-ownership rates between immigrant and non-immigrant households; both had rates of about 60 per cent. For immigrants, however, there was substantial variation by place of birth (fig. 3.13).[16] Of those countries above the average for all immigrants, Italians had the highest rate of home-ownership (95 per cent), followed by immigrants from Hong Kong, Portugal, Germany, China, the Netherlands, the United Kingdom, and India. The list represents both early post-war immigrants and more recent arrivals.

German and Dutch immigrants were among the earliest to arrive in Canada following the war, the majority coming between 1946 and 1961. Both groups found employment in skilled occupations shortly after their arrival and benefited from the economic prosperity of the post-war years. Therefore, they were able to achieve home-ownership at a relatively early stage in their housing career. The majority of British immigrants arrived about the same time, although the immigration flow from the United Kingdom extended through subsequent decades. Like the Germans and Dutch, they generally arrived with skills that enabled them to find relatively well-paid jobs that gave them early access to home-ownership.

Figure 3.13
Home-ownership by immigrant status and place of birth, Toronto CMA, 1996

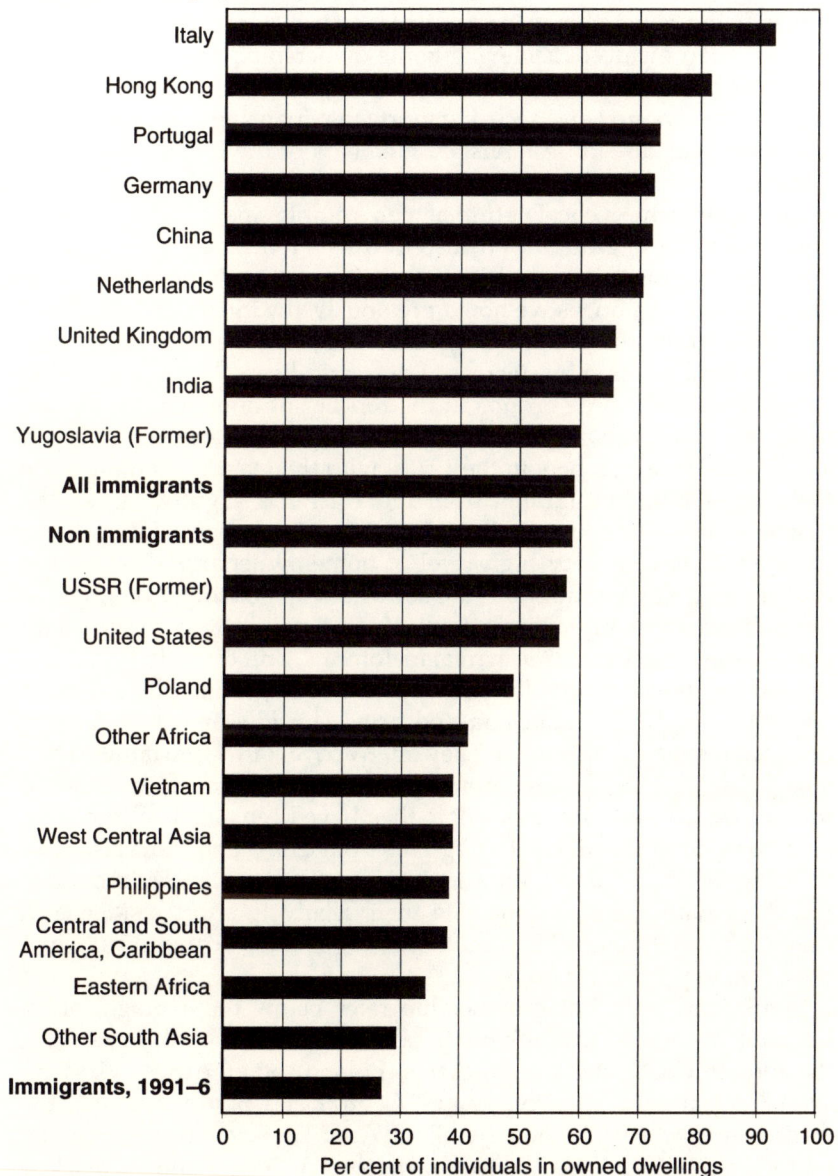

Place of birth	Per cent of individuals in owned dwellings
Italy	~93
Hong Kong	~82
Portugal	~74
Germany	~73
China	~72
Netherlands	~70
United Kingdom	~65
India	~64
Yugoslavia (Former)	~60
All immigrants	~59
Non immigrants	~59
USSR (Former)	~57
United States	~55
Poland	~48
Other Africa	~41
Vietnam	~38
West Central Asia	~38
Philippines	~37
Central and South America, Caribbean	~37
Eastern Africa	~33
Other South Asia	~28
Immigrants, 1991–6	~25

Source: Statistics Canada, *Census of Canada, 1996*, Public Use Microdata File (Individual File).

Italians and Portuguese also arrived at an early period – Italians in the 1950s and 1960s, Portuguese in the 1960s and 1970s. As we indicated earlier, home-ownership was a particularly important objective for these groups. Their means of achieving home-ownership as quickly as possible have been outlined earlier – doubling up in crowded quarters, working long hours, and securing mortgage financing from such informal sources as already established members of the Italian and Portuguese communities. In addition, wages from women's employment helped relieve the cyclical nature of men's employment in the construction trades. These groups were also fortunate to first arrive in Toronto when purchasing a home in the inner city was much more affordable than it is now. Again, as we noted previously, the inner city has undergone substantial social upgrading since then, and the demand for centrally located housing has increased dramatically.

The remaining three groups in the top tier of home-ownership are more recent arrivals. Immigrants from Hong Kong and China began arriving in large numbers in the 1970s, with the majority coming since the early 1980s. Immigrants from India arrived slightly earlier, the largest number coming in the 1970s. Like the Italians, Hong Kong immigrants have a very high level of home-ownership. Over 80 per cent of Hong Kong immigrants are in ownership housing. In contrast to the Italians, most immigrants from Hong Kong moved directly into home-ownership upon first arrival in Toronto. Unlike the Italians, they arrived as independent-class or business immigrants. For the most part, they are highly educated and bring considerable skills and/or financial resources with them. They often arrive with large families and have a high propensity for home-ownership. In general, because of their favourable economic position, they have been able to afford their own home from the outset. Immigrants from China and India also tend to be highly educated, but they do not bring the same level of economic resources with them. Yet, despite their relatively short residence in Canada, many households from these groups have acquired sufficient resources to purchase a house.[17]

Immigrants with home-ownership rates below the average for all immigrants include (in rank order from highest to lowest) those from the former USSR, the United States, Poland, other Africa, Vietnam, West Central Asia, the Philippines, Central and South America, the Caribbean, East Africa, and other South Asia. The seven countries at the bottom, with 40 per cent home-ownership or less, stand in marked contrast to the very high rates for Italy and Hong Kong. The first three countries with relatively low home-ownership rates are rather anomalous. Immigrants from the United States may have lower rates than expected because Americans employed by U.S.-owned firms view their stay in Toronto as transitory. Immigrants from the former USSR and Poland also have lower rates than expected. Given their European origins, they might be expected to have home-ownership rates approximating those of Germany or the Netherlands. The most probable explanation relates to the fact that Toronto has experienced two major waves of immigration from Central and Eastern Europe. The first group arrived in the 1950s and is likely to have achieved a high level of home-ownership, while the second group came in the 1980s and 1990s and is more likely to be renting. This hypothesis is confirmed by further examination of the 1996 census data. Eighty-one per cent of the households in these groups who arrived in Canada between 1946 and 1961 were home-owners in 1996, while only 24 per cent of those who came after 1981 owned their home.

The seven countries or groups of countries with the lowest rates of home-ownership are all economically less-developed countries. For the most part, these immigrants and refugees arrived in Canada with very limited financial resources and, it is, therefore, not surprising that home-ownership rates are low. The limited resources of individual groups are exacerbated by the fact that many came to Toronto very recently and have not had time to build up sufficient equity to purchase a house. For example, 80 per cent of Somalis living in Toronto in 1996 came to Canada in the previous five years. Almost 70 per cent of Sri Lankans, 55 per cent of Iranians, and 50 per cent of Iraqis came during the same period.

In addition to resources and length of stay, family size, commitments in the home country, and the desire to return may be important factors in renting rather than owning. In his study of the residential behaviour of Ghanaian immigrants in Toronto, for example, Owusu (1998) found that many respondents not only had relatively low incomes but were also living as singles or married couples without children. For these immigrants, the tendency was to live in rental accommodation or to share accommodation with other Ghanaian immigrants, a pattern that corresponds with the behaviour of Southern European immigrants such as the Italians and Portuguese when they first arrived in Toronto three decades earlier. In contrast to the Italians and Portuguese, who, overall, have exhibited relatively little return migration, more than 80 per cent of Owusu's sample expressed a desire to return permanently to Ghana, and, for that reason, indicated that they would not buy a house in Toronto, even if they could afford to. Moreover, many had already invested in land and housing in Ghana.

Owusu's findings contrast with Somali renters in Toronto, who, in a recent survey, indicated a strong interest in owning a home in Canada (Murdie 1999). The differences between the two groups are noteworthy. Now that the political situation in Ghana has stabilized, Ghanaians can invest with some security in their home country and make plans to return home. In contrast, the political situation in Somalia is such that refugees from that country see little possibility, at least in the immediate future, of investing in their homeland or returning home.

Variations in Home Ownership by Period of Immigration

Over time, it is expected that immigrants will achieve rates of homeownership that equal or exceed those of the non-immigrant population. Indeed, it has been noted in the previous section and in related studies (e.g., Ray and Moore 1991; Lapointe Consulting and Murdie 1996) that this has happened in Toronto for the immigrant population in general, as well as many individual immigrant groups. From the perspective of immigrant integration, the time needed for immigrants to achieve the rate for Toronto's non-immigrant population – about 60 per cent in 1996 – is of particular interest. Figure 3.14 illustrates home-ownership rates by period of immigration for immigrants living in Toronto in 1996. This diagram indicates that it generally takes about twenty years for immigrants to reach the same level of ownership as non-immigrants. Immigrants to Canada between 1976 and 1980 almost reached the home-ownership rate of the non-immigrant population in 1996. Immigrants arriving between 1991 and 1996 had the lowest ownership rate of 26.6 per cent. Ownership rates climbed thereafter, surpassing the non-immigrant population for those immigrating between 1971 and 1975, and reaching a peak of 81.3 per cent for those immigrating between 1951 and 1955. Rates then dipped slightly for immigrants who came before 1951. This decline in home-ownership can be attributed to the fact that the housing needs of many immigrants in these cohorts change as children leave home and adults reach retirement age.

Immigrant Experiences in Toronto 179

Figure 3.14
Home-ownership rate by period of immigration, Toronto CMA, 1996

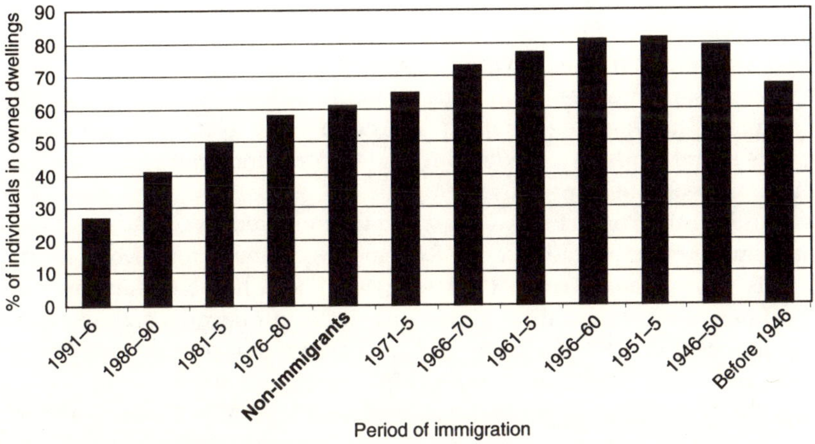

Source: Statistics Canada, *Census of Canada, 1996*, Public Use Master File (Individual File).

The trends in figure 3.14 can be partially attributed to the fact that age of the head of the household is a strong and consistent determinant of home-ownership. In the general population, ownership rates tend to increase until people are in their mid-50s, after which the rates decline slightly as the children leave home and the parents require less housing. Sometimes, the latter is a rental apartment, although condominium ownership is becoming more frequent as the supply of rental housing diminishes and the number of condominiums increases. Another important factor concerns shifts in immigration-source countries. Those who immigrated in the 1950s and 1960s and now have high home-ownership rates are primarily immigrants from Western and Southern Europe. As we noted earlier, these immigrants have done well economically and have a high propensity for home-ownership. In contrast, many newer immigrants entered Canada during a period when it was more difficult to attain a good job, and consequently may have had more difficulty purchasing a house.

Immigrants arriving in Canada since the change in immigration policy in the mid-1960s are a diverse group and because of this diversity, it is useful to track home-ownership trajectories for a representative sample. Figures 3.15a–3.15d provide this information for four groups: persons born in Hong Kong, India, Vietnam, and Central and South America and the Caribbean. These groups are recent arrivals, so information is only shown for households who came after 1966 (after 1976 for the Vietnamese). As figure 3.13 indicates, the four groups reflect a variety of home-ownership rates, from high to relatively low. Two groups (Hong Kong and India) have ownership-rates above the average for all immigrants and the other two (Vietnam, and Central and South America and the Caribbean) lie below this average.

Immigrants from Hong Kong primarily arrived in Canada as business immigrants and reflect one extreme (fig. 3.15a). Hong Kong immigrants who came between 1991 and 1996 had a home-ownership rate (71.3 per cent) almost three times that of all immigrants arriving during this period (26.6 per cent) and well above that of non-immigrants (60.6 per cent). The home-ownership rate of this group increased so rapidly that, within five to ten years of their arrival in Canada, almost 90 per cent of Toronto's Hong Kong immigrants were living in owned dwellings. Households from India have also achieved relatively high rates of home-ownership (fig. 3.15b). Their initial level of home-ownership was slightly above that of all immigrants during the same period and then jumped quickly, within five to ten years, to about the same level as non-immigrants. Thereafter, their rate of home-ownership remained above that for all immigrants, reaching a peak of 80 per cent for those who arrived between 1971 and 1975.

The other two groups, Vietnamese and Central and South American and Caribbean had ownership rates considerably below the average of all immigrants. For the Vietnamese there are substantial variations around the average (fig. 3.15c). Only 4.5 per cent of Vietnamese immigrating to Canada between 1991 and 1996 lived in owned dwellings, while two-thirds of those who arrived between 1976 and 1980 had achieved a similar status by 1996. This is a remarkably quick entry into home-ownership, especially considering the weak economic background of the group. The substantial amount of home-ownership among the first wave of refugees may relate to their relatively high levels of education and their urban background (Pfeifer 1999). In contrast, the second and subsequent waves of Vietnamese came from a greater diversity of geographic and occupational backgrounds. The very low level of home-ownership by recently arrived Vietnamese also reflects the fact that they may have lived with the relatives who sponsored many of these newcomers.

Immigrant Experiences in Toronto 181

Figure 3.15a
Home-ownership by period of immigration, Hong Kong, Toronto CMA, 1996

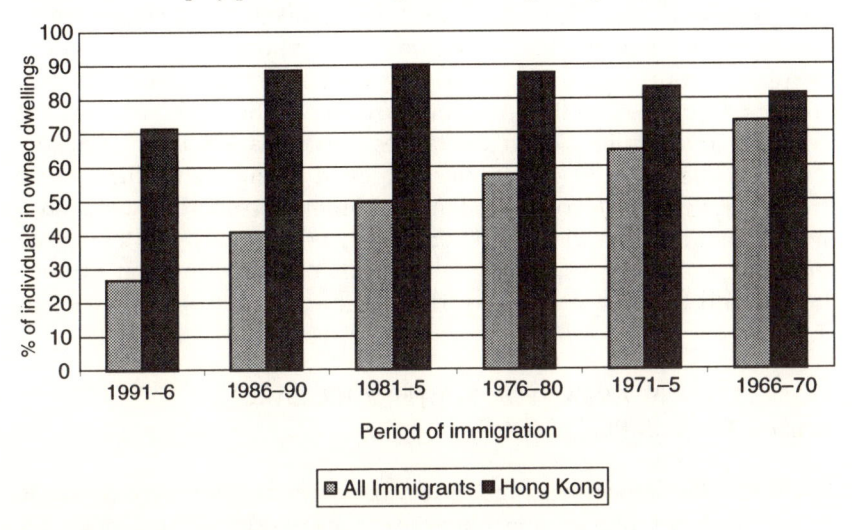

Figure 3.15b
Home-ownership by period of immigration, India, Toronto CMA, 1996

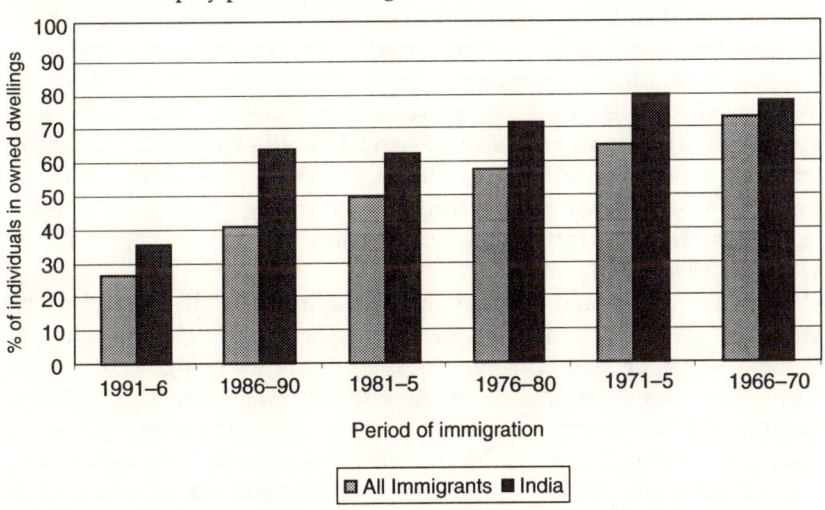

Source: Statistics Canada, Census of Canada, 1996, Public Use Microdata File (Individual File).

In contrast to the Vietnamese, immigrants from Central and South America and the Caribbean have experienced a longer and more gradual path to home-ownership (fig. 3.15d). It has taken this group twenty-five to thirty years to achieve the same level of home-ownership as the non-immigrant population. At no time does the home-ownership rate for this group exceed that of immigrants as a whole. The reasons are complex and, under the circumstances, it is remarkable that a majority from the 1966–70 cohort has achieved home-ownership. Aside from relatively low incomes and limited financial resources, this group, more than any other discussed here, faced a potentially greater degree of social exclusion, especially as a result of discrimination in both labour and housing markets during its initial years of settlement in Toronto.

CONCLUSIONS, AREAS FOR FURTHER RESEARCH, AND POLICY IMPLICATIONS

The settlement experiences and residential patterns of immigrant groups in Toronto have changed considerably in the last century. These changes can be linked to a variety of forces that have taken place, especially during the post–Second World War period, at the global, national, and local levels. An increased flow and greater diversity of migrants have characterized shifts at the international level. In particular, the emphasis on labour migrants in the early part of the period has been replaced by family reunification, refugees, and immigrants with enhanced labour market skills and financial resources. These changes have been reinforced at the national (and provincial) levels by changes in immigration policy, including the number and type of immigrants accepted into the country, continued withdrawal of support for the welfare state, and shifts in labour and housing market opportunities (Murdie 1998).

Global and national changes are also felt at the city level, but are mediated by local conditions. These include the changing structure of Toronto's labour and housing markets, the latter being of particular importance to this discussion. As noted, Toronto's diverse rental-housing market has become relatively smaller and, for the private-rental sector, more expensive during the 1990s. Almost no new rental units have been built since the mid-1990s, while rents have increased at almost twice the rate of inflation. At the same time, the rental vacancy rate has remained below 1 per cent. This, combined with discrimina-

Figure 3.15c
Home-ownership by period of immigration, Vietnam, Toronto CMA, 1996

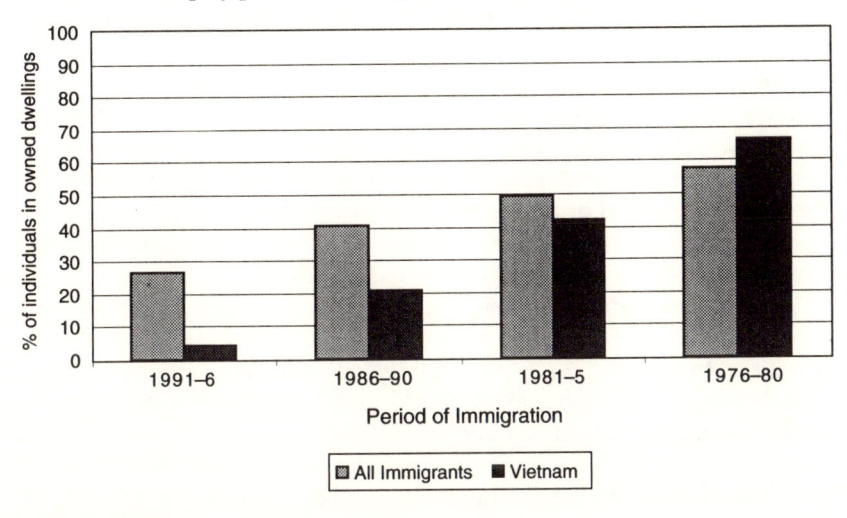

☐ All Immigrants ■ Vietnam

Figure 3.15d
Home-ownership by period of immigration, Central and South America, Caribbean, Toronto CMA, 1996

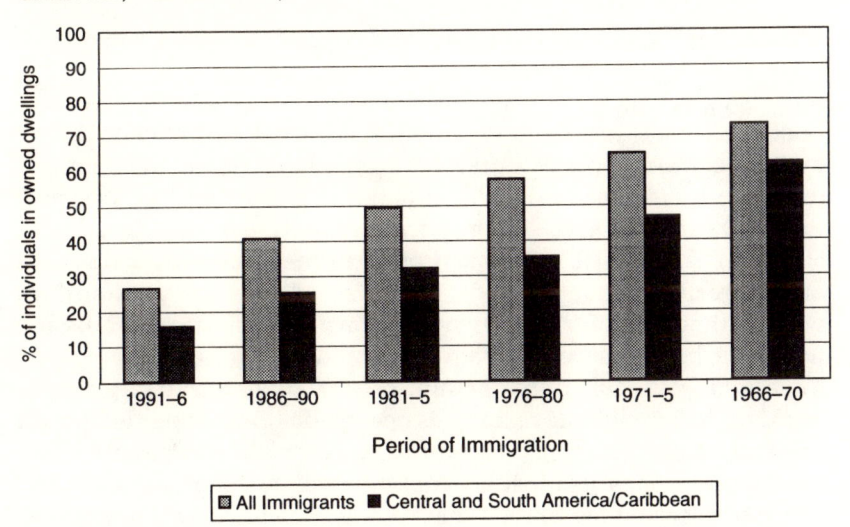

☐ All Immigrants ■ Central and South America/Caribbean

Source: Statistics Canada, *Census of Canada, 1996*, Public Use Microdata File (Individual File).

tory practices in the private-rental market, has reduced the number of housing opportunities available to lower-status new immigrants, many of whom are also visible minorities. In contrast, the problems have not been as severe for higher-income immigrants with greater financial resources, many of whom are able to afford ownership housing upon first arriving in Toronto. It was also demonstrated that most previous immigrant groups have been remarkably successful in attaining high levels of home-ownership over a relatively short time frame. Given the diversity of the recent immigrant groups and the changing nature of Toronto's labour and housing markets, it is likely that many recent immigrants and refugees will not be as successful.

The discussion in this chapter has been based on a selective review of existing literature, augmented by information from the 1996 census. Much of the information, particularly concerning immigrant settlement, comes from graduate student theses. This research is extremely useful, especially in advancing our understanding of the residential patterns of specific immigrant groups. There are, however, gaps in the literature and a need for further research. There is also a need to think about the policy implications of existing findings. It is to these issues that we now turn. We have identified several major themes, but have been selective in doing so.

Ethnic Neighbourhood Formation and Neighbourhood Change

Surprisingly little is known about the formation of ethnic neighbourhoods in Toronto and the ways in which these neighbourhoods change over time. Much more emphasis has been placed on individual immigrant groups than on the neighbourhoods in which they live. We know little, for example, about the multicultural nature of neighbourhoods and the changes that have taken place in these areas over time. We also have little understanding of the social network relationships within ethnic neighbourhoods and the links between immigrants and neighbourhood institutional structures, both ethnic and non-ethnic. In particular, the functions of ethnic organizational structures remain largely unstudied. More research is needed on how immigrant groups construct self-contained, institutionally complete communities and how these groups use institutionally complete communities in the process of social integration. Whether ethnic enclaves will continue to flourish or will gradually disappear within a more assimilative social geography is also an important question for future research. This issue has significant implications for both real estate values and the social fabric of Toronto, especially considering the role of some immigrant groups in establishing thriving commercial and residential districts and thereby playing an important role in neighbourhood revitalization.

A related issue is the way in which neighbourhoods adjust to change in ethnic structure, a point mentioned earlier in the context of new Asian settlements in Toronto's suburbs. This includes not only technical land-use conflicts over monster homes, places of worship (Isin and Siemiatycki 2002), and ethnic theme malls, but also broader fears and racial tensions that emanate from these neighbourhood changes. From a planner's perspective, policy issues concern the most effective way of engaging ethnic groups in the planning process and developing information that best serves these communities. More concretely, planning for ethnic diversity also involves finding the best way to deliver services, including affordable and culturally appropriate housing, to a multicultural community. But as Wallace (2000) notes, there are paradoxes in planning in a multicultural city like Toronto. On one hand, most planners recognize the ways in which immigrants have changed Toronto's physical and social structure, and there have been examples where ethnic communities have been included in the planning process. On the other hand, many planners are not yet ready to fully embrace the idea of planning for multiculturalism. Qadeer (2000) suggests the need for a more comprehensive multicultural planning process rather than a process that deals with issues on a site-specific basis. To that end, he suggests the need for much more detailed research that would examine the relevance of current planning norms and practices in the context of a multicultural society.

The Interplay between Constraint and Choice in Ethnic Concentration

One of the continuing debates in the literature on immigrant groups in North American cities concerns the forces – structural and cultural – that contribute to the spatial concentration or dispersal of these groups. These forces are complex in that they are experienced in different ways by different immigrant groups. In Toronto, both types of forces appear to play a role in sustaining the spatial concentration of immigrant groups and in defining the city's changing ethnic geography. Several interrelated questions arise from this: Is immigrant residential concentration increasing or decreasing over time? Do immigrants want to live in ethnically mixed neighbourhoods, or do they prefer to concentrate in neighbourhoods primarily occupied by their own group? What is the role of urban gatekeepers (for example, landlords in the private and public rental sectors, real estate agents, mortgage lenders) in limiting neighbourhood and housing choices? What is the role of formal and informal sources of information in the search for neighbourhoods and housing, and what is the relative effectiveness of each source? New immigrants and refugees may be in a disadvantaged position when looking for and evaluating housing because of a lack of familiarity with the intricacies of local housing markets, language and cultural barriers, and discrimination by urban gatekeepers. Therefore, they may not be fully aware of all opportunities in the housing market. Particular emphasis needs to be placed on the causes and consequences of discrimination faced by immigrants when looking for housing, as well as on the role and effect of policy initiatives in alleviating discrimination in the housing market.

The Advantages and Disadvantages of Ethnic Concentrations

There has been considerable discussion in the recent literature about the advantages and disadvantages of ethnic residential concentration (e.g., Bolt, Burgers, and van Kempen 1998). The debate, as advanced by Galster, Metzger, and Waite (1999), centres on the extent to which neighbourhood factors support or inhibit the socio-economic advancement of immigrant groups. Neighbourhood factors are variously identified as local ethnic economies, intragroup social networks within the neighbourhood, and the exposure of immigrant groups to people and institutions outside the neighbourhood. Evidence from their research on U.S. cities suggests an association between increased spatial exposure to members of the same ethnic group and more limited socioeconomic advancement. In short, immigrant groups seemed to be harmed economically by residence in an ethnic enclave with members of their own group. As we noted earlier, the limited evidence for Canadian cities is much more muted (e.g., Ley and Smith 1997; Germain and Gagnon 1999; Kazemipur and Halli 2000). However, this issue raises important research and public policy questions about the social exclusion and ultimate integration of immigrants in a complex multicultural city like Toronto.

Gender Differences in the Settlement Experiences of Newcomers

Relatively little is known about gender differences in the settlement experiences of immigrants in Toronto. The 'voices' of immigrant women require further research (e.g., Novac 1999). Important gaps in the literature include (i) the dynamics of settlement and integration of immigrant women, including the barriers they face in the process of adaptation and social integration; and (ii) the social networks that these women develop as an adjustment strategy in their new urban environment (e.g., Ray and Rose 2000).

Immigrant Housing Careers

In spite of the extensive set of studies concerning individual groups, relatively little is known about the long-term nature of immigrant housing careers. This is important because integration is often a slow and arduous process. As we have noted, information is available from the census on the acquisition of home-ownership over a long time. New research has also examined in more depth, especially for the rental market, the barriers that immigrants encounter during the initial few years of settlement and the strategies they used to overcome these barriers (e.g., Hulchanski 1998; Murdie 2002). For most groups, however, less is known about the details of the immigrant residential experience over a longer period. The subsequent residential mobility of immigrants after the initial period of settlement, the factors leading to this mobility, and the extent to which they have made a progressive housing career are of particular interest. Comparative studies between immigrant groups, especially those who arrived in Toronto at about the same time (for example, Portuguese and Jamaicans in the 1970s), would be particularly useful. There are also other groups, especially recently arrived refugees such as Tamils from Sri Lanka, whose housing circumstances are underresearched. As we have said, information from the census suggests that these groups exhibit the most problematic housing conditions. Finally, important research questions also concern the cultural attitudes of immigrants towards housing, including living arrangements and the transformation of a house into a home, the culture of property, and the impact of return migration on attitudes to home-ownership.

Immigrants and the Housing Market

Housing problems particularly affect recent immigrants and refugees who have limited financial resources and who often face various forms of discrimination in Toronto's stressed rental market. The major policy issue is how to accommodate these newcomers in appropriate, secure, and permanent housing. As both provincial and federal governments rely more heavily on the private sector, the need to preserve the existing stock of public-sector housing and expand the supply of low-income housing is critical. On the latter, a number of recommendations involving cooperation between the federal, provincial, and local levels of government and the private sector were suggested in *Taking Responsibility for Homelessness*, the report by the Mayor's Homelessness Action Task Force (Golden et al. 1999). These were echoed more recently in *Where's Home? A Picture of Housing Needs in Ontario* (Ontario Non-Profit Housing Association and Co-operative Housing Federation of Canada – Ontario Region 1999). Since the release of the mayor's report, relatively little progress has been made in implementing the recommendations, especially those concerning the development of more affordable housing. Until action of this sort is taken, there is little possibility of improving the housing circumstances of Toronto's immigrants and refugees, especially those who are most in need of adequate, suitable, and affordable housing. Beyond that, the apparent importance of home-ownership for many immigrant groups and the shortage of appropriate rental housing, suggests a need to consider ways in which access to home-ownership can be accelerated for lower-income immigrant groups who are beyond the initial stage of settlement.

Notes

1 Figure 3.1 and the discussion that follows is adapted from a SSHRC funded project entitled 'The Housing Experiences of New Canadians in Greater Toronto' (Murdie, Chambon, Hulchanski, and Teixeira 1996; Hulchanski 1998).
2 Shelter costs include payments for electricity, fuel, water, and municipal services. For renters, they include the rent, and for owners they include

Immigrant Experiences in Toronto 189

mortgage payments (principal and interest), property taxes, and any condominium fees (Canada Mortgage and Housing Corporation 1999).

3 This point is implied in recent studies commissioned by Canada Mortgage and Housing Corporation (CMHC) within the framework of CMHC's Potential Housing Demand Model. See, for example, Clayton Research Associates Limited (1994) and Lapointe Consulting and Murdie (1996).

4 According to Breton (1964), institutional completeness is achieved by an immigrant group 'whenever the ethnic community [can] perform all the services required by its members. Members would never have to make use of native institutions for the satisfaction of any of their needs, such as education, work, food and clothing, medical care, or social assistance.' This, it should be noted, represents an ideal or extreme model of this phenomenon. In reality, as Breton reminds us, 'in contemporary North American cities very few, if any, ethnic communities showing full institutional completeness can be found' (194).

5 Figure 3.4 is based on census tract data for people identifying Portuguese as their mother tongue. Mother tongue is the language first learned and still understood. The choice of this variable for 1996 permits comparison with a map based on similar data for 1971. Because of a strong commitment to language retention, most first- and second-generation Portuguese likely responded 'Portuguese' to the mother tongue question in the census. Although the highest value for Portuguese mother tongue is 16 per cent of the total population (census tract 615), Portuguese account for the majority in some blocks near the two Portuguese churches in Mississauga.

6 Based on total-ethnic origin (single plus multiple).

7 We might also add immigrants from various Latin American countries. Less is known about the settlement patterns of these groups in Toronto. In general, they have tended to settle in the northwest immigrant corridor, following the Italians and Portuguese, and like the Vietnamese and African groups, are often located in relatively low-cost private-rental accommodation in older suburbs such as North York (Ray 1998).

8 The severity of the problem is indicated in the report of the Mayor's Homelessness Action Task Force (Golden et al. 1999, 25–7). Between 1990 and 1995, the following units from Toronto's purpose-built conventional rental stock shifted into higher rental categories: 4,511 bachelor apartments renting for less than $500 per month; 27,636 one-bedroom units renting for under $600 per month; 22,216 units renting for under $700 per month; and 4,138 three-bedroom units under $800 per month.

9 The federal government stopped funding new social housing units in 1993 and the provincial government in Ontario ended its program in 1995. It

should be noted, however, that the federal government still provides almost $2 billion annually to meet commitments on existing public and social housing units. Also, although the provision of public and social housing programs for new construction is now the responsibility of provincial jurisdictions, Canada Mortgage and Housing Corporation still has some involvement through the Canadian Centre for Public Private Partnerships in Housing and similar initiatives.

10 The public housing component of the Toronto Community Housing Corporation was previously known as the Metropolitan Toronto Housing Authority, an agency of the Ontario provincial government. Public housing became a city responsibility as part of the provincial government's policy to devolve responsibilities from the provincial to municipal levels of government.

11 An economic family includes all persons related by blood, marriage, common-law, or adoption who are living together. It includes households with extended families, but excludes unattached individuals living in a household who are not related to another member of the household. The cut-offs are based on national family expenditure data and are updated annually by changes in the consumer price index (based on Statistics Canada, 1996 PUMF on Individuals/95M0010XCB–User Documentation).

12 These include other South Asia, East Africa, West Central Asia, Vietnam, China, Central and South America and the Caribbean, and other Africa. The following countries dominate the groups of countries listed in Figures 3.8 to 3.13: other South Asia (Bangladesh, Pakistan, Sri Lanka), East Africa (Kenya, Somalia, Tanzania, Uganda), West Central Asia (Afghanistan, Iran, Iraq, Israel, Lebanon), Central and South America and the Caribbean (El Salvador, Guatemala, Guyana, Jamaica, Mexico, Peru, Trinidad and Tobago), and other Africa (Ghana, Morocco, Nigeria, South Africa). In the case of China, it should be noted that persons who state Chinese as their place of birth may have lived in Hong Kong or Taiwan for several years before immigrating to Canada.

13 Major repairs needed is defined by Statistics Canada as defective plumbing or electrical wiring, structural repairs to walls or ceilings, and so on. As with other census data, these figures are based on self-reporting.

14 See note 2.

15 The immigrant groups were rank ordered on each of the three variables and the ranks were totalled to arrive at a composite score.

16 The home-ownership rates calculated from the 1996 Public Use Microdata File are similar in order of magnitude to the rates reported in a 1999 poll of selected immigrant groups in the Greater Toronto Area conducted by

Goldfarb Consultants for *The Toronto Star* (Carey 1999d). In order of magnitude, *The Star* reported the following rates: Italian (85 per cent), Portuguese (85 per cent), Chinese (81 per cent), Filipino (46 per cent), South Asian (39 per cent), Hispanic (30 per cent), Black (24 per cent), and West Asians/Arabs (20 per cent). The census data are based on a much larger sample than *The Star* data and, therefore, are presumably more accurate. The census also provides data for a much broader spectrum of groups.

17 As indicated previously, immigrants who were born in China may have spent time in Hong Kong and Taiwan where they accumulated additional financial resources before coming to Canada.

4 Immigrants' Economic Status in Toronto: Stories of Triumph and Disappointment

Valerie Preston, Lucia Lo, and Shuguang Wang

Since Toronto's inception, immigrants have been a vital ingredient in the local economy. Whether they participate as salaried employees, self-employed individuals, or entrepreneurs, their historical story is one of poverty or near poverty at the time of arrival, followed by social and economic mobility thereafter. The ability to achieve income parity with native-born Canadians is often viewed as the principal measure of economic success and a crucial indicator of socio-economic integration. The buoyant post-war economy was relatively open to immigrants, even those with little formal education. However, the situation changed during the recessions of the 1980s and 1990s. During these periods, immigrants' earnings – one of the most closely watched indicators of inclusion – stalled (DeVoretz 1995; Reitz 1997; Ley 1999). This stagnation in immigrants' earnings may have far-reaching consequences. In the short term, poverty is often associated with exclusion from full social and political participation in Canada. In the long term, persistent poverty will reduce the opportunities available to immigrants' children who will be unable to exercise fully their rights as Canadian citizens.

Although deindustrialization and the steady loss of manufacturing jobs since the 1970s (Norcliffe et al. 1986; Berridge et al. 1995), accompanied by the rise of a bifurcated service economy, have been offered as an explanation for the economic stagnation, they are only part of the story. The generation of immigrants who arrived after 1980 are substantially different from their predecessors in their origins and their entry status. They are also very diverse in terms of their fluency in English, formal qualifications, and educational attainments. Their economic experiences in Toronto are equally varied. Some immigrants struggle in the Toronto economy, while others succeed, rapidly finding employment or creating economic opportunities for themselves through self-employment and entrepreneurship. The diversity of immigrants' economic experiences heightens differences in their experiences of social inclusion and social exclusion.

This chapter outlines the current state of knowledge about the economic experiences of Toronto's immigrants.[1] We explore their economic activities, their economic performance, and their impact on the Toronto economy. Our aims are to examine the extent to which the positive story of the past remains true for recent immigrants and to identify research needs and policy gaps that impede efforts to facilitate immigrants' successful settlement. The chapter is divided into four sections. In the first section, we describe the composition of Toronto's immigrants and their contributions to the Toronto economy. In particular, we compare the taxes they pay as a form of economic contribution to the welfare and unemployment benefits they receive as a form of economic burden. The second section investigates another form of economic contribution by examining immigrants' entrepreneurial activities in Toronto and the nature and structure of various ethnic economies. In the third section, we analyse the industrial division of labour by comparing the distribution of employment of immigrants with that of Canadian-born workers. In the fourth section, we analyse the economic performance of Toronto's immigrants, considering how period of arrival in Canada, age, gender, and ethnoracial background affect earnings, unemployment rates, and poverty rates.

Our attempt to explore immigrants' economic activities, their performance, and their impact on the Toronto economy necessitates the use of information from a variety of sources, including previous research, unpublished studies, and original analyses of census and administrative data. It is inevitable that the data sometimes cover different time periods or use different classification schemes. This is not ideal. Given the complexity of the data, there are bound to be some contradictions in the economic stories of immigrants. As the following sections illustrate, the current situation looks quite worrisome when we examine labour market segmentation, unemployment, and poverty, but more positive when we enumerate tax-benefit differences and entrepreneurial contributions. While some of these issues can be explained, some elements of the story elude us. As the data are never complete, we make do with what we have.

We focus our analysis on the period from 1971 to 1996, the latter being the year for which the most contemporary information was available at the time of preparing this chapter. As the positive story of the past is generally less true for recent immigrants, we find it necessary to qualify the bleak set of results. The 1971–96 period contains the recessions of the early 1980s and 1990s, which were especially punishing for economic sectors such as construction and manufacturing that traditionally hired many immigrants. The second recession was particularly ugly, leading to reductions in government spending and a subsequent contraction of jobs in the public sector. While manufacturing and construction output have rebounded since 1996, detailed information about immigrants' economic activities and performance is not available past this date. Hence, the impact of improving economic conditions on immigrants remains unknown and the potentially positive story for immigrant integration remains untold.

ECONOMIC IMPACTS OF TORONTO'S IMMIGRANTS

Canada's immigration policy is designed to achieve four objectives: demographic balance, economic growth, social well-being, and the fulfilment of Canada's humanitarian obligations (Seward 1987). In practice, however, economic objectives and their consequences, which include both immigrants' economic impacts on the host society and their well-being, have always been debated. While the economic well-being of immigrants may have profound effects on their successful settlement and integration, the general public is often more concerned with immigrants' economic impacts.[2]

The economic impacts of immigrants are a complex mix of the contributions they make to and the burdens they put on the host society. Forms of contributions include the various types of tax they pay to governments, participation in economic production, investment in businesses that inject capital funds into the economy and create jobs for other citizens, and consumption of goods and services. Forms of burdens include welfare/UI benefits they receive, and the cost of language training, job-skills training, education of immigrant children, and medicare. While these economic impacts are an important consideration in immigration policy-making, it is often difficult to quantify them accurately due to a lack of data.

In this section, we explore the economic impacts of Toronto's immigrants.[3] Using the recently released Immigration Data Base (IMDB) data,[4] the analysis compares income taxes paid by Toronto's immigrants in 1995, as a major form of economic contribution, with welfare and unemployment insurance (UI)[5] benefits collected by the same immigrant population in the same tax year, as forms of economic burdens. The immigrant population being studied comprises those who landed in the Toronto Census Metropolitan Area (CMA) between 1980 and 1995 and who were fifteen years of age and over in the 1995 tax year. In this analysis, a 'balance-sheet approach' is used to document per-capita income tax contributions, per-capita welfare benefit receipts, per-capita UI benefit receipts, tax-benefit ratios, and tax-benefit differences. In addition, we look at such indicators as percentage of immigrants reporting income tax, welfare dependency rate, and UI usage rate.[6] We first analyse the data for immigrants as a whole, then for subgroups as distinguished by immigration class, level of education, country of last permanent residence, and length of residence in Canada. We also refer to the general population of Canada to draw out the analysis.

Two limitations must be acknowledged. First, while the balance-sheet approach is a commonly used method in most studies of immigrants' economic impacts, the IMDB does not contain information on all economic impacts. Specifically, it does not include the following contributions: property tax, business income tax, sales tax, business investment, and UI premiums – the main funding source for the payment of UI benefits. Nor does IMDB include such forms of burdens as the public costs of education, training, and medical services. Contributions and benefits are hence narrowly defined in this study as income tax (the largest form of contribution) and welfare and UI benefits (two forms of burdens). Second, the taxation data used for this analysis are for one tax year only. This means that the data identify the numbers of taxpayers and benefit recipients at a point in time, rather than for a continuous period. Therefore, the study results may not accurately reflect immigrants' economic impacts over time.

Profile of Toronto's Immigrants

We begin with a brief statistical portrait of Toronto's immigrants that provides the framework for our analysis of economic impacts of the various immigrant cohorts in Toronto. During the sixteen-year period from 1980 to 1995, over one million (1,001,847) immigrants landed in the Toronto CMA. This was 38 per cent of all the immigrants who were admitted into the country in the same time period. Of the one million immigrants, only 16 per cent came to Toronto in the first half of the 1980s; 27 per cent landed in the second half of the 1980s; and as many as 57 per cent arrived in the first six years of the 1990s (fig. 4.1a). This breakdown clearly shows that immigration to Toronto accelerated significantly in this period, and that more than half of the immigrant population for this study are new arrivals, a fact that has important implications for our subsequent discussions of economic impacts.

Figure 4.1b categorizes the immigrants by world regions of last permanent residence. As the chart shows, only 10 per cent of the one million immigrants came from the traditional source areas of Britain, the United States, Western Europe, and Oceania; another 15 per cent came from other European countries; and the remaining 75 per cent came from Asia (51 per cent), Latin America and Caribbean (18 per cent), and Africa (6 per cent).

Figure 4.1c groups immigrants into three broad categories: economic immigrants, immigrants accepted for family reunification, and those admitted on humanitarian grounds. Overall, 31 per cent of the immigrants were admitted as economic immigrants; 54 per cent were accepted for family reunification; and the remaining 15 per cent were admitted for humanitarian reasons. At another level of aggregation, figure 4.1d shows that 61 per cent of the immigrants came to Toronto with no post-secondary education; 25 per cent came with some post-secondary education, but no university degree; and only 14 per cent came with university degrees.

These statistics are largely consistent with the major changes in Canada's immigration policy since the early 1980s, when more newcomers were accepted from non-traditional source areas and emphasis was shifted from independent, economic immigrants to family reunification applicants (DeVoretz 1995; Green and Green 1995). The changes in the composition of immigrant flows have been the subject of concern, because there are fears that recent immigrants have less ability to contribute economically than their predecessors.

Contributions and Burdens

In 1995, 507,300 immigrants in the Toronto CMA, or 62 per cent of the target immigrant population, filed tax returns. In total, they reported income tax payments to the federal and provincial governments of $1.47 billion. In the same year, 77,800 immigrants, or 9 per cent of the immigrant population, received $607.8 million in welfare benefits; and 66,800 immigrants, or 8 per cent of the immigrant population, received

Immigrants' Economic Status 197

Figure 4.1
Composition of immigrants in the Toronto CMA, 1980–1995

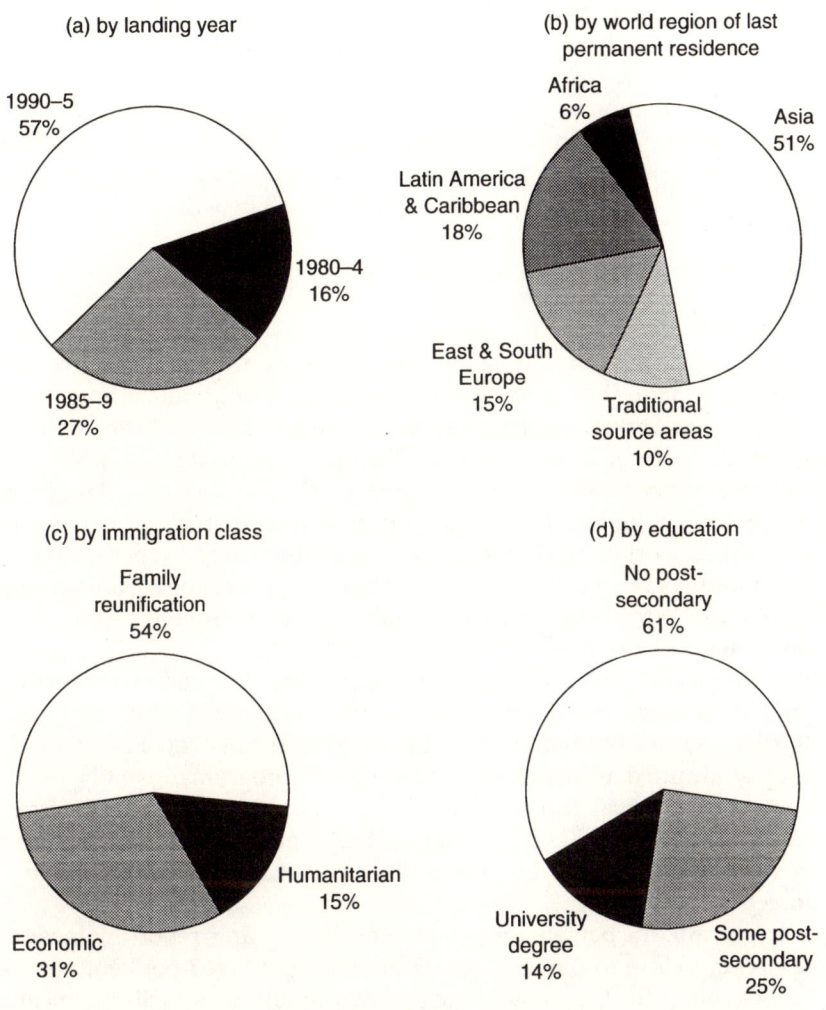

(a) by landing year

- 1990–5: 57%
- 1985–9: 27%
- 1980–4: 16%

(b) by world region of last permanent residence

- Africa: 6%
- Asia: 51%
- Latin America & Caribbean: 18%
- East & South Europe: 15%
- Traditional source areas: 10%

(c) by immigration class

- Family reunification: 54%
- Economic: 31%
- Humanitarian: 15%

(d) by education

- No post-secondary: 61%
- Some post-secondary: 25%
- University degree: 14%

Source: Statistics Canada. 1998. Landed Immigrant Data System, 1980–1995

$281.6 million in UI benefits. Subtracting both types of benefits from total income tax, Toronto's immigrants made a net contribution of $578.2 million to Canada's treasury, with a T–B ratio (ratio of income tax to benefits) of 1.7:1 – for every $1.70 they contributed as income tax, immigrants collected $1.00 in welfare and UI benefits.

Compared with the general population of Canada,[7] a lower percentage of immigrants reported income tax payments (62 per cent versus 89 per cent) and, on average, the immigrant taxpayers paid about $2,000 (40 per cent) less than the average Canadian did. As a result, the T–B ratio of 1.7:1 for immigrants is lower than the ratio of 3.9:1 for the general population of Canada. At the same time, immigrants also exhibited a lower welfare dependency rate and a lower UI usage rate than the general population of Canada: 9 per cent versus 13 per cent for welfare, and 8 per cent versus 16 per cent for UI benefits.

Economic Interests by Immigration Class

In the IMDB, immigrants are grouped into eleven classes that are combined into the same three broad categories that we saw in figure 4.1c and are shown in table 4.1: economic immigrants, immigrants accepted for family reunification, and those admitted on humanitarian grounds. In the economic category, the independent immigrants refers to individuals admitted on the basis of skills, education, language ability, and occupational background; they include both professionals and skilled workers. Retirees are included in this category, because they are admitted on the condition that they bring a required amount of capital funds to spend in Canada and support themselves. In the second category of family reunification, family members include spouses, dependent children, parents, and grandparents of Canadian citizens or landed immigrants; all others are classified as assisted relatives. In the third category of humanitarian, the designated class consists of immigrants admitted under special government programs, usually in response to political upheaval in their home countries. The deferred removal order class (DORC) refers to the immigrants who at one time were ordered to leave Canada but the removal order was never enforced.

In general, the percentage of economic immigrants reporting income tax is very close to the average for all immigrants (63 per cent versus 62 per cent), but they have much greater ability to contribute, meaning that they are able to pay more income taxes than the other two categories of immigrants. On average, economic immigrants each paid $4,323 in 1995 – about 85 per cent more than the amount paid by the other two categories of immigrants. They also have a much lower welfare dependency rate (5 per cent) and a lower UI usage rate (7 per cent), though the recipients, on average, received similar amounts as immi-

Table 4.1
Economic impacts of immigrants in Toronto CMA by immigration class, 1995

Class	% of total immigrants	% reporting income tax	Per-capita income tax ($)	% reporting welfare	Per-capita welfare ($)	% reporting UI	Per-capita UI ($)	T-B Ratio	T-B Difference Amount (m $)	Share %
Economic	**31**	**63**	**4,323**	**5**	**8,013**	**7**	**4,541**	**3.5**	**445.1**	**77**
Independent	24.4	65 (75)	4,977 (5,905)	7 (9)	8,148 (8,102)	9 (11)	4,688 (4,885)	3.4 (3.5)	390.8	68
Entrepreneurs	2.9	63 (94)	1,810 (2,486)	1 (2)	9,276 (9,337)	2 (3)	4,564 (4,815)	6.6 (8.1)	23.2	4
Self-employed	1.1	48 (68)	3,708 (4,750)	2 (3)	7,310 (8,967)	3 (3)	3,774 (5,839)	6.0 (6.7)	13.0	2
Investors*	1.1	74	1,534	3	5,509	13	2,895	2.1	5.1	<1
Retiree	1.5	45 (61)	2,201 (2,294)	1 (2)	3,497 (4,947)	1 (1)	3,908 (–)	9.8 (9.8)	13.0	2
Family reunification	**54.3**	**58**	**2,340**	**8**	**6,925**	**8**	**3,990**	**1.6**	**229.6**	**40**
Family members	42.6	58	2,144	9	6,811	8	3,900	1.4	126.5	22
Assisted relatives	11.7	62	3,120	4	7,862	9	4,332	2.6	103.1	18
Humanitarian	**14.7**	**76**	**2,324**	**24**	**8,777**	**11**	**447**	**0.7**	**-103.5**	**-18**
Refugee (C-R)	6.5	69	1,283	32	8,910	9	4,093	0.3	-129.3	-22
Designated class	7.8	81	3,151	17	8,549	14	4,601	1.2	26.7	5
DORC	<1	77	1,374	<1	–**	<1	–	1.4	0.1	<1
Dependent of (C-R)	<1	61	254	8	10,904	<1	–	0.2	-1.0	-0.2
Average	100	62	2,893	9	7,813	8	4,216	1.7	578.2	100

*Principal applicants for investors cannot be separated from spouses and dependants due to an inconsistency problem in the two special tabulations. That is, the number of principal applicants for investors in the 1995 tax file exceeds the total number of principal investor applicants in the landing files of 1980–95. It seems the principal applicants and non-principal applicants are not separated properly in the tax file.
**A hyphen is used where a per-capita value cannot be calculated because the number of immigrants is small and rounded to zero by Statistics Canada for reasons of confidentiality.
Source: Statistics Canada (1998b).

grants of the other two categories did. Accordingly, the T–B ratio for economic immigrants is the highest of all the categories of immigrants (3.5:1) and is close to the Canadian average (3.9:1). They also made the largest net contributions ($445.1 million) to Canada's treasury. While they account for only 31 per cent of the immigrant population, their net contribution amounts to 77 per cent of the immigrants' total.

Of the various classes of economic immigrants, independent immigrants are able to pay the highest income tax: $4,977 per taxpayer. Entrepreneurs and self-employed immigrants pay less tax than independent immigrants do, probably because they are eligible for tax exemptions for business-related expenses. Still, entrepreneurs and self-employed immigrants pay much more tax than they take from the system, as is evidenced by the high T–B ratios for them: 6.6:1 and 6.0:1, respectively. Even the retirees made a significant net contribution of $13 million in 1995, with a high T–B ratio of 9.8:1. The only surprise comes from the observation that the investor immigrants show a high UI usage rate of 13 per cent, 5 percentage points higher than the average for all immigrants.

It must be pointed out that the economic immigrants in the IMDB include not only principal applicants but also their spouses and dependent children. It is therefore appropriate to have their economic impacts examined separately. After separation, we found that the principal applicants actually make much more in the way of contributions than the combined group. For instance, the percentages of principal applicants reporting income tax are actually as high as 75 per cent for independents, 94 per cent for entrepreneurs, 68 per cent for self-employed, and 61 per cent for retirees; their per-capita tax contribution was also shown to be higher – about $1,000 higher.

As a whole, immigrants accepted for family reunification also made a significant positive contribution to Canada's treasury, with a net contribution of $229.6 million in 1995. While these immigrants account for 54 per cent of the immigrant population, their net contribution accounts for 40 per cent of the immigrants' total. Notably, among assisted relatives, who are subject to the point system, but receive bonus points for having relatives in Canada, a higher percentage pay income tax and are able to pay more dollars than their family members. At the same time, they exhibited a much lower welfare dependency rate, only 4 per cent. This resulted in a much higher T–B ratio for assisted relatives (2.6:1).

Despite the high percentage of humanitarian immigrants making tax contributions (76 per cent), their overall ability to contribute appears low, and both their welfare dependency rate and UI usage rate are high: 24 per cent and 11 per cent, respectively, both being higher than those for economic and family reunification immigrants. This results in a low T–B ratio of 0.7:1, at which point the benefits they received in 1995 exceeded the income tax they contributed in the same year. Apparently, this negative balance was due solely to refugees and their dependants.

By Level of Education

It is generally believed that the more educated the immigrants are at the time of immigration, the more contributions they will make to the host economy, because well-educated immigrants tend to adapt and adjust to the labour market more quickly and require less public money for re-education and training. In fact, this belief is well reflected in the point system embedded in the modern Canadian immigration program, and supported by Swan et al. (1991). In the 1980s and the 1990s, the Canadian economy underwent a transformation from the traditional industrial economy to a service and information technology (IT) economy. Since the transformation has been accompanied by increasingly higher demand for a sophisticated labour force, the above belief about immigrants is more widely accepted now than ever before. While we do not doubt this belief, we intend to find out which immigrants, by level of education, are likely to contribute less to Canada's transformed economy. It should be explained that, in the IMDB, level of education refers to education attainment at time of landing; any subsequent upgrading is not captured.

As table 4.2 shows, except for those with 0–9 years of schooling, immigrants with different levels of education have similar percentages reporting income tax, ranging from 65 to 70 per cent. However, their ability to contribute increases, first slowly, then sharply, with higher levels of education, as reflected by the amount of per-capita income tax and T–B ratios. This is especially true of the immigrants with graduate degrees. For instance, those holding a master's degree each paid $8,000 in income tax in 1995, and those with doctorates each paid $13,229. Both masters and doctorates also have the lowest propensity for welfare and UI benefits, though the recipients on average seem to have collected about the same dollars as other immigrants did. Immigrants with a bachelor's degree are the largest group of net contributors: they account for only 12 per cent of the immigrant population, but their net

Table 4.2
Economic impacts of immigrants in the Toronto CMA by Level of education, 1995

Level of education	% of total immigrants	% reporting income tax	Per-capita income tax ($)	% reporting welfare	Per-capita welfare ($)	% reporting UI	Per-capita UI ($)	T–B Ratio	T–B Difference Amount (m $)	Share %
0–9 years	34	47	1,691	10	7,813	6	4,295	0.82	−50.6	−9
10–12 years	27	69	2,106	12	7,270	9	3,932	1.1	33.7	6
13 years or some university (no degree)	9	69	3,168	9	8,066	9	4,205	2	78.9	14
Trade certificate	10	70	3,317	9	8,012	10	4,389	1.9	92.5	16
Non-university diploma	6	69	3,516	8	8,173	9	4,375	2.3	70.8	12
Bachelor's degree	12	70	4,897	7	8,226	8	4,438	3.9	246.1	43
Master's degree	2	66	8,000	4	8,132	7	4,604	7.3	74.6	13
Doctorate	<1	65	13,229	5	8,939	5	4,557	15.9	32.2	5
Average	100	62	2,893	9	7,813	8	4,216	1.7	578.2	100

Source: Statistics Canada (1998b).

contribution of $246.1 million comprises 43 per cent of the immigrants' total. This is an immigrant group whose T–B ratio is similar to that of the general population of Canada, but they exhibit much lower propensity for welfare and UI benefits.

The only immigrants who received more benefits than the income taxes they paid are those with 0–9 years of schooling. Although the immigrants with 10–12 years of education are able to make a positive net contribution, their T–B ratio approaches 1:1, and their net contribution is much less significant than their share in the target immigrant population (6 per cent versus 27 per cent). It is important to point out that 80 per cent of the immigrants with 0–9 years of schooling and 79 per cent of those with 10–12 years of education were principal applicants and their spouses. These tax filers were all adults at the time of landing and would have completed their education in their home countries. The findings from the IMDB should therefore represent a fairly reliable relation between their level of education (at time of landing) and their economic impact.

By Country of Last Permanent Residence

Table 4.3 summarizes the economic impacts of immigrants by world region of last permanent residence. These regions are broken down into traditional source countries (Britain, the United States, Western Europe, and Oceania); Eastern and Southern Europe; Asia (including the Philippines and India); Latin America and the Caribbean; and Africa. Relatively speaking, immigrants from the traditional source countries have the lowest percentage reporting income tax (50 per cent), yet they show the highest ability to pay income tax ($8,262 per taxpayer in 1995). They also have the lowest welfare dependency rate (2 per cent) and the lowest UI usage rate (5 per cent). This results in a significantly high T–B ratio of 9.7:1. Immigrants from these countries account for only 10 per cent of the immigrant population, but their net tax contribution in 1995 was 48 per cent of the immigrants' total, or $279.5 million.

Although there is a much higher percentage (69 per cent) of immigrants from Eastern and Southern Europe reporting income tax than those from the traditional source areas, their ability to contribute is lower. On average, the taxpayers from Eastern and Southern Europe each paid $3,303 in 1995; in the same year, they showed a higher welfare dependency rate (11 per cent) and a higher UI usage rate (12 per cent). However, despite their low T–B ratio of 1.4:1, their income tax still

Table 4.3
Economic impacts of immigrants in the Toronto CMA by world regions of last permanent residence, 1995

Region	% of total immigrants	% reporting income tax	Per-capita income tax ($)	% reporting welfare	Per-capita welfare ($)	% reporting UI	Per-capita UI ($)	T–B Ratio	T–B Difference Amount (m $)	Share %
Traditional source countries	10	50	8,262	2	7,702	5	4,652	9.7	279.5	48
East & South Europe	15	69	3,303	11	7,887	12	5,039	1.4	78.3	14
Asia	51	62	2,187	8	7,690	7	3,857	1.5	188.5	32
Latin America & Caribbean	18	61	2,490	13	7,957	9	4,055	1.1	21.6	4
Africa	6	72	3,081	20	7,798	9	4,324	1.1	10.5	2
Average	100	62	2,893	9	7,813	8	4,216	1.7	578.2	100

Source: Statistics Canada (1998b).

exceeded the benefits they collected, with a positive balance of $78.3 million in 1995.

Compared with immigrants from Eastern and Southern Europe, Asian immigrants as a whole show a slightly lower percentage reporting income tax (62 per cent), and Asian taxpayers seem to have a lower ability to contribute as well, with each paying $2,187 in 1995. Because they also have a lower propensity for welfare and UI usage (8 per cent and 7 per cent, respectively), Asian immigrants contributed $188.5 million more in income tax than they collected as benefits in 1995. Nonetheless, this represents a relatively low share in the immigrants' total net contribution, compared with the share of Asian immigrants in the target immigrant population. It should also be noted that immigrants from Asian countries vary considerably in their economic impacts. Those from Hong Kong – the largest single source area of the 1980s and the 1990s – exhibited the lowest propensity for welfare and UI usage (1 per cent and 3 per cent, respectively) and the highest T–B ratio (7:1). Immigrants from the Philippines, other East and Southeast Asian countries, and India were also able to make sizeable positive net contributions as they exhibited a relatively low dependency on welfare. Those from West and South Asia (excluding India), who account for 13 per cent of the total target immigrant population, showed lower T–B ratios as a result of higher dependency on welfare.

The percentage of immigrants from Latin America and the Caribbean who report income tax is similar to that of Asian immigrants (61 per cent versus 62 per cent), but they show higher ability to contribute ($2,490 per taxpayer versus $2,187). Despite this, their T–B ratio is measurably lower at 1.1:1, due to a higher welfare dependency rate (13 per cent) and UI usage rate (9 per cent). Their net contribution in 1995 accounts for 4 per cent of the immigrants' total, lower than their 18 per cent share in the target immigrant population. Like the Asian immigrants, those from Latin America and the Caribbean vary considerably in their economic impacts, with those from Central America and Jamaica showing lower T–B ratios than those from other countries in the same region.

At 20 per cent, African immigrants seem to show the highest welfare dependency rate. But because the percentage of African immigrants who make income tax contributions is also high (72 per cent), and the taxpayers on average pay more dollars than immigrants from Asia and Latin America, their net contribution is still positive, with a total of $10.5 million in 1995.

By Length of Residence in Canada

Understandably, it takes time for immigrants to settle in their adopted community, adapt to a new social and economic environment, and find jobs. For some, this process may be longer than for others, but in general, as length of residence increases, immigrants accumulate more local work experience and their English proficiency improves. Accordingly, they should achieve higher levels of economic performance and their ability to contribute to the economy should increase. Therefore, any analysis of immigrants' economic impact must consider immigrants' length of residence in Canada.

To control possible fluctuating effects caused by minor differences between any two consecutive landing years, the sixteen-year period (1980 to 1995) is subdivided into three five-year periods (with the last period covering six years). Our analysis shows that length of residence in Canada has no obvious effects on the percentages of immigrants who report income tax, welfare assistance, and UI benefits (table 4.4). However, it reveals that earlier immigrants are able to pay more income tax and collect fewer welfare dollars. For example, the taxpayers who landed between 1980 and 1984 each paid $3,092 in 1995, and welfare recipients of the same landing period each collected $5,145. Taxpayers who landed between 1985 and 1989 each paid $2,273, and welfare recipients from the corresponding landing period each collected $8,432. Those taxpayers and welfare recipients who arrived subsequently paid $1,221 and collected $8,316 each. Accordingly, T–B ratios for the three groups are in the descending order of 3.6:1, 1.9:1, and 1.1:1, respectively. It is useful to point out that although the immigrants arriving in the second half of the 1980s came to Toronto when there were good employment opportunities, that has not altered the linear descending order of T–B ratios in relation to length of residence in Canada. Since more than half of the immigrants from non-traditional source countries landed in Toronto between 1990 and 1995, compared with only one-third from the traditional source areas, length of residence should provide at least partial explanation for the lower T–B ratios for the immigrants from Asia, Latin America and the Caribbean, and Africa.

The same can be said of refugees. Table 4.4 shows that, as length of residence increases, welfare dependency rate declines sharply from 37 per cent for the 1990–5 cohort to 24 per cent for the 1985–9 cohort and 5 per cent for the 1980–4 cohort. Conversely, the ability of the refugee taxpayers to contribute to Canada's treasury increases significantly, as

Table 4.4
Economic impacts of immigrants in the Toronto CMA by year of landing, 1995 (figures in brackets are for refugees)

Landing period	% reporting income tax	% reporting welfare	% reporting UI	Per-capita income tax ($)	Per-capita welfare ($)	Per-capita UI ($)	T–B ratio
1980–4	61 (22)	10 (5)	7 (2)	3,092 (3,242)	5,145 (8,254)	4,733 (7,277)	3.6 (1.3)
1985–9	63 (72)	10 (24)	9 (11)	2,273 (2,002)	8,432 (8,790)	4,555 (4,377)	1.9 (0.6)
1990–5	61 (72)	9 (37)	8 (9)	1,221 (932)	8,316 (8,953)	3,877 (3,822)	1.1 (0.2)

Source: Statistics Canada (1998b).

is shown by per-capita income tax and T–B ratios. In fact, the 1980–4 refugees, as a whole, were able to make a net positive contribution with a T–B ratio of 1.3:1, suggesting that they are not life-long paupers. However, the data also show that the percentage of the 1980–4 refugees who reported income and income tax was very low – only 22 per cent. It is unclear if the majority of them had left Toronto, or a large proportion of them, while not collecting welfare, in fact live in poverty.

The above results are by and large consistent with the research findings of Akbari (1995), DeSilva (1992), and Fagnan (1995), and suggest that net contributions of immigrants are expected to rise in a period of six to ten years (or ten to fifteen years for refugees). Whether this length is reasonable is subject to debate. Given that it takes time for new immigrants to settle, adjust to the labour market, and integrate, a period of six to ten years is not a long time. But if net contributions for immigrants are expected to be realized immediately upon arrival, then a six- to ten-year delay is certainly considered long.

Subject to the limitations described earlier in this section, our analyses show that Toronto's immigrants admitted between 1980 and 1995 do not obtain social assistance in excess of the income tax they pay. In other words, there is no evidence that these immigrants are an economic drain on the host society. Our analyses also show that Toronto's immigrants in general have not been able to contribute to the governments' coffers at the same level as the average Canadian, an indication that Toronto's immigrants have not achieved levels of economic performance and security comparable to those of the Canadian-born. Among other things, this may be attributed to the fact that 57 per cent of the immigrant population being studied had been in Canada for six or less years when their 1995 tax returns were filed.

While immigrants as a whole make positive net contributions, there remain important internal differences. Economic immigrants have the highest ability to pay income tax (see table 4.1), especially the independent immigrants whose language and jobs skills are subject to full assessment at the time of application under the point system. This proves that the point system has been working to the advantage of Canada's economic well-being. Retirees also make a substantial positive net contribution because they pay income taxes, but receive little social assistance. Entrepreneurs and investors, who are expected to pay high income tax, actually paid less than the average immigrants; and, even more unexpectedly, investors (including their spouses and dependents) also had a high rate of UI usage.

Entrepreneurs and investors may have paid more business income tax than personal income tax, but because business income tax is not included in the IMDB, this part of their contribution cannot be captured in the analysis. It is also possible that entrepreneurs and investors are better able to shelter their income. They may, for example, keep reinvesting their income, thus reducing or postponing income taxes. If this is true, non-immigrant entrepreneurs and investors would have also paid less income tax than employed workers and professionals. Regrettably, we cannot investigate this possibility as we lack data about Canadian-born entrepreneurs and investors. Besides, due to the relative recency of the Investors Program, which was introduced in 1986 (Citizenship and Immigration Canada 1997), 91 per cent of investors had been in Canada for six or less years by the time they filed their 1995 tax returns. Their short length of residence in Canada could have contributed to lower-than-average income tax contributions, as most investments are long-term commitments with little return in the first few years. Finally, low tax contributions may point to a lack of accountability on the part of their Canadian investment managers, and the negligence and fraudulent practices of some immigrant consultants (Kunin and Jones 1995; Marsden 2000).

Contrary to popular belief, immigrants admitted for family reunification, especially assisted relatives, make net positive contributions to government coffers, albeit lower than that for economic immigrants (table 4.1). Family-class immigrants are not economic burdens, as many have perceived. The only classes of immigrants who received more benefits than the amount of taxes they paid are refugees and their dependents. This seems to agree with Lui-Gurr's (1995) observation in her study of British Columbia's immigrants that refugees are at a greater risk of welfare dependency. However, refugees do not seem to be lifelong paupers, as the taxes paid by those who have been in Canada for more than ten years marginally exceed the cost of their benefits. The high rates of welfare dependency among Toronto's refugees may be explained by both their low level of education and their short length of residence in Canada. Sixty-four per cent of them came with no postsecondary education. As well, 66 per cent of all refugees in Toronto arrived in Canada after 1989. Their reliance on welfare is not problematic once we remember that refugees are admitted for political and humanitarian reasons; supporting them while they establish themselves is part of Canada's humanitarian obligations and a price Canadians are willing to pay to fulfil their moral responsibilities. With refugees and their dependents accounting for only 7 per cent of the immigrant population in this study, the cost of providing benefits to them is more than offset by the positive income tax transfers from other immigrants in the Toronto CMA.

The various economic impacts of immigrants from traditional source countries (i.e., Britain, the United States, Western Europe, and Oceania) as compared with immigrants from the rest of the world cannot be fully explained by the former group's better language proficiency. Many immigrants from the Caribbean and Africa speak fluent English or French, yet their economic contributions are lower. Immigrant mix, level of education, and other possible factors (including discrimination) may reduce the ability of immigrants from Asia, Africa, and Latin America and the Caribbean to contribute to the Canadian economy. As the data reveal, the majority of immigrants from Britain, the United States, Western Europe, and Oceania came to Canada as economic immigrants (53 per cent), and only 1.9 per cent were refugees. For other world regions, economic immigrants account for a lower percentage (21 to 33 per cent), whereas between 9 and 30 per cent were refugees.

As for level of education, immigrants from Western European countries have the lowest percentage (30 per cent) with less than secondary education, but the highest percentage with university degrees (24 per cent). In the case of Latin America and the Caribbean, only 4 per cent had university degrees. African immigrants had higher levels of education at the time of landing than immigrants from Latin America and the Caribbean, but nearly one-third of the African immigrants are humanitarian immigrants, who are at the greatest risk of welfare dependency. In sum, immigrants from Africa and Latin America and the Caribbean may have significantly different economic impacts largely because of the human capital – as opposed to financial resources – they bring with them to Canada.

As far as economic contributions (based on tax payments and welfare/UI benefits) are concerned, it appears to be in Canada's best interest, as it will undoubtedly be argued by some, to only accept immigrants from the United States, Britain, Western Europe, and Oceania, and to accept only economic immigrants who possess the most capital funds or human capital (with at least a university degree). However, this is neither possible nor desirable. First, we reiterate that our analysis of economic impacts in this section is only partial. Second, the number of immigrants from these traditoinal source countries would not meet Canada's need for immigrants to shore up its population growth (i.e., to meet its demographic objective). As is shown in the case of Toronto, only 10 per cent of the immigrants arriving between 1980 and 1995 were from these areas, and their share is unlikely to increase in the future. Third, to maximize economic contributions is only one goal of the contemporary immigration policy, which also stresses the importance of family reunion for Canadian citizens and permanent residents and the importance of fulfilling Canada's international commitment to assist refugees. Finally, though economic considerations are a driving force of Canadian immigration policy, there are continuing debates about the moral implications of policies that encourage Canada to select only the best immigrants from countries that are already capital-deprived.

IMMIGRANT SELF-EMPLOYMENT AND IMMIGRANT ENTREPRENEURSHIP

Immigrant self-employment and entrepreneurship refer to the initiative and ability of immigrants to create business entities. Immigrant businesses are often referred to as ethnic businesses if reference is made to a specific cultural group; enterprises that are collectively the result of the efforts of a specific ethnic group are often known as an ethnic economy. Immigrant businesses and ethnic economies not only measure individual success, but also contribute to the economy at large.

In Toronto, the entrepreneurial activities conducted by immigrants are diverse. The rate of self-employment varies tremendously among immigrant groups, ranging from 22.3 per cent for Koreans to 1.6 per cent for Somalis (Statistics Canada 1999c). The most entrepreneurial immigrant groups are generally from Europe, especially people of Jewish and German descent from Poland and Israel. The least entrepreneurial are visible minority immigrants from the Caribbean, Southeast Asia, and Africa. There is an ethnic division of labour in areas of immigrant entrepreneurship (Razin and Langlois 1995): Germans from the former USSR, Jews from Poland, and Italians have a large stake in the manufacturing and construction industries; Korean, Chinese, Greek, Israeli, and Middle Eastern immigrants concentrate in the distributive services – trade, food services, and transportation; immigrants from the U.S., Hungary, Czechoslovakia, and South Africa focus on business, personal, and public services.

Ethnic economies are similarly varied, including everything from a few restaurants and grocery stores that mainly serve a specific ethnic group to a full range of economic activities serving a mixed clientele. The new Somali, Ethiopian/Eritrean, and Maltese economies on the one hand, and the large Chinese and East Indian economies on the other, represent different ends of the spectrum (Lo and Wang 1998; Marger 1989). These ethnic economies are sometimes visible in a single concentration, for example, the Malta Village at St Clair Avenue and Dundas Street, and the Portugal Village bounded by Dundas Street West, College Street, and Spadina and Ossington Avenues. Others extend across several separate locations. In the Toronto Census Metropolitan Area, there are South Asian commercial activities along Gerrard Street in East York, at Markham Road and Highway 401 in Scarborough, at Albion Road and Islington Avenue in Etobicoke, and at Airport and Derry Roads in Malton; Italian businesses abound on St Clair Avenue West and in the town of Woodbridge. Alternatively, ethnic businesses may be dispersed throughout the metropolitan area. For example, Korean-owned convenience stores are all over the city, and not only in Korean Town on Bloor Street West.

In this section, we briefly review the status of immigrant entrepreneurship in Toronto and explore the varying representations of its ethnic economies before examining the impact of immigrant entrepreneurial endeavours on our economy. To clarify the discussions that follow, we refer to 'ethnic' as a specific cultural group, 'co-ethnic' as belonging to the same ethnic group, and 'non-ethnic' as not belonging to that particular group. We define 'minority' as the opposite of majority and visible-minority as the racially distinct. We also note a few empirical studies on Toronto's immigrant entrepreneurs and ethnic economies.

Immigrant Entrepreneurship

Immigrant self-employment not only varies among ethnic groups, it also differs between men and women, with men more likely to be self-employed. While the proportions of self-employment for immigrant men range from 37.1 per cent to 9.7 per cent and those for Canadian-born men range from 37.7 per cent to 5.2 per cent, those for immigrant women range from 20.5 per cent to 3.2 per cent and from 17.6 per cent to 2.7 per cent for Canadian-born women (table 4.5). The variations in the proportions of self-employment among ethnic groups are much greater

Table 4.5
Self-employment by ethnic origin, gender, and birthplace, 1996

	Percentage			
	Women		Men	
Ethnic origin	Immigrant	Canadian-born	Immigrant	Canadian-born
Charter	9.6	7.4	17.4	14.5
Polish	8.7	6.1	16.7	21.7
Ukrainian	8.6	11.4	18.7	17.9
Italian	8.8	5.8	23.8	12.7
South European	6.9	4.6	16.7	9.8
Jewish	20.5	17.6	37.1	37.7
Other European	14.8	8.9	23.3	14.1
African and Caribbean	3.2	5.5	10.3	4.1
West Asian	7.2	2.8	24.1	8.3
South Asian	5.7	2.7	12.9	5.2
Chinese	11.3	9.3	18.2	8.3
East and Southeast Asian	6.8	8.9	10.0	15.3
Central and South American	5.5	9.1	9.7	6.7
Other	8.7	9.2	16.2	14.8

Source: Statistics Canada (1999a).

than the differences between Canadian-born and immigrant workers from the same ethnic background. Self-employment is more common among Jewish, Chinese, and other European immigrants than among any other ethnic group.

However, self-employed immigrants generally do not fare as well as the employed (Wang and Lo 2000). Of the 507,300 immigrants in the Toronto CMA who moved to Canada between 1980 and 1995, and who filed income tax returns in 1995, 10.5 per cent reported self-employment income. Their average self-employment income of $7,105 pales in comparison with the average employment income of $22,373. Toronto's self-employed immigrants earned about one-third the income of employed immigrant workers, a ratio comparable to that of the national population groups. While the previous section has advanced possible explanations for the low self-employment earnings of immigrants, it is striking to see tremendous variations among immigrant groups. Immigrants from Britain, the United States, and Australia, followed by those from Western and Southern Europe, are more prosperous in their self-

Table 4.6
Self-employment income of immigrants of Toronto CMA by countries of origin, 1995

	Self-employment income ($000s)	Number in self-employment	Average self-employment income ($)
All countries	377,985.9	53,200	7,105
Britain	51,389.5	2,900	17,721
Western Europe	10,971.2	1,200	9,143
Eastern Europe (excluding Poland)	34,618.1	5,100	6,788
Poland	39,864.3	6,100	6,535
Southern Europe (excluding Portugal)	10,979.4	1,100	9,981
West Africa	33,205.9	5,000	6,641
Africa	36,450.3	3,600	10,125
Oceania & Australia	4,110.0	300	13,700
South Asia (excluding India)	4,942.6	2,500	1,977
India	29,056.1	3,900	7,450
East & SE Asia (excluding Philippines, Vietnam, Laos Kamp. & Hong Kong)	22,945.4	4,700	4,882
Philippines	5,383.1	1,700	3,167
Vietnam	4,141.2	900	4,601
Hong Kong	26,054.5	4,700	5,544
South America (excluding Guyana)	8,636.2	1,600	5,398
Guyana	3,963.9	1,300	3,049
Central America	3,305.9	500	6,612
Caribbean (excluding Jamaica)	4,922.7	1,300	3,841
Jamaica	2,935.7	1,500	1,957
United States	29,045.3	1,700	17,085

Figures are for those of 15–64 years of age in 1995 who immigrated to Canada between 1980 and 1994.
Source: Statistics Canada (1998b).

employed activities than those from other parts of the world. Immigrants from South and Southeast Asia, and particularly from the Caribbean, fare the worst (table 4.6).

Why, then, are immigrants drawn into self-employment? While past discussions were dominated by the factor of discrimination in the general labour market (Light 1972, 1979; Portes and Bach 1985), there is limited support for this blocked-mobility explanation in Toronto today (Bogue and Shakeel 1979; Rhyne 1982; Marger 1989; Henry 1993; Uneke

1994). The interaction between cultural resources, opportunity structures, and ethnic strategies is now considered to be more important (Waldinger et al. 1990). In particular, class assets such as education, wealth, and knowledge explain the differential business participation rates of our immigrant groups (Chan and Cheung 1985; Marger 1989; Uneke 1994). For instance, compared to Blacks, recent Chinese and South Asian immigrants are wealthier and more educated, have more business experience through participation in family business, and hence higher business participation rates. On the other hand, ability to sustain the business, in varying degrees, depends on ethnic resources. Kinship networks, community ties, co-ethnic workers, and the presence of a relatively homogeneous and institutionally complete ethnic economy all contribute to the success of the Chinese, East Indian, Italian, Jewish, and Portuguese business communities (Chan and Cheung 1985; Marger 1989; Reitz 1990; Teixeira 1998; Ma 1999).

In Toronto, except for highly regulated industries such as public utilities and banking, there are few institutional policies barring access to business ownership. Often it is market conditions that stimulate the entry of immigrant businesses. The rapid growth of the culturally distinct Chinese and South Asian communities in the last two decades explains the proliferation of ethnic shopping malls. There are currently over sixty Chinese and at least four or five South Asian shopping malls or plazas within the Toronto Census Metropolitan Area, all catering specifically to co-ethnic clients. Korean-owned convenience stores and dry-cleaning businesses, Italian-dominated construction companies, South Asian taxi-cab and gas station operations, and the gradual takeover of the garment industry by the Chinese from the Hong Kong are other examples of immigrants establishing a foothold in the open market through sectors that have been abandoned or shunned by the majority population.

Among Toronto's various immigrant communities, the Black community is often portrayed as the least successful. This stance is not necessarily warranted given that the Black community, separated by different cultural origins and historical experiences, is not homogeneous (Head 1975; Uneke 1994). However, while diversity limits the cultural market, and a focus on hairstyling and cosmetics for Black customers competes severely with similar firms in the open market, it is generally true that Black entrepreneurship is constrained by both class and ethnic resources. Black immigrants from the Caribbean islands and Africa often lack capital and business acumen. This bars them from participating more fully in small business loan programs in which the federal or provincial government acts as a guarantor for bank loans on new ventures as long as prospective proprietors provide an equity contribution to qualify.

Despite the varying self-employment rates and entrepreneurial pursuits among immigrant groups, it is important to note that these activities benefit the economy through employment creation and/or the enrichment of sociocultural life.

Ethnic Economies

To examine the role played by immigrant entrepreneurs in the generation of employment opportunities, it is imperative that we briefly turn our attention to ethnic economies. An ethnic economy, broadly defined here as an ethnic-based economic structure consisting of a set of enterprises all owned and managed by members of the same ethnic group, designates a business and employment sector that co-exists with the metropolitan economy. Enclave ethnic economy, non-enclave ethnic economy, and mixed-ethnic economy denote variations in the mix of ethnicity of their workers and clients, in the kind of goods and services they offer, in the market space they command, and in the degree of formality in organizational behaviour such as capital financing and hiring practices (Rhyne 1982; Light et al. 1994; Nee, Sanders, and Sernau 1994; Jones and McEvoy 1996).

There are few studies of ethnic economies in Toronto; any information is usually subsumed in discussions of the history and development of specific ethnic groups (e.g., Zucchi 1988; R. Thompson 1989) or in discussions of immigrant entrepreneurship. Information about the size and composition of immigrant economies is often drawn from surveys and/or ethnic business directories. For example, Rhyne (1982) counted 1,333 Chinese, 501 Black, 247 South Asian, and 139 Japanese businesses in 1979–80. The type of subeconomy to which these businesses belong is related to the composition of those businesses. The Chinese, Black, and South Asian subeconomies consist mostly of service and food-related retail activities, whereas over half of the Japanese businesses are engaged in commercial and professional activities. Within the service sector, Chinese businesses focused on personal, printing, and contractor services; Blacks on personal, entertainment, and real estate; South Asians on insurance and travel services; and Japanese on automotive dealership, and instructional and personal services. The more diverse Japanese businesses showed a more mixed economy than the others. This is probably attributable to two historical events. First, unlike the Chinese and East Indians, early Japanese-Canadians had well-organized religious and social institutions to assist them in their struggle against racism and political persecution, which led to less restricted and more spatially scattered activities. Second, the emergence of Japan as a wealthy industrialized nation after the Second World War, together with its huge foreign investment, improved the economic positions of Japanese-Canadians.

Ethnic businesses are generally small (Rhyne 1982; Reitz 1990). Rhyne (1982) found that 73 per cent of the Black and 92 per cent of the Chinese businesses employed less than twenty workers, and, with the exception of South Asians, only 16 to 28 per cent of the businesses experienced a total sales volume of $1 million. The South Asian subeconomy is less of an enclave and more mixed. Marger (1989) found that the businesses of East Indians who make up the largest percentage of South Asians in Canada, serve both ethnic and non-ethnic populations. The Indian Bazaar on Gerrard Street is patronized by South Asians from the entire metropolitan area. The non-ethnic sector, which is found in dispersed locations, mainly in ethnically mixed areas such as Yonge Street between Bloor and Dundas Streets, sells clothing, small audio/video equipment, housewares, furniture, toys, and accessories. In addition, Jones and McEvoy (1996) found that in 1989, the local ethnic, non-local ethnic, local non-ethnic, and non-local non-ethnic market shares of South Asian businesses in Canada's three largest cities – Toronto, Vancouver, and Montreal – were 8.7 per cent, 29.5 per cent, 33 per cent, and 28.7 per cent, respectively. The relative smallness of the ethnic spaces indicates a non-enclave economy.

Most people agree that, to date, only the Jewish and the Chinese have ever had a well-developed enclave economy in Toronto (R. Thompson 1989; Marger and Hoffman 1992; Hiebert 1993) and their residential concentrations coincide with their business concentrations. Spatial clustering is presumably vital to the success of an enclave immigrant economy. It acts as an incubator, provides a protected market as well as an exclusive labour force, facilitates linkages between co-ethnic suppliers, and gives rise to an agglomeration economy. It can even create a kind of ethnic central place, a cultural and economic focus (Waldinger et al.1990; Logan, Alba, and McNulty 1994; Kaplan 1998; Zhou 1998).

However, immigrant economies are not static. They shift in response to both contextual and structural factors, and the kind of economy associated with an immigrant group at any point in time reflects the integration process (Nee, Sanders, and Sernau 1994). Here we use a case study of the Chinese community in Toronto to illustrate the dynamic relations between immigration policies and ethnic economies.

Chinese Businesses and Their Subeconomy

The first Chinese immigrants in Toronto, like their counterparts elsewhere, faced residential, educational, and occupational segregation. Similar to the experience Kay Anderson (1991) described of Vancouver, institutional discrimination produced the enclave known as Chinatown, prompting their involvement in laundry and restaurant businesses. The enclave economy took shape at the same time that many Chinese entrepreneurs served as intermediaries. In 1923, the year when the Exclusion Act effectively stopped the entry of Chinese into Canada, a population of 2,500 operated 203 restaurants, forty-seven laundries, and nine grocers (Rhyne 1982). The relatively large number of restaurants and laundries indicated a somewhat 'broader than enclave' economy among the earlier generation of Chinese immigrants. The 'success' or sustenance of this subeconomy was due to the extensive use of rotating credit associations, networks based on village kinship, and a diligent work ethic.

The twenty years following the repeal of the Exclusion Act in 1947 was a period of transition. The subeconomy expanded to a size of 448 firms in 1966, the year before the 1967 Immigration Act was introduced. The enclave part of the Chinese ethnic economy expanded to include export/import firms, gift shops, real estate, insurance and travel agents, and a few professionals. The proportion of restaurants declined while that of grocers increased (table 4.7). The 1967 Immigration Act caused considerable change in the size and structure of the Chinese ethnic economy. Chinese business diversified and a true enclave economy emerged. This enclave economy, occurring in multiple locations, was fuelled by demand rather than discrimination. The proliferation of Chinese businesses has been a product of personal rather than group resources, and the emergence of an immigrant middle class has created the consumer demand and capital supply for the expansion of Chinese businesses (Chan and Cheung 1985; P. Li 1992).

The mass immigration of middle-class Hong Kong Chinese since 1984 and the business immigrant program that was promoted in the 1980s caused further significant changes. In 1997, the three Chinese

Table 4.7
Per cent Chinese businesses in Toronto

Type	1923	1966	1981	1994
Laundries and cleaners	18.1	32.6		
Food and grocers	3.5	18.1	18.2	9.3
Restaurants	78.4	38.8	28.0	13.8
General merchandise and other retailing		2.2	30.4	19.2
Financial, real estate, and other business services		1.3	4.8	16.2
Medical and other professional services		3.5	2.8	11.5
Personal and recreational services		0.7	3.6	10.9
Household furniture and services			7.3	11.7
Automotive				4.7
Miscellaneous		2.7	4.4	2.5
Total	100.0	99.9	99.5	99.8

Source: Adapted from Rhyne (1982), Thompson (1989), and Wang (1999).

business telephone directories in Toronto reported over 6,000 Chinese businesses (Lo 1998). While many are retail and service enterprises serving the Chinese community alone, a fair proportion seek and succeed in going beyond the enclave market and intermediary status. The Chinese subeconomy has moved away from a traditional ethnic economy focusing on consumer goods and services to one that covers nearly the whole array of industrial activities, including producer and advanced services.

In a recent study, Lo and Wang (2000) analysed the Dun and Bradstreet Regional Business Directory and made the following observations about recent Chinese business developments in Toronto. First, Chinese businesses are no longer confined to the retail sector. Of the sixty-five industrial categories outside the primary and public administration sectors, Chinese businesses are represented in fifty-two. Chinese enterprises are not found in regulated areas of business such as non-depository credit institutions, and rail and air transportation. Second, the locations of Chinese businesses are shifting. On the one hand, indicative of their enclave nature, many retail, service, finance, insurance, and real estate businesses are located in Chinese settlement concentrations. On the other hand, manufacturing and wholesale firms, not necessarily seeking co-ethnic clients, are dispersed across Toronto. Their location strategy is linked to urban land-use planning and industrial linkages rather than ethnic connections (Zhou 1998). Third, Chinese firms are expanding and multiplant establishments have surfaced. While 57 per cent of Chinese businesses still employ less than twenty employees, 41 per cent have a workforce of more than twenty but less than 200 people, and the remaining 2 per cent, covering a range of business types in wholesale, manufacturing, realty, and accommodation, employ 200 to 750 workers.

In terms of sales volume, while 26 per cent made less than $1 million in 1997, slightly more than 10 per cent of the Chinese firms exceeded the $10 million mark. The study also noted that Chinese firms, while representing 0.1 per cent of the total in Toronto, account for 1 per cent of the top 1,000 Toronto firms in both employment and sales. In particular, one manufacturing firm, ATI Technology Inc., ranked among the top 200 in employment and sales in the whole Toronto sample of almost 650,000 businesses (Dun and Bradstreet Canada 1997, S6, E5). ATI, the third largest high-tech firm in Canada as well as the world's biggest maker of computer graphic chips, was founded by two former Hong Kong residents and is still operated by one who immigrated to Toronto in 1985 (Acharya 1998). This is the largest Chinese-owned computer firm among many that were established by highly skilled, middle-class immigrants from Hong Kong, China, Taiwan, and elsewhere. Similar to Los Angeles (Saxenian 1999), Toronto is seeing the emergence of a knowledge-based ethnic economy.

The Chinese ethnic economy is maturing. Its diversification in size and composition is pointing towards both structural and functional integration of Chinese businesses in Toronto. There is a two-tier ethnic economy or, as Jan Lin (1995) and Yen-Fen Tseng (1994) said of New York and Los Angeles, two circuits of development. Given the macro changes in the world system and the diversity of Chinese immigrants (Lo and Wang 1997), there exists a lower circuit of immigrant labour and petty capitalist incorporation, mostly from China and Vietnam, and an upper circuit of flight capital and highly skilled immigrants, generally from Hong Kong and Taiwan, investing in finance, real estate, advanced services, and technology. The upper circuit is apparent in the suburban proliferation of Chinese shopping malls and industrial plants in the Scarborough, Markham, and Richmond Hill areas of Chinese concentration, as well as in Brampton and Woodbridge. The suburban malls and complexes, many developed or owned by non-Chinese locals, are products of contemporary immigrant societies.

On one hand, however, their 'Chineseness' adds to or detracts from the suburban landscape, depending upon one's perspective (Qadeer 1998; Wang 1999; Preston and Lo 2000). Yet on the other hand, they reflect, in particular, the size of the Chinese ethnic economy and, more generally, the employment opportunities immigrants create. Optimistically, a sizeable mixed economy, with its forward, backward, and lateral linkages, entails continuous exchange of resources, commodities, and information among entrepreneurs, workers, and customers belonging to different ethnic groups; gives rise to a more porous social boundary; and paves the way for social and economic integration. While it is too early to conclude if the Chinese ethnic economy represents a success in terms of its size, composition, and market spaces, its impact on the Toronto economy is apparent.

Economic Impacts of Immigrant Enterprises

The self-employed immigrants and their businesses contribute to metropolitan and national economies in several ways. They generate income (hence national production) and jobs. According to a table reported in Wang and Lo (2000), immigrants in the Toronto Census Metropolitan Area who arrived between 1980 and 1995 generated $377.9 million of income in their self-employed activities. This is 4.6 per cent of the total income reported by all immigrants in Toronto in 1995. In the same year, these self-employed immigrants accounted for 1.7 per cent of all self-employed individuals in the country, and they generated 1.4 per cent of the nation's self-employment income or 0.07 per cent of the national income. Given the recent arrival of this group, this is by no means a small economic contribution, especially as some of them also generate employment income for others and add to the public coffer through other forms of tax contributions.

Immigrant businesses are generally small. But so are the majority of businesses in our general economy. In fact, small non-immigrant firms share many of the attributes characteristic of immigrant enterprises. Their owners often work long hours, recruit from within the family and a close circle of friends, and employ informal economic practices. However small, they generate employment opportunities. While there is no official data on the number of jobs created by immigrant entrepreneurs, we can explore potential impacts based on two recent surveys and the 1996 census data on self-employment (Statistics Canada 1999c; Lo and Wang 2000; Lo, Teixeira, and Truelove 2000). The two groups examined here are Somalis and Chinese, who arrived in Canada under very different circumstances. The Somalis have a shorter history in Toronto; Somali immigrants mostly came as refugees, beginning in the late 1980s. A recently completed survey of fifty Somali businesses in Toronto (ibid.) reveals that they employ an average of 1.8 people in addition to the entrepreneur and the 1996 census reported 135 self-employed Somali immigrants (Statistics Canada 1999c). If we assume that the number of self-employed Somali immigrants remains at 135 today, and if only fifty of them provide an additional 1.8 jobs, the total impact of the Somali ethnic economy is 225 jobs, which is almost 7 per cent of the Somali immigrant labour force in Toronto.

The Chinese have a much longer presence than the Somalis in Canada. The majority of Chinese immigrants came in the last two decades and many arrived as skilled workers and business immigrants. The case study outlined earlier illustrates that the contemporary Chinese ethnic economy in Toronto includes medium- and large-size firms. The sample of 634 Chinese firms recorded in the Dun and Bradstreet Regional Business Directory of Toronto provided 19,546 jobs in 1996 (Lo and Wang 2000), amounting to 30.83 jobs per firm. In 1996, 18,000 Chinese immigrants were self-employed (Statistics Canada 1999c). If only 5 per cent of them were entrepreneurs in the sense that they employed other workers, and if their firms, numbering 900, were structurally similar to the Dun and Bradstreet sample, thereby each employing an average of 30.83 people, together they would provide 44,847 jobs, including their own employment. This is equivalent to 34 per cent of the Chinese immigrant labour force in Toronto, or 2 per cent of the total labour force in the Toronto CMA.

The numbers reported above are conservative calculations of the job impact of immigrant self-employment and entrepreneurship on the metropolitan economy. They are not intended to be prescriptive or predictive estimates. Nonetheless, they illustrate that the myth that immigrants take jobs away from Canadian-born workers is unfounded. To the contrary, they indicate that even the smallest ethnic economies and the newest immigrant entrepreneurs create employment opportunities, and when an ethnic economy grows, it provides jobs not only for some of its co-ethnic workers, but also for the general labour force.

Although immigrant businesses and their ethnic economies create jobs, there are concerns about the quality of these jobs and, in particular, whether they offer appropriate returns to human capital, and hence social and economic mobility. Many critics suggest that ethnic employers especially exploit their co-ethnic employees and that participation in the enclave ethnic market may prevent immigrant workers from ever reaching the general labour market. The empirical record, however, is inconsistent (Portes and Bach 1985; Sanders and Nee 1987). In Toronto, the incomes in enclave employment differ among minority groups. They are lower than average for the Chinese, Portuguese, and West Indians, and higher than average for the Italians (Reitz 1990; Liu 1995; Fong and Ma 1998). Job-event history also shows that immigrant workers can move across ethnic boundaries and market sectors, and away from the informal ethnic domain to the formal market that offers better working conditions and higher income (Nee, Sanders, and Sernau 1994; Liu 1995).

On a more positive note, though, we can view enclave employment as a way that earlier immigrants help later arrivals to establish themselves. Even though the enclave labour market pays lower wages, workers earn more than they would if they were unemployed (Nee, Sanders, and Sernau 1994). Labour market segmentation theory also says that immigrants, as one marginalized group, are often employed in dead-end, low-skill jobs in the secondary market. Even when employed, immigrant workers may end up with little career mobility. An enclave economy at least offers immigrant workers a protected niche with some opportunities for upward mobility, including self-employment (Portes and Bach 1985).

As an ethnic economy expands, ethnic business organizations emerge. In addition to promoting entrepreneurship among their members and forging internal cohesion, the organizations often open trade links and promote business interaction between the communities where immigrants settle and those in their countries of origin. In addition, ethnic businesses can act as important agents for urban renewal, and ethnic economies may have territorial impacts. For example, when the Portuguese community moved from Alexandra Park to the Kensington Market area, Portuguese businesses soon revitalized the area (Teixeira 1998). The northward migration of the Italians from the College/Spadina area to St Clair West changed that area's retail facades, rewriting its territorial history from Little Britain to Little Italy (Buzzelli 2000). In both cases, they have helped the neighbourhoods to develop an identity and to revive their local economies (Zucchi 1988).

Immigrant businesses proliferate, but stories about them are inconsistent. By some, they are hailed as an engine of growth in large urban centres; by others, they are seen as the economic lifeboats for many immigrants. Few studies focus on the economic contribution of the self-employed immigrants and immigrant entrepreneurs. Nonetheless, our limited empirical records indicate that immigrant businesses function positively by contributing to the public treasury and providing easily accessible jobs for immigrants, especially those who are newly arrived and poorly educated. Research in this area is much warranted, given the unnecessarily stereotypical association of immigrant firms as small, insignificant, and non-contributory; the often negative image of immigrants as job-grabbers and welfare dependents, especially in poor economic times; the controversy around business immigration programs; the changing nature of some ethnic economies; and the increasingly transnational nature of some immigrant firms.

Currently, it is almost impossible to assess the full impact of immigrant businesses. Studies of immigrant entrepreneurship, often relying on small-scale and non-random surveys, are mostly exploratory. Investigations of ethnic economies are plagued by data representation problems. The lack of a common database renders proper sampling of ethnic businesses impossible. Ethnic 'yellow pages' lean towards retail trade and are easily outdated due to high rates of business failure and turnover. General business resources such as the Dun and Bradstreet Regional and Business Directory and Scott's Industrial Directories, while more comprehensive in industrial representation, are biased in favour of larger businesses and misrepresent ethnic economies that have a larger share of small businesses than the general economy. A further complication is the presence of an informal economy that makes data less reliable. Inconsistent study outcomes are the norm, leaving many research questions unanswered.

Several observations are important to the analysis of immigrant businesses and ethnic economies. Formal studies and anecdotal discussions of immigrant entrepreneurship and ethnic economies focus on the economic incorporation of immigrants and the social barriers they face. Immigrants are successful if they adopt formal organizational behaviour, hire a moderate and not necessarily co-ethnic workforce, retain diverse establishments, serve a mixed clientele, offer their workers wages comparable to those in the general economy, and generate sizeable income. This assimilation perspective is often glorified. While it is encouraging to see that some ethnic groups have expanded their development path and are serving multiple markets, this approach also has a negative side: it encourages competition among immigrant groups. In addition, within some immigrant groups, there are signs of new ethnic economies in which labour market segmentation is similar to that in the general labour market. This changing market and the nature of ethnic economies have important implications for the future economic performance of immigrants and for the performance of the entire metropolitan economy.

IMMIGRANTS AND EMPLOYMENT IN THE TORONTO LABOUR MARKET

Since 1971, several empirical studies have shown that immigrants living in Toronto often do jobs that Canadian-born workers shun. Although immigrants made up 46.9 per cent of Toronto's employed workforce in 1996, many still work in construction, manufacturing, the garment industry, and child care, often earning low wages and experiencing job insecurity.[8] The goods-producing sectors of manufacturing and construction and specific consumer services, including accommodation, food and beverages, and personal services, are also major employers of immigrants (A. Richmond 1992; Mata 1996; Preston and Giles 1997). However, patterns of industrial concentration vary depending on immigrants' sex and ethnoracial origins. Immigrant men and women often work in different industries, with immigrant women more likely to suffer precarious and poorly paid employment. Ethnoracial background also affects immigrants' industrial division of labour such that visible-minority immigrants have been overrepresented in the least desirable industries (Mata 1996; Preston and Giles 1997; Reitz 1998; Hiebert 1999; Preston and Cox 1999; Ornstein 2000).

Three factors heighten the variation in immigrants' employment patterns. First, length of residence alters immigrants' employment. Although initially concentrated in the least desirable jobs, with the passage of time, immigrants are expected to achieve parity in wages and in the industrial division of employment (DeVoretz 1995; Ley 1999). Second, the qualifications and educational attainments of immigrants have changed as Canadian immigration policy has refined the point system and business migration programs to select attractive immigrants. Among independent immigrants who have arrived since 1980, educational attainments have improved and ability to speak one of Canada's official languages has increased (Badets and Howaston-Leo 1999). At the same time, more business migrants – who are less likely to have formal educational qualifications and who often have limited fluency in either official language – have been admitted (Reitz 1998; Ley 1999).

Third, more selective immigration policies have coincided with a shift in the origins of many immigrants. Asian, African, Caribbean, and Central and South American countries have replaced European countries as the main sources of immigrants. As visible minorities, immigrants from the more recent countries of origin are vulnerable to discrimination in the labour market (Reitz 1998).

Immigrant Men's and Women's Employment

Looking at the composition of the workforce for major industries,[9] we can see long-standing gender differences that are consistent with those reported nationally (Statistics Canada 1999b). Table 4.8 indicates that many women work in service industries – particularly in other services such as hairdressing, domestic help, and various entertainment or recreational services, in health and education services, and finance, insurance, and real estate services, while men are more likely to work in manufacturing, construction, the regulated utilities, and wholesale trade. Employment in accommodation, food, and beverage services is an exception to this pattern of gender differences – among the Canadian-born, women and men have almost equal shares of employment in this sector, 22.8 per cent versus 21 per cent. The relationship is reversed for immigrant workers – women make up 24.5 per cent of the workforce, while immigrant men make up 31.7 per cent. The large number of male immigrant workers in accommodation, food and beverage may be due to the fact that these jobs have low entry costs and minimal skill requirements, and that there are limited job opportunities in other sectors available to them (Waldinger 1996).

Table 4.9 analyses the proportions of immigrant men's and women's total employment in each industry and highlights the importance of manufacturing jobs for immigrant workers. This sector employs 16.8 per cent of immigrant women and 25.5 per cent of immigrant men. Immigrants' continued reliance on manufacturing jobs as a major source of employment, when employment in the sector declined overall between 1981 and 1996, renders them susceptible to layoffs and unemployment. Their vulnerability is underscored by the unstable nature of employment in other industries where they are concentrated. For immigrant men, seasonal and cyclical construction jobs account for 8.9 per cent of all their jobs. Only small proportions of immigrant men and women work in education, government, and business services – service sectors where, traditionally, employment has been well-paid and secure.

Table 4.8
Shares of employment by industry, gender, and birthplace, 1996

	Birthplace			
	Canadian shares		Immigrant shares	
Industry	Women	Men	Women	Men
Manufacturing	14.6	28	20.6	36.8
Construction	7.5	42	4.6	45.9
Regulated utilities	19.1	40.6	11.6	28.7
Wholesale	21	37.2	15.3	26.5
Retail	29	27.5	20.9	22.5
FIRE (fire, insurance, real estate)	31.5	23.8	26.1	18.6
Business	27.7	31.3	18	22.9
Government	29.5	35	18.3	17.2
Education	43.1	19.7	22.7	14.5
Health and social services	41.7	10.3	38	10
Accommodation, food and beverage	22.8	21	24.5	31.7
Other services	28.4	26.4	25.5	19.7
N	263,148	605,124	461,844	546,984

Each row sums to 100.0 per cent.
Source: Statistics Canada (1999a).

Location quotients[10] that compare the proportion of immigrant women's employment in each industry to that of Canadian-born women and the proportion of immigrant men's employment to that of Canadian-born men, confirm the vulnerability of immigrant workers. Immigrant women's jobs are concentrated in manufacturing with lesser concentrations in the accommodation, food, and beverage services (table 4.9). Immigrant men are overrepresented in construction, as well as in manufacturing and accommodation, food, and beverage services. Immigrant workers of both sexes are underrepresented in many service industries, including regulated utilities, wholesale and retail trade, and business, education, and government services.

The location quotients reveal that immigrant women are more likely than immigrant men to work in growing service industries such as finance, insurance, and real estate services (Swan et al. 1991). Immigrant men's proportions of employment in these areas are less than those of Canadian-born men, while immigrant women's proportions of employment in these industries are approximately equal to those of Canadian-born women. Immigrant women's parity with Canadian-

Table 4.9
Percentages of employment and location quotients by industry, gender, and birthplace, 1996

	Canadian		Immigrant			
	Percentage		Percentage		Location quotient	
Industry	Women	Men	Women	Men	Women	Men
Manufacturing	9.8	17.5	16.8	25.5	1.72	1.45
Construction	1.4	7.3	1.1	8.9	0.75	1.21
Regulated utilities	5.3	10.5	3.9	8.2	0.74	0.80
Wholesale	5.3	8.7	4.7	6.9	0.89	0.79
Retail	13.2	11.6	11.6	10.6	0.88	0.91
FIRE (fire, insurance, real estate)	10.6	7.4	10.7	6.5	1.01	0.87
Business	11.4	11.9	9	9.7	0.80	0.81
Government	4.6	5	3.5	2.7	0.76	0.54
Education	10.6	4.5	6.8	3.7	0.64	0.81
Health and social services	13.5	3.1	15	3.3	1.11	1.08
Accommodation, food and beverage	5.3	4.5	6.9	7.6	1.31	1.67
Other services	9	7.8	9.9	6.4	1.09	0.82

Each column of percentages sums to 100 per cent.
Source: Statistics Canada (1999a).

born women's employment in these sectors may be a hopeful sign that the employment circumstances of some immigrant women have improved, although it is worth noting that these service sectors have bifurcated occupational distributions. Although many well-paid and secure positions are found in finance, insurance, real estate, and other services, these industries also employ large numbers of precarious and poorly paid workers in less desirable occupations, such as janitors, cleaners, and filing clerks (Stanback and Noyelle 1984).

Despite the growing importance of self-employment in the Canadian economy (Statistics Canada 1998), the vast majority of immigrant workers in 1996 were employees. In Toronto, the proportion of immigrant women who are self-employed is identical to the proportion of Canadian-born women, 8.4 per cent, while a slightly higher proportion of immigrant men than Canadian-born men are self-employed, 17 per cent versus 14.7 per cent. There is little evidence that, in aggregate, immigrants are more likely than the Canadian-born to be self-employed.[11]

Hours of work are also very similar for immigrant and Canadian-born workers in Toronto. The majority of people work full-time – at least thirty hours per week – although women are more likely than men to work fewer hours. Canadian-born and immigrant women both work part-time at approximately twice the rate of men. For example, more than 20 per cent of immigrant women in Toronto work part-time compared with 10 per cent of immigrant men. Part-time work is slightly more common among Canadian-born women than among immigrant women – 26.9 per cent versus 20 per cent. Economic necessity may account for the slightly lower rate of participation of immigrant women in part-time work.

The Impact of Ethnoracial Backgrounds

Gender structures the industrial division of labour in Toronto, but its effects interact with those of ethnoracial background, and there are substantial ethnoracial differences in immigrants' industries of employment. Location quotients were calculated to identify the industries in which immigrants from each ethnoracial group are overrepresented and those in which they are underrepresented.[12] The importance of manufacturing jobs crosses all ethnoracial and gender groups. For immigrant women, eleven of fourteen location quotients exceed 1.0, and for immigrant men, thirteen of fourteen exceed 1.0 (table 4.10a). Immigrant workers of both sexes are also concentrated in accommodation, food, and beverage services, where the location quotients for nine of fourteen ethnoracial groups exceed 1.0 for men and ten of the fourteen location quotients for women exceed 1.0. Without exception, immigrant men and women are underrepresented in government services where every location quotient is less than 1.0, and are almost equally underrepresented in regulated utilities (table 4.10b). Immigrants from most ethnoracial groups are also excluded from education and business services.

Gender differences, however, do cut across the ethnoracial divisions of labour. Immigrant women often work in health, social, and other services, while the vast majority of immigrant men are excluded from other services. Construction is an important source of employment for immigrant men from several ethnoracial groups – Italian, Polish, Southern European, British, French, and Latin, Central, and South American – while it is relatively unimportant for immigrant women. Even where the location quotients exceed 1.0, the numbers of immigrant women working in the construction industry are small compared with those employed in manufacturing and other services.

Comparing the location quotients among ethnoracial groups rather than industries offers some evidence of the three employment patterns identified in previous research (Mata 1996; Preston and Giles 1997; Reitz 1998). Jewish and charter-group immigrants stand out with location quotients close to 1.0 in business services and finance, insurance, and real estate, while their location quotients in manufacturing are relatively low (tables 4.10a and 4.10b). There are also large concentrations of Jewish immigrant women in health, social services, and education, services where jobs have been stable and well-paid. Ukrainian immigrants, a long-established ethnoracial group, have remarkably similar employment patterns, suggesting that in Toronto they are attaining the same economic success that has been observed for Jewish, British, American, and Northern European immigrants.

The location quotients highlight the persistent concentration of Polish, Italian, and Southern European immigrants in the manufacturing and construction sectors (table 4.10a). The manufacturing location quotients for women from these ethnoracial groups exceed 2.0. These women are also concentrated in construction, perhaps because of involvement in family businesses, particularly on the part of Italian women. Construction is also an important source of men's employment for these ethnoracial groups with location quotients that exceed 1.0 by a wide

Table 4.10a
Location quotients for immigrant women by industry and ethnic origin, 1996

Ethnic Origin	Manu-facturing	Construction	Regulated utilities	Wholesale	Retail	FIRE	Business	Government	Education	Health and social services	Accommodation	Other
Charter	1.28	0.80	1.24	1.17	0.88	1.14	1.03	0.48	0.61	1.29	0.87	1.10
Polish	2.15	1.08	0.52	1.05	0.73	0.59	0.58	0.35	0.36	1.26	3.02	1.26
Ukrainian	1.38	0.00	0.84	0.28	0.79	0.84	0.53	0.00	1.41	1.22	2.83	1.49
Italian	2.45	3.21	0.64	0.80	1.37	1.07	0.30	0.47	0.94	0.68	0.88	0.84
South European	2.51	1.18	0.39	0.59	0.85	0.96	0.58	0.25	0.44	0.89	1.87	1.83
Jewish	0.85	0.31	0.49	0.58	1.06	0.87	0.93	0.23	1.57	1.53	1.16	1.22
Other European	1.24	1.60	0.85	0.65	1.16	1.09	1.02	0.35	1.09	0.98	0.97	1.20
African and Caribbean	1.35	0.49	0.97	0.69	0.79	1.01	0.86	0.46	0.34	2.01	1.38	0.98
West Asian	0.95	0.26	0.40	1.15	1.63	0.84	0.85	0.15	0.88	1.25	2.04	0.92
South Asian	2.56	0.38	0.96	1.29	0.85	1.07	0.88	0.46	0.67	0.92	1.02	0.61
Chinese	2.31	0.42	0.69	1.15	0.85	1.45	0.99	0.33	0.52	0.78	1.47	0.78
East and South-east Asian	1.58	0.25	0.61	0.86	0.95	0.99	0.56	0.22	0.23	1.50	1.76	1.96
Central and South American	1.41	1.02	0.81	1.17	1.15	0.63	0.54	0.41	0.27	1.13	1.44	2.38
Other	1.38	0.49	0.78	0.94	0.85	1.00	1.13	0.55	0.90	1.21	1.19	1.06

Source: Statistics Canada (1999a).

Table 4.10b
Location quotients for immigrant men by industry and ethnic origin, 1996

Ethnic Origin	Industry Manu-facturing	Construc-tion	Regu-lated utilities	Whole-sale	Retail	FIRE	Business	Govern-ment	Education	Health and social services	Accom-modation	Other
Charter	1.34	1.15	1.22	1.13	0.56	1.14	1.04	0.84	1.04	0.87	0.65	0.62
Polish	1.87	2.52	0.98	0.73	0.86	0.40	0.57	0.32	0.59	0.57	1.21	0.68
Ukrainian	1.50	0.91	0.67	0.96	0.85	0.76	0.74	0.62	1.87	1.19	1.31	0.77
Italian	1.32	4.25	0.91	0.56	1.01	0.75	0.25	0.56	0.91	0.37	0.53	0.85
South European	1.63	3.53	0.68	0.65	0.78	0.64	0.31	0.25	0.40	0.55	1.71	1.00
Jewish	1.13	0.85	0.49	0.94	0.97	1.24	1.24	0.46	1.04	2.15	0.96	0.80
Other European	1.54	1.73	0.96	1.00	0.70	0.91	0.91	0.63	0.88	0.81	0.66	0.72
African and Caribbean	1.70	0.91	1.29	0.76	1.02	0.59	0.71	0.53	0.42	1.09	1.46	0.75
West Asian	1.07	0.83	0.92	0.86	1.75	0.70	0.65	0.43	0.62	1.04	2.41	0.73
South Asian	1.93	0.40	0.89	0.96	0.97	0.89	0.81	0.59	0.45	0.86	1.71	0.50
Chinese	1.37	0.51	0.56	1.14	0.89	1.29	0.96	0.45	0.62	0.93	2.71	0.58
East and South-east Asian	2.26	0.34	0.49	0.63	0.98	0.80	0.53	0.41	0.50	1.67	1.83	0.88
Central and South American	2.17	1.61	0.69	0.56	0.87	0.57	0.53	0.14	0.28	0.92	1.34	1.22
Other	1.43	0.83	0.69	0.87	0.91	1.10	0.92	0.62	1.08	1.02	1.46	0.87

Source: Statistics Canada (1999a).

margin (table 4.10b). The reliance on the manufacturing and construction sectors is balanced by underrepresentation in business, government, and health and social services, where the location quotients are low for both men and women. Italian immigrants have the most extreme concentration in manufacturing and construction accompanied by the greatest underrepresentation in services. One example is business services. where the location quotient for Italian immigrant men is 0.25. As skilled tradespeople, many immigrants from Southern and Eastern Europe have enjoyed fairly secure and remunerative employment in the manufacturing and construction sectors. With little formal education, many are prevented from taking jobs in those service industries that are expected to be the economic engines of the future, specifically, business, finance, insurance, and real estate services and health, social, and education services.

Despite the continuing concentration of immigrants from Asia, Africa, the Caribbean, and Central and South America in manufacturing, their employment patterns differ from those of Southern and Central European immigrants in three respects. First, men from Africa, Asia, and the Caribbean are underrepresented in construction, perhaps because of the importance of ethnoracial networks in this industry (Waldinger 1996). Only immigrant men from Central and South America have a location quotient for construction greater than 1.0 (table 4.10b). Second, retail and wholesale trade are important sectors of employment for women from Asia and South and Central America. Chinese men are also involved in these sectors, perhaps a continuation of their historic roles as traders. Third, African, Caribbean, and Chinese immigrants of both sexes have location quotients that approach or exceed 1.0 for finance, insurance, and real estate services, a promising indication that some recent immigrants are finding jobs outside the declining manufacturing sector (tables 4.10a and 4.10b).

Period of Arrival and the Industrial Division of Labour

The time period in which immigrants arrive also exerts an independent influence on their employment patterns. Recent immigrants may be initially concentrated in less desirable jobs in declining sectors because they have difficulty satisfying employers' requirements for Canadian experience and Canadian education and training (Reitz 1990; Boyd 1991). They also have had less time to develop social networks that are crucial sources of information about job vacancies, personal recommendations, and even job offers. Some authors argue that over time as immigrants acquire Canadian experience and wider social contacts, they will achieve parity in wages and in the industrial division of employment (DeVoretz 1995; Ley 1999). Contradicting this benign view, Sassen (1991) has argued that the growth of business and financial services in 'global' cities has increased demand for immigrant workers to fill poorly paid and often insecure jobs in industrial and service sectors.

In Toronto, the vulnerable economic situation of recent immigrants who arrived between 1991 and 1996 is not apparent in their hours of work or their propensity for self-employment.[13] When immigrants are disaggregated by period of arrival, only two effects of years of residence in Canada are discernible. Immigrant women who arrived before 1966 are more likely to work part-time than other female immigrant workers, which may reflect their age. Many of these women are approaching retirement. Iacovetta (1992) has noted the tendency for older Italian immigrant women to reduce their hours of work and to leave the paid labour market as the family's economic position improves. Immigrant men who arrived before 1966 are also more likely than other male immigrant workers to be self-employed. Apart from these early immigrants, period of arrival does not have a significant influence on hours of work or self-employment rates.

Immigrants' industries of employment are influenced slightly by period of arrival,[14] which is related significantly to the proportions of immigrant men and women in each industry. Two trends stand out here, as shown in table 4.11. Among immigrant women, the public sector is a less important employer for recent arrivals than for immigrants who settled in Canada prior to 1986. While 12.2 per cent of immigrant women who arrived before 1966 work in education, of those who arrived between 1991 and 1996, only 6.1 per cent are employed in that sector. Recently arrived immigrant women are also less likely than earlier immigrant women to work in health and social services.

Sectoral shifts are more apparent for immigrant men. Male-dominated industries – construction, transportation, utilities, and wholesale trade – accounted for a much smaller share of the jobs of immigrants who arrived between 1991 and 1996 than for those of earlier arrivals. Employment in education is also lower for recently arrived immigrant men, but the magnitude of the decline is smaller than for immigrant women because jobs in education are dominated by women. Recently arrived immigrant men are also more likely to work in personal serv-

Table 4.11
Percentages of employment by industry, gender, and period of arrival, 1996

Industry	Immigrant women pre-1966	1966–85	1986–90	1991–96	Immigrant men pre-1966	1966–85	1986–90	1991–96
Manufacturing	14.3	16.1	15.3	16.7	20.0	26.2	23.5	26.7
Construction	2.1	1.2	0.8	0.7	14.2	10.1	7.7	6.5
Regulated utilities	4.5	5.0	4.8	4.1	10.2	9.0	9.8	7.5
Wholesale	4.5	4.8	3.3	4.9	6.8	5.7	7.5	5.7
Retail	12.6	9.8	11.6	13.3	8.5	9.4	10.5	12.4
FIRE (finance, insurance, real estate)	11.7	12.4	12.2	12.0	7.8	6.3	7.9	7.3
Business	8.6	8.2	9.6	9.6	9.0	9.7	9.4	9.3
Government	3.9	4.4	5.7	3.7	3.8	3.6	3.8	3.2
Education	12.2	7.7	5.5	6.1	6.1	4.0	3.8	2.8
Health and social services	13.6	17.2	17.5	13.8	3.1	3.6	4.4	3.9
Accommodation	4.3	6.0	5.1	6.3	3.2	6.1	5.8	8.2
Other	7.8	7.2	8.6	8.9	7.2	6.3	5.9	6.6
N	74,052	106,668	76,320	54,072	97,272	123,012	83,268	57,096

Source: Statistics Canada (1996a).

ices, particularly the accommodation, food, and beverage sector than immigrant men who arrived prior to 1991.

The trends in sector of employment are consistent with the hypothesis that, over time, immigrants will obtain better paid and more stable jobs. However, recently arrived immigrants are better educated and more fluent in English than their earlier counterparts. The declining numbers of immigrant men and women working in the public sector may reflect fiscal restraint by the Ontario provincial government that reduced the growth in public spending on health and educational services during the 1990s. Jobs in the public sector were disappearing just as qualified immigrants arrived in Toronto.

Analysis of the 1996 census has confirmed that immigrants in the Toronto labour market are still concentrated in manufacturing, an economic sector that has suffered major job losses over the past three decades. This concentration is accompanied by an almost uniform underrepresentation in business and government services, sectors where job growth has occurred since 1971. There are, however, some encouraging signs of change. Ukrainian immigrants have employment patterns similar to those of Jewish, British, and American immigrants. On the basis of their industries of employment, Ukrainian workers no longer fit with other Southern and Central European immigrants. Among immigrants from Asia and Africa, the proportions of workers from each ethnoracial group employed in finance, insurance, and real estate services are almost equal to the proportions for Canadian-born workers. Chinese immigrants of both sexes along with men and women from selected Asian origins are also having success in retail trade. Employment in these service sectors does not imply that immigrant workers are all in well-paid, secure employment, but their increasing presence in the expanding service industries promises improved economic prospects.

The differentiation of immigrants on the basis of ethnoracial origin and gender continues; even at the aggregate level of thirteen ethnoracial groups, three types of groups are apparent. The composition of these groups has changed slightly with the inclusion of Ukrainians in the first, most successful group, but otherwise the three categories that we described in the section on the impact on employment of ethnoracial background have persisted since 1971.[15] Within the third type, where the majority of recent immigrants are found, a shared concentration of employment in manufacturing and in accommodation, food, and beverage services, and a shared exclusion from employment in business and government services are the main common elements. Employment in other service sectors remains very diverse. Asian, Caribbean, and African immigrants seem to have had more success entering expanding service sectors than have immigrants from Central and South America. In this respect, the findings confirm Mata's (1996) assertion in 1991 that Central and South American immigrants were at the greatest disadvantage in the Toronto labour market.

Immigrants' industries of employment are also influenced by gender effects that cut across ethnoracial differences in complex ways. Immigrant women are the most vulnerable group of workers. More reliant than immigrant men and Canadian-born workers of both sexes on manufacturing jobs, immigrant women are most likely to suffer layoffs and unemployment as jobs disappear in this sector. Furthermore, immigrant women are underrepresented in educational and government services that offer more remunerative and stable employment to Canadian-born women. At the same time, many immigrant women work in accommodation, food, and beverages services that are notorious for precarious and poorly paid jobs. Not all immigrant women are equally vulnerable, however: Jewish, British, Ukrainian, and American immigrant women are employed in reasonable numbers in expanding service sectors.

Our analysis does not allow us to separate the effects of length of residence in Canada from the impact of ethnoracial background. However, Jewish, British, Ukrainian, and American women are most like Canadian-born women from the charter groups. Their relative success contrasts with the economic difficulties of recent immigrants from Asia, Africa, the Caribbean, and Central and South America, who are more qualified than earlier immigrants and most likely to be visible minorities. In light of these findings, discrimination rooted in racism and employers' inability to assess foreign experience and credentials cannot be dismissed as a cause of immigrant women's precarious position in the Toronto labour market.

Period of arrival does influence the employment patterns of immigrants as expected. Immigrants who arrived in Canada between 1991 and 1996, unlike those who arrived earlier, are more likely to be working in personal services, particularly the food, accommodation, and beverage services. Recent arrivals are also less likely than earlier immigrants to be working in the public sector, which is renowned for job security. However, the magnitude of the effects of period of arrival on immigrants' industries of employment are small compared with those of gender and ethnoracial background. In the Toronto economy, social characteristics of immigrants, particularly their sex, ethnicity, and race, place many at a disadvantage. Nonetheless, the findings emphasize the diverse experiences of immigrants whose diverse social characteristics intersect in complex ways with the economic and political circumstances prevailing on their arrival in Canada.

IMMIGRANTS' ECONOMIC ACHIEVEMENTS IN TORONTO

The complex ways that immigrants participate in the Toronto economy are echoed in their varied economic attainments. Using 1996 census data,[16] this section explores the economic achievements of ethnoracial groups in Toronto through an examination of unemployment rates, median employment income, and the incidence of low income. These three indicators provide an indication of employment among different ethnoracial groups, income levels, and the likelihood of different ethnoracial groups experiencing poverty in Toronto.

Our emphasis on ethnoracial groups reflects previous research. Three separate studies of ethnoracial groups in Canada found that people of British origins are overrepresented in higher socio-economic-status positions with associated high incomes (Nakhaie 1995, 1997, 1998). Both 1991 and 1996 data reveal that being an immigrant had a negative impact on the income levels of all visible-minority groups, with the most pronounced effects among recent immigrants (Hou and Balakrishnan 1996; Ornstein 1996, 2000). In this analysis, eleven ethnoracial groups have been categorized as 'visible-minority' groups and all others as 'European' groups. Visible-minority groups consist of Black/African Black, Latin American (visible-minority only), South Asian, Southeast Asian, West Asian/Arab, Chinese, Korean, Japanese, Filipino, and other single visible-minority and multiple visible-minority origins. European groups include British, French, Western European, Northern European, Eastern European, Southern European, Latin American (non-visible-minority only), and multiple non-visible-minority groups.

Just as gender influences the industries in which immigrants work, it also affects income, unemployment, and poverty. Generally speaking, women from non-English-speaking countries are socio-economically disadvantaged (Boyd 1984, 1990; Estable 1986; Basavarajappa and Verma 1990; Preston and Giles 1997; Preston and Man 1999). Visible-minority immigrant women are often employed in occupations that are not commensurate with their experience and skill level. As a result, many have low incomes, high unemployment rates, and, in some cases, high poverty rates.

Recency of immigration is also associated with unemployment, low incomes, and poverty. Structural factors such as social stratification, labour market segmentation, discrimination against visible minorities, and economic cycles at the time immigrants arrive influence the general distribution of immigrant groups in Canada. Indeed, period of immigration may account for some intergroup differences (Dougherty 1999). Demographic characteristics of individual immigrants, such as age at time of immigration, educational attainment, language skills, and family status, contribute to differences in economic achievements within a cohort of immigrants. To understand how recency of immigration affects the economic status of immigrants, we considered five periods of immigration: before 1961, 1961–70, 1971–80, 1981–90, and 1991–6. Although data availability means the last period is shorter, it covers the initial few years of residence in Canada that are the most difficult for recent immigrants.

Unemployment Rates

There is a linear progression of unemployment rates such that recent immigrants have higher rates of unemployment. The most recent immigrant cohort, those who arrived between 1991 and 1996, has the highest unemployment rate, 18.4 per cent, followed by each previous cohort in reverse order of arrival: 1981–90, 12.0 per cent; 1971–80, 8.4 per cent; 1961–70, 6.4 per cent; and before 1961, 5.8 per cent. Those who immigrated before 1971 fared better than non-immigrants, who had an unemployment rate of 7.5 per cent, and better than the Toronto average of 9.1 per cent. This linear progression is apparent for both male immigrants, whose rates ranged from 15.5 per cent to 5.8 per cent, and female immigrants, whose rates ranged from 21.7 per cent to 5.8 per cent (table 4.12). The wide range of unemployment rates for immigrant women is consistent with previous evidence that immigrant women are at a disadvantage in competing for jobs in the Toronto labour market (Preston and Giles 1997; Preston and Cox 1999).

As table 4.13 illustrates, age alters the magnitude of the relationship between unemployment and recency of immigration for both sexes. Within the working-age population of immigrants (all those who are between 15 and 64 years of age), unemployment rates are highest for young workers between the ages of 15 and 29 years, declining steadily thereafter. Unemployment rates fall more quickly for immigrant men than for immigrant women, but in both cases, the decline is notable.

How age affects unemployment depends on the period of immigration. When immigrants are disaggregated on the basis of period of arrival, unemployment rates still decline with age, but the level of unemployment and the speed with which it diminishes as the workforce ages depends on the time of arrival. Among the most recent immigrants, the unemployment rate approaches 25 per cent for immigrant women between 15 and 29 years of age, a much higher level than the 5 per cent reported by women of the same age who arrived between 1961 and 1970. For young immigrant men who arrived in the 1990s, the unemployment rate is also high, 17.1 per cent, compared with only 10.1 per cent for men of the same age who arrived in the 1960s.

The improvement in unemployment rates with age is not sustained for immigrant men and women who arrived after 1980. For these immigrants, unemployment rates declined between the ages of 30 and 44 years and then increased again among older workers between 45 and 64 years of age. In earlier cohorts, unemployment rates for men and women declined steadily – albeit by small amounts – with age. The trends suggest that immigrants who have settled in Toronto since 1980 have encountered structural barriers to employment different from those experienced by earlier arrivals. Certainly, the period from 1981 to 1996 included two recessions – a mild recession in the early 1980s associated with substantial deindustrialization in the former regional municipality of Metropolitan Toronto, and a much more severe recession in the early 1990s when the total employment in the Toronto Census Metropolitan Area contracted. At that time, the manufacturing sector was dramatically restructured and many manufacturing jobs were relocated to the outer ring of the Toronto Census Metropolitan Area (Norcliffe 1996).

Recent immigrants of visible-minority status are more likely to be unemployed than their European counterparts, earlier immigrants, and the Canadian-born (table 4.13). For the most recent cohort of immigrants who arrived between 1991 and 1996, the unemployment rate for all European immigrants is 14.7 per cent compared with 19.5 per cent for visible-minority immigrants. Four visible-minority groups have unemployment rates higher than 19.5 per cent: Black, South Asian, Southeast Asian, and Arab/West Asian. Among recent immigrants, Japanese, Korean, Chinese, Latin American, and Filipino immigrants had unem-

Table 4.12
Unemployment rate by gender, birthplace, and period of arrival, 1996

	Women			Men		
	All	Visible minority	Non-visible minority	All	Visible minority	Non-visible minority
Canadian-born	7.6	18.0	6.9	7.4	18.0	9
Immigrant	12.2	15.2	8.4	9.5	11.7	7.1
Period of arrival						
Pre-1961	5.8	8.7	5.7	5.8	7.7	5.7
1961–70	6.67	6.8	6.6	6.3	6.4	6.2
1971–80	9.26	10.8	6.7	7.7	8.5	6.5
1981–90	13.69	15.0	10.6	10.4	11.5	7.9
1991–96	21.7	22.9	17.8	15.5	16.6	12.0

Source: Statistics Canada (1999c).

Table 4.13
Unemployment rate by gender, period of arrival, visible minority status, and age, 1996

Age/visible-minority status	Pre-1961 Women	Pre-1961 Men	1961–1971 Women	1961–1971 Men	1971–1980 Women	1971–1980 Men	1981–1990 Women	1981–1990 Men	1991–1996 Women	1991–1996 Men
15–29 years										
All immigrants	–	–	5.0	10.1	12.7	13.1	18.6	16.6	23.3	17.1
Non-visible minority	–	–	4.9	10.4	7.9	10.9	12.3	12.5	16.5	12.9
Visible minority	–	–	5.0	9.4	15.6	14.6	21.0	18.3	25.3	18.3
30–44 years										
All immigrants	4.9	4.0	6.9	5.3	8.8	6.4	11.9	8.2	20.5	13.7
Non-visible minority	4.9	4.0	6.9	5.1	6.2	5.5	9.7	6.3	18.0	11.0
Visible minority	8.1	0.0	6.8	5.8	10.3	6.9	12.9	8.9	21.3	14.5
45–64 years										
All immigrants	5.8	6.4	6.6	6.5	7.9	6.5	12.2	9.3	22.5	18.0
Non-visible minority	5.7	6.3	6.5	6.6	6.7	5.4	10.7	7.3	19.6	13.3
Visible minority	8.4	8.7	7.0	6.2	8.6	7.2	12.9	10.4	23.3	19.2

– no valid cases
Source: Statistics Canada (1999c).

ployment rates lower than that for all recent visible-minority immigrants. When these data are broken down by gender, the same ethnoracial groups have higher than average unemployment rates, but, for the most part, women's unemployment rates exceed those of men.

The effects of visible-minority status persist even after period of arrival is controlled. Unemployment rates for men and women tend to be higher for visible-minority immigrants than for European immigrants. The only exception is among immigrants who arrived between 1961 and 1970. In this cohort, the unemployment rates of male visible-minority workers aged between 15 and 29 and between 45 and 64 are slightly lower than those of European immigrants in the same cohort, while for female visible-minority workers, the unemployment rate for 30- to 44- year-olds is slightly less than the unemployment rate for European immigrants of the same age. The differences in unemployment rates are small, ranging from .98 to .15, and they may be due to prolonged residence in Canada. Given their ages in 1996, the majority of visible-minority immigrants who arrived between 1961 and 1970 are likely to have been educated in Canada, and a Canadian education reduces unemployment, even for visible-minority immigrants (Reitz 1998).

Apart from these exceptions for immigrants who arrived in the 1960s, visible-minority immigrants in each cohort had higher unemployment rates than their European, non-visible-minority, counterparts. It is important to note that visible-minority immigrants had higher unemployment rates than their European counterparts during the 1980s and the 1990s when visible minorities were an increasing share of all immigrants settling in the Toronto Census Metropolitan Area. Moreover, the interaction between age and recency of arrival appears to heighten the chances of unemployment for visible-minority immigrants who are the vast majority of recent arrivals.

Median Employment Income

The median employment income of immigrants is related closely to recency of immigration, with more recent immigrants having low median employment incomes. While immigrants who came to Toronto before 1961 earned a median employment income of $31,510, those who arrived between 1961 and 1970 earned $32,060; those who arrived between 1971 and 1980 earned $27,950; those who arrived between 1981 and 1990 earned $21,808; and those who arrived between 1990 and 1996 earned $14,462. For men and women who arrived before 1961, retirement is starting to reduce their incomes, but among immigrant men and women who arrived after 1961, a longer period of residence is associated with higher incomes. The median employment incomes of immigrants who came before 1981 are higher than those of Canadian-born workers ($27,848) and the average workforce income ($25,578). Among immigrants who arrived after 1980, both men and women earn lower median incomes than their Canadian-born counterparts and than the average workforce income.

As with unemployment rates, gender also influences the effects of recency of immigration, as shown in table 4.14. For all immigrant women, their median employment income ($20,079) is less than that of Canadian-born women ($24,031). When the period of immigration is controlled, we see that women who immigrated before 1981 earned more than the median employment income for women in the Toronto CMA. A slightly different pattern is found for men. The median employment income of immigrant men ($28,443) was less than that of Canadian-born men ($31,660). Men who immigrated before 1971 earned more than the median income for all men living in the Census Metropolitan Area, while those who arrived after 1970 earned less than the median employment income of Canadian-born men.

The complex relationships between gender, period of immigration, and median employment income are due in part to aging. In each period of immigration cohort, median employment income peaks between the ages of 30 and 44. Younger workers aged 15 to 29 are more likely to work part-time and seasonally and they lack the work experience that is rewarded by high employment incomes. Older workers between 45 and 64 are beginning to reduce overtime, to work part-time, and even to retire. Both age groups earn lower median employment incomes than workers between the ages of 30 and 44. Immigrant women's median employment income increases relatively more than immigrant men's between the ages of 30 and 44.

The data also reveal low employment incomes among visible-minority immigrants, who earn lower median employment incomes ($21,088) than European (non-visible-minority) immigrants ($28,024) and Canadian-born workers ($27,848). Median employment incomes have similar trends for men and women, but women's employment incomes are lower than those of men, just as they were in 1991 (Preston and Giles 1997). The median employment income of visible-minority immigrant men was $24,013 in 1996, as opposed to $31,660 for Canadian-born men, and $33,855 for European immigrant men. In comparison, the median

Table 4.14
Median employment income by gender, birthplace, and period of arrival, 1996

	Women			Men		
	All ($)	Visible minority ($)	Non-visible minority ($)	All ($)	Visible minority ($)	Non-visible minority ($)
Canadian-born	24,031	8,408	24,981	31,660	9,993	32,704
Immigrants	20,079	19,053	22,779	28,443	24,013	33,855
Pre-1961	26,019	23,922	26,035	38,043	29,981	38,200
1961–1970	27,138	30,069	25,969	38,097	39,960	37,951
1971–1980	24,966	25,019	23,952	31,471	30,056	33,818
1981–1990	18,521	18,734	18,096	25,014	23,978	28,236
1991–1996	11,988	11,971	12,273	16,956	16,002	21,754

Source: Statistics Canada (1999c).

employment income for visible-minority immigrant women was $19,053, almost $5,000 less than that of their male counterparts and of Canadian-born women ($24,031) and European immigrant women ($22,799).

Specific visible-minority groups have below-average employment incomes. For example, South Asian, Korean, Southeast Asian, Filipino, Arab/West Asian, and Latin American visible-minority immigrants have lower median employment incomes than all visible-minority immigrants in the Toronto CMA, as shown in table 4.15. When we examine men's and women's incomes separately for these visible-minority groups, only Southeast Asian male immigrants earned more than the median employment income for visible-minority immigrant men. The low employment incomes of these visible-minority groups contrast sharply with the high median employment income for Japanese immigrant men, who earned more than the median for all immigrant men, Canadian-born men, and European men. No other visible-minority group comes close to the median employment income of Japanese immigrant men.

Median employment incomes for certain visible-minority groups are influenced by gender roles. While Japanese immigrant men had high median employment incomes in 1996, Japanese immigrant women earned close to the average median employment income for visible-minority immigrant women. Cultural practices and high household incomes may contribute to the low employment incomes of Japanese immigrant women. Among Southeast Asian immigrants, women also had low median employment incomes, while men earned as much as or more than other visible-minority immigrants.

The success of Japanese immigrant men was repeated in every period of immigration. At the same time, low median employment incomes persisted across all cohorts for some of the visible-minority groups who had low median employment incomes in 1996. Korean immigrant men and women and Black men, for example, suffer persistent disadvantage in terms of employment income. Each group earned a median employment income below the medians for visible-minority immigrants of both sexes in every cohort. After 1980, just as large numbers of immigrants arrived from Iran and Iraq, among other Middle Eastern countries, the employment incomes of Arab/West Asian men and women also fell consistently below the medians for visible-minority immigrant men and women. Immigrant women in specific visible-minority groups clearly face serious challenges earning an income in the Toronto labour market. Since 1970, Black, South Asian, and

Table 4.15
Ethnocultural groups with median employment incomes below the Toronto median for visible minority immigrants by period of immigration, Toronto CMA, 1996

	Immigrated before 1961	Immigrated 1961–70	Immigrated 1971–80	Immigrated 1981–90	Immigrated 1991–6
All immigrants	Chinese Multiple visible minority	Black Latin American Korean Japanese	Black Latin American Korean Arab/West Asia Multiple visible minority Other visible minority	Black Latin American Korean Arab/West Asian	Black Chinese South Asian Korean Arab/West Asian Multiple visible minority
Median for visible-minority immigrants	$27,653	$34,817	$27,905	$21,009	$13,970
15–29 years	—	Black South Asian Korean Japanese Filipino Latin American	South Asian Chinese Korean Southeast Asian Arab/West Asian Multiple visible minority	Black Chinese Korean Japanese Arab/West Asian Latin American	Black Chinese Korean Japanese Arab/West Asian Multiple visible minority
Median for visible-minority Immigrants	—	$25,074	$15,001	$11,203	$10,011
30–44 years	Black South Asian Filipino	Black Korean Filipino Arab/West Asian Latin American Other visible minority	Black Korean Southeast Asian Arab/West Asian Latin American Other visible minority	Black South Asian Korean Southeast Asian Arab/West Asian Latin American	Chinese Korean Japanese Filipino Arab/West Asian Multiple visible minority
Median for visible-minority immigrants	$30,037	$34,960	$29,984	$24,988	$16,008
45–64 years	Chinese Other visible minority Multiple visible minority	Black Korean Japanese Latin American Other visible minority	Black Korean Latin American Multiple visible minority	Chinese Korean Southeast Asian Latin American Other visible minority Multiple visible minority	Chinese Arab/West Asian
Median for visible-minority immigrants	$27,828	$34,951	$30,007	$22,434	$13,992

Source: Statistics Canada (1999c).

Latin American visible-minority women have had median employment incomes below the median for visible-minority immigrant women and, since the recession of 1990, Chinese and multiple-origin visible-minority women have also earned low incomes. Our analysis does not indicate the causes for the growing numbers of visible-minority immigrants earning low employment incomes, but their numbers have increased since 1980, when visible minorities began to dominate immigration to Canada. The prevalence of low employment incomes among visible-minority immigrants suggests systemic patterns of income discrimination and systemic underemployment for visible minorities.

Men and women from visible-minority and European immigrant groups earn less than the average Canadian-born worker until they have resided in Canada for approximately fifteen years. These trends for immigrants in the Toronto Census Metropolitan Area mirror those described by Ornstein (2000) for residents of the City of Toronto.

Poverty as Indicated by the Low-Income Cut-off (LICO)

Given the trends in unemployment rates and employment incomes, it is not surprising that recent immigrants have a large chance of experiencing poverty in the Toronto Census Metropolitan Area. Unfortunately, the data only allow us to distinguish between the households of immigrants who arrived in Canada before 1986 and those who arrived between 1986 and 1996. In the pre-1986 cohort, 21.2 per cent of immigrant households had incomes below the poverty line.[17] This percentage more than doubles for immigrants who arrived between 1986 and 1996, to 45.4 per cent of all immigrant households. Those who immigrated before 1986 'fared better' than later arrivals, even though the percentage of all immigrant households whose incomes fell below the low-income cut-off is higher than the percentage for Canadian-born households – 23.1 per cent versus 16.7 per cent.

As we might expect on the basis of the earlier analysis of un-employment trends and employment income, visible-minority immigrant households fared worse than immigrant households headed by a primary income earner of European, non-visible-minority origin. More than one-third of immigrant households headed by a visible-minority income earner had incomes below the cut-off (36.9 per cent), more than double the 18.3 per cent for European immigrant households.

Table 4.16
Percentage of households with incomes below LICO by birthplace and visible-minority group, Toronto, 1996

	Canadian-born	Immigrant Pre-1986	Immigrant 1986–96
Total	16.7	21.2	45.4
Non-visible minority	16.3	19.0	36.5
Visible minority	29.8	25.3	48.5
Black	44.1	32.2	59.5
South Asian	26.9	19.3	45.8
Chinese	19.0	22.3	45.1
Southeast Asian	37.4	31.2	55.6
Filipino	36.8	14.1	34.4
Arab/West Asian	32.8	26.2	57.1
Latin American	44.9	36.4	49.8
Other visible minority	16.6	26.2	43.7

Source: Statistics Canada (1999c).

Among visible-minority households, the percentage living in poverty varied substantially among ethnoracial groups. Black, Southeast Asian, Arab/West Asian, and Latin American households had higher percentages of households living in poverty than the visible-minority immigrant population as a whole. These are the same visible-minority groups who had low median employment incomes and high unemployment rates. In general, the percentage of households from each ethnoracial group whose incomes fell below the low-income cut-off is higher among immigrants than among Canadian-born Torontonians. For example, about one-third of Chinese immigrant households had incomes below the cut-off compared with only 19 per cent of Chinese households headed by a Canadian-born primary maintainer (table 4.16).

The exceptions are Black and Latin American immigrants. Being Canadian-born does not reduce the proportions of poor households headed by Black and Latin American income earners. For both ethnoracial groups, the proportions of households reporting incomes below the low-income cut-off are the same for those headed by immigrants and those headed by Canadian-born. For these two visible-minority groups who are 'darkest' in terms of skin colour, race rather than place of birth appears to affect the chances of living in poverty. The poverty rates for Filipino households, in which immigrant households have lower proportions of adults reporting incomes below the cut-off than Canadian-born households, also contradict the notion that the Canadian-born always have higher incomes than immigrants (table 4.15). Many immigrant Filipinos enter Canada as live-in caregivers whose admission depends on a prior guarantee of employment. Although the incomes of live-in caregivers are too low to attract Canadian-born workers, the jobs do ensure a small employment income. Small households dictated by employment contracts that require caregivers to live with their employers may also reduce the chances of living in poverty. Filipinos who are Canadian-born are more likely to experience the same systemic barriers to employment as Blacks and Latin Americans.

Recent arrival increases the chances of living in poverty for immigrant households from all ethnoracial backgrounds. Consistently, the percentages of households with incomes below the low-income cut-off were 1.5 to 3 times higher among immigrants who arrived after 1985 than for those who arrived earlier (table 4.16). The levels of poverty are startling. Among Black, Arab/West Asian, and Southeast Asian households who arrived after 1985, more than half lived in poverty: 59.5 per cent, 57.1 per cent, and 55.6 per cent, respectively. Even among European non-visible-minority immigrants, 36.5 per cent of households who arrived after 1985 lived in poverty.

The size and composition of immigrant households may reduce the likelihood of living in poverty. According to Ley (1999), large immigrant households that include multiple families and adult children pool the incomes of several wage earners and thereby offset the effects of the low employment incomes discussed earlier. Certainly, the percentage of households with multiple wage earners living in poverty was lower than the percentage of households with only one wage earner. The percentages of immigrant households with incomes below the low-income cut-off ranged from 12 per cent for couples without children to 15 per cent for multiple-family households. In every instance, the poverty rates for immigrant households exceeded those for Canadian-born households, although the differences in the percentages of households living in poverty were smaller for large households with many adults than for couples with children and single-parent households.

Household composition magnifies the effects of period of immigration in the likelihood that single-parent immigrant households and unattached immigrants are living in poverty. The percentages of small immigrant households who arrived after 1985 and were living in poverty ranged from 69.1 per cent of single-parent households to 54.1 per cent of unattached individuals. Among couples with children and multiple-family households, 43.1 per cent and 26.4 per cent of households who arrived after 1985 had incomes below the low-income cut-off.

The differences in poverty rates among ethnoracial groups are sometimes small compared with the effects of household composition and recency of arrival. For example, 69.1 per cent of single-parent immigrant households that arrived between 1986 and 1996 live in poverty; the percentages of single-parent households living in poverty were almost identical for visible-minority immigrants and those of European, non-visible minority status, 69.5 per cent and 67.5 per cent, respectively. We can see the same results among unrelated individuals, whose poverty rates for visible-minority and European immigrants were equally high, 55.7 per cent and 50.2 per cent, respectively. Ethnoracial differences were more noticeable for recently arrived immigrant households with more potential wage earners. It is important to remember that fewer of these households have incomes below the low-income cut-off. For example, among couples without children who arrived between 1986 and 1996, the percentage of visible-minority households living in poverty was 39.1 per cent, much higher than the 26.5 per cent for European households. Differences of similar magnitude were found between visible-minority and European non-visible-minority households consisting of multiple families and couples with children and additional people (table 4.17).

Two major patterns emerge from the analysis. First, recent immigrants have higher unemployment rates, lower employment incomes, and a greater tendency to be poor than earlier immigrants, and also fare worse than Canadian-born residents of Toronto. Second, visible-minority immigrants often fare worse than European non-visible-minority immigrants, even after the effects of the period of immigration are considered. The findings raise an important question regarding the integration of immigrants. At what length of residence do immigrants experience the same or better economic circumstances than the Canadian-born population? Depending on the indicator, parity between immigrants and Canadian-born workers occurs at different times. Immigrants who arrived before 1971 had low unemployment rates that were similar to those of the Canadian-born Torontonians. The median employment incomes and poverty rates of immigrants who arrived

Table 4.17
Immigrant households below LICO by visible-minority status, period of arrival, and household type, Toronto, 1996

Household Type	Unattached Individuals Pre-1986	Unattached Individuals 1986–1996	Couples without children Pre-1986	Couples without children 1986–1996	Couples with children Pre-1986	Couples with children 1986–1996	Single-parent households Pre-1986	Single-parent households 1986–1996	Couples with children & others Pre-1986	Couples with children & others 1986–1996	Multiple family households Pre-1986	Multiple family households 1986–1996
Non-visible minority	40.5	50.2	13.3	26.5	9.3	31.0	24.2	67.5	7.0	20.4	8.1	17.5
Visible minority	43.1	55.7	20.1	39.1	15.4	48.3	44.7	69.5	11.5	34.7	11.3	27.3
Black	40.8	60.7	15.0	39.3	15.8	49.3	49.1	75.0	11.4	41.8	9.7	34.6
South Asian	40.3	50.0	18.6	39.8	14.2	50.7	34.9	62.9	12.9	34.7	10.6	29.5
Chinese	47.0	55.4	24.2	43.2	14.7	47.2	30.3	59.1	11.5	37.3	13.2	29.1
Southeast Asian	45.5	60.4	16.6	32.2	23.5	53.2	66.9	81.9	14.0	31.9	9.4	22.4
Filipino	30.5	41.1	19.3	23.4	7.1	32.8	28.3	63.8	4.2	21.5	7.2	15.7
Arab/West Asian	43.0	61.9	21.0	46.4	19.4	59.1	46.8	68.1	12.0	41.8	16.3	29.1
Latin American	52.2	51.6	17.8	31.3	26.4	47.2	59.2	76.9	16.7	24.9	21.4	20.0
Other visible minority	50.7	56.5	24.9	34.6	15.5	41.3	39.4	60.8	12.0	34.2	8.4	18.9
Total	41.3	54.1	14.6	34.6	11.5	43.1	34.6	69.1	9.4	32.8	9.8	26.4

Source: Statistics Canada (1999c).

before 1980 were also similar to those of the Canadian-born. Although not conclusive, the data suggest that it probably takes immigrants about fifteen years to be 'on par' with the Canadian-born. In other words, socio-economic parity with the Canadian-born population, a primary indicator of social inclusion, is achieved after ten to fifteen years of residence in Canada.

The high levels of unemployment, low employment incomes, and high poverty levels experienced by many visible-minority immigrants have persisted since 1980. Our analysis does not indicate the causes of visible-minority immigrants' economic disadvantage, but, the overall economic picture for visible-minority immigrants is bleak. The trends are unexpected to improve, in light of recent government efforts to recruit more qualified and well-educated immigrants. The 1996 data may not have captured the impact of this policy change. An alternative and far more troubling explanation is that visible-minority immigrants are the victims of racial discrimination and systemic barriers in the Toronto labour market.

Our analysis reveals differences in the economic circumstances among visible-minority immigrant groups themselves. Specifically, Korean, Black, Southeast Asian, Arab/West Asian, and Latin American visible-minority immigrants have higher unemployment rates, lower incomes, and higher poverty rates than other visible-minority immigrants. The economic achievements of Chinese, multiple-visible-minority, and other-visible-minority immigrants are representative of all visible-minority immigrants, while Japanese, Filipino, and Southeast Asian immigrants are more successful than all visible-minority immigrants. The various economic attainments of different visible-minority immigrant groups suggests that minority status and the discrimination that often accompanies it is only one of the factors contributing to the economic exclusion of visible-minority immigrants: gender, period of immigration, and household composition also influence economic attainments. However, more detailed information is needed to specify the interactions between these demographic characteristics and the effects of visible-minority status and immigrant status.

CONCLUSIONS

Our analyses demonstrate that immigrants contribute to the Toronto economy through market participation, income generation, and job creation. The empirical findings indicate that upward mobility is still intact for immigrants as a whole. On average, employment incomes improve and unemployment and poverty rates decline with increased length of residence in Canada. In the long run, immigrants have achieved social inclusion in terms of economic criteria. It is, however, disappointing that it takes immigrants fifteen to twenty years to achieve economic parity with the Canadian-born population. Immigrants who arrived after 1980 are also suffering unacceptably high poverty and unemployment rates. Visible-minority immigrants and immigrant women also have relatively low employment incomes. Among small immigrant households, particularly single-parent households, poverty rates are outrageous. The jury is out as to whether the economic attainments of these immigrant cohorts will improve. Their current economic problems may be due to cyclical trends. Since 1980, Toronto has suffered two recessions, the most severe and far-reaching occurring in 1990 and 1991 (Norcliffe 1996). Immigrants in Toronto may be bearing the brunt of local economic decline that only reversed after the census was collected in the last half of the 1990s. More troubling is the alternative possibility that structural changes in the labour market, such as increased competition from Canadian-born workers whose educational attainments have improved substantially, and systemic discrimination towards visible-minority immigrants may be contributing to immigrants' current economic stagnation.

Our findings underscore the heterogeneity of immigrants' economic experiences. We found a number of intergroup and intragroup patterns in both paid employment and self-employment. With only a few exceptions, recent immigrants work in a wider range of industries and experience higher unemployment rates and lower incomes than earlier immigrant counterparts. As yet, the varied industries of employment in which recent immigrants work have not insulated them from the effects of the economic downturn in Toronto at the beginning of the 1990s, as we might have expected. Moreover, the industrial division of labour for immigrants is still tilted towards manufacturing and construction for the employed and towards retail and personal services for the self-employed and entrepreneurs. Although certain manufacturing subsectors, for example, computer manufacturing, may be expanding, other manufacturing subsectors are still contracting. While the economic prospects of immigrant workers clearly depend on the subsector in which they are working, the continued reliance on work in the manufacturing and personal service sectors, where many jobs are poorly paid and insecure and where many businesses experience low returns, has probably contributed to the economic stagnation suffered by immigrants who arrived after 1979.

The disappointing experiences of recent immigrants suggest that it may be useful to review the assistance provided during the initial phases of settlement. We need to determine if current settlement programs in Toronto prepare recent immigrants for the contemporary job market, in which greater educational, skill, and language requirements are the norm (Reitz 1998). In Australia, the provision of specialized language training designed for physicians, nurses, engineers, and other professionals has facilitated accreditation and recognition of foreign credentials enabling immigrants to re-engage in their chosen professions (Hawthorne 1999). It may be useful to adapt these programs to the Canadian context.

Some recent immigrants may require more assistance than others. European immigrants fare better on our economic indicators than visible-minority immigrants. Many visible-minority immigrant groups have below-average self-employment and business participation rates, above-average unemployment and poverty rates, and below-average median employment incomes. For example, Blacks have low self-employment rates, low employment incomes, and high levels of poverty; Koreans and visible-minority Latin Americans have low employment incomes; and West Asians have high levels of poverty. Effective strategies are needed to reduce the current gap between the incomes and unemployment rates of European and visible-minority immigrants. The task, however, is complex. Incomes and employment rates do not increase regularly with years of residence in Canada, although business participation rates may. The complicated relationships between incomes and unemployment rates, on the one hand, and length of residence, on the other, illustrate the need for sophisticated policies that take into account the diverse immigrant realities. These policies may have to include regulation of systemic labour market barriers, as well as settlement programs.

Immigrants' economic attainments often depend on access to a number of public programs. The changes in the provision of language training illustrates the importance of considering how policies affect immigrants' chances. In the early 1990s, Citizenship and Immigration Canada attempted to increase the availability of language-training courses by eliminating training, transportation, and child-care allowances and redirecting the funds to providing more language classes. Subsequent research demonstrated that, without the allowances, many women were unable to attend language training (Preston and Man 1999).The interrelationships among settlement services, public education initiatives, skills-development programs, and other settlement infrastructure need to be considered when services are being designed.

The example of language training also indicates how gender affects the connections between the economic indicators: unemployment, incomes, and poverty, recency of immigration, and visible-minority status. In general, immigrant women are less successful economically than immigrant men. The impact of gender is apparent in every ethnoracial group and across immigrants from all periods of immigration. For example, visible-minority and non-visible-minority European immigrant women have higher unemployment rates than their male counterparts. Among recent immigrants, who arrived between 1991 and 1996, women have much lower median employment incomes than men. The disparity between the economic achievements of immigrant men and those of immigrant women point to inadequate settlement policies that fail to take into account men's and women's different domestic roles and the gender division of labour in paid employment.

The wide gaps among immigrant cohorts suggest that service agencies should have a repertoire of strategies targeted to each demographic component of their communities. To target services successfully, government funding formulae may need to permit more local autonomy, while requiring increased representation for immigrants themselves in the policy process. More attention to community consultations with immigrant groups and inclusion of immigrants themselves in the governing bodies of service agencies are essential first steps to designing and implementing services that will reduce the employment barriers faced by recent immigrants, visible-minority immigrants, and immigrant women. Variations in business participation rates among immigrant groups may indicate the presence of similar institutional barriers to business development. Financial institutions and federal and provincial agencies should implement policies promoting business development by recent immigrants.

The varied experiences of immigrants reveal the incongruity between immigration selection policies and integration policies. The concentration of many working immigrants in manufacturing and other declining sectors and the long period of time required for immigrants to achieve parity in income and employment are two indications that the skills and work experiences of many immigrants carefully selected under the current points system are not fully utilized. The seeming inability of self-employed and investor immigrants to achieve comparable economic status as the employed points to the possibility of problems in the administration and management of our business immigration programs. The underutilization of a skilled immigrant labour force has adverse implications for national productivity, regional and local economic development, and commercial and consumer markets.

Education is a good predictor of immigrants' partial economic contributions. When we only take into account income and use of social benefits, economic immigrants are more likely than other classes of immigrants to make positive net economic contributions to the Canadian economy in the short run. However, our findings demonstrate conclusively that over time, all classes of immigrants – economic, family reunification, and humanitarian – make positive net economic contributions, even according to our limited measures. A fuller accounting may well uncover earlier economic benefits from all classes of immigrants.

Further Research

To effectively address the current economic difficulties facing immigrants, researchers need more detailed information about immigrants' employment experiences. Census information adequately describes aggregate trends in the labour market, but qualitative research examining the work histories of immigrants is needed to understand the social and economic processes that contribute to their persistent vulnerability in the Toronto labour market. Research should consider the work histories of immigrants who have succeeded in obtaining remunerative jobs commensurate with their qualifications, as well as of those who struggle to find and keep appropriate employment. Such comparative research may reveal the factors contributing to economic success and inclusion more readily than many previous studies that have concentrated on the least successful immigrants.

The emergence of a large immigrant middle class and the expansion of the immigrant working class, together with the growth of a variety of ethnic economies and varying degrees of ethnic niching and economic incorporation, provide a rich context for studies of immigrant entrepreneurship. However, the activities of only a few groups have been studied and compared. Little is known about the determinants of entrepreneurialism and its relative merits in the Canadian context. We still do not know what social and economic factors promote entrepreneurialism among immigrants from different backgrounds. A few studies have examined social barriers to entrepreneurship, but none have considered policy or institutional barriers. We need comparative research focusing on the interplay between ethnicity, race, and gender and successful entrepreneurialism. In particular, the role of women has hardly been discussed.

The role of space and place in ethnic entrepreneurship has also been overlooked. We do not know the significance of changes in the locations of ethnic economies. For example, the reasons for the relocation of Italian businesses from Kensington Market to Corso Italia and most recently, to the northern suburbs of the Toronto metropolitan area, as well as the impact of relocation, are open to interpretation. The assumption is that businesses followed the Italian population's move to the suburbs. However, much residential development in Toronto's outer suburbs is preceded by commercial development. This pattern of development suggests that the suburbanization of Toronto's Italian population may be due in part to the relocation of the community's ethnic economy. The meaning of changes in the location of an ethnic economy is also unclear. Does a change in location indicate that the ethnic economy is becoming more diversified and more integrated into the larger urban economy? What factors contribute to the persistence of ethnic economies at one location, even as one immigrant group is succeeded by another? How do changes in the locations and sizes of ethnic economies affect the relations among immigrant groups?

Our study demonstrates that regardless of their entry status, all immigrants and refugees contribute to the Canadian economy. This is a significant finding because our analysis has not taken into account many forms of economic contributions, both tangible and intangible. Among the most significant may be the contributions of immigrants to establishing and maintaining international business links. A full accounting in this area is likely to underscore the importance and magnitude of immigrants' contributions to the Canadian economy. All contributions need to be considered in light of recent recommendations that Canada's immigration program be designed to maximize its economic impacts (Citizenship and Immigration Canada 1998).

Our research has highlighted the diversity of immigrant experiences in Toronto's economy, a story of differential inclusion and exclusion. Recent immigrants, immigrant women, and many, but not all, visible-minority immigrant groups are experiencing economic difficulties. Immigrants from European countries who arrived in Canada before 1980 report remarkable economic achievements. Additional research is needed to specify the processes contributing to the economic difficulties of some immigrants and the economic success of others. The research imperative is urgent. While economic success is only one aspect of social inclusion, it is of increasing importance in contemporary Toronto. Reductions in social assistance, combined with cut-backs in public services, mean the burden of integration is increasingly borne by immigrants themselves. In this context, a better understanding of the factors that facilitate the economic success of immigrants is essential to developing policies and programs that will foster social inclusion of all immigrants.

Notes

1 We wish to acknowledge detailed comments from Dan Hiebert, A.R. Richmond, and two anonymous reviewers who helped us to restructure and improve the chapter. Dr Hiebert's commentary on an earlier version was especially helpful. We alone are responsible for any errors and omissions that remain. This chapter is a greatly revised version of an earlier working paper entitled 'Immigrants' Economic Status in Toronto: Rethinking Settlement and Integration Strategies,' by Lucia Lo, Valerie Preston, Shuguang Wang, Katherine Reil, Edward Harvey, and Bobby Siu. We are grateful for the assistance of Michael Romeiro, Derrek Eberts, Andy Charles, and Susan Rainey.
2 In 1994, in response to criticism from opposition parties and the public, the Liberal Government of Canada launched a nation-wide consultation for revision of Canada's immigration program. During the eight-month-long consultation with more than ten thousand Canadians, the immigration minister at the time, Sergio Marchi, was told repeatedly that economic impacts of immigrants were the most important public concern and, therefore, should be the primary consideration in immigration policy-making and reform. Specifically, Canadians who were consulted expressed clearly that, while our society welcomes immigrants, it does not want to accept immigrants who will be supported by taxpayers. They argued that Canada needs immigrants whose education, language, and job skills allow them to adjust quickly to changes in the labour market (*Bill Graham Report* 1994). As a result of the consultation, the immigration minister introduced the federal government's long-term immigration strategy with adjusted selection criteria in 1995. The most significant change was to tighten the defini-

tion of family class to make it harder to sponsor parents and grandparents as landed immigrants, and to allow the government to use quotas to bring in more economic immigrants – skilled workers, entrepreneurs, and investors. A landing fee of $975 was also introduced for all landed immigrants, including refugees. (In a news release on February 28, 2000, Citizenship and Immigration Canada announced it would abolish the landing fee for refugees only. The fee remains for all other immigrants.)

3 This section is a short version of a longer paper first published by Shuguang Wang and Lucia Lo, 'Economic Impacts of Immigrants in the Toronto CMA: A Tax-Benefit Analysis,' *Journal of International Migration and Integration* 1, no. 3: 273–303. The shortened version is used in this chapter with *JIMI*'s permission.

4 The database consists of several relational databases maintained by Citizenship and Immigration Canada and Statistics Canada. Two special tabulations were analysed in this section. The first provides detailed information on demographic, social, and economic characteristics of all the immigrants in the Toronto CMA who landed between 1980 and 1995, including immigration class, age, gender, family status, country of last permanent residence, and level of education at time of immigration. The second tabulation, based on the 1995 federal tax returns filed by the same immigrants, contains total income, employment income, self-employment income, investment income, federal income tax, social welfare benefit, unemployment insurance benefit, and number of immigrants who reported each type of income, tax, and benefit. Provincial income tax was not included in the original database, but it was easily recovered using the rate of 58 per cent of federal income tax, which was provided in the 1995 Ontario Tax Return Guide. The IMDB contains detailed information about most of the immigrants who have settled in Toronto, however, it does not include immigrants residing in Toronto while their claims to refugee status are being adjudicated, students, and other temporary residents.

5 In 1996, UI was changed to EI – employment insurance.

6 The proportion of immigrants reporting income tax and welfare dependency rates are calculated for the immigrants who were 15 to 80 years old in 1995 (those above 80 are excluded to control mortality effect), whereas UI usage rate is calculated for those who were 15 to 65 in 1995, as they were the immigrants legally eligible for UI benefits in that year. In consideration that some immigrants might have moved out of the Toronto CMA after they first landed here, rates of secondary migration are estimated for each subgroup using a similar IMDB table for the province of Ontario. The

Ontario table records the number of immigrants who originally landed in Ontario, but were residents of other provinces in 1995. Using the Ontario data, various emigration rates were calculated for each subgroup of immigrants and applied to the Toronto study. While not perfect, they are the best estimates possible.

7 Statistics for the general population of Canada are also for those 15 years of age and over. They are calculated from the following sources: Minister of Industry (1998a and 1998b); Minister of National Revenue (1998); National Council of Welfare (1997); and Revenue Canada (1995).

8 Unless otherwise stated, all data are from the 1996 Public Use Microdata Sample that provides detailed information about individuals residing in the Toronto Census Metropolitan Area. For more information, see Statistics Canada (1999a).

9 The typology of industries was largely dictated by the information available in the Public Use Microdata Sample. To increase sample size and facilitate comparison with previous research, information is reported for thirteen industries. Following the typology proposed by Stanback and Noyelle (1984), service industries are combined into ten categories: distributive services that include wholesale trade and the regulated transportation, communications, utilities industries, producer services that include business services and finance, insurance and real estate services, social services that consist of health and social services, government administration, education, and finally, consumer services that include retail trade, accommodation, food and beverage services, and all other services not classified elsewhere.

10 The marked gender division of labour means it is more appropriate and more informative to compare immigrant women's employment patterns with those of Canadian-born women than with those of the total labour force. The value of location quotients range from 0.0 upwards. A value of 1.0 indicates that the two proportions are identical, while values less than 1.0 reveal that immigrant women's proportion of employment in the industry is less than that of Canadian-born women. Values greater than 1.0 reveal an overrepresentation of immigrant women in the industry.

11 The aggregate information may mask substantial differences in the propensity for self-employment among immigrants from different birthplaces and ethnoracial groups (Reitz 1998).

12 Location quotients were also calculated in which the divisor was the proportion of all Canadian-born workers in an industry. The resulting location quotients largely reflected the effects of gender, rather than ethnoracial

origin. The small size of the samples for several ethnoracial origins meant it was impossible to compare separately immigrant and Canadian-born workers from the same ethnoracial background.
13 Relationships were tested by t-tests of proportions calculated for each period of arrival.
14 For each period of arrival, the numbers of immigrant men and women working in each industry were computed. Chi-squared tests were then calculated.
15 The first group includes Jewish and charter-group immigrants in the financial, insurance, and real estate service sectors; the second group includes immigrants from Central and Southern Europe in the construction and manufacturing sectors; and the third group includes African and Asian immigrants in the manufacturing and trade sectors.
16 The socio-economic characteristics of the population used for this study were derived from a 20 per cent sample of households that excluded residents of institutions such as prisons, orphanages, and nursing homes. The analysis uses special tabulations data provided to the Joint Centre of Excellence for Research on Immigration and Settlement–Toronto by Statistics Canada (1999c).
17 LICO measures the proportion of households whose income falls below an absolute amount roughly equal to 56 per cent of the median income for households of similar size living in municipalities of specific sizes. Poverty of households is determined on the assumption that household members pool their incomes.

5 Immigrant Students and Schooling in Toronto, 1960s to 1990s

Carl E. James and Barbara Burnaby

This chapter explores ways in which immigrants and refugees have been inserted into the Toronto educational system, and how immigrants have inserted themselves into the system in their efforts to establish themselves in Canada. With reference to educational policies and programs of governments, school boards, post-secondary institutions, and non-governmental organizations (NGOs) that were designed to address issues arising from the arrival of large numbers of immigrants to Toronto, we present an analysis of trends, over time, of educational outcomes for immigrant learners, particularly young immigrants.[1] These outcomes represent, to the extent possible given the limitations of the available data, a measure of the success of the programs put into place to integrate and accommodate these students. In this context, we will discuss, within a four-decade time frame, educational participation, experiences, aspirations, and outcomes of immigrants and, where information allows, refugees.

Given the complex relationship of race, ethnicity, language, religion, and immigrant and refugee status, as well as the tendency for information and data about immigrants to be confounded by these factors, it is difficult for us to discuss the experiences of, and issues pertaining to, immigrant students without reference to these diverse groupings. Indeed, much of the available information upon which we rely is both about and related to ethnoracial-minority Canadians, some of whom are newcomers and some not. We remain cautious of the conclusions we are able to draw, knowing that what applies for ethnoracial-minority students does not necessarily apply to immigrant students.[2] It is with these cautions in mind, and with an awareness of the importance of obtaining a picture of the issues related to the education of immigrants in Toronto, that we endeavour to represent salient issues regarding the responses of educational institutions to immigrants in Toronto.

Before proceeding, we want to clarify the understanding we bring to the following key terms used in this discussion, because we understand that multiple meanings and issues are embedded in these terms.

In this chapter, the term 'immigrant' refers to recently arrived residents of Canada and to their immediate offspring. This is not to suggest that the offspring of immigrants are not 'Canadians,' with all the attendant cultural nuances. However, we suggest that there are particular issues and needs that evolve from their background growing up with immigrant parents. We also underline that discussing immigrants and refugees collectively is not intended to underestimate the social, economic, and political differences between groups subsumed under those terms. Nevertheless, there are many issues and experiences that they share as newcomers to Canada, and to Toronto in particular. As just noted, it is important to appreciate that immigrants in the city are a widely divergent group, the composition of which is constantly changing both demographically and in many other ways – length of time in the country; gender and age; the social, cultural, and political context into which they are expected to settle (and from which they have come); and their patterns of community and institution-building. We also emphasize that examining the educational needs, issues, interests, experiences, and attainment of immigrants must be considered not only in terms of their status as immigrants but as Canadian citizens who are part of our diverse society.

'Refugees' are taken to be individuals who claim to have, and according to the United Nations Convention have been judged to have, 'a well-founded fear of persecution for reason of race, religion, nationality, or membership in a particular social group or political opinion' that prevents them from living in their country of origin – recognized as 'refugee-producing' – and hence are allowed to settle in Canada (James 1999, 169). Yau (1995) points out that after the initial stages of relief and enthusiasm, refugees undergo a difficult process of adjustment that includes not only the struggle of adapting to a new language and culture but also the reality of dealing with post-traumatic stress and fear; dealing with a precarious residency status during a sometimes long bureaucratic process to ensure their status in Canada; trying to reintegrate their families; frequent relocations; and financial difficulties. While, as Yau found, teachers are often unable to distinguish between refugees and immigrants, there are times, nevertheless, when the physical scars, limited schooling, unusual social behaviours, and poor health of refugees make their differences from immigrants more apparent. James and Haig-Brown (2001), in their research into the experiences of immigrant and refugee university students, demonstrate that it was the refugee students who felt a responsibility to 'give back' to their immediate geographic and ethnic communities and to show their gratitude to the country by 'returning the dues.'

The scope of the term 'education,' for our purposes, has been largely restricted to activities carried out in schools under the Education Act of Ontario and to the first years of university and college programs. We make only brief mention of non-government-funded education programs in schools, colleges, or other institutions such as NGOs (for example, mainstream and ethnic settlement agencies). In light of this restricted scope within the larger field of education, the students we refer to are mostly children or young adults. Because the term education has very wide applications, encompassing most institutions in society, many topics that could be considered educational (such as health and community) are dealt with in other chapters of this book. The more formal and regulated education is, the easier it is to document and assess. However, it should be noted that much of education is also self-directed learning on the part of individuals, a process that is probably not recognized as education elsewhere in this volume, but which we would like, nevertheless, to acknowledge if not explore more fully.

'Policy,' 'activities,' and 'programs' are also important terms in this exploration of immigrants, refugees, and schooling. We interpret policy to mean legislated activities or other programs supported at least in part by government(s). The term activities represents those significant actions on which we report that would not normally be seen as a policy in the formal sense, for example, as in a one-time event. Policies and activities are considered, as much as possible, from the well-documented perspectives and interests of initiators – the state in the form of government and school board policies and programs – as well as from the less well-described perspectives of those affected – the parents, children, and educators. The fact that the interventions are more likely to be documented from the initiators' point of view than from the perspectives of those affected by the policies reflects the relative positions of these stakeholders in initiatives in formal education.

In the first section of this chapter, we discuss the role of education in immigrant-host relations; in the second section, we provide an overview of public initiatives in the education of immigrants in Ontario, in general, and Toronto, in particular, from 1960 to the 1990s. In the third section, we address responses to the educational issues of immigrants and refugees in terms of access to English as a second language (ESL) training for adults, and research on activities, aspirations, and attainments of immigrant and refugee students in Toronto schools, colleges, and universities. Finally, we draw conclusions and suggest implications in terms of policy trends and impacts on educational institutions and their clientele.

THE ROLE OF EDUCATION IN IMMIGRANT-HOST RELATIONS IN TORONTO

Our examination here of the role of education in immigrant-host relations is informed by two key discourses in theory and research. The first focuses on the aspirations and experiences of immigrants; the second, on state-dominated power structures and relations into which immigrants are inserted. Educational institutions are one site where this insertion, or 'integration,' occurs. As we indicated in our definition of the term 'immigrant,' we see that the term masks a great deal of diversity – a diversity we acknowledge while at the same time recognizing, as Ogbu (1983) and others (Kao and Tienda 1995; Gibson 1997; Cummins 1997) have established, that there are some patterns and consistencies among immigrant groups.

A wide range of studies of the aspirations and experiences of immigrants (Anisef et al. 2000; James 1990; Gibson and Ogbu 1991; Ogbu 1991; Lam 1994; Simmons and Plaza 1999), and refugees (Opoku-Dapaah 1995; Yau 1995; Barnhard and Freire 1996; Pacini 1998; James and Haig-Brown 2001) show that many, motivated by what some refer to as 'the immigrant drive' (Anisef et al. 2000), come to Canada hoping for economic and social success for themselves and their children, and are willing to work hard to fulfil this ambition. Correspondingly, with the support of their parents, immigrant children tend to have high educational and occupational aspirations; in some cases, where parents may not succeed in their own ambitions, they seek to ensure that their children do (James 1999). As Moodley (1995) notes:

> On the whole, competence, not culture, is the major concern of minority-group parents. While the two are not mutually exclusive, it is foremost the

mastery of modern knowledge, as well as the retention of functional aspects of their own traditional knowledge, to which parents most aspire (Musgrove 1982). The former serves their instrumental, survival needs, which are the priority in the country of adoption, and the latter their expressive needs, for which they themselves assume responsibility. Whereas diverse cultural inclusion in the school curriculum is an important device for raising the self-concept of minority children, most minority parents see their children as educationally deprived rather than culturally deprived ... In many instances, these expectations [of minority parents for access to mainstream educational success] were the prime reasons for leaving the country of origin. (817)

According to the research and discourse on immigrant aspirations, immigrants generally tend to place confidence in the fact that education will enable them to access opportunities and extend possibilities, thus ensuring attainment of their occupational and/or career goals. To this end, therefore, they hold high educational aspirations with the expectation that, having achieved their goals, they will gain upward social mobility. Given such hopes and expectations, indeed desire, to participate fully and successfully in Canadian society, it is reasonable to assume that immigrants would see the acquiring of Canadian academic credentials as critical. On this basis, we can presume that they would expect to access educational programs and engage with educators who would be responsive to their needs and aspirations during their transition period. The value of education, especially for children but also for adults,[3] then, is axiomatic in contemporary Canadian society. However, in our view, it remains open to question whether education should merit the trust and high expectations of educators and immigrant communities.

The existing policy documents and research reports we refer to in this exploration provide an occasion to reflect on what has been happening in particular areas of education, whether it is fulfilling parent, community, and educator expectations, and what changes in policy and practice might help us to better plan for future generations of immigrants. Clearly, one chapter can do no more than touch the surface of this complexity. This discussion, then, is presented largely through the most visible events supported by selected documents. Where possible, we bring in highlights of research and cover the most prominent aspects into our analysis.

Our discussion is also informed by the discourse on immigrants and the state that emphasizes the dynamics of power and hegemony in structuring relationships between, as well as within, ethnocultural groups. Canada is a society into which immigrants have entered for more than five hundred years, and one to which various ethnic groups have contributed and participated in varying ways. Hence, the 'host society' into which immigrants have entered is one that is culturally diverse and complex, and itself structured by inequitable economic and power relationships. The resultant policies and programs that are set up to accommodate or integrate the immigrant population are likely to be reflective of the relative power and influence of the dominant ethnoracial group, and, importantly, what the ethnoracial-minority groups have managed to negotiate through their struggles against unequal treatment, particularly in the areas of immigration and education. To some extent, then, various 'host ethnoracial' groups have contributed to the development of educational policies and programs that speak to the needs and issues of their respective groups. So while white English-speaking Canadians have been constructed for many centuries as the 'host society,' in fact, the 'host society' has always been heterogeneous and in constant change (James 1999).

This understanding of the heterogeneity and dynamism of the host and immigrant populations is missing from Canada's 'cultural policy' of multiculturalism 'within a bilingual framework,' established in 1971[4] 'as the most suitable means of assuring the cultural freedom of Canadians' and as a way of assisting 'all Canadian cultural groups ... to grow and contribute to Canada.' These 'cultural groups' to which the policy refers are, in fact, racial and ethnic minority Canadians. These minorities are constructed as immigrants whose cultures are static and who have to be 'integrated' into Canadian society, particularly if they wish to acquire 'at least one of Canada's official languages in order to become full participants in Canadian society' (James 1999, 200).

Significant to this integration is the role of education and training, both in meeting the objectives of the state and in understanding and interpreting the needs and aspirations of immigrants. Thus, when Ontario endorsed the policy of multiculturalism in 1977 and established multicultural education policies and programs for its immigrant population, it initially focused on language socialization through language (including dialects) classes. In later years, multicultural programs were based on the promotion of sensitivity to and respect for ethnocultural differences; they were also based on the integration of immigrant minority students using, as Ghosh (1996) points out, 'the dominant educational framework of a monocultural pedagogy in which other [earlier] ethnocultural groups have been accommodated' (1). Evidently, the integration of various immigrant groups into the imagined host group is unrealistic and unjust. Furthermore, as James (2001) argues, the multicultural discourse, with its emphasis on integration into the dominant ethnoracial group culture, has been so pervasive that the educational policies and programs that have been developed over the years have been ineffective in meeting the diverse needs and aspirations of racial and ethnic minority Canadians and immigrants alike (see also Ghosh 1996; Bannerji 1997; Roman and Stanley 1997).

Given this context, therefore, we may ask, Whose specific interests are served by the kinds of policy and program interventions initiated or not initiated for the immigrant population? Is assimilation of immigrants to the mainstream an obvious goal? Are immigrants' specific needs addressed so that they may gain access to mainstream system(s)? Are alternative systems being created and interventions designed for growth and accommodation on the part of the mainstream as well as the immigrant population?

In the next sections, we explore two of these questions: (1) How does or should education merit the trust we have in it to achieve the results expected by so many parties? (2) Whose specific interests are served by the kinds of policy and program interventions initiated or not initiated for the immigrant population? Through an analysis of selected documentation during the period from 1960 to the 1990s, we are able to outline some answers to these questions.

OVERVIEW OF PUBLIC ACTIONS IN THE EDUCATION
OF IMMIGRANTS IN TORONTO

Some of the findings of the first phase of the study by Burnaby, James, and Regier (2000), which we look at here, give us a framework for considering certain actions taken by federal and provincial governments, as well as school boards and NGOs, to deal with issues created by the arrival of immigrants and, to some extent, meeting the needs and interests of the immigrants.

Historical and Social Factors in Response to Diversity in Canada and Toronto

Three factors that have greatly influenced social and educational policy in Canada and Toronto are the centrality of French–English relations, economics, and the constitutional division of powers. The first significant factor in the education policies relating to immigration in Toronto has been the prevailing paradigms or priorities in the country as a whole. In 1867, when the British North America Act was signed as Canada's original constitution, the political focus was on making social and legal provisions that took into account citizens of British and French origins. According to Neatby (1992, v–ix), in the nineteenth century, the legal expression of rights for the 'English' and the 'French' populations focused on religion rather than language, culture, race, class, political affiliation, or other possible distinctions. However, political attention on the identification of differences between groups largely shifted by the middle of the twentieth century to language, and even later there was increased attention focused on culture, race, gender, and sovereignty. This identification is not entirely paralleled in the United States, where, for example, race was a high-profile issue at the same time the central focus in Canada was on language. The point here is that the Canadian federal preoccupation with language in French–English relations has been a powerful influence, although the focus has more recently moved towards sovereignty and race. Most importantly, the ongoing, but changing, character of federal negotiations has influenced a great deal of decision-making at all levels of state-sponsored activities.

A second important factor influencing Canada's immigration policies and actions has been economics. According to Chiswick (1992), 'Economics was more important for shaping immigration policy in Canada than in the United States, and American policies were more closely tied to foreign policy questions than were Canadian ... [Canadian] immigration has been dealt with in the same ministry as manpower or employment matters, whereas most immigration issues are handled by the Justice Department in the United States' (5). As is noted in this chapter and elsewhere in this volume, the federal interest in economics has had varying impacts on immigration policies over time.

Given the importance placed by Canada on the role of immigrants in the labour force, it was to be expected that the training of immigrant adults specifically for roles in the workplace would be a major policy initiative. Also, policies on immigrant selection have been influenced by expectations not only about the effects of immigrants on the economy, but also about the absorptive capacity of the mainstream population in receiving those immigrants. A salient point here is the extent to which government provides enough or the right educational support in preparing the host populations to accept and accommodate the newcomers.

With Canada's focus on language and economics, the accommodation of immigrants, as in most Western countries, has tended to be assimilationist because of the power differential between the newcomers and the mainstream and, sometimes, because of the integrative motivations of some immigrants. Given the current urban, globalized ethos of Western societies, an ability to speak the dominant language of the society afforded priority over all the other ways in which immigrants are pressured to assimilate. In other words, the host country expects immigrants to bring with them transferable skills and knowledge in most aspects of life, but identifies communication in the dominant language as a prerequisite skill and immigrants, on the whole, are expected to meet this prerequisite. Thus, training in English as a Second Language is the major component of education initiatives for non-English-speaking immigrants, as contrasted with skills training, multicultural, or anti-racism initiative in many of the Western, English-dominant countries (Herriman and Burnaby 1996).

A third critical factor in the development of policies and actions on education relating to immigration has been the formal and informal governing structure of the country. In the British North America Act, 1867, and its renewed form, the Constitution Act, 1982, divisions of power between the federal and provincial governments were clearly laid out. Of significance to this discussion is that responsibility for education was vested in the provinces, while responsibility for citizenship and immigration were given to the federal government. In practice, what this division of powers means is that, in situations where issues that relate to both immigration and education arise, responsibility has to be negotiated. Possible approaches to such situations include both sides claiming that the issue is the responsibility of the other; one side or the other negotiating to act on the other's territory; or both sides acting on the issue in a coordinated or uncoordinated way. The division of power between education and immigration is a greater stumbling block for accommodating diversity in Toronto than are the federal–provincial divisions of power related to the other areas covered in this volume.

More fundamental than this constitutional particularity is the impact of demographics and political activity on the voting potential of various groups in the population of a democratic society, with each level of government having a different mix of voters within its constituency. Thus, the facts and issues considered in this chapter are strongly influenced by the perceived and real voting and political lobbying power of the immigrant population as a whole or of groups within each level. Throughout the period under consideration, changes occurred in the proportions of immigrants in Toronto, their characteristics, (for example, race, level of education, past political experience), and the numbers who had obtained the right to vote. Communities of immigrants have also developed various levels of institutional development along ethnic lines (Breton 1990), including organizing political bodies to act on their own behalf. This factor, while not elaborated on in this discussion, has contributed to policy development over time in this city.

Demographic characteristics and economics have influenced Canadian immigration and settlement policy and how the host population receives immigrants. The learning of official languages by immigrants has been the highest priority in the training of immigrants. The constitutional division of power, giving education to the provinces and immigration to the federal government, has resulted in complex struggles in the arrangement of educational interventions for immigrants. The changing demographic and social character of immigrant communities continues to exert fluctuating influences on local and central political scenes. These are some of the many factors in the political economy of Toronto that provide a complex, rich, and active matrix in which to search for immigration and education patterns.

An Overview of Government Agencies, Educational Policies, and Public Actions

In the 1960s, the majority of the federal government's voter base did not urge support for immigrants; indeed, the federal government was under pressure to support national unity (assimilate immigrants and even express xenophobia) and labour development. Thus, the federal government managed to hide its expenditure on immigrant education (all for adults) from public notice. Instead, political attention in terms of language, culture, and national unity was focused on French–English relations, the Royal Commissions on Bilingualism and Biculturalism (drawing on many sources of expertise in intergroup relations), and the Official Languages Act, 1969. On these matters, the government was under intense pressure from voters, and every detail of the implementation of the Official Languages Act was closely watched. Any deviation of federal attention from supporting the status of the French language, such as supporting ESL for immigrant children or the retention of heritage languages (languages other than English, French, or Aboriginal languages), was avoided.

The Government of Ontario, like the federal government, receives little voter pressure to support immigrant needs and interests. Exceptions included a few constituencies with high numbers of immigrants. Ontario constrained its reactions to the impact of immigration on education to the Education Act, which was a particular target of public interest during the baby-boom years (the 1950s to the 1970s). The provincial government probably became more aware of issues that could be contentious through the school boards and NGOs, which reported on issues of language, culture, access, and racism arising in schools and the community, than through the electorate. Individual school boards, schools, and teachers, having no ready-made models to refer to, researched and created responses based on their own experiences. The province responded with some services for adult immigrants, teacher training, and considered designated funding for school boards with special needs. It avoided any solution that would influence the structure of the Education Act, such as creating policy on ESL for schools or even hiring department staff with ESL expertise, since that would raise the issue in the public consciousness and might create long-term obligations for spending specifically on immigrants. The Royal Commission on Bilingualism and Biculturalism (1970) hinted at federal funding for ESL for immigrant children, but this was not forthcoming.

Expertise for deciding what kinds of interventions would be effective was scarce at most levels in this educational scenario. The people who had and were developing experience in the field were the front-line personnel in the schools and NGOs. Academia had no appropriate pedagogical solutions. Theories about second-language teaching for adults were evolving in the United States and Britain along rigid linguistic and psychological lines. They were largely based in theory, or were developed from situations of adults learning English as a foreign language overseas or in American and British graduate schools. Questions of how marginalized groups of children could access mainstream institutions, much less the concept of the mainstream institutions integrating diversity, were not directly addressed.

If we assume that mainstream institutions in the simplest terms wanted immigrants to fit into the social and economic life of the country to the benefit of mainstream goals, and that immigrants wanted access to the social and economic life of the country but not at the cost of their essential identity and values, then any attempt to resolve differences arising out of this scenario could result in a virtually bottomless pit of human and/or economic costs to be paid by both or either side. The responses from mainstream institutions – at least the ones we can easily document – were (1) to provide minimal resources, mostly directed at assimilation; (2) to minimize the public visibility of these actions; (3) to avoid entrenching these gestures in instruments such as legislation that would be hard to change; and (4) to maintain control of the amount spent so that willingness to spend, rather than need, dictated the budget.

Throughout the 1970s, the federal government maintained the low profile of its funding for immigrant education, again only for adults. A major federal priority was the implementation of the Official Languages Act; it supported French and English schooling and second-official-language learning in terms of the Act, but there was still no federal funding for immigrant children who spoke neither French nor English. The federal multiculturalism policy of 1971 failed in its promise to support ESL and FSL for immigrants, although for a time it funded projects to develop non-official languages through school programs. However, public sympathy for refugees made it possible to launch the Immigrant Settlement and Adaptation Program, which provided settlement services through NGOs. Clearly, more pluralist influences were reaching the government and taking their place alongside the older, more assimilationist ones.

In Ontario, specific needs in the education of immigrants as communicated through school boards and NGOs were forcing the provincial government to take overt action. The Ministry of Education normalized ESL teacher training for teachers with certificates, published ESL guidelines for high-school courses, and provided extra funding for school boards with high immigrant populations. It became embroiled in a conflict, largely with the Board of Education for the City of Toronto, over the teaching of heritage languages. The result was a guideline for a Heritage Languages Program, but the ministry resisted pressure from that board to make changes in the Education Act that would allow non-official languages as medium of instruction.

One outcome of the 1970s was the professionalization of ESL teachers. Their skills were officially recognized for employment purposes through the school boards and, to some extent, in other educational institutions. ESL teacher training for certified teachers and others was expanded and consolidated and, with help from the Citizenship Branch, ESL teachers organized their own professional organization. Another development was the growth and expansion of NGOs to provide language training and settlement services that provincial and federal levels of government wanted to provide through them. While this served to move many educational and settlement services into the community where immigrants could better access them, it also created the risk of dependency by NGOs on core, sustained funding. NGOs lobbied governments on issues related to immigrants, and were consulted to a considerable extent by the 'softer' units in government such as the Settlement Branch of the Canada Employment and Immigration Commission (CEIC) and the Newcomer Services Branch of the Ontario Ministry of Culture and Recreation and, to a great extent, by school boards.

In the 1980s, public awareness of immigration and concern about changes in the economy forced governments to openly recognize literacy and language issues for marginalized groups, such as non-English-speaking immigrants and people with low levels of literacy. However, particularly at the federal level, ESL support was kept strictly apart from adult literacy so that ESL learners would not (be seen to) be filling up adult literacy programs. Apparently, government still felt that it would be more popular to support a domestically created 'problem' (literacy) than one related to 'imported problems' through immigration. The same could not be said of the schools in Ontario, where it appears that a large proportion of non-English-speaking immigrant children were still being treated as if they had the same kinds of language problems as mother-tongue English-speaking children. Concerns about the economy were also appearing in calls for deficit reduction through cuts in federal government spending on social programs. NGOs stood to be weakened in a market in which they were forced to compete with one another with no core funding and potentially high demands for accountability.

Also in the 1980s, the Canadian Charter of Rights and Freedoms (1982) required that attention be paid to matters of equity, and provided recourse through the courts. On the federal side, the most visible result seemed to be the Canadian Multiculturalism Act, which concentrated on general equity matters. The local school boards finally settled their dispute with the Ministry of Education over heritage-language teaching, but the ministry managed this without making changes to the Education Act and without letting heritage languages become a significant part of any school's curriculum. Lobbying by local school boards and national organizations for federal funding of ESL classes for elementary- and secondary-school immigrant children went unheeded.

By the end of the 1990s, racial, ethnic, and linguistic diversity was still increasing in Toronto, and the lack of coordination and coherence among programs for immigrants was intensifying. At the beginning of the new millennium, not much in the federal multiculturalism program relates to education, but anti-racism and equity work at the level of the provincial government, the Ministry of Education and Training, and the school boards is evident. The heritage language programs are holding their own in schools with community links, and they can now be offered at the secondary level for credit.

As for ESL and standard English as a second dialect (ESD) in schools, the structure and size of programs and their applications are very difficult to analyse because of the ways in which data on them are or are not kept. Administrators feel, however, that ESL programs are adequate, but that ESD and FSL programs are not. Changes in the numbers and characteristics of immigrant students entering the school system bring increased pressures to schools. While schools in Toronto are making efforts to deal with equity and economic issues, students see more that can be done. As with adult ESL programming, research is greatly needed on the relationship between supply of and demand for programs, and, especially, on needs as perceived and expressed by students themselves.

Between the 1960s and the 1990s, major changes were made at all levels of government and in other social organizations with respect to openness to and action on the presence of immigrants in Toronto. Overall, governments' attitudes changed from regarding immigrants as a necessary evil and foreign threat to regarding them seriously as an important economic and social force affecting Canadian society as a whole. At the same time, the devolution of responsibility from more to less senior levels of government has had implications for service provision. Programs and policies addressing immigrants' needs and interests are vastly more numerous than they were in the 1960s and somewhat more sensitive to the new social reality. Nonetheless, much more needs to be done.

EDUCATIONAL NEEDS AND ISSUES: INTERPRETATIONS AND EXPERIENCE

In this chapter, five main areas illustrate the ways in which the educational needs and issues of immigrants and refugees have been accommodated by federal, provincial, and non-government organizations. The first is the professionalization and then discounting of teachers of ESL for immigrant adults, the history of which strongly reflects the changing valuations of immigrants over the decades, as well as changing economic times and government strategies. The second is the research that has been done and not done to assess the impacts of various educational programs for immigrants since the 1960s, and the possible reasons for either action or inaction. The third encompasses the studies conducted by the Toronto Board of Education that report on the experiences, aspirations, and attainments of students, and, in particular, of racial- and ethnic-minority, immigrant, and refugee students. We spend considerable time exploring this research since we believe that, starting in 1970, the Toronto Board of Education (TBE) has provided the most comprehensive data on the ethnocultural, ethnoracial, and linguistic backgrounds of students (excluding adults) attending school in the Toronto area. (Note that this material refers to actions prior to the 1998 merger of the various school boards to become the Toronto District School Board as per the Fewer School Boards Act of 1997.) The fourth covers studies that were conducted by independent researchers who attempted to provided some interpretations of the experiences and situation of immigrant, ethnic- and racial-minority students in Toronto schools that have high proportions of immigrant students. The fifth explores how colleges and universities have responded to the post-secondary needs, interests, and aspirations of students.

Access to English Language Training through Government and Non-Government Programs

ESL programs for adult immigrants developed in Canada early in the twentieth century with programs offered by NGOs and school boards. Federal government funding entered the scene, administered under provincial government auspices, in the 1940s with an agenda of assimilating immigrants and readying them for the labour force. When the economic boom of the 1960s and 1970s slowed down and the need for labour changed, the federal government began to alter its granting structure so that educational delivery agencies had to compete for ESL and training contracts. Throughout this period, ESL teaching came into being as a distinct form of teaching, was professionalized in the 1970s, but then suffered a decline in job security and professional status as a result of policy changes.

The early-twentieth-century programs for teaching English to immigrants were run by non-governmental organizations such as Frontier College, the YMCA, churches (Pal 1993; Burnaby 1998a), school boards, and individual citizens. Federal policy created a series of programs in 1947 called the Citizenship and Language Instruction and Language Textbook Agreements (CILT) to fund adult ESL in school boards and NGOs through provincial departments of education. One part of the program paid the entire cost of textbooks for citizenship and language classes, while the other paid half of the direct costs for instruction. The ostensible focus was preparing immigrants with the language, knowledge, and allegiance to pass the citizenship test, but it is difficult to know how this intention actually translated into class-room instruction. It is almost impossible to trace the expenditures under this program, nor can we tell what volume of ESL programming and orientation training generated through CILT was actually delivered. Demand for both ESL and settlement information by immigrants certainly exceeded supply. In line with constitutional provisions, the federal government stood back from the provincial responsibilities of deciding the educational content of such programs and from delivering the services.

In 1967, the federal government, concerned about human resources for the country's booming economy, built into the Immigration Act an emphasis not only on the selection of the most suitable workers but also on the provinces' cooperation in bearing the costs of immigration. A year earlier, in 1966, the government had created what will be called here the Manpower ESL program, providing funding for a range of full-time occupational and pre-occupational training for immigrant and other Canadian adults. In taking this step, the federal government came close to trespassing on the provincial governments' constitutional rights to education, but sidestepped the problem by retaining the right of federal officials to select the students and by purchasing the training from provincial organizations (A. Thomas 1987, 112). The ESL for immigrants component, in which ESL students received about twenty-four weeks of full-time training with a living allowance, comprised a considerable proportion of the training offered. These programs were in very high demand by immigrants because of the training allowance and the possibility of being sent for further training after the basic ESL course was finished.

The province of Ontario had to find ways of implementing these two federal initiatives for adults (CILT and Manpower ESL), as well as responding to the needs of immigrant children and their teachers in the school system. The Ministry of Education did not have a policy on accommodating immigrants, nor did it have experts in this field among its staff. It was up to the school boards to deal with specific issues such as ESL, but like the Ministry of Education, these teachers and administrators had little expertise with ESL other than-on-the-job experience gained by actually working with immigrant students (Mewhort et al. 1965). NGOs such as the settlement houses, however, continued to provide and develop expertise and models for teaching ESL from their own work in this area.

With the incentive of CILT funding, in the late 1950s, the provincial government created a Citizenship Branch of the provincial office of the Secretary of State that initiated, among other programs, a series of supports for ESL teachers of adults such as newsletters, conferences, and textbooks. In the 1960s, it also piloted ESL classes for immigrant parents and preschool children, taught by volunteers who were trained by ESL and preschool program supervisors under contract. In school boards, a good deal of what became adult ESL in evening and adult day classes started with adaptations of adult basic education and business English classes. The Toronto Board of Education had three adult day schools for academic-upgrading subjects and basic business-related courses. In 1965, one school was dedicated to teaching ESL to adults on a full-time basis; other adults took ESL in evening classes in schools. In 1958, the Ministry of Education started a summer program to train ESL teachers, employing the expertise of members of the Citizenship Branch, many of whom had had experience in teaching adult ESL. Throughout the 1960s, the students in these courses were mostly people intending to teach adults, although a growing number of elementary and secondary teachers took the course (Mewhort et al. 1965, 42).

Although the focus on training teachers of adults was clear, since the students were not required to have a teaching certificate, it was not clear what teaching methods should be presented. Academia had few appropriate pedagogical approaches at that time, and the people who had developed experience in the field were the front-line personnel in the NGOs and the schools. As we will see, however, the professional standing of teachers in these adult programs, at one time the pedagogical pioneers in the field, would eventually be eroded by subsequent government restructuring of funding and the changes in ESL programs for adults, which the new funding structures entailed.

In 1970, the Citizenship Branch supported the creation of TESL Ontario, an organization of ESL teachers and other interested parties to support the provision of ESL to immigrants, and provided a good deal of the funding to keep the organization and its conferences going until about 1978. In 1973, TESL Ontario studied provisions in TESL teacher training and standards. The summer programs funded by the Ministry of Education and conducted by the Citizenship Branch continued, but the study raised questions about the ways in which certified teachers who took the course would be credited in relation to their certification. Eleven other ESL teacher-training courses in post-secondary institutions were in place or were about to begin, increasing the need for coordination of the program offerings and standards. In order to fully appreciate the complexity of efforts involved in teacher training for ESL at this time, we need to take into account that the decision was then being made that would require elementary school teachers to have an undergraduate degree (which took effect in 1980). This decision meant the creation of standards by which teachers would be credited with specialized learning.

The final outcome for ESL, starting around 1976, was the evolution of the old Ministry of Education ESL summer course into the three-part Additional Qualification program in ESL, which still exists today, taught by the faculties of education. By completing all three parts of this program, a certified teacher becomes an ESL specialist. The impact of this teacher certification was substantial in that school boards and other institutions could now assess candidates for teacher positions for skills in ESL, and even require qualifications. These developments, in effect, constituted the professionalization of ESL teachers and their integration into the schools, with significant but lesser impact on the colleges and NGOs.

Also in the 1970s, the province divided education and training delivery first into two and then into three ministries. The first had responsibility for the schools; the second, responsibility for post-secondary education and training credit programs and the implementation of the Manpower adult ESL programs in the colleges; and the third, responsibility for non-credit training relating to the labour force, including adult literacy and private-sector interests. All three of these jurisdictions still included adult non-credit programs for immigrants and others. In 1980, the Ontario Ministries of Education and Colleges and Universities published a discussion paper on continuing education, which is non-credit formal education that is neither elementary/secondary nor post-secondary (colleges and universities). This paper focused rather narrowly on the need for employment-related training and adult literacy. It did not mention ESL. The underlying issue appeared to have been which ministry or ministries would carry the fiscal burden for continuing education. The matter then disappeared from public view for six years, during which time the low levels of adult literacy as a purported damper on the economy became a high profile issue both federally and provincially.

In 1986, the Ontario Ministry of Colleges and Universities responded to this concern by publishing *Continuing Education Review Project: Project Report: For Adults Only*, which established separate responsibilities for secondary schools, colleges, and universities with respect to adult literacy, ESL and FSL, Franco-Ontarians, older adults, and people with special needs. It ensured that school boards could not charge a tuition fee for adult basic education or ESL and that universities and colleges would be restricted in the amount that they could charge (26). A clear distinction was drawn between credit and non-credit courses; ESL and adult literacy were largely in the latter category. One result of this division of responsibilities was that people teaching adult non-credit courses did not have to be certified teachers. Although the report comments on the need for well-trained ESL teachers, it does not specify what suitable qualifications might be (38).

Coordination in the arcane and complicated system of language-training funding and delivery has been an ongoing problem since the 1960s (see, for example, Canada Employment and Immigration Advisory Council 1991, 51–4; Burnaby 1992). The federal ESL Manpower program had been criticized on a number of serious grounds, including discrimination and poor quality (Burnaby 1998b, 250). Therefore, in 1983, the Canada Employment and Immigration Commission (CEIC) sent out a discussion paper proposing the amalgamation of the Manpower ESL program and CILT to create one new program. The main program would provide one basic curriculum for newly arrived immigrants. Stipends would not be available, but services such as child care and transportation might be arranged. A second and smaller part would be made available for those who needed specific language training before they could enter the labour force (CEIC 1983). The delivery model for this proposed program was based on contracting directly with NGOs or an educational institution rather than going through a provincial government. Such a change would permit the federal government (1) to make its own decisions about service programs and delivery agencies; (2) avoid the wage scales of unionized teachers in provincial educational institutions; and (3) keep delivery agencies competitive and accountable on one-year contracts while being reimbursed for fewer administrative costs.

In 1986–7, CEIC launched a pilot of the general program for newly arrived immigrants, called the Settlement Language Training Program, which was judged to be successful for the most part, except for delays in the financing that caused severe problems for some of the delivery agencies (Burnaby et al. 1987). Meanwhile, the CILT program was eliminated, thus reducing the federal programs from two to one. The reality was that the federal government had been getting very little recognition for its expenditures through CILT and had little control over what the provinces would charge back against the program.

Despite this experiment towards a more general, yet flexible, federal language-training program, the federal government revamped the Manpower program in the late 1980s. Then, in 1990, the federal government introduced a new immigration plan that included a revised adult language-training program, replacing the Manpower ESL program with Language Instruction for Newcomers to Canada (LINC), available to all immigrants in their first three years in Canada, and a smaller program for LINC graduates called Labour Market Language Training (LMLT). Delivery agencies and their teaching programs were selected as they were for the Settlement Language Training Program, through an annual competition of proposals from suitable agencies (universities, school boards, NGOs, or private agencies), thus bypassing the community colleges unless they come in with a competitive bid (Employment and Immigration Canada 1993). In addition, all immigrants who wanted to enter the program were assessed on the basis of national language benchmarks, including a level for those not literate in their first language. The benchmarks also related to curriculum programs across the country for easier coordination. After assessment, immigrants were given a list of local programs that could serve their needs.

The LINC program has been criticized for only serving immigrants in their first three years in the country; for an annual proposal and reporting structure that causes a great deal of stress to delivery agencies, especially small organizations; and for the use of national benchmarks that may provide a good description of language levels but do not address the many different requirements (particularly the lack of literacy skills) that immigrant language-learners bring to the classroom (Goldstein 1993; Cray 1997). Flemming (1998) objects to the benchmarks on the grounds that they are a throw-back to the era of experts imposing themselves on teachers' autonomy and professionalism, and adds that benchmarks pose potential dangers if they are proposed as a reliable indicator of what actually is needed in ESL classrooms.

In 1998, the Ontario government commissioned a study of all adult ESL/FSL services in Ontario. Among training providers who served adult immigrants (rather than universities and private sector firms who largely serve foreign students), LINC programs accounted for 39 per cent of all the Ontario programs, and 48 per cent of the programs combined LINC with ESL supported from other sources. Unfortunately, it is not possible to work out the extent to which LINC classes took over from the Manpower program. We do know that community agencies provided most of the LINC programs and half of the combined LINC/ESL programs. School boards offered almost all of the ESL programs, and about 35 per cent of the combined LINC/ESL programs, but very few of the LINC-only ones. The ESL only classes were about 80 per cent non-credit. Classes typically had about seventeen students; almost all had continuous intake of students; a quarter were multilevel classes; and few used alternative forms of delivery. Four percent of students had had no education at all, and 13 per cent had not reached high school (Power Analysis Inc. 1998). Women comprised 69 per cent of the students. These educational conditions, except for the class sizes, were significantly challenging (Cray 1997).

As for the teachers, school boards employed 70 per cent of the LINC/ESL instructors, while community agencies employed only 10 per cent because many of the teachers in the agencies were already supplied by the boards. For all types of programs, 86 per cent of the teachers were women, 35 per cent were not native speakers of English, and 56 per cent considered themselves fluent in another language as well as English. Although they were almost universally highly qualified, the teachers averaged 20.6 hours of teaching a week; only 29 per cent were permanent employees; the average hourly wage was $28.65; 40 per cent had no benefits (most of those who did only had sick days); and 42 per cent belonged to a union. The teachers and administrators agreed that funding was by far the biggest problem (Power Analysis Inc. 1998).

Whatever the strengths and shortcomings of LINC, the federal government has already devolved its responsibility for adult ESL programs in British Columbia and Manitoba but not in Ontario. Work continues federally at the Centre for Canadian Language Benchmarks, now an arm's-length federal agency, to determine how these standards will be used by the provinces. Ontario has simplified its own adult ESL operations. By 1996, it had closed down all of the ESL programs in the Citizenship Branch of the Ontario government, except for those which were settlement-related, such as language training for the professions and trades in Ontario. The government funded TESL Ontario to produce a set of standards for non-credit adult ESL instructors in the province, during the course of which it became clear, as it did in the Power Analysis Inc. (1998) report, that current teachers of adult non-credit ESL are generally very well qualified (Sanaoui 1996, 1997, 1998). The TESL standards will be used in LINC programs and future provincial programs to improve content and accountability.

In sum, then, the federal government started in the 1940s to fund the provinces for ESL for adult immigrants through NGOs and school boards, for settlement purposes, and in the 1960s through community colleges, for labour development. As economic problems arose in the 1980s, it sought to reduce its costs by contracting out adult ESL, not through the provinces, but directly through delivery agencies, thus bypassing union wages and the power of the provinces themselves. As a result, the federal government has transferred its whole enterprise of ESL delivery for adults in Ontario to community programs, mainly in school boards and NGOs, most of which have challenging teaching conditions. The employment conditions for the teachers under LINC (and other adult ESL programs) are highly unfavorable despite the high qualifications of the teachers, and funding is precarious.

Like the federal government, the Ontario government began by working through the Ministry of Education to offer educational programs for adult immigrants through school boards and NGOs, then expanded its programs in the 1960s into other areas under the Citizenship Branch and other government bodies. The Ministry of Education has fiercely and effectively guarded itself against any changes that would impinge on the Education Act directly and on its legislated responsibility for the qualifications of teachers. Teachers of non-credit adult ESL in school boards do not have to have the same credentials as those teaching regular school programs. The school boards' continuing education programs are now much more like those offered by NGOs than programs under the Education Act. (One partial advantage that they have over NGOs in the competition for training dollars is that they have a somewhat more secure infrastructure to sustain them in the competitive process as long as the boards consider it worthwhile to continue to compete.) The Citizenship Branch and the school boards once supported NGOs and developing outreach programs, but the Citizenship Branch was closed down in the mid-1990s in anticipation of a blanket provincial ESL and settlement program.

In this whole process, both levels of government have been instrumental in the early professionalization of ESL teachers overall, but eventually teachers of non-credit ESL teachers were deprofessionalized and their job conditions deteriorated. Once the flow of money in the 1980s had slowed down and the federal government started to fund on a competitive basis, both mainstream and immigrant group-specific NGOs programs and adult ESL programs in school boards had to struggle harder in order to survive under the competitive and accountability exigencies of ESL funding (Owen 1999). Similar circumstances for adult ESL have been reported in the U.S. (Chisman, Wrigley, and Ewen 1993).

Research on the Activities, Aspirations, and Attainments of Students in Toronto Schools

1950 to 1970
The tremendous increase in post–Second World War immigration to Canada contributed to a significant expansion of the Canadian education system, particularly in Ontario, where student enrolment increased over 200 per cent between the 1950s and 1970s. Lind (1974) shows, as does Harold Troper in chapter 1 of this book, that in the first twenty years following the war, the predominantly white Anglo-Saxon city of Toronto became increasingly populated with non-Anglo-Saxon immigrants from Hong Kong, Southern Europe, and the Caribbean. According to Lind, unlike immigrants to the U.S. who lived in the ethnic and racial enclaves or ghettos of American cities, immigrants in Toronto lived in relatively heterogeneous neighbourhoods largely in part because of their diversity, continuous influx and mobility aspirations. It was, therefore, unlikely for schools to have new arrivals from only one country; instead, Toronto schools often had clusters of students who were, for example, Greek, Portuguese, Italian, and Chinese.

Lind (1974) also contends that while the Toronto Board of Education did make attempts to respond to the increasing criticisms of their treatment of immigrant students, they did so within the framework of 'New Canadianism,' an approach to education that emerged out of the liberal-progressive thinking of those board administrators who emphasized the interconnections between language and culture – an approach 'well-suited to the political organization of the system' (32). So, while claiming to recognize the cultural, racial, religious, linguistic, and ethnic differences of Toronto's immigrant students, the board had the expectation that the students would simply 'adjust to our city, our ways, and our classrooms.' Lind cites Joseph Sterioff, the principal of an experimental program for immigrant students, as someone who exemplified this doctrine of 'New Canadianism.' Acknowledging that the experience of learning a new language was a cultural process, Sterioff went on to suggest that the best way of doing so was to be immersed in the new culture. In other words, 'the simple expedient of somehow getting the new immigrant schoolboy [sic] to sound, write, or recognize signals we use to represent our language is not going to do anything at all about his mastering the language, let alone his integrating the culture which developed it into his nervous system. Invite him to the culture and he will acquire the language for himself, as well as the trappings that make it sensible' (ibid.).

These views of language learning became the basis for the development of teaching strategies and programs, and determined the way in which non-English-speaking immigrants were to be educated: to adapt immigrants to the language and culture of Anglo-Saxon Toronto (Lind 1974). Immigrants were defined as problems rather than viewed as specially advantaged. Within this framework, the trustees of the board were able to ignore diversity, arguing that a focus on minority cultures would undermine the goals of the education system and would be unfair to non-immigrant students. The chairman of a curriculum guideline series of the Ministry of Education claimed, 'It's a question of seeing the school as the institution of social cohesion as over against seeing it as the agency for personal fulfillment as the ethnic groups desire' (cited in Lind 1974, 114). Social cohesion, Lind argues, 'is a code word for stamping children with the New Canadian image belittling their native cultures, familial ties and personal inclinations, for the socialization purposes of the state' (116).

Within this context, and concerned with the progress and placement of students, particularly immigrants, in the education system, the Toronto Board of Education initiated a study in 1970 that reported on the relationship between students' backgrounds and their participation within the education system. Since then, the board has conducted and reported on seven system-wide surveys.[5] The 1970 *Every Student Survey: Student's Background and Its Relationship to Class and Programme Placement in School #91* reported that the largest number of non-Canadian-born students in the board were from Italy (7,015), followed by Portugal (3,982), Greece (2,382), England (1,883), West Indies (1,643), and China and Hong Kong (1,614) (Wright 1970). A similar study in 1975 found a decrease (5 per cent) in the number of Canadian-born students, an increase in non-English speakers (40 to 46 per cent), and an increase in the number of students from low socio-economic families. There was a significant increase in the number of students from Portugal, China and Hong Kong, and the Caribbean. In both surveys, students learning English as a second language were most often first language speakers of Portuguese, Italian, Greek, and Chinese.

The 1970 and 1975 data showed that Canadian-born elementary school students whose first language was not English and non-Canadian-born students for whom English was a second language were represented in similar proportions in opportunity and vocational classes.[6] Dual-language Canadian-born students[7] tended to be placed in vocational classes, while immigrant students who were learning English tended to be found in health-related-problem classes. Males of all language groups were found in greater numbers than females in all special classes, but twice as likely in behavioural classes. In 1970, Canadian-born secondary school students whose first language was not English were found to have the largest proportion of students in the academically oriented program. Polish, Ukrainian, and German students were the most likely to be found in academically oriented programs, and similar to the findings at the elementary level, secondary students who were born in Canada and whose first language was not English were the least likely to be in a special vocational program or non-university-destined program. By comparison, the non-English-speaking immigrants, females more than males, were the most likely to be placed in a special vocational or opportunity classes and non-university program than any other group, and they were the smallest proportion of students to be enrolled in academically oriented courses.

Among the immigrant groups, Chinese- and German-speaking students were enrolled in large numbers in academic programs, and in relatively small numbers in vocational non-academic programs. By contrast, the Italian, Greek, and Portuguese-speaking students were the most likely to be in the vocational non-academic programs. The situation remained essentially the same in 1975 for Canadian-born students whose first language was not English. They were the largest proportion of students taking academic courses, while non-English-speaking foreign-born students were the smallest proportion of students taking such courses. What can be concluded from the 1970 data is that non-English-speaking immigrant students were likely to be below grade level, while Canadian-born English as a Second Language students were more likely than any other group of students to be above expected grade level.

Both the 1970 and 1975 data indicated that age of arrival was a significant factor in the program placement of students. English-speaking immigrants who arrived later in their high school years were more likely than their younger counterparts to be placed in special education classes and the non-academic-stream program. Non-English-speaking immigrant students who arrived between the ages of 7 and 12 were most likely to be found in vocational classes, while those who were older (arriving between ages 12 and 15) were the most likely to be in the non-academic-stream program and the least likely to be in the academic program. The data from both surveys also revealed that students who arrived before the age of 6 and after age 16 were less likely to be found in special education classes, and more likely to be found in the academic program.

Further, the 1970 and 1975 data demonstrated that there was a relationship between socio-economic status (SES) and program placement across all immigrant/language groups. Lower socio-economic students were more likely to be found in special education classes. For example, 'among the Canadian-born students with English as a first language, students with parents as labourers, taxi drivers, packers, etc. had 4 out of 10 chances of being enrolled in level 5 [academic] courses; by comparison, students whose parents were accountants, engineers, etc. had 9 chances out of 10 of being enrolled in such courses' (Deosaran 1976, 7). Therefore, as socio-economic status increased, the proportion of students in academic-stream courses steadily increased and student placement in special classes was less likely. These differences in program placement were more dramatic in secondary than elementary schools. According to Deosaran, Wright, and Kane (1976), 'In both 1970 and 1975 a much higher proportion of students from high-income homes were enrolled in level 5 [academic] courses' (44).

From further analysis of the relationship between parents' occupations, a student's mother tongue and immigrant status, Wright and McLeod (1971) concluded that language background was a significant factor in determining parents' occupational status, and hence the placement of students. Those for whom English was their parents' first language had an advantage. Likewise, Deosaran (1976), in his analysis of *The 1975 Every Student Survey*, showed that the differences in occupational status were related to a student's language background rather than his/her country of birth. As Deosaran said, 'Regardless of where they were born, students with English as first language were much more likely than those with English as Second Language to have parents in a higher occupational category and much less likely to have parents in the lowest occupational category' (6). However, a more detailed analysis of the Every Student Survey data undertaken by Wright (1971) revealed that, regardless of country of birth and mother tongue, there was a distinct and direct relationship between program placement and occupation of household. The trend that emerged from the 1970 and 1975 surveys demonstrated that socio-economic status was a better predictor of special class placement than either language or country of birth.

But the relationship between English as a first language, occupational status, and academic-stream student placement did not hold for Caribbean students. For instance, Wright (1971) found that 'a much larger percentage' of students born in the Caribbean, compared with those born in Great Britain and the United States, were found in vocational programs. Deosaran demonstrated that this had to do with the fact that the parents of Caribbean students were 'vastly underrepresented within the professional occupations' while parents of students from the other two countries were 'over-represented in such occupations' (14). Caribbean parents tended to be labourers, porters, and kitchen helpers.

In an examination of the post-secondary aspirations of students, it was found that in addition to social class, school programs, and grade point averages, such aspirations were also related to family size, socio-economic status, student area of residence (urban versus suburban), community characteristics, and occupational aspirations. Insofar, then, that immigrant students tended to attend inner-city schools (Costa and

Di Santo 1972) where they were half as likely to be in academic programs, they were less likely to aspire to pursue post-secondary education. Research showed that students' aspirations for post-secondary education were directly linked to their ability to pay their way through, as well as the role that educators and guidance counsellors, in particular, played in the dissemination of information about post-secondary education (Deosaran 1975). Based on his findings, Deosaran suggested that providing post-secondary information to students should move beyond the classroom and 'be accompanied by a careful analysis of how and why some students reject, perhaps inadvertently, the message for further education' (81), and that guidance counsellors should actively seek out students who may not be aware of available resources and occupational options.

Using the 1970 and 1975 data, Cheng, Wright, and Larter (1980) examined in their report, *Streaming in Toronto and Other Ontario Schools*, the relationship between streaming and academic achievement, country of birth, language, social origin, and future placement of students. Streaming was referred to as 'the placement of pupils in groupings according to a criterion such as ability, achievement, interest, need, or a combination of these factors for the purposes of providing instruction so that pupils can proceed toward appropriate educational goals at an appropriate pace' (1–2). The data showed that Canadian-born, English-speaking students were much more likely to be placed in special education classes than students from other language/immigrant groups. However, this finding was not consistent across all programs. For instance, at the elementary school level, a disproportionately large percentage of Canadian-born, English-speaking students were enrolled in special education programs including learning centres, home instruction, and hospital programs. Italian-speaking immigrants, however, were overrepresented in hearing/deaf, language, and health, and other related special programs. The authors also confirmed earlier findings, that foreign-born secondary school students, particularly those arriving before age 6 and after age 16, were least likely to be placed in academic-stream educational programs.

The 1980s and Later
In the 1980s, the Every Student Surveys continued to be a major source of student information for the Toronto Board of Education. The Grade 9 student surveys undertaken in 1982 and 1983 revealed very little change

in the demographic make-up of schools. One small change was noted – the approximately 2 per cent increase in students of Asian background. Findings showed that students' age of arrival continued to be a factor in their program of study at the secondary-school level. Specifically, English- and French-speaking students, who were in the school system longest, were most likely to be enrolled in advanced-level programs. However, immigrant students whose first language was not English or French were also most likely to be at the advanced level. Consistent with earlier studies, students born in the Caribbean tended to be represented in high proportion in the basic and general level programs. And similar to previous studies, a clear pattern emerged showing that students with parents in the higher occupational categories were almost twice as likely to be taking advanced level courses than students whose parents were in lower occupational categories (Wright and Tsuji 1983, 1984). A subsequent Every Secondary Student survey was conducted in 1987 and showed little changes in some areas, but useful to us here are the comparative analyses that were carried out using the data from 1987 and 1991.

The surveys of 1987 and 1991 found that academic achievement was related to 'such socio-demographic characteristics as race, academic level, gender, socio-economic status, home language, birthplace, and parental presence in the home' (Brown 1993, 4). It was also found that there was a decrease in the white and an increase in the Black and Asian student populations (from 7 to 9 per cent, and 24 to 30 per cent, respectively), an increase in the proportion of non-English- and non-French-speaking students, an increase in students not living with parents (from 10 to 16 per cent), and a greater percentage of all students' families in higher SES categories.

A follow-up study of a 1987 Grade 9 student cohort five years later categorized the data such that, at the end of five years, students in the Toronto Board of Education were shown as having either graduated (considered to be a cohort graduation rate), remained as students, or left the educational system without a diploma (considered to be a drop-out rate[8]). Brown (1993) found that of 4,077 students who started Grade 9 in 1987, 56 per cent had graduated with their Ontario secondary school diploma (OSSD) or had completed thirty or more credits; 11 per cent were still attending school in the board; and 33 per cent had left school without graduating. The cohort drop-out rate then was considered to be 33 per cent. Understandably, the graduating students were largely in the advanced-level program and tended to have accumulated an average of seven credits each year, compared with the three accumulated by those leaving school without graduating. And while there were similar graduation rates for Canadian-born and foreign-born students, there were notable differences. It was found, for instance, that in terms of the ethnic backgrounds of the students completing school, the graduation/drop-out rates were as follows: 44 to 42 per cent for Blacks, compared with 59 to 32 per cent for whites, and 72 to 18 per cent for Asians. Quite significant was the number of Black males who left school without graduating. Black males had a drop-out rate of 48 per cent compared with 35 per cent and 20 per cent for whites and Asians, respectively. Of linguistic groups, Chinese and Vietnamese students (72 per cent each) had the highest graduation rate, followed by Greek (63 per cent), English-only and Italian (53 per cent each), and Portuguese students (48 per cent).

In 1991, nearly half of the students were native speakers of a language other than English or French. Of the non-English mother-tongue students, the largest linguistic groups were Chinese (14 per cent), Portuguese (7 per cent), and Vietnamese (5 per cent). Over half (57 per cent) of the secondary school students were born in Canada, nearly a quarter (24 per cent) were born in Asia, and the remainder (19 per cent) were born in other regions, including Europe (7 per cent), Africa, South and Central America, and the Caribbean (3 per cent each). African students came mainly from Ethiopia and Somalia; the Central American students came mainly from El Salvador and Nicaragua; and the Middle Eastern students came mainly from Iran; all came to Canada no earlier than 1987 (Brown 1992).

A follow-up study of the 1991 data by Cheng, Yau, and Ziegler (1993a) reported on the profiles of the secondary-school students, their aspirations, and their perceptions of the school climate. The study revealed that Greek (86 per cent), Portuguese (85 per cent), and Korean students (81 per cent) were most likely to come from two-parent homes. These students were more likely to have higher SES backgrounds, enrol in advanced-level courses, and aspire to go to university. By comparison, Canadian-born and Caribbean-born Blacks (40 and 41 per cent, respectively), and Aboriginals (34 per cent) had the highest proportion of students living in mother-only households. These students were found to spend less time on homework than other students, and were overrepresented in general and basic-level courses. Those students who were overrepresented in basic-level courses were Canadian-born Blacks

(14 per cent) and Portuguese (9 per cent, same as Aboriginals). It is worth noting that the students from lower SES families with unemployed parents were mostly non-white immigrants for whom English was their second language.

In terms of the ethnicity, it was found that Asians, particularly Chinese and Koreans (75 and 86 per cent, respectively) were most likely to indicate that they planned to attend university. This was less the case for Tamils (56 per cent) and students from Indochina (51 per cent). For Black students, post-secondary aspirations varied according to birthplace, with 50 per cent of Canadian-born students planning to attend university compared with 41 per cent of African-born and 29 per cent of Caribbean-born students. While the report did not find any connections between students' aspirations and their perceptions of school climate, it is something worth exploring. Black students were the most likely to indicate that their school did not treat all races fairly. Among Asian students, Tamils were most positive about the school climate, while Koreans gave the least positive responses. Interestingly, Asians, at all program levels, reported spending more time on homework than all other racial groups.

In their report on students' performance and achievement between 1987 and 1991, Cheng, Yau, and Ziegler (1993b) found that foreign-born students were slightly overrepresented in general and basic-level courses. However, while the number of Asians in the higher program levels were dropping (i.e., from advanced to basic level by 1991), they remained the students most likely to be in the higher-level program. By contrast, the representation of Black (and Aboriginal) students in general and basic-level courses was more than double their presence in advanced-level courses. Asians also tended to be achieving well in school and were least likely to be at risk (i.e., failing to accumulate credits to graduate within five or six years of high school) compared with Black students who, second to Aboriginal students (46 per cent), were most at risk ('over a third [36 per cent] were identified as at risk'). But generally, between 1987 and 1991, there was an increase in the number of Black students who achieved well in English and mathematics. And while Canadian and foreign-born students were evenly distributed in the four achievements indicators (from having sufficient credits and doing well in English and mathematics to not having earned levels of sufficient credits and potentially being at risk), Canadian-born Asians and Blacks were seen to have a slight advantage over their foreign-born peers. Foreign-born students who arrived after 1987 were more likely to be at risk than their Canadian-born counterparts. For all language and racial groups, the proportion of students who were at risk was lowest among the dual-language speakers.

As in the *1991 Every Secondary Student Survey*, the 1997 survey showed that about half of the students in the Toronto Board of Education were racial minorities, the majority of whom were first-generation immigrants, born in different parts of Asia, the Caribbean, South and Central America, the Middle East, and Africa (Cheng and Yau 1999). The more recent immigrant students were Tamils, Iranians, Filipinos, Somalis, and Vietnamese. And although one in four students were from single-parent families, they were mainly from the newer immigrant groups, specifically Latin Americans (51 per cent), Filipinos (47 per cent), Caribbeans (38 per cent), and Africans (20 per cent). The parents of the more recent immigrants student were in unskilled occupations or unemployed.

Almost a quarter (23 per cent) of the secondary school students – most of whom were Tamils, Filipinos, African-born Blacks, and Iranians – were reported to be enrolled in ESL classes (64 to 54 per cent of each group). As in 1991, students reported how they felt about the climate of their schools. Foreign-born students evaluated the curriculum more positively than Canadian-born students. In fact, over 80 per cent of the more recent immigrant students (Tamils, African-born Blacks, and Filipinos) felt that school prepared them for their future, compared with nearly half of Canadian-born English-speaking students. And it was also these same immigrant students (Tamils and Africans) who reported spending more time on homework and part-time work and less time on leisure activities. Asians continued to be the group that spent most of its time on homework (13 hours per week).

Overall, 'the level of parental involvement in school was consistently higher for parents with professional jobs compared to those with lower status jobs or were unemployed' (Cheng and Yau 1999, 8). Ethnolinguistic backgrounds also played a role in parental involvement in schools. For example, Vietnamese, Chinese, and African parents were less likely than other groups to be involved in school activities, such as participation in parent interviews. Further, students with English as their home language were more likely to receive help with their school work at home, while a disproportionately high number of Africans (22 per cent), Tamils, Iranians, and Koreans (some 7 to 8 per cent) compared with others (3 per cent) reported using library resources to complete their homework. Understandably, access to computers was an issue for students from low-income families; those of immigrant backgrounds reporting lack of access were mostly Portuguese, foreign-born Blacks, and Latin Americans.

The *1997 Every Secondary Student Survey* also asked students to rate themselves in terms of oral, writing, research, problem-solving, leadership, and social skills. Results showed that students' languages and cultural backgrounds influenced the way in which they perceived their competence in different skills. For example, in addition to feeling considerably less comfortable than their English-speaking peers speaking up in class, Chinese, Korean, Vietnamese, and Filipino students – the largest groups of English as a Second Language – rated their abilities as much lower than their peers, except in two categories: organizational skills and being responsible. Students of Chinese origin were reported as having the lowest levels of self-confidence compared with students of Caribbean, Latin American, Eastern European, and South Asian backgrounds. Students who rated themselves lower in oral communication skills (Chinese, Filipinos, Vietnamese, and Tamils) were more likely to show preference for mathematics, science, and technology. By comparison, students who rated themselves highly in oral communication skills were more likely to aspire to careers in teaching and law. In terms of aspirations, compared with the overall student population, foreign-born Black and Filipino students were more likely to plan to attend community college, and a larger proportion of Portuguese and Caribbean-born Black students said that they intended to work full-time after high school.

Refugee Students
A 1995 study that explored the experiences of refugee students in the Toronto Board of Education who arrived in Canada between 1991 and 1994[9] (Yau 1995), found that nearly 6,900 refugee students were in the school system. This was an increase of about 25 per cent over the number that had been in the schools between 1988 and 1991 (5,500). A large percentage (47 per cent) of refugee students were over 19 years old, about half of them reported being on their own, and about half were either unemployed or employed in unskilled, manual jobs. It was common to find refugee students working part-time. Further findings indicated that the majority of the students left their homelands because of life-threatening situations and/or dissatisfaction with their home governments due to 'unfavourable political, economic, military, or religious conditions' (Yau, 1995, 15). These pre-immigration and migration

experiences, Yau notes, not only affected the students' previous schooling experiences but also their post-migration adjustment to schooling in Canada. As Yau writes: 'Former schooling for many refugee students was often interrupted or disrupted by the pre-migration situations in their homeland, and by the long and transitory nature of their migration journeys. Furthermore, the trauma many refugee students went through in their home countries and during their exodus had its impact on their emotional well-being even after settling in a new country' (21).

Generally, refugee students have tended be less critical of the Toronto school system than other students (Brown 1992; Cheng, Yau, and Ziegler 1993a, b; Yau 1995). For example, while it was noted that teachers needed to be more understanding and sensitive towards the feelings and unique circumstances of refugee students, the 1995 study showed that all reported that they enjoyed their school experiences and were generally pleased with their teachers – mostly their ESL teachers rather than their regular classroom teachers. These positive responses even came from students who reported that they had experienced racial incidents, ranging from verbal to physical abuse. Experiences with racial incidents were most often reported by students at the elementary-school level, usually among recent immigrants who were vulnerable and least able to defend themselves (Yau 1995).

Yau also reports that slightly less than two-thirds (63 per cent) of the total refugee population were enrolled in advanced-level courses compared with nearly three-quarters of the foreign and Canadian-born secondary students, and that their level of aspiration tended to be lower than that of other students. Specifically, 45 per cent of refugee, 57 per cent of immigrant, and 61 per cent of Canadian-born students aspired to go to university. But particularly disturbing was the mismatch between the aspirations and program enrolment of refugee students; this was most evident among those from Central American, Somalia, and Ethiopia (recent refugees), and, specifically, among those identified as most at risk of dropping out of high school. For example, of the refugee students aspiring to attend university, nearly 20 per cent were enrolled in general or basic-level programs – programs that would not have qualified them to attend university. This, as Yau contends, was likely a reflection of their being misinformed about the education system.

With the increasing diversity of metropolitan Toronto in the twenty years following the Second World War, the Toronto Board of Education, working within the framework of New Canadianism and giving attention to the interconnections of language and culture, initiated programs that would integrate immigrants to the language and culture of Anglophone Toronto. Years later, responding to increasing criticisms regarding their treatment of immigrant students, the board introduced system-wide surveys that provided comprehensive information about the demographic, social, and academic characteristics, as well as the progress, placement, aspirations, activities, and perceptions of elementary and secondary students attending Toronto schools. The results from surveys covering more than twenty-five years, from 1970 to 1997, indicated that students' academic achievement was influenced by various sociodemographic factors, including immigrant or refugee status, program placement, post-secondary aspirations, socio-economic status, parental education, language, birthplace, and composition of family. Canadian-born students, regardless of language spoken, were more likely to be in university-bound programs and least likely to be in special education classes. Conversely, immigrant students, the highest proportion of whom were from Portugal, Italy, Greece, China, and the Caribbean, were more likely to be placed in special education classes and least likely to be enrolled in advanced level programs.

Data from the 1991 and 1997 surveys also showed that as socio-economic status increased, the proportion of students in university-bound (or advanced-level) courses steadily increased, and student placement in special education or lower-level programs became less likely. Further, post-secondary aspirations were shown to be directly related to family size, grade point averages, socio-economic and immigrant or refugee status, and occupational aspirations, as well as to the information that students, and immigrants in particular, received from educators and guidance counsellors.

Interpretations of Immigrant Students' Situation, Experiences, and Aspirations

Researchers – primarily non-school-based researchers – have conducted a number of studies that report on the situation and experiences of students in relation to their immigrant status, as well as their race, ethnicity, social class, and aspirations. Most of this research demonstrates that social stratification and inequality are sustained by the complex relationship between social class, race, ethnicity, immigrant and refugee status, racism, and discrimination. Furthermore, the stratification and inequality contribute to the ways in which schools accommodate students' needs, interests, and aspirations, which, in turn, influence their educational and occupational outcomes (Ramcharan 1975; James 1990; Curtis, Livingston, and Smaller 1992; James and Haig-Brown 2001).

We have already seen, in the above discussion of the findings from the Toronto Board of Education studies, that the social class of parents often determines whether the student enters a five-year academic-oriented, university-geared program; a four-year general level college-oriented program; or a basic-level, work-directed program (see also Curtis, Livingston, and Smaller 1992). In fact, as Porter (1965) states, 'The class position of the family determines to a great extent whether or not a young person will go to university ... [and] the kind of course he [sic] will take when he gets there' (184). Other studies of Toronto students also show that the higher the social class background of students already in university-preparatory programs, the greater their chances of actually entering university (Anisef 1975; Buttrick 1977; Larter et al. 1982; James 1990).

The Toronto Board of Education studies also indicate that race, ethnicity, English language skills, immigrant and refugee background, and social class all play a role in the schooling and educational process of students. For instance, the studies show that ethnic- and racial-minority immigrant students whose first language is not English tend to come from lower socio-economic backgrounds. Nevertheless, while students from higher SES families were more likely to aspire to university than students from lower SES families, for many immigrant students, social class did not appear to pose the same problems for them as it did for Canadian-born students, particularly when we think of immigrant students' high educational and career aspirations. Indeed, a number of studies throughout the decades under consideration here have shown this to be the case. In a study of the occupational and educational expectations of Toronto high school students, for example, Calliste (1982) found that Black Caribbean and Southern European students had high post-secondary expectations and were more likely than Anglo-Canadians to believe that 'university education is very important to help young people get ahead in Canada and to achieve prestige' (15). She explains that 'education may be the most important, if not the only, mobility channel for West Indians and Southern Europeans. Therefore, manifestations of success in education such as high grades, high self-concept of ability, and high educational and occupational expectations may be relatively more important for them than Anglo-Canadians' (ibid.).

Calliste further notes that, despite the fact that the Caribbean and Southern European students were characterized by low socio-economic status, they were 'less entrenched in their class position and [were] more highly motivated, more achievement oriented and more upwardly mobile than working class Anglo-Canadians' (15). It is possible that the high motivation of Southern European students, as Calliste points out, is related to family expectations. For as Danziger (1978) found in his analysis of the patterns of socialization among predominantly lower-class Italian immigrant boys in Toronto, family was a major source of motivation. The boys' aspirations tended not to be their own individual goals, but represented those of their parents and their concern that they be worthy of their parents' goals. Danziger writes that 'this fact will often counterbalance the inability of foreign-born parents to provide the child with all the cognitive skills needed in the new society' (156).

Studies of Black students also show that, despite their low-income background and low parental participation in school, their tendency to be in non-university-oriented courses, their years within the school system, and their low credit accumulation that often led to their dropping out of school, they nevertheless voiced commitment to education (Head 1975; James 1990; Dei et al. 1997). In fact, a Toronto Board of Education study of Grade 8 students showed that even though Black Caribbean students were overrepresented in special education classes (between 20 and 35 per cent) and came from single-parent households, they still held high educational aspirations because they saw education as an opportunity for self-realization (Larter et al. 1982, 53). Similarly, James (1990), in his study of Black students in Toronto, found that while they acknowledged that racism was an obstacle for them, they nevertheless tended to hold high educational and career aspirations, optimistically believing that with their strategies of hard work, determination, and education, they would be able to overcome the 'hurdles' and attain their career aspirations. James argues that the high educational and career aspirations of minorities in general, and Black youth in particular, are, in part, constructed in relation to their perceptions of their position within the social structure. It is possible, he points out, that they hold high aspirations believing that they will not achieve their goals. Yet they are prepared to hold such aspirations, reasoning that they have to aim high in order to compensate for the racism and discrimination that they will face.[10]

The discriminatory practices of schools, which result from racism as well as from xenophobia and ethnicism, act as barriers to educational access and opportunities for some students and are also evident in the assessment, streaming, and counselling of students (Ramcharan 1982; Head 1984; Board of Education for the City of Etobicoke 1993; Special Committee of Parliament 1984; Dei 1996). During the 1970s, for instance, psychological assessment tests for recent immigrants were identified as having a negative impact on students' placement in school. According to Cummins (1984), a study of psychological assessment of recent non-English-speaking immigrant students demonstrated that academic performance and program placement were substantially lower for students whose first language was not considered during the interpretation of test scores. That is, students whose primary languages were carefully considered and accommodated during the interpretation of test scores performed much better than students whose first language was not taken into account.

Interestingly, language also played a role in the assessment of Caribbean students – students for whom English might be considered to be their first language (Coelho 1988). Studies conducted in the 1970s showed that language, accent, pronunciation, and intonation created problems for Caribbean students, thus creating learning difficulties (Anderson and Grant 1975). As with other immigrant groups, these difficulties were further complicated by the inability of teachers to understand the cultural backgrounds of the students and, as Roth (1976) claims in relation to Caribbean students, the students' orientation to schooling.

Another noteworthy point regarding Caribbean students has to do with the families' pattern of migration. Researchers point out that Caribbean parents, mainly mothers, tend to immigrate first and are sometimes separated from the children for many years. This means that when the children eventually come to Canada, they are likely to have double-adjustment problems – they simultaneously must adjust to the new society and school life *and* to a new family situation with parental expectations that they become high educational achievers (Roth 1976; Anderson and Grant 1975; Beserve 1976; daCosta 1976). Furthermore, researchers like Head (1975) have claimed that the inappropriate assessment and resultant placement or streaming of academically capable Black Caribbean students into vocational and special-education classes had to do with the stereotypes of these students as 'slow learners' and intellectually inferior. Such practices have contributed to students feeling humiliated, resulting in negative attitudes, hostility towards school, and rebellious behaviours. A further consequence is that some students come to have little faith in education as a means of self-fulfillment or career advancement.

In analyzing issues faced by immigrant students (East Indians, Greeks, Italians, Portuguese, and Caribbeans), Ashworth (1975) reports that, coupled with limited access to school facilities, immigrant students had teachers who were not sufficiently aware of their culture and often lacked sensitivity to the problems that they faced in adjusting to a new environment. And as Masemann (1975) explains, lack of access to educational programs that would maximize immigrant students' skills and help them to fulfil their high aspirations was an issue for many first-generation immigrant students who were more likely to be in vocational programs at schools because they tended to settle in areas where schools disproportionately offered vocational programs. Given such a situation, it is understandable that immigrant youth tend to be underrepresented in post-secondary institutions. In fact, in 1978, the Economic Council of Canada (1978) in it annual report, *A Time for Reason*, mentioned that 'Canada has proportionately more of its young people in post-secondary educational institutions than does any OECD country except the United States, however, the participation of recent immigrants needed substantial improvement' (107).

Research findings have also identified the pivotal and problematic role played by guidance counsellors in the assessment and academic placement of immigrant students, especially when we consider that many parents might not have the appropriate skills and relevant knowledge to negotiate the educational system and support their children. The parents might also come from societies or cultures where teachers are considered to know what is best for their children and hence participate in a limited way in the education system (Head 1975; Brathwaite 1989; Lam 1994). Researchers such as Cummins (1984) and Chodzinski (1986) have called for cultural sensitivity and have pointed out that counsellors need to be aware that English-speaking and non-English-speaking immigrant students require alternative approaches to the traditional standardized tests when being assessed. Chodzinski (1986) further asserts that counsellors needed to avoid the racism and ethnocentrism promoted by the tests, and 'must restructure the delivery of services to avoid institutional, structural, technical, and psychometric attitudes which contribute to inequalities in schools and society in general' (82). Based on his findings that immigrant students often resisted social interactions with teachers and have negative attitudes towards school, Wolfgang (1975) also suggests that guidance counsellors require special training to develop the skills necessary to work with immigrant students. On this basis, he suggests that students and their parents be invited to orientation programs in their native languages, and that counsellors familiarize themselves with the methods of communication and parenting styles of various cultures, such as physical cues, touching, non-verbal communication, and appropriate facial expressions.

Almost a decade later, amid growing dissatisfaction with the streaming of students and the placing of a disproportionately large number of newly arrived students in basic-level programs, a Provincial Advisory Committee to the Ministry of Education, which was established after a race relations conference in 1986, set about to address these problems. The committee noted that many recently arrived immigrant students were placed in special-education classes because their language difficulties were misinterpreted as learning problems. Hence, they advanced the idea that the period of adjustment for immigrant students, even for those of high academic ability, may be one in which they encounter difficulties, particularly in the area of language. Further, based on their findings, they recommended that the assessment and placement of students into educational programs be done after giving students sufficient time for adjustment to a new environment; that materials be made available to students and parents in a variety of languages; that appropriate records and data on students' previous educational and personal experiences be obtained and assessed in order to establish equivalent placement levels; and that parents be informed, through a translator when necessary, of their children's education. Accordingly, the committee wrote, 'The Ministry of Education encourages all school boards to put policies in place to monitor the assessment and placement of children, facilitate the involvement of parents in this process and assess the equity of student services' (Ontario Ministry of Education and Training 1987, 18).

Five years later, in the face of very little changes, the ministry again recommended in its 1992 document, *Changing Perspectives: A Resource Guide for Anti-racist and Ethnocultural-Equity Education*, that the placement of immigrant students be preceded by a period of time in which the students' learning behaviours could be examined; that an assessment be done in the students' first language; that modifications be made to the students' program; and that this be followed up with a carefully documented assessment of the students' progress. The document went on to say that when a student's performance is being evaluated, the assessor must take into consideration problems of adjustment and that evaluation procedures should be clear, given orally, involve an ESL/ESD teacher, and distinguish between second-language and content-area needs, and that translators should be involved to help parents understand the results.

While the special situation of refugees, compared to immigrants, has not been extensively researched, one study of Somali refugees, one of Canada's most recent refugee groups, reveals that only 25 per cent of the study participants (roughly 50 per cent fewer males than females) pursued formal education or upgrading during their time in Canada (Opoku-Dapaah 1995). Opoku-Dapaah found that, on the one hand, there was 'a positive relationship between access to educational counselling and pursuit of education. Nearly two-thirds of all those who completed some formal education/upgrading did receive information and counselling; on the other hand, 85 per cent of those who had not undertaken any academic training have had no access to counselling and information on education' (4). The reason for this limited access to educational counselling and information was, among other things, lack of knowledge about institutions that provide such services. While over half of the participants (some 60 per cent females) were not aware of the availability of government funding for education, the majority (40 per cent) of those Somalis who pursued education in Canada did so with the assistance of government loans and grants.

Despite the obstacles to education, we have seen through the TBE studies as well as those of Danziger (1971), James (1990), and others that immigrant students have consistently aspired to attain high educational and occupational goals, which many have realized.[11] But as Anisef (1975) observed, there are differences between generations. Specifically, in his analysis of Grade 12 Ontario students, he found that first-generation Canadians were more likely than foreign-born and second-plus-generation students to expect to enrol in postsecondary education. However, foreign-born students were more likely to continue with part-time studies or to enrol in trade schools or apprenticeship programs. Unfortunately, Anisef did not disaggregate the foreign-born population data; doing so is important since, as researchers (M. Zhou 1997; James forthcoming) indicate today, and as the TBE studies demonstrate, one-and-a-half-generation immigrant students, particularly those entering the school system between the ages of 6 and 16 years, tended to do better academically, had higher educational aspirations, and were more positive about the school climate (Cheng, Wright, and Larter 1980; Cheng and Yau 1999) than their first- and second-generation counterparts. Not only were the high educational aspirations of the immigrant students based on their desire to satisfy both their parents' expectations of them and their own career ambitions (Danziger 1971; James 1990; Lam 1994), but as Masemann (1975) notes, immigrant students perceived a clear link between school training and their subsequent employment. They were aware of the menial jobs their parents held and were determined to achieve a higher level of employment.

For some immigrant students, sports was used as a means of negotiating the alien school system. With reference to Black students in the Toronto area, James (1995) and Solomon (1992), like Head (1975) before them, ascertained that working-class immigrant Black youth, and males in particular, tended to be keenly interested in sports. They believed that it was through their successes in sports that they would be able to gain respect in school, be recognized by their teachers and peers, obtain an education – and even a post-secondary education – through scholarships, and eventually attain upward social mobility. This was not peculiar to Black youth, however, for as Anisef et al. (2000) found in their follow-up study of 1973 Grade 12 students, working-class immigrant students, in this case Italians, were able to stay in school and obtain scholarships to study at an American university because of their interest and successes in sports. Today, these former high school athletes are well-established in their chosen careers.

These studies show that, undeterred by their experiences with xenophobia, classicism, racism, and discrimination, immigrant and refugee students, particularly those who were first-generation, constructed high educational and career aspirations. And even though their educational circumstances – being streamed into non-university oriented programs – seemed to be contrary to the possibility of attaining their aspirations, they projected an optimism that showed their confidence in their capacity to overcome the 'hurdles' that might stand in their way. Motivated by family support, their desire to satisfy their family expectations, and their determination to succeed, many immigrant and refugee students employed strategies they knew would help them attain their high educational and career aspirations.

The Response of Schools, Colleges, and Universities to the Diverse Needs of Students

Ministry of Education and boards of education documents indicate that, over the years, educators have made attempts to respond to the diverse needs, concerns, interests, and aspirations of students. In addition to the Toronto Board of Education Every Student Surveys, the boards also initiated other studies,[12] or allowed other studies to be conducted within schools, and worked with community organizations and parents to produce reports that not only documented the concerns and needs of immigrant and refugee students and parents but also developed ways of addressing the problems. In this section, we examine some of the initiatives by school boards, community colleges, and universities, noting a few of the outcomes for students.

Debates on accessibility to post-secondary education in Canada, and in Ontario in particular, indicated that low-income, immigrant, and racial-minority students were limited in their access to post-secondary education (Ontario Federation of Students 1984). In reviewing studies that reported on students' participation in post-secondary education, the Ontario Federation of Students noted in its 1984 presentation to the Ontario Economic Council that

> Countless studies in Canada ... have provided ample evidence illustrating that the school system operates in a discriminatory fashion by transferring disproportionate amount of low socio-economic and ethnic minority students to low level programs. The effects on these students are the development of low expectations, alienation from the school system, and a decline in educational achievement. (10)

This view was supported by the Special Committee of Parliament on the Participation of Visible Minorities in Canada. In its *Equity Now!* report (1984), the Committee wrote that 'research suggests that they [visible minorities] are faced with a number of obstacles to participation, including discrimination, non-acceptance, low expectation by teachers and lack of respect for, and recognition of, the learners' past experience' (133).

A number of publicly funded colleges and universities responded to these and other reports. These institutions understood education as an important mechanism for promoting social justice, enhancing equality of opportunity, and providing citizens with the knowledge and skills that would enable them to participate effectively in society. As they became conscious of shifts in policies and customs around questions of cultural diversity (for example, contract compliance and employment equity policies), they initiated access programs to address the needs of historically disadvantaged groups of students who were not gaining access to post-secondary education. This was pointed out by Dr. James Hall, Jr. at the 'Conference on Strategies for Improving Access and Retention of Ethno-Specific and Visible Minority Students in Ontario's Post-Secondary Institutions.' In his keynote address (1990), he said: 'The challenge ... of diversity ... is upon us. ... There are four things that I identify, four reasons that motivate institutions to do something about this diversity ... It is good for education, it is the proper Christian thing to do, it is mandated ... it is good economics.' It is probably these four reasons that inspired a number of colleges and universities to establish access initiatives. However, an examination of these initiatives reveals that they vary considerably in terms of how they define and operationalize access and the support systems that are in place to sustain students' participation and retention. So while the access programs at the University of Toronto and York University enable students to gain entry into some undergraduate, graduate, and professional programs leading to regular degrees, there tends to be little support that ensures their participation and retention (Allen 1996; James 1997).

The access program at the University of Toronto, known as the Transitional Year Program, began in September 1970, following summer programs in 1969 and 1970 that prepared Black and Aboriginal students for university. The majority of the students from the summer programs enrolled at York University. As Allen (1996) writes, 'These two summer programs were part of the efforts made by the Black community in Toronto to increase the numbers of Blacks, and other visible minorities, in universities in Toronto. The organizers of the summer programs had some support from progressive members of both the University of Toronto and York University' (249). Moreover, as Calliste (1996) and Brathwaite (1996) claim, this access program came about as a result of the 1960s and 1970s struggles of Blacks, many of whom were immigrants to Toronto and were demanding human rights, equality, and full participation in society. The programs continue today, responding to the educational needs and social situation of university aspirants in the Toronto community.

York University has access programs, which have been in existence since the 1980s, in four faculties: the Faculty of Law (Osgoode Hall Law School), the Faculty of Arts, the Faculty of Education, and the Faculty of Environmental Studies. The programs are independent of one another and address the particular access needs of potential applicants who do not meet the necessary entry requirements. In targeting applicants of working-class, minority racial and ethnic backgrounds, each of the programs, in effect, tends to capture a significant proportion of people of immigrant and refugee backgrounds. The Faculty of Education, however, is the only faculty that also names refugees in its target population for recruitment.

While the access initiatives are intended to remove systemic barriers to entry into universities, they are not without their limitations. For instance, with reference to the access initiative in the Faculty of Education at York University, James (1997) notes that, in applying for entry through the access program, applicants are asked to state their gender, race, and so on, and identify any 'barriers' that might have prevented them from obtaining the necessary entry requirements. In his study of the experiences of African-Canadian students, all of whom were immigrants or children of immigrants who entered the York University education program through the access initiative, James found that the applicants were often ambivalent and conflicted about responding to these requirements. The applicants were skeptical about how the admissions personnel would assess their file and conflicted about giving the impression that they were incapable of gaining entry through the normal stream and were gaining entry out of sympathy. At issue here was their distrust of the institution and the rules under which they were expected to function. Nevertheless, despite their experiences with trying to secure entry into university, many students agreed with the need for access programs because, since racism and discrimination exist, it is a way for them to pursue post-secondary education and attain their educational and career aspirations.

James (1997) also found that the conflicts and tensions that many students experienced in applying through the access programs continued once they were in university. Even for those Black students who did not enter the university via the access route, the very fact that they were racial minorities and that such a program existed in the faculty (and to an extent the university), meant that they were perceived to be 'access students' and were treated accordingly, most often in subtle, disrespectful ways. Skin colour was often used as a signifier of access and was a factor in the ways in which many racial minorities negotiated their existence within the academe. Many were well aware of the rhetoric of universities that only the 'most qualified' gained entry and, hence, felt that it was important for them to demonstrate that they were qualified, legitimate, and worthy students. For this reason, they were in constant fear of not getting good grades; this, in turn, produced much anxiety (James 1997; James and Mannette 2000).

James (1997) further suggests that the African-Canadian students' experiences with stereotyping, racism, and discrimination within the university contributed to their frustrations, ambivalence, and anger. Nevertheless, the students considered themselves to be 'involved in a critical process of change,' not only within the education faculty, but in the university as a whole, and in the education system generally. Some saw themselves as 'role models,' as advocates and change agents, people with a mission to 'diversify education' and establish 'an inclusive curriculum' that would speak to the diversity of today's student population (James 1997; James and Mannette 2000). James (1997) also found that these experiences produced 'contradictory tensions' that were apparent in the students' constructed narratives of their university experiences – narratives that indicated their disenchantment with the institution and its educational practices, while simultaneously justifying their participation, their presence in the institution despite attitudes that their attendance appeared to be contradictory, and their successes through a view of themselves as individuals who were resisting erasure.

In terms of graduate programs, indications are that there is growing diversity among the student population. At York University, for example, a 1995 survey of graduate students by Professor Michael Ornstein (1996), found that about one-quarter, 23.8 per cent, of graduate students were not of European background. Nearly half of all non-European graduate students were East Asians, who accounted for 11.6 per cent of all graduate students. The next largest groups were South Asians, accounting for 4.3 per cent of all graduate students, and Africans and Blacks, accounting for 3.1 per cent. A further 2.5 per cent of graduate students were of Middle Eastern origin, and 1.1 per cent were of Southeast Asian origin. Fully 42.2 per cent of the students in science were non-European, with 25 per cent of East Asian and 7 per cent of South Asian backgrounds. About one-quarter of the administrative studies and MBA program students were of non-European origin, with 15 per cent East Asian MBA students and 6.2 per cent South

Asians. In the social sciences, 6.6 per cent were East Asian and 3.1 per cent African or Black, about 1 per cent were South Asian, East Asian, and Middle Eastern. The education program was the only one with a significant proportion of African and Black students, about 14 per cent (8).

Ornstein (1996) also found that over one-quarter, 26.2 per cent, of graduate students who were African or Black felt that they had been disadvantaged in their studies at York University as a result of their race. Concerns about disadvantage were also cited by 11.3 and 14.1 per cent of South Asian and East Asian students, respectively, along with 6.7 per cent of Middle Eastern and 5.5 per cent First Nations students (13). Ornstein quotes one student as saying:

> I believe that the faculty I am currently attending does not offer a variety of courses that cover race and gender issues, i.e., it is not an important element to consider when completing an MBA degree. Also I believe that there are serious employment equity problems at York FAS [Faculty of Administration Studies]. Their current staff is reflective of the business world reality. There are very few women in positions of power and fewer visible minorities with any authority. As with all faculties, administration is riddled with politics and nepotism. I strongly believe that equitable policies will not be enforced or effective until the positions that dictate/develop these practices are felt by individuals who understand what equity means. (36)

The diversity that is to be found within educational institutions, and, in particular, the diversity that relates to the presence of racial-minority students in post-secondary institutions, is, no doubt, as James and Mannette (2000) argue, disruptive to the notions of neutrality, objectivity, meritocracy, scholarship, excellence, and colour-blindness that have traditionally characterized the claims of our educational institutions. They are disruptive insofar as the differential participation and outcomes of immigrant students indicate how these institutions produce and reproduce gender, race, ethnic, and class hegemonies. To address this situation, educational institutions must change, and in doing so, universities must make structural, not cosmetic, changes, particularly if they are to make their resources and services fully accessible and responsive to the needs, interests, aspirations, and expectations of all students. Equity, then, requires a situation in which educational programs, particularly the curricula, pedagogy, and social relationships are structured in ways that speak to the particular needs of, and social justice for, immigrant students.

The evidence shows that colleges and universities have been making their post-secondary education more accessible to immigrant and minority students. Having acknowledged the inherent social and cultural structures that have operated as barriers to individuals' attainment of post-secondary education, and recognizing the social and economic benefits of an expanded and diverse student population, universities and colleges have initiated access programs that have brought many immigrants and refugees into the institutions. However, there still remains the need to address the resulting problems, tensions, and conflicts that accompany any new program, and, most of all, one that seeks to redress inequity, injustice, and discrimination within institutions that have hitherto claimed that they are founded on principles of objectivity and meritocracy.

TOWARDS ACCOMMODATING IMMIGRANTS WITHIN EDUCATIONAL INSTITUTIONS

At this point, under the weight of all the data presented above, we return to the two basic questions with which we started: (1) How does or should education merit the trust we have in it to achieve the results expected by so many parties? (2) Whose specific interests are served by the kinds of policy and program interventions initiated or not initiated for the immigrant population?

To answer the first question, our information indicates that governments and educational institutions, by and large, have moved from a position of trying to force immigrants into an imagined mould of 'the real Canadian' to a position of recognizing that changes must be made on the parts of all stakeholders and that ignoring or neglecting differences and tensions is dangerous. The host communities and their governing structures were dragged along, sometimes kicking and protesting, to this position. Their efforts have always come a considerable time after problems and issues have developed and been identified. Also, human and material resources that have been developed to respond to the needs, issues, and concerns of immigrants have usually fallen short of these identified needs, issues, and concerns.

The information we were able to gather in this chapter reveals relatively little about the effects of education on immigrants and the rest of the population. Policy initiatives relating to immigration and education are fairly well documented, and they form the bulk of the contents of our earlier report (Burnaby, James, and Regier 2000). However, time and again we encountered complaints about the lack of coordination and program data, and found that funding was impossible to trace. Even the census has only recently been asking questions that permit researchers to gauge the complex relationship between factors of language, ethnicity, and race and factors of immigration date, education, and other personal characteristics. Only in the 1990s did studies attempt to provide general descriptions of programs across the city and province. Some of these were frustrated by the poor quality of the data available (e.g., Spencer 1991; Cumming et al. 1993), while Power Analysis Inc. (1998) was able to give only the most simple figures about programs. Reports by Sanaoui (1996, 1997) and Power Analysis Inc. (1998), however, have provided a more detailed account of the characteristics, qualifications, and teaching conditions of ESL teachers of adults, and Power Analysis Inc. even offered perspectives from these teachers and administrators.

In the end, the most detailed information came from the Toronto Board of Education's Every Student Surveys and Every Secondary Student Surveys (e.g., Wright 1970; Deosaran 1976; Wright and Tsuji 1983, 1984). Since the 1970s, these data have become increasingly richer in their ability to provide a picture of the students themselves. Even though, in the past decade, these surveys have been restricted to secondary school students, they have been expanded to include students' evaluation of their education. While a few studies have given us students' views (Cheng and Yau 1998a, b; 1999; Spencer 1991), it is rare to get a glimpse of the perspectives of learners, especially adults. The potential ramifications for education have come out in government commissions such as R. Abella (1984), the Special Committee of Parliament on the Participation of Visible Minorities in Canadian Society (1984), and the Task Force on Access to Professions and Trades in Ontario (1989).

The implications for research here, then, is that it is imperative that more studies be done that provide overall, detailed information about the current programs – including funding; numbers of programs; types of programs; numbers of teachers, students, and administrators; intake; output; timeframes – that can be compared directly with program objectives in terms of delivery and outcomes. It is especially important that research be conducted to learn the views of the students in the program, and even those of potential learners. We know very little about the satisfaction of learners, much less about immigrants' perspectives on their own needs. There is no lack of rhetoric about the intentions and generosity of service delivery, but we need results to show that any of this has been worthwhile.

Having said this, we must recognize that it is difficult to conduct meaningful research on the process and outcomes of education. It is hard enough to obtain the nuts-and-bolts information about numbers of classrooms and students. But attempts at descriptive research, especially on a large scale, easily become bogged down in qualitative problems, even on such fundamental issues as the definition of an ESL student (e.g., Cumming et al. 1993) or how national ESL curriculum levels can be described to fit the needs and characteristics of real learners (e.g., Cray 1997; Flemming 1998). Nonetheless, we have indeed found some helpful case studies (e.g., D'Oyley 1976; James 1990; Cheng 1996). By narrowing the scope, researchers can deal in depth with questions of definition and shed light on qualitative issues. An iterative approach is needed that falls somewhere between large-scale and quantitative research, and small scale and qualitative research, in order to get a sense of the scope and the impact of educational programming relating to immigration in Toronto.

A further, but related, research concern is linking cause and effect realistically. Learners enter educational programs with an entire set of constantly changing personal characteristics, undergo experiences in their program (which are intended and unintended in the objectives), and leave with an altered set of characteristics. Educational research does what it can to account for program effects, but confidence about establishing causality is elusive. Researchers must be realistic in their claims about the role that education, as opposed to many other personal influences, plays in determining students' later attributes and behaviour. We also need research that will yield in-depth information about learners' knowledge, skills, and attitudes that are specifically related to details about the teaching they received and the objectives of the program – in other words, precisely how learners change in relation to what the program provided. Gathering the views of learners as well as data from 'objective' tests of their abilities is essential.

Finally, research programs must be planned to take into account the slow process of educational, social, and personal change. Groups in society recognize a problem and identify education (and perhaps other strategies) as a solution. Then they pressure the system to design and incorporate a suitable response in education. (Sometimes the system resists and the community has to create its own solutions.) Any response from the system requires implementation that includes recruiting the right human and material resources and fitting them into the rest of the system. Once the program is in place, it takes time for results to emerge. In the Canadian political enterprise, with its four- to five-year cycles in the lives of governments and senior officials, the reality of the lifespan of educational change is often overridden in both the implementation of programs and the assessment of their effects. Academic time frames, too, interfere with good timing in research. In some cases, research is neglected because it is not needed to serve a political purpose; at other times (unsuitable) research is conducted when it is politically expedient. In very few cases are programs designed to incorporate ongoing data collection to monitor program outcomes in line with intended outcomes for the learners and outreach to the intended learners. Our study demonstrates clearly the need for long-range planning in both programming and the assessment of its outcomes.

Notes

1 In an earlier phase of this inquiry, we discussed in more detail the wide variety of issues and the initiatives (e.g., multiculturalism and anti-racism) that were introduced by governments, educational institutions, and NGOs to address them from the 1960s to the 1990s (see Burnaby, James, and Regier 2000).
2 We say this conscious of the debates by scholars, community members, and immigrants themselves on the tendency for these individuals to be constructed as 'other' Canadians – people with different race, ethnicity, and cultural backgrounds (James and Shadd, 1994; Walcott 1997; James 1999) in comparison with the presumed 'raceless' mainstream Canadians. This is a construction to which many object and against which many struggle.
3 In a survey of adult education in Canada, Devereaux (1985) reported that there was a 4 per cent difference in Canadian-born (20 per cent) and foreign-born (16 per cent) adults' enrollment in adult education. Further, 'those who came during the eighties and were 35 and over were more likely to enrol [in adult education] than the native-born population. On the other hand, rates were lowest among people over 35 who arrived before 1970' (11). But while the enrollment of foreign-born men and women in adult education was similar, compared to their Canadian-born counter-

parts, they tended to enrol in courses that seemed to be related to their participation in the society. Specifically, foreign-born males tended to enrol in 'personal development' courses and foreign-born females tended to enrol in 'personal development' and job-related courses. Canadian-born females were just as likely to enrol in these two course areas, plus hobby courses (29).

4 Recall that the Multiculturalism Policy of 1971 was revised in 1988 and became the Canadian Multiculturalism Act.
5 The earlier surveys examine both elementary and secondary school population, while the later ones focus only on students at the secondary level.
6 Opportunity and vocational classes were classes with non-university-streamed programs.
7 Dual-language Canadian-born students refers those for whom English was not their first language. Included within this definition are students who learned English as a second language; students who learned another language and English at the same time; and students who were recent arrivals, for example, students from Portugal, Italy, Greece, and China.
8 Brown (1993) points out that there is no consistent definition of drop-out rate in Canada or the United States. He used two methods to calculate drop-out rates: a cohort study, and an annual completion/drop-out rate after five years, a time when students would normally have completed the five-year program.
9 According to the Immigration and Refugee Board of Canada (1990) the nine main countries from which immigrants were coming into Canada were Sri Lanka, Vietnam, China, Iran, Somalia, Ethiopia, El Salvador, Guatemala, and Nicaragua (cited in Yau 1995, 8).
10 This point is corroborated by studies such as D. Byrnes (1982) and Pelham and Fretz (1982), which assert that racial-minority students in the United States tend to hold high career goals, albeit unrealistic, at times, insofar as they 'had less measured ability than that required by their expressed career choice' (Pelham and Fretz 1982, 38). Interestingly, as Byrnes (1982) also found, racial-minority students tended to hold attitudes and ideas that they felt were necessary for them to survive a tough social environment, such as high school, in order to protect their social and cultural situation (see also James 1990; Solomon 1992; Dei et al. 1996).
11 The Special Committee of Parliament on the Participation of Visible Minorities in Canadian Society states that minority-group members look to education as a means whereby they can increase their participation in society and thus ameliorate the problems caused by race (1984, 116). But the committee goes on to point out that visible-minority-group members

encounter interpersonal and organizational obstacles to their participation in post-secondary institutions.
12 See for example, reports by Schreiber (1970), Stewart (1975), and the Consultative Committee on the Education of Black Students in Toronto Schools (1988); studies by Fram et al. (1977); Coehlo (1988); and Handscombe and Becker (1994); Roth (1976); Board of Education for the City of Etobicoke, *Students' Perspectives on Current Issues* (1993). Many of these studies report on issues affecting Black Caribbean students, which indicates that these students, much more than others, have been an ongoing concern for the various boards of education.

6 Diversity and Immigrant Health

Samuel Noh and Violet Kaspar

Demographic projections show significant transformations in composition and social characteristics of the Canadian population, brought about primarily by post–Second World War immigration. As Harold Troper has illustrated in chapter 1, and Clifford Jansen and Lawrence Lam further break down in their sociodemographic overview in chapter 2, people from non-European nations (for example, in Asia, Africa, and the Middle East) have constituted most of Canada's post-war immigrants during the past three decades. According to the 1996 Canadian census, 11.2 per cent of Canadians are visible minorities, more than double the figure of 5 per cent based on the 1981 census; the province-wide figure for Ontario in 1996 was 15.8 per cent. If current immigration and fertility trends persist, visible minorities will comprise one-third of the Canadian population within the next three decades. A large majority of non-European immigrants (42 per cent) have made the Greater Toronto Area their permanent place of residence. Each year, 70,000 immigrants resettle here, representing over one-third of the annual influx into Canada. Currently, 50 per cent of Toronto's population comprises foreign-born immigrants and visible minorities from 170 nations, speaking more than one hundred languages.

Toronto is likely to remain an important player on the immigration scene and continue to be a model of cultural pluralism and multiculturalism in the new millennium. *Together We Are One*, a report prepared by the Task Force on Community Access and Equity for the Toronto city council, includes a statement that the city does not simply recognize and tolerate its diversity, but respects, values, and intends to nurture that diversity as an integral part of its collective identity (Rees 1993). 'Integrated diversity' is a popular phrase used to express Toronto's self-identity and pride. And while few would disagree that Toronto is a city of diversity and a model for other cities attempting to integrate a diverse population with all the ensuing complexities, Toronto has had a long history of intolerance. A riot at Christie Pits during the summer of 1933 was an overt and violent expression of the cultural intolerance and intergroup tensions that existed in Toronto during the Depression. Moreover, a recent media report suggests that inequities based on race cannot be relegated to Toronto's past: 'Racial segregation is alive and well in Toronto, a city so proud of its rich and growing ethnic mix that it adopted the motto "Diversity, Our Strength" only a few years ago. In neighbourhoods across the city, racial minorities are confined to living in the shabbiest buildings and working in some of the lowest-paid jobs, no matter what their level of education' (Philip 2000, A15).

As the authors of the first two chapters have noted, Canada's immigration history has also been tarnished by racist practices in selecting immigrants and by self-serving economic motives. Until a few decades ago, Canada was extremely reluctant to accept immigrants from Southern or Eastern European countries and was also opposed to admitting Jews, Asians, and Africans. All of these immigrants were considered 'unassimilatable' and 'undesirable.' Moreover, the perception that these immigrant groups could not contribute to the Canadian economy through service jobs or trades, or that national spending to offer education or training to immigrants would place excess burden on the Canadian economy, were used to rationalize racially biased admitting practices. The contemporary treatment of newcomers to Toronto, while more subtle, continues to reveal an intolerance and ambivalence toward immigrants. The most recent opinion polls show that a majority of Canadian residents continue to believe that the influx of immigrants (from non-traditional source countries) should only be justified based on economic needs (Palmer 1997). However, while their economic contributions are welcome, immigrants become scapegoats and targets of resentment and animosity at times of economic decline.

Even after the introduction of less discriminatory immigration policies in Canada following the Second World War (Beaujot 1991), Toronto was not free of its legacy of racial exclusion, cultural segregation, pervasive inequalities, and systemic discrimination against racial minorities and other cultural and ethnic groups. Immigrants settling in Toronto were kept in isolation, relegated to the confines of 'reception areas' (see chapter 3 on housing). The residential segregation of ethnic groups became a highly prominent and durable feature of Toronto's geography throughout the 1950s and 1960s. And although we now find large pockets of ethnic concentrations in all regions of Toronto, a large majority of immigrants and refugees continue to experience contemporary forms of systemic and institutional discrimination in housing, employment, education, legal systems, and the public media (Reitz and Breton 1994; Henry et al. 1995). Children and youth of ethnic minorities also report daily exposure to unfair treatment in school by teachers and fellow students; older youth experience discrimination on the job (Philip 2000). Even Toronto's *Together We Are One* cited 'huge inequalities' in employment, income, education, housing, and legal justice for visible, non-white immigrants.

This chapter provides an overview of the literature addressing immigrant health and mental health. Often, the general public feels threatened that liberal immigration policies will create social, economic, and health problems for Canada. Do immigrants bring illnesses and diseases to Canada (and Toronto)? Do they impose a burden on our healthcare and economic systems? Do immigrants and refugees show more psychological distress symptoms, adjustment disorders, or mental disorders? Do the children of refugee and immigrant families exhibit serious emotional and adjustment problems, antisocial behaviour, or social incompetence?

It is important to note at least three limitations that we encountered in our research. First, there are only a small number of empirical research findings reported in peer-reviewed publications on immigrant health. Although research on population health has accumulated exponentially over the last three decades, the knowledge base about immigrant health is not extensive. This intellectual lag is due in part to a lack of systemic and stable support for research on immigrant and minority population health (Sue and Morishima 1982). This is particularly the case in Canada, as evidenced by the relative scarcity of scientific data on immigrant health compared with the data available in the United States. Health statistics on immigrants living in Toronto are extremely rare. While Toronto data will be used where possible in this chapter, we will also have to rely on national data. Second, because a large majority of recent immigrants are members of racial- or ethnic-minority groups, it is often difficult to separate the experiences and circumstances of immigrants from those of racial and ethnic minorities. Third, readers must be aware of the fact that simple summaries of the literature on complex social issues inevitably tend to oversimplify the degree of complexity of the issues. This chapter is, therefore, necessarily limited in its scope.

IMMIGRATION AND HEALTH

Based on a series of both successful and failed attempts by human smugglers to bring illegal migrants into Canada, the *National Post* carried articles by Diane Francis (1999a, b) who blatantly concluded that immigrants and refugees pose significant threats to the health of the Canadian public, claiming that immigrants and refugees bring such serious infectious diseases as tuberculosis and HIV to Canada. Perhaps because of a lack of information, coupled with the fear and anti-immigrant attitudes of the public, media reports about a few cases have not only evoked strong emotional reactions and controversy but have also perpetuated myths that immigrants pose a health risk to Canadians.

Research findings to date have not supported perceptions that immigrants are unhealthy. Empirical results of immigrant health studies in Canada (Noh et al. 1992a, b; Chen, Ng, and Wilkins 1996a), Australia (Donovan et al. 1992), and the United States (Burnam et al. 1987; Stephan et al. 1994; Vega et al. 1998; Landale, Oropesa, and Gorman 2000) have provided evidence that is difficult to dispute – immigrants are at least as healthy, and sometimes healthier, than the non-immigrant population.

Statistics Canada researchers (Chen, Wilkins, and Ng 1996b; Chen 1999) have provided some of the most comprehensive reports on Canadian immigrant health. Using population data from three national databases – the census, vital statistics, and the Health and Activity Limitation Survey (HALS) – Chen and his colleagues compared functional disability (disability and dependency for role performance) and vital statistics (mortality and life expectancy) across three subpopulations of Canada: (1) Canadian-born non-immigrants (Canadians), (2) immigrants born in Europe (European immigrants), and (3) immigrants born outside Europe (non-European immigrants). The results primarily demonstrated that, during the late 1980s (1985–91), non-European immigrants had the lowest rates of mortality, disability, and dependency, and showed the highest life expectancy.

The age-adjusted prevalence rates of disability and dependency are summarized in figures 6.1 and 6.2, respectively (Chen, Wilkins, and Ng

320 Samuel Noh and Violet Kaspar

Figure 6.1
Prevalence of disability, by severity, sex, and immigrant status, Canada, 1991

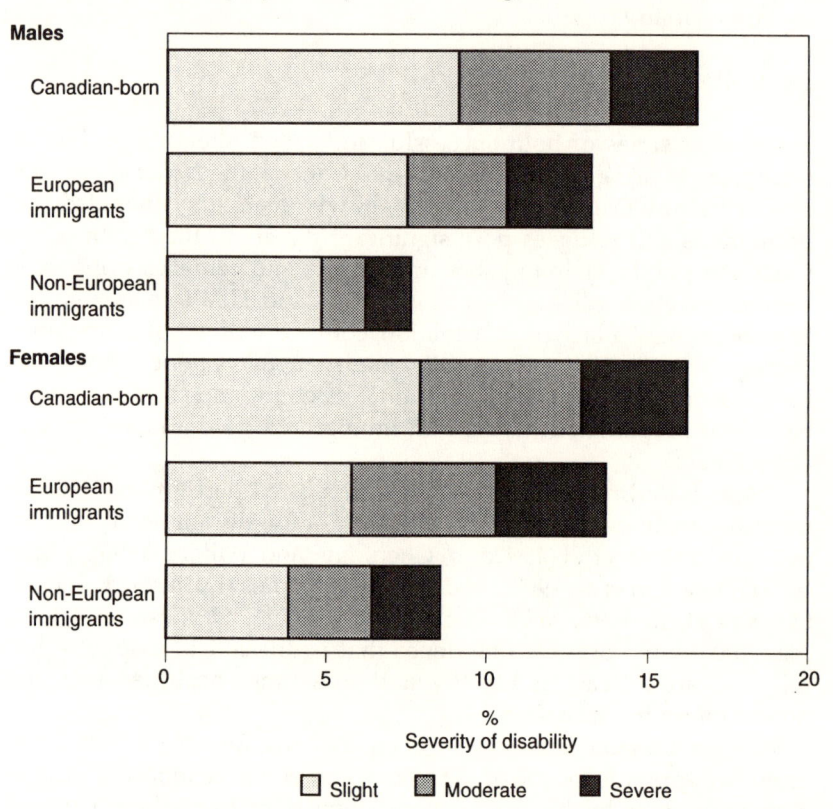

Source: Chen, Wilkens, and Ng (1996).

1996). The results show clear linear patterns of significant and substantial variations in the rates of disability within males and females. Among males, the Canadian-born were more than twice as likely to have disability than non-European immigrants; the prevalence rates were 16.5 per cent and 7.6 per cent, respectively. For women, the respective rates were 16.2 per cent and 8.6 per cent. European immigrants, males and females, were situated between the Canadian-born and non-Europeans. The patterns of variations between Canadian-

Figure 6.2
Prevalence of dependency, by severity, sex, and immigrant status, Canada, 1991

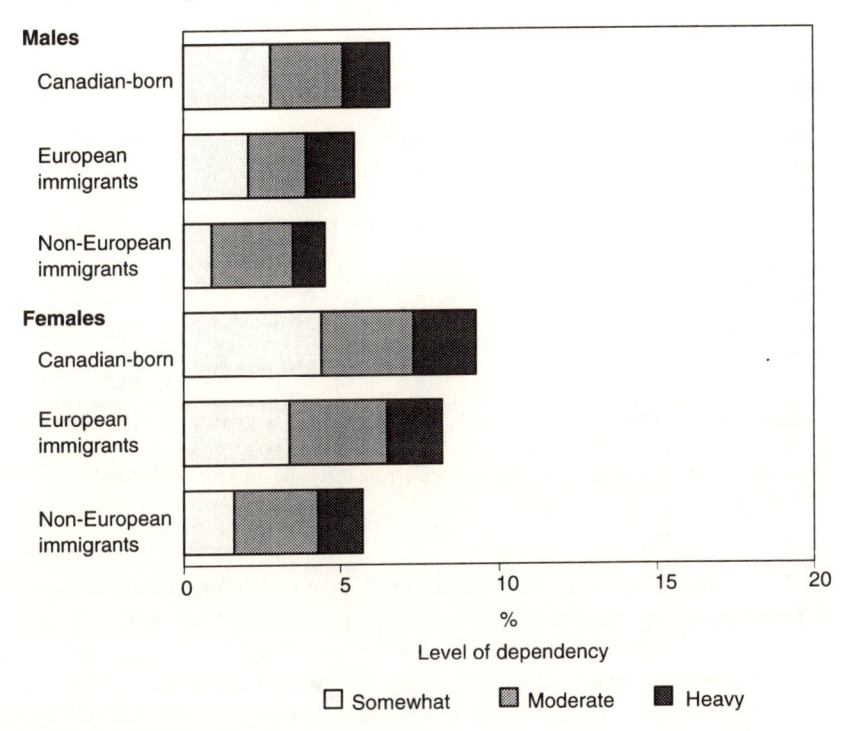

Source: Chen, Wilkens, and Ng (1996).

born and non-European immigrants were consistent when re-examined for severe disability only. The rates of severe disability for male and female European immigrants were almost identical to the rates for Canadian-born residents. Although the contrasts are less dramatic, the association between immigration status and dependency, at all levels of dependency, was consistent with that reported with respect to disability (fig. 6.2).

Vital statistics also reveal the health advantages of immigrants, especially those from non-European nations. As shown in table 6.1, the estimated life expectancy at birth in 1986 was about five years longer for non-European immigrant males than for Canadian-born males.

Table 6.1
Life expectancy in years, by sex and immigration status, Canada, 1986 and 1991

	Males		Females	
	1986	1991	1986	1991
At birth				
Canadian-born	72.3	73.6	79.3	80.4
European immigrants	75.6 (3.3)[1]	76.3 (2.7)	81.0 (1.7)	81.8 (1.4)
Non-European immigrants	77.4 (5.1)	80.3 (6.7)	83.4 (4.1)	85.7 (5.3)
At age 65				
Canadian-born	14.6	15.3	19.0	19.7
European immigrants	15.7 (1.1)	16.2 (0.9)	19.7 (0.7)	19.9 (0.2)
Non-European immigrants	17.3 (2.7)	19.5 (4.2)	21.5 (2.5)	23.8 (4.1)

Source: Chen, Wilkins, and Ng (1996). Figures were estimated based on 1986 and 1991 Canadian census, and Canadian Vital Statistics Data Base, 1985–7, 1990–2.
[1] Numbers in parentheses show the difference from the estimates for Canadian-born.

In 1991, the difference increased to 6.7 years. Among women, non-European immigrants were expected to live about four to five years longer than non-immigrant Canadian women. At the age of 65, non-European immigrant men and women were both expected to live three to five years longer than the Canadian-born cohort. The differences between estimates for Canadian-born and European immigrants were substantially reduced; however, in all cases, European immigrants were expected to outlive Canadian-born cohorts.

Undoubtedly, the findings reported by Chen, Ng, and Wilkins (1996a) are convincing. At least in Canada, it seems safe to conclude that immigrants, especially non-European immigrants, outperform Canadians on major vital and disability statistics. However, it is not clear whether these health advantages based on the estimates hold true on other measures. In their subsequent work, Chen and his colleagues (Chen, Wilkins, and Ng 1996) used the National Population Health Survey (NPHS) data to examine variations in key health indicators and health behaviours, including chronic health conditions, hospitalization, frequent visits to physicians, dental care, smoking, and physical activities. The investigators also examined the effects of acculturation, the result, for our purposes, of living in Canada for more than ten years.

Table 6.2
Age-adjusted prevalence of chronic conditions and never smoked among adults (18 years or older), by immigration status, sex, income, and education

	Canadian-born	European immigrants 0–10 years	European immigrants 11+ years	Non-European immigrants 0–10 years	Non-European immigrants 11+ years
Chronic conditions	56.8	46.7	57.7	37.2*	51.2
Male	53.0	39.8	54.7	33.8*	46.7
Female	60.5	52.3	60.5	40.1*	55.6
Income of less than					
$30,000	59.7	46.3	59.5	37.4*	55.5
$30,000 or more	54.7	46.4	56.8	39.0*	48.7
No high school					
education	56.3	55.2	58.8	37.0*	58.3
High school +	56.2	45.8	57.0	35.8*	50.1
Never smoked	34.4	55.7*	37.6	74.9*	61.7*
Male	29.8	–	32.7	58.7*	48.2*
Female	38.2	69.1*	43.8	87.9*	75.4*
Income of less than					
$30,000	28.3	53.8	31.6	69.1*	65.7*
$30,000 or more	36.4	55.4	38.7	81.1*	61.5*
No high school					
education	24.3	57.2*	30.3	80.6*	57.8*
High school +	37.0	55.0	37.6	70.9*	62.3*

Source: Chen, Ng and Wilkins (1996a), table 2 and table 5, based on the National Population Health Survey, 1994–5.
Notes: The prevalence rates marked by * are significantly different from the corresponding rates for the Canadian-born.

By and large, the conclusions were consistent with their earlier work, except that immigrants tended not to hold onto their health advantages over time. For example, as shown in table 6.2, the age-adjusted prevalence rates of chronic health conditions, including joint conditions, allergies, hypertension, headaches, asthma, and heart problems and stroke, were substantially higher among the Canadian-born than among non-European immigrants. European immigrants looked similar to the Canadian-born. However, the difference between the immigrants and Canadians diminished substantially among those who had been in Canada more than ten years.

The data also appeared to suggest that changes in health among immigrants were likely to be the consequence of changes in health behaviours. At the bottom of table 6.2, we can see that considerable proportions of immigrant men and women started smoking following their settlement in Canada.

These findings have been shown to be robust across countries and across ethnocultural groups, and have been attributed to selection criteria and stringent health examinations that ensure the healthiest individuals are admitted to Canada. However, results show clearly that immigrants failed to maintain their health advantages over the years and generations in Canada. A rigorous health screening includes passing the Immigration Medical Examinations (IME).[1] The enforcement of a point system means that Canada is admitting the most physically healthy,[2] educated, and linguistically and economically advantaged individuals. Although Canadian immigration policy is multi-purposed, the primary motive for accepting new immigrants is to serve the Canadian economy by filling a need for skilled workers in specified industrial sectors. For the last four decades, Canada has adopted a point system that focuses on age, education, language (the ability to speak one of the two official languages), occupation (and experience), and adaptability. The selection system includes specific details of the educational requirements and occupational or business requirements for individual applicants. Although conditions may be relaxed for sponsored applicants and refugee claimants, in practice, the same criteria are applied for the selection and admission of almost all cases. Given the stringent selection and admission criteria, it is not clear what accounts for the observed deterioration in immigrant health. Based on the literature to date, as reviewed below, we suggest that any explanation must incorporate a wide variety of contextual and personal influences. For example, the evident downward trend in immigrant health may be due to an unwillingness or inefficiency of the receiving community in meeting the needs of newcomers. One illustration of this is the significant fact that a favourable IME does not ensure the approval of provincial health-care coverage in Canada.[3] The deterioration in immigrant health may also be a function of the stressful nature of migration and resettlement. Finally, the decline in health may be an integral aspect of an acculturation process by which immigrants come to more closely resemble the host group.

'HEALTHY IMMIGRANT EFFECT'

With such rigorous selection of potential future citizens, it may not be surprising to find reports demonstrating the 'healthy immigrant effect.'

Chen, Ng, and Wilkins (1996) compared the foreign-born and Canada-born individuals participating in the National Population Health Survey. Their analyses, which examined an array of health indicators, including chronic illness and disabilities, past-month sick days, and the frequency of using health-care services, illustrated clearly that, compared with native-born respondents, immigrants were significantly less likely to have long-term health conditions or disabilities, had fewer sick days, and less absenteeism. The rates of long-term use of health-care services varied little between the native- and foreign-born respondents. These health advantages were found despite severe life strains prevalent among foreign-born Canadians. For example, unemployment and poverty rates among immigrants were two to three times greater than the Canadian rates (Beiser et al. 2000, 2002; Ornstein 2000).

It would seem as if the healthy immigrant effect observed in Canada is not easily disputable, given that the same effects have been reported in receiving countries – such as Australia and the United States – using a similar point (selection) system and IMEs. Researchers have attributed the phenomenon to selection-immigration systems based on points, which emphasize employability, sound physical health, and psychological hardiness. In addition, medical examinations and screenings that are part of the immigration process block admission of the less healthy to Canada.

Nonetheless, conclusions regarding a healthy immigrant effect should be tempered. First, although the healthy immigrant effect is an accurate generalization when all things are put together, immigrants consist of populations whose health behaviours and lifestyles are extremely diverse. To suggest an all-encompassing effect of healthy immigrants tends to ignore the acute needs of such extremely disadvantaged populations as visible-minority immigrants. Second, careful attention must be given to *changes* in immigrant health, not only to health *status*. Health researchers refer to the deterioration of immigrant health as a part of the natural course of 'becoming us' (for example, the adoption of the poor aspects of a North American lifestyle such as an unhealthy diet, drinking, and smoking). However, it may also suggest the presence and effects of stress, including the stress of living in poverty, living in substandard conditions, and living with systemic and persistent discrimination against new immigrants and refugees. Finally, although immigrants are, in general, healthier than the native-born population, some immigrant or refugee groups may exhibit significantly increased rates of specific health problems. The relative risk of tuberculosis, to cite one example, is many times greater among immigrants than it is among the general population, and is especially high among refugees from selected areas of the world, such as Southeast Asia, sub-Saharan Africa, the Indian subcontinent, Latin America, the former Soviet Union, and Eastern Europe. Given rigorous screening procedures, it is critical to consider the role of post-migration stress, including poverty and poor living conditions, as contributing to the deterioration in immigrant health.

ACCULTURATION AND IMMIGRANT HEALTH

The healthy immigrant effect is strong and difficult to dispute, and it runs contrary to the conventional wisdom that highlights the stressful nature of settlement. But the effect does not endure for long; as we have already noted, as immigrants learn and adopt new ways of life (Canadian or American), their health tends to deteriorate, a process independent of the health consequences of aging. Matched on age and developmental stage, the health status of immigrants is better than that of their Canadian- or American-born counterparts of the same ethnic origin. The fact that this decline in immigrant health appears to be due to the settlement process, or acculturation, also seems to run contrary to both conventional wisdom and sociological assumptions. Intuitively, although we think of the early settlement period as stressful, surely acculturation should ease the burden of life strains among immigrants, and the children of immigrants should face less stressful events and circumstances.

One explanation of the declining health status in immigrants is based on the premise that the acculturation process naturally includes the adoptions of Canadian and American behavioural norms for diet, smoking, drinking, and sexuality. A classic study of the health influence of changes in lifestyle examined the rates of coronary heart disease (CHD) among Japanese Americans in Hawaii (Kagan et al. 1975; Syme et al. 1975; Marmot and Syme 1976). Research findings based on this study showed a gradient in the CHD incidence, with the highest rates observed among those in California, and the lowest rates among those living in Japan; Japanese-Americans in Hawaii had intermediate rates. The variations in CHD rates could not be explained by standard CHD risk factors, including obesity. However, the retention of traditional Japanese values and heritage was related to reduced rates of CHD (Syme et al. 1975), because it encouraged a low-fat diet and discouraged smoking, drinking, and sex, especially among youth and women. A case-control study by the National Cancer Institute of the U.S. among Japanese-, Chinese-, and Filipino-American women, found that lower cancer rates were observed among new immigrant women from these countries than among women whose grandmothers were born in the United States (Saphir 1997).

According to the 1994–5 NPHS data, 18.1 per cent of European immigrants and 13.2 per cent of non-European immigrants have tried, or started, smoking tobacco after their first ten years in Canada (table 6.2). The rate of change in smoking behaviours was largest for female European immigrants (25.3 per cent) and European immigrants with less than a high school education (26.9 per cent). In fact, the percentage of 'never smoked' among immigrants of longer residence (ten years or longer) was no different from that for Canadian-born residents. The 1993 California Tobacco Survey showed that the rate of smoking among Hispanic women (10 per cent) was significantly lower than the rate for non-Hispanic white women (20.7 per cent); rates for men, however, were similar between the two groups (23.3 per cent and 23.5 per cent). But among adolescents, a greater proportion of Hispanic girls were smoking than white non-Hispanic girls. Thus, compared to their white counterparts, the immigrant children or children of immigrants were at greater risk for smoking, while their parents were at lower risk. In Canada and the U.S., acculturation is often linked to increased rates of smoking and drinking, especially among women and adolescents (Karno et al. 1987; Burnam et al. 1987; Rumbaut 1988; Pierce et al. 1994; Vega et al. 1998).

Empirical data supporting the post-settlement deterioration in immigrant health have typically been derived from cross-sectional epidemiological surveys that compare the health status of foreign-born and native-born host populations, compare adult immigrants, child immigrants, and children of immigrants, or compare variations in the length of residence in the host country. Based on positive associations with the place and length of residence or generational status, the differential health status across generations and cohorts of immigrants who arrived at different times were attributed to differential degrees of acculturation among the populations. In all these studies, acculturation has been rarely well defined.

While they provide some essential information, these research designs, in our view, are limited in their lack of attention to changes in health status according to the changing ways of life and health behaviours that occur during the resettlement period. Acculturation is also the process of acquiring and incorporating such aspects of a new culture as codes of behaviour and, accordingly, undoubtedly includes changes in health care and help-seeking behaviour. The contemporary demographies of most urban centres in Canada and the United States suggest the need to develop systematic research focusing on the links between acculturation and health. We need reliable information about the effects of changes in behaviour on specific health-indicators in order to plan health services and health promotion and illness-prevention programs for immigrants, refugees, and their children.

A crucial first step is contextualizing the acculturation process. At the time of their arrival, many immigrants, especially refugees, lack most social and material resources. They begin resettlement in the neighbourhoods where they find affordable housing, as Robert A. Murdie and Carlos Teixeira explain in chapter 3. Unfortunately, residential neighbourhood segregation, whether created by institutionalized coercion or formed voluntarily by ethnic groups, manifests an exclusive and persistent form of inequality (Williams 1997). As they begin to learn English and earn their living – most commonly in unskilled manual jobs – immigrants learn the Canadian way of living from their co-workers and neighbours, as well as from members of the same ethnic community who have been in Canada longer. A significant number of non-European refugees are rarely in contact with the Canadian middle-class population until many years or decades into their resettlement. They also have considerably more difficulty with the official languages and in finding a job related to their profession than migrants of European background. European immigrants often experience an immediate promotion in socio-economic status and improvement in their standard of living. Thus, the course and colour of acculturation for new Canadians can be categorically different depending on the country of origin.

Gender is another factor. The data suggest that the course and health impacts of acculturation may be significantly different for men than for women. Smoking and depression are taken as examples here. The rate of smoking is significantly higher among Chinese males when compared with the overall rate of smoking in Canada, but few Chinese females smoke. Among Chinese immigrant males, there seems to be no significant change in smoking behaviour over time, while there is a significant increase in cigarette smoking among Chinese immigrant women (Marin, Perez-Stable, and Marin 1989). In a study of the mental health of Southeast Asian refugees, and Beiser and Hou (2001) reported that depression was significantly more prevalent among men than women during the first three years of settlement in Canada. This pattern of gender difference is an unusual observation in population health research, and has been attributed to stress in finding employment, which may be of particular importance for males. Interestingly, during the next five years, the pattern observed in the Southeast Asian sample became consistent with epidemiological findings of depression in Canada. At follow-up, the rate of depression was significantly higher among women than men. The mental health of refugee males appeared to improve substantially, while refugee females experienced a considerable deterioration in their mental health. Incorporation of these considerations in research would improve the validity and specificity of empirical results regarding changes in migrant health and health behaviour, as well as of the psychosocial determinants of such changes.

Accurate conceptualization and measurement of an acculturation construct is also important since acculturation is multi-dimensional; its different components may help to explain some of the variability in population health indicators that cannot be accounted for by simply using the length of stay as a proxy measure of acculturation. It is difficult to hypothesize the health implications of adopting intrinsic cultural traits (arts, music) and beliefs (religion, political ideology, social equity). Another dimension of acculturation, however, is related to the adoption of instrumental traits of Canadian culture such as language, education, skills training, participating in job searches, and learning how to use media and social services. Deficits in these areas may have negative effects on mental or physical health. And adaptation to certain lifestyle behaviours – especially more risky ones such as drinking, smoking, and sexual behaviour – presents a dimension of acculturation that may have more direct health consequences.

Despite considerable interest, research on acculturation and health has not been grounded in well-defined theories. Noh, Kaspar, and Hou (1997) presented a model for linking acculturation and immigrant mental health (see figure 6.3) that is consistent with the theoretical paradigm of the stress process (Pearlin et al. 1981), and views acculturation as a process of constantly facing demands for learning new skills and making adjustments. According to the model, acculturation either ameliorates or impairs mental health, depending on the nature and appraisals of acculturative experiences. For instance, as a survival skill

Figure 6.3
Acculturation and acculturative stress in the stress process

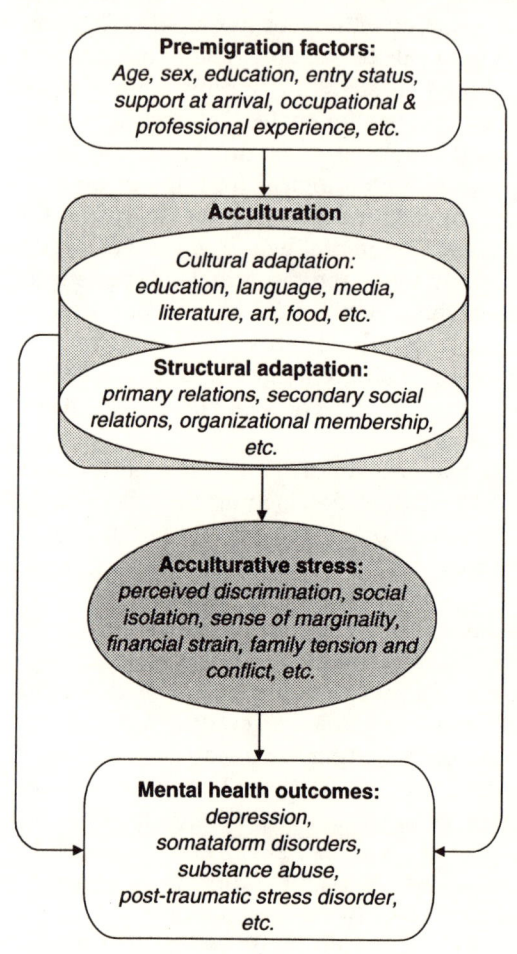

Pre-migration factors:
Age, sex, education, entry status, support at arrival, occupational & professional experience, etc.

Acculturation

Cultural adaptation:
education, language, media, literature, art, food, etc.

Structural adaptation:
primary relations, secondary social relations, organizational membership, etc.

Acculturative stress:
perceived discrimination, social isolation, sense of marginality, financial strain, family tension and conflict, etc.

Mental health outcomes:
depression, somataform disorders, substance abuse, post-traumatic stress disorder, etc.

Source: Noh, Kaspar, and Hou (1997).

critical to the cultural and economic adjustments of immigrants, (English) language ability promotes better mental health because it facilitates immigrants' success in economic domains, decreases social isolation and dependence on others for communications, and contributes to the development of social resources and new coping strategies (Montero and Dieppa 1982; Westermeyer, Neider, and Vang, 1984; Ying and Miller 1992; Nicassio et al. 1986). As immigrants acculturate and show improved ability in English and improved economic status, however, their acquisition of a better understanding of various shortcomings and realities within the new cultural milieu (for example, through subtle discriminations) contributes to negative mental health symptoms (Portes 1984; Noh et al. 1999). Noh, Kaspar, and Hou (1999) hypothesized that increased levels of acculturation may have positive effects on health, while the extent of stress perceived by new immigrants to derive from acculturative demands may exert adverse influences. Analyses of data from the Chinese American Psychiatric Epidemiological Study by Shen and Takeuchi (2001) have shown results that are consistent with this argument.

An important feature of this model (Noh et al. 1997) is that it incorporates variations in acculturative experiences across different ethnocultural immigrant and refugee groups. That is, the model specifies how the effects of race and ethnicity on immigrant health are mediated by acculturation. For immigrants whose values, religion, occupation, and language deviate sharply from those of the host society, the repercussions of failing to meet the demands of the acculturation process can result in extremely taxing resettlement contexts characterized by unemployment, poverty, poor housing, and racial discrimination. Accurate assessment of immigrant health must take into account that negative life events arising in such poor contexts are disproportionately distributed across ethnic and racial groups.

SETTLEMENT STRESS AND HEALTH

Stress and Infectious Diseases: The Case of Tuberculosis

Despite strong empirical evidence to the contrary, concern and controversy persist over whether immigration puts public health in jeopardy. As we noted earlier in this chapter, some experts and the public media portray immigrants as host carriers of such infectious diseases as tuberculosis (TB) and HIV. Tuberculosis, in particular, provides an interesting case study of this question, given the striking results of the incidence of the disease in relation to the immigration status of those affected. Beiser (unpublished) acknowledges that immigration undoubtedly helps account for TB's tenacity. He notes that, in 1980, 50 per cent of all cases of tuberculosis occurred among the Canadian-born, non-Aboriginal population. The proportion dropped to 22 per cent in 1991. During the same period, the proportion of all cases of TB in the foreign-born population increased from 35 per cent to 58 per cent; remaining cases either occurred in the Aboriginal population or were of unknown origin.

Toronto's population accounted for 25 per cent of TB cases in Canada, and the prevalence of TB in Toronto has reached an alarming level of 23 occurrences per 100,000 (in 1990–5); 81 per cent of those cases were among the foreign-born population of Toronto. Similar trends have been observed in the United States (McKenna, McCray, and Onorato 1995). In England, foreign-born residents account for only 5 per cent of the total population, but make up over 50 per cent of all TB cases (Tocque et al. 1998).

This rapid increase in the incidence of TB in immigrants was contemporaneous with a decrease in incidence among the native-born population. This is also the period when massive economic restructuring took place in most industrial countries and cities, which resulted in immense changes in labour demand (see Valerie Preston, Lucia Lo, and Shuguang Wang's discussion of immigrant economic status in chapter 4). While many Canadians and Torontonians had been affected by the industrial downsizing, visible-minority immigrants arriving after 1980 were forced to absorb most of it (Lian and Matthews 1998; Reitz 1998; Akbari 1995; Kazemipur and Halli 2000). There is statistical evidence that immigrants belonging to the charter groups from Western and Northern Europe and the United Stated assumed relatively little of the consequences. Even those from Southern and Eastern Europe showed a fair amount of stability in their economic performance (Preston, Lo, and Wang, chapter 4, this volume).

The statistics alone appeared to suggest that immigrants account for the majority of TB cases. But, did the statistics show that immigrants brought disease with them? In Canada, the U.S., and the UK, most cases of TB among the foreign-born developed within the first five to ten years following landing (McKenna, McCray, and Onorato 1995; Binkin et al. 1996; Kerbel 2000). The mean latency period was significantly shorter for refugee than immigrant groups.

Beiser (unpublished) sees two possible explanations for the high incidence of TB among immigrants and refugees during the early resettlement period. Inadequate screening for the disease is a possibility; however, the data do not support this explanation. One study of TB cases in Manitoba (Orr, Manfreda, Hershfield 1990) found that almost

80 per cent of TB cases among new immigrants were among patients whose IME found negative, stable chest X-rays and negative sputum. Even among immigrants placed under public-health surveillance because they showed a trace of active or inactive TB upon screening, only 22 per cent were eventually detected as cases. Clinically, those under surveillance have a 4.5 to 6 times greater risk for developing active TB compared with persons with negative test results (Nolan and Elarth 1988).

Thus, inadequate medical screening cannot account for the fact that an overwhelming majority of post-migration TB cases were new cases with a negative pre-migration condition. Beiser has suggested that the surge of TB in the foreign-born population might be explained by considering how the stress of resettlement may reduce immunology defence. Shorter mean latency periods for TB in refugee compared with immigrant populations is consistent with this explanation. Relative to immigrants, refugees are exposed to more severe life stress prior to landing, and they lack established like-ethnic community support systems in Canada. The population health data that is currently available do not provide information about whether harsh and stressful living conditions early in the resettlement period could partially account for the high incidence of TB in immigrant and refugee pop-ulations. Although immigrants as a whole are a relatively healthy population, they are exposed to greater health risks than the general population to the extent that they experience severe and enduring poverty. Poverty is one of the most powerful determinants of health, and is among the most profound causes of inequities in mortality, morbidity, and disability (Krieger 1999). Many new immigrants and refugees, especially those from non-European countries, find such basic requirements as earning a sufficient income and getting adequate housing in Toronto are not as easily achieved as they dreamed when they arrived in Canada.[4]

One recent report by the U.S. Centers for Disease Control and Prevention (2001) revealed that, while the rates of TB in some areas in the United States ranked higher than in some developing countries, treatment programs fail to incorporate procedures for identifying individuals who are vulnerable to acquiring TB, including those who are in close contact with those infected with TB, as well as those with HIV. Poor immune functioning with HIV is associated with an 800-time increased likelihood of developing active TB upon exposure to it. Moreover, there is a lower probability of detecting infection through standard TB testing among those with HIV. The CDC study found that only one in seven people with close contacts with TB patients were screened for HIV infection, and that at least 25 per cent were not fully tested for TB. Given that over 80 per cent of TB cases were among foreign-born people, the lack of comprehensive detection and prevention programs places those in contact with these patients at high risk for contracting diseases. Unfortunately, the public, as well as governments, media, and some medical professions have focused on solutions aimed at reducing rates of such infectious diseases as TB through restricting entry to Canada of immigrants from non-European countries. Rarely has there been support for formulating policies and programs directed at enhancing resettlement services, as well as medical surveillance and treatment of infected patients and their families.

Social Stress and Mental Health: The Case of Discrimination

There is a long tradition of scientific inquiry into the significance of social inequity as a primary source of differential distributions of health and well-being (Pearlin 1989; Aneshensel 1992). In the U.S. and in Canada, race is a principal determinant of access to social status and resources, of personal identity, and of mortality and morbidity (for example, Williams 1997). The extent to which minorities and foreign-born residents feel that they are being treated unfairly, excluded, ignored, or rejected on the basis of their race or ethnicity is a good indicator of Toronto's competence in dealing with diversity. Discrimination does not simply refer to evaluating personal treatment based on indicators of ascribed status (for example, race, gender, age, disability, and religion), but it also includes both a systemic denial of basic human rights and exclusion from and access to one's share of social benefits and resources.

Canadian studies show that minorities and immigrants in Canada are the frequent targets of racism and discrimination (Head 1975, 1981; Pitman 1977; Ubale 1977; Breton 1978; Robson and Breems 1985; Lewis 1992; Henry et al. 1995; Noh et al. 1998). In addition, ethnoracial groups encounter racism at different rates of frequency and in different ways. For example, South Asians and Blacks in Canada have been the most frequent targets of extreme and overt forms of racism. According to one study, about 50 per cent of South Asians living in Vancouver experienced at least one discrimination-related incident, and 14 per cent were victims of property damage or vandalism (Robson and Breems 1985). In a Toronto study, 67 per cent of South Asians and 64 per cent of Blacks reported personal experiences of racial discrimination, mainly in housing and employment (Head 1991).

An earlier study by Breton (1978) also revealed inter-ethnic variations in perceptions of discrimination. Breton found that 75 per cent of West Indians living in Toronto reported experiences of job-related discrimination. Among Chinese, the corresponding statistic was only 29 per cent. The rates of discrimination perceived by Asians in Breton's study approximated those reported in a Vancouver study of Southeast Asian refugees conducted more than a decade later in 1991 (Noh et al. 1999). Approximately one-quarter (26 per cent) of the Southeast Asian respondents reported one or more experiences of perceived discrimination.

Results based on our own research in Toronto showed that less than 16.5 per cent of Korean immigrant respondents said they had never been discriminated against because of their ethnic background. A possible reason for the high rate of discrimination in this study relative to other studies is that we asked respondents to rate their experiences of a variety of discrimination-related events. In other studies, respondents typically endorsed their agreement with a single item. This suggests that self-reports on single items may underestimate the actual rates of experienced discrimination among immigrants (Noh et al. 1999).

It is worth noting that the rates found in Canadian studies are not lower than the rates found in American studies. Jackson, Antonucci, and Gibson (1995), based on their analysis of the Americans' Changing Lives Survey data, found consistent rates across diverse racial minority groups. Rates of being treated badly because of their race or ethnicity were, respectively, 47 per cent, 45 per cent, and 34 per cent for Black, Asian, and Native Americans. Polish and Italian Americans had rates of 16 per cent and 10 per cent, respectively. Kuo (1995), who studied Asians living in Seattle in 1982, reported similar rates of discrimination. Fifteen per cent of the respondents in Kuo's study said that they had experienced discrimination when looking for housing, and 30 per cent when looking for work. A. Roberts (1988) studied perceived discrimination among Vietnamese refugees in northern California and the U.S. Gulf states, and reported a prevalence of 33 per cent.

If many people of colour, especially new refugees and immigrants, find it difficult to avoid racial prejudice and stigma, there is a serious threat to their successful resettlement and good health (Lieberson 1982; Portes 1984; Canadian Task Force 1988). This assumption is consistent with sociological traditions that emphasize the significance of social inequity as the primary source of differential distributions of health and well-being (Pearlin 1989; Aneshensel 1992). The research indicates that experiences of unfair treatments based on one's racial or ethnic backgrounds have negative consequences for physical and mental health. Discrimination constitutes a significant social stressor for racial minorities (Rabkin and Struening 1976; Kessler and Neighbors 1986; V.L. Thompson 1996) with negative physical and mental health consequences (Williams 1997). According to the results of qualitative studies and community surveys, the experience of discrimination is significantly related to increased levels of psychological distress among immigrants and visible minorities in Canada (Dion 1975; Essed 1991; Noh et al. 1999), New Zealand (Pernice and Brook 1996), and the United States (Amaro, Russo, and Johnson 1987; Salgado de Snyder 1987).

Research on the psychological and physical health consequences of discrimination has been relatively more active in the United States than in Canada, with U.S. studies focused primarily on the experiences of African Americans. Several of these large scale epidemiological community studies have demonstrated significant associations between the experience of racial discrimination and psychological well-being. Williams and colleagues (Jackson, Williams, and Torres 1997; Williams and Chung 1997; Williams et al. 1997) used data from two U.S. national surveys (National Study of Black Americans and Americans' Changing Lives) and a regional study (Detroit Area Study) to examine the impacts of discrimination on an array of health outcomes. Their results showed that the self-reported experience of discrimination during the previous month was associated with increased levels of chronic health problems, physical disabilities, self-reported physical symptoms, and diagnosed depression. Self-reported discrimination was also related to a reduced degree of life satisfaction, happiness, and psychological distress (Jackson, Williams, and Torres 1997; Williams and Chung 1997).

Professor Kenneth Dion, a psychologist at the University of Toronto, reported a direct link between discrimination and higher levels of psychological symptoms among Jewish and Chinese university students in Toronto (Dion and Earn 1975; Pak, Dion, and Dion 1991). Poor self-esteem was related to discrimination among female university students, supporting the 'double jeopardy' hypothesis (Dion 1975). Noh et al. (1999) reported that the discrimination-depression connection was, in part, conditioned by the presence (and extent) of emotional arousal invoked by the perception of discrimination. Discrimination with mini-

Table 6.3
Regression of depression on perceived discrimination, and two types of coping (forbearance and confrontation) among Southeast Asians living in the Greater Area of Vancouver (N = 643)

Predictors in the model	Metric regression coefficient	Standard error
Age	−.038*	.021
Sex: Female = 1; Male = 0	.501	.407
Marital status: Married = 1; Else = 0	−.752	.484
Employment status: Employed = 1; Else = 0	−1.499*	.618
Years of education	−.159*	.066
Discrimination: ever discriminated in Canada = 1; Else = 0	1.566***	.429
Coping: forbearance	−2.494***	.457
Coping: confrontation	.414	.304
Constant	24.894***	1.428

*p < .05; ** p < .01; *** p < .001
Source: Noh et al. (1999).

mal emotional arousal was not associated with higher depression; however, there was a substantial hike in depressive symptoms if perceptions of discrimination were associated with higher emotional strain.

Noh et al. (1999) also examined the role of coping and ethnic identity as stress-buffering moderators within a large sample of Southeast Asians (so-called boat people) in British Columbia. Like Jackson et al. (1995) in the United States, Noh et al. (1999) found a significant direct influence of perceived racial/ethnic discrimination on depression. As shown in table 6.3, controlling for the effects of common social correlates of depression, perceived discrimination had a substantial impact on depression (b = 1.566, se = .429, p < .001). Also observed was the significant stress-buffering effect of forbearance coping; those who accepted and ignored racial events as part of life, and reserved direct responses, showed little increase in depressive symptoms following experiences of racial incidents. As illustrated in figure 6.4, this buffering effect of forbearance coping was significantly more pronounced among those Asian refugees who maintained a strong sense of ethnic adherence and salience. Among those who did not have strong attach-ment to ethnic culture, forbearance did not help ease their psychological distress related to racism.

Figure 6.4
Moderating effect of ethnic identity for the effect of forbearance coping on depression

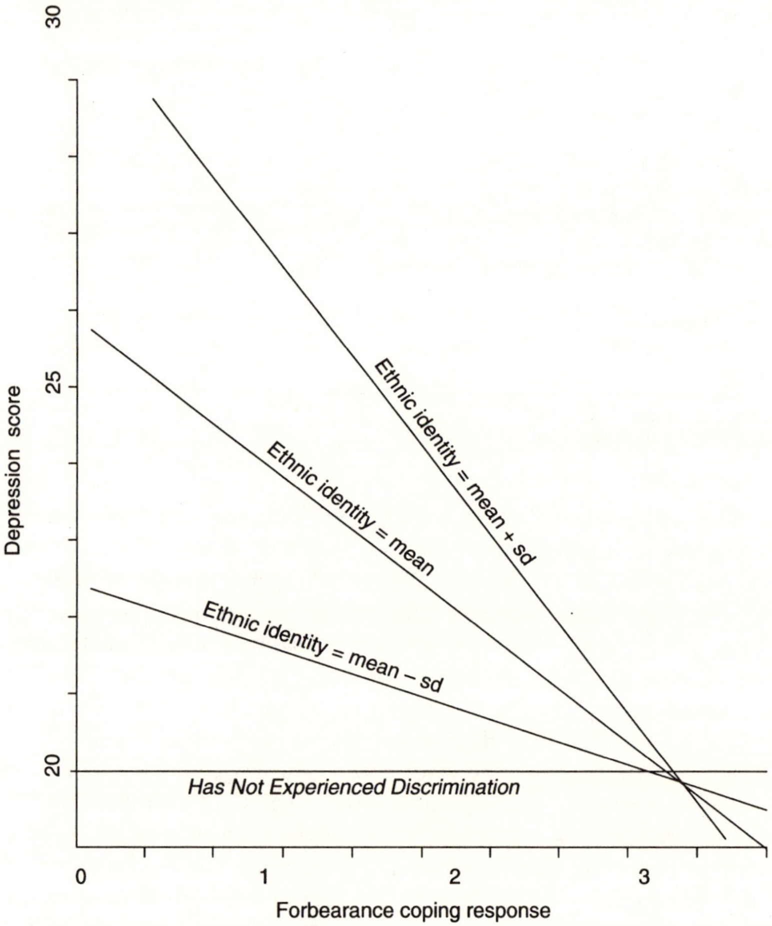
30
25
20
Depression score
Ethnic identity = mean + sd
Ethnic identity = mean
Ethnic identity = mean – sd
Has Not Experienced Discrimination
0
1
2
3
Forbearance coping response

Source: Noh et al. (1999), figure 2.

In summary, a large majority of visible minorities and immigrants in Canada (and Toronto) feel that they are often treated unfairly. Most of the discrimination appears to occur in housing and job markets. The research indicates that experiences of unfair treatment based on one's racial or ethnic background have negative consequences for physical and mental health through three identified pathways to ill health (Krieger 1999; Williams et al. 1994, 1997). First, racism and ethnic discrimination affect the well-being of immigrants by placing and keeping them under social and economic deprivation. Segregated neighbourhoods across racial or ethnic distinctions is an extreme form of structural discrimination. Not only is residential segregation not possible without systemic cooperation at the levels of economic, political, private and public institutions (including government, media, the legal system, police, banks, and realtors), its impact cuts across many indicators and determinants of health and well-being (including financial, industrial, educational, environmental, and personal health). Second, exposure to discrimination is a serious stressor. Williams and Morris (2000) have demonstrated that frequent and repeated exposures to excessive stressors reduce human immune functions and increase vulnerability to physical and mental disorders. Exposure to discrimination also exerts adverse effects through socialization processes by which members of minority groups accept the stereotypes and prejudices about their group.

Clearly, research on racism, discrimination, and health is in its infancy. Although the adverse influence of discrimination on the physical and mental health of minority groups (females, racial/ethnic minorities, and immigrants) has been widely assumed, little empirical evidence has ever been presented (Williams 1997; Krieger 1999). It is critical at this point to consider the possibility of alternative pathways:

> While the findings of the current study are consistent with the hypothesis that exposure to discrimination is associated with elevated levels of depressive symptoms, and that forbearance, particularly when adopted by individuals with strong ethnic identification, reduces the emotional impact of the exposure for ... Southeast Asian refugees in Canada, the issue of causal order remains an important consideration ... The possibility remains that depressed individuals are more likely than the psychologically comfortable to recall experiences of discrimination and to blame them for their current unhappiness. Similarly, strong ethnic identification may increase the likelihood of recalling or perceiving discrimination. (Noh et al. 1999, 203)

For a more valid assessment of the impact of discrimination, the development of a longitudinal, prospective cohort study and appropriate experimental study is paramount. The consistency and magnitude of the cross-sectional association provides a rationale for extending efforts to implement prospective and experimental studies.

ACCOUNTING FOR VARIATIONS IN IMMIGRANT HEALTH

For decades, researchers held 'disease' or 'deficit' perspectives on immigrant and minority health (Hull 1979; Fitinger and Schwartz 1981; Sue and Morishima 1982; Kuo 1984). Concepts used to depict sources of immigration- and resettlement-related stress include the uprooting process (Handlin 1951), culture shock (Oberg 1960), culture fatigue (Guthrie 1975), language shock (Smalley 1963), role shock (Byrnes 1966), perspective ambiguity (Banchevska 1981), and acculturative stress (Berry et al. 1987; Noh and Avison 1996). During the last three decades, however, research findings on immigrant and refugee populations have contradicted the expectation based on the deficits models (Beiser and Fleming 1986; Noh et al. 1992a, b; Noh and Avison 1996; Wu and Kaspar 2000). In general, reliable research findings invariably suggest either physical and mental health advantages of immigrants, or little difference between immigrant and non-immigrant Canadians. The research supports the resilience of immigrants and refugees in spite of their experiences of extreme forms of risk situations, including severe poverty, disruption in family unity due to migration, and systemic barriers to educational and occupational/professional ambitions. There is relatively less certainty about what protects immigrants and refugees from the tolls of life stress. The literature offers only ad hoc explanations, including the protective effects of (a) the ethnic community and extended family social support; (b) upward mobility; and (c) cultural and personal coping resources. We present research findings related to these views next, along with some research findings on the mental health of children and youth from immigrant and refugee families. The developmental adjustments of these youth are among the most critical indexes of the long-term effects of settlement processes and policies in Canada.

Like-Ethnic Community Support

An epidemiological study by Beiser and his colleagues (Beiser and Fleming 1986; Beiser et al. 1995) focused on the socio-economic adaptations and mental health of Southeast Asian refugees in British Columbia. These were refugees from Vietnam, Laos, and Cambodia who settled in and around Vancouver between 1979 and 1981. In order to evaluate the relative risk for psychiatric tolls in this high-risk group, the researchers also obtained data from a random sample of non-immigrant Vancouver residents. The results of the study showed little difference in mental health symptoms between the sample of boat people and the comparison sample of Vancouver residents, and the investigators speculated about the protective effects of the presence of a large Asian community in Vancouver. This hypothesis was, in fact, partially supported. Refugees of Chinese origin received instrumental and informational social support and a sense of historical-cultural continuity from Vancouver's Chinese community, whereas other refugees (mostly Vietnamese) did not have access to such like-ethnic community support. During the first three years, Chinese refugees demonstrated significantly reduced levels of anxiety and depressive symptoms when compared with other refugees.

Noh and his colleagues conducted an epidemiological study of psychiatric symptoms among Korean immigrants living in the Greater Toronto Area, referred to as the Korean Mental Health Study (KMHS). A sample of adult immigrants (those who immigrated after the age of 16) was interviewed in 1990–1 (N = 860). Follow up data were collected twelve to sixteen months following the baseline interviews (N = 690). Psychiatric symptoms were measured by the revised form of the Symptom Checklist-90 (SCL-90-R) and the Centre for Epidemiologic Study of Depression (CES-D) scale. The translated (and back-translated) scales were provided with excellent psychiatric properties including reliability, construct validity, and cross-cultural appropriateness (Noh, Avison, and Kaspar 1992; Noh and Avison 1996; Noh, Kaspar, and Chen 1998). The confirmation of the psychometric and cross-cultural adequacy of these instruments is a critical step because Asians are more likely to present their somatic symptoms to clinicians as, for example, 'fire in the chest,' while not reporting their emotional or psychological distress or symptoms (Kleinman 1977, 1988). However, most rigorous analyses of Asians' responses reveal that, when questioned specifically, they do acknowledge, and respond accurately to having emotional symptoms (Noh and Avison 1996; Noh, Avison, and Kaspar 1992; Lin and Cheung 1999; U.S. Public Health Services 2001). Social support was measured using three indicators: (1) presence of confidence; (2) quality of social relations; and (3) perceived social support, with ratings repeated for supports derived within ethnic (Korean) networks and outside ethnic networks.

Like the Vancouver study, results based on this community survey of Korean immigrants showed that the prevalence of depression (4.5 per cent for the total sample, 2.6 per cent for males, and 6.7 per cent for females), despite economic and social hardships, approximated rates reported in large sample surveys of general populations of Americans and Canadians (Noh et al. 1992a, b). The results of that research also showed that, although a variety of social coping resources seemed to play a less significant part in the process through which Korean immigrants experienced distress, ethnic social support, nevertheless, had a direct effect on affective and psychotic symptom levels. Data shown in Panel A of table 6.4 are unequivocal in demonstrating substantial and significant effects of life stress and ethnic support, and the minimal influence of non-ethnic support, on both measures of psychological symptoms. It is also clear from the results presented in Panel B that the impact of life stress on affective symptoms is substantially moderated for those with a higher level of reported ethnic support (4.624) than for those with lower support (6.900) – a 33 per cent reduction in impact. The corresponding effect of non-ethnic support is a 19 per cent reduction in impact (6.400 against 7.915). The data seem to suggest no moderating effect of non-ethnic support on psychotic symptoms.

Through the longitudinal analysis of their data, Noh and Avison (1996) also found that ethnic (Korean) social support reduced exposure to subsequent life stressors. Ethnic social networks and support may protect new immigrants and refugees from experiencing stressful life difficulties, which in turn may reduce personal and psychological resources such as mastery, self-esteem and hardiness. Should this pattern of effects be demonstrated through a more rigorous research design, a generalization of the findings may have significant implications for planning and delivering social and health-care services. For example, social and health-care services developed and delivered by like-ethnic members and organizations may find more positive outcomes.

The KMHS findings do not warrant the conclusion that social support from the broader community has no role to play in the mental health of Korean Canadians. However, the mental-health-promoting effects of social support from the ethnic community observed in the KMHS provided empirical evidence that not all sources of support are equally effective in reducing psychological distress in immigrants. This finding can only be understood in the context of our sample of immigrants. Because Koreans born in Canada were not included in the study,

Table 6.4
Direct effect of life stress and social support on mental health, and stress-moderating effects of social support

Predictors	Mental health symptom clusters[a]	
	Affective symptoms[b]	Psychotic symptoms[c]
	Standardized beta coefficients	
A:		
Ethnic (Korean) social support	−.322 (5.844*)	−.339 (6.011*)
Non-ethnic social support	−.020 (.550)	−.011 (.256)
Stressful life events: All	.336 (6.378*)	.351 (6.041*)
	Metric beta coefficients of stressful life events	
B:		
Higher ethnic support	4.624 (6.896*)	.240 (6.376*)
Lower ethnic support	6.900 (8.284*)	NE[d]
Higher non-ethnic support	6.400 (9.425*)	.423 (9.780*)
Lower non-ethnic support	7.915 (8.881*)	.460 (8.447*)

Notes: Reported estimates are standardized and unstandardized beta matrix, with t-values in parentheses, estimated by the LISREL VII. Estimation controlled for the effects of age, sex, marital status, income, education, and length of residence in Canada on all latent factors in the analysis (i.e. social support measures, stressful life events, and mental health outcomes. Those t-values notes with * suggest statistical significance ($p < .001$).
[a] Mental health outcomes were assessed by adopting the CES-D, SCL-90-R, and a culture-specific somatic symptom scale for Koreans.
[b] Latent variable 'affective symptoms' were derived from CES-D, SCL-90-R subscales (depression, somatization, and anxiety) and Korean somatic symptom scale.
[c] Latent variable 'psychotic symptom' scores were derived from the SCL-90-R subscales (phobic anxiety, psychosis, paranoia).
[d] Model was not identified for the subsample of lower ethnic support.
Source: Noh, Wu, and Avison (1994).

the potential impact of general social support on the mental health of Korean Canadians is probably attenuated. That is, limiting this study to immigrants probably underestimated the effects of acculturation and its contributions to mental health benefits derived through support from the broader community. This is a good example of how our knowledge of immigrant health is relatively less extensive than that of the health of the native-born Canadian population.

New Mobility Effect

A recent report (Tracey-Wortley and Wheaton 1997) based on random community samples of adults in Toronto compared white respondents and samples of racial minorities immigrants or refugees. Among men at the lower end of the socio-economic (SES) continuum (income and education), rates of mental disorder were higher compared with the sample of white males. Among upper-SES minority males, rates of disorders were substantially lower than the rates found among whites. Tracey-Wortley and Wheaton (1996) hypothesized a 'new money' or 'mobility' effect (Davis 1984), a highly relevant point for understanding immigrant mental health. Upper income and education levels among racial minority immigrants and refugees may have indicated recent upward mobility, and recent increases in financial security could have more health promoting and buffering effects than having a high income (see Davis 1984, as cited by Tracey-Wortley and Wheaton 1997).

The effect was not repeated among women. Among women, the respondents of minority immigrants fared better across all measures of psychiatric symptoms and disorders. East Asian women showed the most advantages relative to white women; the same trend was evident among Black women, but the size of their relative advantage over white women was smaller. The gender difference seemed to show the differential significance of economic and occupational mobility (either downward or upward), which could have affected men substantially more than women.

Culture-Specific Responses and Coping

A limited amount of research points to the possible effects of culture-specific ways of responding to settlement stress, as well as the effects of culture on coping success. In their analysis of national health data (National Population Health Study), Wu and Kaspar (2000) reported that Asian immigrant respondents experienced better mental health than non-Asian immigrants or non-immigrants in the NPHS. Their explanation of this finding was framed in terms of cultural characteristics specific to Asians that may contribute to their ability to cope better with, and be less susceptible to psychological and physical stress related to migration. Better mental health in the Asian sample may have represented an Asian cultural orientation towards calm responses to stressful circumstances. Alternatively, cultural prohibitions may have discouraged Asian respondents from admitting psychological distress or a need for psychiatric services (Takeuchi et al. 1988).

An analysis of longitudinal data of Korean immigrants in Toronto (Noh and Avison 1996) highlighted the role of coping resources. The findings demonstrated that mental health (as measured by depressive symptomatology) was directly linked to the level of life stress, including the experiences of employment, financial strain, unfair treatment, and family problems. However, the study also showed that a significant portion of the stress effect was suppressed or buffered by coping resources. Two aspects of personal resources were found to be particularly important. Those immigrants who maintained a strong sense of efficacy in mastering one's life conditions showed significantly fewer symptoms of depression than other immigrants who were exposed to the same levels of life stress, but lacked the sense of mastery. In the same way, self-esteem, another important coping resource, protected immigrants' mental health from the potential toll of the life stress. The study provided an empirical confirmation of the independent effects of the two coping resource variables.

One pivotal finding from the longitudinal analysis was the critical role played by stress. Noh and Avison (1996) reported that repeated or cumulated experiences of resettlement stress and other negative life events each exerted direct effects diminishing the level of these essential coping resources – mastery and self-esteem. The finding was consistent with the previously noted immigrant health deterioration during the post-migration settlement and acculturation. Although new immigrants may have anticipated and prepared for the challenges of the new environment, their experiences of persistent stress, systemic barriers and bias towards immigrants and racial minorities, and the inadequacy of personal efforts could have corroded their confidence in their own effectiveness and, consequently, their self-esteem and self-worth. They also suggested that ethnic social support played the most critical role in mitigating this stress process.

Finally, despite research evidence supporting lower pathology in immigrant populations, research to date cannot confirm a better state of well-being among immigrants. Unfortunately, little research has concentrated on the positive mental health aspects of immigration and immigrant well-being. As we discussed earlier, immigrants failed to retain their health advantage with extended residence in Canada. Our own research shows that settlement stress and other forms of life strains erode resilience in immigrants and compromise their health and well-being. This suggests a less encouraging scenario of immigrant health. Data highlighting the importance of social support systems among coethnic members sharing compatible cultural values and situational experiences (for example, racial stigma) should be a priority for developing preventive interventions.

Children of Immigrant and Refugee Families

Research findings on the well-being of foreign-born children and children of immigrants are inconsistent, depicting both maladaptation and a healthier image of immigrant children compared with age cohorts of indigenous populations (see Rutter et al. 1974; Bradly and Sloman 1975; Amaral-Dias et al. 1981; Burke et al. 1982; Skhiri and Allani 1982; Morgan, Wingard, and Felice 1984; Krener and Sabin 1985; Sack 1985; Steinhausen 1985; Kinzie et al. 1986; Monroe-Blum et al. 1989; M. Zhou 1997; Zhou and Bankston 1998). Nonetheless, authorities in this field support the view that, on most criteria, children of im-migrants and child immigrants are as well-adjusted as non-immigrant children – and often surpass the national health status – despite increased rates of most major risk factors including poverty, functional illiteracy, living in high-risk neighbourhoods, and lower socio-economic status (Beiser et al. 2000, 2002; Hernandez and Charney 1998).

Although research findings are consistent with this conclusion, the scientific assessment of childhood mental health is not as well advanced, and we cannot draw any definitive conclusions regarding the mental health of immigrant and refugee youth. To examine the viability of the healthy immigrant effect in Canadian children and youth, we conducted some preliminary analyses of data from a national Canadian survey, the National Longitudinal Study of Children and Youth (NLSCY). The NLSCY was designed for a longitudinal investigation of a nationwide probability sample of 25,000 Canadian children, ranging from newborns to 12 year olds. Parents provided all information on all children up to the age of ten10. For children ten to eleven years of age, data were obtained from both children and parents. The analysis (unpublished) supported the view that immigrant children are healthier than later-generation children or native-born children of the host population. Parental assessments revealed a substantially lower mean emotional distress score in immigrant children than in second-generation and non-immigrant children. Sample means of conduct disorder for these groups also revealed an identical pattern of variation. The findings of parental reports closely replicated the general conclusions among the experts depicting healthy images of immigrant children.

We also obtained, from a random sample of immigrant youth and young adults (aged 10 to 25) in Toronto, data on depressive symptoms, antisocial behaviour, and two measures of perceived competence. The primary goal of the project was to compare the adolescent and young adult children of Korean immigrants in Toronto with neighbourhood peers of the same sex and age. Overall, the data did not support the conclusion of better health of immigrant children and youth (Noh et al. 1999). For example, as shown in figure 6.5, as far as the self-reported data were concerned, the adolescent and young adult children of Korean immigrants appeared to experience higher levels of depression than non-immigrant controls. However, as figure 6.5 clearly illustrates, according to parental assessments, immigrant youth and young adults showed a substantially lower mean depression score than second-generation and non-immigrant children. Sample means of anti-social behaviour also revealed an identical pattern of contrast.

The Korean immigrant sample, however, reported less competence in social and instrumental tasks. These results directly contradicted the conclusions of many recent studies, and seemingly well-accepted conclusions in the field. Furthermore, using NLSCY data, we examined the trends among children eleven and twelve years of age. Analysis of the self-reported adolescent data showed results that were consistent with those reported in the study of Korean youth; an exception was that ratings on hyperactivity showed better-adjusted immigrant youth in both self-reports and parental assessments.

These findings point to the critical issue of examining multiple sources of ratings in order to advance the current state of knowledge about the health of immigrant children and youth. The generally poor correspondence between youth self-reports and ratings made by proxy informants (usually the mother) in assessing childhood mental health (Achenbach, McConaughy, and Howell 1987) may be exaggerated in some refugee populations (Rousseau and Drapeau 1998). Rousseau and Drapeau's research found that not only did parents tend to assess their children's mental health more positively, and report significantly fewer symptoms compared to youth self-reports, but that this tendency varied across cultural groups.

Regarding such internal conditions as depression and anxiety, experts have suggested that adolescents may provide more reliable information than either parents or teachers (Achenbach, McConaughy, and

Figure 6.5
Depression for Korean immigrant adolescents and control samples

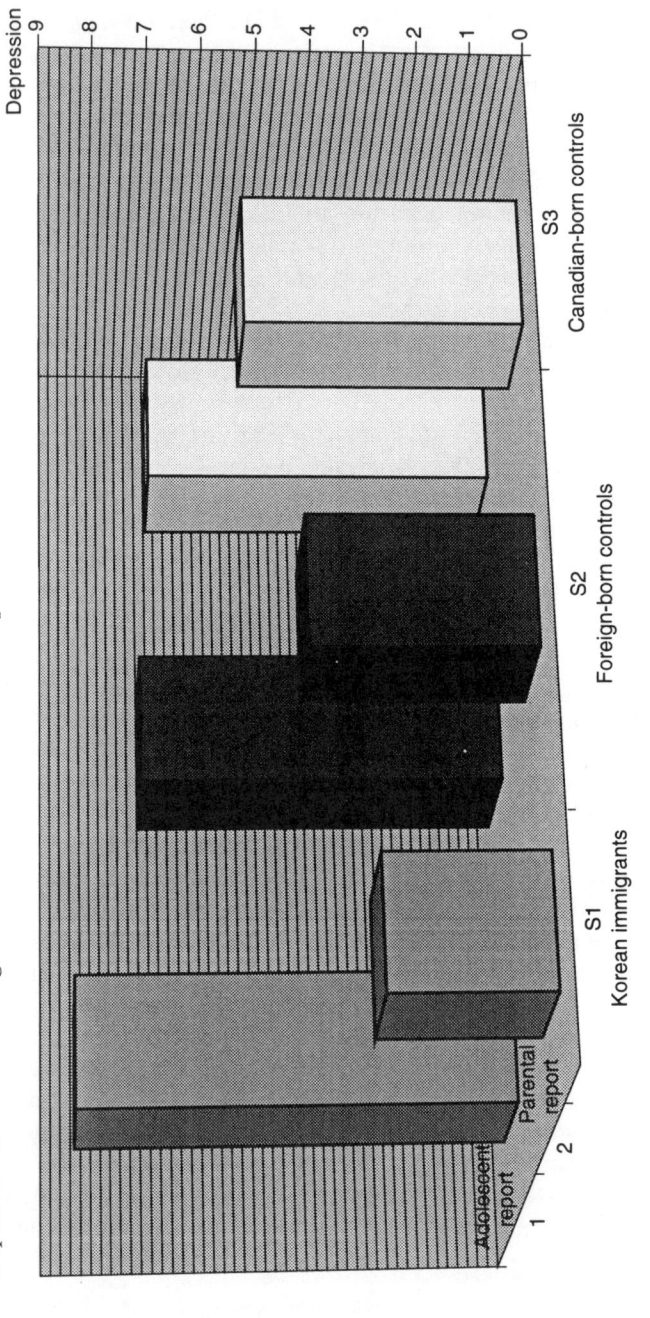

Source: Noh, Kaspar, and Hou (1998).

Howell 1987). If this assumption is reasonable, the discordance issue represents a source of bias that raises serious concern about underestimations of mental disorders and distress among immigrant children and adolescents. Is the mental health advantage of immigrant children more pronounced when the evaluation is based on parental reports than when it is based on children's self-reports? Is the parent-child discordance greater between children and immigrant parents than non-immigrant parents? Age and nature of symptoms are important considerations. Is response discordance greater in the assessment of adolescents when compared with the assessments of children, and is the assessment of internalizing symptoms more seriously discordant than the assessment of externalizing behaviour? Until these methodological issues are resolved, it would be premature to conclude that immigrant children are better adjusted than non-immigrant youth.

CONCLUSION

Toronto's response to the roughly 70,000 new immigrants and refugees – nearly one-third of Canada's total annual influx of newcomers – who make the city their final destination each year has been to adopt 'Diversity, Our Strength' as its motto, acknowledging that newcomers benefit the city by bringing with them new cultural and economic strengths. Toronto has been recognized by international organizations, such as the World Health Organization, for its desire to create a new model of a cosmopolitan city where people of all colours, languages, ethnic origins, beliefs, and socio-economic backgrounds may build a secure and safe life. To a large extent, the city has achieved most of this goal. Nonetheless, the challenges continue as new waves of immigrants continue to arrive in Toronto; the task of integrating them has not been completed.

Accommodating newcomers requires more than offering an orientation and involves more than playing the role of host. Integrating diversity means entering into a process by which strangers are becoming us, as described by Morton Beiser. It can be an exciting and dynamic process, but it requires an extraordinary commitment to constantly reshaping our identity – demographic, political, and cultural. Integrating diversity implies that all Torontonians, both collectively and individually, have equal access to the city's social, economic, political, and cultural resources. Integrating diversity in health requires planned acts to ensure the equal distribution of illness-prevention and health-promotion services across all ethnoracial communities and among newly arriving immigrants and refugees, and the implementation of new programs that specifically target newly arising health problems – even if the problems are only endemic in isolated communities. Moreover, these specialized programs and services should not only be directed towards the specific needs of minority groups but should also be delivered in culturally appropriate methods and languages. Ideally, the long-term outcome of integration in health-care policy and services would be manifested in minimal discrepancies in health status across diverse ethnoracial groups and between old and new communities.

This chapter has focused on immigrant health and selected determinants of health that are found to be particularly relevant for immigrants and refugees. The evidence is clear. Overall, new immigrants show fewer health problems, either physical or mental, than native-born Canadians. Although the conclusions pertaining to children need to be read with some caution, children of immigrants show good performance in most areas of development, including educational attainment and psychological well-being. These findings are inspiring because a large majority of immigrants and refugees and their children are exposed to most critical risk factors, including poverty, living in high-risk neighbourhoods, and excessive stress due to the social disadvantages of racial/ethnic groups (for example, discrimination). In fact, their better health, their willingness to take undesirable and underpaid work that is largely avoided by most native-born Canadians and their eagerness to become Canadian citizens are invaluable social and cultural resources.

Successful integration is, as we have said, an ongoing challenge and, in the interest of meeting that challenge, this chapter has illustrated two main themes. First, social and epidemiological research demonstrates that the more 'they' become more like 'us,' immigrants and immigrant children fail to maintain their initial health advantages. Either immigrants are adopting our poor health behaviours and lifestyles or the settlement process wears down their hardiness and resilience. Another possibility is that the deterioration of immigrant health may be attributable to the resources that immigrants left behind in the home country (social networks, cultural practices, employment in their field of training, and so on). Currently, this process is not well explained. It is, however, difficult to negate the adverse effects of acculturative stress. Although acculturation itself may accommodate improved social status and well-being, the process of acculturation inevitably induces a degree of stress that may be responsible, at least in part, for losses of health advantages. Systemic discriminations in housing, employment, denial of foreign credentials, and daily interactions take their tolls through psychological strain. Clearly, new immigrants and refugees of non-European origins suffer disproportionately from severe poverty and chronic unemployment. Current data show that the income differences across ethnic and racial groups is worse in Toronto than in other major cities in Canada, and the gap has been widening during recent surges of economic wealth in Toronto.

While research finds that immigrants are healthy, or healthier immigrants may be screened for admission, some immigrant ethnic groups bring with them special health problems. Tuberculosis, HIV, and hepatitis are our most serious health problems. As the leading host city of Canada, Toronto currently houses a large majority of the immigrants and refugees carrying these diseases. The Toronto Public Health Department is responsible for managing any carriers of disease and for protecting other residents from these serious health diseases. Monitoring and providing adequate case management requires an effective coordination of policies and financial resources among federal, provincial, and municipal levels of government. Given the limited commitment from upper levels of government, it would be difficult to expect the Toronto Public Health Department to be fully accountable for its mandate.

Demographic projections suggest a continuing or increasing influx of immigrants and refugees in the new millennium. Canada cannot sustain declining population growth without immigration and immigration policy is critical for the country's economic performance. To date, immigration policy has focused almost exclusively on the selection of 'ideal' or 'fit' immigrants; little attention has been directed to the post-migration settlement process. Despite its motto and reputation, Toronto does not appear to do better than other cities in helping the healthy immigrants remain healthy. At this point, we cannot explain well why this happens. There is an urgent need for strategic support for more rigorous and systematic research on post-migration settlement processes and health among immigrants, refugees, and their children.

Although, in principle, universal health-care systems provide fair and equal access and services to all residents, regardless of their place of birth and ethnic and racial origin, basic care, as well as expensive specialist care, are not equally accessible to all Canadians (Canadian Institute for Health Information 2000). Indeed, it has been claimed that the Canadian health-care system has always been a multi-tiered system

(Crowley, Zitner, and Faraday-Smith 1999). People of middle and upper SES receive expensive, specialized medical care significantly more often than those of lower SES. The former may be more articulate in demanding care and convincing physicians to provide it than the latter. New immigrants and refugees are, therefore, exposed to 'multiple jeopardy.' They know less about the Canadian health-care system and social programs, are less articulate – or even functionally illiterate – in health-care settings, and are the least likely to receive cooperation from physicians and other health-care workers.

Finally, these issues are not independent of Canada's continued refusal to allow foreign-trained medical doctors to practise in Canada, except for those trained in the U.S. This policy contributes to the current shortage of medical professionals in Ontario and potentially denies immigrants access to culturally sensitive care. Under the changing public and government attitudes that lean towards reducing public health care – for example, Toronto's public health budget was $325,000 lower in 2000 than it was in 1999 (Philip 2000) – new immigrants in Toronto can only face further disadvantages.

Notes

1   Independently of the point system for selection, all applicants seeking permanent residence in Canada, regardless of age, gender, and entry status (immigrant or refugee), are subject to immigration medical examinations (IME). These examinations are performed by 1,300 physicians *in situ* worldwide (they are designated medical practitioners appointed by the Citizenship and Immigration Canada). The IME results are valid for twelve months – that is, applicants who pass the IME must enter Canada within twelve months following the examination. Refugee claimants within Canada are not exempted from this procedure. In this case, the claimants must complete the IME within sixty days of their claim. All individuals are subject to the same medical examination. The IME consists of taking an exhaustive and detailed history and a physical examination, including a chest X-ray, testing for sexually transmitted diseases, and hearing tests. Children are not exempted from the IME. Urinalysis is required for children five years or older (dipstick for protein, sugar, and blood, and, if positive, microscopy). A chest X-ray is required for youth eleven years of age or older, and syphilis serology is required for all individuals fifteen years or older.
2   Two independent medical officers must provide certification to refuse any

applicant admission to Canada on a medical basis. Medically unfit persons are not granted visas, although exceptions can be made through a minister's permit. Contentious cases among persons holding this permit may be handled at a medical officers' conference. Cases are sometimes referred to the Immigration Advisory Board, made up of ten private health-care professionals across Canada. Some medically admissible individuals may need to be under medical surveillance for specified health conditions, such as inactive tuberculosis.

3 In Ontario, a ninety-day qualification period is required for all immigrants and refugees. During this period, individuals may obtain private health-care insurance. However, these plans may not cover pre-existing conditions. Refugee claimants are normally issued a photo-identified document that acknowledges the card-bearer's eligibility for the Interim Federal Health Program (IFH). The IFH covers (1) essential health services only for the treatment and prevention of serious medical and/or dental conditions; (2) contraception, prenatal, and obstetrical care; (3) essential medications; and (4) emergency dental care. Diagnostic and high-cost care (including high-cost medications) are not covered by the IFH. Dental care IFH is limited to a maximum coverage of $250 during the entire eligibility period.

4 When compared on crude rates, families of European background experienced a poverty rate of 14 per cent, while 49 per cent of Black African families were poor. Estimated rates were 35 and 45 per cent for South Asians and Arab/West Asians, respectively. For the two charter groups, British and French, family poverty rates were 11 and 16 per cent, respectively. Most alarming, 87 per cent of Ghanaians and 70 per cent of Ethiopians in Toronto had family incomes below the low-income cut-off (LICO). So did 78 and 63 per cent of Afghan and Somali families, respectively. Other poverty stricken ethnoracial communities included Tamil, Pakistani, Bangladeshi, other African, Central American, Sri Lankan, and other Arab/West Asian communities. More than 50 per cent of the families in these communities were poor. In fact, among all non-white groups, only the Japanese (9 per cent) and Armenian (20 per cent) had poverty rates below the Toronto rate (23 per cent). Inequalities in the rates of child poverty showed similar patterns across ethnoracial compositions. However, non-white or non-European groups were even more disadvantaged. To simply note that poverty is more prevalent among ethnoracial minorities than among those from the U.S. and West European countries would be to minimize the extent of racial and ethnic disparities in Toronto's socio-economic conditions, and to disguise the fundamental causes (as argued by Link and Phelan 1996) and consequences of these inequalities.

7 Images of Integrating Diversity: A Photographic Essay

Gabriele Scardellato

When the editors of *The World in a City* asked me to compile a photographic essay for the volume, I eagerly accepted, regarding the invitation as an opportunity to contribute to an important research undertaking. Toronto has inspired some wonderful photography over the years and much of it is available in various city repositories. Also, given the more contemporary focus of some of the themes in the volume, the requested essay provided an occasion to photograph aspects of city life that suggest its diversity or to use photographs that I had taken already. The photographs in this compilation, then, attempt to provide a pictorial narrative of the growing diversity of the Greater Toronto Area, and the significant contribution of immigration to that diversity.

This photographic essay follows some impressive precursors, in particular a volume co-authored by Harold Troper (himself one of the contributors to *The World in a City*) and the late Robert Harney titled *Immigrants: A Portrait of the Urban Experience.* Although long since out of print that volume was, and remains, a ground-breaking historical overview of the immigrant presence in Toronto. The use of photographs to suggest diversity either in the past or in the contemporary city, however, should be undertaken with some care.

While photographs might be more powerful than words they might also be more problematic as conveyors of information. It is unlikely, for example, that any two viewers will see and interpret the contents of a photograph in the same way. Worse, the act of recording diversity photographically usually requires the selection of what is visibly different and thus suggests, or perhaps even helps to create, a norm that renders the subject of the photograph itself as diverse or as 'other.' Commercial or similar signage that incorporates Urdu or Hebrew script, or Chinese or Japanese ideograms, for example, might signal 'otherness' only to those who are not familiar with these writing systems. What if, however, some of these scripts (Hebrew, for example, or various types of ideograms) have been part of cityscapes for several generations, as is true for Toronto? Do they suggest the presence of immigrants, or simply historical diversity in the city's population, and perhaps a 'backdrop' against which contemporary immigration unfolds? These are important questions to keep in mind when viewing the photographs selected to illustrate *The World in a City*.

The images that I have included are intended to illustrate a number of different points. First, some effort has been made to proceed chronologically in an effort to re-create some of the history of immigration to the city, beginning, for example, at the turn of the last century with the arrival of British and other immigrants, and moving to the present. Of course in some cases, two or three generations later, the individuals depicted cannot now be thought of as immigrants, which is as true for the British arrivals shown in 1909 as it is for the African-Canadian women posed in front of the Young Women's Christian Association, or for other ethnically anonymous individuals shown in photographs from this relatively early period. The point, though simple, is worth emphasizing: cultural diversity as a result of immigration has a long and often complex tradition in Toronto, and the creation of *The World in a City* has been a long-term undertaking.

The chronological approach is also combined with an effort to show, to some extent, how immigrant groups have followed one another into Toronto, though this progression has rarely been linear. The sequence of occupation of the Shaarei Shomayim synagogue, for example, apart from signalling diversity, also suggests changes in immigration and settlement in the city. In this case, Hungarians are seen to be following the settlement pattern of Jews as their numbers in the city swelled, in particular after the events of 1956 in Hungary. This photograph cannot show, however, all of the complexities of the interplay between Jewish and Hungarian settlement, including the more recent arrivals of Jews, the continued resettlement of Hungarians in the city, and so forth. A reminder of some of that complexity – evidence of a much earlier settlement of Hungarians in the city – is provided in the 1932 photograph of the young students of the Grange Road Hungarian school. Also, various uses of the Shaarei Shomayim building itself – as a place of worship, one of several depicted in this photograph collection, or as a community centre – reflect important aspects of immigrant community life, a major theme of *The World in a City*.

For the photograph of the young African-Canadian women, the available information does not allow us to specify whether they are themselves immigrants or whether they represent an internal migration from other locales in Ontario. If the latter is true it is possible that their families may have settled in the province following their escape from slavery in the United States. Thus, they may be the descendants of immigrants who easily pre-date, for example, the British immigrants shown arriving in 1909. Further, their portrait should warn us against simplistic assumptions, as noted above, based on an uncritical viewing of a given image.

The other important criterion for the inclusion of photographs is their ability to address some of the themes covered in the chapters of this book and to illustrate these themes over time. Thus, Toronto's St John's Ward (long since expunged from the cityscape) with its proximity to important transportation routes into and across the city was a preferred immigrant and migrant settlement area, preferred in the sense that its often decrepit housing was at least affordable for newcomers. A contemporary immigrant settlement area, though with housing stock that is of much better quality, is the area known as St Jamestown, and it is included here for comparison and as an illustration to the volume's chapter on immigrant housing.

Other themes in the volume include education, enterprise, health, and community life, and most of the photographs included in this essay suggest aspects of some of these areas of the immigrant experience. Many immigrants, on reflection, note that an important impetus for leaving their homeland was the desire to provide their children with a better future, a goal usually achieved by the toil of their 'hardened hands' and expressed in terms of opportunities for their children to achieve higher education levels. In the immigrant experience, however, education can have both positive and negative possibilities. Education can provide opportunities for betterment; it can also be an inclusionary experience in those cases where it brings together students from diverse backgrounds and provides them with opportunities for learning about the 'others' in their midst. At the same time, education might also serve to separate not only parents from their children but also children from the society in which they are trying to integrate. Education might raise concerns for immigrants about their children retaining important aspects of their culture of origin, especially language and religion. In some cases these needs are fulfilled in the place of worship, which can provide a locale where something of the community life of the country of origin can be re-created. This might be the locus, for example, where language (and culture) is learned or retained. Alternatively, separate language schools might be created to ensure that the mother tongue is not forgotten. Thus, education in this case might serve to isolate students from the society in which they and their parents have settled.

Immigrant enterprise is another important theme in *The World in a City* and is reflected in a number of historic photographs, including that of the Hebrew-language sign of the 1920s advertising poultry for sale in what was then referred to as the city's 'Jewish quarter,' now Kensington Market. Today, streetscapes where a wide variety of services are advertised in Chinese ideograms and other scripts reflect the cultural diversity of commercial activity in the city. Enterprise is also suggested where various markets, large and small, spill out into public spaces and in effect enrich many aspects of neighbourhood life. In some instances, the photographs represent more than one of the volume's themes. The Chinese-Canadian moose in one of the photographs, for example, is decorated with the Chinese yin-yang symbol of good health and is used to advertise herbal remedies: this multipurpose display illustrates how the health needs of an immigrant or ethnocultural group can provide opportunities for entrepreneurs.

Some of the photographs, such as those of the Caribana parade, Good Friday procession, or the Polish Constitution Day parade, not only reflect the city's diversity but also suggest the desire of some immigrant groups (or their descendants) to celebrate aspects of their culture in public spaces. These are manifestations of community life and through them immigrants are able to claim some of the city's public space as their own, something that groups have been doing for a long time, as suggested in the 1911 photograph of the Chinese-Canadian members of the YMCA enjoying a Sunday picnic. Events such as these also allow the larger society to participate, and thus ease a group's inclusion into the broader cultural fabric.

One of the photographs included here – the 1938 image of young women holding an anti-Semitic sign – shows that inclusion has not always been the guiding principle in the City of Toronto. Of course, since that photograph was taken, and in particular over the last thirty years or so, the city has become much more culturally diverse. As a consequence, and as some of the photographs suggest, an interesting and enormously rich cultural amalgam is emerging, and we need to continue to ensure that this occurs in an inclusive environment.

Immigrants arriving in Toronto from Great Britain, c. 1908. (City of Toronto Archives [CTA], William James Fond [WJF], SC 1244-104)

Images of Integrating Diversity 359

Newly arrived and perhaps in search of lodgings, c. 1910.
(CTA, WJF, SC 1244-47.8)

Young African-Canadian women in pre–First World War Toronto
posed in front of the YWCA's Ontario House, a residential facility
maintained for 'coloured girls.' (CTA, WJF, SC 1244-71.22)

Accommodations for migrants new to the city sometimes could be a challenge, as seen in downtown Toronto's St John's Ward in 1914. (CTA, Health Department collections, RG 8-32-326)

Second annual picnic of the Chinese YMCA and the Toronto Chinese Sunday Schools, 1911. (Multicultural History Society of Ontario [MHSO])

Images of Integrating Diversity 361

Some newcomers may have been just passing through: Romany camp on the banks of the Humber River, 1918. (National Archives of Canada)

A sign in Hebrew for Shechat's poultry in the 'Jewish quarter,' now Kensington Market, in the 1920s. Advertising is suggestive of a neighbourhood's ethnic contours. (CTA, WJF, SC 1244-39.4)

362 Gabriele Scardellato

The *Globe* published this photo in 1922 of boys of Greek, Hebrew, and Polish origin on Toronto's Elm Street. (William James; Toronto Public Library, T12276)

Anti-Semitism in Toronto in 1938, though reflecting an era, unfortunately survived the Second World War. (CTA, SC 1266-52350)

Images of Integrating Diversity 363

Toronto's first Hungarian school, Grange Road, 1932. Then, as now, education in the language (and usually culture) of the homeland might be combined with dual loyalties. The population of the city's Hungarian immigrants would swell considerably after the events of 1956 in Hungary. (MHSO)

Like thousands before and after them, some new arrivals, including these Portuguese pioneers posing for the camera in 1957, arrived in the city in response to economic and other needs. They were in search of opportunity, and the city sought them out to fill its demand for labourers with 'hardened hands.' (MHSO)

The settlement of various groups across the city often can be traced in the history of their buildings. Although the Shaarei Shomayim congregation began construction of its synagogue in 1936 on St Clair Avenue West, it was completed only after the Second World War. By 1966, the congregation had built a new synagogue further north on Glencairn Avenue. The original building was sold in 1970 and became the Hungarian Cultural Centre in 1974. (Gabriele Scardellato)

After the Second World War, the arrival of displaced persons, including many Poles, swelled the ranks of several groups already established in the city. By the early 1960s, as shown in this photograph of a Polish Constitution Day parade, the groups were flourishing as never before. (MHSO)

Images of Integrating Diversity 365

Neighbourhoods change as the groups occupying them do. Gardens and their proud cultivators can reflect diversity in interesting ways. (Vincenzo Pietropaolo)

Foodstuffs displayed in local shopping areas reflect the cultural diversity of neighbourhood clientele. (Gabriele Scardellato)

Signage reflects cross-cultural influences and varieties of entrepreneurial inventiveness. (Gabriele Scardellato)

The integration of diversity in mainstream institutions is clearly reflected at Spadina and Dundas, downtown Toronto. (Gabriele Scardellato)

A Chinese-Canadian moose, decorated with the yin-yang of good health, stands behind a bilingual City of Toronto street sign in the midst of Chinese- and Vietnamese-Canadian enterprises (restaurants, herbalists, and others) in the city's downtown core. (Gabriele Scardellato)

Images of Integrating Diversity 367

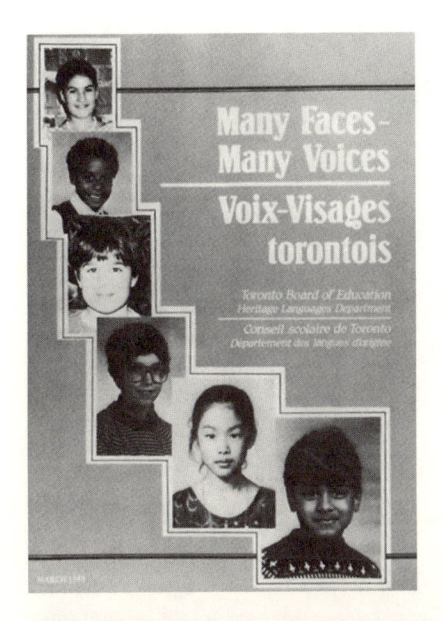

Some of the faces of diversity in the City of Toronto's education system in the mid-1980s. (MHSO)

Professional Indian dancer Menaka Thakkar instructing young Torontonians in the intricacies of her art form. Education can provide cross-cultural insights. (MHSO)

Italian-Canadian Good Friday procession, near intersection of Shaw and Dundas Streets, Toronto, 1998. Some celebrations provide opportunities for community affirmation. (Gabriele Scardellato)

Caribana 2000 celebrations, Toronto. Transplanted and sometimes reinvented, some celebrations come to surpass those in their countries of origin and are embraced by a broad spectrum of groups and peoples in their new settings. (fetenet.com)

Images of Integrating Diversity 369

The Madina Mosque on Danforth Avenue. In modern-day Toronto there are more Muslims than Presbyterians. (Gabriele Scardellato)

The Rajahari convenience store (foreground bottom right) serving the highrise housing complex in downtown Toronto known as St Jamestown, where 60 per cent of the resident population of some 20,000 are said to be ESL learners. (Gabriele Scardellato)

Hindu temples in a religious complex under one roof built by craftsmen from the homeland. This building adaptation allows for styles of worship otherwise not possible in a difficult climate. (Gabriele Scardellato)

Little India, on Toronto's east side, in the Gerard and Coxwell neighbourhood – enterprising diversity. (Gabriele Scardellato)

Danforth diversity in the 1990s, 'Flowers on the Danforth.' (Alex Macdonald)

8 Integrating Community Diversity in Toronto: On Whose Terms?

Myer Siemiatycki, Tim Rees, Roxana Ng, and Khan Rahi

Few cities have become so multicultural so quickly. Within a few decades, global migration has transformed Toronto into a remarkably diverse ethnic, racial, linguistic, and religious metropolis. Consider the lived experience of Toronto urban affairs reporter John Barber. Writing near the end of the twentieth century in the *Globe and Mail*, Barber observed: 'I grew up in a tidy, prosperous, narrow-minded town where Catholicism was considered exotic; my children are growing up in the most cosmopolitan city on Earth. The same place' (Barber 1998, A8).

Yet few places – few cities – could have been less prepared for immigrant diversity than Toronto. From its late-eighteenth-century origins to the middle of the twentieth century, a single ethnic community predominated in Toronto. In 1931, for instance, 81 per cent of the city's population of 631,207 was British in origin. This prompted one historian of the day to conclude that 'no other city of comparable size ... is as homogeneous' (Lemon 1985, 50). Indeed, the city was frequently referred to as the 'Belfast of Canada,' a British bastion of Orange Protestantism. As recently as 1971, almost six of ten Toronto-area residents still claimed British ethnic origin (Breton et al. 1990). However, by the time Toronto celebrated its 150th anniversary of municipal incorporation in 1984, the city's 'most salient feature,' according to immigration historian Robert Harney, was 'its preferred target of migration for people from every corner of the globe, its polyethnic character, and its reputation for tolerance of human variety' (1985, 1).

By 1996 only 16 per cent of the Toronto Census Metropolitan Area (CMA) population of 4.2 million self-identified as exclusively British

(Statistics Canada 1998d); two years later the newly amalgamated City of Toronto – with its population of 2.4 million citizens residing in the core of the CMA – adopted as its motto 'Diversity, Our Strength.' The Toronto CMA is now home to immigrants from 169 different countries of origin, with forty-eight ethnic groups having at least 5,000 members across the city region, and 106 groups claiming at least 1,000 members (Simich 2000). Toronto is presently distinguished, therefore, by a wide range of immigrant and diaspora *communities*.

In scholarly literature, there is no general agreement on what 'community' actually means. It is a contested term that has been applied to everything from geographic areas to groups of people who share a common bond, real or imagined. Ng, Walker, and Muller (1990) identified two overall approaches to the study of communities. The first they characterize as the standard or definitional approach, which proceeds by defining and redefining the concept. The criteria of what constitute a community include shared territory or space, and common needs, interests, and concerns that unite people. This approach focuses on the positive elements in a community, but does not investigate how a community arises in the first place. The second approach is the descriptive or relational approach, which is aimed at describing and discovering the social forces involved in the constitution of community. This approach seeks to understand the dynamics that lead to the formation of communities, be they around common places of origin, shared identity, or space.

For the purposes of this chapter, we lean towards the second approach. While we identify the common elements that give immigrant communities their cohesion, we do so by situating these elements in their historical contexts and their relation to the host society. Accordingly, the first section of this chapter begins with an assessment of the experiences of four major immigrant groups that illustrate the history of twentieth-century immigrant-community formation in Toronto: Jewish, Italian, Caribbean, and Chinese. Common themes emerge across these experiences, including the hardships newcomers faced, the diversity within each community, the resilience of newcomer communities adapting to and making claims on their new homeland, and how these communities developed and changed in relation to the larger society they settled into.

In the second section, we provide an overview of the contemporary configuration of immigrant diversity in Toronto. The data presented paint a disturbing profile of gaps and inequalities (in terms of income, education, political representation, and so on) among distinct ethnic and newcomer communities in the city, as well as between men and women.

This adverse economic, social, and political landscape has produced new forms of resistance and modes of protest and solidarity among diverse newcomer groups. This emerging pattern of community mobilization is the subject of the third section. Here we examine issues that led to the formation of new movements and alliances that cut across traditional ethnic and racial boundaries. We have selected four issues that illustrate patterns of immigrant cross-community coalescence and mobilization transcending ethnic, racial, and social differences: gender equity, antiracism, access to services, and political representation. We are not suggesting these are the only issues of concern to immigrant groups. Rather, we use them to highlight the tensions inherent in Toronto's growing pains from a city dominated by a single group to one characterized by diversity. We use these 'cases' as examples to show that traditional boundaries once imposed on group cohesion are no longer adequate to address the emerging issues that confront immigrants in Toronto.

In the fourth section, we turn our attention to how government policy has responded to the increasing heterogeneity of Toronto's population. While we make reference to federal and provincial initiatives, our chief interest lies in the municipal level. Over the years, local governments in Toronto have charted a distinct orientation to immigrant diversity and we assess this 'made-in-Toronto' government response to diversity.

Finally, in our conclusion, we address the significance of Toronto's experience of global migration and diversity. In our contemporary 'age of migration,' countries and cities around the world are increasingly characterized by unprecedented diversity of population (Castles and Miller 1993). 'Multi-ethnic, multi-racial, and multi-national populations are becoming a dominant characteristic of cities and regions across the globe,' Leonie Sandercock (1998) has observed, 'and this is causing a profound disturbance to the values, norms, and expectations of many people' (164). What the world desperately needs are urban role models, examples of cities that can make diversity work. Iris Marion Young (1990) defines contemporary life (largely due to global migration) 'as the being together of strangers' (237). Successful cities, she contends, will affirm group difference without any attendant inequalities and exclusion. For her part, Leonie Sandercock (1998) invokes both a name and a prescription for successful urban diversity. Her imagined urban utopia is *cosmopolis* – a city characterized by genuine respect for differing human identities as well as a recognition of the common destiny and intertwined fate of diverse groups; a city devoted to inclusive democracy and the social justice claims of its more marginalized, less powerful communities.

Is there such a *cosmopolis* anywhere in the world? In her book, *Towards Cosmopolis*, Sandercock (1998) assesses and rejects the claim of six cities to this exalted status: New York, London, Paris, Frankfurt, Istanbul, and Jerusalem. What about Toronto? Its claim on *cosmopolis* hinges on our assessment of a host of factors. Is Toronto a significant site of diversity? How has the city received the 'strangers' who have come to call it home? Are there recurring, structural inequalities confronting newcomer communities? What opportunities have newcomer communities had to advance their claim to belonging in Toronto? How well have local institutions responded to diversity? These are issues we address throughout this chapter. As we demonstrate, diverse immigrant communities have always sought to influence the terms and circumstances under which they would integrate into Toronto. In the process – despite adversities – they have transformed Toronto.

BECOMING TORONTONIAN: IMMIGRANT
COMMUNITY EXPERIENCES

Embedded in Toronto's transformation from homogeneity to diversity are a host of important dynamics and questions. How were immigrant newcomers received in Toronto? How did immigrants establish institutions and a sense of community? How have immigrant communities been changed by Toronto? How have newcomer communities changed the city? How, in short, did Toronto go about integrating immigrant diversity? One way to explore these issues is to historically examine the experiences of the largest groups of non-British immigrants who arrived in Toronto through the course of the twentieth century: Jewish immigrants during the first half-century; Italians during the 1950s and 1960s; Caribbeans during the 1970s; and Chinese immigrants who have arrived since the 1980s. By their religion, ethnicity, and racialization these four groups represent – sequentially over the past one hundred years – the newcomers who most explicitly challenged Toronto's self-definition by expanding the city's diversity. These four communities therefore constitute an interesting test of how immigrant communities developed and were treated in twentieth-century Toronto. What emerges from their experience, as reviewed in this section, is a city opening itself to the world, but uncertain of the role and status newcomers should be afforded.

The Jewish Community

Throughout the first half of the twentieth century, Jews comprised by far the largest non-British ethnic group in Toronto. Thanks to a huge wave of immigration during the first quarter of the century, the city became home to a flourishing Jewish community. Jews were Toronto's first large community of newcomers to test the warmth of welcome to be accorded immigrants who brought to the city a distinctly foreign culture, language, religion, and identity. Their experience up to 1950 did not reflect a host city open to diversity and difference. Through adverse circumstances, however, Jews in Toronto succeeded in building a resilient and dynamic community.

While the earliest Jewish presence in Canada dates back to the eighteenth century, the community's significance is a twentieth-century story. From 1831 until 1901, Canada's Jewish population grew only modestly, from 107 to 16,401 (Kage 1981; Tulchinsky 1992). Over the next quarter-century, soaring levels of immigration would create a community of over 125,000 Jews across the country. Most of these newcomers left persecution and poverty in Eastern and Central Europe (particularly in Russia and Poland), and, overwhelmingly, they settled in Canada's largest cities: Montreal, Toronto, and Winnipeg. Accordingly, the City of Toronto's Jewish population rose by over 1,000 per cent in the first two decades of this century! Its numbers climbed from 3,090 in 1901 to 34,619 in 1921; by mid-century the City of Toronto and its expanding suburbs were home to 59,448 Jews (Breton et al. 1990). More revealing than these total numbers, however, is the relative place of this growing Jewish community in the total composition of Toronto's society.

Jews stood out in Toronto. In 1931, for instance, when 80.9 per cent of the population claimed British ethnic origin, the city's Jewish population of 45,305 represented the largest non-British group, at 7.2 per cent of the city population (Levitt and Shaffir 1987). Next in rank stood the Italian community at just 2.1 per cent of Toronto's population. For over fifty years, from 1901 until the mid-1950s, Jews were the only non-British ethnic group with more than 5 per cent of the city's population. The Jewish experience in the first half of this century reminds us how much Toronto would have to change before it could accommodate diversity.

Early-twentieth-century Jews migrated and settled in a Toronto most typically characterized as dour, narrow-minded, xenophobic, and anti-Semitic. Levitt and Shaffir (1987) contend, for instance, that 'Toronto in the early thirties was a parochial, provincial, and puritanical city that still felt a strong attachment to the British Empire,' a place where ethnic minorities such as Jews 'were outsiders ethnically, religiously, linguistically, culturally, and economically' (23). Sundays, in particular, marked the city as a distinctive urban community. As Robert Fulford (1995) has observed, 'The 1907 Lord's Day Act, which forbade almost all public activity on Sunday except churchgoing, was obeyed with a dedication that visitors thought excessive' (2). Far more scathing were the judgments of two unhappy writers who lived in the city for a time. As a young reporter for the *Toronto Daily Star*, the American author Ernest Hemingway felt himself incarcerated in Toronto, which he characterized as a 'City of Churches' where '85 per cent of the inmates attend a protestant church on Sunday' (Lemon 1985, 57). Writing to his poet friend Ezra Pound in 1923, Hemingway was at a rare loss for words to describe Toronto: 'It couldn't be any worse. You can't imagine it. I'm not going to describe it' (Columbo 1987, 382). Twenty years later, in the 1940s, the English writer Wyndham Lewis wrote of Toronto as 'a sanctimonious ice-box ... this bush-metropolis of the Orange Lodges' (Fulford 1995, 2).

The Orange Order represented the dominant culture and tone of city life in Toronto. Founded in Ireland in 1795 amidst violent clashes between rival Protestant and Catholic groups, the Order's mission was to champion Protestantism and the ties to Britain. Transplanted to Canada, the Order was strongest in Toronto where an unwritten rule of city politics gave the Order considerable influence in electing mayors and aldermen to council and control of appointments to the civic workforce – particularly police and firefighters. The Orange Order espoused a narrow definition of Canadian and Toronto identity based on a particular blend of religion (Protestant), nationality (British), language (English), and culture (restrained to the point of repression, in 'Toronto the Good'). Inevitably other identities and cultures were regarded as suspect, threatening, and potentially divisive. And as we have seen, few large cities anywhere outside of Britain had indeed succeeded in building such an ethnically homogeneous society.

Multicultural Toronto was many years into the future. Jewish immigrants arrived in a proud outpost of the British Empire determined to be 'more British than the British,' and 'along with this hyper-Britishness went a suspicion of foreigners' (Levitt and Shaffir 1987, 28). The dilemma facing Jews in Toronto during the first half of the twentieth century is acutely captured by an observation of historian D.C. Masters. Toronto at the time, Masters has written, was a society in which conventional public opinion believed that for citizens 'to be on the streets on the Sabbath, for reasons other than church-going, placed their souls or their social positions in jeopardy' (Houston and Smyth 1980, 156–7). This could only create double jeopardy for Jews who worshipped on Saturday not Sunday, and did so in synagogues not churches.

Anti-Semitism proved to be a pervasive by-product of this prevalent, restrictive definition of Canadian and Toronto identity. Gerald Tulchinsky (1992) is correct in noting that hostility towards Jews in Canada's past flowed from a 'fairly generalized distrust of and dislike for foreigners at that time.' Yet unlike Asians who were barred from entering Canada, many Jews were at least able to migrate to Canada during the early decades of this century (233, 232). Still, what is striking about the early experiences of Jews in Toronto is how blatant and pervasive were the prejudice and discrimination they faced.

According to Tulchinsky (1992), Toronto was home to 'Canada's best-known Jew-hater in the late nineteenth century,' Goldwin Smith. (The same could be said a century later, when anti-Semite and Holocaust-denier Ernst Zundel called the city home.) It was a sign of the times that Smith – a University of Toronto professor, essayist, and journalist and Canada's leading intellectual until his death in 1910 – peppered his lectures and publications with references to Jews as 'Christ-killers,' who were devoted to 'wealth-worship' and pursuing 'Jewish domination,' and concluded for good measure that 'Jews are no good anyhow' (231–8). Smith appears to have had significant influence on at least one University of Toronto graduate who would go on, we will see, to have a profound impact on Canadian immigration policy and the fate of Jews in the twentieth century. Writing in his diary in 1946, near the end of his career as Canada's longest-serving prime minister, William Lyon Mackenzie King thought again of his old professor: 'I recall Goldwin Smith feeling so strongly about the Jews. He expressed it at one time as follows: that they were poison in the veins of a community ... the evidence is very strong, not against all Jews ... that in a large percentage of the race there are tendencies and trends which are dangerous indeed' (Tulchinsky 1992, 238). Not even the Holocaust could dislodge such views from Canada's prime minister. King, in this respect, was a product of his society, where disregard and contempt for Jews was commonplace.

Prejudice seemed to intrude into many dimensions of Jewish existence in Toronto. They routinely faced discrimination in employment, in high-level professional positions such as hospital doctors and university professors, as well as in retail sales positions serving the public (Speisman 1979; Tulchinsky 1992). Desirable neighbourhoods in the city were off-limits to Jews (Colton 1980; Lemon 1985; Levitt and Shaffir 1987; Speisman 1979). Signs warning No Jews or Dogs Allowed, or the more genteel Gentiles Only were common at Toronto beaches, dance halls, and nearby summer resorts (Levitt and Shaffir 1987). The reluctance of many Torontonians to do business with Jews was reflected in an extraordinary 1923 advertisement in the *Star* for a company run by the Glass family informing the public that contrary to 'erroneous impression,' the family was not Jewish and assuring Toronto consumers that 'without prejudice or intended offense, we beg to state that this house is strictly gentile, owned and managed by Canadians in Canadian interests' (Speisman 1979).

Newspaper editorials were another forum for anti-Jewish sentiment, none more vehement than the Orange-inclined *Telegram*. Calling for curbs on Jewish immigration in 1925, the paper railed, 'An influx of Jews puts a worm next to the kernel of every fair city where they get hold. These people have no national tradition ... They are not the material out of which to shape a people holding a national spirit.' Deeming Jews not fit to be Canadian, the *Telegram* recommended that a poll tax be levied on Jewish immigrants that was steep enough to assure that only 'a baker's dozen per annum' could gain entry (Speisman 1979, 321).

Toronto's municipal officials and institutions were no more hospitable towards Jewish immigrants. In 1920 alderman John Cowan asserted during a debate on a motion to ban non-English (meaning Yiddish) advertising signs, 'If foreigners who came here to make a living could not conform to English ways and customs they could return to their native countries' (Lemon 1985, 53). Four years later, a Board of Education trustee responded to complaints that Jewish children in the city's public schools were being compelled to sing Christian hymns by declaring, 'Are we a Christian nation or a Jewish nation? As long as we remain a Christian nation we are not to be dominated by the Jewish people' (Speisman 1979, 327). And three years later, in 1927, a police officer's kick in the *derrière* of a Jewish youth on a Toronto street, followed by the order 'You little Jew bastard move on,' reinforced the Jewish community's belief that anti-Semitism was prevalent in the police force (Levitt and Shaffir 1987, 38–9).

The worst eruption of public anti-Semitism in Toronto's history occurred during the summer of 1933. The timing was precipitated by a variety of factors, both international and local in origin. The lingering economic depression of the 1930s unleashed a mixed brew of desperation and resentment easily directed against 'foreigners.' Hitler's rise to power in Germany months earlier gave unprecedented publicity and legitimacy to anti-Semitism. Within weeks, confrontations erupted in two Toronto locations where Jews had only recently become significant visitors or residents. In the east end of town, the Balmy Beach Swastika Club was formed at the start of August, ostensibly devoted to keeping the Beaches area prim and proper. The fact that this included keeping 'obnoxious visitors' from the area, led the *Star* to headline the club's formation as 'Nazi Organization Seeking to Oust non-Gentiles off Beach' (Levitt and Shaffir 1987, 78). The club's tactics included displaying swastikas and Hail Hitler signs in its beach clubhouse, using swastika badges for its members, and dozens of club supporters holding parades and chanting anti-Semitic songs and slogans. Within days there were several instances of physical attacks on Jews in the Beaches neighbourhood.

Two weeks later, the real showdown came in the west-central area of Christie and Bloor Streets at the Christie Pits baseball fields where a predominantly Jewish team was playing in the city softball quarter-finals. Jews had recently begun moving into the neighbourhood, much to the dismay of some local youths who banded together as the 'Pit Gang.' During the first playoff game on August 14, 1933, spectators in attendance unfurled a five-foot-long swastika banner; that night Hail Hitler was painted onto the park clubhouse. When the swastika reappeared at the next game, on August 16, the Christie Pits Riot was on. For six hours, hundreds of Jews, reinforced by Italian sympathizers, did battle with mobs who were opposed to foreigners in their city and their parks. Baseball bats and metal pipes were the weapons of choice, putting over a dozen combatants in hospital and prompting the *Globe* to conclude that it was 'a miracle that more were not seriously hurt' (Levitt and Shaffir 1987, 157). Perhaps harder to fathom was a Toronto magistrate dismissing charges against those alleged to have incited the riots, on the grounds that the provocation of Jews was intended as a joke (Speisman 1979).

Despite – or perhaps because of – the marginalized position accorded them in Toronto, Jews succeeded in forging a remarkably dynamic community grounded in shared space, spirituality, language, culture, employment, and oppression. If Toronto could not quite bring itself to accept Jews as full and equal citizens, Jews created their own neighbourhoods and institutions to advance their identity and interests. Thus Stephen Speisman refers to the city's first Jewish neighbourhood – an area known early in the 1900s as the Ward, bounded by Yonge Street, University Avenue, and Queen and College Streets – as 'a miniature Jewish civilization in the heart of Anglo-Saxon Toronto,' a part of town which 'had become virtually a self-contained community as regards Jewish services and cultural, religious and educational facilities' (Speisman 1985, 107, 112). While municipal officials and the local press typically condemned the Ward as an overcrowded slum, the neighbourhood nourished a vibrant sense of Jewish community identity. This would not be the last time outsiders and insiders regarded immigrant neighbourhoods through different lenses.

The Ward was an affordable neighbourhood adjacent to the city's clothing and garment industries where the majority of Jewish immigrants worked, typically in exploited sweatshop conditions. As early as 1898, reports and news stories abounded of underpaid, overworked Jews toiling in unsanitary and dangerous conditions in clothing production. Not surprisingly these conditions would give rise to decades of union organizing and militancy among Toronto's Jewish garment workers. One indication of the extent to which the Ward had become a Jewish enclave was in local school enrollment. By 1912, 87 per cent of students in the area's two public elementary schools were Jewish (Tulchinsky 1992). Another was the presence of many synagogues, which Speisman identifies as the 'most ubiquitous institution in the Ward' (Speisman 1985, 113). Setting a pattern to be emulated by subsequent newcomer non-Christian faiths in Toronto, some early Jewish places of worship were newly built, some occupied converted churches or commercial sites and others gathered in residential homes. Jewish stores, restaurants, health clinics, private schools and day nurseries, theatres, and newspapers dotted the neighbourhood.

Institutionally, the growth of mutual benefit societies was perhaps the strongest indication of the ties of community and solidarity among Toronto Jews. In an era before the emergence of the welfare state, unemployment, strikes, illness, and death could spell utter destitution for individuals and families. Immigrant Jewish communities across

North America – exemplified by Toronto's experience – formed an extensive network of mutual benefit societies to provide members with emergency assistance in hard times, and social activities in good times. By 1925, there were thirty such organizations in town, ranging from eighty to five hundred dues-paying members. Some societies, like the venerable Toronto Hebrew Benevolent Society (over a century old and still functioning today), were open to Jews of all national origins and occupations, religious or non-affiliated. Others united immigrants from the same town or region in the Old Country.

Trade union and socialist organizations were other important defining elements of Toronto's Jewish community. Jews constituted much of the garment industry workforce, where, as we have said, poor wages and working conditions often prevailed. In response, Toronto Jews joined unions and a variety of left-wing political parties. Toronto's twelve branches of the *Arbeiter Ring* (Workmen's Circle) comprised a unique association of workers devoted to mutual aid, education, and social change. Even more important were unions in the garment industry, such as the Amalgamated Clothing Workers and the International Ladies Garment Workers Union, whose membership in Toronto was overwhelmingly Jewish. As historian Ruth Frager (1992) has written, during the first half of the twentieth century Jews in Toronto 'formed a dynamic movement, born out of the vigorous reactions of a displaced people who fled from the persecutions of the Old World to find themselves thrust out of necessity into the sweatshops of Spadina Avenue' (211). Unwilling to remain passive victims of their new environment, Jewish workers embraced unions and workplace strikes as the surest means of improving their conditions in the New World. Frager also describes the prominent role played by women as workers, trade unionists, and strikers as a crucial element of the Jewish labour movement. This was an immigrant community in which women took a lead role in advancing claims for equal treatment.

All the organizations previously cited – synagogues, schools, theatres, newspapers, mutual benefit societies, unions – confirm Speisman's characterization of Toronto Jews as 'a community of "joiners"' (Speisman 1985, 96). These organizations were the institutional mechanisms through which a Jewish community was created in Toronto. When Toronto's garment industry moved west to Spadina Avenue after the First World War, the Jewish community also migrated westward from the Ward to the Kensington Market area. Here, Toronto's Jewish community elected its first federal and provincial politician during the 1930s – despite prominent publications such as *Saturday Night* proclaiming, 'Imagine a gang with names like that running a white man's country!' (Lemon 1985, 53).

While the Jewish community succeeded in getting its own members elected in predominantly Jewish constituencies, however, they were unable to secure favourable government policy when it mattered most. As Irving Abella and Harold Troper (1982) have shown, throughout the 1930s, the Canadian government turned a deaf ear to the Jewish community's pleas for Canada to provide haven for Jewish refugees of Nazi persecution. Mackenzie King's government would not open the doors. And even after the Second World War, Canada remained reluctant to take in survivors of the Holocaust. As Canada prepared to open wide its doors to post-war immigration from Europe, the lingering anti-Semitism of Canada's political, economic, and social elite was expressed by the anonymous senior Canadian official who, in 1945, responded to a journalist's query of how many Jews would be admitted to Canada after the war by declaring, 'None is too many' (Abella and Troper 1982, ix). Jews were about to be supplanted as Toronto's largest minority group.

Ironically, the Jewish community's greatest advance in Toronto society would come in the last half of the twentieth century, when other immigrant groups came to vastly outnumber Jews in the city. During the past fifty years, Toronto's Jewish community has generally prospered and succeeded by advancing in the city's business and professional ranks. In the public domain as well, Jews have held a prominence of place scarcely conceivable to earlier generations of Torontonians. Toronto has had three Jewish mayors over the past four decades, including Nathan Phillips, after whom the landmark civic square at City Hall is named, and Mel Lastman, the first mayor of the amalgamated City of Toronto. The election of Jewish mayors reflects not only the social mobility of Jews in Toronto over the twentieth century, but the extent to which massive multicultural migration to the city since 1950 has transformed assumptions of who is fit to play a lead role in the city's affairs.

The Italian Community

In 1961 Pierre Berton wrote a book entitled *The New City*. The book celebrated the demise of the staid 'Toronto the Good,' which Berton described as 'this town of quiet homes and quiet Sundays, of smug, satisfied Anglo-Saxons.' To Berton's delight, a more dynamic and cosmopolitan Toronto was emerging. The first sign – and agent – of the transformation Berton identified in the book was the city's bursting 'Italian Town' along College Street in the west end of Toronto (19, 39). Yet the experience of Toronto's Italian community demonstrates the adversity and resilience involved in changing a city's prevailing values and customs.

Following the Second World War, elements of both certainty and uncertainty characterized Canada's immigration prospects. It was clear that for the first time in two decades, the doors would have to be opened wide to newcomers. Since the mid-1920s, immigration into Canada had virtually come to a halt. By the mid-1940s, Harold Troper (1993) writes, 'for the first time in thirty years Canada faced a peacetime shortage of workers' (258). Canada's low birth rate – occasioned by both the Depression and the war – meant the country lacked the workforce required by its booming post-war economy. As Troper discusses in chapter 1 of this book, companies lobbied the government to bring in more immigrants. But where should they come from? In 1945, under prevailing policy, only a limited category of immigrants were allowed into the country: British and American citizens and farmers with sufficient means to farm in Canada (Hawkins 1972). Nor was there popular or political sentiment to cast the immigration net wider; a Gallup poll in 1946 showed 61 per cent of Canadians opposed to permitting mass migration from Europe (Iacovetta 1992), and the strongest opposition in this poll was expressed against Japanese, Jewish, and Italian newcomers.

A year later, in 1947, Prime Minister Mackenzie King reassured a sceptical public that 'careful selection' would be exercised in determining who could enter the country. 'The people of Canada,' King declared, 'do not wish, as a result of mass immigration, to make a fundamental alteration in the character of the population' (Ramcharan 1982, 13). One official in the immigration department made it clear in a memo that Italians were not on the welcome list, saying that Canadians 'are not now anxious to receive an influx of Italians whom they do not regard as the most desirable type of immigrant.' With insufficient numbers of immigrants arriving from traditional source countries, however, business continued to press the government to look further afield. The Canadian Manufacturers Association, for instance, urged Ottawa to recruit 'husky unmarried men' from Italy 'to fill the gap' (Iacovetta 1992, 23).

The first step towards a new outlook on immigration that would transform Toronto came in 1947. That year, Italy was finally removed from the wartime enemy alien list. (During the war some Italians were stripped of their citizenship, while a smaller number were interned as suspected aliens.) Then entry was extended to immigrants from across Europe who were able to work in resource and manufacturing industries. Once again, Canada's immigration policy responded to economic demands. Initially the number of arrivals from Italy rose modestly. During the 1950s and 1960s, however, they climbed to record numbers year after year. From 1946 to 1972, over three and a half million immigrants came to Canada; the second-largest group (after British arrivals) came from Italy. They numbered almost half a million in total, or one in every eight newcomers over this period.

By far the greatest proportion of Italians – 70 per cent – came from the south of Italy, forsaking the struggles of agricultural subsistence for the promise of a better life across the ocean. Interestingly, Canadian immigration officials aggressively tried to recruit northern Italians as immigrants, regarding them as a better 'fit' into a Canadian society dominated by Western and Northern European peoples. Yet the great majority came from the south, illustrating yet again how migration movements can evade the micro-management of nation-state policy preferences. Toronto was, by far, the preferred place of settlement for Italian immigrants to Canada, becoming home to 40 per cent of the new arrivals. Between 1951 and 1971, the number of Italians in the Toronto CMA increased ten-fold, from 27,000 to over 270,000. By 1961 Italians ranked as the largest non-British ethnic group in Toronto (Lemon 1985; Ramirez 1989; Iacovetta 1992; Tomasi 1997; N. Harney 1998).

The post-war period also saw the growth of other large 'non-traditional' immigrant communities in Toronto, with the arrival of Greek, Portuguese, and Eastern European immigrants. But by their massive numbers, it was Italians who symbolized the changing face of Toronto through the 1950s and 1960s and who helped to propel Toronto past Montreal as Canada's largest metropolitan centre. By settling into older, central-city neighbourhoods emptied by the exodus to post-war suburbs such as North York and Scarborough, Italians played a crucial role in preserving the central city as both a viable and vibrant residential space. This would prove a major virtue for Toronto, in contrast to the demise of the central core in many American urban areas. And as we will see, much of Toronto's extensive post-war city-building was built on the backs of Italian immigrants.

It should be noted, however, that Toronto's Italian community predates the massive post-war influx. Italian explorers and adventurers, of course, were instrumental in the European colonization and settlement of North America. Though their names have long been anglicized, Cristoforo Colombo and Giovanni Caboto both played crucial parts in opening the New World to the Old. Yet, as Clifford Jansen (1988) has noted, not until the 1880s, when work began on building the Canadian Pacific Railway and other construction projects, did significant permanent Italian settlement occur in Canada. The image of Italians as a hard-working, cheap, and docile workforce took hold early when most Italians were drawn to work outside large cities on railway construction, mining, and logging sites. The expansion of Canadian manufacturing in the late 1890s gave rise to the first significant Italian communities in Canadian cities. Estimates suggest Toronto was home to perhaps 1,000 Italians in 1900; 10,000 in 1914; and just under 20,000 in 1941 (R. Harney 1983; N. Harney 1998).

Language, nationality, and religion set Italians apart from Toronto's dominant (English, British, Protestant) culture in these years, and relegated them, like Jews, to outsider status. Indeed, during the first half of the twentieth century, Italians and Jews had much in common. They shared neighbourhood space – first the downtown area known as the Ward, then College Street west of Spadina. Close friendships and unlikely bilingualism were often forged by Jewish families leaving their children with Italian neighbours during Saturday synagogue services and reciprocating to care for Italian children during Sunday morning mass. One unexpected result of these child-care arrangements was the number of Jewish children who learned to speak Italian, and Italian children who became conversant in Yiddish. Interestingly, too – motivated by their own sense of victimization – many Italian youths rushed to join the fray in support of embattled Jews during the Christie Pits mêlée of 1933. And, finally, Italians also demonstrated from the outset a strong inclination to build distinctive communities in keeping with their traditions. As John Zucchi (1988) has shown, prior to the Second World War, Toronto had three 'Little Italy' neighbourhoods, three Catholic parishes, and a number of Italian clubs, associations and mutual benefit societies. 'From the earliest stages of Italian settlement in Canada,' Bruno Ramirez notes, 'one may observe the presence of ethnic associations' (15). These organizations provided not only tangible services such as illness and death benefits, language classes, and social and cultural activities; they were networks through which immigrant *community* was established and reproduced.

Despite the fact that a significant Italian community had existed in Toronto as far back as 1900, a recurring theme in academic writing about the post-war Italian immigrants is the discrimination they faced upon arrival. Franca Iacovetta (1992), for instance, contends that Toronto proved to be 'an extremely cold and unfriendly place,' where Italians were treated 'as a target of scorn.' More ominous still, she notes, 'in the years before the large number of immigrants of colour from Asia, Africa, and the Caribbean – a migration that would not reach significant proportions for another decade – the southern Italians, by virtue of their darker skin colouring, were at times virtually ascribed the status of a visible minority.' Few voices expressed this view more directly or crudely than the member of the Orange Lodge who wrote Ontario's premier in 1954 complaining of the recent infestation of 'these ignorant, almost Black people,' born in 'a Vatican controlled country,' and whose young men were typically 'armed with knives and ... continually holding up people and especially ladies near parks and dark alleys' (xi, 103, 106). Italians were neither the first nor the last immigrant group to be racialized and stigmatized in Toronto.

Discrimination against Italians in Toronto manifested itself in two prime domains: at work (affecting adults) and at school (affecting children). Italian immigrants in the 1950s and 1960s found work, as Jansen (1988) notes, 'in the lowest occupational categories' (139). Italian men were overwhelmingly concentrated in construction and public infrastructure building, while women worked in manufacturing, particularly in the garment and food industries. The work experience of both Italian men and women was aptly described by Iacovetta's (1992) assessment that Italians 'performed the dangerous or low-paying jobs that others shunned' (x). The massive Italian migration coincided with the most extensive period of construction and public infrastructure development in the city's history. A new two-tier metropolitan system of government was established in Toronto in 1954 to expedite the building of expressways, subways, and sewer systems to accommodate continued suburban development. Toronto had never seen a building boom like it; Italian immigrants became its prime workforce and tragic victims.

Construction companies seemed to spring up overnight, and disappear just as fast. Wages went unpaid and Italians were regarded as a cheap, disposable workforce. Working conditions were often dangerous; safety enforcement, lax or non-existent; unsafe work sites, poor wages, and even threats of deportation characterized the newcomers' working lives. In March 1960, fire swept through a sewer tunnelling project in north Toronto, leaving five Italian workers dead. Torontonians read newspaper headlines charging that Italian immigrant labourers were being 'treated like animals' (Bagnell 1989, 147). First the Italian community mourned its dead, and then thousands rallied to form new unions in the construction sector, culminating in two bitter, though ultimately successful strikes in the summers of 1960 and 1961. Underlying both strikes was the workers' determination to be treated as full and equal members of Canadian society. One strike leader told a rally of Italian labourers, 'Canada is a free country and immigrants should be treated the same as Canadians!' Another cried out for 'an end to immigrant slavery,' as the rally ended with mass chanting of the strike slogan, 'Canadian wages, Canadian hours!' (Iacovetta 1992, 169). Unionization became a means of not only improving wages and working conditions for Toronto's Italian immigrants, but of advancing their collective identity as Canadian citizens. One strike leader described the strikes as 'a peaceful revolution by men who have been treated with disgrace' (Bagnell 1989, 156).

The stereotyping of Italian immigrants as a cheap labour workforce negatively impacted on their children's life opportunities as well. Kenneth Bagnell argues that during the 1960s prejudice against Italians 'had its most harmful expression in the country's educational system' (Bagnell 1989, 178). As Carl E. James and Barbara Burnaby describe in chapter 5, Ontario's school system was based on a philosophy of 'streaming,' whereby high school students pursued either vocational or preparatory college/university studies. While streaming was supposedly determined by academic performance, many immigrant communities in Toronto – the Italians first! – complained that selection criteria had more to do with ethnicity and racial identity. Many school teachers and guidance councillors routinely shipped Italian students off to vocational schools in accordance with the mainstream society's image of this immigrant community. As with their employment difficulties, Italians responded by organizing to advance their rights. Community and parent groups lobbied school boards to stop discriminatory streaming and become more diversity-friendly through such initiatives as heritage-language programs.

Even more so than those who came before them, post-war Italian immigrants demonstrated a tremendous capacity for community-building. This took two forms. The first was claiming urban space and territorializing it to reflect the community's culture and values. 'Little Italy' neighbourhoods in the city's west end along College Street, Davenport Road, and St Clair Avenue turned traditional streets into *piazzas*, transforming Toronto's use of street space. Long regarded as simply corridors for moving cars and pedestrians, streets now became public gathering and dining spaces as outdoor cafés proliferated. Second, Italians established a vast network of institutions to recreate and preserve their distinct identity in Toronto. Indeed, by the 1980s, 'an unusual degree of institutional completeness would be attained' by Toronto's Italian community (R. Harney 1983, 357). The term 'institutional completeness' refers to a minority community's capacity to create its own institutions – religious, educational, cultural, and so forth – and therefore meet its community members' needs internally. Italians in Toronto proved adept not only at meeting the physical challenge of city-building, as we have seen, but also at meeting the social challenge of community-building.

The number of Italian community organizations in Toronto – spanning a remarkable range of traditions, services, and activities – climbed from thirty-eight in 1954, to 240 in 1984, and to over 400 in the 1990s (N. Harney 1998). Together they constitute the organizational foundation of Toronto's Italian community and warrant a brief discussion. The Italian Immigrant Aid Society was established in 1952 to provide a range of settlement services and support to newcomers. Two years later the Italian newspaper *Corriere Canadese* began publishing. In 1961 *Centro Organizativo Scuole Technice Italiane* (COSTI) was established to teach newcomers English and work skills. Four decades later, inspired by its motto 'Integration through Education,' COSTI has provided teaching and training to well over one hundred thousand learners drawn from every immigrant community that has made Toronto home. In the words of an early president, Lino Magagna, 'COSTI is an expression of deep human feelings in our society. It is a way of reaching out by human beings and saying, "Here I am, don't be afraid, here's how you take the first step, let me help"' (Bagnell 1989, 176).

In 1974 the National Congress of Italian Canadians was formed, based in Toronto, as the umbrella organization and voice of Italian Canadians. Two years later, the city's Italian community officially opened Villa Columbo, a multiple-facility complex including seniors' housing, an athletic facility, an art gallery, and a community centre. The project was largely financed through internal community fundraising and was regarded by many Italians as an opportunity to overcome negative impressions existing in the broader society. Nicholas Harney (1998) notes that Italians in Toronto were typically regarded 'either as *cafoni* (rural louts) or Mafiosi.' More than one Italian who was active in building Villa Columbo saw it as a means of achieving community acceptance in the city: 'I felt we needed to prove we were good and hardworking Canadians, but of Italian extraction. What better way to do it than show some sort of civic responsibility, taking care of your own, by building an old-age home' (158, 60). While some community institutions were built to win social acceptance, others were only established by overcoming exclusionary barriers.

Interestingly, it took something of a battle before Toronto's Italian community felt fully at home within the Catholic Church here. Over 90 per cent of Italian immigrants to Toronto were Catholic and, by 1971, Italians comprised one-third of the city's 841,000 Catholics and belonged to thirty-three different parishes. Yet, within the church, Italians complained bitterly of second-class treatment as evidenced by overcrowded churches, insufficient opportunities and advancement for Italian priests, and inferior access to space. As one parishioner recalled, 'It was a disgrace, the way we were herded into the basement, and the English get to have a real church, to worship with dignity' (Iacovetta 1992, 134). Ethnic tensions within the church persisted for years, with the archdiocese gradually providing more resources for Italian worshippers in the face of complaints from older Canadian parishioners that too much was being given to the newcomers. Accordingly, churches became important gathering points for the Italian community in Toronto.

Nicholas Harney (1998) also describes 'the ubiquity of social clubs' – typically located in storefronts sparsely equipped with a basic kitchen, a TV set, and playing card tables – that constituted an even more grassroots community institution (142). Frequently organized on the basis of common home-town origin, these clubs kept old networks alive and renewed in the 'new city of Toronto,' which Italians not only now inhabited in huge numbers but, as Pierre Berton had noted, were transforming. In striving to make a place for themselves in the city, Italian immigrants confronted employers, teachers, school boards, and the church establishment. As Iacovetta (1992) observes, post-war Italian immigrants to Toronto 'showed a tremendous capacity to pool their resources together and a talent for finding ways to recreate culture and community in the new environment' (201).

The Caribbean Community

During the 1970s and 1980s, over a quarter of a million Caribbean immigrants settled in Canada. This was the first substantial increase in the country's Black community since the mid-nineteenth century. These newcomers would confront a problematic legacy of racialized exclusion and discrimination in their new homeland. Historian James Walker (1980) has observed that 'Black history in Canada goes back to our very roots, and that it was a history that began in oppression' (10). By the end of the twentieth century, the Caribbean community's experience in Toronto was characterized – in the subtitle of the foremost study of the subject – as 'learning to live with racism' (Henry 1994). This section explores the travels, troubles, and triumphs of Blacks who migrated to Toronto.

Slavery in Canada has been described as 'one of our best-kept historical secrets' (Walker 1980, 19). For over two hundred years, slavery – more than any other phenomenon – defined the Black experience in Canada. As we will see, this entailed two very different dimensions: first, the lengthy record of slavery in Canada itself; and second, Canada's stature in the mid-nineteenth century as a refuge for escaped slaves from the United States.

The first Black Canadian arrived as a slave in 1628. By 1759, when the British captured New France, over one thousand Black slaves had been brought to the colony. Further east, there were Black slaves at the French outpost of Louisburg and – numbering over one hundred in 1767 – among the first settlers of Halifax (Walker 1980, 19). When Toronto was founded in 1793, the first Black settlers were slaves belonging to British officials and military officers. In 1799, fifteen of the town's four hundred residents were Black (Hill 1985). Compared with the United States and the Caribbean, slavery in Canada was relatively limited and short-lived. Slavery was most widespread and brutal in plantation economies involving agricultural production and the need for a large rural workforce. The Canadian climate and geography were not conducive to such economic activity, nor was slavery a feasible means of supplying workers to the major Canadian resource industries of the day, such as the fur, fish, and lumber trades. Most slaves in Canada performed domestic and servant duties, and Ontario (then known as Upper Canada) became the first British territory to legislate against slavery. In 1793 the colonial legislature prohibited the entry of any more slaves into the colony and provided for the gradual elimination of slavery. Any new slaves brought in would immediately be freed, any children born to resident slaves would go free at age twenty-five; already-resident slaves, however, would remain captive their entire life. The last generation of Ontario slaves lived through the first part of the nineteenth century.

Blacks who migrated freely to Canada early in its history often encountered disappointment at the end of their journey. The first refugees to arrive in Canada were the Loyalists in the 1780s, residents of the United States who preferred to stay loyal to the British Empire following the American Revolution and who moved up to Canada. Beyond patriotism, promises of free land lured many northwards. Most settled in the Maritimes, with smaller numbers heading to Ontario. Ten per cent of all Loyalists, thirty-five hundred arrivals, were free Blacks who were typically either denied land grants or allocated less fertile property in remote segregated areas (Walker 1980). Despite Toronto's rapid growth, the Black population remained small during the first decades of the nineteenth century, growing from eighteen persons in 1802 to some fifty families in 1837. Some were the community's last slaves, others worked in services, as tradesmen, or owned successful businesses. Early nineteenth-century Toronto provides confirmation of Cecil Foster's (1996) observation that '[a]s long as there have been Blacks in Canada, there has been a church at the heart of the community' (54). A number of Black churches, particularly Baptist and Methodist, were thriving by the 1840s.

During the 1840s and 1850s, growing numbers of Black slaves fled the United States for Canada through the Underground Railroad, a secretive network of supporters that helped thousands of slaves escape, with most settling in southwestern Ontario. By the mid-1850s, Toronto's population of fifty thousand included twelve hundred Blacks (Hill 1985, 88). The city quickly established a reputation for tolerance – or at least an aversion to explicitly bigoted behaviour. One Black journalist described the treatment of Blacks in the city as follows: 'Here there is no difference made in public houses, steamboats, railroad cars, schools, colleges, churches, ministerial platforms, and government offices. There is, no doubt, some prejudice here, but those who have it are ashamed to show it. This is at least true of Toronto' (ibid., 89). Indeed, the abolitionist cause, devoted to eliminating slavery in the United States, was particularly strong here. The Toronto Anti-Slavery Society was formed in 1851 to provide support to runaway slaves and to advocate an end to slavery. Heading the society were some of Toronto's wealthiest and most prominent citizens, including George Brown, publisher of the *Globe* and a future 'Father of Confederation.' The society sometimes held its meetings at City Hall, chaired by the mayor, with one of its meeting described in the *Globe* as 'the largest and most enthusiastic meeting we have ever seen in Toronto' (ibid., 90).

Why was mid-nineteenth-century Toronto a bastion of abolitionism and human rights? Four factors may have contributed to this. First, Toronto's own Black community carried considerable credibility. Loyal to the British Empire, many had left the United States after its independence, and even fought with the British against the Americans in the War of 1812. Economically the community in Toronto was well-established, earning compliments from the likes of Toronto's first mayor, William Lyon Mackenzie, for their contribution to Toronto society. Second, for a few years during the 1850s, Toronto was home base for Canada's first Black abolitionist newspaper, the impressive *Provincial Freeman* established by Mary Ann Shadd Cary. Consequently many leading figures of the Black abolitionist movement lived in or passed through Toronto. Third, the fact that Britain had outlawed slavery in the 1830s now made abolitionism a major ethical divide between the British Empire and its renegade former colony, the United States. Abolitionism in other words, became one way of asserting a British rather than American set of values in what was then called British North America (to become Canada in 1867). And few places were more determined to display their British roots, we have already seen earlier in this chapter, than Toronto. Finally, it should be noted that opposing slavery in the United States made good economic sense for Toronto's civic elite. Slavery provided the competing American economy to the south a comparative advantage, thanks to its low-cost labour force. So a host of factors placed Toronto in the vanguard of the nineteenth-century anti-slavery movement.

Ironically, perhaps, the end of slavery in the United States led to a sharp drop in Toronto's Black population. Following the American Civil War, many recently arrived Blacks in Canada returned home. By 1871, Toronto's community had shrunk to 551 persons, and then reached an all-time low of only 408 in 1911 (Hill 1985). Much of this had to do with the lure of larger Black communities within the more prosperous American economy. But another factor was the impossibility of Blacks entering Canada as immigrants. Between 1896 and 1907, for instance, one and a half million immigrants arrived in Canada – of these, fewer than one thousand were Black. From the days of the Underground

Railway until the 1960s, Canadian immigration policy targeted Blacks for non-entry. In the 1890s, for instance, the Canadian government reacted quickly when its promotion of Prairie settlement attracted American Blacks northward. Canada sent government officials to the Southern U.S. to discourage migration, and Blacks who persisted were turned back at the border (Walker 1980).

For much of the twentieth century, Canada's immigration policies were explicitly racist, seeking to establish a 'white settler' society (Stasiulis 1995). Canada's Immigration Act of 1910 specifically provided for the prohibition of 'any race deemed unsuited to the climate or requirements of Canada' (Walker 1980, 94). A year later, Prime Minister Sir Wilfrid Laurier's government applied the law to exclude 'any immigrants belonging to the Negro race' (Alexander and Glaze 1996, 26). Almost fifty years later, the Immigration Act of 1952 reaffirmed that immigrants could be barred from Canada because of their 'ethnic group' identity, their 'geographic area of origin,' or their 'probable inability to become readily assimilated' (cited in Walker 1980, 94). Strangely, these guidelines were used to exclude Blacks who had been living in Canada since the 1700s.

Indeed, Blacks faced more prejudice and institutionalized forms of discrimination in the first half of the twentieth century than during the nineteenth century. This stemmed largely from the rise of pseudoscientific, untruthful assertions of racial purity and superiority that became fashionable and led to a host of discriminatory practices against non-white peoples. Thus, for the first half of this century, it was legal and common for Blacks in Toronto to be barred from certain jobs, theatres, hotels, dance halls, residential neighbourhoods, public beaches, and skating rinks. In his memoir, native Jamaican Harry Gairey (1981) recalls arriving in Toronto at the end of the First World War and being informed at numerous factories displaying Help Wanted signs that there were no jobs 'for coloured people.' Gairey describes the extent of segregation in interwar Toronto, during the 1920s and 1930s, by noting that as a Black, 'you couldn't go to Eaton's and ask for a job, or to the Bell Telephone. It was unheard-of to go to a restaurant or a public dance.' A generation later, when the first graduate nurse from the Caribbean was allowed into Canada, it would take fourteen months for her to gain hospital employment, 'and the only place that would hire her was the Jewish hospital, Mount Sinai' (7, 9, 35). Interestingly, a hospital that was established earlier in the century to provide Jewish doctors and nurses a place to practise now offered the same opportunity to a another immigrant spurned by mainstream hospitals. Until the middle of the twentieth century, there were no laws prohibiting discrimination, and the courts routinely upheld segregationist practices.

On the immigration front, until the 1960s, Blacks were allowed into Canada only as a 'last-resort' supply of cheap labour or skilled workers. This particularly applied to two periods when special programs were established to bring in Caribbean women as domestic household workers. From 1922 to 1931, 74 per cent of the 768 Caribbean Blacks who immigrated to Canada came as domestics; from 1955 to 1961, 44 per cent of the 4,219 Caribbean immigrants were female domestics (Calliste 1991). At the more skilled end of the job spectrum, Caribbean nurses were allowed into Canada in the 1950s, provided they could demonstrate 'exceptional merit' and prospective hospital employers were aware of their racial origin (Calliste 1996a). As Alexander and Glaze (1996) conclude, these limited and tightly regulated entry programs 'did nothing to eradicate the underlying principle of Canada's Immigration Act: that there are superior and inferior races of people' (179).

Following the Second World War, Toronto's Black community became increasingly active in lobbying for more open, equitable immigration policies on Black immigration. This mobilization of community stemmed from three sources: a sense of injustice; the belief, among ex-veterans especially, that since Blacks had fought for Canada in the war, they should not be discriminated against; and the emergence of a number of Black organizations able to speak on their community's behalf. Like Jews and Italians before them, Blacks relied on trade unionism as a vehicle of collective identity and expression.

While Jews and Italians predominated in the garment and construction industries respectively, the occupation most associated with Black men from 1900 to the 1950s was the railway car porter – the railways did not hire Black men in more responsible positions and confined them to lower-paid, stereotypical service employment. Harry Gairey, for instance, worked for decades as a railway sleeping car porter. Despite being demeaned and segregated into the lowest rung of rail industry employment, the Black porters succeeded in building an important community organization on the basis of their occupational exploitation. The 'Black porters' struggle for unionization and equality,' Alexander and Glaze (1996) write, 'is one of the great achievements of Canadian Black history' (135). As a way to challenge powerful railway corporations and prevailing anti-Black prejudices, the Canadian porters formed branches of the Sleeping Car Porters Union and affiliated with the large Canadian Brotherhood of Railway Workers. By the 1950s, the union had succeeded in raising wages for porters and pressing their employers to open more lucrative occupations (including that of conductor) to Blacks.

The union and its leaders also rallied to condemn Canada's discriminatory immigration policies. Joining the campaign were other Black union activists who had begun moving into labour leadership positions in other manufacturing sectors, such as the auto and steel workers' unions. In 1951, Harry Gairey and a number of other Black union and community activists in Toronto formed the Negro Citizenship Association to press for equal access to immigration for Blacks. Many organizing meetings later, in 1954, thirty-five Black community activists from the Sleeping Car Porters Union and the Negro Citizenship Association took a historic trip to Ottawa. There they met with and petitioned federal cabinet ministers to allow Caribbean Blacks to enter Canada through the expansive post-war immigration doors on an equal footing with other British subjects. Their call for redress was not heeded. An opinion poll of the day showed that nearly 60 per cent of Canadians were in agreement with the proposition that immigration to Canada should be more difficult for some groups than others (Winks 1997). It was a view held – and expressed with particular vigour – by Canada's director of immigration, the senior civil servant overseeing the country's immigration policies, who wrote in 1955:

> It is not by accident that coloured British subjects other than the negligible numbers from the United Kingdom are excluded from Canada. It is from experience, generally speaking, that coloured people in the present state of the white man's thinking are not a tangible community asset, and as a result are more or less ostracized. They do not assimilate readily and pretty much vegetate to a low standard of living. Despite what has been said to the contrary, many cannot adapt themselves to our climatic conditions. (Carty 1994, 217)

Because whites did not regard Blacks as 'a tangible community asset,' another group of twentieth-century prospective immigrants was met with the response 'none is too many.' Rooted in racial and racist stereotyping and prejudice, Canada's immigration welcome mat remained reserved for white Europeans and Americans. As Troper has already noted in chapter 1, in 1960 not one of Canada's twenty-seven immigration offices outside North America was located in the Caribbean or Africa.

Other authors in this book have already argued that Canada's opening of doors to migrants from around the world in the 1960s was motivated less by ethics than by economics. Diplomacy considerations also came into play as Canada's stature in international arenas such as the Commonwealth and the United Nations, was being undermined by its discriminatory immigration provisions. These various pragmatic forces culminated in the amended Immigration Act of 1962, which specified that, henceforth, every prospective immigrant would be considered 'entirely on his own merit, without regard to race, colour, national origin or the country from which he comes' (Winks 1997, 443). And, again, as Troper explains in the first chapter, the introduction five years later of the entry-by-merit approach, known as the 'points system,' transformed Canadian society in very short order by allowing all prospective immigrants to be assessed on the same objective considerations related to their education, occupation, employment prospects, and knowledge of English or French.

Caribbeans were by far the largest group of 'non-traditional' immigrants to first capitalize on a merit system of immigration. Canada's doors opened at precisely the time that Britain began curtailing Caribbean immigration, so many now flocked to Canada in hopes of improving their economic circumstances. In 1961, there were 12,000 Caribbean-born individuals living in Canada; by 1981 the number had soared to over 200,000; and by the early 1990s, the Caribbean community in Canada (including both immigrants and Canadian-born children) was estimated at 455,000. Almost three-quarters of all Caribbean immigrants settled in Ontario, with most drawn to the Toronto area. While the Caribbean consists of a large number of independent countries, four, in particular, provided almost 90 per cent of the 309,585 Caribbean-born Canadian residents in 1992: Jamaica, 102,440; Guyana, 66,055; Trinidad and Tobago, 49,385; and Haiti, 39,880. As we will see, these differing national origins have contributed to the establishment of diverse, rather than homogeneous, Caribbean communities in Toronto.

Another significant aspect of the Caribbean migration to Canada was the preponderance of women, in sharp contrast in the experience of most other immigrant groups to Canada, where men outnumbered women. By the early 1980s, there were ten Caribbean women for every eight men in Canada; the ratio for Jamaican Canadians was ten to seven. This gender imbalance reflected both the legacy of the domestic-workers program of the 1950s and the continuing pattern in subsequent decades for more women than men to migrate to Canada (Walker 1985; Henry 1994). Regardless of their gender, regardless of which country they were leaving, many Caribbean immigrants likely shared the 'romantic image' that drew writer Cecil Foster (1996) to Canada: 'a place of pristine snow and streams, a home of tolerance, a country in the forefront of racial harmony' (48). Once they had arrived in Toronto, however, the daily experiences of many Caribbeans would belie this idyllic image.

Frances Henry (1994) adopts the concept 'differential incorporation' to describe the Caribbean experience in Toronto. The term, she explains, 'refers to their unequal treatment and differential access to the economic, social, political, and cultural rewards offered in a plural society' (17). A host of markers identify the difficulties Caribbeans and other Blacks have faced in Toronto, including discrimination in employment and housing; alarmingly high school drop-out rates; insensitivity from cultural institutions; barriers impeding the establishment of community institutions; and disproportionate confrontations with police. The following examples, drawn from experiences in recent years, suggest the scope of marginalization that Caribbeans face in Toronto.

An early 1980s study of job hunting in Toronto found that when whites and Blacks had the same qualifications, white applicants received three times as many job offers. Subsequent data showed that, despite higher levels of education, visible-minority workers were paid less than other Canadians. And evidence has also surfaced that visible minorities were still being relegated to less desirable occupations, despite having consistently higher levels of education than other workers in lower-paying positions (Henry 1994). Writing in 1990, Jeffrey Reitz contended that the prevailing underemployment of Caribbeans (affecting not only whether they held jobs, but also what positions and wages they secured), could only be attributed to discrimination. Their place in the labour market lagged behind their educational and job qualifications. Caribbean males were predominantly employed in health care (often as hospital orderlies and janitors), in industry, as taxi drivers and security guards, and in clerical positions; Caribbean females were disproportionately employed in personal services, clerical, and nursing positions (Breton et al. 1990). In fact, as discussed later in this chapter, labour market and income discrepancies have persisted, even intensified. Next, however, we briefly identify indicators of the Caribbean community's 'differential incorporation' into Toronto.

- In education, as Carl E. James and Barbara Burnaby discuss in chapter 5, there were signs of a serious mismatch between Toronto schools and Black students. In the 1990s, 60 per cent of Black stu-

dents quit high school before graduating; disproportionately large numbers who did graduate had been streamed into non-postsecondary vocational programs; and Black youth commonly complained of having their academic potential undervalued by teachers and guidance councillors (Henry 1994; Foster 1996).
- Two major cultural events, the Royal Ontario Museum's *Out of Africa* exhibit and Livent's production of the musical *Show Boat*, offended the Toronto Black community because of cultural bias and misrepresentation. These cultural productions were widely condemned in Toronto's Black Community for perpetuating negative stereotypes and for misappropriating voice and experience.
- Reflecting on the struggle against resistance from neighbouring property owners and the North York city council that delayed construction of a new community centre by the Jamaican Canadian Association (JCA) for years, JCA President Herman Stewart confided, 'I wouldn't wish it on my worst enemy' (Siemiatycki and Isin 1998, 96).
- Many Torontonians of Caribbean heritage believe that they are particularly poorly served by the city's police. Eighty per cent of Black survey participants told York University researchers they believed the police in Toronto treated Blacks worse than whites; many Black motorists regard themselves as charged with DWB (Driving While Black) to explain why they seem to be stopped so often by police; and, most tragically, a string of police shootings of Black men – resulting in eight deaths between 1988 and 1992 alone – have left Toronto's Black community feeling angry and vulnerable (Foster 1996; Croucher 1997).

In his 1992 *Report on Race Relations in Ontario*, former Canadian ambassador to the United Nations Stephen Lewis reviewed the experience of Toronto's Black community (by far the largest portion being of Caribbean origin) and concluded, 'What we are dealing with, at root, and fundamentally, is anti-Black racism' (Alexander and Glaze 1996, 115). Two years later, based on the most comprehensive study of Toronto's Caribbean community to date, Frances Henry arrived at a similar conclusion, writing that the prime factor 'to explain the differential incorporation of the Caribbean community in Toronto is that *societal racism* affects all aspects of the lives of Caribbean people in Canada' (Henry 1994, 16, original emphasis). An American political scientist made the same point a few years later, contending that, despite the city's widespread image of multicultural tolerance, 'Toronto is not an ethnic and racial paradise' (Croucher 1997, 320).

As for Torontonians of Caribbean origin themselves, many believe that a subtle, but pervasive, pattern of prejudice inhibits their life in the city. Cecil Foster speaks of encountering 'racism with a smile on its face' in Toronto; a Black lawyer contrasts the U.S. style of 'dim-witted racism' with its 'much more subtle, more finessed' manifestation in Canada; and many Caribbeans echo the experience of the Toronto community legal services worker who told a public enquiry that only after arriving in Toronto did her Black identity become significant. 'I am Black,' Beverly Folkes told the 1989 Task Force on Race Relations and Policing. But, she continued, 'I never became aware that I was Black until I set foot on the shores of this country. It was always there, but it was never important until now ... I have become one of the people who is guilty until proven innocent, a total reversal of what the law should have been. I hurt. I feel helpless. I feel frustrated' (Foster 1996, 14; Croucher 1997, 332, 338–9). The Caribbean diaspora in Toronto is a reminder that the city has not yet achieved integration on equal terms for all its immigrant communities.

Frustrations among Black youth, primarily of Caribbean-origin, in Toronto proved an important element in the events of May 4, 1992, which came to be known as the Yonge Street Riot. On that day a demonstration was organized at the U.S. consulate building in downtown Toronto to protest the acquittal in Los Angeles of police officers accused, and videotaped, in the beating of Black motorist Rodney King. As fate would have it, just days before the planned protest, Toronto police shot and killed a Black man. Emotions ran high among many demonstrators at the demonstration, exploding on the city's downtown commercial thoroughfare when protestors embarked on a wave of storefront vandalism and looting along Yonge Street. Canada's leading news magazine, *Maclean's*, headlined the rioters as 'Black and Angry,' but other media and participants emphasized the multiracial nature of the protest (Kaihla and Laver 1992). While Blacks were certainly not the only participants in the riot, the event fundamentally challenged Toronto's prevailing image of ethnoracial harmony (Croucher 1997).

Frances Henry (1997) has concluded that while racism is the most significant cause of the adversity Caribbeans have faced in Toronto, there are a number of 'cultural values and institutions that Caribbean people bring with them that do not work to their advantage in the new society' (17). Among the problematic patterns Henry identifies are a high proportion of single-parent families, prevailing rivalries that divide Caribbeans from different islands and countries, and a relatively low rate of political participation among Caribbeans in Toronto. 'People of Caribbean origin,' Henry concludes, 'have not yet reached the level of cohesion necessary to enter the political process' (244). This is attributable to a variety of factors, including the relative recency of migration (compared, for example, with the more established Jewish and Italian communities); the preoccupation with day-to-day economic and social pressures; the widely scattered residential pattern among Caribbeans that prevents them from numerically dominating electoral constituencies; and the divisions among Caribbeans based on island or national origin. Indeed, as Henry asserts, 'The Caribbean community in Toronto is not homogenous. In fact, the term "community" is misleading and "communities" is a more accurate description of a group that is clearly segmented by a number of factors' (ibid., 268).

Social class and birth country have been the major divides within the 'community.' Associational life, for instance, has largely been organized by country of origin, leading to the creation of groups such as the Jamaican Canadian Association and the Trinidad and Tobago Association. While these organizations have provided a variety of support services and activities, they have also reinforced the institutional fragmentation of Caribbeans in Toronto. It is a divide some regard as problematic and needing to be overcome. 'What I would like to live long enough to see is one Black organization,' octogenarian Harry Gairey said in 1981, 'like the Canadian Jewish Congress, that would speak for all Blacks and appoint a spokesman, instead of all these little splinter groups' (Gairey 1981, 42–3). Gairey's hope remains to be realized.

The Chinese Community

Chinese migration to Toronto originated in the late nineteenth century. A century later, Chinese newcomers constituted the largest wave of immigrants ever to settle in the city in a short period of time. The city's recent emergence as the North American urban area with the largest Chinese population constitutes a dramatic renewal of multicultural Toronto (Nipp 1992). While Toronto's Chinese community numbered no more than five thousand in 1950, by 1996 their numbers had soared to 380,000 and Chinese had displaced Italian as the second most commonly spoken language in the Toronto area (Cannon 1989; Carey 1999c; T. Wong 1999). As Lo and Wang (1997) note, the Chinese community is

Canada's 'fastest growing ethnic group' thanks to its 'accelerated immigration' in recent years (49). However, opening the door to Chinese newcomers has not necessarily meant a warm welcome for the newest Torontonians. 'Aside from the indigenous people,' Peter Li (1998) has written, 'no racial or ethnic group in Canada has experienced such harsh treatment as the Chinese' (5).

While weighing and comparing oppression among different groups is inherently problematic, Li's assertion reflects the adverse treatment of Canadian Chinese-origin peoples. Certainly, the limited size of the Chinese community in Canada for most of its history stemmed from a series of government measures designed to keep the Chinese out. Those allowed in were often recruited as a vulnerable, easily exploited workforce. Ironically, now that Chinese immigrants are more likely to be well-educated and affluent, they too, like their poorer Chinese predecessors, have had to integrate into a new society that at times both resents and requires their presence.

Chinese immigration to Canada began in the late 1850s, with settlement overwhelmingly concentrated in British Columbia. There the first Chinese Canadians, numbering a few thousand at most, worked either in mining or domestic service as cooks and cleaners. The largest arrival of Chinese immigrants (until the late twentieth century) occurred during the 1880s, when some fifteen thousand Chinese labourers were brought in to work on the construction of the Canadian Pacific Railway that ran from central Canada to the Pacific Ocean. The shocking fact that over three thousand of these labourers died on the job – an average of one fatality for every mile of track laid – reflected both the treacherous task of blasting a railway through the Rockies, as well as the disregard and devaluing of Chinese lives by builders, contractors, and governments of the day. Adjacent to one of Toronto's contemporary landmark contemporary sites, the SkyDome stadium, is a stunning, recently built monument that pays belated tribute to the Chinese labourers who sacrificed so much to build a ribbon of steel across Canada.

The Chinese Canadian community of the late nineteenth and early twentieth century was dealt one blow after another. These setbacks of government policy were designed to admit as few Chinese newcomers as possible, and to assure that those in the country did not attain full equality and citizenship. As soon as the Canadian Pacific Railway was completed in 1885, the federal government moved swiftly to restrict Chinese immigration. That year the government introduced a head tax of $50 on all persons of Chinese origin entering the country. Ships travelling to Canada could carry no more than one Chinese person for every fifty tons of vessel weight. In 1900 the head tax was hiked to $100, and then to $500 in 1903. As intended, Chinese immigration to Canada fell sharply. Canadians of the day, and their government, racialized and demonized the Chinese as a foreign people unwanted in Canada unless they could be of some particular use, such as building the railway.

But not only were the Chinese often ruthlessly exploited in the worst, poorest-paid jobs, they were vilified for working for low wages and for depriving native Canadians of a living wage. Anger against the Chinese occasionally manifested itself in full-scale assaults on their community. Several such riots – which in another context would be termed pogroms, targeted attempts to destroy and evict a minority community – took place in Vancouver. The worst occurred in 1907, when a parade organized by the Asiatic Exclusion League marched through the Chinese district carrying banners proclaiming, A White Canada and No Cheap Asiatic Labor, and White Canada – Patronize Your Own Race and Canada. Before long, the march degenerated into a full riot, leaving a trail of ransacked and ruined Chinese businesses and homes.

In 1923 came the most decisive move of all, when Canada's Parliament passed the Chinese Immigration Act, barring all Chinese immigration into Canada. The Act was not repealed until 1947. This was the same year the right to vote was finally extended to Chinese residents of British Columbia, who for decades had been denied basic political rights and the right to work in a host of occupations and professions (Cannon 1989; Li 1998). Through much of Canada's history, then, the Chinese were singled out as unworthy and unwanted Canadians. According to sociologist Peter Li (1998), this perception continues to shape Canadian attitudes. 'The image of Chinese or Chinese-Canadians as belonging to a foreign race,' he observed, 'is ingrained in the cultural fabric of Canada' (xiii). Chinese immigrants, therefore, faced particular challenges in becoming accepted as fully Torontonian.

By 1900 Toronto was home to a fledgling Chinese community of some two hundred residents. Self-employment in laundries, cafés, and groceries was the predominant source of livelihood. Even such a small presence, however, was grounds for concern among some upstanding Torontonians. The city's very first neighbourhood association – the Rosedale Ratepayers Association – cited among its founding missions at the start of the twentieth century the need to keep Chinese laundries out of the neighbourhood. By 1921, on the eve of the exclusionary Chinese Immigration Act, the city's Chinese population had reached a modest 2,176, representing .4 per cent of Toronto's population (Breton et al. 1990). During the 1930s the first organization to advocate an end to discriminatory Canadian immigration policies towards the Chinese was established in Toronto. Leaders in the local Chinese community formed the Committee for the Movement to Abolish the Canadian Restrictive Immigration Policy Towards Chinese (P. Li 1998). The committee lobbied the federal government, but to no avail. Canada would change its immigration policy not when the Chinese community requested, but when an open door served Canada's own interests.

Repealing the Chinese Immigration Act in 1947 did not usher in a sudden wave of Chinese newcomers. Nor was this the government's intent, as Prime Minister Mackenzie King informed the House of Commons. 'Large-scale immigration from the Orient would change the fundamental composition of the Canadian population,' he declared (King 1947, 2646). Until the 1960s, sponsored immediate relatives of Chinese Canadians were the only Chinese able to enter Canada. From 1949 to 1967, 2.7 million persons immigrated to Canada; less than 2 per cent, just 43,106, were Chinese. Only when a 'race-blind' universal point system was adopted in 1967 to assess all prospective immigrants to Canada were large numbers of Chinese persons able to enter Canada. However, as we have seen earlier in this volume, the adoption of objective entry criteria based on education, skills, and occupation was prompted by Canada's own needs.

By the final third of the twentieth century, Canada's economy faced labour shortages and a shrinking stream of migrants from traditional source countries in Europe. Canadian domestic economic interests, combined with a desire to retain strong relations with non-European states and economies, required opening the doors to global migration. No group has capitalized better on a situation of being judged on their merits than the Chinese. In the thirty years since the introduction of the points system, almost 750,000 immigrants have arrived in Canada from Hong Kong, China, and Taiwan. The 1990s have been the greatest period of Chinese migration in Canadian history, with the largest numbers arriving from Hong Kong. It was in this decade that Chinese surpassed Italian as the third most commonly spoken language across Canada, and, as we mentioned earlier, the second most common across the Toronto metropolitan area (P. Li 1998; Citizenship and Immigration Canada 1999).

Several factors account for the sharp rise in Chinese migration to Canada in recent decades. Since the largest number of Chinese immigrants have arrived from Hong Kong, we will address the particular circumstances of this region first. The return of Hong Kong to China's sovereignty in 1997 unleashed widespread anxiety among residents of the former British colony. In the years leading up to the transfer, many Hong Kong residents feared the prospect of their free-wheeling, entrepreneurial, capitalist society reverting to the control of the Communist People's Republic of China. The more affluent Hong Kong families, in particular, were eager to secure a safe haven. The earliest wave of migration began in the late 1960s, when political turmoil raised fears of a mainland Chinese invasion and Hong Kong was put under martial law for four months. The next wave began in 1982 when Prime Minister Margaret Thatcher declared that Britain would not contest the end of its control over Hong Kong, as specified by the late-nineteenth-century treaty that had turned the city into a colony of the British Empire. Political uncertainty weighed heavily on many. Ronald Skeldon (1999) estimates that, by the early 1990s, 585,000 Hong Kong residents, 10 per cent of the colony's population, had already migrated. Record numbers more would leave in the years just before 1997. Margaret Cannon (1939) has identified 'fear and desperation' as the 'engine driving the Hong Kong exodus.' For his part, Skeldon (1999) contends that 'Hong Kong migrants are as much bold pioneers in transnational commerce as they are reluctant exiles' (68). To be sure, it has generally been the wealthier sections of Hong Kong's community who were able to emigrate before 1997. And Canada proved to be their destination of choice.

In the last decades of the twentieth century, Hong Kong emigrants constituted the advanced world's preferred immigrant pool. As affluent, educated, entrepreneurial, and globally connected business migrants, people leaving Hong Kong were actively courted by every traditional country of immigration, including the United States, Australia, New Zealand, and Canada. From the mid-1980s onward, Canada attracted by far the most emigrants from Hong Kong. Thus, in 1994, Canada received 43,651 Hong Kong migrants, compared with the 11,949 who went to the United States and the 4,075 who emigrated to Australia. A significant element of Canada's success was its aggressive recruitment of Hong Kong immigrants through newly established business-immigrant categories established in the mid-1980s. With federal and provincial government agents in Hong Kong actively promoting businessperson's migration to Canada, it was not surprising that, from 1986 to 1996, 40 per cent of all entrepreneur immigrants and 47 per cent of all investor immigrants to Canada came from Hong Kong.

How the Chinese presence changed in Canada since the late nineteenth century! Then, as we have seen, Chinese newcomers were only allowed in as a menial, exploitable workforce to assume the most hazardous or poorest-paid jobs in the country. They were now being courted to invest in businesses and resource interests. In both instances, economic self-interest guided Canada's outreach, yet affluent Chinese newcomers would encounter as chilly a reception as their impoverished predecessors.

It is important to note, however, that diversity – not homogeneity – has characterized Chinese migration to Canada in recent years. Certainly, not all immigrants from Hong Kong are wealthy. In 1990, for instance, 25 per cent of Hong Kong immigrants earned less income than the Statistics Canada low-income cut-off, compared with 15 per cent of the Canadian-born population and 19 per cent of all immigrants (Statistics Canada 1996a). But the variety of countries of origin represents the greatest heterogeneity in Canada's Chinese population. By the mid-1990s, Toronto's Chinese community was a microcosm of the globalized Chinese diaspora: 40 per cent of all Chinese immigrants were born in Hong Kong; 30 per cent in mainland China; 4 per cent in Taiwan; 10 per cent in Vietnam; 9 per cent elsewhere in Asia; 3 per cent in the West Indies; and 4 per cent in the rest of the world (Lo and Wang 1998). The removal of emigration prohibitions in the People's Republic of China over the past two decades has resulted in a surge of newcomers to Canada. This cohort is characterized by incomes that are significantly below both Canadian-born and other immigrants in the country (Statistics Canada 1996b).

Geographically, the Chinese presence in Canada has undergone a dramatic shift with the tremendous growth in Chinese immigration over the past few decades. Changing settlement patterns have been manifested both *between* and *within* urban areas. Toronto, not Vancouver, now contains the largest Chinese community in the country. Historically, British Columbia had hosted Canada's largest Chinese community. In 1901, for instance, 86 per cent of Canadian residents of Chinese origin lived in BC; in 1961, BC still had the largest share at 41.6 per cent compared with Ontario at 26 per cent. But once the point system of the late 1960s opened the doors fully to Chinese migration, the tide turned to Ontario, thanks to Toronto's appeal to Chinese newcomers. By the 1981 census, Toronto had eclipsed Vancouver (and Ontario led BC) as home to the largest number of Chinese. In 1991, Toronto's metropolitan area was home to 231,820 Chinese-origin residents, compared with 167,425 in Vancouver; in the same year, Ontario was home to 46.7 per cent of Canada's Chinese population compared with 30.9 per cent in BC (W.C. Ng 1999). Several factors account for Toronto's appeal: its greater size; its stature as the country's economic centre; its strong tradition of public and post-secondary educational institutions that corresponded to the great value many Chinese immigrants placed on their children's education; and the fact that most immigrants were now flying into Canada (as opposed to previous cross-Pacific boat travel), which eliminated access difficulties to the country's mid-continent metropolis.

Within the Toronto area, too, Chinese settlement patterns have changed dramatically in recent decades, as Robert A. Murdie and Carlos Teixeira examine in chapter 3. The downtown core had been the site of a small 'Chinatown' since the early 1900s, but within a few years in the late 1990s, four more Chinatowns sprang up thanks to the great upsurge of Chinese migration. The new settlement areas reflected the diversity among ethnic Chinese coming to Toronto. Less affluent newcomers – predominantly from mainland China and Vietnamese-born ethnic Chinese – settled to the east of the downtown core; more affluent recent immigrants – primarily from Hong Kong – settled in the postwar suburb of Scarborough or the new edge cities of Markham and Richmond Hill. Differences of gender, class, language, nationality, religion, income, and residential location now characterize Toronto's huge Chinese population. Distinctions may manifest themselves over matters ranging from homeland politics to preferred choice of restaurants, as Toronto writer Robert Fulford discovered. 'In the northwest corner of Scarborough,' he wrote in 1995, 'wealthy immigrants from Hong Kong dine at magnificent oriental restaurants, and explain that they find the cuisine in the old downtown Chinatown around Spadina Avenue unsophisticated' (103). But riches may carry risk as well, with north Scarborough's Chinese community subsequently declared Toronto's 'carjack central,' the area most prone to theft of luxury vehicles (Abbate 2000, A16).

Toronto's Chinese community is sufficiently large and affluent, in sections, to promote an impressive commercial, media, and marketing presence. In addition to its five Chinatowns, the Toronto area has dozens of distinctive 'Asian-style' malls and plazas, three Chinese-language daily newspapers, two Chinese-language television stations, several high-profile English-language magazines that publish Chinese editions, and a host of businesses and advertisers engaged in niche marketing to sell to a Chinese clientele. A major client is the Ford Motor Company, eager to convince Chinese newcomers that driving a Ford has its own social cachet. In the words of Patrick Fong, head of Can-Asian Advertising in Toronto, 'You turn social change into a marketing opportunity' (as quoted in Heinzl 1999). Chinese media, marketing, and retailing have undoubtedly combined to strengthen the sense of community among Toronto residents of Chinese origin.

Ironically, perhaps, the more affluent Chinese immigrants who have come to Toronto at the end of the twentieth century have not been spared the prejudicial treatment their poorer predecessors faced earlier in the century. A 1999 survey found that 65 per cent of Chinese respondents in the city believed there was discrimination against their community; 38 per cent claimed they had personally experienced prejudice or discrimination. Verbal abuse and taunts were the most frequently reported difficulties encountered by both males and females, with Chinese women reporting far higher denial of service, access, or promotion rates than men (Carey 1999c). Perceptions of prejudice and exclusion are relatively widespread, then, within Toronto's Chinese community and several public, high-profile incidents have raised particular concerns within the community about Toronto's – and Canada's – openness to diversity.

In 1979, a national television program, CTV's *W5*, appeared to brand all Chinese as foreigners taking advantage of Canada. The broadcast – a report on foreign students at Canadian universities entitled 'Campus Giveaway' – contended that foreigners were preventing Canadian students from attending university, and claimed that Chinese students, in particular, were overrepresented on Canadian campuses. The program somehow overlooked the fact that many of the Chinese students shown were actually Canadian citizens; clearly many Canadian institutions, including the media, have been slow to recognize that full-fledged Canadians could be of Chinese ancestry. The Chinese community in Toronto rallied in a mass mobilization to protest prejudice stereotyping and formed the Chinese Canadian National Council (CCNC) to express its opposition to the program. CTV issued a public apology for its racist programming, and the Chinese community gained strength from having defended both its right to fair media coverage and to equal access to Canadian institutions.

Fifteen years later, members of Toronto's Chinese community were again labelled as 'foreigner.' In 1995, Carole Bell, the deputy mayor of Markham (an edge city north of Toronto) warned that the prevalence of Chinese-language signs in the area's malls was prompting longtime residents to move out of town. Again it appeared that even in multicultural Canada, using a language other than English could brand Chinese newcomers as outsiders taking over a neighbourhood. Protests from the Chinese community and their supporters followed, but Ms Bell remained adamant in her views. The town ultimately appointed an advisory committee to address the public's concerns and, without condemning her remarks, the committee's report called for all newcomers to be welcomed to Markham. In reality, however, Markham has responded by using its planning and development regulations to pressure new Chinese commercial establishments to use English in their public signs (Cousens 1998).

While suburbs have occasionally faltered in fully accepting Chinese newcomers, the City of Toronto has also periodically stumbled, despite its longer history of Chinese settlement. A number of controversies in recent years have intensified police relations with the community. The 1997 police shooting of a homeless, mentally ill Chinese man prompted the Chinese Canadian National Council to actively challenge systemic racism in the treatment of the mentally ill by Toronto's police force. And twice in 1999, Toronto police had to apologize for describing a crime suspect as 'yellow,' a derisive term commonly associated in earlier years with the term 'yellow peril' (Immen 1999, A1).

Toronto's Chinese community is both vigilant and active in promoting equity, racial, and social justice, primarily through the CCNC. The Council operates both at the national level, to address issues of federal government responsibility, and locally, to lobby municipal governments. In recent years, the CCNC has pursued a large and varied advocacy agenda. Interventions at the national level have included preparing a court challenge seeking redress for the Chinese head tax and exclusionary immigration policies; filing complaints with the CRTC regarding either the invisibility or stereotypical portrayal of Chinese Canadians in television broadcasting; submitting reports on immigration law reform; and educating the community about federal election issues. The CCNC has both a Toronto chapter and a York Region chapter (comprising Markham and Richmond Hill) to deal with municipal issues. Over the years the council has addressed policing, municipal restructuring, social service cuts, and local election education (Chinese Canadian National Council 1997, 1998).

Undoubtedly, one impediment facing the CCNC in the political arena is the underrepresentation of Chinese Canadians among elected politicians in the Toronto area. Across the region, there are no politicians of Chinese origin in either the federal or provincial Parliament. The municipal record is marginally better with four of the 263 municipal politicians elected into municipal councils across the Greater Toronto Area being of Chinese origin – two in the City of Toronto (one woman and one man) and two male councillors in Markham. The Chinese community has the potential electoral advantage of strong residential concentration; large Chinese Canadian residential communities can be a natural base of support for politicians of Chinese origin. But even municipally, the community remains underrepresented in elected offices. This is still, in large measure, a community of relative newcomers who lack both strong roots in Canada's political system and extensive familiarity with competitive liberal-democratic elections from their homeland experiences. Increasing rates of citizenship among Chinese immigrants, combined with civic education campaigns by organizations like the Chinese Canadian National Council should raise the number of Chinese-origin candidates seeking public office.

Meanwhile, despite adversities, most immigrants to Toronto who are of Chinese origin appear pleased to have a new urban home. Ninety-four per cent of survey respondents agreed that the Chinese community has generally found acceptance in the city. As one respondent declared, 'Toronto has become the best of both worlds. You can have the tastes of many different cultures and still be part of a wonderful city' (T. Wong 1999, B3).

Plus Ça Change? ...

'The more things change, the more things remain the same,' goes the famous French saying. What conclusions are we to draw from this survey of newcomer settlement in Toronto over the course of the twentieth century? The experiences of Jewish, Italian, Caribbean, and Chinese immigrants reflect both continuity and change.

To be sure, these four groups represent less than a handful of the many newcomer communities from around the world who have chosen to make Toronto their home. However, because of their great numbers, Jewish, then Italian, then Caribbean, and, finally, Chinese settlers comprised the four immigrant communities who have most dramatically represented the changing face of Toronto through the twentieth century. Each group had to contend with discriminatory Canadian immigration policies restricting their entry to Canada. The doors opened to each group only when the country felt these newcomers could be economically useful, typically as a low-wage workforce, or more recently as wealthy, globally connected investors. Once in Toronto, each group experienced discrimination and racialization as they were treated as an exploitable workforce, regarded as unfit for higher status positions, excluded from various civic facilities, negatively portrayed in the media, and poorly served by various municipal government departments.

These four newcomer communities responded to adversity through community solidarity and organization. They founded or joined a host of organizations to advance their rights and sense of belonging in Toronto. These included trade unions, synagogues, churches, temples, fraternal societies, social service agencies, and community advocacy organizations. In each of these communities, women have played important leadership roles, and each was far more *internally diversified* across lines such as gender, national origin, religion, occupation, and income than resident Torontonians generally recognized. In times of particular crisis (for example, the Christie Pits Riot or the Chinese community's difficulty gaining acceptance in new suburban areas), an embattled newcomer group could find allies among members of other minority communities. As we will see in further detail below, a pattern of *multi-community* mobilization has now emerged in multicultural Toronto.

Without question, the civic outlook towards diversity in Toronto today is unrecognizable from the city's defining values of a hundred years ago. Immigration has made Toronto a truly global city, home to the world's population. Accordingly, the city exhibits no outward signs of its past xenophobic, anti-foreigner sentiments. And yet, as we show in the following section, Toronto continues to display a surprising tolerance for inequalities rooted in identity. Advantage and disadvantage remain starkly divided in present-day Toronto.

PRESENT-DAY CONFIGURATION OF TORONTO'S DIVERSITY

Changing Policy Framework

Over the course of the twentieth century, three policy frameworks have shaped the integration of newcomers into Toronto's civic society. The period from 1900 to the 1950s may be characterized by immigrant self-reliance in a society that regarded non-British residents as foreigners.

The period from the 1950s to the early 1980s ushered in a different framework of newcomer integration with the rise of the welfare state and multiculturalism policies. Finally, the period since the mid-1980s has seen a retreat from government commitments to social services, multiculturalism, and equity initiatives. These differing policy orientations have set the context for newcomer integration in Toronto.

Throughout the first half of the twentieth century, unequal access to public resources and policy-making forced the onus of integration into Canadian society on immigrant communities themselves. The economic and political power structure was exclusionary, dominated by the British charter group; institutional rigidities prevented access and opportunities for mobility to new immigrant communities.

As we described in the first section of this chapter, the history of settlement services for migrants in Toronto has largely been one of voluntary self-help from community-based immigrant and ethnic associations and religious organizations that have long existed to provide immigrant economic assistance and integration services. Until the rise of the welfare state in the middle of the twentieth century, governments were not the primary providers of health care and income support to Canadians, in general, which placed particular onus on individual and community self-reliance to care for people's needs. Among immigrants in particular, mutual aid was a powerful imperative; voluntary fraternal societies and community health clinics flourished and filled a critical gap.

Following the Second World War, governments came to play an increasingly important role in the fields of health, education, and social services. With the turn towards a Keynesian welfare state in Canada, governments themselves assumed the principal role of building a network of both universal and needs-targeted services and programs for Canadians. Through to the early 1980s, the state became the primary provider of public education, public health care, and income support for the poor, the elderly, and the unemployed; governments also provided substantial funding for a wide range of immigrant, ethnic, and minority group services, as well as for advocacy groups. This community-based sector was financially supported by the state to fulfil their role in delivering targeted settlement services. There was a well-developed community-based settlement service infrastructure in place through which government support could be channelled into the provision of language programs and contracted services and grants to the community settlement agencies.

It was not until the 1960s that significant measures were taken to protect and defend the human rights of all citizens. The Canadian Bill of Rights was adopted in 1960, and the Ontario Human Rights Commission was established. And, as has been noted previously, the restrictive and outright discriminatory nature of Canadian immigration regulations was changed in 1967 with the introduction of the points system. From the 1970s on, these new regulations led directly to a dramatic increase in the number of non-white immigrants from the Caribbean, Asia, and Africa. In addition to these measures designed to curb (or give the appearance of stopping) discriminatory practices, Canada adopted multiculturalism policies in the 1970s that had more proactive implications.

The principles encoded in the multicultural policies adopted by the federal, provincial, and municipal governments throughout the 1970s included a commitment to the full and equal participation of all citizens in the cultural, economic, political, and social life of the country. The ideal that the circle of life should embrace all citizens equally, advanced the principles of equality of access, equality of opportunity, and equality of all cultures. Espousal of these principles also implied that all individuals should have access to societal resources – and should be treated equitably by societal institutions – irrespective of their race, ethnicity, immigrant status, or national origin (Breton 1998). The refusal, inability, or disinclination on the part of societal institutions to respond to the needs of immigrant communities or to the differential needs of a diverse population was no longer tenable. Together, the development of welfare state and multiculturalism policies shifted relations between immigrant communities and the 'mainstream' in Canada.

A host of factors propelled governments to this more pluralistic and rights-based approach to Canadian society and citizenship: labour-market needs for a growing pool of immigrants; rising immigrant expectations; and a host of political calculations, such as government designs on winning electoral support among newcomer communities, securing the goodwill of important immigrant-sending states, and reducing the primacy of Quebec's claims on the country's political agenda by identifying multiculturalism as a defining characteristic of Canadian society. All these forces contributed to formal, articulated commitments to human rights, access, and equity. While such commitments and principles might be described as providing important symbolic support, they are essential in setting the tone of what is acceptable. They have provided the cornerstone for a political and public policy basis for action, and have sent out clear signals in support of justice, equality, and inclusiveness.

The pursuit of equality was reflected, for example, in new human rights legislation, employment equity, public education campaigns, and an opportunity structure of grants, research, policies, and consultative processes that legitimized and supported ethnically based activities. In this environment, community-based organizations moved beyond self-help activities to broader advocacy campaigns (several of which are examined in the third section of this chapter). The goal was often to transform or 'multiculturalize' mainstream institutions; that is, to define them as common spaces in which all individuals and communities could participate on an equal footing. Typically, this involved newcomer communities pressing institutions such as schools, hospitals, social service agencies, governments, the media, and employers to become more inclusive, accountable, and equitable. Among the results, we will see, was the creation of a host of consultative mechanisms through which community voices could be heard, if not listened to.

The last decade of the twentieth century, however, has seen a significant pulling back of the public sector. Governments at all levels undertook deep cuts to their spending and services. A political culture of public and state responsibility for services and citizen well-being turned into a belief in markets as optimal distributors of services and self-reliance as a primary human virtue. The impact on immigrants to Toronto over the past decade has included federal government cuts to programs such as unemployment insurance, health care, and immigrant-settlement services; provincial government cuts to welfare and health care, and the outright disbanding of such initiatives as Immigrant Welcome Houses, employment equity legislation, and the Anti-Racism Secretariat; and municipal government cuts to community grant programs, hikes in user fees for a variety of services, and the closure of local institutions such as schools and libraries. Significantly, this retreat in government commitment to social spending has occurred when Canada's immigrant newcomers were more diverse than ever, with the fewest arriving from Europe, the most from Asia and Africa.

The neo-liberal assault on Keynesian public policy has also created a crisis for immigrant community organizations. Already overextended, these agencies are expected to step up their level of service to replace retreating government support. While all areas of public sector activity have experienced government downsizing and downloading, the immigrant and refugee sector has been particularly hard hit. A 1997 study of the impact of government funding cuts on community agencies, entitled *Profile of a Changing World*, showed very clearly that settlement services received the largest funding cuts and were most at risk in terms of sustainability. This survey found that 43 per cent of all programs for immigrants or refugees were at a high risk of being eliminated (Municipality of Metropolitan Toronto 1997). While public sector funding probably peaked around 1994, funding cuts have varied from 20 per cent for some of the larger multi-service agencies to 40 per cent for some of the smaller, ethno-specific agencies, many of whom have since closed (T. Richmond 1996). Community-based settlement agencies have become accustomed to operating in a climate of instability and chronic shortages in key areas at a time of growing need (Simich 2000).

This change in public policy and the consequent change in funding patterns have come at a time when the settlement of new communities in Toronto is becoming increasingly suburbanized. As Robert A. Murdie and Carlos Teixeira point out in chapter 3, settlement patterns in Toronto no longer conform to the earlier and traditional urban patterns of initial settlement downtown, where institutions and self-help groups have developed over time to facilitate the integration of newcomers. Since the 1970s, Toronto's inner city has no longer been the exclusive reception area for new immigrants. Indeed, by 1996, eight municipalities in the Greater Toronto Area had higher proportions of residents who were foreign-born than the (former pre-amalgamated) central city of Toronto! These municipalities with greater immigrant concentration were, from highest to lowest level of concentration, North York, Scarborough, York, Markham, Etobicoke, Mississauga, Vaughan, and Richmond Hill (Siemiatycki and Isin 1997). Some of the factors contributing to this suburbanization process have been the diminishing supply of inexpensive housing in the central area; the availability of financially accessible large-scale suburban apartment complexes; the attraction of edge city suburbs to more affluent recent migrants; and the absence of established support networks in the central area for new groups who come from very different parts of the world.

The suburbs of Toronto, however, have generally been unprepared to serve as settlement areas for new immigrants. With inadequate immigrant information resources and services, limited resources in the school system to serve the special learning and adjustment needs of immigrant children, limited availability of child care, and limited public environments in which to meet and mix, suburban newcomers are experiencing very limited formal and informal supports that or are required and have traditionally existed. In addition, the sprawled pattern of suburban settlement can impede the development of communal and mutual forms of support among newcomers themselves. This suburban dispersal is further compounded by the diversity of source countries of immigrants to Toronto. No longer is there a compact, concentrated reception area in Toronto for immigrants arriving from the same cultural, racial, or religious background. Today's immigrants are culturally, linguistically, religiously, and racially heterogeneous.

As a consequence of all these factors, the newer and smaller immigrant communities in Toronto, inevitably, have a somewhat fractured presence. The vast majority of African associations, for example, have only formed within the last decade. The greatest problem they face is chronic underfunding, as well as problems with lack of facilities and lack of recognition (by both government and the mainstream service-providing organizations) of the services they provide. A study of settlement services for African newcomers noted that even if new organizational infrastructures to coordinate the activities of different African ethnocultural organizations and service providers were to be established, it would still not, in itself, guarantee effective settlement services to African newcomers (George and Mwarigha 1999). This example clearly suggests the need to take a very careful look at whether we can continue to assume that all ethnoracial communities, no matter how small, can devote the resources and develop the capacity to build effective community-based infrastructures through which to provide appropriate services to their members, or whether we should expect them to.

The sheer numbers of immigrants coming to Toronto, the composition of immigrants coming from all parts of the world, the very different skills and expectations of the modern immigrant, the suburban and dispersed nature of settlement, the diminishing and redefining role of the public sector in supporting the settlement process, and the increasing racialization of inequality and immigrant poverty raise some very serious and urgent questions as to how immigrant communities will develop and relate to the larger society as we move into the new millennium. Recent research points to causes for concern.

The Social, Demographic, and Economic Picture

Data from the1996 census confirms how dramatically Toronto's population is changing. In 1996, 48 per cent of the population of the City of Toronto were foreign-born. With over 70,000 immigrants and refugees coming to Toronto every year, it is safe to say that today, those not born in Canada comprise the majority of the city's residents. One in five of Toronto residents arrived in Canada after 1981; one in ten after 1991. As of 1996, Toronto residents came from over 169 countries of origin; this represents over 91 per cent of the current members of the United Nations (Doucet 1999). Before 1961, virtually all of Toronto's immigrants came from Europe, including Britain; today, European-born comprise less than 2 per cent of Toronto's recent immigrants (Ornstein 2000). In 1961, people of colour represented just 3 per cent of Toronto's population; today, they are estimated to comprise the majority – 53 per cent – of the city's population (Municipality of Metropolitan Toronto 1995; Carey 2001). Over one hundred languages are spoken by the people of Toronto and over one-third of all Torontonians speak a language other than English in the home. A very significant proportion of newcomers, over 40 per cent, speak neither official language in the initial stages of settlement.

How do living conditions and life chances of newcomer groups in Toronto compare with the city's overall population? Recent research points to stark contrasts, underlining how unequal the lives of our diverse population have become. The most comprehensive recent study of ethnoracial inequalities in Toronto was published in 2000 by Michael Ornstein of York University's Institute for Social Research. 'In education, employment, and income,' Ornstein concluded, 'the census data reveal pervasive inequality among ethno-racial groups in Metropolitan Toronto' (122). His study demonstrated, for instance, that Toronto's adult (aged 25 to 64) residents of non-European origin had an *80 per cent higher* unemployment rate than adults of European origin (61). While 6.9 per cent of the latter group were unemployed, the non-European adult rate stood at 12.5 per cent. Some specific communities are particularly disadvantaged. Combining data for both youth (aged 15 to 24) and adults, the unemployment rates among Torontonians of African, Black, and Caribbean origin was 19 per cent, almost twice the city's unemployment rate at the time.

Poverty is distressingly widespread and ethnoracially clustered in Toronto. Ornstein (2000) concluded that in 1996 more than one in five Toronto families lived in poverty: approximately 135,900 families (22.7 per cent) of the city's 600,000 families. While the poverty rate for European-origin families was 14 per cent, the toll was much higher for non-Europeans. For example, 32.1 per cent of Aboriginal families, 34.6 per cent of South Asian, 44.6 per cent of African, Black, and Caribbean, and 45.2 per cent of Arab and West Asian families live in poverty. Combining all the non-European groups, the family poverty rate is 34.3 per cent – more than twice the figure for those Torontonians who self-identify as Canadian or European in origin. Non-Europeans make up 36.9 per cent of all families in Toronto, but account for 58.9 per cent of the city's poor families.

The impact on children is especially severe, with some communities bearing particular hardship. One in five children of European origin in Toronto (21 per cent, or 43,285 children) lived in poverty in 1996. This compares with 35 per cent for those of East and South Asian origin; 42 per cent of Aboriginal children; 43 per cent of South Asians; 52 per cent of Latin Americans; 57 per cent of Arab and West Asian children; and 59 per cent of all children of African, Black, and Caribbean origin. It is surely remarkable that a majority of children drawn from these last three composite global regions live under impoverished conditions in Toronto. The actual numbers of impoverished children involved are great: projections from the 1996 census place the totals at 41,585 African, Black, and Caribbean children; 10,795 Arab and West Asian children; 10,300 Latin American children; and 23,060 South Asian children. If we examine the figures by nationality of origin, an even more troubling picture emerges. Among Somalis, Ethiopians, and Ghanaians in Toronto, family rates of poverty in 1996 stood at staggering thresholds: 62, 70, and 87 per cent, respectively. More than 70 per cent of Somali children, 75 per cent of Ethiopian children, and 91 per cent of Ghanaian children live below the poverty line. These figures suggest a desperate degree of impoverishment, disadvantage, and need (Ornstein 2000).

The socio-economic polarization in Toronto can be characterized, with little oversimplification, as a division between Toronto's white European-origin population and the non-white population from every other continent. Constructing a hierarchy of deprivation, Ornstein (2000) concludes that the most 'extremely' disadvantaged in Toronto are those of African and Afghani descent; next, with 'severe' disadvantage are Vietnamese, Iranians, Tamils, and Sri Lankans; finally, a variety of groups face 'significant' disadvantage, including Aboriginal people, Jamaicans, West Indians, Guyanese, Turks, and Central and South Americans. Toronto today appears to have its own litmus (colour) test of advantage and disadvantage. The link between low socio-economic status and immigrant or racial status is intensifying. Regrettably, Frances Henry's (1994) assessment of Caribbean newcomers' disadvantageously 'differential incorporation' in Toronto also describes the experiences of more recent, racialized minority newcomers to the city.

This conclusion is reinforced by a number of other studies. Valerie Preston, Lucia Lo, and Shuguang Wang note in chapter 4 that recent European immigrants fare better in Toronto than recent non-white immigrants from every other continent. Jean Lock Kunz et al. (2000) in a report published by the Canadian Race Relations Foundation, demonstrate that both Canadian-born and foreign-born visible minorities experience higher unemployment, fewer promotions, and lower wage levels, despite comparable or superior educational achievement. Indeed, the higher unemployment rates and lower employment earning levels of visible minorities in Toronto has become a well-established theme of recent labour market research (Akbari 1995; Ley 1997; Reitz 1998). Now, in a housing market void of rent controls – thanks to provincial government deregulation – Toronto is witnessing a distinct ghettoization of visible minority residents into substandard high-rise apartment complexes scattered across Toronto's downtown core, in its post-war suburbs, and in isolated edge-city pockets (Carey 2001). Worse, concerns are growing that a racialized underclass is being created in Toronto.

Within visible minority communities themselves, many believe that discrimination is a major cause of disadvantage. A poll conducted by the *Toronto Star* in 1999 found that 29 per cent of all Torontonians claimed to have experienced discrimination based on their ethnic or racial origin. Among specific, readily identifiable communities, the rates were considerably higher: Chinese (37 per cent), Hispanic (37 per cent), Filipino (40 per cent), and Black (62 per cent). Thirty-five per cent of Black respondents reported that their children had been victims of verbal assaults or taunts and 10 per cent had been subjected to physical attack. Fifty-nine per cent of all Blacks surveyed said they felt unfairly treated by the media, and nearly three-quarters of Jamaicans polled believe they are unfairly treated by Toronto's police (Carey 1999d).

The data clearly show that Toronto is a society segmented and segregated by ethnic, racial, and immigrant status. Critical voices are increasingly raising concerns about immigrant and ethnoracial inequalities in Toronto. The Ontario Council of Agencies Serving Immigrants (OCASI) is a coalition of community organizations providing programs and services to a wide variety of newcomer groups. In 2000, OCASI issued a statement describing Toronto's current experience of diversity as 'a picture of widespread and deepening suffering and marginalization of the racialized majority of the city.' Many of these communities have been in the city for decades, yet they find themselves living in segregated and ghettoized neighbourhoods. The combination of unemployment, poverty, and segregation have resulted in apartheid-like economic conditions (OCASI 2000).

In October 2000, over one hundred people drawn from the diversity of Toronto's communities attended a forum organized by OCASI to address and confront 'Economic Apartheid in Ontario.' These divisions are eroding the city's self-image of successful immigrant integration. Reflecting on the findings of Michael Ornstein's study, the *Toronto Star's* Haroon Siddiqui (2000) lamented, 'We can no longer ignore such well-substantiated evidence of entrenched inequality based on race, and pretend that all is well in our beloved Canada, and peddle feel-good multiculturalism to the world' (A34). Not surprisingly, as we will now discuss, immigrant groups in Toronto have actively mobilized to challenge their subordinate social position.

IMMIGRANT COMMUNITIES MOBILIZING FOR CHANGE

Immigrant community organizations have typically been group-specific in focus. Advocacy or service organizations were established by each newcomer group to serve its own members' needs. But as Toronto became more ethnically, racially, and culturally diverse, organizational alliances began to be built across immigrant communities. Some of the most innovative and energetic immigrant community mobilization now involves solidarity movements that transcend the confines of segmented communities to unite members of diverse communities in common cause. This broader scope of mobilization reflects significant changes both within immigrant communities themselves, and in the circumstances they face in Toronto.

Individual immigrant communities are hardly monolithic; rather, differences of gender, class, sexual orientation, national origin, language, and religion have revealed fragmentation and tension within them. Indeed, the very notion of 'community' has become increasingly elusive. It is also erroneous to consider the city's ethnoracial communities as homogenous, each with its fixed internal ties and strongly defined boundaries distinguishing its immutable core identity. Immigrant groups are not locked into unchanging traditions, but interact at many levels with the wider society, thereby transforming both themselves and their city. This process of mixing and hybridization will increasingly be the norm (Madood et al. 1997). Thus, for instance, the 1996 census revealed that close to one-third of Toronto residents now self-identify as belonging to multiple ethnic origins (Ornstein 2000). And within many ethnoracial communities, members are increasingly prone to recognizing the significance of differences rooted in such divisions as gender, class, sexual orientation, ideology, and religion. All this heightens the prospects for political mobilization that transcends traditional boundaries of community.

Immigrant communities are now moving from the institutional completeness characteristic of an earlier period, to an ever-greater complexity and multiplicity of needs. In this section, we present four examples of intercommunity organizing around issues of gender and sexism, racism and anti-racist struggles, access to services, and campaigns for equitable political representation. These cases serve as illustrations of how immigrants create new forms of alliances and organizations out of the changing experiences they encounter in an evolving host environment. They are by no means the only forms of organizing found in Toronto. Among the missing pieces, which will need to be filled by future research and case studies, are, for example, issues of dis/ability and sexuality. Additionally, much valuable service delivery and advocacy work continues to be done by organizations representing particular newcomer groups. The four cases discussed below, however, point to new forms of immigrant community mobilization. Perhaps most importantly, these diverse ethnoracial movements portray the globalization of political life in a cosmopolitan city like Toronto.

Immigrant Women's Organizing

For as long as there were immigrants in Toronto, women have organized themselves, their families, and their communities to alleviate the strains of displacement through migration. During the early periods of immigration, with, perhaps, the exception of domestic workers from the Caribbean, many communities were so-called bachelor societies, in that only men were permitted to enter Canada to fill gaps in the labour market. This applies especially to racial minority groups such as the Chinese (see A. Chan 1983), in order to preserve Canada as a white, Christian nation. In Toronto, for example, (male) construction workers were recruited from Italy in the post-war period, when the economy began to improve, but they were not allowed to bring their families. Thus, many ethnic organizations were what may be called benevolent associations, formed to assist men to overcome their isolation as immigrant workers without their families. With the liberalization of immigration policy, especially since 1967, men brought their wives and other family members over, thus increasing the number of immigrant women in the city of Toronto.

In the earlier periods, organizing took the form of support groups. Women got together socially in their homes or at a convenient location to break the isolation experienced in the immigration process. A notable example of this form of organizing was the Caribbean Club. As early as 1958, single West Indian women, who came to the city as domestic workers, got together on a weekly basis, first at 21 McGill Street and then at the YWCA's McPhail House. These Thursday evenings came to be known as the 'maid's day out.' A worker at the YWCA provided counselling for the women and facilitated group activities. The club lasted for twenty-two years (Das Gupta 1986). Since informal support groups had little documentation, it was difficult to determine how extensive they were. Thus, we do not know a lot about this form of organizing, except to say that they must be more numerous than the few documented cases we do have.

Another form of organizing was service-oriented. Despite Canada's reputation as an immigrant country, the settlement of immigrants was never the state agenda at either the federal or provincial level, and ethnocultural communities have traditionally looked after the newcomers through organizations, such as benevolent associations, that mainly catered to the needs of men (see Knocke and Ng 1999). Immigrant women were the silent and neglected minorities within many minority groups. The 1960s, however, saw the emergence of special services for immigrant women. A notable example is the English classes and nursery schools that were organized for homebound Italian women and their children by a number of women from the Faith United Church near the Dufferin and St Clair area in 1964. This initiative led to the formation of the Community Committee on Immigrant Children of the Social Planning Council of Metro Toronto, which started more classes in other locations in 1966 with funding from the Ontario Department of the Provincial Secretary and Citizenship. This effort was the first to make English classes available to women who were not in the paid labour force. Another project that combined social support with language instruction and child care was the YWCA's Multi-Ethnic Women's Program. This informal program, started in 1969 by two volunteers, served as a model for many later immigrant women's groups (Das Gupta 1986).

The 1970s is a critical decade in terms of immigrant women's organizing. In the wake of an increasingly vocal and militant feminist movement in Canada, immigrant women, especially those living in larger urban centres such as Toronto and Vancouver, also broke their silence and began to organize across racial and cultural boundaries. By the mid-1970s, it had become obvious that apart from racial, ethnic, and cultural diversity, immigrant experiences within particular ethnoracial communities were further differentiated by gender, age, family status, and so forth. Many immigrant women organized services to meet their specific needs. These organizations were either specific to an ethnocultural community (such as the Centre for Spanish-Speaking People formed around 1973 and the Women's Group of the Chinese Interpreter and Information Services formed in 1978), or across community boundaries. The range of services also broadened, from employment counselling (such as the Women's Community Employment Centre established in 1974) and job training (such as the Working Skills Centre formed in 1978), to health concerns (such as the Immigrant Women's Centre formed in 1975) (Das Gupta 1986).

While many of these services were located in the downtown area, groups were also formed in the suburbs, signalling the fact that immigrants did not only live in the city centre; they lived and continue to live in areas outside the downtown core. One example is the Rexdale Women's Centre, which was initiated by social services workers in the northwestern part of Toronto (north Etobicoke) in 1978–9. It began as an outreach project and self-help group, with workers and women meeting in their own homes, and developed into different groups based on language and ethnicity (for example, Spanish, Italian, and South Asian). The centre itself was formalized in 1982 (Das Gupta 1986).

A notable feature of these organizations is that, in contrast to mainstream service organizations where the staff were white Canadian women, both the 'clients' and the workers were immigrants, indicating that immigrant women were by no means passive 'victims' of the migration process. In a sense, the organizing that took place and the organizations that were established in the 1970s formed the backbone of the immigrant women's movement in Toronto. Although agencies providing services to immigrant women and the types of services have proliferated and changed since then, immigrant women have established their presence in the social, cultural, and political fabric of Toronto.

With the emergence of service organizations geared towards the specific needs of immigrant women, other issues began to surface.

Here, we outline some of the key issues and organizations to display the range of activities in which women were engaged; they are by no means representative of the multiplicity of activities occurring since the 1970s. A major desire felt by many workers and activists was the need to develop skills, and share information on the service-delivery system and their experiences working with immigrants women who were less educated and non-English speaking.

In 1974, an informal group of women who called themselves 'Women Working with Immigrant Women' (WWIW), began to meet. This group evolved into an umbrella organization and has become a focal point of the immigrant women's movement in Toronto. Initially begun as a volunteer and informal group, by the late 1970s, WWIW had a formal committee structure and paid staff to oversee the group's increasing activities. WWIW is unique in that it serves as a mechanism for the network of agencies and individuals working with immigrant women to support each other and to strategize together. Many worthwhile programs that service organizations would not consider because of their service mandate were developed through WWIW. It also co-sponsors projects of other organizations. One example was a widely used kit produced in 1978 and entitled *By and About Immigrant Women*, the result of a survey of the needs of immigrant women and subsequent workshops based on the survey (Das Gupta 1986). This was the first comprehensive kit with analytical and experiential articles on, and resources available to, immigrant women in Toronto, and was used by organizations and individuals throughout the 1980s, indicating its significance and utility.

In addition to its networking function, WWIW also serves as an advocacy organization, speaking out on behalf of immigrant women and those in other organizations who are unable to lobby on their own behalf (for example, many service organizations are restricted by their service mandate and are not able to lobby). It also joins with other networks and coalitions, such as and the International Women's Day Coalition (see below) and the Ontario Immigrant Women's Network, to raise public awareness and to improve the status of immigrant women. Although its activities are drastically reduced due to decreased funding, it is still a core player in the immigrant women's movement in Toronto today.

As the immigrant population increased, and with more immigrants coming from non-European countries from 1970s onward, there was also an increasing awareness of discrimination against racial minorities in the city. This awareness was, in part, a consequence of the changing demographic reality of the city, and, in part, informed by the changing discourse on race and racism associated with the civil rights and other movements. Immigrants, especially those from racial minority backgrounds, were beginning to organize specifically around the issue of racism. Antiracism and antidiscrimination are persistent themes in the organizing efforts of the Caribbean community and among domestic workers (through a nation-wide group called Intercede based in Toronto).

Although not exclusively an immigrant women's project, the Cross-Cultural Communication Centre (CCCC), first established in 1975, deserves special mention. Beginning with a Local Initiative Project (LIP) grant, CCCC developed a special collection of resources on immigrant women. Even with diminished funding, the centre houses one of the best audio-visual and print libraries on immigrant women, racism, immigrant settlement, and related topics (Das Gupta 1986). Many of the materials are unpublished (such as reports, essays, and student term papers) and not found elsewhere. It is widely used by lay people and researchers alike. The staff members, many of them immigrant women, were and continue to be active in actions affecting immigrant women, including in advocacy and coalition work.

Meanwhile, especially since the early 1980s, there was a growing recognition that, although women across ethnic, racial, religious, linguistic, and class divides were victims of violence, notably domestic violence, immigrant and racial minority women experienced special difficulties when they used existing shelters. Among some of these barriers were communication problems due to the workers' unfamiliarity with the victims' cultural background and the victims' lack of proficiency in English, as well as problems of racism and other forms of discrimination. As well, immigrant women were not always aware of the fact that they could go to a shelter in the event of domestic violence. Immigrant women who worked within the shelter movement also reported on the silencing they experienced when they tried to raise concerns (see Kohli 1993). A task force, initiated by WWIW, was formed in 1983 to look into the possibility of forming a special shelter for immigrant women. After years of outreach, planning, and lobbying, the Shirley Samaroo House officially opened its door in 1986. Although no longer in existence, the struggle for a separate shelter for immigrant women represents both the division among women and the ability of immigrant women to organize based on their own needs and agenda.

In addition to organizing to create a stronger and larger immigrant women's movement, immigrant women (together with Aboriginal women) also individually and collectively challenged the racism and cultural myopia inherent in other social movements, notably the feminist movement and organized labour. For example, in the 1970s, the Toronto International Women's Day Coalition (IWDC)[1] was dominated by white, middle-class women to the exclusion of women from other groups and social classes. Since the 1980s, immigrant women and women of colour began to challenge the narrow focus among the IWDC organizers and the underrepresentation of women of colour. Writing in 1982, activist Winnie Ng (1982) characterized immigrant women as the silent partners of the women's movement and posed three demands to their white Canadian sisters: making English-language training a basic right similar to child care, making immigrant women's need a priority by providing interpretation in meetings, and recognizing the contributions of immigrant women. An immigrant women's committee was formed within the IWDC in 1981. As a result of these challenges, many annual celebrations since the mid-1980s had, as their major themes, racism or anticolonialism. It is in this way that immigrant women made their presence felt within the mainstream feminist movement and made a contribution to the struggles for equality for all Canadian women.

These challenges have reshaped the discourse of the feminist movement (see Srivastava 2000). The term 'women of colour' emerged in the 1980s as a result of immigrant and other minority women's growing awareness of the interlocking effects of racism and sexism. Whereas 'immigrant women' points to women's legal status and place of origin, 'women of colour' is a political designation created by women who are minorities, regardless of their legal status and birthplace, to indicate their collective identity based on their experience of marginalization and discrimination in society (see also Kohli 1993). Thus, although many services still retain 'immigrant women' in their organizations' titles, individually and collectively many immigrant women began to identify with and call themselves 'women of colour.'

Immigrant women and women of colour have also been working relentlessly within the union movement to make its concerns and actions more inclusive of minority women, in general. Although this challenge is not specific to Toronto, many of the key players, such as June Veecock (see Leah 1993) and Winnie Ng, were activists in the immigrant women's and antiracist movements in Toronto. Their challenge to and work within the labour movement were and continue to be supported by immigrant women and women of colour outside organized labour, demonstrating the interconnection of issues and networks that go beyond the local setting.

An interesting case that illustrates the interconnection between the local and extra-local is the organization of homeworkers (women who sew garments at home). Since the post-war period, Toronto has been a major centre of garment production, which employs mostly immigrant labour. With globalization and industrial restructuring, many garment plants in Toronto scaled down their operation in the 1980s and 1990s, and reverted to the use of homeworkers to maximize profit. Working with local activists concerned about the situation of these homeworkers, many of whom were immigrant women from Asia, the Toronto region of the International Ladies Garment Workers Union (ILGWU) launched a series of actions to publicize the exploitative use of immigrant workers and organize them into the Homeworkers' Association, which was formally established in 1992 (Borowy, Gordon, and Lebans 1993; Ng 2000). This is a unique case because the union movement, including the central office of the ILGWU, is generally hostile to homeworkers, seeing them as undermining union solidarity. The initiative taken by the Toronto office was, therefore, an innovative and courageous move; it suggests that immigrant women's activism has created an awareness of the plight of this group of workers, at least in the Toronto area, that has an impact on the labour movement beyond Toronto.

Today, the number of immigrant women's organizations and programs run and controlled by immigrant women themselves have proliferated. New programs are always emerging, with old ones falling by the wayside, as new needs are identified and funding is secured. While the change of the provincial political climate, from a social democratic to a conservative government in 1995, and the merging of the Toronto-area municipalities into a mega-city, have had serious repercussion for the services available to immigrant women due to major funding cuts, immigrant women have made their presence felt in Toronto. They have become an important and vocal group in the city's increasingly multicultural and diverse landscape. Their visibility as a group attests to the creative alliances that can be and are forged among people across racial, ethnic, gender, and cultural lines in their attempt to work towards a better world.

Combatting Racism

The existence of racism has been a long-standing undercurrent of attitude and practice throughout Toronto's history. For much of the twentieth century a variety of groups including Jews, Catholics, Blacks, Chinese, and other minorities, have experienced overt discrimination and adverse treatment because of their identity. Yet Toronto's racist legacy was rarely a publicly acknowledged fact of history in this city. Indeed, as Frances Henry (1995) observes, identifying Toronto's racially based exclusions 'was not subject for public discussion nor was it part of the political discourse' (12). It was not until the mid-1970s, when the media began to report a number of particularly vicious racial assaults, that racist behaviour became part of Toronto's consciousness. Since then, several community organizations have emerged to challenge racist attitudes and actions in the city. Some of these have been movements within specific communities. Particular recognition must be given to the Black Action Defence Committee for its determined efforts in recent decades to hold Toronto civic institutions, especially the police, accountable for discriminatory treatment against Blacks.

The most enduring and wide-ranging attempt to forge a broad coalition to combat racism in Toronto is the Urban Alliance on Race Relations (UARR). Few issues affecting immigrant communities have escaped the alliance's attention, which came into being in 1975, as a reflection of the rising concern among people from a wide diversity of racial and cultural backgrounds over escalating racial violence and tensions directed at newcomers in the city. The first president of the Urban Alliance, Wilson Head, noted in his memoir (1995) that 'a major feature of the new organization was that it was designed to be interracial in character.' Accordingly, wrote Head, 'it would not be "ethnospecific," a focus which required making specific and determined efforts to recruit members from groups who had not been accustomed to working in an interracial or multicultural context' (297). Its board of directors was an alliance of ordinary citizens reflecting the diversity of modern society in Toronto. With the goal of promoting 'a stable and healthy multiracial environment in the community,' the Urban Alliance has carried out its public education mandate for more than a quarter-century by developing educational materials, producing award-winning posters and public service announcements, and organizing seminars and conferences for many different sectors of Toronto's community. It has initiated and participated in literally hundreds of workshops with religious groups, community organizations, and professional associations and carried out training sessions with educators, social workers, the police, and community leaders.

Over its history, the Urban Alliance's approach to combatting racism has evolved. Initially, racism and discrimination were regarded as the behaviour of misguided individuals acting out their prejudice or ignorance. Accordingly, the Alliance responded to racism as a human relations problem that could be solved by sharing a body of intercultural knowledge. While minority communities continue to be asked to provide this public-education role, and while education and training initiatives continue to be an important organizational response to the changing demographics, community organizations like the Urban Alliance began to recognize that they did not have much of an impact on changing organizational systems. From public education and staff development activities, the second strategy that emerged for community mobilization to address racism was action research.

In the late 1970s, several studies and reports of racism were published. The Urban Alliance began its own research on policing, education, human rights in Ontario, employment, and media. All of these studies contributed to a growing body of both objective data and subjective experience that together indicated that the main structures and systems of society were directly responsible for racial discrimination. Racial discrimination was woven into the policies and practices of the major structures and systems in society. Even if individuals responsible for translating policy into practice were not themselves prejudiced, the established and conventional modes of organizational operation often had an adverse and discriminatory impact on people of colour.

Community initiatives, therefore, began to focus on identifying and pursuing advocacy strategies that would more directly affect the policies and practices of institutions. Based upon the needs and concerns articulated by minority groups, community organizations like the Urban Alliance worked on several fronts simultaneously: educational institutions, media, police, social services, and employment. The involvement of community advocacy groups with institutions such as police, boards of education, and radio stations was aimed at establishing the kinds of corporate, consultative, monitoring, and employment practices that are equitable and responsive to the needs of minorities. Pursuing this institutional change and policy-development process has involved, for community advocacy groups like the Urban Alliance on Race Relations, the preparation of briefs on almost every major issue in the area of race equity. The Alliance has appeared before every task force, inquiry committee, and commission dealing with race equity over the last twenty-five years, and has made innumerable presentations to all levels of government on issues affecting the rights of minorities (Tator and Rees 1991).

The results of all these activities clearly suggest that the achievement of racial equity in Toronto will not come about as a result of a rational, intellectual process of understanding. Nor will it occur through some kind of 'invisible hand' of organizational dynamics. Community-based antiracism strategies continue to be needed to identify and address institutional behaviours, as well as the occupational ideologies and values underlying the constantly evolving expressions of racism in different sectors and organizations. Although national and international conditions can precipitate social change, experience in Toronto over the last quarter-century suggest that a major impetus has been and will continue to be community pressure. It is the victims who are continuing to force the public to come to terms with racism. The ex-slave Frederick Douglass insisted that freedom is only won when there is effective demand, words that clearly suggest that minority groups must move beyond begging the white power elites for freedom and equality. Reflecting on Frederick Douglass's counsel, Wilson Head of the Urban Alliance contended that 'effective demand requires the application or the threat to exert social, economic, or political power. It would be foolish to expect the power elite to relinquish domination in the absence of that pressure. It is my firm belief that minority groups must achieve the power, ability, and determination to make demands which cannot be ignored' (Head 1995, 27). In a similar vein, David Theo Goldberg (1993) concludes that 'resistance to racisms cannot merely be moral or sustained merely by moral appeal narrowly construed. In general, the struggle against racisms must be played out on the political terrain' (213).

One of the most important conclusions that can be drawn from community-based antiracism activities in Toronto over the last two decades is that immediate, consistent, and well-developed community mobilization and action strategies can be highly successful in influencing political, institutional, and social action. At the same time, one is also able to conclude that progress towards race equity is unlikely to be attained unless concerned citizens and communities are able to cooperate to combat racism. The longevity and success of much of the work of the Urban Alliance on Race Relations as advocate, educator, researcher, and coalition-builder can, perhaps in part, be ascribed to this cooperation. As former president, Kamala Jean Gopie noted, 'For too long many of us had endeavoured to work separately in our diverse communities, dealing with situations which impacted directly on our particular group. We all felt like isolated victims. What the UARR caused to happen was a bringing together of like-minded citizens to pool energies and resources' (Gopie 1995, 23).

In comparing Los Angeles with Toronto, Mark Nakamura has observed that the various communities that comprise Los Angeles tend to reside in and focus their lives on their own ethnoracial communities (Nakamura 1995). The roots of this phenomenon find their origins in dynamics that run the gamut from survival tactics, to exclusionary practices, to an exercise in choice. The result is some kind of free-market ethnoracial force field that has the effect of propelling groups of people further apart.

Rather than accentuating racial differences and exacerbating competition between groups, community mobilization in Toronto to combat racism has, to some extent, managed to overcome these tendencies and, to a some extent, focused on similarities, sharing, and working together. Apart from the experience of the Urban Alliance on Race Relations, other broad coalitions include the Metro Network for Social Justice, the Ontario Coalition of Agencies Serving Immigrants, and the network that has come together to push for action in response to the results of the Ornstein (2000) report. Recent experiences of partnerships also include the Hispanic Development Council (HDC), the Chinese Canadian National Council (CCNC), and the Coalition of Agencies Serving South Asians (CASSA), who are working together on joint research and social-planning initiatives.

Another recent cooperative initiative was the coming together of community organizations in the preparatory meetings leading up to the UN World Conference on Racism held in South Africa in 2001. In Toronto, this involved the partnership of the African Canadian Coalition against Racism, the Ontario Young People's Alliance, the Assembly of First Nations, the National Anti-Racism Council, and the Women of Colour Council. These organizational networks suggest a movement towards the difficult process of pooling resources and of joining in a common struggle against the complexities of racism.

Community mobilization activities in Toronto, as we move into the twenty-first century, indicate an increasing challenge to the politics of traditional multiculturalism that has tended to ignore the system of power and the inequalities that prevail in the city. These community networks also suggest a rejection of static concepts of identities and communities as fixed sets of experiences, meanings, and practices. Racialized communities are moving beyond the narrow understanding of identity imposed by notions of multiculturalism and, instead, are seeking out new alliances and affiliations based on mutual needs and shared objectives as reciprocal processes that include rather than exclude. These initiatives illustrate a growing trend in social activism that is recognizing the need for painstaking and deliberate efforts to fashion egalitarian community mobilization movements, 'which respect and recognize difference and diversity, while simultaneously being able to forge common ties and strategies to advance individual group as well as broad causes for equality and social justice' (Smith 1999, 23).

The Struggle for Access and Equity in Human Services

The flow of immigrants and refugees into Toronto has had a profound influence on the delivery of public and community-based services, ranging from mental health and social services to economic development, social planning, housing, and education. It has also helped reshape Toronto's social policy and civic development. At the community level, concerns about the service-delivery systems and advocacy of community-based modes of delivery and equity have brought forward mixed results. Too often the human services system has been characterized by differential treatment of newcomer immigrants and limited opportunities for diverse communities to shape policies and programs (Doyle and Rahi 1991). The documentation on access and equity offers the basis for understanding the persistent existence of gaps in the access to human services between newcomers and Canadian-born services users.

In recognition of these community concerns, the Social Planning Council of Metropolitan Toronto took the lead during the 1980s and initiated a four-year study to examine the extent to which members of cultural and racial groups lacked access to health and social services offered by mainstream service providers. The study, led by Robert Doyle and Livy Visano in 1987, focused on two key service-delivery issues: the inadequacy and insensitivity of the mainstream response to particular cultural and linguistic needs of immigrants and the inadequacy of existing language-training programs. The study came up with a number of groundbreaking recommendations to address systemic barriers in human-service systems and structures, program planning, and service delivery.

More significantly, it set out a framework for action for the mainstream agencies in a number of important areas, including developing policies in hiring, the 'twinning' of mainstream and ethnospecific agencies, funding to support the operation of ethnospecific services and data collection on the needs of ethnoracial clients. (Mainstream organizations are those offering services to all members of the community, regardless of their identity; ethnospecific organizations, by contrast, target their programs and services to members of a particular ethnoracial group.) Further, the study urged the development of access and equity policies and practices in mainstream service-delivery systems. It also promoted the adoption of new models for collaboration between ethnospecific and mainstream organizations, and for the development of public education campaigns on the status and needs of minority communities.

As the study proceeded, it became apparent that the health and social services system, at least for members of diverse cultural and racial groups, could be characterized as a situation of two solitudes – mainstream and ethnospecific agencies existing side by side, but hardly taking account of one another in their effort to plan and deliver services, with little coordination of plans or activities.

Arguing that 'access' encompasses two distinct elements – access both to needed services and to the decision-making structures that underpin them – Doyle and Visano identified a range of barriers preventing minority groups from making use of available health and social services, including a lack of culturally sensitive or appropriate programming, the non-availability of services in languages other than English, high transportation and child-care costs, the physical inaccessibility of services, the lack of information on available programs and services, the long waiting lists, and the lack of commitment on the part of agencies to 'effect change beyond the identification of barriers' (Doyle and Visano 1987). 'A Program for Action' spurred activity in all these areas. Not only was it the first major survey undertaken in Toronto on minority access to human services, but it became a template for similar work undertaken elsewhere in Ontario and Canada (Reitz 1997). It also led to the creation in 1987 of the Access Action Council (AAC), a nonprofit independent agency that has been a catalyst for change on access and equity issues affecting Toronto's minority and newcomer communities (CERIS Newsletter 1997).

The Access Action Council was mandated to act on the key recommendations of the Social Planning Council's access study. Recognizing the particularly pressing needs of Toronto's most recent newcomers, AAC moved beyond the access report and began to shift its focus to the service and organizational needs of more recent and smaller communities of immigrants and refugees in the Toronto area. Specifically, AAC promoted two key approaches to improving access to human services: first, by advocating full citizen participation and strengthening the organizational capacities of these communities to form their own service-delivery systems, and second, through innovative strategies to effect organizational change within the mainstream service-delivery system. The Council's advocacy and public-education work was instrumental in a number of areas, including promoting the language of 'access' and helping to prod municipal and provincial governments into launching new initiatives to improve access in the delivery of services. In 1988 the Municipality of Metropolitan Toronto adopted an AAC recommendation to establish a Multicultural Funding Policy and develop multicultural policy for services delivered directly by the Metro government (Municipality of Metropolitan Toronto 1990). Both the municipal and provincial governments also provided funding to assist ethnospecific and mainstream service agencies to collaborate in the joint delivery of services to targeted communities.

Meanwhile, the principles underlying the establishment of the Access Action Council were echoed in a national symposium on settlement organized by the Canada Employment and Immigration Advisory Council in 1990. At this meeting, participants called upon policy-makers to adopt an approach to settlement and integration that was based on the 'twin principles of full equity and unqualified acceptance of diversity, rather than the now-inadequate principle of "tolerance"' (Canada Employment and Immigration Advisory Council 1991b, 10). In another initiative, the United Way of Greater Toronto committed itself in 1993 to broadening its base of support, and since then has admitted at least thirty-five new organizations serving Toronto's multicultural communities, while at the same time requiring all of its agencies to adhere to strict antiracist guidelines (United Way of Greater Toronto 1991).

However, even as one acknowledges the efforts made by the United Way and others to address access barriers in human service delivery, it is clear that more needs to be done. A recent study by the Access Action of Metropolitan Toronto (1997) identified gaps in services and resources available to the Somali, South Asian, Chinese, and Hispanic communities of Toronto. The most recurring problems were access to employment, health care, social services, housing, and funding for community organizations. All four communities identified these shortcomings as barriers to full integration into Canadian society. Two years later, community organizations in Toronto stepped up their call for redress. Community advocates involved in a consultation organized by the Toronto Task Force on Community Access and Equity (2000) asserted that while 'naming racism as a cause of systemic discrimination is an important first step,' it must be accompanied by concrete measures to alleviate such discrimination (48). Due to shifts in government outlook, this has proven to be a challenging goal to achieve.

The 1990s have seen a fundamental restructuring of the welfare state, signalling the reversal of the state intervention approach that helped to create the existing immigrant services structure. The growing policy reliance on market definitions of service provision and effectiveness have stressed privatization, contracting out, and quantitative measures of outcomes over more qualitative results. By the mid-1990s, funding cuts and downloading measures of senior governments were severely constraining the capacities of community-based organizations (Municipality of Metropolitan Toronto et al. 1997). Thus for instance, in 1995 and 1996, fifty-four social service agencies ceased operations in the city, compared with a total of just seven closures during the previous two years (United Way of Greater Toronto 1997).

The current climate is not conducive to advances in access and equity. In order to continue operating, community-based services and settlement agencies have to endure increased competition as a result of the process of downloading and devolution. This new political phenomenon challenged the capacity of the non-governmental organizations to accommodate the forces of change and compete for a more restricted funding base. The pressure has been especially acute on agencies with limited administrative structures and staff size. As we noted, more community organizations – both long-standing and relatively new – are simply caving in and closing shop. Recent examples of closed or dramatically streamlined organizations include the Latin American Community Centre, the Iranian Association of Ontario, the Coalition of Visible Minority Women, and other less-known organizations throughout the city. Among remaining community agencies, a variety of approaches continue to be applied to increase access to services and effect organizational change, with mixed results and an uneven impact on capacity-building. The campaign for access and equity in Toronto that began near the end of the twentieth century remains on the agenda for newcomer communities in this new century.

Campaigning for Equitable Political Representation

Diversity challenges traditions of citizenship and belonging. As Sharon Zukin (1995) has observed, the task confronting ethnoracially diverse societies is 'whether [they] can create an inclusive political culture' (44). And as Daiva Stasiulis (1997) has noted, global migration patterns 'pose a fundamental challenge to develop morally defensible, inclusive forms of citizenship' (197). The emergence of an immigrant/minority community campaign to influence the creation of the provincially imposed municipal amalgamation of Toronto in 1997 reflected a significant assertion of claims to citizenship and political participation.

In 1997, Ontario's Conservative government announced its intention to amalgamate the six federated municipalities that had comprised Metro Toronto since 1954: Toronto, York, East York, Etobicoke, North York, and Scarborough. The decision was prompted by a variety of provincial interests including downsizing government, eliminating an adversarial central City of Toronto, and creating a larger municipality that could absorb the downloading of service costs previously paid for by the province. To many local residents, amalgamation raised the spectre of accessible local governments giving way to a remote megacity burdened with additional service costs. The opposition galvanized the largest citizens' movement in Toronto's history. Journalist Joe Chidley (1997) captured the city's ensuing passion-play well. 'The city is in the grip of Mega-Madness,' he wrote in March 1997, 'and a riveting drama is being played out on the civic stage' (46). Initially, immigrants and diverse ethnoracial communities were missing from this movement, but eventually they launched their own, autonomous intervention into mega-city politics.

First, a quick overview of the scale of citizen mobilization. The mega-city protest was organized around a non-partisan organization called Citizens for Local Democracy, typically revered or reviled under its acronym C4LD. The group held weekly meetings that routinely attracted between 800 and 1,200 citizens. The group's largest rally was a full house of 2,600 at the venerable concert venue, Massey Hall. February 1997 was, conveniently, the 160th anniversary of the Upper Canadian Rebellion, and a crowd variously estimated at between 10,000 and 15,000 people re-enacted the march of an earlier generation of dissidents down Yonge Street. Then came provincial hearings into the mega-city legislation, which drew over 600 deputants, most speaking passionately against the proposed legislation. And, finally, a referendum on amalgamation in March across the six Metro Toronto municipalities generated a 76 per cent rejection of the mega-city plan.

With remarkably few exceptions, the anti-mega-city movement represented a mobilization of white, British-stock Toronto. This is a point acknowledged by the leaders of C4LD. Kathleen Wynne (1997) was a member of C4LD's steering committee, and she chaired the group's weekly mass meetings. Reviewing the movement's campaign, she acknowledged at that time that 'we have not reached out, we have not succeeded in bringing in people from other ethnic communities. We are an Anglo group, white Anglo. It was mostly an Anglo WASP, or WASC (there were Catholics, too!), community that rose up against the mega-city.'

Why was that? A variety of factors account for the movement's ethnoracial homogeneity in this remarkably diverse city. First, an explanation of why white, Anglo Toronto did rise up. Kathleen Wynne identifies most C4LD participants as preponderantly downtowners, elderly, well-educated and literate; as she observed, 'people who when you said John Ralston Saul was coming got on their feet and cheered' (Wynne 1997). And they cheered in a large downtown church where the movement's weekly meetings were held. The 2,300 people on C4LD's mailing list lived in the former central city of Toronto, and fully 60 per cent lived south of Bloor Street in the downtown area. The movement was galvanized by an assortment of both principled and pragmatic concerns: the elimination of local governments that these residents felt some ownership of, the prospect of higher property taxes, and the feared erosion of a host of local services across the city's social and physical infrastructure. As Wynne (1997) says, this was 'a constituency that felt comfortable coming into the halls of power and then felt entitled to organize this citizen's movement ... Nobody had the authority to stop them.' Toronto's shrinking population of British ethnics comprised the vast majority of those who initially resisted the imposition of municipal government restructuring.

The anti-mega-city movement proved inaccessible and scarcely relevant to the large immigrant and ethnoracial communities across the six municipalities targeted for amalgamation. Ever scrambling to respond to a bulldozing and blustering provincial government, C4LD did little to mobilize the city's diverse communities. Except for a short-lived initial attempt, materials were not translated into other languages. The meetings' downtown location – in a church at that – was a mismatch for many communities. No effort was made to identify amalgamation's threat to issues of concern to immigrant and minority communities such as service access, employment equity, and policing.

As a result, the anti-mega-city movement never spoke to the city's diverse composition and communities. Some believe this stemmed from Toronto's own experience of two solitudes. The coordinator of the Mayor's Committee on Community and Race Relations in the former city of Toronto, Augusto Mathias (1997), observes that 'C4LD was very mainstream, Canadian-born, white European. We [visible minorities] have always been in isolation from the mainstream.' Another leader from the South Asian community feels that the absence of immigrants from the struggle reflected their political marginalization. Viresh Fernando (1997), a lawyer who would subsequently be instrumental in mobilizing a distinctive immigrant and visible minority presence in the debate over Toronto's political future, says immigrants didn't participate in C4LD 'because they feel powerless ... They feel that it's all decided elsewhere.'

To this point, then, the struggle against the mega-city may be seen as the old Toronto – remnants of its 'white settler' urban society – rising to defend its familiar and trusted system of municipal government, while newer Torontonians stood on the sidelines. But political participation and citizenship are not static phenomena. As the debate over Toronto's restructuring reached its provincially imposed conclusion, immigrant and visible minority groups mobilized on two fronts: first, through the formation of a new coalition called New Voices of the New City; and second, through an assertive campaign to promote a continued commitment to access, equity, and antiracism work in the new mega-city.

New Voices of the New City originated from the provincial hearings into the mega-city legislation. One of the few visible minority presentations was by Viresh Fernando, on behalf of the Council of Agencies Serving South Asians (CASSA). Preparing the submission, it became clear to Fernando and CASSA that immigrant communities could be particularly vulnerable in a new mega-city. Their brief identified a variety of risks: downloading would lead to cuts in services and funding for community agencies; an increase in user fees for municipal services would have an adverse impact on immigrants and minorities; ethnoracial groups were better off dealing with seven local governments more attuned to neighbourhood needs than with a more remote, centralized institution; a single large council would be harder to lobby for its interest in community concerns; municipal-sector job losses caused by amalgamation would hit designated equity groups hardest; and the mega-city might not follow equity principles in making appointments to its assorted agencies, boards, and commissions.

CASSA's deputation did not deter the provincial government's amalgamationist mission, but it did convince CASSA of the need to mobilize the marginalized voices in mega-city politics. By the summer of 1997, CASSA had pulled together an impressive coalition of sixty-three diverse community organizations under the banner of New Voices of the New City. Affiliated groups included the Canadian Arab Association, the Chinese Canadian National Council, the Ethiopian Association of Toronto, the Jamaican Canadian Association, the Canadian Sri Lankan Association, the Somali Canadian Association, and the Vietnamese Association of Toronto, as well as a number of women's organizations and unions. Recent-immigrant groups predominated, and most were spatially concentrated not in the former central city of Toronto, but in the three post-war suburbs of North York, Scarborough, and Etobicoke. A civic alliance on this scale was unprecedented, as New Voices co-chair Viresh Fernando (1997) noted, 'most of the sixty-three groups had never come together voluntarily on any issue.'

Its founding document served notice that New Voices of the New City (1997a) was intended to promote more engaged and effective forms of urban citizenship among traditionally marginalized communities: 'Increasing the participation of First Nations, visible minorities, immigrant groups, socially disadvantaged persons in the political process is the main aim of this project ... The purpose of this project is to strengthen civic society by ensuring that these voices are heard and that the future Mayor and Council of the Mega-city will respond to these concerns' (1).

Specifically, and perhaps too minimally, New Voices of the New City committed itself to organizing a mega-city mayoralty debate on issues of access, equity, and antiracism. Their objectives were to raise these issues in the election campaign, press the candidates to take a stand, and raise community participation and voter turn-out in the election. New Voices (1997b) may have set a record for the longest title attached to a political forum: the mayoralty debate was billed as 'Defining the Spaces and Roles of First Nations, Immigrants, People of Colour, Disadvantaged Women, and Other Marginalized Groups in the Mega-City.' The two mayoralty front-runners, as well as an African-Canadian candidate, from a field of seventeen 'also-rans,' were invited to participate. Several hundred people attended, media coverage was strong, and

Viresh Fernando (1997) of New Voices deemed the event a great success, saying, 'We brought [the candidates] face to face with diversity, and the politics of diversity.'

Paradoxically, then, the creation of the mega-city of Toronto – denounced for undermining local democracy – stimulated unprecedented civic mobilization among immigrant and visible minority communities. In the politics of amalgamation, immigrant communities were less concerned with preserving a jurisdictional status quo than with attempting to assure that an enlarged city government was responsive to their distinct concerns.

Yet a demographic profile of Toronto's mega-city council makes it clear that newcomer and minority communities remain on the margins of power in the new city. The first fifty-eight-member mega-city municipal council elected in 1997 was comprised of twenty-six members of British ethnic origin (44.8 per cent of the council); ten of Italian origin (17.2 per cent); six Jewish members (10.3 per cent); nine of other European origin (15.5 per cent); and seven visible-minority members (12 per cent of council). The latter group included three members of Caribbean origin, three Chinese members, and one Korean. In the subsequent 2000 municipal election, the representation of visible minorities in local government declined further. For this vote, the provincial government ordered a reduction of Toronto's municipal council from fifty-eight members to forty-five. Elected onto council were twenty members of British origin (44.4 per cent); nine Italians (20 per cent); four Jews (8.9 per cent); seven of other European origin (12 per cent); and five visible-minority members (11.1 per cent), including two members of Caribbean origin, two Chinese members, and one Korean member. These numbers reflect entrenched differences primarily constructed on racial lines.

While visible minorities now constitute over half of the City of Toronto's population, they hold barely one in ten council seats. Conversely the city's British-origin population holds almost half the seats on council while comprising a quarter of the city's population. Visible minorities face a number of barriers to equitable political representation. These include reduced numbers of available council seats, the venerable advantage to incumbents in municipal elections, the relative recency of migration, the disadvantaged economic position of visible minority communities, and perhaps, a lingering impulse among Toronto voters to keep political authority in white hands (Siemiatycki and Saloojee 2000). Electoral equity remains a distant goal in Toronto.

MUNICIPAL RESPONSES AND IMPLICATIONS

Few of Toronto's institutions in recent years have been able to avoid addressing issues of diversity. Global migration has transformed the complexion of the city's citizenry, workforce, consumers, and service clientele. Also, as we have seen, newcomer community mobilization has prompted both public and private organizations to reassess their response to diversity. Indeed, in responding to new demographic realities, institutions have become very adept at appropriating the language of equity. Concepts such as equity, racism, inclusiveness, access, and so on have become misused and suffered further obfuscation in the linguistic worlds of political rhetoric and bureaucratese. Institutions have also used the paraphernalia of organizational systems to create the appearance and illusion of adapting and acting in response to diversity. They have become adept at implementing a *process* of change (typically involving staff training and new corporate guidelines and goals), without producing significant changes in outcome.

How can one move the issues of diversity from the margins of institutional life to a central and integral part of organizational culture? What are the right attitudes, the right systems and procedures that simply do not permit the continued marginalization of large sections of the population and their exclusion from fully participating in the social, cultural, and political life of the city?

The Municipal Response

As the level of government that is closest to its residents, it is useful to look at the role of the City of Toronto as a case study of an institutional response to the needs of its diverse communities. What has been the City of Toronto's role in developing inclusive policies and programs that are accessible and equitable for all sectors of its dramatically changing population? What is the City of Toronto doing to ensure that all members of the community are able to derive equal benefit from municipal services when the nature of our population is changing so rapidly? What is the city's role in ensuring the full participation of everyone in its dramatically changing population? What is the city's incorporation strategy to 'multiculturalize' its services, that is, to define them as common spaces in which all individuals participate on an equal basis?

As was just noted, in 1998 the new amalgamated City of Toronto replaced seven former municipalities against the wishes of the majority of its residents. The amalgamated city has a population of close to 2.5 million people. It was established by an Ontario government whose ideology is to diminish and dismantle government – an ideology that looks to the market, the private sector, and self-reliance as the prime sources of required goods and services. It is also a provincial government that looks to municipalities – especially Ontario's largest, Toronto – as fiscal lifelines on which to offload provincial costs. With this enormous weight of ideological and fiscal downloading, the City of Toronto has been clearly restricted in its manoeuverability and its ability to seize any new vision of equity and inclusiveness. How is the City of Toronto responding when the political and fiscal amalgamating pressures clearly indicate a counter-direction to the principles of diversity and equity?

The very first international event in early 1998 that the new mayor of the amalgamated city, Mel Lastman, attended was the G8 'Summit of the Cities' in Birmingham, England. He was invited to talk to other big-city mayors from around the world specifically about how Toronto was responding to its diversity. That Toronto's new mayor was requested to address this topic is indicative, perhaps, of the international image and recognition of Toronto as a city based on diversity. In reflecting and capturing this sense of the city, one of the first actions of the newly amalgamated Toronto was to adopt 'Diversity, Our Strength' as its official motto. The first point that needs to be made, then, is that the City of Toronto formally recognizes the benefits of its diversity and recognizes the contributions of immigrants and refugees who have enriched the fabric of life for us all. Far from being a drain on the municipal purse, far from impoverishing the city, it is an official and proud recognition that this diversity defines and enriches the city.

From the perspective of municipal governance issues, it is of interest to note that the City of Toronto has adopted an inclusive framework towards equity. Diversity has been defined to include not just characteristics such as immigrant status, ethnicity, race, and language, but also age, gender, sexual orientation, and mental and physical disability. In addition, the definition recognizes the further layers of increasing diversity in the city in terms of lifestyles, values, power relations, and life chances (Scotti 2000).

Diversity is a useful concept because it describes all the differences and dissimilarities among people – differences and the resulting expectations that are based on any characteristic that helps shape a person's attitude, behaviour, and perspective. No matter what differences and dissimilarities there are among Toronto residents, they should all have access to municipal resources and be treated equitably by municipal institutions. The concept of diversity is also useful, then, because it includes and is about everyone. And city government serves everyone.

From schools to health care, parks, policing, social services, zoning, and infrastructure, municipal institutions and services in many ways define the immigrant and refugee experience. Conversely, the needs of immigrant communities converge with virtually every aspect of municipal service from economic development, emergency services, physical planning, and recreation to housing. The City of Toronto, as a civic leader and policy-maker, as a contractor of good and services, as a service planner and deliverer, as an employer, and as a grants provider, plays an important and direct role in determining whether all the people who share our civic space really feel at home here. Having said that, one needs to also say that the City of Toronto does not directly fund or deliver 'settlement services' as they may be defined by the other levels of government. Nor does the city target services or grants programs specifically to immigrants and refugees. Instead, immigrants, refugees, and other city residents receive a wide range of programs and services delivered or funded by the city to support all residents of Toronto.

It is within the framework of diversity that the City of Toronto considers the settlement needs of immigrants and refugees. The city takes the position that in Toronto, it would be artificial and not useful to regard immigrant settlement as a separate, discrete area of program activity. It is viewed, instead, as a major element within the paradigm, within the framework of responding to diversity. And diversity is regarded as a core and integral principle that impacts and influences every area of city life and every area of the city's policy and program activity.

For example, with respect to its public-education role, the city continues to commission and disseminate research and public-education materials on diversity issues. It sponsors a number of special events such as the commemoration of the International Day for the Elimination of all Forms of Discrimination, Black History Month, International Women's Day, Access Awareness Week for persons with disabilities, Gay Pride Week, the United Nations Human Rights Day, Aboriginal Week, and so on.

With respect to communications, city departments usually advertise in the ethnic media, and work in partnership with ethnoracial community-based agencies. In addition to the second-language skills of staff, the AT&T interpretation service is used to ensure access for people who require assistance in a language other than English. Access to appointments to boards of the city's agencies and commissions, for example, is a result of a specific council policy aimed at increasing representation by diverse groups on these bodies.

The city also provides training on diversity issues and human rights to front-line, middle and senior management. These include, for example, an intensive training program for senior management, workplace harassment training workshops, and human rights seminars for both management and unionized staff. The Children's Services Division in the Community and Neighbourhood Services Department has undertaken a comprehensive program that includes training for all staff, a code of conduct for staff, parents and children, a multicultural newsletter distributed to all child-care centres, and a yearly multi-ethnic calendar. The Buildings Division provides in-house training for buildings inspectors to improve their awareness of how people may use and or alter their house to accommodate their cultural or religious beliefs.

The City of Toronto provides grants totalling in excess of $40 million a year to community services, the arts, public health, economic development, and access and equity. To ensure that recipients of municipal grants are responding to and serving all sectors of the city's diverse population, Toronto City Council adopted an antiracism, access, and equity policy in 1998 that is specifically directed at grant recipients, requiring them to demonstrate how they are reflecting the city's diversity on their board, and among their staff, clients, or audience. Despite the current pressures of restraints and reduced funding available, this policy initiative is a clear recognition that proactive initiatives are necessary to ensure access for all sectors of the diverse community to organizations and programs that are supported by tax dollars.

Several initiatives have been implemented to improve awareness by ethnoracial businesses of the various contract opportunities available from city departments and special-purpose bodies. The Purchasing Division, for example, has a video entitled *How to Do Business with the City of Toronto* that is available in eight languages. It arranges for presentations to minority business groups, also in several languages, and annually advertises in over twenty ethnic newspapers, as well as in the mainstream media, to attract new suppliers. By more widely advertising the option of alternative bond and security requirements in its contracts, the Works Department was able to address a major barrier for small and minority-owned businesses in being able to bid on municipal contracts.

With respect to non-discriminatory human-resource policies and practices and equal opportunities in employment, the City of Toronto is looking at issues not only of representation, but also in such areas as occupational choice, positions of authority and decision-making, job security, employment conditions, and pay and benefits. Present priorities, for example, entail improving the accessibility of city government premises and increasing jobs for persons with disabilities.

An example of how the city's ambulance service has responded to diversity is the relationship it has developed with Hatzoloh, a volunteer organization providing emergency response and other community-related services concerning to the unique medical and social needs of the Orthodox Jewish community. Particular religious and cultural beliefs can, at times, pose difficulties for ambulance paramedics who are trained to provide medical intervention in a generally accepted manner. Language barriers, combined with strict religious beliefs, can impede the immediate notification of and access to emergency medical services when required. In this case, Hatzoloh has created a volunteer community-based emergency medical service. Through newsletters and community programming, subscribers within the Jewish community are able to contact Hatzoloh at any time of the day. Volunteers are able to provide interpreter services, access to other Jewish community agencies, medical assistance for the paramedics, and, most importantly, the ability to assist city-employed paramedics in situations where the religious beliefs of patients complicates the delivery of accepted medical practice. One example of optimizing the use of community-based resources, the Toronto ambulance service is working with Hatzoloh and has developed appropriate protocols to ensure the safety of on-scene volunteer responders, in compliance with legislation such as the Highway Traffic Act, the provision of training, and the continued promotion of appropriate first-response services.

In the absence of adequate support for immigrant and refugee settlement services in Toronto, newcomers increasingly are relying on municipal services. It is estimated for example, that 450 refugee claimants are accommodated in the city's emergency shelter system on any given night, and some 8,000 refugees rely on social assistance each month. An additional 6,000 immigrants receive social assistance because of sponsorship breakdown. The approximate net cost to the

City of Toronto for providing these services is estimated at over $30 million dollars annually.

A high proportion of recently arrived immigrants and refugees continue to use public health services today. Toronto's Public Health Department calculates that approximately 30 per cent of children participating in its dental program are immigrants and refugees, while 90 per cent of tuberculosis cases in Toronto occur in those who were born outside Canada. The total cost of public health services for immigrants and refugees is estimated to range from $3 million to $3.8 million annually (City of Toronto 2000).

Political Leadership

The former municipalities that now comprise the amalgamated City of Toronto first dealt with the issue of its changing population in the late 1970s. Recognizing the need for a concerted intergovernmental, corporate, and public commitment, all the former municipalities adopted policy statements on multiculturalism and race relations. Since then, the former municipalities continued to adopt further specific policies to ensure that all municipal activities address its diverse populations. These policies have included employment equity, access to services, workplace accommodation, human rights, immigrant and refugee settlement, and others.

Beyond these value and policy statements, municipal governments in Toronto have also established political structures to strengthen ties to their newcomer communities. All seven municipalities that were amalgamated into the new City of Toronto as of January 1, 1998, had well-established advisory committees on community, race, and ethnic relations. For example, the present mayor of the City of Toronto and former mayor of North York, Mel Lastman, established the North York Committee on Community, Race and Ethnic Relations in 1979 in order to promote appropriate responses to the significant changes in the racial, religious and ethnic, make-up of Toronto.

In addition to these community advisory committees, in 1990 the Metropolitan Toronto Council established a committee that was originally called the Council Action Committee to Combat Racism. Renamed the Anti-Racism, Access, and Equity Committee, it was the first municipal committee in Canada comprised solely of elected councillors who reported directly to the municipal council on issues dealing with diversity between 1994 and 1997.

As a political body, this committee not only demonstrated the city government's public commitment but also enabled it to formally and structurally assume a political leadership role in pursuing diversity with the broader community. It also assisted the municipality in ensuring the implementation and integration of its diversity policies into its own governmental policies and practices. In 1997, for example, in response to a considerable number of reports and community deputations received by this committee, Metro Toronto Council – perhaps more than any other political body in Canada – debated and made recommendations on a number of diversity issues, including immigrant and refugee settlement issues, accountable policing, combating hate activity, the urban Aboriginal community, education, and health services.

Municipal Structures

In order to follow through on its policy commitment, the new Toronto City Council established a Task Force on Community Access and Equity on March 4, 1998, to devise an action plan for the newly amalgamated city. Made up of five councillors and thirteen community members, the Task Force proceeded to undertake an extensive consultation process, holding over fifty sectoral community consultations and also meeting monthly to receive presentations, written submissions, letters, and other comments from a broad range of community stakeholders concerned with access and equity. The final recomendations (City of Toronto 1999b) were adopted in a unanimous decision by Toronto City Council in December 1999. The final report was adopted early in the new year (Task Force on Community Access and Equity 2000).

In adopting the task force's recommendations, Toronto City Council created five city-wide access and equity policy advisory committees for:

- Aboriginal Affairs
- Disability Issues
- Status of Women
- Race and Ethnic Relations
- Lesbian, Gay, Bisexual, and Transgender Issues

Each of these committees is made up of community members and at least one elected member of council. They report to city council through the appropriate standing committee on issues within the mandates of the respective standing committees. These five committees replace the access and equity committees of the former municipalities.

While the Task Force report was adopted unanimously, some of its recommendations were not received with unanimity by all stakeholder groups. The work of the Task Force and the establishment of these five citizen advisory committees might, in many ways, be said to run counter to the directions the city is taking as described earlier in this section. The City of Toronto, in this dilemma, represents an interesting case study, if not a battleground, of conflicting approaches to diversity within the same institution. Addressing access and equity issues by creating official categorizations of different population groups may have the unintended consequence of reinforcing the very boundaries that their establishment is aimed at removing or reducing. Observers suggest that there may be a danger in structuring such a process of institutionalizing, rather than reducing, boundaries (Breton 1998).

These different structural approaches by the city reflect, perhaps, some ambiguity between group rights versus individual rights, between the particular and universal principles. Addressing equity through discrete groupings, as critics of multiculturalism have argued, can too often lead to a process of static cultural relativism where group membership is ascribed and linear. At several Task Force meetings, some groups made it clear that they did not see any commonality between the issues each had to address (Smith 1999). To further exacerbate the problem, the Task Force elected to consult with each group separately, which resulted in each group bringing forward their own issues and concerns and making recommendations addressing their own needs.

Other criticisms of the citizen advisory model suggest they are flawed and empty tools (Tator 1998), and that they are 'out-of-date, irrelevant, and inappropriate mechanisms for the City of Toronto to use to take us into the twenty-first century' (Urban Alliance on Race Relations 1999). Such restrictive structures have also been criticized for failing to capture the dynamic and interactive process by which human identity is managed over time (Shelton 1998). In conclusion, as a city in a state of rapid transition, it is perhaps inevitable that the city government itself reflects some of the contradictions and uncertainties with regard to addressing the dynamics and challenges of a diverse population.

In addressing diversity, the newly amalgamated City of Toronto has begun to show leadership in some areas, and has, at the same time, understood the need to deal with the issues more comprehensively. Since adopting its motto 'Diversity, Our Strength' the city council has moved forward in approving its strategic plan, which restates that diversity is recognized, accepted, and promoted as a core strength. The principles that guide the city's actions include:

- Being advocates on behalf of our city's needs with other orders of government.
- Responding to and supporting diverse needs and interests and working to achieve social justice.
- Facilitating active community involvement in all aspects of civic life, both locally and city-wide.
- Seeking out partnerships with constituents, community groups, businesses and other public institutions, and orders of government.

The adoption of these principles is part of the process of embedding access and equity into the everyday thinking of all municipal government action. While the city continues to develop, test, and adjust its approaches, it is interesting to recollect the nature of municipal 'settlement' services 150 years ago. A historic plaque on the site of Metro Hall (a major municipal government building) recognizes the 100,000 Irish immigrants who arrived in Canada in 1847 fleeing famine and disease. Many thousands died in transit on the 'coffin' ships; many more died at the quarantine station at Grosse Île in Quebec. Of the approximately 40,000 who made it to Toronto, the healthy were assisted to leave the city as soon as possible. The city's Public Health Department constructed twelve 'fever sheds' (72 feet long by 25 feet wide) at the present site of municipal government at King and John Streets. In the summer of 1847, 863 Irish immigrants died of typhus in those sheds. In the array of services now provided by the City of Toronto, 150 years later, to support the settlement of newcomers, it is a reassuring measure of progress that the City of Toronto does not consider it necessary to help immigrants to leave the city as quickly as possible. Nor are 'fever sheds' and burial programs common newcomer services. Then again, the city government is building no accommodations to house its growing homeless population. Basic human needs continue to go unmet in modern-day Toronto.

RESEARCH AND POLICY GAPS

Much remains to be known and done in response to Toronto's remarkable demographic transformation brought on by global migration to the city. While the past decade has seen sustained growth in immigration research, we believe research is particularly needed in two broad spheres: the first to enrich our understanding of Toronto through the eyes and lives of newcomers; and the second to support the capacity for creative and effective policy responses to diversity.

Since the end of the Second World War, immigrants to Canada have displayed a decided preference for settling in Toronto. One in three immigrants in all of Canada now resides in the Toronto area. Yet surprisingly, there has been little research done on what draws migrants to this city. Improving our understanding of the city's appeal to global migrants would help the city's institutions prioritize its response to diversity. Other Canadian cities might also benefit from a clearer identification of how an urban place on Lake Ontario came to establish a global appeal for migrants the world over.

While this chapter began by exploring the experiences of four particular newcomer communities to Toronto through the twentieth century, little research has been done on a host of more recent immigrant arrivals to the Toronto area. Indeed, it is presently impossible to write a comprehensive narrative of immigrant settlement in Toronto. The case studies, monographs, and histories of such varied communities as Filipinos, Vietnamese, Koreans, Indians, Pakistanis, Poles, Russians, Turks, Kurds, Iranians, Afghanis, Somalis, Ghanaians, and Latin Americans remain to be written.

Additionally, it is important for studies of immigrant communities, both recent and more settled, to portray their *internal diversity*. No community is a monolith, and we need to know more about how variables such as gender, race, class, age/generation, sexual orientation, disability, language, religion, and ideology can fragment identity, experience, and interests within what may be portrayed as a homogenous community. At the same time, we need research that reminds us of the circumstances under which cohesive solidarity is expressed by newcomer communities, typically in the face of adverse treatment from the larger society. The tension between belonging and separation, in other words, can manifest itself both within an immigrant community, and in its relationship to the larger society. We need more research that is attentive to such complexities.

Transnationalism and citizenship have been key themes of recent immigrant research. The former seeks to explain the global networks and attachments that continue to link migrants to their country of origin; the latter notion of citizenship explores how newcomer communities participate in the life of their new society. Both concepts suggest fruitful lines of research into Toronto's immigrant communities. We need to know more about how such varied factors as sports, politics, fashion, religion, family, the arts, and business continue to tie Toronto's newcomers to their homelands and to other destinations in their community's global diaspora. Similarly, we need to better understand how newcomers negotiate their sense of belonging in Toronto: through work, neighbourhood, volunteerism, education, recreation, religion, politics, and their children. Particularly important is the need to be attentive to gender differences in the experience of both transnationalism and citizenship. Enhanced research along these lines would help to identify improved newcomer settlement resources and services.

Lastly, we emphasize the importance of grass-roots, community-based research. Very few studies have carefully explored the record of newcomer community organizations. What lessons and best practices exist among service and advocacy organizations in immigrant communities? What can identity-based and mainstream organizations learn from each other? What kinds of policies, programs, and services do most to advance access, equity, integration, and well-being? Research is a crucial ally in this and other challenges of newcomer integration.

The policy challenge facing Toronto is to enhance inclusion and equity among the city's diverse communities. But in recent years, disparities among Toronto's many communities have intensified. Unemployment, poverty, neighbourhood stigmatisation, and electoral underrepresentation are increasingly common among newcomer, visible minority communities. A host of factors are adding to the marginalization of recent immigrants: economic globalization and restructuring have produced a more segmented and precarious labour market; reduced unionization and heightened reliance on contingent (part-time, seasonal, and contract) labour are eroding earnings; a steady diet of government spending cuts has had a particularly negative impact on newcomer communities; immigrant settlement houses have closed, community organizations have seen their funding slashed, interpretive services have been dropped, and no more social housing is being built. Simultaneously, the provincial government's relentless commitment to neo-conservative principles has eliminated such measures as employment equity legislation, the Anti-Racism Secretariat, and rent controls. Escalating rents and diminished public policy attentiveness to discrimination have been the results. The forced amalgamation of the

City of Toronto into a single municipality of almost 2.5 million people has reduced the number of available seats on local council and created a far less accessible system of local-government decision-making.

Improving the terms of newcomer integration into Toronto, therefore, requires policy interventions on a wide variety of fronts. Earlier generations of newcomers settled into a Toronto with an ample social infrastructure of accessible services and resources. Children's recreational programs were free, roads could be freely navigated, and university tuition fees were set at a modest level. Today, newcomers are faced with recreational user fees, toll roads, and unprecedented post-secondary tuition costs. Government retrenchment is creating a more difficult environment for newcomers.

As for the policy preferences of the stakeholders themselves, decentralization appears to be a common appeal. Toronto's municipal government is pressing for 'a seat at the table' – consultation and input into immigration policies from which they are now largely excluded due to constitutional lack of status. Organizations representing newcomer communities, such as voluntary-sector service or advocacy groups, are pressing for greater powers and funding at the grass-roots level. And across many immigrant communities, there is dissatisfaction over local political institutions (municipal council, local school board, and municipal special-purpose bodies) whose decision-makers are not reflective of the city's rich demographic diversity. After a difficult decade in which amalgamations and centralization of resources and power have been the norm, it is time to experiment with creative exercises in devolution.

CONCLUSION

'No great North American city can be understood,' wrote Robert Harney (1940), Toronto's pioneering scholar of immigration, 'without being studied as a city of immigrants, of newcomers and their children, as a destination of myriad group and individual migration projects' (229). One of the great ironies of twentieth-century Toronto is that immigration and diversity have come to define the place and to confer on it a measure of global recognition. For much of the past century, Toronto was a parochial society promoting conformity to a monolithic dominant culture. It was typically suspicious of newcomer identities. Today, Toronto stands out as one of the world's foremost immigration cities, with a reputation for successfully integrating its new-found diversity.

Indeed global migration has finally put this insecure, ambitious city 'on the map,' fulfilling its craving for 'world-class' civic stature.

Some cities are acclaimed for their geographic setting, economic dynamism, or cultural or architectural treasures. If Toronto resonates at all in global consciousness, it is as a city where diversity has been fashioned into an urban strength. For the past two decades, international media coverage of Toronto has typically praised, even glorified, the city for its successful multiculturalism. Thus *U.S. News and World Report* in the mid-1980s described Toronto as 'home to hundreds of thousands from around the world who share their cultures and live in harmony.' Ten years later, a popular American travel magazine waxed rhapsodic in describing Toronto as 'a mulligan stew with an international blend of ingredients – a touch of this culture, a pinch of that custom – which has created a spectacular mixture of sight and sound, color and style along the once-staid shores of Lake Ontario' (as quoted in Croucher 1997, 326). So lavish and recurrent have been these tributes to Toronto's diversity, that an 'urban legend' took hold in the city at the end of the twentieth century. Local politicians, the media, and city boosters routinely asserted that the United Nations had declared Toronto the world's most multicultural city. The claim seemed so attuned to the city's newfound image, that it was embraced, cherished, and, above all, repeated as an uncontested truth. That was, until the relentless probing of geographer Michael Doucet (2001) demonstrated that no such declaration of Toronto's exalted stature had ever been issued by the United Nations.

A city's mystique does not always reflect its reality. Is Toronto the world's *cosmopolis*? A city that is home to the world, devoid of undue barriers to integration, where all newcomer communities can imprint their identities and aspirations on the urban landscape? We believe that *quantitative* and *qualitative* variables offer conflicting verdicts.

Toronto, we saw, was an unlikely candidate to serve as a model for urban diversity recognition. Until at least the middle of the twentieth century, the city was overwhelmingly characterized by ethnic homogeneity and a fixed dominant culture. Over the past fifty years, changes in both Canadian immigration policy and global migration patterns have brought the world to Toronto. Set against its blatantly xenophobic past, the peaceful settlement over the past fifty years of literally *millions* of newcomers from Southern Europe, Eastern Europe, the Caribbean, Asia, Africa, and Central and South America marks a significant achievement for Toronto. Few cities in the world can match its immigrant threshold, with half the population of some 2.5 million persons having been born outside Canada. To be sure, enlightened self-interest has played an important part in the city's opening up to diversity. Immigrants have filled important gaps in the local labour market, they have become major investors and entrepreneurs in the city economy, and, most recently, were harnessed to the city's failed bid for the 2008 Olympic Games. Thus the city's Olympic-bid Web site emphasized Toronto's stature as 'a place where you can literally tour the globe without ever leaving the city' (Carey 2000, F1).

Toronto has proven adept at capitalizing on its diversity. A significant factor in its success was the relative ease with which the city changed its rhetoric, discourse, and policy orientation towards demographic difference and diversity. Within a generation, the city that had signs banning Jews and Blacks from public beaches was proclaiming its commitment to tolerance, pluralism, and multiculturalism. As we have seen, municipal government leadership has played an important part in transforming Toronto's civic culture. Yet beyond the official rhetoric of inclusion and diversity, entrenched differences endure. Neither political nor economic power is equitably distributed. Stark divisions exist in the living standards of Toronto's diverse communities that are rooted in immigrant status, ethnoracial identity, and gender, *not* in differences of education or training. Minority communities also continue to feel aggrieved over their treatment by a host of municipal services including policing, schooling, and land-use planning; and by a variety of private sector forces, including the media, housing, and employment markets.

Toronto is often praised as a tolerant place. Yet we believe there is too great a tolerance for inequalities to qualify Toronto as *cosmopolis* gained. Indeed the most tolerant Torontonians are its newcomers! Immigrants typically accept their own social and economic setbacks as a necessary investment for their children's subsequent advancement in a new country and city. Toronto's reputation for multicultural harmony owes much to the stoicism, determination, and faith in the future shown by immigrants themselves. Its progress towards *cosmopolis*, we believe, will best be advanced by the emerging mobilization and solidarity of diverse movements challenging inequalities of gender, race, resource access, and political influence. The energies so many individuals and organizations devote to forging diversity on equitable terms may one day create fully realized *cosmopolis* in Toronto.

Notes

The authors gratefully acknowledge the excellent research assistance provided by Shannon Ryan.

1 IWDC was and is a loose network of individuals and groups who organize the annual Women's Day march through downtown Toronto and the information sessions that celebrate women's struggles worldwide and raise public awareness about women's concerns.

9 World in a City: A View from Policy

Meyer Burstein and Howard Duncan

Note: The thoughts contained in this chapter are those of the authors at the time of writing. They are not to be taken to represent the policy of the Government of Canada. They do not necessarily represent the thoughts of the authors tomorrow.

SOME FIRST WORDS

The preceding chapters of this book tell a tale of Toronto in transition, a tale of rapid population growth and ethnic, racial, and religious diversification. Although this tale is perhaps most profound when told of Toronto, it can be repeated for many Canadian cities and towns. What is happening in Toronto is already or will be happening elsewhere in Canada, and the lessons learned here will be worth all of our attention. The central theme of the story is integration, how the many newcomers to Toronto have been able to adjust to life in Canada's most populous and diverse city. The story is, in comparison to many other cities in the world, a largely happy one – although it is not without its sorrier subplots. By many measures, Toronto is a healthy city, a good place to live, a place where immigrants, refugees, and other migrants have been able to forge good lives. It is for this reason, we must suppose, that Toronto remains a destination of choice for so many of the world's migrants. Although some real challenges remain, integration in Toronto appears to be working well, and the people who live there have reason to feel good about this.

Of course, not all immigrants are from backgrounds that are ethnically dissimilar from the majority population and the government is just as concerned with their well-being as with the well-being of those who are different. It is easy these days to make a special case of ethnic diversity – to regard it as the key to managing immigration – but diversity is not the entirety of the immigration story, nor is ethnic diversity the only diversity that we need to attend to. Nonetheless, the integration of people from ethnically diverse backgrounds is important to social stability, to social order, and to peace in our cities, and there is no question that a measure of the success of Canada's immigration program is success in social integration.

What we in the immigration business mean by 'integration' remains tentative, and the contributors to this book are decidedly nervous in their use of the term, although careful to distinguish it from the now-avoided 'assimilation.' More recently, commentators on social well-being have been incorporating various concepts such as social cohesion, social exclusion, and social inclusion in their attempts to bring new insights to our understanding of how our societies are working and how some of its members can be at a comparative disadvantage. Writers on immigration have adopted these terms to elucidate the situation that immigrants and refugees find themselves in, and we see this in *The World in a City*. The terminological flux will continue in the migration literature, we can assume, as commentators struggle to eke out new insights from the data and from the everyday experiences of newcomers to Canada.

Although we have no strong terminological preferences, we will use the older term 'integration' in this chapter. This is partly because we believe that it will enjoy a greater staying power within policy circles; time will tell. Terminology choices in the literature have become highly political and we will sidestep the academic debates that can accompany one's choice of wording. Similarly, whether integrating is a good thing or a bad thing, something that is or should be done by the newcomer, immigrant, refugee, or relocating Canadian, or something that is done by the receiving society, by those who are already there, is not an issue of great moment for us in these pages. What is clear enough is that adjustments are in fact made by both the newcomer and those already living in the country. This is the way it happens, willingly or grudgingly, rapidly or slowly, easily or with tension. No matter what the current politics of integration, the streets of Toronto are two-way streets.

The contributors to this book have examined the central aspects of integration that are covered in the immigration literature: employment and economic well-being, social and cultural integration, housing, education, health, and so on. There are other aspects that we could look at, other elements of life that we can take as indicators of how well immigrants are settling into their new home and how the arrival of newcomers is affecting the lives of Torontonians who were already there. Some of these include sports and recreation, the retail environment, entertainment, the use of public spaces, political discourse, religious behaviour, the activities of transnational or diasporic communities, crime, the underground economy, public attitudes, and many, many more. But what the previous chapters give us is a good, if standard, beginning from which to understand and assess the situation in Toronto and elsewhere in Canada.

In this chapter, we will look at things from the perspective of government policy – at the importance of events and changes in Toronto for policy decisions at a national level, the importance of the information that research provides for discussing, debating, and setting these policies. We will take a step back from the exciting dynamics of Toronto and from the wealth of detail that the research has generated, and consider what it means for those who must govern the entire country, according to the procedures that we Canadians have adopted over the past 134 years.

For the purposes of this discussion, we will take it that integration, despite its ambiguity, refers, at least, to something that people do or something that communities of people do. It refers to life as it is lived on the streets of our cities and towns and rural areas. Whatever its precise meaning, integration is *not* a government service or program. Social engineering is hardly an area where governments, at least democratic governments, have been especially effective in the past. Having social integration take place in Toronto is not like collecting taxes, opening a national park, or sending the armed forces to a peacekeeping mission abroad. As with many of Canada's social objectives, creating socially integrated cities is something that government can help along through policies and programs, but it cannot be done unilaterally – it cannot be delivered in an envelope or announced at a ribbon-cutting ceremony.

In the field of public debate and academic discussion, we often hear the constitutional truism that (outside Quebec) the federal government sets immigration policy, thereby determining the annual number of new arrivals, while the cities of destination, left out of federal decision-making, carry the weight of the decisions, pay the costs of integration, and deal with the problems. This, it is often suggested, is unjust. We will resist the temptation to wade into constitutional waters, but will acknowledge the obvious, that immigrants to Canada settle in our cities, just as most Canadians have done. Cities are, for this reason, of increasing importance; they are where the people live. And the federal government recognizes this. Its programs, for the benefit of the people of Canada, are at the same time for the benefit of those people of Canada who live in our cities. They are, for the most part, one and the same people. So here we will aim to avoid a municipal form of parochialism and shy away, too, from the questions of which level of government should pay for what. These are, inevitably, political discussions and we will not engage in political advocacy here.

For our final opening comment, let us step back and observe that cities are made up of groupings of people – people linked by a physical infrastructure, social networks, and institutional systems. They are, in a free society, a dynamic nexus of activity and opportunity. Government policy makes a difference, but the life of a city is largely the product of the actions and choices of the people who live in it; were this not the case, the impact of immigration would be small. When it comes to integration, then, we emphasize the actions of people over the actions of 'the city' or of the government. And we will all do well to remember that immigrants are individuals, as well as members of groups, whether they are gathered socially or merely statistically. Like all individuals, what happens in their lives is a result of a complex of social and historical factors and choices they themselves make. The extent to which government action is or could be a significant factor in their lives is often, we think, overstated or overestimated, whether from naïveté or from hopeful advocacy. Government has a role in creating social cohesion, certainly and seriously, but it is decidedly limited and ought to be so.

THE ROLE OF THE FEDERAL GOVERNMENT
IN MANAGING DIVERSITY

Canada is a federation of provinces and territories. The provinces and their regions and cities, it is important to remember, have considerable constitutionally enshrined autonomy. They are proud of their heritage, culture, and traditions that have been allowed to develop, in part, because of the nature of Canada's constitutional agreements. Ottawa's broad role with regard to integration in our cities, in addition to what is delineated in the constitution, might be described as providing a national framework within which cities and provinces can run their affairs. This role will often be facilitative, with the 'lead' being played by cities like Toronto, not by the federal government. The constitutionally defined autonomy that the provinces, in this case Ontario, and the cities have is especially strong with regard to immigration and the integration of immigrants into Canadian society.

Section 95 of the Constitution reads:

> In each Province the Legislature may make Laws in relation to Agriculture in the Province, and to Immigration into the Province; and it is hereby declared that the Parliament of Canada may from Time to Time make Laws in relation to Agriculture in all or any of the Provinces, and to Immigration into all or any of the Provinces; and any Law of the Legislature of a Province relative to Agriculture or to Immigration shall have effect in and for the Province as long and as far only as it is not repugnant to any Act of the Parliament of Canada.

In the spirit of shared jurisdiction, the federal government consults with the provinces regarding integration. (Quebec, it should be noted, has special authorities originating in the British North America Act.) Section 108 (1) of the Immigration Act reads: 'The Minister shall consult with the provinces respecting the measures to be undertaken to facilitate the adaptation of permanent residents to Canadian society and the pattern of immigrant settlement in Canada in relation to regional demographic requirements.'

What, then, does this mean for the role of our federal government in managing diversity in major cities such as Toronto? The efficacy of a democratic government in managing integration in a free and pluralistic society is going to be limited anyway, but the division of responsibilities and authorities in Canada means that the federal government will play a somewhat background role of creating conditions within which our cities and their residents can flourish.

To a certain extent, this can be construed as removing barriers to integration, something that can be aided through legislation, public education, and programming such as second-language instruction. Also to be considered is the role of the federal government in managing immigration and internal migration, for it is out of these that much of Toronto's diversity arises. In broad outline, there is widespread consensus within Canada on what the government's role is; there is considerable disagreement about the details and the instruments, some are along ideological lines, some are more practically grounded. But let us start from the fundamental Canadian precept that our elected federal officials and their supporting bureaucracies are to provide peace, order, and good government. When applied to our immigration, refugee, and related programs, including those that facilitate integration, this requires the government to do things like establish an appropriate number of immigrants to admit annually, and to establish means and criteria for selecting and admitting immigrants and refugees through programs that meet economic, social, and humanitarian objectives – that they be effective and efficient – and are in accord with the values in Canadian society. In other words, that they be just and democratic programs.

The framework for the federal legislative, policy, and program framework is made up, in part, by these programs, initiatives, and institutions:

- Selection, recruitment, and admission
- Settlement assistance
- Integration assistance
- Citizenship
- Law enforcement
- Planning and research
- Legal instruments such as the Charter of Rights and Freedoms, the Multiculturalism Act, anti-discrimination provisions in labour laws, housing laws, education laws, and so on

This set of initiatives with their attendant policies, laws, and regulations, comprises a framework within which immigrants enter Canada and settle here, mostly in the three municipalities of Toronto, Vancouver, and Montreal. This framework is fluid – arising from parliamentary decisions (including the passing of legislation such as the Immigration Act) that are, we will assume, responsive to society's development – and has, in fact, changed over the decades in significant ways, many of which have been carefully described in the preceding chapters. It is through this evolving framework – a mix of measures designed to provide incentives, to promote certain behaviours and attitudes, and to provide the force of law where this is appropriate and necessary – that the federal government affects diversity in Canadian cities and the degree to which people of different ethnic, racial, and religious backgrounds are integrated into the life of the cities. This framework, then, is the primary instrument of the federal government for supporting the integration of the diverse peoples in our country; to a large extent, it is a framework within which the people of Canada integrate themselves.

Where does the integration process begin? We suggest that the immigrant and refugee selection system that Canada uses is the first step in the process of integrating newcomers, for it is the job of the selection system to try to establish a good fit between the person admitted and the nature of Canadian society, its labour markets, social climate, business climate, and so on; errors made in selection can mean later difficulties in integration. Numbers matter; the Canadian economy and its various sectors need and can employ only so many people at a time. The rapidity with which change occurs matters; Canadians can adapt to only so much social change at a time. Our cities and their social and physical infrastructures can handle only so many people; of growing interest is the capacity of our sometimes fragile natural environments to withstand the pressures of growing populations. The skills and personal characteristics of the immigrants and refugees matter; whether they will find a place in the economy or will be able to live in harmony in their new communities. And public attitudes and institutionalized values make an enormous difference to the degree to which newcomers are accepted, welcomed, admitted to the job market, to our neighbourhoods, to our schools and other social institutions, and eventually welcomed as new citizens to Canada.

Government must understand the social and economic forces at play in deciding who and how many newcomers to admit, for what purpose, and for what length of time. Government must also be ready to make adjustments as society and the economy change, adjustments to the selection system and to the rest of the framework that can affect the degree to which Canada and Canadians will welcome newcomers. A selection system that functions well will, all other things being equal, help smooth the way to integration; it is the first step in the integration process.

Government can also help the cause of integration for those it admits into the country, we believe, by such measures as:

- Fostering the appropriate social values through policy and law (such as the Charter of Rights and Freedoms, antidiscrimination laws for the workplace, education systems, and so on)
- Creating expectations that people and institutions behave in supportive ways towards immigrants and refugees

- Creating expectations that immigrants and refugees will come to regard Canada as their home and take out citizenship and assume the responsibilities that this brings
- Influencing the social climate, public debate, and public attitudes through education programs and other interventions that promote successful integration
- Setting standards in the housing market, the labour market, the workplace, in health care, in social services
- Offering directly, or financing services for, language training, settlement and housing, job searches, cultural and community orientation, and related matters

All of these can be helpful to the integration process; but none offers guarantees.

Ensuring social order is a major responsibility of government. Without a basis of social order, little can function well in any society, prosperity will be hard to come by, and peace will be elusive. Part of government's responsibility for ensuring social order concerns integrating newcomers. Doing this well requires sound empirical research.

THE DIFFERENCE THAT RESEARCH ON TORONTO MAKES

Having an effective framework for social integration means, ultimately, that our diverse newcomers become well-integrated into their new societies so that they and their new neighbours, schoolmates, employers, and employees can flourish and lead good lives. It is important for the federal government to monitor how well Canada is integrating its immigrants and refugees, to examine the trends for various aspects of integration, to investigate the conditions that are affecting these trends, to identify emerging issues of concern, and to decide what aspects of integration are working well and can be replicated elsewhere in Canada, and so on. Responsible governments will look to research for this information.

For simplicity's sake, we affirm that the primary value of the researcher in this context lies in providing facts that policy-makers can consider as they go about their business. Furthermore, it is important that there be discussions about these facts, their interpretation, and their implications for Canadian society so that policy interventions can be developed to support our goals. We emphasize the role of facts, notwithstanding current academic debates that dismiss the concepts of objectivity and objective factual evidence. The realism–relativism debate aside, research can tell policy-makers what is actually taking place in Canadian society with respect to immigration, integration, and diversity. This type of information, when it is balanced, comprehensive, and free (so far as possible) of ideology, can help the policy-maker assess where adjustments are needed in the federal framework sketched above and how radical the adjustments need to be. (It would be a rare case, we submit, in which the research findings require a massive restructuring of the framework; this is why we will normally speak of *making adjustments* to a framework whose basic features remain in place.) This requires a complex set of judgments by the decision-maker, beginning with whether the economic and other social conditions are of such a magnitude as to warrant an adjustment to program expenditures, regulations, or legislation, and whether it is at the federal, provincial, or municipal level that the adjustments would be most appropriate or most effective. And these are preliminary, of course, to the judgments of what the adjustments ought to be, from the points of view of both effectiveness and justice.

Of course, research is often accompanied by social or political values, sometimes by evident and stridently held ideologies, sometimes by an ignorance of what government in Canada can or even should do. In government, we are often led to feel that researchers too readily draw conclusions in the absence of independent argument, that a social condition requires government remedial action, usually in the form of additional spending. In other words, there appears to be a propensity to uncritically assume that social problems are usually best solved through government action or spending; indeed, it is often assumed that social problems are the result of government error, even malevolence. Such assumptions are made far too quickly and cannot be sustained, nor may government efficacy be so great as this suggests. Further, we must note with caution that nothing is easier for government to do than to transfer funds to others in order to be seen to be acting in the public interest.

Unfortunately, the simple logic of increasing government spending to solve social problems is very often ineffective at solving anything at all in the absence of a clear understanding about the problem, the remedies that could help, and about the agents who are best able to bring about effective solutions. It is hardly axiomatic that all social problems can be solved by governments, let alone through a simple transfer of public funds to those who are 'close' to the problem.

Assessing a problem and its magnitude carefully to determine if government action is needed at all or is the most effective way to alleviate a social condition is essential to responsible governance. Research can be extremely valuable when it considers the actual impact of government interventions and assesses the likely impact of potential future interventions; it is even better when it offers a comparison of alternative courses of action, say, at the community level, or even the option of no action at all. Social forces are often in themselves powerful agents of progressive societal change. Therefore, we need research that tell policy-makers more than that a problem exists; we also need a sober assessment of its gravity, where effective solutions may lie, and, correlatively, where they do not.

Toronto is an especially interesting case for assessing the federal framework for integrating diversity because of its exceptionally high degree and long history of diversity, which was culminated in the current situation in which it is often immigrants who are integrating immigrants. The large and quickly growing population makes it an important test case for the government's approach. But Toronto is also anachronistic for these same reasons. It may not be representative enough of the Canadian situation to be a major source of lessons for other cities, and its economic power is also a factor not shared by all. These, too, are matters to be determined by empirical research and careful analysis of the results.

The research presented in this book is, to a large degree, about Toronto's past and reflects the amazing achievement that the city has made in its reception of immigrants and refugees from over one hundred countries. Seeing the historical context alongside the current situation allows those of us in the policy world to more subtly assess what is happening today. Many of the contributors suggest that Toronto is making progress and, significantly, is doing so in part because of the efforts of immigrants and refugees themselves, their grass-roots organizations, their churches, and their economic activities. The governments involved have created some conditions and provided some funding and other supports that have allowed newcomers to act in their own and their communities' best interests, whether those actions are to directly assist themselves or to lobby for institutional or governmental change. For example, the move towards having social services such as education and health care delivered in ways that are more appropriate to their cultures surely has something to do with the effective lobbying efforts of the cultural minorities.

Exercising their voices in their own behalf is, we feel, a healthy response – one made possible, in part, by the particular governmental framework that Canada has adopted and adapted as social conditions have changed. An important aspect of social change in Toronto and in Canada is the increasing self-confidence that the immigrant communities express when dealing with government; their eagerness to make demands on government and their new societies was not as evident in the past. While this has, at times, been challenging for government officials and politicians, it is encouraging to see this growing ability to grapple with the difficulties of being an immigrant. And, again, we are now witnessing the phenomena of immigrants integrating with immigrants and not just with native-born Canadians or native-born Torontonians; we need to assess anew who the 'host society' is in Toronto, the society *into which* and *by which* future new arrivals will be integrated.

The research that places today's conditions into historical context is helpful; we would also find it helpful if the researchers could provide serious speculations on where we are headed. Given current social and economic trends, what does the future hold for integrating immigrants of diverse backgrounds? Will the future Toronto, with its fantastically diverse population a matter of historical record, deal even better with this fact? Will the children of immigrants growing up in such a diverse environment come to take it for granted, come to embrace mixed-race and mixed-ethnicity friendships and love relationships to the point where diversity no longer matters? Will today's concerns about integrating diversity simply dissipate into irrelevancy? We can hold out hope.

In the meantime governments must ensure that the framework through which both new Canadians and old lead their lives supports the trends towards successful integration, operates realistically to remove the remaining hindrances, to prevent new ones from forming, and to promote the peaceable and prosperous lives that most of us seek.

THE RESEARCH FINDINGS

We cannot comment here on the wide range of findings presented in the preceding chapters; we will leave that to specialist policy analysts. Our comments here are more general. The research, in chapter after chapter, identifies the important role of culture and ethnicity in the integration process, shaping where people live, work, study, and play.

There are strong and persistent influences of culture and ethnicity on participation in the labour market and on the creation of business enclaves. There is at least as strong an influence on community and neighbourhood development. And the evidence indicates that ethnicity is strongly related to the opportunities that immigrants and minorities find open to them, as well as to the assets – the financial and the knowledge assets – that they bring to the task of integration. More important than the differences, however, is what the research tells us about the Canadian playing field. As much as we would like to believe that the playing field is level, it is not. This suggests that Canadians are interested – and here the interest clearly extends to public policy – in finding ways to redress the inequalities.

At the same time, what complicates the situation and hampers direct intervention is the fact that the Charter of Rights and Freedoms, prevailing ideology, and the nature of public discourse in Canada do not support the organization of public policy on a racial or ethnic basis. One way out of this dilemma would be to develop a more thoughtful and purposeful relationship between government and non-governmental organizations (NGOs). Such organizations do, in fact, structure themselves along ethnic and racial lines and are, for this reason, potentially well-equipped to take on direct service roles. Research could indicate where and how public policy should seek greater NGO involvement.

The findings in this book are unequivocal in pointing out that more attention should be paid to particular subpopulations that are at risk. Structural changes in the Canadian economy resulting from globalization and North American economic integration have led to declining economic performance by recent immigrant cohorts. This would appear to be a departure from the dominant tale of harsh beginnings, hard struggle, and eventual success, if not for the first generation then for their children and for the integrated communities that follow. The recent emergence of homelessness as a major public policy issue along with poverty that seemingly extends across generations, belies the generally well-founded optimism that pervades most accounts of immigration to Canada. Based on the research that is emerging, there would appear to be a clear need for a coordinated and sustained 'public investment strategy' that would focus on much better access to training and education by groups who are at risk. The creation of socio-economic opportunities, accompanied by strategies that would enable these groups to take advantage of such opportunities is critical to success in all sectors, including health, housing, and education. A challenge for policy-makers, not only at the federal level, but at all levels, is to organize such an investment strategy without stigmatizing the groups in need of help and without losing public support for immigration and for continued social investment.

One critical point that emerges over and over again in the research and that constitutes a subtext for much of the proposed public policy agenda concerns discrimination and, to a lesser extent, overt racism. This point is fundamental for three reasons. First, the vast majority of immigrants to Canada are 'visible minorities,' so there is little doubt that the already substantial presence of visible-minority communities in Canada's major cities will continue to grow rapidly. Second, there is a strong division of opinion across Canada as to the prevalence and significance of discrimination: most white Canadians discount the negative effects, in contrast with the strongly held views of Canadians who are members of minority groups. And third, the research is unequivocal in showing that visible minorities, especially Black and South Asian Canadians (and Aboriginal Canadians) pay a 'penalty' in terms of their incomes, employment, and, thus, access to opportunities for advancement for themselves and their children.

The scope for government intervention in these areas is limited, in part because legal and other remedies are already in place. Nonetheless, the importance of these issues, the cost of their failure, and their centrality to Canada's multiculturalism and immigration policies tell us that much more attention will need to be devoted to remedial interventions. The research also points out the importance of reassessing the role of institutions, both public and private, in shaping public attitudes and in producing change. Policy-makers will need to devote particular attention to targeted education, training (especially language training), health and justice programs, and to the institutions that deliver these programs and services. In general, program targeting for immigrant and minority groups, which has fallen into disfavour, will need to be re-examined to consider whether it is an important element in addressing emerging problems.

Paradoxically, the research suggests that the growing heterogeneity in Toronto and in other major Canadian cities is itself complicating the integration process and confounding earlier policy and program strategies. The fact that new arrivals are exhibiting new settlement and clustering patterns and are frequently being integrated within communities that are themselves largely composed of newcomers suggests that earlier assumptions about the nature of communities and their role in the integration process may no longer hold and may need to be rethought. In this context, governments need to reassess their relationships with cultural and ethnic networks and need to develop better strategies for helping groups who are at risk. Research on this topic and on the changes that are taking place within the receptor communities would be extremely helpful, especially at a time when government is evaluating strategies for increasing immigration and for expanding the absorptive capacity in larger cities and in smaller centres.

Perhaps the most important policy finding to emerge from this research – and one that confirms the fundamental premise of the Metropolis Project and the establishment of the Toronto Centre of Excellence – is that the same challenges manifest themselves in domains that span housing and neighbourhood development, education, health, employment, and civic engagement. This adds no small amount of seriousness to the findings in each sector as it suggests a common cause. It must be said, however, that this does not in itself demonstrate a need for involvement by the federal government, or, indeed, by any other level of government. At the same time, in the Canadian political context, with our constitutionally defined jurisdictions over public issues, it suggests that one of the major challenges in the area of immigration and diversity is governance itself.

Unlike governments, issues are not confined by the jurisdictional boundaries that circumscribe federal, provincial, and municipal actions. Another significant challenge confronting all stakeholders – the host community, the groups or individuals who are the subject of analysis, and the policy-makers and practitioners who are implicated in the solutions – over and above the issues themselves, is the difficulty of sorting out jurisdictions, identifying responsibilities, and developing a shared understanding of the problems and the need for remedial action. What is clear is that newcomers and disadvantaged individuals and groups lack the knowledge and resources to solve this puzzle, which places an onus on governments to coordinate their efforts and to produce a more collaborative form of governance around migration and diversity issues. This should not be impossible; throughout Canada, unlike other countries, there is broad agreement on the vision.

OTHER RESEARCH

No single selection of essays could possibly convey the richness that research might reveal about the ways in which immigrants have and have not been integrated into life in the city of Toronto. In addition to the work presented here, there are, inevitably, further areas of study in this complex set of phenomena that would be of interest to government policy-makers and policy analysts. What follows are some ideas that empirical studies might explore:

1 Perspectives on integration and diversity from the hosts, the Canadian-born residents of Toronto: the employers, the school administrators, the health-care administrators, the city administrators, the police, the social workers, and the community associations. As we said at the outset, integration is a two-way street in Toronto; along with the point of view of immigrants, we need to hear from other voices.
2 The experiences of native-born Canadians migrating to Toronto, both those with specific jobs to go to and those relocating in the hopes of finding work. How well do they integrate? Data about this could provide a comparison of a different and important sort. How well do internal-to-Canada migrants integrate to life in Toronto compared with immigrants?
3 What government interventions are effective in regard to ethnic and racial disadvantage, discrimination, long-term poverty (especially among dysfunctional groups)? What government interventions are effective in resolving conflicts (for example, regarding property and land use, and cultural practices) between immigrant and non-immigrant groups? Which subgroups are at particular risk of long-term disadvantage? Are refugee claimants at a disadvantage when their claims are years in the processing?
4 The unreported economic and social impacts of the underground economy (industrial sweatshops, smuggling/trafficking networks, organized crime, terrorism) among immigrants is something that is studied much more frequently in the United States and Europe than in Canada. To what extent do immigrants work in a Toronto-based underground economy?
5 The economies of diasporas and other types of transnational communities. The unemployment/employment levels, and earnings analyses that we usually see from academic research do not normally include contemporary transactions involving transnational organizations, the workings of globalization at the local level. We anticipate that there is significant transnational economic activity involving residents of Toronto, activity that goes well beyond traditional remittances.
6 Political activity, both home-grown and here, including such political activity of diasporas as support for those engaged in conflict in the homeland.

7 What migrants do for themselves to settle and integrate, including how they integrate with family, friends, and co-nationals, and how they interact with migrant organizations. To what extent is government assistance necessary? Where is it best targeted? What are the comparative effects of immigrants helping themselves versus receiving government assistance. Where are governments most helpful? Where should they leave things to others?

8 What is it about Toronto that has gone so well? What has the city government done, what have its residents done over the years that has brought about the level of integration that it enjoys? We need general conclusions and lessons about cities that have succeeded in this respect.

9 The net economic benefits and costs to Toronto resulting from immigration, either primary or secondary. Much contemporary discussion refers to the costs that, it is suggested, are downloaded to the municipalities, yet little work has been done on the overall economic benefits that Toronto (its employers, businesses, and families) reaps. Any comparisons between the benefits accruing from the arrival of immigrants and the arrival of Canadian-born migrants to Toronto would be interesting.

10 Has the strength of Toronto as a magnet for immigrants become a problem for other Canadian cities which might reap similar benefits from immigrants locating there?

11 Do we expect more of immigrants than we do of the Canadian-born? Great disparities also exist among native-born Canadians. Do we regard or treat immigrants differently from native Canadians when they fall into poverty?

12 How does immigration affect Toronto's physical environment and its sustainability?

13 How does immigration to Toronto affect Canada's economic and demographic adjustment to globalization, including our international competitiveness?

REFLECTIONS ON CLOSING

Reflecting on the research that appears in this book brings us back to the questions of the fundamental role that governments ought to play in seeing cohesive societies develop, of the extent to which governments ought to attempt to 'engineer' the attainment of social values, of the extent to which governments should attempt to determine the nature of a society. In this setting, we want to ask where should the government set its sights for social integration? What counts as an acceptable degree of social cohesion? How much disparity must we accept as a trade-off for living in a pluralistic and free society? In general, how far should government intervene in the city's life or communities in order to protect the social good?

These are especially difficult considerations for a democratic society that prides itself on pluralism and freedom. When should government act and when should it let the residents and their local organizations work things through? Of course, there is no guarantee that government intervention will always bring benefits, not to mention benefits that are worth their costs. We would argue that a certain amount of patience is advisable; when the local residents bring about change for the better themselves, we are inclined to think that the benefits will be more durable than if they were brought about by government intervention. In a liberal democracy, there is always a serious issue of the circumstances under which a government should intervene in the life of a community. These are matters for broad-based discussion and debate that, ultimately, will be decided – and re-decided – in Parliament and at the ballot box.

The research tells a largely happy tale – again, with some sorrier subplots. Nothing in the research would suggest a radical reformulation of the framework through which the federal government contributes to the social integration of Toronto's diverse population. The framework will need to be fine-tuned to respond to emerging social conditions, some of which are described in this book. One example, and a frequent concern of the research represented here, is with equality of outcome, whether it be in earnings, in living conditions and housing, in health status or access to services, or in education. Although we would argue that there is more to integration than this, performance here is a significant indicator of how well integration is taking place in Toronto. Canadian society, with its emphasis on liberty, favours equality of opportunity over equality of outcome. This speaks to limited government intervention. However, when outcomes become excessively polarized, we see this as a sign of something going wrong, as a sign that opportunity itself might be polarizing – and this demands considered and careful action. But the framework for success seems to be in place, the various communities of newcomers are increasingly taking charge to everyone's benefit, and we hold out hope for a bright future, led, perhaps, by the young people for whom diversity is becoming simply a matter of everyday life.

Epilogue: Blockages to Opportunity?

Michael Lanphier and Paul Anisef

The World in a City represents an initial, but comprehensive, inquiry into the reciprocal impact of immigration on Toronto as a metropolis and the social arrangements of the metropolis on the lives of newly arrived immigrants. It has highlighted that, since 1970, there has been an impressively extensive accommodation of people from diverse backgrounds and impressive patterns of adaptation on the part of newcomers. Authors in this volume, for the most part, agree that the broad outlines of Canada's admission policy during this recent period has attempted to maintain a shifting, if at times uneasy, balance of priorities. These priorities include an interest in receiving economic (independent) immigrants on the basis of their potential contribution to the Canadian economy, an interest in family reunion, and an interest in humanitarian (refugee) intake on the basis of Canada's international commitments.

We have argued that, within the immigration policies enunciated by the federal government since 1965, Canada's 'points' system and related policies have widened the inclusiveness of intake to admit applicants from worldwide sources, according to educational and occupational achievement-related criteria. Despite annual target numbers that invariably limit the number of admissions, the selection can no longer categorically exclude applicants on the basis of national origin, ethnicity, or religion. Although these specifications have varied from time to time, this signal feature has distinguished Canadian (and, in turn, Australian) intake policy as socially inclusive, however infused it may be with enlightened self-interest on the part of the nation-state.

Similarly, Canada's 1976 Immigration Act enunciated a broad policy directive to the minister of immigration to provide an annual report on immigration 'levels' to Parliament, including not only targets for independent ('points' system) applicants, but also family and humanitarian classes. While the yearly announcement of these 'target' numbers frequently incites critical comment from advocacy groups throughout Canada, especially among NGOs that serve immigrants, it is acknowledged that Canada's intake levels, internationally, have been higher, proportional to its population, than most other countries.

Although Canada lagged in formally signing the UN refugee convention in 1969 – some eighteen years after its inauguration – it was among the first to set forth clear criteria for determining eligibility of refugees abroad. Annual target numbers for acceptance since 1979 have, again, been proportionally higher than for nearly every other postindustrial nation-state. After several detailed policy documents in the 1980s, with regard to inland refugee (asylum) claimants, Canada adopted an elaborate and costly system of determination of claims that has garnered respect worldwide for its incorporation of human rights principles of applicants. Once again, Canada has embraced broadly inclusive principles to inform its policy of determination.

Although provincial policies on immigration in Ontario have not been formally enunciated, certain features generally reflect a similar pattern of inclusiveness. While there are attempts to 'spread' immigrants through the province, arrivals may move to the city of their choice sometime after arrival. This relatively open policy of 'secondary' migration has significantly augmented the number of newcomers in the Toronto area; to an important extent then, newcomers have 'chosen' to live in the Toronto area.

We note in this volume, however, important differences in perspective with respect to expectations of settlement policy. Authors of the research chapters on the different domains have pointed to gaps between expectation and outcome. Researchers in all the domains we have surveyed have detailed significant instances in which newcomers appear disadvantaged in comparison with other residents of the Toronto area. These illustrations of inclusion and exclusion arise less from instances of overt interpersonal discrimination against peoples of minority backgrounds, and far more often from forms of structural discrimination.

Let us review a sample of these findings to illustrate the variety of structural barriers encountered on arrival in Toronto.

1 Murdie and Teixeira's analysis of the availability of housing stock demonstrates a notable difficulty for newcomers. While lower-cost rental housing has always been a commodity in short supply because of low profit margins and relatively high maintenance costs, even that supply virtually disappeared during the 1990s. Consequently, newcomers cannot locate affordable housing that is adequate for their family needs.
2 Similarly, Preston, Lo, and Wang report that, on the basis of recent census and related data, newcomers experience difficulty in locating occupations in fields appropriate to their training. Occupational profiles reveal large numbers of newly arrived immigrants in service-related occupations with few obvious prospects for advancement.
3 In their analysis of language programs and policy in recent decades, James and Burnaby have found that few English- (or French-) language programs have been adapted to the needs and lifestyle requirements of adult newcomers. Educational administrators have difficulty securing funding, and there are few policy guidelines for such programs.
4 In their extensive review of community programs for newcomers, Siemiatycki and colleagues note that the development of groups for immigrant women have arisen out of necessity. They not only provide assistance and information for members of their own origin but they also help to circumvent apparent blockages in access to needed resources from the wider community.
5 Noh and Kaspar document that the mental health of newcomers – such as experiences of prolonged periods of depression – shows little improvement over the years since arrival. These findings, which have appeared consistently as indicators, have become increasingly applicable to cross-cultural comparisons.

The above examples arouse concern that resources and deliveries of goods and services considered common for all residents have apparently failed to reach newcomers. The editors and authors in this volume have attempted to explain such findings within the frame of processes of social inclusion and exclusion – a patterned means of (positive and negative) discrimination among a variety of peoples inhabiting the same community or area.

The authors have offered a variety of possible interpretations for findings concerning unequal distribution of resources, goods, and services to newcomers to the Toronto area. First, newcomers may not be informed about certain services, either through lack of adequate information in media or other community sources. Second, newcomers may not be attentive to such information, either because they lack facility in English (or French) or because they are unfamiliar with commonly accepted channels of communication. Third, goods and services may be unevenly delivered across the Toronto area and, as demonstrated repeatedly in the literature on ethnic social stratification, across socio-economic strata (Boyd 1984; Reitz 1990, 1998; Ornstein 2000). Each of the above reasons evokes a somewhat different implication for policy change. Unfortunately, our understanding of the underlying causes of such maldistribution among newcomers is less firm than the data documenting it in this book. In any event, policy implications to remedy these shortfalls abound.

By contrast, commentary from the federal policy perspective has rendered a somewhat different interpretation. Burstein and Duncan prefer to understand settlement within the framework of 'integration.' In their sense, processes of 'inclusion' and 'exclusion' appear as subprocesses within the larger 'integration' framework. From that perspective, they remind us that federal policy serves as an overall umbrella to cover not only intake but also settlement. They note, moreover, that settlement issues and policies fall largely to provincial and local jurisdictions. The federal role lies in providing very general conditions for the provincial and metropolitan implementation of settlement strategies. Burstein and Duncan remind us that it is neither appropriate nor possible for the federal government to 'deliver [settlement] programs in an envelope.' The federal role, they assert, does include an obligation to 'manage diversity' through programs, initiatives, and the provision of facilitative instruments, including settlement assistance.

Federal policy analysts acknowledge the consistent and increasing predilection of newcomers to gravitate to metropolitan centres. Burstein and Duncan point out the federal government has an obligation to set standards for 'the housing market, the labour market, the workplace, in health care, in social services.' Viewed from the federal angle, however, settlement strategies and programs in the metropolis should be locally determined. Disparities in distribution of services become part of a regularized political and civic process of give and take. These disparities reflect less systematic structural discrimination, as many researchers argue, and more an evolution of policy and practice that has become more difficult with the proliferation of interests of newcomers to compete against existing priorities.

We judge that this difference in perspective requires closer attention. If the role of federal oversight is to assume cogency, strategies of implementation are no less a component than are guidelines. Disparities in outcome cannot be relegated solely to differences in perspective – oversight versus grounded. It appears off the mark to assert that the state should concern itself with equality of opportunity more than equality of outcome. In this connection, the findings in this volume repeatedly demonstrate blockages in opportunity through low resource bases and inadequate service deliveries. Consequently, the metropolis does not provide a level 'playing field' to ensure equality of opportunity. Furthermore, if this analysis is correct, this state of disequilibrium cannot escape governmental policy attention at any level – federal, provincial, or municipal.

We conclude, therefore, that while perspectives may differ, our analysis of patterns of inclusion and exclusion has revealed an agenda of needed reforms in policies as well as practices of implementation. These policy gaps call out for sustained attention of all policy-makers in Canada. It is not possible to claim distance and separation of powers as sufficient reason to maintain merely a perspective of dispassionate oversight. An agenda of action commends attention and engagement. This agenda calls for more dialogue, re-examination settlement policy formulation, and implementation at the federal level, no less than at the provincial and municipal levels. Continued and even more sustained dialogue between policy-makers and researchers is in order to ensure conditions of maximal inclusiveness in heterogeneous metropolitan areas.

References

Abbate, Gay. 2000. Carjackers target Agincourt, police warn. *Globe and Mail*, 10 March, A16.
Abella, Irving, and Harold Troper. 1982. *None Is Too Many: Canada and the Jews of Europe, 1933–1948*. Toronto: Lester and Orpen Dennys.
Abella, Rosalie S. 1984. *Report of the Commission on Equality in Employment*. Ottawa: Supply and Services Canada.
Access Action of Metropolitan Toronto. 1997. Making human services more accessible. Unpublished Report Submitted to the City of Toronto, Access and Equity Centre.
Acharya, Madhavi. 1998. Turning a vision into a reputation. *Toronto Star*, 9 October, D1, D5.
Achenbach, Thomas M., Stephanie H. McConaughy, and Catherine T. Howell. 1987. Child/adolescent behavioral and emotional problems: Implications of cross-informant correlations for situational specificity. *Psychological Bulletin* 101, no. 2: 213–32.
Adelman, Howard. 1980. Changes in policy. In *The Indochinese Refugee Movement: The Canadian Experience*, edited by H. Adelman, 23–7. Toronto: Operation Lifeline.
– 1982. *Canada and the Indochinese Refugees*. Regina: L.A. Weigl Educational Associates.
– 1991. Refugee determination. *Refuge* 11, no. 2 (December): 1–4, 8–18.
– ed. 1980. *The Indochinese Refugee Movement: The Canadian Experience*. Toronto: Operation Lifeline.
Akbari, Ather H. 1995. The impacts of immigrants on Canada's Treasury, circa 1990. In *Diminishing Returns: The Economics of Canada's Recent Immigration Policy*, edited by Don J. DeVoretz. Toronto: C.D. Howe Institute.

Alba, Richard D. 1990. *Ethnic Identity: The Transformation of White America*. New Haven: Yale University Press.

Alexander, J. 1997. The paradoxes of civil society. *International Sociology* 12, no. 2 (June): 115–33.

Alexander, Ken, and Avis Glaze. 1996. *Towards Freedom: The African-Canadian Experience*. Toronto: Umbrella Press.

Allen, Keith. 1996. The transitional year programme at the University of Toronto: A life-line for blacks seeking a university education. In *Educating African Canadians*, edited by Keren S. Brathwaite and Carl E. James, 234–50. Toronto: Lorimer.

Amaral-Dias, C.A., T.N. Vicente, M.F. Cabrita, and A.R. de Mendon. 1981. Transplantation, identity and drug addiction. *Bulletin of Narcotics* 33: 21–6.

Amaro, H., N.F. Russo, and J. Johnson. 1987. Family and work predictors of psychological well-being among Hispanic women professionals. *Psychology of Women Quarterly* 11: 505–21.

Anderson, Grace, M., and David Higgs. 1976. *A Future to Inherit: Portuguese Communities in Canada*. Toronto: McClelland and Stewart.

Anderson, Kay J. 1991. *Vancouver's Chinatown: Racial Discourse in Canada, 1875–1980*. Montreal: McGill-Queen's University Press.

Anderson, Wolseley W., and Rudolph W. Grant. 1975. *The New Newcomers: Problems of Adjustment of West Indian Immigrant Children in Metropolitan Toronto Schools*. Toronto: York University.

Aneshensel, Carol S. 1992. Social stress: Theory and research. *Annual Review of Sociology* 18: 15–38.

Angus Reid Group. 1991. *Multiculturalism and Canadians: Attitude Study 1991, National Survey Report*. Ottawa: Multiculturalism and Citizenship Canada.

Anisef, Paul. 1975. Consequences of ethnicity for educational plans among grade 12 students in Ontario. In *Education of Immigrant Students*, edited by A. Wolfgang. Toronto: Ontario Institute for Studies in Education.

Anisef, Paul, Paul Axelrod, Etta Baichman, Carl E. James, and Anton H. Turrittin. 2000. *Opportunity and Uncertainty: Life Course Experiences of the Class of '73*. Toronto: University of Toronto Press.

Anisef, Paul, and Kenise Murphy Kilbride. 2000. *The Needs of Newcomer Youth and Emerging 'Best Practices' to Meet Those Needs*. Toronto: Joint Centre of Excellence for Research on Immigration and Settlement.

Ashworth, Mary. 1975. *Immigrant Children and Canadian Schools*. Toronto: McClelland and Stewart.

Aun, Karl. 1985. *The Political Refugees: A History of the Estonians in Canada*. Toronto: McClelland and Stewart in association with the Multiculturalism Directorate, Department of the Secretary of State.

Badets, Jane, and Linda Howatson-Leo. 1999. Recent immigrants in the workforce. *Canadian Social Trends* (Spring): 16–22.

Bagnell, Kenneth. 1989. *Canadese: A Portrait of the Italian Canadians*. Toronto: Macmillan.

Banchevsak, R. 1981. Uprooting and settling: The transplanted family. In *Strangers in the World*, edited by Leo Eitinger and David Schwarz, 107–32. Bern: H. Huber.

Bannerji, Himani. 1997. Geography lessons: On being an insider/outsider to the Canadian nation. In *Dangerous Territories: Struggles for Difference and Equality in Education*, edited by Leslie G. Roman and Linda Eyre, 23–41. New York: Routledge.

Barber, John. 1998. Different colours, changing city. *Globe and Mail*, 20 February.

Barnhard, J.K., and M. Freire. 1996. Latino refugee children in childcare: A study of parents and caregivers. *Canadian Journal of Research in Early Childhood Education* 5, no. 1: 59–71.

Barrett, Stanley. 1987. *Is God a Racist? The Right Wing in Canada*. Toronto: University of Toronto Press.

Basavarajappa, K., and B.P. Verma. 1990. Occupational composition of immigrant women. In *Ethnic Demography: Canadian Immigrant, Racial and Cultural Variations*, edited by Shiva S. Halli et al. Ottawa: Carleton University Press.

Beaujot, Roderic. 1991. *Population Change in Canada: The Challenges of Policy Adaptation*. Toronto: McClelland and Stewart.

Beiser, M. 1988. Influences of time, ethnicity, and attachment of depression in Southeast Asian refugees. *American Journal of Psychiatry* 145: 46–51.

– n.d. Tuberculosis in immigrants. Unpublished.

Beiser, M., R. Dion, A. Gotowiec, and I. Hyman. 1995. Immigrant and refugee children in Canada. *Canadian Journal of Psychiatry* 40, no. 2: 67–72.

Beiser, M., and J.A. Fleming. 1986. Measuring psychiatric disorder among Southeast Asian refugees. *Psychological Medicine* 16, no. 3: 627–39.

Beiser, M., and F. Hou. 2001. Language acquisition, unemployment and depressive disorder among Southeast Asian refugees: A ten-year study (Canada). *Social Science and Medicine* 53: 1321–34.

Beiser, M., F. Hou, I. Hyman, and M. Tousignant. 2002. Poverty, family processes and the mental health of new immigrant children in Canada. *American Journal of Public Health* 92: 220–7.

Beiser, M., F. Hou, V. Kaspar, and S. Noh. 2000. Changes in poverty status on developmental behaviors of 4- to 11-year-old children in Statistics Canada's National Longitudinal Survey of Children and Youth. Paper submitted to Human Resources and Development Canada, Directed Research Program,

Income Security and social Development Studies, Applied Research Branch, Strategic Policy.
Beiser, M., and I. Hyman. 1997. Refugees' time perspective and mental health. *American Journal of Psychiatry* 154, no. 7: 996–1002.
Berridge, Joe. 1995. Is Toronto different from U.S. cities? Was it planned that way? *Globe and Mail*, 10 April, A13.
Berridge Lewinberg Greenberg Dark Gabor Ltd., and M. Gerler. 1995. *Adapting to the New Realities: Industrial Land Outlook for Metropolitan Toronto, Durham, York, Halton, Peel, Hamilton-Wentworth and Waterloo.* Report prepared for the Muncipality of Metropolitan Toronto. Toronto: Municipality of Metropolitan Toronto.
Berry, J.W., Uichol Kim, Thomas Minde, and Doris Mok. 1987. Comparative studies of acculturative stress. *International Migration Review* 21, no. 3: 491–511.
Berton, Pierre. 1961. *The New City: A Prejudiced View of Toronto.* Toronto: Macmillan.
Beserve, Christopher. 1976. Adjustment problems of West Indian children in Britain and Canada: A Perspective and a review of some findings. In *Black Students in Urban Canada*, edited by Vincent D'Oyley and Harry Silverman. Toronto: Ministry of Culture and Recreation, Citizenship Branch.
Bill Graham Report, The. 1994. Toronto: Bill Graham's Constituency Office.
Binkin, N.J., P.L. Zuber, C.D. Wells, M.A. Tipple, and K.G. Castro. 1996. Overseas screening for tuberculosis in immigrants and refugees to the United States: Current status. *Clinical Infectious Diseases* 23, no. 6: 1226–32.
Blau, Peter M. 1964. *Exchange and Power in Social Life.* New York: Wiley.
Board of Education for the City of Etobicoke. 1993. *Students' Perspectives on Current Issues.* Toronto: Etobicoke Board of Education.
Bogue, Charles A., and G. Sabir Shaleek. 1979. *Labour Market Experiences of Recent Immigrants to Canada.* Toronto: Research Branch, Ontario Ministry of Labour.
Bolt, G., J. Burgers, and R. van Kempen. 1998. On the social significance of spatial location, spatial segregation and social inclusion. *Netherlands Journal of Housing and the Built Environment* 13, no. 1: 83–95.
Borowy, Jan, Shelley Gordon, and Gail Lebans. 1993. Are these clothes clean? The campaign for fair wages and working conditions for homeowners. In *And Still We Rise: Feminist Political Mobilizing in Contemporary Canada*, edited by Linda Carty. Toronto: Women's Press.
Boyd, Monica. 1984. At a disadvantage: The occupational attainments of foreign-born women in Canada. *International Migration Review* 18, no. 4: 1091–119.

- 1990. Sex differences in occupational skill: Canada, 1961–1986. *Canadian Review of Sociology and Anthropology* 21, no. 3: 285–315.
- 1991. *Gender, Visible Minority and Immigrant Earnings Inequality: Reassessing an Employment Equity Premise.* Departmental working paper 91-6, Department of Sociology and Anthropology, Carleton University, Ottawa.

Bradley, Susan, and Leon Sloman. 1975. Elective mutism in immigrant families. *Journal of the American Academy of Child Psychiatry* 14, no. 3: 510–14.

Brathwaite, Keren S. 1989. The black student and the school: A Canadian dilemma. In *African Continuities / L'Heritage Africain*, edited by Simeon Waliaula Chilungu and Sada Niang. Toronto: Terebi.
- 1996. Keeping watch over our children: The role of African Canadian parents on the educational team. In *Educating African Canadians*, edited by Keren S. Brathwaite and Carl E. James, 107–30. Toronto: Lorimer.

Breton, Raymond. 1964. Institutional completeness of ethnic communities and personal relations of immigrants. *American Journal of Sociology* 70, 193–205.
- 1978. The structure of relationships between ethnic collectivities. In *The Canadian Ethnic Mosaic: A Quest for Identity*, edited by L. Driedger, 55–73. Toronto: McClelland and Stewart.
- 1979. From a different perspective: French Canada and the issue of immigration and multiculturalism. *TESL Talk* 10, no. 3: 45–56.
- 1990. The ethnic group as a political resource in relation to problems of incorporation: Perceptions and attitudes. In *Ethnic Identity and Equality: Varieties of Experience in a Canadian City*, edited by R. Breton, W.I. Isajiw, W. Kalbach, and J. Reitz, 196–255. Toronto: University of Toronto Press.
- 1992. *Report of the Academic Advisory Panel on the Social and Cultural Impacts of Immigration: Meeting on Indicators of Integration.* Ottawa: Research Division, Strategic Planning and Research.
- 1998. Ethnicity and race in social organization: Recent developments in Canadian society. In *The Vertical Mosaic Revisited*, edited by Rick Helmes-Hayes and James Curtis, 60–115. Toronto: Univerity of Toronto Press.

Breton, Raymond, Wsevolod Isajiw, Warren Kalbach, and Jeffrey Reitz. 1990. *Ethnic Identity and Equality: Varieties of Experience in a Canadian City.* Toronto: University of Toronto Press.

Brouwer, Andrew. 1999. *Immigrants Need Not Apply.* Ottawa: Caledon Institute of Social Policy.

Brown, Robert Craig. 1996. Full partnership in the fortunes and future of the nation. In *Ethnicity and Citizenship: The Canadian Case*, edited by Jean Laponce and William Safran. London: Frank Cass.

Brown, Robert S. 1992. *The 1991 Every Secondary Student Survey: Initial Findings #200.* Toronto: Research Services, Toronto Board of Education.

- 1993. *A Follow-Up of the Grade 9 Cohort of 1987 Every Secondary Student Survey Participants #207*. Toronto: Research Services, Toronto Board of Education.
Burke, J.D., J.F. Borus, B.J. Burns, K.H. Millstein, and M.C. Beasley. 1982. Changes in children's behavior after a natural disaster. *American Journal of Psychiatry* 139, no. 8: 1010–14.
Burnaby, B. 1992. Official language training for adult immigrants in Canada: Features and issues. In *Socio-Political Aspects of ESL*, edited by B. Burnaby and A. Cumming. Toronto: Ontario Institute for Studies in Education.
- 1998a. English as a second language for adult immigrants. In *Learning for Life: Canadian Readings in Adult Education*, edited by S.M. Scott, B. Spencer, and A.M. Thomas. Toronto: Thompson Educational Publishing.
- 1998b. ESL policy in Canada and the United States: Basis for comparison. In *Language and Politics in the United States and Canada: Myths and Realities*, edited by T. Ricento and B. Burnaby. Mahwah, NJ: Lawrence Erlbaum.
Burnaby, B., M. Holt, N. Steltzer, and N. Collins. 1987. *The Settlement Language Training Program: An Assessment*. Report on behalf of the TESL Canada Federation. Ottawa: Employment and Immigration Canada.
Burnaby, B., C.E. James, and S. Regier. 2000. *The Role of Education in Integrating Diversity in the Greater Toronto Area*. Toronto: Joint Centre of Excellence for Research on Immigration and Settlement – Toronto, Working Papers Series.
Burnam, M. Audrey, Richard L. Hough, Marvin Karno, Javier I. Escobar, and Cynthia A. Telles. 1987. Acculturation and lifetime prevalence of psychiatric disorders among Mexican Americans in Los Angeles. *Journal of Health and Social Behavior* 28, no. 1: 89–102.
Burnet, Jean. 1976. Ethnicity calling: Canadian experience and policy. *Sociological Focus* 9, no. 2: 199–207.
- 1979. Myths and multiculturalism. *Canadian Journal of Education* 4, no. 4: 43–58.
Burstein, M. 1991. *Immigration in Canada: A Statistical Report for the Continuous Reporting System on Migration of the OECD*. Ottawa: Employment and Immigration Canada, Strategic Planning and Research Branch, Immigration Policy Group.
Buttrick, John. 1977. *Who Goes to University from Toronto?* Toronto: Ontario Economic Council.
Buzzelli, Michael. 2000. Toronto's postwar little Italy: Landscape change and ethnic relations. *Canadian Geographers* 44: 298–305.
Byrnes, Deborah. 1982. Hard battles ahead: A note on the future perspectives of minority children. *Psychology in the Schools* 19 (October): 513–16.
- 1999. *Social Exclusion*. Buckingham: Open University Press.
Byrnes, F.C. 1966. Role shock: An occupational hazard of American technical

assistants abroad. *Annals of the American Academy of Political and Social Science* 368: 95–108.

Calliste, Agnes. 1982. Educational and occupational expectations of high school students. *Multiculturalism* 5, no. 3: 14–19.

– 1991. Canada's immigration policy and domestics from the Caribbean. *Socialist Studies* 5: 136–68.

– 1996a. African Canadians organizing for educational change. In *Educating African Canadians*, edited by Keren S. Brathwaite and Carl E. James, 87–106. Toronto: Lorimer.

– 1996b. Anti-Racism organizing and resistance: Blacks in urban Canada, 1940s–1970s. In *City Lives and City Forms: Critical Research and Canadian Urbanism*, edited by Jon Caulfied and Linda Peake. Toronto: University of Toronto Press.

Canada Employment and Immigration Advisory Council. 1991a. *Immigrants and Language Training: A Report Presented to the Minister of Employment and Immigration*. Ottawa: CEIAC.

– 1991b. *National Symposium on Settlement and Integration: Recommendations*. Ottawa: CEIAC.

– 1991c. *Immigrants and Language Training*. Ottawa: CEIAC.

Canada Employment and Immigration Commission. 1987. *A Discussion Paper on a New Framework for Immigrant Language Training*. Ottawa: CEIAC.

Canada Mortgage and Housing Corporation. 1999. *Special Studies on 1996 Census Data: Canadian Housing Statistics*. Socio-economic Series 55-1. Ottawa: Canada Mortgage and Housing Corporation.

Canadian Council for Refugees. 1998. Best settlement practices: Settlement services for refugees and immigrants in Canada. Based on workshops conducted by the CCR conferences held in Edmonton.

– 2001. Refugee claimants via USA. <http:www.web.net/nccr>. 3 Oct.

– 2002. Press Release: Scrapping of refugee appeal makes a mockery of parliamentary process. <http:www.web.net/nccr>. 29 April.

Canadian Ethnic Studies. 1975. Special issue on the green paper 7, no. 1.

Canadian Institute for Health Information. 2002. Discharge Abstract Database. Data quality re-abstraction study: Combined findings for fiscal years 1999/2000 and 2000/2001. Ottawa: Canadian Institute for Health Information. <http://dsp-psd.communication.gc.ca/Collection/H118-10-2002E.pdf>.

Canadian Institute of Public Opinion. 1946. Public Opinion News Service Release, 30 October.

Canadian Task Force. 1988. *Review of the Literature on Migrant Mental Health*. Canadian Task Force on Mental Health Issues Affecting Immigrants and Refugees. Ottawa: Minister of Supply and Services Canada.

Cannon, Margaret. 1989. *China Tide: The Revealing Story of the Hong Kong Exodus to Canada*. Toronto: Harper Collins.
Carey, Elaine. 1997. Toronto magnet for immigrants. *Toronto Star*, 5 November, A1.
– 1999a. Black pride, city prejudice: Discrimination lingers on. *Toronto Star*, 3 July, A1, A4.
– 1999b. Close-knit Portuguese community starts to spread its wings. *Toronto Star*, 13 June, A1, A6.
– 1999c. Poverty rising among Chinese, professor says Chinese community feels prejudice. *Toronto Star*, 10 May, A1, A8.
– 1999d. The 'city that works' could be even better. *Toronto Star*, 1 May, A1, A10, A11.
– 2000. City's diversity key to Olympics sales pitch. *Toronto Star*, 1 September, F1.
– 2001. High-rise ghettoes. *Toronto Star*, 3 February, G1.
Carroll, W. 1974. The response of the Canadian academic community to the Chilean crisis. *Bulletin of the Association of University Teachers* (October): 1.
Carty, Linda. 1994. African Canadian women and the state: 'Labour only' please. In *We're Rooted Here and They Can't Pull Us Up: Essays in African Canadian Women's History*, edited by Peggy Bristow et al., 193–229. Toronto: University of Toronto Press.
Castles, Stephen, and Miller, Mark. 1993. *The Age of Migration: International Movements in the Modern World*. New York: Guilford Press.
Caulfield, Jon. 1994. *City Form and Everyday Life: Toronto's Gentrification and Critical Social Practice*. Toronto: University of Toronto Press.
Centre of Excellence for Research on Immigration and Settlement (CERIS). 1997. Access Action Council of Metropolitan Toronto. *Newsletter*. Toronto: Centre of Excellence for Research on Immigration and Settlement. December.
Chan, Anthony. 1983. *Gold Mountain: The Chinese in the New World*. Vancouver: New Star Books.
Chan, Janet B.L., and Yuet-Wah Cheung. 1985. Ethnic resources and business enterprise: A study of Chinese business in Toronto. *Human Organization* 44: 142–54.
Chen, J. 1999. Health of immigrants in Canada: A longitudinal perspective. An invited paper presentation to the Fourth National Metropolis Conference, Toronto, 22 March.
Chen, J., E. Ng, and R. Wilkins. 1996. The health of Canada's immigrants in 1994–5. *Health Reports* 7, no. 4: 33–45.
Chen, J., R. Wilkins, and E. Ng. 1996. Health expectancy by immigrant status. *Health Reports* 8, no. 3: 29–37.

Cheng, Maisy. 1996. *Anti-Racist Education Project: A Summary Report on the Extent of Implementation and Changes Found in Wards 11/12 Schools: 1991–92 to 1994–95 #223*. Toronto: Toronto Board of Education.

Cheng, M., and M. Yau. 1998a. *The 1991 Every Secondary Student Survey: Preliminary Findings #207*. Toronto: Toronto Board of Education.

– 1998b. *The 1997 Every Secondary Student Survey: Preliminary Findings #227*. Toronto: Toronto District School Board.

– 1999. *The 1997 Every Secondary Student Survey: Detailed Findings #230*. Toronto: Toronto Board of Education.

Cheng, Maisy, Edgar Wright, and Syliva Larter. 1980. *Steaming in Toronto and Other Ontario Schools: A Review of the Literature #157*. Toronto: Toronto Board of Education for the City of Toronto.

Cheng, Maisy, Maria Yau, and Suzanne Ziegler. 1993a. *The 1991 Secondary Student Survey. Part II: Detailed Profiles of Toronto's Secondary Students #204*. Toronto: Toronto Board of Education.

– 1993b. *The 1991 Every Secondary Student Survey. Part III: Program Level and Student Achievement #205*. Toronto: Toronto Board of Education.

Chidley, Joe. 1997. The fight for Toronto. *Maclean's*, 15 March, 46–50.

Chimbos, Peter D. 1980. *The Canadian Odyssey: The Greek Experience in Canada*. Toronto: McClelland and Stewart; Ottawa: Multiculturalism Directorate.

Chinese Canadian National Council. 1997. *Generous Together*. Toronto: CCNC.

– 1998. *Image Revision*. Toronto: CCNC.

Chisman, F.P., H.S. Wrigley, and D.T. Ewen. 1993. *ESL and the American Dream*. Washington, DC: Southport Institute for Policy Analysis.

Chiswick, Barry R. 1992. Introduction. In *Immigration, Language, and Ethnicity: Canada and the United States*, edited by B. Chiswick. Washington, DC: AEI Press.

Chodzinski, R. 1986. The role of the school counsellor in multicultural education. In *Multicultural Education: Programmes and Methods*, edited by R.J. Samuda and S.L. Kong, 11–88. Kingston, ON: Intercultural Social Sciences Publication.

Citizenship and Immigration Canada. 1993. *Immigration Consultations. 1993: The Federal Immigration Integration Strategy in 1993: A Progress Report*. Ottawa: Employment and Immigration Canada.

– 1997. *Not Just Numbers: A Canadian Framework for Future Immigration*. Ottawa: Minister of Public Works and Government Services Canada.

– Business Immigration Division. 1997a. *Business Immigration Program Review*. Ottawa: Citizenship and Immigration Canada.

– 1998. *Building on a Strong Foundation for the Twenty-first Century: New Directions for Immigration and Refugee Policy and Legislation*. Ottawa: Minister of Public Works and Government Services Canada.

- 1999a. *Facts and Figures 1998: Immigration Overview.* Ottawa. Citizenship and Immigration Canada.
- 1999b. *1999 Facts and Figures: Immigration Overview.* <http:www.cic.gc.ca/english/pub/index-2.html#statistics>.
- 2000a. Bill C-11: Immigration and Refugee Protection Act. <http:www.cic.gc.ca/english/about/policyc11-reg.html>.
- 2000b. News Release: Caplan tables new Immigration and Refugee Acts. <http: www.cic.gc.ca/english/press/00/0009-pre.html>. 6 April.

City of Toronto. 1998. *Profile Toronto: Immigrants in Toronto.* Toronto: Urban Planning and Development Services.
- 1999a. Framework for citizen participation in the City of Toronto. Report no. 2 of the Special Committee to Review the Final Report of the Toronto Transition Team. Adopted by Toronto City Council. 2 March.
- 1999b. Final recommendations of the task force on community access and equity. Report no. 11 of the Policy and Finance Committee. Adopted by Toronto City Council. 14 December.
- 2000. Terms of reference – Immigration and settlement policy framework. Report no. 5 of the Community Services Committee. Adopted by Toronto City Council. 7 June.

C.I.P.S. 1974. *Immigration Policy Perspectives, The Immigration Programme, Immigration and Population Statistics, and Three Years in Canada.* Ottawa: Manpower and Immigration Canada.

Clark, William. A.V. 1998. *The California Cauldron: Immigration and the Fortunes of Local Communities.* New York: Guilford Press.

Clayton Research Associates Limited. 1994. *Immigrant Housing Choices, 1986.* Ottawa: Canada Mortgage and Housing Corporation.

Coelho, Elizabeth. 1988. *Caribbean Students in Canadian Schools.* Toronto: Carib-Can Publishers.

Colton, Timothy J. 1980. *Big Daddy: Frederick G. Gardiner and the Building of Metropolitan Toronto.* Toronto: University of Toronto Press.

Columbo, John. 1987. *Columbo's New Canadian Quotations.* Edmonton: Hurtig Publishers.

Commission of Inquiry on War Criminals. 1986. *Report, Part I: Public.* Ottawa: Minister of Supply and Services Canada.

Consultative Committee on the Education of Black Students in Toronto Schools. 1988. *Final Report of the Consultative Committee on the Education of Black Students in Toronto Schools.* Toronto: Toronto Board of Education.

Contenta, Sandra. 1986. Rebel chief ready for the unexpected. *Toronto Star*, 7 December, H4.

Costa, Elio, and Odoardo Di Santo. 1972. The Italian child, his family, and the

Canadian school system. In *Must Schools Fail? The Growing Debate in Canadian Education*, edited by N. Byrne and J. Quarter, 242–50. Toronto: McClelland and Stewart.

Cousens, Don. 1998. Interview. Toronto, Ontario, 30 July.

Cousins, C. 1999. Social exclusion in Europe: Paradigms of social disadvantage in Germany, Spain, Sweden and the UK. *Policy and Politics* 26, no. 2.

Cray, E. 1997. Teachers' perceptions of a language policy: 'Teaching LINC.' *TESL Canada Journal* 15, no. 1: 238.

Croucher, Sheila. 1997. Constructing the image of ethnic harmony in Toronto, Canada. *Urban Affairs Review* 32: 319–48.

Cumming, A., D. Hart, D. Corson, and J. Cummins. 1993. *Provisions and Demands for ESL, ESD, and ALF Programs in Ontario Schools*. Toronto: Modern Language Centre, Ontario Institute for Studies in Education.

Cummings, Peter, Enid Lee, and D.G. Oreopoulos. 1989. *Access! Task Force on Access to Professionals and Trades in Ontario*. Toronto: Ontario Ministry of Citizenship.

Cummins, Jim. 1984. *Bilingualism and Special Education: Issues in Assessment and Pedagogy*. Clevedon, UK: Multilingual Matters.

– 1997. Minority status and schooling in Canada. *Anthropology and Education Quarterly* 28, no. 3: 411–30.

Curtis, Bruce, David Livingstone, and Harry Smaller. 1992. *Stacking the Deck: The Streaming of Working-class Kids in Ontario Schools*. Toronto: Our Schools/Our Selves Education Foundation.

daCosta, Granville A. 1976. Counselling and the Black child. In *Black Students in Urban Canada*, edited by V. D'Oyley and H. Silverman. Toronto: TESL Talk, Ministry of Culture and Recreation, Citizenship Branch.

Danys, Milda. 1986. *DP: Lithuanian Immigration to Canada after the Second World War*. Toronto: Multicultural History Society of Ontario.

Danziger, Kurt. 1971. *The Socialization of Immigrant Children*. Research Report. Toronto: York University Ethnic Research Programme, Institute for Behavioural Research.

– 1978. Differences in acculturation and patterns of socialization among Italian immigrant families. In *Socialization and Values in Canadian Society*, edited by E. Zureik and R.M. Pike. Toronto: McClelland and Stewart.

Das Gupta, Tania. 1986. *Learning from Our History – Community Development by Immigrant Women in Ontario, 1958–1986: A Tool for Action*. Toronto: Cross Cultural Communication Centre.

Davis, James A. 1984. New money, an old man/lady, and two's company: Subjective welfare in NORC general social surveys, 1972–1982. *Social Indicators Research* 15: 319–41.

Dei, George S. 1996. Black/African Canadian students' perspectives on school racism. In *Racism in Canadian Schools*, edited by I. Alladin. Toronto: Harcourt Brace.

Dei, George S., J. Muzza, E. McIsaac, and J. Zine. 1997. *Reconstructing 'Dropout': A Critical Ethnography of the Dynamics of Black Students' Disengagement from School*. Toronto: University of Toronto Press.

Dennis, R. 1997. Property and propriety: Jewish landlords in early twentieth-century Toronto. *Transactions of the Institute of British Geographers* 22: 377–97.

Denovan, Kevin. 1986. Dragon centre a hub for Chinese traffic problems ample evidence the 70 shops are big attraction. *Toronto Star*, 7 July, A6.

Deosaran, Ramesh. 1975. *Educational Aspirations, What Matters: A Literature Review #135*. Toronto: Toronto Board of Education.

– 1976. *The 1975 Every Student Survey: Parent's Occupation, Student's Mother Tongue and Immigrant Status #139*. Toronto: Toronto Board of Education.

Deosaran, R., E.N. Wright, and T. Kane. 1976. *The 1975 Every Student Survey: Student's Background and Its Relationship to Program Placement #138*. Toronto: Toronto Board of Education.

Department of Manpower and Immigration Canada. 1974a. *A Report of the Canadian Immigration and Population Study*. Vol. 1: *Immigration Policy Perspectives*; Vol. 2: *The Immigration Program*; Vol. 3: *Immigration and Population Statistics*; Vol. 4: *Three Years in Canada*. Ottawa: Department of Manpower and Immigration.

– 1974b. *Green Paper on Immigration and Population*. Vol. 1. Ottawa: Information Canada.

DeSilva, Arnold. 1992. *Earnings of Immigrants: A Comparative Analysis*. Ottawa: Economic Council of Canada.

Devereaux, M.S. 1985. *One in Every Five: A Survey of Adult Education in Canada*. Ottawa: Statistics Canada, Department of the Secretary of State, and Education Support Sector.

DeVoretz, Don J. 1995. New issues, new evidence, and new immigration policies for the twenty-first century. In *Diminishing Returns: The Economics of Canada's Recent Immigration Policy*, edited by Don J. DeVortz. Toronto: C.D. Howe Institute.

Dion, K.L. 1975. Women's reactions to discrimination from members of the same and opposite sex. *Journal of Research in Personality* 9: 294–306.

Dion, K.L., and B.M. Earn. 1975. The phenomenology of being a target of prejudice. *Journal of Personality and Social Psychology* 32, no. 5: 944–50.

Dion, K.L., and A.W. Pak. 1992. Personality-based hardiness as a buffer for discrimination-related stress in memberrs of Toronto's Chinese community. *Canadian Journal of Behavioral Sciences* 24: 517–36.

Dirks, Gerald. 1977. *Canada's Refugee Policy: Indifference or Opportunism?* Montreal: McGill-Queen's University Press.
- 1985. Canadian refugee policy: Humanitarian and political dimensions. In *Refugees and World Politics*, edited by E.G. Ferris, 120–35. New York: Praeger.
Donelan, K., R.J. Blendon, C. Schoen, K. Davis, and K. Binns. 1999. The cost of health system change: Public discontent in five nations. *Health Affairs* 18, no. 3: 206–16.
Donovan, J., E. d'Espaignet, C. Merton, and M. VanOmmeren. 1992. *Immigrants in Australia: A Health Profile*. Australian Institute of Health and Welfare: Ethnic Health Series, No. 1. Canberra: AGPS.
Doucet, Michael. 1999. *Toronto in Transition: Demographic Change in the Late Twentieth Century*. Toronto: Joint Centre of Excellence for Research on Immigration and Settlement.
Dougherty, C. 1999. New entrants to the labor market: a comparison of the labor market performance of immigrants landed in the 1980s and 1990s. Paper presented at the Fourth Annual International Metropolis Conference, Washington, DC, December.
Doyle, Robert, and Khan Rahi, eds. 1991. *Organizational Change Toward Multiculturalism*. Toronto: Access Action Council of Metropolitan Toronto.
Doyle, Robert, and Livy Visano. 1987. *A Time for Action: Access to Health and Social Service for Members of Diverse Cultural and Racial Groups*. Toronto: Social Planning Council of Metropolitan Toronto.
D'Oyley, V. 1976. Entering urban education: The case of the Black student. *TESL Talk* 7, no. 1: 1–34.
Dreisziger, N.F. 1982. *Struggle and Hope: The Hungarian Canadian Experience*. Toronto: McClelland and Stewart in association with the Multiculturalism Directorate, Department of the Secretary State, and the Canadian Government Publishing Centre, Supply and Services Canada.
Duffy, K. 1995. *Social Exclusion and Human Dignity in Europe*. Cedex, France: Council of Europe.
Dun and Bradstreet Canada. 1997. *1997 Regional Business Directory of Toronto*. Mississauga: Dun and Bradstreet Canada.
Ebersold, S. 1998. *Exclusion and Disability*. Organization for economic cooperation and development centre for educational research and innovation. Available from <http://www1.oecd.org/els/pdfs/EDSCERIDOCA029.pdf>.
Economic Council of Canada. 1978. *A Time for Reason: Fifteenth Annual Review of the Economic Council of Canada*. Hull, QC: Supply and Services Canada.
- 1991. *New Faces in the Crowd: Economic and Social Impacts of Immigration: A Statement*. Ottawa: ECC.
Eitinger, Leo, and David Schwartz. 1981. *Strangers in the World*. Bern: H. Huber.

Employment and Immigration Canada. 1980. *Indochinese Refugees: The Canadian Response, 1970 and 1980*. Ottawa: Employment and Immigration Canada.
- 1987. *Profiles of Canadian Immigration*. Ottawa: Employment and Immigration Canada.
- 1990. *Annual Report to Parliament: Immigration Plan for 1991–1995*. Ottawa: Minister of Supply and Services Canada.

Employment and Immigration Canada. Public Affairs Branch. 1990. *Report on the Consultations on Immigration for 1991–1995*. Ottawa: Employment and Immigration Canada.
- 1992. *Managing Immigration: A Framework for the 1990s*. Ottawa: Employment and Immigration Canada.
- 1993. *The Management of Immigration*. Ottawa: Employment and Immigration Canada.
- 1999. *Report on the Consultations on Immigration: A Framework for the 1990s*. Ottawa: Employment and Immigration Canada.

Escobar, J.I. 1998. Immigration and mental health: Why are immigrants better off? *Archives of General Psychiatry* 55, no. 9: 781–2.

Escobar, J.I., and E.T. Randolph. 1982. The Hispanic and social networks. In *Mental Health and Hispanic Americans: Clinical Perspectives*, edited by R.M. Becerra, M. Karno, and J.I. Escobar, 41–57. New York: Grune and Stratton.

Essed, Philomena. 1991. *Understanding Everyday Racism: An Interdisciplinary Theory*. Newbury Park, CA: Sage Publications.

Estable, Alma. 1986. Immigrant women in Canada: Current issues. Background paper prepared for the Canadian Advisory Council on the Status of Women, 21–4. Ottawa: Canadian Advisory Council on the Status of Women.

Evenden, L.J., and G.E. Walker. 1993. From periphery to centre: The changing geography of the suburbs. In *The Changing Social Geography of Canadian Cities*, edited by L.S. Bourne and D.F. Ley. Montreal: McGill-Queen's University Press.

Fagnan, Sheila. 1995. Canadian immigrants' earnings, 1971–1986. In *Diminishing Returns: The Economics of Canada's Recent Immigration Policy*, edited by Don J. DeVoretz. Toronto: C.D. Howe Institute.

Farah, M. 1999. Immigrants experience in accessing housing in Metropolitan Toronto: A case study opf the Somali population. Master's thesis, Environmental Studies, York University.

Fennel, T., and DeMont, J. 1989. *Hong Kong Money: How Chinese Families and Fortunes Are Changing Canadian Business*. Toronto: Key Porter.

Fernando, Viresh. 1997. Interview. 19 November.

Fitinger, L., and Schwartz, D. 1981. *Strangers in the World*. Bern: Hans Huber.

Fleming, Douglas. 1998. Autonomy and agency in curriculum decision-making: A study of instructors in a Canadian adult settlement ESL program. *TESL. Canada Journal* 16, no. 1: 19–35.

Fong, Eric, and Ambrose Ma. 1998. Chinese ethnic economy in Toronto. Research Report to the Toronto Joint Centre of Excellence for Research on Immigration and Settlement.

Foster, Cecil. 1996. *A Place Called Heaven: The Meaning of Being Black in Canada*. Toronto: HarperCollins Publishers.

Frager, Ruth A. 1992. *Sweatshop Strife: Class, Ethnicity, and Gender in the Jewish Labour Movement of Toronto, 1900–1939*. Toronto: University of Toronto Press.

Fram, I., G. Broks, P. Crawford, J. Handscombe, and A.E. Virgin. 1977. *'I Don't Know Yet' – West Indian Students in North York Schools: A Study of Adaptive Behaviours*. Research Report. Toronto: North York Board of Education.

Francis, Diane. 1999a. These refugees and immigrants can be deadly. *National Post*, 24 July, D3.

– 1999b. Illegal aliens should be sent back. *National Post*, 24 August C3.

Freiler, C. 2000. Social inclusion as a focus of well being for children and families. Paper prepared for the Advisory Committee, Children's Agenda Program, Laidlaw Foundation, Toronto.

Frideres, J., and W. Reeves. 1989. The ability to implement human rights legislation in Canada. *Canadian Review of Sociology and Anthropology* 26: 311–32.

Fulford, Robert. 1995. *Accidental City: The Transformation of Toronto*. Toronto: Macfarlane, Walter and Ross.

Gairey, Harry. 1981. *A Black Man's Toronto, 1914–1980: The Reminiscences of Harry Gairey*. Toronto: Multicultural History Society of Ontario.

Galster, G., K. Metzger, and R. Waite. 1999. Neighbourhood opportunity structures and immigrants' socioeconomic advancement. *Journal of Housing Research* 10, no. 1: 95–127.

Gates, Paul W. 1934. Official encouragement to immigration by the province of Canada. *Canadian Historical Review* 15: 24–38.

George, Usha, and M.S. Mwarigha. 1999. Consultation on Settlement Programming for African Newcomers. University of Toronto.

Germain, A., and J.E. Gagnon. 1999. Is neighbourhood a black box? A reply to Galster, Metzger and Waite. *Canadian Journal of Urban Research* 8, no. 2: 172–84.

Ghosh, Ratna. 1996. *Redefining Multicultural Education*. Toronto: Harcourt Brace.

Gibson, Margaret. 1997. Complicating the immigrant/involuntary minority typology. *Anthropology and Education Quarterly* 28, no. 3: 431–54.

Gibson, Margaret, and John Ogbu, eds., 1991. *Minority Status and Schooling: A Comparative Study of Immigrant and Involuntary Minorities*. New York: Garland Publishing.

Globe and Mail. 1999. Anger over the illegals. 14 August, D11.

Goldberg, David Theo. 1993. *Racist Culture: Philosophy and the Politics of Meaning.* Cambridge, MA: Blackwell.

Golden, A., W.H. Currie, E. Greaves, and J. Latimer. 1999. *Taking Responsibility for Homelessness: An Action Plan for Toronto.* Toronto: Mayor's Homelessness Action Task Force.

Goldstein, T. 1993. Working with learners in LINC programs: Asking ourselves some questions. Contact: *Newsletter of the Association of Teachers of English as a Second Language of Ontario* 18, no. 2: 12–13.

Gopie, Kamala Jean. 1995. Partnerships. *Currents: Readings in Race Relations* 8, no. 3: 23–4.

Green, A.G., and D.A. Green. 1995. Canadian immigration policy: The effectiveness of the point system and other instruments. *Canadian Journal of Economics* 28: 1006–41.

Guthrie, G.M. 1975. A behavioral analysis of culture learning. In *Cross Cultural Perspectives on Learning,* edited by R.W. Brislin, S. Bochner, and W.J. Lonner. Beverly Hills, CA: Sage Publications.

Hagan, J.M. 1998. Social networks, gender, and immigrant incorporation: Resources and constraints. *American Sociological Review* 63: 55–67.

Hall, James, Jr. 1990. *Proceedings of the Conference on Strategies for Improving Access and Retention of Ethno-Specific and Visible Minority Students in Ontario's Post-Secondary Institutions.* Toronto: Ryerson Polytechnic Institute.

Hamilton, Robert M., ed. 1952. *Canadian Quotations and Phrases: Literary and Historical.* Toronto: McClelland and Stewart.

Handlin, Oscar. 1951. *The Uprooted: The Epic Story of the Great Migrations that Made the American People.* New York: Grosset and Dunlap.

Handscombe, Jean, and Nancy Becker. 1994. *A Week in School.* Research Report. North York: North York Board of Education.

Hansen, Marcus Lee, and John Bartlet Brebner. 1940. *The Mingling of the Canadian and American Peoples.* New Haven: Yale University Press.

Harney, Nicholas. D. 1998. *Eh, Paesan! Being Italian in Toronto.* Toronto: University of Toronto Press.

Harney, Robert. 1983. The Italian community in Toronto. In *Two Nations, Many Cultures: Ethnic Groups in Canada,* edited by J.L. Elliot. Scarborough, ON: Prentice-Hall.

– 1985. Ethnicity and neighbourhoods. In *Gathering Place: Peoples and Neighbourhoods of Toronto, 1834–1945,* edited by Robert Harney. Toronto: Multicultural History Society of Ontario.

– 1990. Ethnicity and neighbourhoods. In *Cities and Urbanization: Canadian Historical Perspectives,* edited by Gilbert Stelter. Toronto: Copp Clark.

Harris, R. 2000. Housing. In *Canadian Cities in Transition: The Twenty-first*

Century, 2nd ed., edited by Trudi Bunting and Pierre Filion. Toronto: Oxford University Press.

Hawkins, Freda. 1972. *Canada and Immigration: Public Policy and Public Concern*. Montreal: McGill-Queen's University Press.

– 1988. *Canada and Immigration: Public Policy and Public Concern*. 2nd ed. Montreal: McGill-Queen's University Press.

– 1991. *Critical Years in Immigration: Canada and Australia Compared*. 2nd ed. Montreal: McGill-Queen's University Press.

Hawthorne, L. 1999. Female, mobile and skilled: The migration process and professional integration of ESB and NESB nurses in Australia, 1986–1996. Paper presented at the Fourth Annual International Metropolis Conference, December, Washington, DC.

Head, Wilson. 1975. *The Black Presence in the Canadian Mosaic: A Study of Perception and the Practice of Discrimination against Blacks in Metropolitan Toronto*. Toronto: Ontario Human Rights Commission.

– 1980. *Adaptation of Immigrants: Perceptions of Ethnic and Racial Discrimination*. Toronto: York University.

– 1984. Historical, social, and cultural factors in the adaptation of non-white students in Toronto schools. In *Multiculturalism in Canada: Social and Educational Perspectives*, edited by Ronald J. Samuda, John W. Berry, and M. Laferriere. Toronto: Allyn and Bacon.

– 1991. *A Life on the Edge: Experiences in 'Black and White' in North America*. Toronto: University of Toronto Press.

– 1995. Toronto: Polite racism and marshmallow politics. *Currents: Readings in Race Relations* 8, no. 3: 26–7.

Heinzl, John. 1999. Ford tries to tap Chinese community. *Globe and Mail*, 14 July, M1.

Henry, Frances. 1993. *A Survey of Black Business in Metropolitan Toronto*. Toronto: Multicultural and Race Relations Division of Metropolitan Toronto.

– 1994. *The Caribbean Diaspora in Toronto: Learning to Live with Racism*. Toronto: University of Toronto Press.

– 1995. Racism revisited in Toronto the good. *Currents: Readings in Race Relations* 8, no. 3: 12–15.

Henry, Frances, Carol Tator, Winston Mattis, and Tim Rees. 1995. *The Colour of Democracy: Racism in Canadian Society*. Toronto: Harcourt Brace.

Hernandez, Donald, and Evan Charney. 1998. *From Generation to Generation: The Health and Well-Being of Children in Immigrant Families*. Washington, DC: National Academy Press.

Herriman, Michael, and Barbara Burnaby, eds. 1996. *Language Policies in English-Dominant Countries: Six Case Studies*. Clevedon, UK: Multilingual Matters.

Hiebert, Dan. 1993. Jewish immigrants and the garment industry of Toronto,

1901–31: A study of ethnic and class relations. *Annals of the Association of American Geographers* 83: 243–71.
- 1997. *The Colour of Work: Labour Market Segmentation in Montreal, Toronto, and Vancouver, 1991*. RIIM Working Paper Series 97. Vancouver: RIIM.
- 1999. Local geographies of labour market segmentation: Montreal, Toronto, and Vancouver, 1991. *Economic Geography* 75: 339–69.

Hill, Dan. 1985. The Blacks in Toronto. In *Gathering Place: Peoples and Neighbourhoods of Toronto 1834–1945*, edited by Robert Harney. Toronto: Multicultural History Society of Ontario.

Holdsworth, D.W. 1993. Evolving urban landscapes. In *The Changing Social Geography of Canadian Cities*, edited by Larry S. Bourne and David F. Ley. Montreal: McGill-Queen's University Press.

Hou, Feng, and T.R. Balakrishnan. 1996. The integration of visible minorities in contemporary Canadian society. *Canadian Journal of Sociology* 21, no. 3: 307–26.

Houston, Cecil J., and William J. Smyth. 1980. *The Sash Canada Wore: A Historical Geography of the Orange Order in Canada*. Toronto: University of Toronto Press.

Hulchanski, J.D. 1994. *The Use of Housing Expenditure-to-Income Ratios: Origins, Evolution and Implications*. Background Paper #2 for the Ontario Human Rights Commission. Toronto: Ontario Human Rights Commission.
- 1998. Immigrants and access to housing: How welcome are newcomers to Canada? In *Metropolis Year II: The Development of a Comparative Research Agenda*, edited by M. McAndrew and N. Lapierre Vincent. Proceedings of the Second National Conference, 1997. Montreal: Inter-University Research Centre of Montreal on Immigration.

Hull, Diana. 1979. Migration, adaptation, and illness: A review. *Social Science and Medicine* 13: 25–36.

Iacovetta, Franca. 1991. Ordering in bulk: Canada's postwar immigration policy and recruitment of contract workers from Italy. *Journal of American Ethnic History* 11: 51–80.
- 1992. *Such Hardworking People: Italian Immigrants in Postwar Toronto*. Montreal: McGill-Queen's University Press.

Immen, Wallace. 1999. Police apologize for second 'yellow' slur. *Globe and Mail*, 16 February, A1.

Immigration. 1974. *International Canada* (April): 28.

Infantry, Ashante. 1995. Little Jamaica competition is stiff in the shopping area that has sprung up along Eglinton Ave. to cater to the taste of a growing West Indian community. *Toronto Star*, 7 August, C1, C3.

Isajiw, Wsevolod. 1999. *Understanding Diversity: Ethnicity and Race in the Canadian Context*. Toronto: Thompson Educational Publishers.

Isin, Engin F., and Myer Siemiatycki. Making space for mosques: Struggle for urban citizenship in diasporic Toronto. In *Race, Space, and the Law: Unmapping a White Settler Society*, edited by Sherene H. Razack, 185–210. Toronto: Between the Lines.

Jackson, J.S., T.C. Antonucci, and R.C. Gibson. 1995. Ethnic and cultural factors in research on aging and mental health: A life-course perspective. In *Handbook on Ethnicity, Aging, and Mental Health*, edited by Deborah K. Padgett, 22–46. Westport, CT: Greenwood Press.

Jackson, James S., David R. Williams, and Myriam Torres. 1997. *Perceptions of Discrimination: The Stress Process and Physical and Psychological Health*. Washington, DC: National Institute of Mental Health.

James, Carl E. 1990. *Making It: Black Youth, Racism, and Career Aspirations in a Big City*. Oakville, ON: Mosaic Press.

– 1995. Negotiating schooling through sports: African Canadian youth strive for academic success. *Avante* 1, no. 1: 20–36.

– 1997. Contradictory tensions in the experiences of African Canadians in a faculty of education with an access program. *Canadian Journal of Education* 22, no. 2: 158–74.

– 1999. *Seeing Ourselves: Exploring Race, Ethnicity and Culture*. Toronto: Thompson Educational Publishing.

– Forthcoming. Achieving desire: Narrative of a Black male teacher. *International Journal of Qualitative Studies in Education*.

James, C.E., and C. Haig-Brown. 2001. 'Returning the dues': Community and the personal in a university/school partnership. *Urban Education* 36, no. 22: 226–55.

James, C.E., and Adrienne Shadd, eds. 1994. *Talking about Difference: Encounters in Culture, Language and Identity*. Toronto: Between the Lines.

James, Royson. 2001. Lastman 'native' joke sparks fury. *Toronto Star*, 21 June, A1, A16.

– 2001. Sorry Sorry Sorry ... but scripted lines aren't good enough. *Toronto Star*, 22 June, B01.

Jansen, Clifford. 1988. *Italians in a Multicultural Canada*. Lewiston, NY: Edwin Mellen Press.

Jones, Trevor, and David McEvoy. 1996. Commerce and context: South Asian retailers in Britain and Canada. Paper presented at the annual meeting of the Association of American Geographers, Charlotte, North Carolina, April.

Kagan, A., T. Gordon, G.G. Rhoads, and J.C. Schiffman. 1975. Some factors related to coronary heart disease incidence in Honolulu Japanese men: The Honolulu Heart Study. *International Journal of Epidemiology* 4: 271–9.

Kage, Joseph. 1981. Able and willing to work: Jewish immigration and occupational patterns in Canada. In *The Canadian Jewish Mosaic*, edited by

Morton Weinfeld, William Shaffir, and Irwin Cotler. Rexdale, ON: John Wiley and Sons Canada.
- 1999. *With Faith and Thanksgiving: The Story of Two Hundred Years of Jewish Immigration and Immigrant Aid Effort in Canada, 1760–1960*. Montreal: Eagle Publishing.

Kaihla, P., and R. Laver. 1992. Black and angry. *Maclean's*. 18 May, 24–9.

Kalbach, Warren E. 1970. *The Impact of Immigration on Canada's Population*. Ottawa: Dominion Bureau of Statistics.

Kalbach, M.A., and W.E. Kalbach. 1999. Demographic overview of ethnic origin groups in Canada. In *Race and Ethnic Relations in Canada*, 2nd ed., edited by Peter S. Li. Toronto: Oxford University Press.

Kao, Grace, and Marta Tienda. 1995. Optimism and achievement: The educational performance of immigrant youth. *Social Science Quarterly* 76, no. 1: 2–19.

Karno, M., R.L. Hough, M.A. Burnam, and J.I. Escobar. 1987. Lifetime prevalence of specific psychiatric disorders among Mexican Americans and non-Hispanic whites in Los Angeles. *Archives of General Psychiatry* 44, no. 8: 695–701.

Kaplan, David. 1998. The spatial structure of urban ethnic economies. *Urban Geography* 19: 489–501.

Kaufman, Maurice. 1968. Will instruction in reading Spanish affect ability in reading English? *Journal of Reading* 11: 521–7.

Kazemipur, A., and S.S. Halli. 1997. Plight of immigrations: The spatial concentration of poverty in Canada. *Canadian Journal of Regional Science* 20: 11–28.
- 2000. *The New Poverty in Canada: Ethnic Groups and Ghetto Neighbourhoods*. Toronto: Thompson Educational.

Kelly, Ninette, and Michael Trebilcock. 1998. *The Making of the Mosaic: A History of Canadian Immigration Policy*. Toronto: University of Toronto Press.

Kenridge, J. 1998. Jewish families put down new roots in old parts of city. *Globe and Mail*, 8 September, A12.

Kerbel, D. 1997. Epidemiology of tuberculosis in Ontario, 1995. *PHERO*, no. 4: 81–93.

Kessler, Ronald C., and Harold W. Neighbors. 1986. A new perspective on the relationships among race, social class, and psychological distress. *Journal of Health and Social Behavior* 27, no. 2: 107–15.

Kinzie, J.D., W.H. Sack, R.H. Angell, and S.M. Manson. 1986. The psychiatric effects of massive trauma on Cambodian children: I. The children. *Journal of the American Academy of Child and Adolescent Psychiatry* 25, no. 3: 370–6.

Klasen, S., 1998. Social exclusion and children in OECD Countries: Some conceptual issues. Munich: Department of Economics, University of Munich.

Kleinman, A. 1977. *Depression, Somatisation and the 'New Cross-Cultural' Psychiatry.* Medical Vol. 11, 3–10. Oxford: Pergamon Press.
- 1988. *The Illness Narratives.* New York: Basic Books.
Knocke, Wuokko, and Roxana Ng. 1999. Women's organizing and immigration: Comparing the Canadian and Swedish experience. In *Women's Organizing and Public Policy in Canada and Sweden,* edited by Linda Briskin and Mona Eliasson. Montreal: McGill-Queen's University Press.
Kobasa, S.C., and S.R. Maddi. 1977. Existential personality theory. In *Current Personality Theories,* edited by Raymond J. Corsini, 243–76. Itasca, IL: F.E. Peacock Publishers.
Kohli, Rita. 1993. Power or empowerment? Questions of agency in the shelter movement. In *And Still We Rise: Feminist Political Mobilization in Contemporary Canada,* edited by Linda Carty. Toronto: Women's Press.
Kralt, J. 1990. Ethnic origins in the Canadian census, 1987–1986. In *Ethnic Demography,* edited by Shiva S. Halli, Leo Driedger, and Frank Trovato. Ottawa: Carleton University Press.
Kreiger, N. 1999. Embodying inequality: A review of concepts, measures, and methods for studying health consequences of discrimination. *International Journal of Health Services* 29: 295–352.
Krener, P.G., and Sabin. 1985. Indochinese immigrant children: Problems in psychiatric diagnosis. *Journal of American Academy of Child Psychiatry* 24, no. 4: 453–8.
Kunin, Roslyn, and Cheryl L. Jones. 1995. Business immigration to Canada. In *Diminishing Returns: The Economics of Canada's Recent Immigration Policy,* edited by Don J. DeVoretz. Toronto: C.D. Howe Institute.
Kunz, Jean Lock, Anne Milan, and Sylvain Schetagne. 2000. *Unequal Access: A Canadian Profile of Racial Differences in Education, Employment and Income.* Toronto: Canadian Race Relations Foundation.
Kuo, W.H. 1984. Prevalence of depression among Asian-Americans. *Journal of Nervous and Mental Disease* 172: 449–57.
- 1995. Coping with racial discrimination: The case of Asian Americans. *Ethnic and Racial Studies* 18: 109–27.
Kuo, W.H., and Yung-Mei Tsai. 1986. Social networking, hardiness and immigrant's mental health. *Journal of Health and Social Behaviour* 27, no. 2: 133–49.
Lai, Chuen-Yan David. 1992. Emigration to Canada: Its dimensions and impact on Hong Kong. In *Migration and the Transformation of Cultures,* edited by Jean Burnet et al., 241–52. Toronto, ON: Multicultural History Society of Ontario.
- 1988. *Chinatowns: Towns within Cities in Canada.* Vancouver: UBC Press.

Lam, L. 1994. Immigrant students. In *Learning and Sociological Profiles of Canadian High School Students: An Overview of 15–18 Year Olds and Educational Policy Implications For Dropouts, Exceptional Students, Employed Students, Immigrant Students, and Native Youth*, edited by P. Anisef. Lewiston, NY: Edwin Mellen Press.

Landale, Nancy S., R.S. Oropea, and Bridget K. Gorman. 2000. Migration and infant death: Assimilation or selective migration? *American Sociological Review* 65: 888–905.

Lanphier, C. Michael. 1979. *A Study of Third-World Immigrants*. Ottawa: Economic Council of Canada.

Lapointe Consulting and Robert A. Murdie. 1996. *Immigrants and the Canadian Housing Market: Living Arrangements, Housing Characteristics, and Preferences*. Ottawa: Canada Mortgage and Housing Corporation.

Larter, Sylvia, M. Cheng, S. Capps, and M. Lee. 1982. *Post Secondary Plans of Grade Eight Students and Related Variables*. Toronto: Board of Education for the City of Toronto.

Leah, Ronnie. 1993. Black women speak out: Racism and unions. In *Women Challenging Unions: Feminism, Democracy and Militancy*, edited by Linda Briskin and Patricia McDermott, 157–71. Toronto: University of Toronto Press.

Lemon, James T. 1985. *Toronto since 1918: An Illustrated History*. Toronto: Lorimer.

Levitt, Cyril, and William Shaffir. 1987. *The Riot at Christie Pits*. Toronto: Lester and Orpen Dennys.

Lewis, S. 1992. Report on race relations in Ontario. Unpublished letter to the premier of Ontario, Bob Rae, 9 June.

Ley, D. 1993. Past elites and present gentry: neighbourhoods of privilege in the inner city. In *The Changing Social Geography of Canadian Cities*, edited by Larry S. Bourne and David F. Ley. Montreal: McGill-Queen's University Press.

– 1997. *Is There an Immigrant 'Underclass' in Canadian Cities?* Vancouver: Vancouver Centre of Excellence, RIIM. Working Paper Series No. 97–108.

– 1999. Myths and meanings of immigration and the metropolis. *Canadian Geographer* 43, no. 1: 2–19.

Ley, D., and H. Smith. 2000. Relations between deprivation and immigrant groups in large Canadian cities. *Urban Studies* 37, no. 1: 37–62.

Ley, D., and J. Tutchener. 2001. Immigration, globalisation and housing prices in Canada's gateway cities. *Housing Studies* 16, no. 2: 199–223.

Li, Peter S. 1988. *The Chinese in Canada*. Toronto: Oxford University Press.

– 1992. Ethnic enterprise in transition: Chinese business in Richmond, BC, 1980–1990. *Canadian Ethnic Studies* 24: 120–38.

- 1994. Unneighbourly houses or unwelcome Chinese: The social construction of race in the battle over 'monster homes' in Vancouver, Canada. *International Journal of Comparative Race and Ethnic Studies* 1: 14–33.
- 1998. *The Chinese in Canada*, 2nd ed. Toronto: Oxford University Press.

Li, Wei. 1998. Anatomy of a new ethnic settlement: The Chinese *ethnoburb* in Los Angeles. *Urban Studies* 35, no. 479–501.

Lian, J.Z., and D.R. Matthews. 1998. Does the vertical mosaic still exist? Ethnicity and income in Canada, 1991. *Canadian Review of Sociology and Anthropology* 35: 461–81.

Lieberson, S. 1982. Stereotypes: Their consequences for race and ethnic interaction. In *Social Structure and Behavior: Essays in Honor of William Hamilton Sewell*, edited by Robert M. Hauser, D. Mechanic, A.O. Haller, and T.S. Hauser, 47–68. New York: Academic Press.

Light, Ivan. 1972. *Ethnic Enterprise in America: Business and Welfare among Chinese, Japanese and Blacks*. Berkeley: University of California Press.
- 1979. Disadvantaged minorities in self-employment. *International Journal of Comparative Sociology* 20: 31–45.

Light, Ivan, Georges Sabaghs, Mehdi Bozorgmehr, and Claudia Der-Matrirosian. 1994. Beyond the ethnic enclave hypothesis. *Social Problems* 41: 65–80.

Lin, Jan. 1995. Polarized development and urban change in New York's Chinatown. *Urban Affairs Review* 30: 332–54.

Lin, K.M., and F. Cheung. 1999. Mental health issues for Asian Americans. *Psychiatric Services* 50: 774–80.

Lind, Loren Jay. 1974. *The Learning Machine: A Hard Look at Toronto Schools*. Toronto: Anansi.

Link, B.G., and J.C. Phelan. 1996. Understanding sociodemographic differences in health – the role of fundamental social causes. *American Journal of Public Health* 86: 472.

Liu, Xiao Feng. 1995. New mainland Chinese immigrants: A case study in Metro Toronto. PhD diss., York University.

Lister, R. 2000. Strategies for social inclusion. *Social Inclusion, Possibilities and Tensions*. London: Macmillan.

Lo, Lucia. 1998. Unpublished research data.

Lo, Lucia, and Shuguang Wang. 1997. Settlement patterns of Toronto's Chinese immigrants: Convergence or divergence? *Canadian Journal of Regional Studies* 20: 49–72.
- 1998. Immigration, ethnic economies and integration: A case study of Chinese in the Greater Toronto area. Research Report to the Toronto Joint Centre of Excellence for Research on Immigration and Settlement.

- 2000. Chinese business in Toronto: A spatial and structural anatomy. Paper presented at the Conference on Comparative Perspectives on Chinese Ethnic Economies, September, Toronto, Ontario.
Lo, Lucia, Carlos Teixeira, and Marie Truelove. 2000. Survey of Somali Businesses. Unpublished research report.
Logan, John, Richard D. Alba, and Thomas L. McNulty. 1994. Ethnic economies in metropolitan regions: Miami and beyond. *Social Forces* 72: 691–724.
Luciuk, Lubomyr. 1984. Searching for place: Ukrainian refugee migration to Canada after World War II. PhD diss., University of Alberta.
Lui-Gurr, Susanna. 1995. The British Columbia experience with immigrants and welfare dependency, 1989. In *Diminishing Returns: The Economics of Canada's Recent Immigration Policy*, edited by Don J. DeVoretz. Toronto: C.D. Howe Institute.
Lupul, Manoly. 1983. Multiculturalism and Canada's white ethnics. *Canadian Ethnic Studies*: 99–107.
Ma, Ambrose. 1999. Study of Chinese shopping malls/plazas. Fact sheet prepared by Goldfarb Consultants. June.
MacCharles, Tonda. 2002. Canada, U.S. near deal on refugees. *Toronto Star*, 7 May, A6.
Madood, T., R. Berthoud, J. Lakey, J. Nazroo, P. Smith, S. Virdee, and S. Beishon. 1997. *Ethnic Minorities in Britain: Diversities and Disadvantage*. London: Policy Studies Institute.
Malarek, Victor. 1986. Immigration racket suggested as reasons for floods of Turks. *Globe and Mail*, 2 December, A1.
- 1987. *Heaven's Gate: Canada's Immigration Fiasco*. Toronto: Macmillan of Canada.
Mandres, M. 1998. The dynamics of ethnic residential patterns in the Toronto Census Metropolitan Area. PhD diss., Department of Geography and Environmental Studies, Wilfrid Laurier University.
Marger, Martin N. 1989. Business strategies among East Indian entrepreneurs in Toronto: The role of group resources and opportunity structure. *Ethnic and Racial Studies* 12: 539–63.
Marger, Martin N., and Constance A. Hoffman. 1992. Ethnic enterprise in Ontario: Immigrant participation in the small business sector. *International Migration Review* 26: 968–81.
Marin, G., E. Perez-Stable, and B.V. Marin. 1989. Cigarette smoking among San Francisco Hispanics: The role of acculturation and gender. *American Journal of Public Health* 79: 196–9.
Marmot, M.G., and Syme, S.L. 1976. Acculturation and coronary heart disease in Japanese Americans. *American Journal of Epidemiology* 104: 225–47.

Martin, Paul. 1983. *A Very Public Life*. Ottawa: Deneau.
Marsden, W. 2000. Citizenship for sale. *The Gazette* (Montreal), 13 May.
Masemann, Vandra. 1975. Immigrant students' perceptions of occupational programs. In *Education of Immigrant Students: Issues and Answers*, edited by Aaron Wolfgang. Toronto: Ontario Institute for Studies in Education.
Mata, Fernando. 1992. The recognition of foreign degrees in Canada: Context, developments and issue relevance. Paper presented at the Conference on Migration, Human Rights and Economic Integration, 19–22 November, at Centre for Refugee Studies, York University, Toronto.
– 1996. Birthplace and economic similarities in the labour force: An analysis of Toronto's census microdata. In *Immigration and Ethnicity in Canada*, edited by Anne Laperriere, Varpu Lindstrom, and Tamara Palmer Seiler. Montreal: Association for Canadian Studies.
Matas, David, and Susan Charendoff. 1987. *Justice Delayed: Nazi War Criminals in Canada*. Toronto: Summerhill Press.
Mathias, Augusto. 1997. Interview, Toronto, Ontario, 7 October.
McKenna, M.T., E. McCray, and I. Onorato. 1995. The epidemiology of tuberculosis among foreign-born persons in the United States, 1986 to 1993. *New England Journal of Medicine* 332, no. 16: 1071–6.
Mead, George H. 1934. *Mind, Self, and Society*. Chicago: University of Chicago Press.
Metropolitan Toronto Planning Department. 1993. *Metro's Changing Housing Scene, 1986–1991*. Toronto: Municipality of Metropolitan Toronto.
Mewhort, D.S., A.B. Milloy, N.A. Sweetman, and G.M. Gore. 1965. Untitled Report. Toronto: Board of Education of the City of Toronto, Office of the Director of Education.
Ministry of Industry Canada. 1998a. *Canadian Economic Observer: Historical Statistical Supplement*. Ottawa: Ministry of Industry.
Ministry of Industry Canada. 1998b. *Canada Year Book 1999*. Ottawa: Ministry of Industry.
Ministry of National Revenue Canada. 1996. *Income Statistics 1996–1998 Tax Years*. (T4133 Rev. 98). Ottawa: Ministry of National Revenue.
Modiano, Nancy. 1973. *Indian Education in the Chiapas Highlands*. New York: Holt, Rinehart and Winston.
Momryk, Myron. 1992. Ukrainian DP immigration and government policy in Canada, 1946–1952. In *The Refugee Experience: Ukrainian Displaced Persons after World War II*, edited by Wsevolod W. Isajiw, Yury Boshyk, and Roman Senkus, 413–34. Edmonton: Canadian Institute of Ukrainian Studies, University of Alberta.
Monroe-Blum, H., M.G. Boyle, D.R. Offord, and N. Kates. 1989. Immigrant

children: Psychiatric disorder, school performance and service utilization. *American Journal of Orthopsychiatry* 59: 510–19.
- Montero, D., and I. Dieppa. 1982. Resettling Vietnamese refugees: The service agency's role. *Social Work* 27: 74–81.
- Moodley, K.A. 1995. Multicultural education in Canada: Historical development and current status. In *Handbook of Research on Multicultural Education*, edited by James A. Banks and Cherry A. McGee Banks. New York: Macmillan.
- Moore, E., and B. Ray. 1991. Access to homeownership among immigrant groups in Canada. *Canadian Review of Sociology and Anthropology* 28: 1–27.
- Morgan, M.C., D.L. Wingard, and M.E. Felice. 1984. Subcultural differences in alcohol use among youth. *Journal of Adolescent Health Care* 5, no. 3: 191–5.
- Municipality of Metropolitan Toronto. 1990. *A Review of Ethno-Racial Access to Metropolitan Services*. Toronto: Municipality of Metropolitan Toronto.
- 1995. *The Composition and Implications of Metropolitan Toronto's Ethnic, Racial and Linguistic Populations, 1991*. Toronto: Municipality of Metropolitan Toronto.
- Municipality of Metropolitan Toronto, City of Toronto, and Social Planning Council of Metropolitan Toronto. 1997. *Profile of a Changing World: 1996 Community Agency Survey*. Toronto: Social Planning Council.
- Munro, J.A. 1971. British Columbia and the Chinese evil: Canada's first anti-Asiatic immigration law. *Journal of Canadian Studies* 6, no. 4: 42–51.
- Murdie, Robert. 1991. Local strategies in resale home financing in the Toronto housing market. *Urban Studies* 28: 465–83.
- 1992. Social Housing in Transition: *The Changing Social Composition of Public Sector Housing in Metropolitan Toronto*. Ottawa: Canada Mortgage and Housing Corporation.
- 1994. Blacks in near-ghettoes? Black visible minority population in Metropolitan Toronto Housing Authority public housing units. *Housing Studies* 9, no. 4: 435–57.
- 1996. Economic restructing and social polarization in Toronto. In *Social Polarization in Post-Industrial Metropolises*, edited by John O'Loughlin and Jurgen Friedrich. New York: Walter de Gruyter.
- 1998. The welfare state, economic restructuring and immigrant flows: Impacts on sociospatial segregation in Greater Toronto. In *Urban Segregation and the Welfare State: Inequality and Exclusion in Western Cities*, edited by S. Musterd and W. Ostendorf. London: Routledge.
- 2002. The housing careers of Polish and Somali newcomers in Toronto's rental market. *Housing Studies* 17, no. 3: 423–43.
- Murdie, R., A. Chambon, J.D. Hulchanski, and C. Teixeira. 1996. Housing

issues facing immigrants and refugees in Greater Toronto: Initial findings from the Jamaican, Polish and Somali communities. In *Housing Question of the 'Others,'* edited by Emine M. Komut. Ankara: Chamber of Architects of Turkey.

Musgrove, Frank. 1982. *Education and Anthropology: Other Cultures and the Teacher*. Chichester: Wiley.

Musterd, Sako, and Wim Ostendorf, eds. 1998. *Urban Segregation and the Welfare State: Inequality and Exclusion in Western Cities*. New York: Routledge.

Nakamura, Mark. 1995. Race relations in Toronto and Los Angeles. *Currents: Readings in Race Relations* 8, no. 3: 35–44.

Nakhaie, R. 1995. Ownership and management position of Canadian ethnic groups in 1973 and 1989. *Canadian Journal of Sociology* 20, no. 2: 167–92.

– 1997. Vertical mosaic among the elites: The new imagery revisited. *Canadian Review of Sociology and Anthropology* 34, no. 1: 124.

– 1998. Ethnic inequality: Well-paid employees of the Ontario public bureaucracy. *Canadian Ethnic Studies* 30, no. 1: 119–39.

Nash, Alan. 1987. *The Economic Impact of the Entrepreneur Immigrant Program*. Ottawa: Institute for Research on Public Policy, Studies in Social Policy.

National Council of Welfare. 1998. *Welfare Incomes 1996*. Ottawa. The Council.

National Institute of Mental Health: National Advisory Mental Health Council. 1995. *Basic Behavioral Science Research for Mental Health*. US Department of Health and Human Services: National Institution of Health (NIH Publication No. 95-3682).

Neatby, B. 1992. Introduction. In *Our Two Official Languages over Time*. Ottawa: Office of the Commissioner of Official Languages.

Nee, Victor, Jimy M. Sanders, and S. Sernau. 1994. Job transitions in an immigrant metropolis: Ethnic boundaries and the mixed economy. *American Sociological Review* 59, no. 6: 849–72.

Nesdale, D., R. Rooney, and L. Smith. 1997. Migrant ethnic identity and psychological distress. *Journal of Cross-Cultural Psychology* 28: 569–88.

Neuwirth, G. et al. 1985. *Southeast Asian Refugee Study: A Report on a Three-Year Study on the Social and Economic Adaptation of Southeast Asian Refugees to Life in Canada, 1981–1983*. Ottawa: Carleton University.

New Voices of the New City. 1997a. Background Information. 21 September.

– 1997b. Mayoralty Candidates Debate Brochure. 14 October.

Ng. Roxana. 2000. Globalization, recolonization and worker resistance: The case of garment workers in Toronto. Public Lecture delivered at McMaster University, Hamilton, ON. 1 March.

Ng, Roxana, Gillian Walker, and Jacob Muller. 1990. *Community Organization and the Canadian State*. Toronto: Garamond Press.

Ng, Wing Chung. 1999. Canada. In *The Encyclopedia of the Chinese Overseas*, edited by Lynn Pan. Cambridge, MA: Harvard University Press.

Ng, Winnie. 1982. Immigrant women: The silent partners in the women's movement. In *Still Ain't Satisfied! Canadian Feminism Today*, edited by Maureen Fitzgerald, Connie Guberman, and Margie Wolfe. Toronto: Women's Press.

Nicassio, P.M., G.S. Solomon, S.S. Guest, and J.E. McCullough. 1986. Emigration stress and language proficiency as correlates of depression in a sample of Southeast Asian refugees. *International Journal of Social Psychiatry* 32, no. 1: 22–8.

Nipp, Dora. 1985. The Chinese in Toronto. In *Gathering Place: Peoples and Neighbourhoods of Toronto, 1834–1945*, edited by Robert Harney. Toronto: Multicultural History Society of Ontario.

– 1992. For the love of the family. *Toronto Star*, 15 October, E2.

Noh, S., and W.R. Avison. 1996. Asian immigrants and the stress process: A study of Koreans in Canada. *Journal of Health and Social Behavior* 37, no. 2: 192–206.

Noh, S., and V. Kaspar. 2003. Perceived discrimination: Moderating effects of coping, acculturation, and ethnic support. *American Journal of Public Health* 93: 232–8.

Noh, S., W.R. Avison, and V. Kaspar. 1992. Depressive symptoms among Korean immigrants: Assessment of a translation of the Center of Epidemiologic Studies–Depression Scale. *Psychological Assessment* 4, no. 1: 84–91.

Noh, S., M. Beiser, V. Kaspar, F. Hou, and A. Rummens. 1999. Perceived racial discrimination, coping, and depression among Asian refugees in Canada. *Journal of Health and Social Behavior* 40: 193–207.

Noh, S., V. Kaspar, and X. Chen. 1998. Measuring depression in Korean Immigrants: Assessing validity of the translated Korean version of the CES-D scale. *Cross Cultural Research: Journal of Comparative Social Science* 32, no. 4: 358–77.

Noh, S., V. Kaspar, and F. Hou. 1997. *Measuring Acculturative Stress among Immigrants: Validation of the Acculturative Stress Index*. Montreal: Canadian Ethnic Studies Association.

Noh, S., V. Kaspar, and F. Hou. 1998. Mental health of children and youth of immigrant families. Paper presented at the Third National Metropolis Conference, Vancouver, January 15.

Noh, S., M. Speechley, V. Kaspar, and Z. Wu. 1992a. Depression in Korean immigrants in Canada: I. Method of the study and prevalence of depression. *Journal of Nervous and Mental Disease* 180, no. 9: 573–77.

Noh, S., Z. Wu, and W.R. Avison. 1994. Social support and quality of life:

Sociocultural similarity and the efficacy of social support. *Advances in Medical Sociology* 5: 115–37.
Noh, S., Z. Wu, M. Speechley, and V. Kaspar. 1992b. Depression in Korean immigrants in Canada: II. Correlates of gender, work, and marriage. *Journal of Nervous and Mental Disease* 180, no. 9: 578–82.
Nolan, C.M., and A.M. Elarth. 1988. Tuberculosis in a cohort of Southeast Asian refugees. A five-year surveillance study. *American Review of Respiratory Disease* 137: 805–9.
Norcliffe, Glen. 1996. Mapping deindustrialization: Brian Kipping's landscapes of Toronto. *Canadian Geographer* 40: 266–72.
Norcliffe, G., M. Goldrick, and L. Muszynski. 1986. Cyclical factors, technological change, capital mobility, and deindustrialization in Metropolitan Toronto. *Urban Geography* 7: 413–36.
Novac, Sylvia. 1999. Immigrant enclaves and residential segregation: voices of racialized refugee and immigrant women. *Canadian Woman Studies* 19, no. 3: 88–96.
Oberg, Kalervo. 1960. Cultural shock: Adjustment to new cultural environments. *Practical Anthropology* 7: 177–82.
Ogbu, John U. 1983. Minority status and schooling in plural societies. *Comparative Education Review* 27, no. 2: 168–90.
– 1991. Immigrant and involuntary minorities in comparative perspective. In *Minority Status and Schooling: A Comparative Study of Immigrant and Involuntary Minorities*, edited by M. Gibson and J. Ogbu. New York: Garland Publishing.
Olson, S.H., and A.L. Kobayashi. 1993. The emerging ethnocultural mosaic. In *The Changing Social Geography of Canadian Cities*, edited by Larry S. Bourne and David F. Ley. Montreal: McGill-Queen's University Press.
Ondaatje, Michael. 1987. *In the Skin of a Lion*. Toronto: Vintage Canada.
Ontario Council of Agencies Serving Immigrants (OCASI). 2000. Press Statement. 8 August.
Ontario Federation of Students. 1984. Ontario's universities: Social elitism or social responsiveness? Paper presented to the Ontario Economic Council.
Ontario Ministry of Colleges and Universities. 1986. *Continuing Education Review Project. Project Report: For Adults Only*. Toronto: Ontario Ministry of Colleges and Universities.
Ontario Ministry of Education and Training. 1987. *The Development of a Policy on Race and Ethnocultural Equity: Report on the Provincial Advisory Committee on Race Relations*. Etobicoke: Borough of Etobicoke Board of Education.
– 1992. *Changing Perspectives: A Resource Guide for Antiracist and Ethnocultural Equity Education*. Toronto: Queen's Printer for Ontario.

Ontario Non-Profit Housing Association and Co-operative Housing Federation of Canada – Ontario Region. 1999. *Where's Home? A Picture of Housing Needs in Ontario*. Toronto: Ontario Non-Profit Housing Association and Co-operative Housing Federation Canada – Ontario Region.
- 2001. *Where's Home? 2000 Update*. Toronto: Ontario Non-Profit Housing Association and Co-operative Housing Federation Canada – Ontario Region.
Opoku-Dapaah, Edward. 1995. *Somali Refugees in Toronto: A Profile*. Toronto: York Lanes Press.
- 1996. *Ethno-racial Inequality in Metropolitan Toronto: Analysis of the 1991 Census*. Toronto: Access and Equity Centre, Municipality of Metropolitan Toronto.
- 2000. *Ethno-racial Inequality in the City of Toronto: An Analysis of the 1996 Census*. Toronto: Access and Equity Unit, City of Toronto.
Orr, P.H., J. Manfreda, and E.S. Hershfield. 1990. Tuberculosis surveillance in immigrants to Manitoba. *Canadian Medical Association Journal* 142, no. 5: 453–8.
Ornstein, Michael. 1996. *A Survey of Graduate Students and Contract Faculty at York University*. Toronto: Institute of Social Research, York University.
- 2000. *Ethno-Racial Inequality in Metropolitan Toronto: An Analysis of the 1996 Census*. Toronto: Municipality of Metropolitan Toronto, Access and Equity Centre.
Owen, Thomas Yaw. 1999. The view from Toronto: Settlement services in the late 1990s. Paper presented at the Third National Metropolis Conference, January, Vancouver.
Owusu, T. 1996. The adaptation of Black African immigrants in Canada: A case study of residential behaviour and ethnic community formation among Ghanaians in Toronto. PhD diss., University of Toronto.
- 1998. To buy or not to buy: determinants of home ownership among Ghanaian immigrants in Toronto. *Canadian Geographer* 42, no. 1: 40–52.
- 1999. Residential patterns and housing choices of Ghanaian immigrants in Toronto, Canada. *Housing Studies* 14, no. 1: 77–97.
Pacini, M. 1998. The language of power: Interactions between Latino parents and the Canadian school system. MEd thesis, York University.
Pak, A., K.L. Dion, and K.K. Dion. 1991. Social-psychological correlates of experienced discrimination: Test of the double jeopardy hypothesis. *International Journal of Intercultural Relations* 15: 243–54.
Pal, Leslie A. 1993. *Interests of State: The Politics of Language, Multiculturalism and Feminism in Canada*. Montreal: McGill-Queen's University Press.
Palmer, D.L. 1997. Canadians' attitudes and perceptions regarding immigration: November and December 1996, and February 1997 surveys. Citizen-

ship and Immigration Canada. Program Support, Strategic Policy, and Planning and Research Branch, June.
Pal, Leslie A. 1993. *Interests of State: The Politics of Language, Multiculturalism and Feminism in Canada*. Montreal: McGill-Queen's University Press.
Palmer, D.L. 1997. Canadians' attitudes and perceptions regarding immigration: November and December 1996, and February 1997 surveys. Citizenship and Immigration Canada. Program Support, Strategic Policy, and Planning and Research Branch, June.
Paugam, S. 1996. A new social contract? Poverty and social exclusion: A sociological view. EUI Working Papers RSC 96, 37.
Pearlin, Leonard I. 1989. The sociological study of stress. *Journal of Health and Social Behavior* 30, no. 3: 241–56.
Pearlin, Leonard I., Elizabeth G. Menaghan, Morton A. Lieberman, and Joseph T. Mullan. 1981. The stress process. *Journal of Health and Social Behavior* 22, no. 4: 337–56.
Pelham, Judy P., and Bruce R. Fretz. 1982. Racial differences and attributes of career choice unrealism. *Vocational Guidance Quarterly* 31, no. 1: 36–42.
Pernice, Regina, and Judith Brook. 1996. Refugees' and immigrants' mental health: Association of demographic and post-migration factors. *Journal of Social Psychology* 136, no. 4: 511–19.
Petersen, William. 1955. *Planned Migration: The Social Determinants of the Dutch-Canadian Movement*. Berkeley: University of California Press.
Pfeifer, Mark Edward. 1999. Community, adaptation, and the Vietnamese in Toronto. PhD diss., University of Toronto.
Philip, M. 2000. Poor? Coloured? Then it's no vacancy. *Globe and Mail*, 18 July, A15.
Pierce, J.P., N. Evans, A.J. Farkas, S.W. Carvin et al. 1994. *Tobacco Use in California: An Evaluation of the Tobacco Control Program, 1989–1992*. La Jolla, CA: University of California Press, San Diego.
Pitman, W. 1977. *Now Is Not Too Late*. Toronto: Report to the Council of Metropolitan Toronto by the Task Force on Human Relations.
Porter, John A. 1965. *The Vertical Mosaic: An Analysis of Social Class and Power in Canada*. Toronto: University of Toronto Press.
– 1972. Dilemmas and contradictions of a multiethnic society. *Royal Society of Canada*: 193–205.
Portes, Alejandoro. 1981. Models of structural incorporation and present theories of labor immigration. In *Global Trends in Migration*, edited by Mary Kritz, Charles B. Keeley, and Silvano M. Tomasi, 279–97. New York: Center for Migration Studies.
– 1984. The rise of ethnicity: Determinants of ethnic perceptions among Cuban exils in Miami. *American Sociological Review* 49, no. 3: 383–97.

Portes, Alejandro, and Robert L. Bach. 1985. *Latin Journey: Cuban and Mexican Immigrants in the United States*. Berkeley: University of California Press.

Power Analysis Inc. 1998. *Study of ESL/FSL Services in Ontario: Final Report*. London, ON: Power Analysis Inc.

Preston, Valerie, and Joseph C. Cox. 1999. Immigrants and employment: A comparison of Montreal and Toronto between 1981 and 1996. *Canadian Journal of Regional Science* 22: 87–112.

Preston, Valerie, and Lucia Lo. 2000. 'Asian theme' malls in suburban Toronto: Land use conflicts in Richmond Hill. *Canadian Geographer* 44, no. 2: 182–90.

– Forthcoming. The local territorial impact of federal immigration policy: A case study of 'Asian theme' malls in suburban Toronto. *Canadian Geographer*.

Preston, Valerie, and Guida Man. 1999. Employment experience of Chinese immigrant women: An exploration of diversity. *Canadian Woman Studies* 19: 155–22.

Preston, Valerie, and Wenona Giles. 1997. Ethncity, gender, and labour markets in Canada: A case study of immigrant women in Toronto. *Canadian Journal of Urban Research* 6: 135–59.

Qadeer, Mohammed. 1998. *Ethnic Malls and Plazas: Chinese Commercial Developments in Scarborough, Ontario*. Toronto: Joint Centre of Excellence for Research on Immigration and Settlement.

– 2000. Urban planning and multiculturalism: Beyond sensivity. *Plan Canada* 40, no. 4: 16–18.

Rabkin, Judith G., and Elmer L. Struening. 1976. Life events, stress and illness. *Science* 194, no. 469: 1013–20.

Radloff, L.S. 1977. The CES-D Scale: A self-report depression scale for research in the general population. *Applied Psychological Measurement* 1: 385–401.

Ramcharan, Subhas. 1975. Special problems of immigrant children in the Toronto school system. In *Education of Immigrant Students*, edited by Aaron Wolfgang. Toronto: Ontario Institute for Studies in Education.

– 1982. *Racism: Nonwhites in Canada*. Scarborough, ON: Butterworth.

Ramirez, Bruno. 1989. *The Italians in Canada*. Ottawa: Canadian Historical Association.

Ramirez, B., and M. Del Balzo. 1981. The Italians of Montreal: From sojourning to settlement, 1900–1921. In *Little Italies in North America*, edited by Robert F. Harney and J. Vincenza Scarpaci. Toronto: Multicultural History Society of Toronto.

Ray, B. 1998. *A Comparative Study of Immigrant Housing, Neighbourhoods and Social Networks in Toronto and Montreal*. Ottawa: Canada Mortgage and Housing Corporation.

- 1999. Plural geographies in Canadian cities: Interpreting immigrant residential spaces in Toronto and Montreal. *Canadian Journal of Regional Science* 22, nos. 1 and 2: 65–86.
Ray, B., and D. Rose. 2000. Cities of the everyday: Socio-spatial perspectives on gender, difference, and diversity. In *Canadian Cities in Transition: The Twenty-First Century*, 2d ed., edited by Trudi Bunting and Pierre Filion. Don Mills, ON: Oxford University Press.
Ray, B., and E. Moore. 1991. Access to homeownership among immigrant groups in Canada. *Canadian Review of Sociology and Anthropology* 28: 1–27.
Razin, Eran, and Andre Langlois. 1996. Metropolitan characteristics and entrepreneurship among immigrants and ethnic groups in Canada. *International Migration Review* 30, no. 3: 703–27.
Rees, Tim. 1998. Together we are one: A summary paper on diversity in Toronto. Toronto: Access and Equity Centre, City of Toronto.
Reitz, Jeffrey G. 1990. Ethnic concentrations in labour markets and their implications for ethnic inequality. In Raymond Breton et al., *Ethnic Identity and Equality: Varieties of Experience in a Canadian City*, 135–95. Toronto: University of Toronto Press.
- 1997. Institutional structure and immigrant earnings: A comparison of American, Canadian, and Australian cities. Paper presented at the annual meeting of the American Sociological Association, Toronto.
- 1998. *Warmth of the Welcome: The Social Causes of Economic Success for Immigrants in Different Nations and Cities*. Boulder: Westview Press.
- 1999. Immigrant success in the knowledge economy. *Toronto Star*, 21 November, A18.
Reitz, J.G., and R. Breton. 1994. *The Illusion of Difference: Realities of Ethnicity in Canada and the United States*. Toronto: C.D. Howe Institute.
Reitz, J.G., and S.M. Sklar. 1997. Culture, race, and the economic assimilation of immigrants. *Sociological Forum* 12, no. 2: 233–77.
Relph, Edward. 1997. *The Toronto Guide: The City, Metro, the Region*. Toronto: Centre for Urban and Community Studies, University of Toronto.
Revenue Canada. 1995. *Tax Statistics on Individuals*. <www.rc.gc.ca/`bvt/gb95/pts/t1_inc.htm>.
Rhyne, Darla. 1982. *Visible Minority Business in Metropolitan Toronto: An Exploratory Analysis*. Downsview, ON: Institute for Behavioural Research, York University.
Richmond, Anthony H. 1967. *Post-War Immigrants to Canada*. Toronto: University of Toronto Press.
- 1972. *Ethnic Residential Segregation in Metropolitan Toronto*. Toronto: Institute for Behavioural Research Program, York University.

- 1976. Recent developments in immigration to Canada and Australia: A comparative analysis. *International Journal of Comparative Sociology*: 188.
- 1991. Foreign-born labour in Canada: Past patterns, emerging trends, and implications. *Regional Development Dialogue* 12, no. 3: 145–61.
- 1992. Immigration and structural change: The Canadian experience 1971–1986. *International Migration Review* 26, no. 4: 1200–21.

Richmond, Anthony H., and Warren E. Kalbach. 1980. *Factors in the Adjustment of Immigrants and their Descendants: 1971 Census Monograph*. Ottawa: Statistics Canada.

Richmond, Anthony H., and G. Lakshmana Rao. 1977. Recent developments in immigration to Canada and Australia: A comparative analysis. *International Journal of Comparative Sociology* 17, nos. 3/4: 183–205.

Richmond, Anthony H., G. Lakshmana Rao, and Jerzy Zubrzycki. 1984. *Economic Adaptation*. Vol. 2: *Immigrants in Canada and Australia*. Downsview, ON: Institute for Behavioural Research, York University.

Richmond, Ted. 1996. *Effect of Cutbacks on Immigrant Service Agencies: Results of an Action Research Project*. Toronto: City of Toronto.

Roberts, Alden E. 1988. Racism sent and received: Americans and Vietnamese view one another. *Research in Race and Ethnic Relations* 5: 75–97.

Roberts, R.E., and S.W. Vernon. 1983. The center for epidemiological studies depression scale: Its use in a community sample. *American Journal of Psychiatry* 140, no. 1: 41–6.

Robson, R., and B. Breems. 1985. *Ethnic Conflict in Vancouver*. Vancouver: Civil Liberties Association.

Rodgers, G. 1995. What is special about a social exclusion approach? In *Social Exclusion: Rhetoric, Reality, Responses*, edited by G. Rodgers, C. Gore, and J. Figeiredo. Geneva: International Labour Organization.

Roman, Leslie G., and T. Stanley. 1997. Empires, emigres, and aliens: Young people's negotiations of official and popular racism in Canada. In *Dangerous Territories: Struggles for Difference and Equality in Education*, edited by Leslie G. Roman and Linda Eyre, 205–31. New York: Routledge.

Room, G. 1995. *Beyond the Treshold: The Measurement and Analysis of Social Exclusion*. Bristol: Polity Press.

Roseman, Curtis C., Hans-Dieter Laux, and Günter Thieme. 1996. *EthniCity: Geographic Perspectives on Ethnic Change in Modern Cities*. Lanham, MD: Rowman and Littlefield Publishers.

Roth, John. 1976. *West Indians in Toronto: The Student and the Schools*. Toronto: MERS Learner Characteristic Committee, Board of Education for the Borough of York.

Rousseau, Cecil, and Aline Drapeau. 1998. Parent-child agreement on refugee

children's psychiatric symptoms: A transcultural perspective. *Journal of the American Academy of Child and Adolescent Psychiatry* 37, no. 6: 629–36.
Royal Commission on Bilingualism and Biculturalism. 1970. *The Cultural Contributions of the Other Ethnic Groups.* Ottawa: Queen's Printer.
Ruimy, Joel. 1986. New system lets 90 per cent of refugees remain here. *Toronto Star*, 12 December, A1.
Rutter, M., W. Yule, M. Berger et al. 1974. Children of West Indian immigrants: Rates of behavioral deviance and psychiatric disorder. *Journal of Child Psychology and Psychiatry* 15: 241–62.
Sack, W.H. 1985. Post-traumatic stress disorders in children. *Integrative Psychiatry* 3, no. 3: 162–4.
Salgado de Snyder, V.N. 1987. Factors associated with acculturative stress and depressive symptomatology among married Mexican immigrant women. *Psychology of Women Quarterly* 11, no. 4: 475–88.
Sanaoui, R. 1996. Characteristics of instructors teaching non-credit adult ESL in Ontario: A progress report on TESL Ontario's research study. *Contact* 21, no. 2: 28–30.
– 1997. Professional characteristics and concerns of instructors teaching English as a Second Language to adults in non-credit programs in Ontario. *TESL Canada Journal* 14, no. 2: 32–54.
– 1998. The development of a protocol and uniform standards for the certification of instructors teaching non-credit ESL to adults in Ontario: Phase 3: Draft report on the Steering Committee's recommendations. Submitted to TESL Ontario, February 1998.
Sanati, M. 1999. Little Italy counts the cost of being hip. *Globe and Mail*, 4 January, A10.
Sandercock, Leonie. 1998. *Towards Cosmopolis: Planning for Multicultural Cities.* New York: John Wiley.
Sanders, Jimy M., and Victor Nee. 1987. Limits of ethnic solidarity in the enclave economy. *American Sociological Review* 52: 745–67.
Sanders-Thompson, and L. Vetta. 1996. Perceived experiences of racism as stressful life events. *Community of Mental Health Journal* 32, no. 3: 223–33.
Saphir, A. 1997. Asian Americans and cancer: Discarding the myth of the 'model minority.' *Journal of the National Cancer Institute* 89: 1572–4.
Sassen, Saskia. 1991. *The Global City: New York, London, Tokyo.* Princeton, NJ: Princeton University Press.
Satzewich, Vic. 1989. Racism and Canadian immigration policy: The government's view of Caribbean migration, 1962–1966. *Canadian Ethics Studies* 21, no. 1: 77–97.

- 1991. *Racism and the Incorporation of Foreign Labour: Farm Labour Migration to Canada since 1945*. New York: Routledge.
Saxenian, AnnaLee. 1999. *Silicon Valley's New Immigrant Entrepreneurs*. San Francisco: Public Policy Institute of California.
Schreiber, Jan. 1970. *In the Course of Discovery: The West Indian Immigrants in Toronto Schools*. Toronto: Board of Education for the City of Toronto.
Scotti, Rosanna. 2000. Access, equity, civic participation and municipal government: A Toronto perspective. Presentation to the Fourth National Metropolis Conference, March, Toronto.
Sen, Amartya. 2000. Social exclusion: Concept, application and scrutiny. Social Development papers 1. Manila, Philippines: Office of Environment and Social Development, Asian Development Bank.
Seward, Shirley B. 1987. *The Relationship between Immigration and the Canadian Economy*. Ottawa: Studies in Social Policy, Institute for Research on Public Policy.
Shelton, Antoni. 1998. Challenging urban cultural tribalism. *Currents: Readings in Race Relations* 9, no. 2: 4–6.
Shen, B., and Takeuchi, D.T. 2001. A structural model of acculturation and mental health status among Chinese Americans. *American Journal of Community Psychology* 29: 387–418.
Shields, John, and B. Mitchell Evans. 1998. *Shrinking the State*. Halifax, NS: Fernwood.
Siddiqui, Haroon. Immigration policies hurt Torontonians. *Toronto Star*. <http:www.thestar.com/thestar/edi...nion/991114NEW02c_OP.Haroon14.html>. 14 November.
- 2000. Immigrants should boycott Canada. *Toronto Star*, 14 September, A34.
Siemiatycki, Myer, and Engin Isin. 1997. Immigration, diversity and urban citizenship in Toronto. *Canadian Journal of Regional Science* 20, nos. 1/2: 73–102.
Siemiatycki, Myer, and Anver Saloojee. 2000. Ethno-racial political representation in Toronto: Patterns and problems. Paper presented to the Fifth International Metropolis Conference, Vancouver.
Simich, Laura. 2000. *Towards a Greater Toronto Charter: Implications for Immigrant Settlement*. Toronto: Maytree Foundation.
Simmons, Alan. 1990. The origin and characteristics of 'New Wave' Canadian immigrants. In *Ethnic Demography: Canadian Immigrant, Racial and Cultural Variations*, edited by Shiva S. Hall, Frank Trovato, and Leo Driedger, 141–60. Ottawa: Carleton University Press.
- 1993. Latin American migration to Canada. *International Journal* 48, no. 2: 282–309.

Simmons, Alan, and Kieran Keohane. 1992. Canadian immigration policy: State strategies and the quest for legitimacy. *Canadian Review of Sociology and Anthropology* 29, no. 4: 421–52.

Simmons, Alan, and Dwaine E. Plaza. 1999. Breaking through the glass ceiling: The pursuit of university training among African Caribbean migrants and their children in Toronto. *Canadian Ethnic Studies* 30, no. 2: 165–85.

Skeldon, Ronald. 1999. The case of Hong Kong. In *The Encyclopedia of the Chinese Overseas*, edited by Pan Lynn. Cambridge, MA: Harvard University Press.

Skhiri, Annabi, and Robert Allani. 1982. Enfants d'immigrants: Facteurs de liens ou de rupture? *Annales Medio Psycholoques* 140, no. 6: 597–602.

Smalley, William A. 1963. Culture shock, language shock, and the shock of self-discovery. *Practical Anthropology* 10: 49–56.

Smith, Charles. 1999. The restructured landscape: Politics and social change at the start of the new millennium. Unpublished paper.

Soberman, Liane. 1999. Immigration and the Canadian federal election of 1993: The press as a political educator. In *Ethnicity, Politics, and Public Policy: Case Studies in Canadian Diversity*, edited by Harold Troper and Morton Weinfeld, 253–81. Toronto: University of Toronto Press.

Solomon, Patrick. 1992. *Black Resistance in High School: Forging a Separatist Culture*. Albany: State University of New York Press.

Sorenson, J. 1999. Somalis. In *Encyclopedia of Canada's Peoples*, edited by Paul Robert Magocsi. Toronto: University of Toronto Press.

Special Committee of Parliament on the Participation of Visible Minorities in Canadian Society. 1984. *Equality Now!* Ottawa: House of Commons.

Speisman, Stephen. 1985. St John's Shtetl: The ward in 1911. In *Gathering Place: Peoples and Neighbourhoods of Toronto, 1834–1945*, edited by Robert Harney. Toronto: Multicultural History Society of Ontario.

– 1979. *The Jews of Toronto: A History to 1937*. Toronto: McClelland and Stewart.

Spencer, Robert. 1991. *Adult ESL in the City of Toronto: An Issue Paper*. Toronto: George Brown College.

St John-Jones, L.W. 1973. Canadian immigration trends and policies in the 1960s. *International Migration*: 141.

Stanback, Thomas M., and Thierry J. Noyelle. 1984. *The Economic Transformation of American Cities*. Totowa, NJ: Rowman and Allanheld.

Stasiulis, D. 1985. Racism and the Canadian state. *Explorations in Canadian Ethnic Studies*: 13–32.

– 1995. 'Deep Diversity': Race and ethnicity in Canadian politics. In *Canadian Politics in the 1990s*, 4th ed., edited by Michael Whittington and Glen Williams. Toronto: Nelson Canada.

- 1997. International migration, rights, and the decline of 'actually existing liberal democracy.' *New Community* 23, no. 2: 197–214.
Statistics Canada. 1990. *Immigrants in Canada, Selected Highlights*. Ottawa: Statistics Canada.
- 1996a. *Profiles: Hong Kong*. Ottawa: Statistics Canada.
- 1996b. *Profiles: China*. Ottawa: Statistics Canada.
- 1998a. 1996 Census: Labour force activity, occupation and industry, place of work, mode of transportation to work, unpaid work. *The Daily*, 17 March.
- 1998b. *Immigration Database (IMDB): A Special Tabulation*. Ottawa: Statistics Canada.
- 1998c. *Landed Immigrant Data System 1980–1995 (CD)*. Ottawa: Statistics Canada.
- 1998d. 1996 Census: Ethnic origin, visible minorities. *The Daily*, 17 February.
- 1999a. *The 1996 Census of Canada, Public Use Microdata File, User Documentation*. Ottawa: Statistics Canada.
- 1999b. *Special Tabulations: 1996 Census of Canada*. Ottawa: Statistics Canada.
- 1999c. *Special Tabulations: 1996 Census of Canada*. Toronto: Statistics Canada Regional Office.
Stephan, E.H., K. Foote, G.E. Hendershot, and C.A. Schoenborn, C.A. 1994. Health of the foreign-born population: United States, 1989–90. *Advance Data from Vital and Health Statistics* 241: 1–10.
Steinhausen, H.C. 1985. Psychiatric disorders in children and family dysfunction. A study of migrant workers' families. *Social Psychiatry* 20, no. 1: 11–16.
Stewart, A. 1975. *See Me Yah: Working Papers on Newly Arrived West Indian Children in the Downtown School*. Toronto: Toronto Board of Education.
Sturino, Franc. 1990. *Forging the Chain: A Case Study of Italian Migration to North America, 1880–1930*. Toronto: Multicultural History Society of Ontario.
- 1999. Italians. In *Encyclopedia of Canada's Peoples*, edited by Paul Robert Magocsi. Toronto: University of Toronto Press.
Sue, Stanley, and James K. Morishima. 1982. *The Mental Health of Asian Americans*. San Francisco: Jossey-Bass.
Swan, Neil, Ludwig Auer, Densi Chenard, Angelique dePlaa, Arnold deSilva, Douglas Parlmer, John Serjak, and Lorraine Milobar. 1991. *Economic and Social Impacts of Immigration: A Research Report Prepared for the Economic Council of Canada*. Ottawa: Economic Council of Canada.
Syme, S.L., M.G. Marmot, A. Kagan, H. Kato, and G.G. Rhoads. 1975. Epidemiological study of coronary heart disease and stroke in Japanese men living in Japan, Hawaii and California: Introduction. *American Journal of Epidemiology* 102: 477–90.
Takeuchi, David T., Philip J. Leaf, and Hsu-sung Kuo. 1988. Ethnic differences

in the perception of barriers to help-seeking. *Social Psychiatry and Psychiatric Epidemiology* 23, no. 4: 273–80.
Task Force on Access to Professions and Trades in Ontario. 1989. *Access!* Toronto: Queen's Printer.
Task Force on Community Access and Equity. 2000. *Diversity Our Strength, Access and Equity Our Goal. Final Report.* Toronto: City of Toronto.
Task Force on Human Relations. 1977. *Now Is Not Too Late.* Submitted to the Council of Metropolitan Toronto by Task Force on Human Relations. Toronto: Task Force.
Tatla, Rupinder K. 2000. Acculturation and perceptions of anti-smoking interventions in immigrants in Canada. Unpublished thesis, Department of Community Health, University of Toronto.
Tator, Carol. 1998. Community and race relations at the local level in the United States. *Currents: Readings in Race Relations* 9, no. 2: 7–8.
Tator, Carol, and Tim Rees. 1991. Advocacy and race relations. In *Making Knowledge Count: Advocacy and Social Service*, edited by P. Harries-Jones. Montreal: McGill-Queen's University Press.
Teixeira, C. 1995. The Portuguese in Toronto: A community on the move. *Portuguese Studies Review* 4: 57–75.
– 1998. Cultural resources and ethnic entrepreneurship: A case study of the Portuguese real estate industry in Toronto. *Canadian Geographer* 42, no. 3: 267–81.
Teixeira, C., and Murdie, R.A. 1997. The role of ethnic real estate agents in the residential relocation process: A case study of the Portuguese homebuyers in suburban Toronto. *Urban Geography* 18: 497–520.
Thomas, A.M. 1987. Government and adult learning. In *Choosing Our Future: Adult Education and Public Policy in Canada*, edited by Frank Cassidy and Ron Faris. Toronto: Ontario Institute for Studies in Education.
Thompson, Allan. 2002. Ottawa rebuked over refugee plan. *Toronto Star*, 30 April, A6.
Thompson, Richard H. 1989. *Toronto's Chinatown: The Changing Social Organization of an Ethnic Community.* New York: AMS Press.
Thompson, V.L. 1996. Perceived experiences of racism as stressful life events. *Community Mental Health Journal* 32, no. 3: 223–33.
Tocque K., M.J. Doherty, M.A. Bellis, D.P. Spence, C.S. Williams, and P.D. Davies. 1998. Tuberculosis notifications in England: The relative effects of deprivation and immigration. *International Journal of Tuberculosis and Lung Disease* 2, no. 3: 213–18.
Tomasi, Lydio F. 1977. The Italian community in Toronto: A demographic profile. *International Migration Review* 11, no. 4: 486–513.

Tracey-Wortley, J., and Wheaton, B. 1997. Assessing mental health differences among ethno-racial groups in Toronto: A comparison of East Asians, South Asians, Blacks, and Whites. Paper presented at the 92nd Annual Meeting of the American Sociological Association, Toronto.

Troper, Harold. 1972. The Creek-Negroes of Oklahoma and Canadian immigration, 1909–1911. *Canadian Historical Review* 48, no. 192: 255–81.

– 1978. Nationalism and the history of curriculum in Canada. *History Teacher* 12: 11–27.

– 1987. Jews and Canadian immigration policy: 1900–1950. In *The News of North America*, edited by Moses Rischin, 44–61, 51–2. Detroit: Wayne State University Press.

– 1993. Canada's immigration policy since 1945. *International Journal* 48 (Spring): 255–81.

– 1999. Multiculturalism. In *Encyclopedia of Canada's People*, edited by Paul Robert Magocsi, 997–1006. Toronto: University of Toronto Press.

– 2000. *History of Immigration since the Second World War: From Toronto 'The Good' to Toronto 'The World in a City.'* Toronto: Joint Centre of Excellence for Research on Immigration and Settlement – Toronto. Working Paper Series.

Troper, Harold, and Morton Weinfeld. 1989. *Old Wounds: Jews, Ukrainians and the Hunt for Nazi War Criminals in Canada.* Chapel Hill: University of North Carolina Press.

Tseng, Yen-Fen. 1994. Chinese ethnic economy: San Gabriel Valley, Los Angeles County. *Journal of Urban Affairs* 16, no. 2: 169–89.

Tulchinsky, Gerald. 1992. *Taking Root: The Origins of the Canadian Jewish Community.* Toronto: Lester Publishing.

Turner, R. Jay, and Lloyd, Donald A. 1998. The stress process and the social distribution of depression. Paper presented to the Seventh International Conference on Social Stress Research, 26 May, Budapest, Hungary.

Ubale, Bhausaheb. 1977. *Equal Opportunity and Public Policy: A Report on Concerns of the South Asian Canadian Community Regarding their Place in the Canadian Mosaic.* Toronto: Indian Immigrant Aid Services.

Uneke, Okori Akpa. 1994. Inter-group differences in self-employment: Blacks and Chinese in Toronto. PhD diss., University of Toronto.

United Way of Greater Toronto. 1991. *Action, Access, Diversity.* Toronto: United Way of Greater Toronto.

– 1997. *Metro Toronto: A Community at Risk.* Toronto: United Way of Great Toronto.

Urban Alliance on Race Relations. 1999. Anti-racism, access and equity in the new City of Toronto. Occasional paper no. 1. Toronto: Author.

U.S. Centers for Disease Control and Prevention. 2001. *Surveillance Reports: Reported Tuberculosis in the United States, 2001.* <http://www.cdc.gov/nchstp/tb/surv/surv2001/default.htm>.

U.S. Public Health Services. 2001. *Mental Health: Culture, Race and Ethnicity – A Supplement to Mental Health: A Report of the Surgeon General.* Rockville, MD: US Department of Human Services, Substance Abuse and Mental Health Services Administration, Center for Mental Health Services.

Valji, Nhla. 2001. Women and the 1951 Refugee Convention: Fifty years of seeking visibility. *Refuge* 19: 25–35.

Vega, William A., Bohdan Kolody, Sergio Aguilar Gaxiola, Ethel Alderete, Ralph Catalano, and Jorge Caraveo-Anduaga. 1998. Lifetime prevalence of DSM-III-R psychiatric disorders among urban and rural Mexican Americans in California. *Archives of General Psychiatry* 55, no. 9: 771–8.

Walcott, Rinaldo. 1997. *Black Like Who? Writing Black Canada.* Toronto: Insomniac Press.

Waldinger, Roger, 1996. Immigrant integration in the postindustrial metropolis: A view from the United States. Paper prepared for the Working Group Session on Urban Economic Restructuring: Implications for Immigrants and Other Marginalized Groups, First Annual Conference, Metropolis Project, November, Milan, Italy.

Waldinger, Roger, Howard Aldrich, and Robin Ward. 1990. *Ethnic Entrepreneurs: Immigrant Business in Industrial Societies.* Newbury Park, CA: Sage Publications.

Walker, James W. St. G. 1980. *A History of Blacks in Canada. A Study Guide for Teachers and Students.* Hull, QC: Minister of State Multiculturalism.

– 1985. *Racial Discrimination in Canada: The Black Experience.* Ottawa: Canadian Historical Association.

– 1997. *'Race,' Rights and the Law in the Supreme Court of Canada: Historical Case Studies.* Waterloo, ON: Wilfrid Laurier University Press.

Wallace, M. 2000. Where planning meets multiculturalism: A view of planning practice in the Greater Toronto Area. *Plan Canada* 40, no. 4: 19–20.

Wang, Shuguang. 1999. Chinese commercial activity in the Toronto CMA: New development patterns and impacts. *Canadian Geographer* 43: 19–35.

Wang, Shuguang, and Lucia Lo. 2000. Economic impacts of immigrants in the Toronto CMA: A tax benefit analysis. *Journal of International Migration and Integration* 1: 273–303.

Watson, J. 2001. Where planning meets multiculturalism: A view of planning practice in the Greater Toronto Area. *Plan Canada* 40: 19–20.

Weinfeld, M. 1999. Jews. In *Encyclopedia of Canada's Peoples*, edited by Paul Robert Magocsi. Toronto: University of Toronto Press.

Weinfeld, M., and L. Wilkinson. 1999. Immigration, diversity, and minority communities. In *Race and Ethnic Relations in Canada*, 2nd ed., edited by Peter S. Li. Toronto: Oxford University Press.

Westermeyer, Joseph, John Neider, and Tou-Fu Vang. 1984. Acculturation and mental health: A study of Hmong refugees at 1.5 and 3.5 years postmigration. *Social Science and Medicine* 18, no. 1: 87–93.

Whitaker, Reginald. 1987. *Double Standard: The Secret History of Canadian Immigration*. Toronto: Lester and Orpen Dennys.

Wittington, Michael S., and Glen Williams, eds. 1995. *Canadian Politics in the 1990s*, 4th ed. Toronto: Nelson Canada.

Williams, David R. 1997. Race and health: Basic questions, emerging directions. *Annals of Epidemiology* 7: 322–33.

Williams, David R., and An-Me Chung. 1997. Racism and health. In *Health in Black America*. Rose Gibson and James S. Jackson. Thousand Oaks, CA: Sage Publications.

Williams, D.R., and Williams Morris. 2000. Racism and mental health: The African-American experience. *Ethnicity and Health* 5: 243–68.

Williams, David R., Risa Lavizzo Mourey, and Rueben C. Warren. 1994. The concept of race and health status in America. *Public Health Reports* 109: 26–41.

Williams David R., Yan Yu, James S. Jackson, and Norman B. Anderson. 1997. Racial differences in physical and mental health: Socio-economic status, stress, and discrimination. *Journal of Health Psychology* 2, no. 3: 335–51.

Winks, Robin W. 1997. *The Blacks in Canada: A History*. 2nd ed. Montreal: McGill-Queen's University Press.

Wolfgang, Aaron. 1975. Basic issues and plausible answers in counselling new Canadians. In *Education of Immigrant Students: Issues and Answers*, edited by Aaron Wolfgang, 139–48. Toronto: Ontario Institute for Studies in Education.

Wong, Lloyd. 1984. Canada's guestworkers: Some comparisons of temporary workers in Europe and North America. *International Migration Review* 18, no. 1: 85–9.

– 1991. Business immigration to Canada: Social impact and racism. Paper presented at the Conference on Immigration, Racism and Multiculturalism. 1990 and Beyond, sponsored by the Social Research Unit, 22–23 March, Department of Sociology, University of Saskatchewan.

Wong, Tony. 1988. The new, upscale Chinatown prospering in Scarborough. *Toronto Star*, 21 November, A6.

– 1999. Family's success mirrors community. *Toronto Star*, 10 May, B3.

Wright, E.N. 1970. *The Every Student Survey: Student's Background and its*

Relationship to Class and Programme Placement in School #91. Toronto: The Toronto Board of Education.
– 1971. *Programme Placement Related to Selected Countries of Birth and Selected Languages: Further Every Student Survey Analyses #99*. Toronto: Board of Education for the City of Toronto, Research Department.
Wright, E.N., and D.B. McLeod. 1971. *Parents' Occupations, Student's Mother Tongue and Immigrant Status: Further Analyses of the Every Student Survey #98*. Toronto: Board of Education for the City of Toronto, Research Department.
Wright, E.N., and Gerry Kazuo Tsuji. 1983. *The Grade Nine Student Survey: Fall 1982 #173*. Toronto: Board of Education for the City of Toronto, Research Department.
– 1984. *The Grade Nine Student Survey: Fall 1983 #174*. Toronto: Board of Education for the City of Toronto, Research Department.
Wu, Z., and V. Kaspar. 2000. The mental health of Asian immigrants in Canada. *University of Victoria/National Sun Yat-sen University Symposium*. Victoria, BC: University of Victoria Press.
Wynne, Kathleen. 1997. Interview with Myer Siemiatycki. Toronto. 11 November.
Yau, Maria Y.M. 1995. *Refugee Students in Toronto Schools: An Exploratory Study #211*. Toronto: Research Services, Toronto Board of Education.
Ying, Yu-Men, and Leonard S. Miller. 1992. Help-seeking behavior and attitude of Chinese Americans regarding psychological problems. *American Journal of Community Psychology* 20, no. 4: 549–56.
Young, Iris Marion. 1990. *Justice and the Politics of Difference*. Princeton, N.J: Princeton University Press.
Young, Ken, and Naomi Connelly. 1981. *Policy and Practice in the Multi-Racial City*. London: Policy Studies Institute.
Zhou, Min. 1997. Growing up American: The challenge confronting immigrant children and children of immigrants. *Annual Review of Sociology* 23: 63–95.
Zhou, Min, and Carl L. Bankston. 1998. *Growing up American: How Vietnamise Children Adapt to Life in the United States*. New York: Russell Sage Foundation.
Zhou, Yu. 1998. Beyond ethnic enclaves: Location strategies of Chinese producer service firms in Los Angeles. *Economic Geography* 74, no. 3: 228–51.
Zucchi, John E. 1988. *Italians in Toronto: Development of a National Identity, 1875–1935*. Montreal: McGill-Queen's University Press.
Zukin, Sharon. 1995. *The Cultures of Cities*. Cambridge, MA: Blackwell.

Contributors

Paul Anisef is professor of sociology at York University. For well over a decade, he has conducted extensive research on accessibility to Canadian higher education, the transition from school to work at the secondary and post-secondary levels of education, settlement and integration of immigrant youth, and careers for Canadian youth. He is co-author of *Opportunity and Uncertainty: Life Course Experiences of the Class of '73* (with P. Axelrod, E. Baichman Anisef, C. James, and A. Turrittin) (2000), among other publications. He is currently associate director of the Centre of Excellence for Research on Settlement and Immigration.

Barbara Burnaby is a professor in the Faculty of Education, Memorial University of Newfoundland. She has been involved professionally with English as a foreign language (EFL) teaching in Japan and in the People's Republic of China, English as a second language (ESL) teaching in Canada, and teacher training and materials development for ESL and the teaching of Canadian Aboriginal languages. Her research includes topics such as ESL for adult immigrants, adult literacy, language and literacy in Aboriginal education, and language policy. Her teaching focuses on adult education and qualitative research methods.

Meyer Burstein is the co-founder of and develops the overall strategic directions for the International Metropolis Project. He co-chairs the Metropolis International Steering Committee, representing Canada, and is the chair of the Canadian Interdepartmental Working Group. He was director general of the Strategic Research and Analysis Branch in the

Department of Citizenship and Immigration. He was responsible for a major redesign of the Immigration Act's provisions governing the management of immigration flows.

Howard Duncan received his PhD in philosophy from the University of Western Ontario. He taught philosophy at the University of Ottawa and the University of Western Ontario and then he turned to consulting in strategic planning, policy development, and program evaluation. He joined the federal Department of Health and Welfare (now Health Canada) in evaluation, planning, and policy. In 1997, he joined the Metropolis Project as its international project director and recently was appointed executive head. He has concentrated on increasing the project's benefits to the policy community with direct exchanges between researchers, practitioners, and policy makers. As head of the Metropolis International Secretariat, he has increased Metropolis's geographic reach and expanded its range of issues.

Carl E. James teaches in the Faculty of Education at York University. His teaching areas include foundation of education, urban education, and practitioner research. In his research and publications he explores issues of accessibility and equity in education and employment as well as issues related to multiculturalism and immigration. He is the author of a number of publications including *Seeing Ourselves: Exploring Race, Ethnicity and Culture* (1999).

Clifford Jansen is Emeritus Professor at York University. Born in South Africa, he was educated in Italy, Belgium, and England before coming to York University in 1968. Recent publications include a co-authored book, *Sociological and Economic Change in the Peasant Society of Troina, Sicily*, and articles on Italians in Canada in the 1990s and issues of race in employment among Caribbean women in Toronto.

Violet Kaspar is assistant professor with the Department of Psychiatry, University of Toronto, and research scientist with the Centre for Addiction and Mental Health. Her research on the determinants of children's mental health and adjustment examines trauma exposure, social stress, and material deprivation manifested as physical or mental pathology in racial or ethnic minorities.

Lawrence Lam is associate professor in the Department of Sociology at

York University. His research interests include race and ethnic relations, migration and refugee studies, and refugee resettlement in Canada. His most recent project is on the settlement experience of Kosovar refugees in Ontario and the experience of sponsors of Kosovar refugees in Ontario.

Michael Lanphier is professor of sociology and deputy director, Centre for Refugee Studies, York University. He has authored numerous articles and book chapters on immigrant and refugee resettlement in Canada and, comparatively, in Australia, the United States, and France. He was the founding chair of the Centre of Excellence for Research on Settlement and Immigration Management Board. He served as president of the Canadian Ethnic Studies Association (2000–2). He is currently principal investigator of a major collaborative project, 'Social Cohesion and International Migration in a Globalizing Era,' which studies transnational solidarities and institutional bases of newcomer incorporation in Canada.

Lucia Lo is associate professor of geography at York University. Her varied research interests span quantitative analysis and spatial choice modeling, economic and social aspects of migration and immigration, and the impact of retail restructuring on consumer preferences. Having co-investigated a project on immigrant entrepreneurship, she is principal investigator of several projects on ethnic and immigrant consumer preferences, settlement services, and Canada's foreign banks.

Robert A. Murdie is professor of geography at York University and the housing and neighbourhoods domain leader for the Joint Centre of Excellence for Research on Immigration and Settlement – Toronto. During the past decade he has undertaken several studies of immigrant experiences in the housing market and is currently co-investigator of a major research project entitled 'Housing Experiences of New Canadians: Comparative Case Studies of Immigrants and Refugees in Greater Toronto.' He maintains close links with researchers in Sweden and has published several articles on metropolitan residential segregation and housing segmentation of immigrants in Sweden.

Roxana Ng is a researcher, feminist, anti-racist activist, and educator specializing on gender, race, and class issues as they pertain to immigrant women. Among her publications are *The Politics of Community Services: Immigrant Women, Class and State* (1988, reprinted in 1996) and

Community Organization and the Canadian State (1990, edited with G. Walker and J. Muller). Her current research is on globalization, immigrant garment workers and their learning. She teaches in the Adult Education and Community Development Program at the University of Toronto.

Samuel Noh is a professor with the Department of Sociology at the University of Akron (Ohio). His research examines social status and conditions as determinants of health among immigrants and refugees, with emphasis on Asian mental health, and culture-specific contextual interpretations of mental health risk factors, as well as cross-cultural validation of widely used psychiatric and epidemiologic mental health measures in clinical and community studies.

Valerie Preston is a professor and director of the graduate program in geography at York University. Her research interests include the geography of women's employment in North American cities, the economic and social integration of immigrants in Canada, and the social geography of restructuring in single-industry towns. The author of many publications, she is currently co-investigator of several research projects exploring the transnational behaviours of recent immigrants and their settlement experiences in Canadian metropolitan areas.

Khan Rahi has an MA in the sociology of development. A community-based researcher and consultant specializing in human and settlement services and in the social and political impact of environmental issues, he is executive director of the Access Action Council of Metropolitan Toronto and research consultant with York Region Neighbourhood Services and the Massachusetts-based Loka Institute.

Tim Rees is a coordinator of Access and Equity with the City of Toronto. He has worked in the settlement, race relations, and equity program and policy development fields for over thirty years in the public sector as well as private and voluntary sectors.

Gabriele Scardellato is currently the research fellow with the Mariano A. Elia Chair for Italian Canadian Studies and teaches Italian-Canadian Studies in the Department of Italian Studies, University of Toronto and the Department of Languages, Literatures, and Linguistics, York University. He is also past editor of *Ontario History*, the journal of the

Ontario Historical Society, and has a strong interest in photography. From 1988 to 1997 he was director of research resources for the Multicultural History Society of Ontario.

Myer Siemiatycki is professor of politics and public administration at Ryerson University. He is leader of the Community Domain of the Centre of Excellence for Research on Immigration and Settlement. His particular area of interest is urban citizenship – the civic engagement of immigrant and minority communities.

Carlos Teixeira teaches in the Department of Geography at the University of Toronto. His research interests include urban and social geography, migration processes, community and neighbourhood change, ethnic entrepreneurship, and the social structure of Canadian cities.

Harold Troper is professor of history in the Department of Theory and Policy Studies at the University of Toronto. He teaches and researches the history of immigration, and ethnicity and inter-group relations. He has been honoured with a John Simon Guggenheim Memorial Fellowship, the American Jewish Book Award, and the Sir John A. Macdonald Prize for the best book published in Canadian history. His long publication list includes *Immigrants: A Portrait of the Urban Experience; None Is Too Many; Old Wounds; Friend or Foe?* and, most recently, *The Ransomed of God*. He is currently conducting research into issues of ethnic identity in Canada during the late 1960s.

Shuguang Wang is associate professor of geography at Ryerson University in Toronto. His research interests include ethnic economy, the economic consequences of immigration, and the geography of retailing. Among his recent publications are 'Chinese Commercial Activity in the Toronto CMA: New Development Patterns and Impacts,' 'Settlement Patterns of Toronto's Chinese Immigrants Convergence or Divergence?' (with Lucia Lo), and 'Economic Impacts of Immigrants in the Toronto CMA: A Tax-Benefit Analysis' (with Lucia Lo).

Index

Abella, I. 384
Abella, R. 311
Aboriginal Awareness Week 444
Aboriginal peoples: and tuberculosis 332; and anti-racism 432
access: to educational programs 301, 305–7; to public institutions 36; to training and education 467
Access Action Canada (AAC) 434, 435
Access Action of Metropolitan Toronto 435
Access Awareness Week 444
accommodation. *See* housing
accreditation 255
acculturation 322, 326–31; and coping strategies 330–1
acculturative stress 340, 350
adjustment: disorders 318; economic and demographic 472; problems with 303
Africa 64; immigration from 196, 203, 210, 223
African immigrants 20; housing for, 134; in Toronto 20, 388; 415; restrictions against 317. *See also* Blacks; Caribbean
African Canadian Coalition against Racism 432
Agincourt 153
Akbari, A.H. 208
Alexander, J. 7, 396
Allen, K. 306
Amalgamated Clothing Workers 383
American cities: immigration to 22–3
Amercians' Changing Lives Surveys 335
American Civil War 22, 394
Amin, I. 43
Anderson, K. 218
Anglo-Protestant élite 22
Anisef, P. 3–17, 303, 474–8
Anti-Racism Secretariat 415, 452
Anti-Racism, Access, and Equity Committee 447
anti-Semitism 317, 357, 362, 378–82
Antonucci, T.C. 335
Arbeiter Ring (Workmen's Circle) 383
Ashworth, M. 301

Asia 41; immigration from 196, 223
Asian immigrants: and housing 134; in Toronto 388, 415
Asiatic Exclusion League 404
aspirations of immigrants 297; educational and occupational 266
Assembly of First Nations 432. *See also* Aboriginal
assimilation 277, 458
Australia 29, 220, 255, 325, 406
Avison, W.R. 342, 345

Bagnell, K. 389
Balmy Beach Swastika Club 381
Barber, J. 373
Beiser, M. 331-3, 340, 349
Bell, C. 409
Berton, P. 384-5, 391
Black Action Defence Committee 429
Black History Month 444
Blacks: immigration to Toronto 355-6, 359, 392-7; racial prejudice against 400, 401. *See also* Africa; African immigrants; Caribbean; Caribbean immigrants
Board of Education for the City of Toronto 274
Bosnia-Herzegovina 76
Brampton 153, 156, 220
Brathwaite, K. 306
Breton, R. 139, 335
Britain 69, 196, 210; immigrants from 355, 358
British Columbia 41, 209, 337, 340, 403-4, 407
British Commonwealth: immigration from 31
British North America 394
British North America Act 270-1, 461
Brown, G. 291, 394

Burnaby, B. 15, 389, 399, 476
Burstein, M. 17
business-class immigrants 50-1, 222. *See also* Hong Kong immigrants
businesses: Chinese 218-21; ethnic 216-8; Italian 258
Byrne, D. 7, 314

Calliste, A. 298-9, 306
Canada: Caribbean immigration to 398-9; Chinese immigration to 403-8; Cold War immigration policies 30-1, 37-8; economic conditions and immigration 40; effects of immigration on 63-4, 68, 174; immigration to 19-27; and immigration categories 49-51; immigration health studies in 319-24, 331-40; and intake of refugees 42-4, 57-8; Italian immigration to 32-3; and Jewish refugees 384; and managing diversity 461-4; multiculturalism in 44-6, 414-15; post-war immigration 27-30, 316; and racial restrictions 41-2
Canada Census (1996) 20, 316
Canada Employment and Immigration Advisory Council 435
Canada Employment and Immigration Commission (CEIC) 281
Canada Mortgage and Housing Corporation (CMHC) 138, 165, 189-90
Canadian Arab Association 440
Canadian Bill of Rights (1969) 414
Canadian Brotherhood of Railway Workers 396
Canadian Charter of Rights and Freedoms 55, 275
Canadian Council for Refugees 84

Canadian Council of Churches 43
Canadian Jewish Congress 402
Canadian Labour Congress 40
Canadian Manufacturing Association 385
Canadian Pacific Railway 403
Canadian Race Relations Foundation 420
Canadian Sri Lankan Association 440
Cannon, M. 406
Caplan, E. 80
Caribbean: immigration from 49, 134, 196, 203, 210, 388
Caribbean immigrants 285; and Caribana 356, 368; and the education system 300–1; and housing 169; in Toronto 155–7; settlement in Canada 392, 395–402; support groups for 423. See also Africa; African immigrants; Blacks
Central and South America 169, 223
Central Europe 20, 377
Centre for Epidemiology Study of depression (CES-D) 341
Centro Organizativo Scuole Technice Italiane (COSTI) 390
Chen, J. 319, 322, 325, 331
Cheng, M. 290, 292–3
Chile: refugees from Pinochet regime 43–4
China: immigration from 51, 405–8
Chinatown: in Toronto 145–6, 218–19; in Vancouver, 22, 218. See also Chinese immigrants
Chinese American Psychiatric Epidemiological Study 331
Chinese Canadian National Council (CCNC) 409, 410–11, 432, 440
Chinese immigrants 51, 100, 102, 360; businesses 218–22, 357, 366; barriers against 403–5; community 402–12; and home-ownership 174–6, 180; illegal migrants 56–8; in Toronto 20, 51, 145–6, 152–5, 408–11
Chinese Immigration Act 404–5
Chiswick, B. 270
Chodzinski, R. 301
Christie Pits Riot 317, 381–2, 412
Citizens for Local Democracy 437–9
Citizenship, Canadian 462; and immigration policy 51; institution of 35–6, 46; protection under 36–7
Citizenship and Immigration Canada 67, 81, 255
Citizenship and Language Instruction and Language Textbook Agreement (CILT) 278–9
City of Toronto 374, 445
City of Vaughan 145
Coalition of Agencies Serving South Asians (CASSA) 432
Coalition of Visible Minority Women 436
co-ethnic 212, 222
Cold War: and immigration policies 30–1, 37
collective identity 317
Committee for the Movement to Abolish the Canadian Restrictive Immigration Policy Towards Chinese 405
Community Committee on Immigrant Children 423
community: definition 374; support 340–3
Confederation 22–3
Conference on Strategies for Im-

proving Access and Retention of Ethno-Specific and Visible Minority Students in Ontario's Post-Secondary Institutions 306
Constitution Act (1982) 271
Co-operative Commonwealth Federation (CCF) 36
Co-operative Housing Federation of Canada – Ontario Region 163
Core Housing Need model 138, 169–74. *See also* housing
Corriere Canadese 390
cosmopolis 34, 376, 454–5
Council Action Committee to Combat Racism 447
Council of Agencies Serving South Asians (CASSA) 439
Cowan, J. 380
Cross-Cultural Communication Centre (CCCC) 426
cross-sectional epidemiological survey 327
cultural: compatible values 346; diversity 356; homogeneity 21; intolerance 317; pluralism 268, 316
culture: and the integration process 467–8; shock 340
Cummins, J. 300–1
Czechoslovakia 69, 211

Danzinger, K. 299, 303
deindustrialization 192
demography: projections of 316; and regional requirements 461; socio-demographic overview of 63–131
Deosaran, R. 289–90
Department of Citizenship and Immigration 30, 68
Department of Manpower and Immigration 48, 69, 71

dependency and disability rates 319–22
DeSilva, A. 208
Devereaux, M.S. 312
diasporas: of the Chinese 51; economies of 471
Dion, K.L. 336
disability: and rates of dependency 319–21, 333. *See also* health
discrimination 27; economic 218, 239, 248, 253–4; in education 297, 299, 300, 308; ethnic 41; in health care, 325, 334–40; in housing 153, 182, 186; prevalence and significance, of 469; racial 41, 331; systemic 317–18
displaced persons (DP) 42; admission programs for 28–30; camps for 32
diversity 90, 316–53, 473; federal government management of 460–4
division of labour (ethnoracial, gender, industrial) 211, 226–33, 235–6, 254
double jeopardy hypothesis 336
Doucet, M. 454
Doyle, R. 433–4
drop-out rates in education: 291–2, 296, 314. *See also* education
Duffy, K. 7
Duncan, H. 17

Eastern bloc 32
Eastern Europe 20, 28, 203 326, 377
economic: achievement and contributions of immigrants 221, 223, 238, 253; benefits and costs of immigration to 472; disadvantages 418–21; expansion in Canada 25; impact of immigration on 194–8,

221; parity for immigrants 253–4; well-being 459
Economic Council of Canada 301
economic-immigrant class 198–201
economy Canadian 317; ethnic enclaves in 211–12; 216–23
education: and accommodating migrants 310–13, 356–7; discrimination in 318, 300–4; and drop-out rates 291–2, 196, 314; equity in 275–6, 305–10; formal 265; and guidance counselling 302; and multicultural programs 272, 276; needs and issues of 277–310; non-academic streams 288; policies 263, 270; public actions 269–77; public education 461; role of 65–9, 265–9
Education Act (Ontario) 265, 273, 276
Education Improvement Commission 67
education, secondary: access to 305–7; graduate programs 308
education, special: 297, 302
educational characteristics of immigrants 102–3; comparisons by gender 107, 110,
Egypt: immigration office in 41
empirical research 466, 471–2
employment 105, 111, 318, 458; concentration of 229–30; and job fairs 37
Employment and Immigration Canada 78
England 332, 443
entrepreneur 211–12, 216, 221–2, 365; entrepreneur-class immigrant 50
epidemiological research 350
equality of outcome 473

equity: in education 275–6, 305–10; policy gaps in implementing social equity 452–3
ESD programs (standard English as a second dialect) 276
ESL (English as a second language): access 265; adult programs in 276–7; funding for 284–5; Manpower program 278; qualification programs in 280; teachers of 273, 283–4; training 271
Ethiopian Association of Toronto 440
ethnic: barriers to immigration 41–2; businesses 151, 211, 217; diversity 458; economy 211–12, 216–22; leaders 40; origins 88–90; pluralism 68; selectivity 27; subeconomy 33
ethnicity 158, 160–1, 297, 467
ethnocultural: differences 268; groups 324
ethnoracial division of labour 229–33
Etobicoke 161, 212, 416, 440
Europe: decrease in immigration from 55; entrepreneurial groups from 211–12; immigrants from 19, 41, 68–9, 320, 405, 415
Every Secondary Student Survey 291–5, 311
Every Student Survey 289, 290, 311
exclusion 6–11, 68, 138, 174, 182, 186–7, 475–7, 458
Exclusion Act (1947) 218

Fagnan, S. 208
family reunification 33, 40; regulations 41; economic impacts of 198,
federal government. *See* government, federal
Fernando, V. 439–41

fertility: rates in Canada 48; trends 316
Fewer School Boards Act 277
Filipino-American 327. *See also* Phillipines
First World War 23, 30, 64, 144, 395
Flemming, D. 283
Fong, P. 409
foreign: citizenship 103; credentials 255; foreign-born 316
foreigner(s) 22, 23, 26
Foster, C. 399, 401
Francis, D. 319
Franger, R. 383
Fulford, R. 378, 408

G8 Summit of the Cities 443
Gairey, H. 395, 396–7, 402
Galster, G. 186
Gander: illegal migrants in 55
Gay Pride Week 444
gender 187, 225, 226–9, 237
gentrification 151, 161
Germany 28, 75, 102, 110,
Ghana: immigrants from 157
Ghanaian immigrants 157–8, 177–8; population in Toronto, 159
Ghosh, R. 268
Gibson, M. 335
Glaze, A. 396
globalization 467
Globe and Mail 373, 394
Goldberg, D.T. 431
Gopie, K. J. 431
government 464; changes in 466; funding education 265; intervention, 469, 471, 473; managing diversity 470, 477; measures to foster integration, 463–4; spending 465
government, federal 477; legislative framework of 462; policies of 457, 459; role of 461
government, municipal: and immigration 442–50
Great Depression 27, 64, 317
Greece: immigration from 149–51, 286, 314
green paper on immigration 46–9
Greater Toronto Area (GTA): increase in immigration to 67; Korean immigrants in 341; multiethnic population in 20, 316; opposition to amalgamation 437–41. *See also* City of Toronto; Toronto

Haig-Brown, C. 265
Halifax: Black settlement in 392 immigration to 19
Hall, J. 306
Hamilton 23
Harney, N. 391
Harney, R. 354, 373, 453
Hatzoloh: servicing Orthodox Jewish community 446
Head, W. 300, 429, 431
health and health care 318, 351, 459; anti-social behaviour 318; authorities 34; coronary heart disease 326; coverage, provincial 324; determinants 333; differential distribution 334; healthy immigrant effect 324–7; hepatitis 351; HIV 319, 331–4, 351; indicators 325; long-term conditions 325; risks to 319; smoking 327; statistics of 318; status of 325, 327; stress and anxiety 341; tuberculosis 319, 325, 331–34, 351. *See also* mental health
Health and Activity Limitation Survey (HALS) 319

hegemonies 309
Hemingway, E. 378
Henry, F. 399–402, 419, 429
Heritage Language Program 273
Hindu temple 370
Hispanic Development Council (HDC) 432
Holocaust 28, 144, 379, 384
homelessness 467; Mayor's Homelessness Action Task Force 188
home-ownership 139, 147–8, 162, 174–82, 190–1
Hong Kong immigrants: business-class 51, 76, 220, 405–6; and home-ownership 174, 180; in Toronto 59, 152, 285, 408
host society: Toronto as 467
Hou, B. 329
household 101; size of 167–8
housing 187–8, 318, 459; anti-discrimination legislation 37; appropriate 132, 126, 138–9; conditions of 169–70, 174, 356; constraints and opportunities 161–82, 185–6; Limited Dividend Housing 164–5; market 161–82, 188; municipal 54; private-rental 162–3; public 163–4; quality 331
human rights: agenda 36–7; systemic denial of 334
humanitarian-class immigrants 72, 75, 198; and Convention against Torture 83
Hungarian immigrants 355, 363
Hungary 69, 211; uprising in 37

Iacovetta, F. 388, 391
immigrant and Adaptation Program 273
immigrants 457: agricultural 23–6; communities 37; defined 264; entrepreneurship of 211–12, 216, 221–2; health of 316–53; and host relations 266; landed 39; nominated class 40; pre–Second World War 21–7; reception areas 160; and selection policies 56, 270, 461, 463; self-employment 211–13, 222; service deliveries 433–6; service providers in Toronto 50; settlement areas 22; settlement patterns 461; status 297; students and schooling 263–315; women and organizing initiatives 422–8
immigration 3–4, 20, 21; appeal division of 80; bureaucracy 30; chronological photographic history of 354–72; history of 317; law 30, 39; policies 21, 23–6, 30, 47, 194, 225, 317–18, 324, 474–5; post-war 27–30, 36; priorities 28; procedures 42, 57; recruitment program 24; regulations 53; urban-friendly 30–3
Immigration Act 52, 56, 70, 396, 461; (1910) 395; (1952) 47, 68, 70; (1962) 398; (1967) 218; (1976) 71, 74, 78; (1978) 81; Bill C-11, the Immigration and Refugee Protection Act (2000) 80–1; Bill C-55 55, 74, 79–81, 84, 86; Bill C-86 79
Immigration and Refugee Board (IRB) 74, 83, 314
Immigration and Refugee Protection Act (2001) 76
Immigration Appeal Board 71
Immigration Branch of the Department of Mines and Resources 30
Immigration Medical Examination (IME) 324
Immigration Museum, Canadian 19
inclusion 68; social 6–11, 475–7

income 113–14, 120, 123–5, 318; from self-employment 213, 243
independent-migrant class 51
India 102, 110; immigration from 31; refugees from 326
Indian immigrants 367, 371; and home-ownership 174, 180–1
Indo-Chinese 72–4
industrial: development of 25; and division of labour 225–38
inequality 297, 317
infectious diseases 331–4. *See also* health
institutional barriers 256, 258
integrated diversity 317, 373–456; framework for 466
integration 4–6, 218, 220–1, 256, 457–8, 462, 463, 471, 477; cultural and social, 459; defined 459; patterns of 33
intermarriage 91
International Day for the Elimination of all Forms of Discrimination 444
International Ladies Garment Workers Union (ILGWU) 383, 428
International Women's Day 444
International Women's Day Coalition (IWDC) 427, 456n1
interpretation of research on immigrant students 297–305
intolerance 317
investment strategy 469
investor class 50
investors program 209
Iranian Association of Ontario 436
Ireland 378: immigrants from 450
Italian Immigrant Aid Society 390
Italian immigrants 32; in Toronto 20, 151, 368, 384–91, 411–12
Italy 28; immigrants from 32–3

Jackson, J.S. 334
Jamaican Canadian Association (JCA) 400, 402, 440
James, C.E. 15, 265, 269, 299, 303, 307–9, 389, 399, 476
Jansen, C. 13, 316, 387
Japan: immigration office in 41; immigrants from 28
Japanese Americans 326
Japanese Canadians 217
Jewish immigrants: barriers against 28, 317, 377–84, 411–12; in Toronto 20, 34, 142–5, 355–6, 364
Jones, T. 217

Kalbach, M. and W. Kalbach 128
Kane, T. 289
Kaspar, V. 15–16, 476
Kensington Market 22, 142–3, 148–9, 223, 258, 357, 361, 383
Keynesian public policy 413, 415
King, Mackenzie 27, 30
King, R. 401
King, William Lyon Mackenzie 379, 384–5, 405
knowledge 267
Korea 78
Korean Mental Health Study (KMHS) 341
Korean Town 212
Kralt, J. 130
Kunz, J.L. 420
Kuo, W.H. 335

labour force 25, 69, 467; division of 211, 226–34, 239; recruitment of workers for 28, 30
Labour Market Language training (LMLT) 282–5
Lai, C-Y D. 145

Lam, L. 13, 316
language 331; ability 330; education 269; mother tongue 85; shock 340. *See also* ESD, ESL
Language Instruction for Newcomers to Canada (LINC) 282–5
Lanphier, M. 70, 474–8
Larter, S. 290
Lastman, Mel 3–4, 67, 384, 443, 447
Latin America 189, 196, 203, 210, 326
Latin American claimants 56
Latin American Community Centre 436
Laurier, Sir Wilfrid 395
law: enforcement of 462; justice under 318
Lebanon: immigration office in 41
Legislative Advisory Group: and changes to immigration law 80
Levitt, C. 378
Lewis, S. 400
Lewis, W. 378
Ley, D. 162, 165, 250
Li, P. 403–4
Li, W. 152
Liberal government 45
life: expectancy 319, 320; satisfaction 336
lifestyle behaviours 329
Lin, J. 220
Lind, L.J. 285–6
Little Britain 223
Little Caribbean 155
Little Greece 151
Little Italy 144, 148, 151, 223
Little Portugal 148–9
Little Somalia 157
Lo, L. 14–15, 153, 402, 420, 476
Local Initiative Project (LIP) 426
Lord's Day Act (1907) 378

Low-Income Cut-Off (LICO) 165–7, 190, 248–51
Loyalists 393
Lui-Gurr, S. 209

Madina Mosque 369
Magagna, L. 390
Manitoba: tuberculosis in 332
Marger, M. 217
Markham 152–3, 220, 409–10, 416
Martin, P. 35
Masemann, V. 301
Masters, D.C. 379
Mathias, A. 439
Mayor's Committee on Community and Race Relations 439
Mayor's Homelessness Action Task Force 188
McEvoy, D. 217
McLeod, D.B. 289
medical screening 332–3; surveillance 334. *See also* health
mental health 330, 340; anti-social behaviour 318; depression 341; distress symptoms 18, 336; emotional adjustments 318; stress and anxiety 341. *See also* health
Metro Network for Social Justice 432
Metropolis Project 470
Metropolitan Toronto Council 447, 448
Metropolitan Toronto Housing Authority 157
Metzger, R. 186
Middle East 64, 76, 294; oil embargo against (1973) 48, 71
Ministry of Education 273, 276, 279, 280, 281, 284, 286, 302, 305
Ministry of Education and Training 276

minorities: racial and ethnic 318; Roman Catholic 22; visible 316;
Mississauga 416; Chinese settlement in 152–3; Portuguese settlement in 149–50, 160
Montreal 22, 23, 64; foreign-born immigrants in 66, 67; ethnic economies in 217; immigration to 73, 462; Jewish settlement in 377; refugees in 76
Montreal *Gazette* 84
Moodley, K.A. 266
Morris, W. 339
mortality rates 48, 319, 333
Muller, J. 374
multicultural 20; education policies 268; education program 272, 276; funding policy 435; planning for 185
multiculturalism 44–6, 316, 414, 469; policy (1971) 314; rhetoric of 46
Multiculturalism Act 462
Municipality of Metropolitan Toronto 435
Murdie, A.M. 328
Murdie, R.A. 13–14, 408, 416, 476

Nakamura, M. 432
National Anti-Racism Council 432
National Cancer Institute of the U.S. 327
National Congress of Italian Canadians 390
National Longitudinal Study of Children and Youth (NLSCY) 346
National Population Health Survey (NPHS) 322, 325
National Post: and anti-immigration 319
Neatby, B. 270

Negro Citizenship Association 397
neighbourhoods 22; formation of 139–61, 184–5; and integration 132, 136–8
Neighbourhood Services Department 445
neo-conservatism 413, 415–16
Netherlands 27, 68, 100, 102, 174
New Canadianism 297; doctrine of 286
New Canadians 37
New Voices of the New City 439–41
New Zealand 336, 406
Newcomer Services Branch of the Ontario Ministry of Culture and Recreation 275
Ng, R. 16–17, 322, 325
Ng, W. 427
Nicaragua 292, 314
Noh, S. 15–16, 316–53, 476
North York 161, 416; African settlement in 157; amalgamation into GTA 437, 440; Italian settlement in 145, 386; Vietnamese settlement in 153
North York Committee on Community, Race and Ethnic Relations 447
Nova Scotia: illegal migrants in 55, 75. *See also* Halifax

Oceania 196, 210
Official Languages Act 272, 273
Ogbu, J. 266
Ontario 68; abolition of slavery in 392–3; Caribbean settlement in 398; funding for immigrant services 67–8; government of 129; jurisdiction over immigration 461;

racial discrimination in 430; visible minorities in 316
Ontario Council of Agencies Serving Immigrants (OCASI) 420–1, 432
Ontario Department of the Provincial Secretary and Citizenship 423
Ontario Economic Council 305
Ontario Federation of Students 305
Ontario Human Rights Commission 414
Ontario Ministries of Education and Colleges and Universities 281
Ontario Non-Profit Housing Association 163
Ontario Secondary School Diploma (OSSD) 291
Ontario Young People's Alliance 432
Opoku-Dapaah, E. 303
Orange Lodge 378, 388
Orange Order 20, 378
Ornestein, M. 128, 248, 308–9, 418–21, 432
Ottawa 27–28, 32, 35, 38–41, 43, 52–53, 385, 397, 460
Owusu, T. 177–8

Pakistan: immigration from 31; immigration office in 41
Parliament of Canada 461
Parliamentary Committee on Immigration 39
Paugam, S. 7
Pelham, J. 314
period of arrival 233–8
Philippine immigrants: and housing 169
Philippines: immigration office in 41
Philips, N. 384
photographs: as historical narrative 354–72

Pickersgill, J. 38
pluralism: ethnic and racial 41–2, 49
point selection system 41, 81, 325
Poland 20, 100, 110, 211
Polish Constitution Day parade 357, 364
political representation: equity in 437–41
Porter, J. 298
Portugal 120, 100, 102, 151, 174, 314
Portuguese immigrants: in Toronto 212, 363; settlement in Kensington Market 223
Pound, E. 378
poverty 114, 120, 128, 331, 467; rates of 238, 248–53, 325
Prague Spring (1968) 42
Preston, V. 14–15, 420, 476
prevention programs 334
Provincial Advisory Committee to the Ministry of Education 302
Provincial Freeman 394
Public Health Department 450

Qadeer, M. 185
Quebec 68, 450
quota system 50

racial: exclusion 317; mix 59; pluralism 68; prejudice 335; segregation 317; selection criteria 49
racism 217, 297, 299–300, 308, 317, 334
Rahi, K. 16–17
Ramirez, B. 387
Ray, B. 132
realism–relativism debate 465
Rees, T. 16–17
Reform Party 56
refugees 42–4, 263, 305, 457: admission and regulation of 53, 55–6;

children 54; Czechoslovakian 42, 43; Chilean 43; definition of 264; Hungarian 38, 42; integration of 52; policy 42, 43, 52–8; reception of 466; rights to sanctuary 43; sponsorship of 53; status 297; students 295–7; Ugandan Asian 43; Vietnamese 53
Refugee Appeal Division 84
Regier, S. 269
Reitz, J. 128, 399
religion 86–8, 331
rent-to-income ratio: based on persons per room 171, 174
Report of the Canadian Immigration and Population Study (1974) 47, 71
Report on Race Relations in Ontario (1992) 400
research: findings 467–70; gaps in 450–2; importance of 464–7; planning of 312
resettlement: of boat people 53; of Czechs 43; of Hungarian refugees 38; services 334
residential property: acquisition of 33
residential segregation 318
responsible governance 466
Rexdale Women's Centre 424
Rhyne, D. 216
Richmond Hill 144, 152–3, 220, 408, 416
Riverdale 149, 151
Roberts, A. 335
Robillard, L. 67, 80
Rodgers, G. 10
Romany immigrants 361
Rosedale Ratepayers Association 404
Roth, J. 300

Royal Commissions on Bilingualism and Biculturalism 272
Royal Ontario Museum 400

St Jamestown 356, 370
St John's Ward 142–6, 356, 360
Sandercock, L. 375–6
Saskatchewan 37
Saul, J. R. 438
Scarborough 152–3, 161, 212, 220, 386, 408, 416, 440
Scardellato, G. 16
Second World War 64; entry of war criminals in post-war peri-od 31; immigration during 69; neighbourhoods in pre-war period 22; post-war immigration 58, 133–4, 144, 296, 451; post-war immigration policies 317, 396
security: checks 30; service in Canada 43
segregation 144, 153
selection 462
self-esteem 345
Sen, A. 9–10
service industry 226
settlement 326, 475; agricultural 23, 25, 30; assistance for 462; patterns of 469; policy for 475–7; services 19; stress related to 331–40
Settlement Branch of the Canada Employment and Immigration Commission (CEIC) 275
Settlement Language Training Program 282
Shadd Carry, M.A. 394
Shaffir, W. 378
Shaarei Shomayim synagogue 355–6, 364
Shen, B. 331

Shirley Samaroo House 426
Siddiqui, H. 421
Siemiatycki, M. 16–17
Sifton, C. 24
Simmons, A. 72
Singh v. Minister of Employment and Immigration 55
Skeldon, R. 406
Sleeping Car Porters Union 396–7
Smith, G. 379
social assistance 54; access to or exclusion from 334
social change: in Toronto 467
social characteristics of immigrants 316
social class of immigrants 297
social: cohesion 287, 458–60, 473; development of resources 330; incompetence 318; inequity 335–6; integration 458–9, 473; isolation 330; networks 137, 148; problems 465; social order 458, 464; stability 458; stratification 297; stress 334–40; support 340–4, 346, well-being 458–9
Social Planning Council of Metro Toronto 423, 433–4
socio-economic: adaptation 340; opportunities 467; status (SES) 288, 328
socio-economic continuum (SES) 344
Somali Canadian Association 440
Somalia 157, 178
South Africa 211, 432
South America 41
South and Central America 64
South Asia 76, 169
Southeast Asia 326
Southern Europe 203, 223, 285, 317

Soviet Union 28, 326
Special Committee of Parliament on the Participation of Visible Minorities in Canada 305, 311, 314
special education 288, 297, 302. *See also* education
Speisman, S. 382
Sri Lanka 151
Stasiulis, D. 437
Statistics Canada 165, 319
stereotyping 308
Sterioff, J. 286
stigma 335
stress 325; post-migration 326. *See also* health
structural discrimination 339
students: drop-out rates 291–2, 296, 314; defined as 'slow learners' 300–1. *See also* education
subeconomy 216–18
Sub-Saharan Africa 326
suburban 59, 220–1
suburbanization 416–17
Suez Crisis 69
symptom checklist 90, 341

Taiwan: immigrants from 51, 78, 405
Taiwanese immigrants: in businesses 220; in Toronto 152
Takeuchi, D. 331
Taking Responsibility for the Homeless 188
Task Force on Access to Professions and Trades in Ontario 311
Task Force on Community Access and Equity 316, 448
Task Force on Race Relations and Policing (1989) 401
tax-benefit ratio 197

teachers: non-credit ESL 285. *See also* ESL
Teixeira, C. 13–14, 328, 408, 416, 476
Telegram 380
tension: interethnic and interracial 59
TESL Ontario 280
Thatcher, M. 406
Thornhill 144
Together We Are One 316, 318
Toronto Anti-Slavery Society 393
Toronto Board of Education 277, 286–90, 295–9
Toronto Census Metropolitan Area (CMA) 373–4; study of immigrants in 195–248
Toronto Centre of Excellence 470
Toronto 3–4, 19; City Council 94; community 373–456; educational system 263–315; health of citizens in 316–53; history of immigration in 19–62; immigration policy 457–73; Old City Hall 142; sociodemographic overview 73, 100. *See also* Greater Toronto Area
Toronto Community Housing Corporation 164
Toronto District School Board 277
Toronto Hebrew Benevolent Society 383
Toronto Public Health Department 351
Toronto *Daily Star* 378
Toronto *Star* 155, 381, 420, 421
Toronto Task Force on Community Access and Equity 436
Tracey-Wortley, J. 344
Trial Division of the Federal Court 79–80

Trinidad and Tobago Association 402
Troper, H. 12–13, 63–4, 68, 285, 316, 354, 384–5, 398
Trudeau, P. E. 45
Tseng, Y-F. 220
tuberculosis 319, 325, 331–4, 351. *See also* health
Tulchinsky, G. 379

Uganda 43
Ugandan Asians 52
underemployment 248
underground economy 471
Underground Railroad 393
undesirable 317
unemployment 26, 110, 238–43, 325, 331
United Kingdom 41, 174
United Nations 20, 42, 454
United Nations Convention for Refugees (1951) 52
United Nations Convention on Refugees 42
United Nations Human Rights Day 444
United Nations World Conference on Racism 432
United Way 28, 435
Universal Declaration of Human Rights 37
University of Toronto 336; access program (Transitional Year Program) 306
university-geared programs 298
Upper Canada Rebellion 437
uprooting process 340
Urban Alliance on Race Relations (UARR) 429–33

U.S. Centers for Disease Control and Prevention 333
U.S. News and World report 454

values 25, 331
Vancouver: Chinese community in 51, 341, 404, 407; ethnic businesses in 217–18; immigration population in 22, 64, 67, 165, 462
Vaughan 160, 416
Veecock, J. 427
Vienna 38
Vietnam: immigrants from 20; and boat people crisis 52–3
Vietnamese Association of Toronto 440
Vietnamese immigrants: and health issues 340–1; and housing outcomes 169
Villa Columbo 390, 391
Visano, L. 433–4
visible minorities 238–43, 318, 469
vital statistics 319, 320

Waite, R. 186
Walker, J. 374
Wallace, M. 185
Wang, S. 14–15, 153, 402, 420, 476
Ward, The 382
Weinfeld, M. 5–6
West Central Asia 169
West Indies: immigration office in 41
Western Canada 24, 25
Western Europe 41, 196, 210

white paper on immigration 38–40
Wilkinson, L. 5–6, 128
Williams, D.R. 339
Winnipeg 22, 377
Wolfgang, A. 302
women, immigrant 372; organizing initiatives 422–8
Women of Colour Council 432
Women Working with Immigrant Women (WWIW) 425
Woodbridge 145, 212, 220
work-directed program 298
Works Department 446
World Health Organization 349
Wright, E.N. 289, 290
Wu, Z. 344
Wynne, K. 438

xenophobia 26, 34, 300

Yau, M. 264–5, 292–3, 296
YMCA 278, 357, 360
Yonge Street Riot 401
York University 400; access programs of 306–10; Institute for Social Research 418
Young, I. M. 375
Yugoslavia 76, 110
YWCA's Multi-Ethnic Women's Program 423

Ziegler, S. 292–3
Zukin, S. 437
Zundell, E. 379